D1430012

Alexander Peabody 11/88
Western Intellectual
Thought

Introduction to the
HUMAN SCIENCES

Introduction to the HUMAN SCIENCES

An Attempt to Lay a
Foundation for the Study
of Society and History

Wilhelm Dilthey

Translated with an Introductory Essay
by Ramon J. Betanzos

Wayne State University Press   Detroit   1988

Einleitung in die Geisteswissenschaften, vol. I of *Wilhelm Diltheys Gesammelte Schriften,* copyright © 1923 by B. G. Teubner, Leipzig and Berlin, © 1959, 1979 B. G. Teubner, Stuttgart. English
translation copyright © 1988 by Wayne State University Press,
Detroit, Michigan 48202. All rights are reserved.
No part of this book may be reproduced without formal permission.
92 91 90 89 88   5 4 3 2 1

Library of Congress Cataloging-in-Publication Data

Dilthey, Wilhelm, 1833–1911.
  [Einleitung in die Geisteswissenschaften. English]
  Introduction to the human sciences : an attempt to lay a
foundation for the study of society and history / by Wilhelm Dilthey
; translated with an introductory essay by Ramon J. Betanzos.
    p. cm.
  Translation of: Einleitung in die Geisteswissenschaften.
  Includes index.
  ISBN 0-8143-1897-5 (alk. paper). ISBN 0-8143-1898-3 (pbk. : alk.
paper)
  1. Humanities. I. Betanzos, Ramon J., 1933– . II. Title.
B3216.D83E413 1988
001.3—dc19   88-52
                                                CIP

Grateful acknowledgment is made to the following Wayne State University divisions for financial assistance in the publication of this volume: the Office of the Vice-President for Research and Dean of the Graduate School; the Office of the Dean, College of Liberal Arts; and the Department of Humanities.

Contents

Acknowledgments

Many people have helped me bring this project to fulfillment, and it is my pleasant duty to recognize at least the main contributors. At Wayne State University Professors Yates Hafner of the English department and Marc Cogan of the Humanities department have read significant parts of the manuscript and have made valuable suggestions about how to render Dilthey's often tortuous philosophical prose into what I hope is a reasonably tolerable English equivalent. All my colleagues in the Humanities department, especially the chairman, Professor Martin Herman, and Professor Sara Leopold, have been supportive and encouraging. Javan Kienzle typed and transcribed a first complete draft of the notes with their mélange of languages and provided other technical assistance. Susan McNamara typed the entire manuscript. My sincere thanks go to all of them.

Professor Stephen Tonsor of the University of Michigan, helpful mentor and friend over many years, first led me to a serious interest in nineteenth-century German philosophy and especially historicism. His counsel and kindness have been unstinted and have benefited me greatly. I am grateful.

The Office of Research and Sponsored Programs Services at Wayne State University has assisted this project substantially by research grants in 1981 and 1985 as well as by a publication subvention in 1987.

Finally, my thanks to "the home front"—Kay, Beth, and Mary—for their loving acceptance of my being away from them for many hours in favor of a task that must have seemed so far from home.

Wilhelm Dilthey: An Introduction

Dilthey's Life and Style

A reader's first extensive contact with the work of Wilhelm Dilthey might well create the impression that Dilthey, like Friedrich von Schlegel, was a man who "began everything and finished nothing," or perhaps that Dilthey was the proverbial man who "jumped on his horse and rode off in all directions." Dilthey did elaborate and develop an immense array of projects in his enormously industrious lifetime of seventy-seven years; the sheer quantity and diversity of his enterprises are simply astounding. Here is a man who wrote many outstanding historical essays and much pioneering speculation about the theory of history itself. He did extensive serious work in philosophy, psychology, sociology, anthropology, hermeneutics, biography, poetry, music, law, economics, and pedagogy; in short in virtually everything that man has ever done in the cultural sphere.

Dilthey's work is so varied and incomplete not just because in his mind, inevitably, "one thing led to another," nor just because he proceeded in an historical, fact-gathering, descriptive manner, but mainly because his overriding interest and concern was nothing less than *human life itself*: the infinitely varied and multiform life of man, the individual and the race, through all specifically human expressions and objectifications of life beginning as far back as the earliest records can take us, on to Dilthey's time, and into the future. In other words, Dilthey tried to do the impossible. In H. Stuart Hughes's words: "Dilthey laid out a program that no mortal . . . could hope to bring to completion. . . . He attempted a synthesis too mighty for the human mind."[1] But evidently he could not help it: "Expansion of my studies is after all my nature, and I do not wish to change that even if I could."[2]

The fascination with human life in toto, the conviction that "man" is to be found not in some abstract philosophical definition but amid a historical-cultural process that continuously "defines" him and then partially "undefines" him by way of a continually expanding process of "redefinition" meant in effect that whatever success Dilthey might achieve in his enterprise must be provisional, partial, and permanently corrigible. This should not surprise anyone. Every attempt to deal with man as a whole has ended in results that are provisional, partial, and corrigible. But naturally, like any other thinker, Dilthey hoped for something more. Different as he was in many respects from Hegel, he was one with him in the view that "the truth is in the whole" and that the proper sort of philosophy could validly establish scientific guidelines for studying man and his place in the universal scheme of reality.

Dilthey's personal life was the relatively staid and placid life of a German professor. He was born November 19, 1833, at Biebrich am Rhein, the son of a Calvinist (Reformed) church pastor. His early upbringing and studies were intended to prepare him to follow his father's footsteps in the ministry. After finishing his *Gymnasium* schooling in nearby Wiesbaden in 1852, Dilthey studied theology for three semesters at the University of Heidelberg. Actually he was more interested in the *history* of theology and of Christianity than he was in theology in the traditional sense, just as he was more interested in the history of philosophy than he was in abstract systems. As a twenty-five-year-old student he envisioned a "history of the Christian *Weltanschauung* of the West" as a major lifetime project (V:xxiii-xxiv). (Throughout this introduction, references to Dilthey's work are to the *Gesammelte Schriften* [Leipzig and Berlin: Verlag von B. G. Teubner, 1923–], 19 vols. Roman capitals refer to volume numbers, including volume I, and roman lowercase and arabic numbers refer to pages.) Dilthey always regarded history rather than abstract speculation as the key to understanding all things human. His chief mentor at Heidelberg was the pantheistically oriented historian of philosophy, Kuno Fischer, and his move to Berlin in 1864 brought him under the influence of another historian of philosophy, especially Aristotelianism, Friedrich Adolf Trendelenburg. It became increasingly clear to the young Dilthey that theology was not his proper field although, for his parents' sake, he passed the state theological examination in 1864. However, he also passed the state philosophical examination in the same year. He was now outfitted for an academic career.

A scholarly academic career was indeed the story of his life. Dilthey spent virtually all his adult life in research, writing, and teaching, with great intensity and unflagging dedication. He received appointments to chairs of philosophy at Basel (1866), Kiel (1868), and Breslau (1871), before receiving his most prestigious appointment to the chair of philosophy in Berlin (1882) to replace Lotze. Dilthey stopped his university teaching in 1905 to devote his time exclusively to scholarly contemplation, research, and writing in a desperate effort to pull together the major strands of his thought into a systematic foundation for the human sciences and the "critique of historical reason" to which he devoted his life. He never fully achieved these supreme career ambitions. Dilthey died October 1, 1911, at Seis am Schlern near Bolzano.

There is ample testimony that Dilthey was highly esteemed in his time as a man of vast erudition and original scholarship. He had a loyal, loving band of students and followers on whom he made a powerful lifelong impression. The publication of his writings and the introductions written for some of them give testimony to that. His close friendship with Count Paul von Yorck, to whom he dedicated the *Einleitung,* is an admirable example of a fruitful philosophical collaboration over many years. And yet, as one of Dilthey's students and the editor of some of his works wrote of him: "I do not know whether anyone can say that he knew Dilthey. Despite the many things he produced, people experienced his effects, they felt the living power which emanated from him rather than being able to give an account of the personality which created those effects."[3] Herman Nohl, another of his students, wrote of him: "What Dilthey praises in Hegel, namely his immersion in the objective matter at hand with no thought whatsoever for his own person, was in fact his own quintessential character!" (IV:vi). Even to those who stood close to him and knew him well, "Dilthey" was almost synonymous with "Dilthey's work."

There are doubtless many reasons why, despite the important influence he has had on several leading twentieth-century thinkers and the growing attention paid him in the English-speaking world, Dilthey's work is still not as well known, nor as well received, nor as accessible as it might be. We have already alluded to the enormous scope of the work, which extends over the whole range of the human sciences. His *Collected Works* run to nineteen volumes, and there are thousands of pages of notes, sketches, and essays in the *Nachlass,* only a small part of which has found its way into the *Collected Works.* Even the work that has been published in orderly fashion has invariably appeared in partial or introductory form. For example, he never supplied the missing second volume to the *Leben Schleiermachers* or the second (and crucial) volume to the *Einleitung in die Geisteswissenschaften.* Many of his major essays are of the "Contributions toward . . ." or "An Introduction to . . ." variety. Hence Groethuysens's comment: "And if one then read his writings, this impression was strengthened: the beginnings of great projects, preliminary sketches for comprehensive works, scattered essays, which have the effect of announcements of something to come."[4] Dilthey confessed to Edmund Husserl that he was largely responsible for the misunderstandings his work occasioned because he had the habit of allowing preliminary thoughts on a topic to be published and then holding back the development of these "for further reflection." "This quality earned him the unflattering title of 'man of the half-volume' and 'the great fragmentist'; it is said that he provided not introductions but 'introductions to introductions.' "[5] Ortega y Gasset justifies the need for going beyond what Dilthey actually wrote to do justice to his own intentions because "it is characteristic of Dilthey that he never succeeded in thinking through to the end, in shaping and mastering his own intuition. . . . In the pursuit of his own idea Dilthey stopped midway. Hence the lack of fullness and precision, of cogency in all his formulations. It would be pointless to discuss them if we left them in their own inadequacy."[6] (This is a point of view that Dilthey, along with many others, held about Kant's works: these needed to be "completed" by a further development. Dilthey, too, believed that one could understand an author better than he understood himself.) The nature of his work and thought is suggestive of the title of a large part of Franz von Baader's work in the early nineteenth century: *Fermenta Cognitionis.*[7] Perhaps it is partly because of Dilthey's inability to crystallize his thought as a whole into anything like a single "major work" or "system" that his work is widely regarded as merely *transitional,* as leading to later, more substantial, philosophies and systems.[8]

Part of the problem of reading Dilthey is his style. He writes in a relentlessly abstract idiom, preferring such expressions as "psychophysical units," "dynamic complexes," "socio-historical," "nexus of purposes," and the like, to more concrete language. Much of what he intends to say he merely suggests, but does not formulate clearly. Often he repeats favorite ideas or turns of phrase in his convoluted style; at times he covers the same topic several times in proximity to one another, for example, his treatment of "cultural systems" and "external organizations of society" in the *Einleitung.* On occasion he almost leaves the reader with the sense that he is writing in a stream-of-consciousness technique.[9]

Although there is a substantial unity of direction in Dilthey's thought and work, his personal history of development led him at various stages of his career to prefer different approaches, topics, and emphases in dealing with his lifetime project. Thus his search for a foundational science for the human sciences led him first to favor psychology as the pivotal discipline, then phenomenology and its allied doctrine of the intentionality of ideas, and finally hermeneutics; all this makes it important to distinguish the order and date of his writings. These are but some of the reasons why there are many interpretations about what Dilthey "really" said and thought. There is a measure of hermeneutical challenge in dealing with any philosopher's work; Dilthey's is no exception. Thus this word of caution may be superfluous: This introduction does not claim to be a comprehensive or completely adequate presentation and critique of Dilthey's work. It is but a summary of some of its salient and most important features followed by a general critical assessment.

Basic Philosophical Concepts and Influences

Although the foregoing suggests several reasons why Dilthey's thought and work are not easy to understand and analyze, it is far from being the case that they are a mere hodgepodge of disjointed and random mental exercises. Dilthey's thought and purpose do have a unity and direction about them as a whole. The purpose of this section will be to identify and describe a complex of some of Dilthey's most distinctive and critical ideas and attitudes that, taken together, characterize his philosophical work as a whole.

Philosophy of Life

Dilthey's *Grundgedanke,* or kernel idea, is expressed in several different but connected formulations in his writings. The most all-encompassing and adequate of these is that his work is first and foremost a "philosophy of life," more specifically a philosophy of the meaning of the mind's manifestations or "objectifications" of life. "The dominant impulse in my philosophical thought is my desire to understand life in its own terms [*aus ihm selber*]," says Dilthey (V:4). His "everythingism" was confined within the parameters of "life," which is coterminous with human reality and functions as an absolute. He rejects Kant's view that time is merely phenomenal because that would make life itself merely phenomenal. So Dilthey concludes forcefully:

> Thus arose the thesis [*Satz*] that thought cannot go behind life. To view life as appearance is a contradiction in terms, for in the process of life, in growing out of the past and stretching forward into the future, we encounter the realities which constitute the dynamic system and value of our life. If there were a timeless something which existed behind life which courses forward in past, present, and future, then this would be an antecedent of life; it would therefore be something which would be a condition of the course of life in its entire organization. This antecedent would then be precisely that which we have not had living experience of and would thus be merely a realm of shadows. (V:4)

While evaluating Lotze's epistemology in his essay "Erfahren und Denken," Dilthey makes the point in a different way:

> Life itself, the living reality [*Lebendigkeit*] behind which I cannot go, contains connections which hold the key to explaining all experience and thought. *And it is here that the decisive point lies for the entire possibility of knowledge*. We have knowledge of reality only because life and experience contain the framework which we find in the forms, principles, and categories of thought, only because we can show that framework analytically in life and experience. (V:83; Dilthey's italics)

Dilthey stands foursquare on "the standpoint of life" (V:136) in his thought. "Here is life itself. It is always its own proof" (V:131). Such expressions about life course through all Dilthey's work like a leitmotiv.

In going back to life as the foundation of all reality for human beings Dilthey was registering his profound feeling that rational speculation and metaphysical theories had utterly failed to explain the meaning of human life in the world. Otto Bollnow summarizes the point: "The loss of faith in reason as the supportive basis [*den tragenden Grund*] of the external world as well as one's own life indicated the decisive point which determines our current philosophical situation, and it is the presupposition without which it is fundamentally impossible to understand Dilthey."[10] Dilthey's animus against abstract speculation and arid reason comes to evidence constantly in his writings. Despite his admiration for the modern classical philosophers in some respects, Dilthey shows in his preface to the *Einleitung* how far he believed they had strayed from the core of life in their thought:

> The human sciences constitute a system which is independent in its own right. If it is true that on such matters I found myself to be in agreement on many counts with the epistemological views of Locke, Hume, and Kant, nevertheless I was compelled to conceive of this relationship of the facts of consciousness, in which all of us agree to recognize the whole basis of philosophy, in a different way than they did. If one sets aside some impulses, few in number and never developed scientifically (such as those of Herder and Wilhelm von Humboldt), earlier epistemology, both empirical and Kantian, explains experience and knowledge on the basis of a framework which is purely ideational. *There is no real blood flowing in the veins of the knowing subject fabricated by Locke, Hume, and Kant, but only the diluted juice of reason as mere mental activity.* But dealing with the whole man in history and psychology led me to take the whole man—in the multiplicity of his powers: this willing-feeling-perceiving being—as the basis for explaining knowledge and its concepts. (I:xviii; my italics)

It is not thought or reason that is at the core of life; on the contrary "the core of what we call life is instinct, feeling, passions, and volitions" (V:xc). Thought is unquestionably important in life and is the power that makes it possible for man to develop science, which Dilthey prizes. But thought is nevertheless *about life* and must try to explain life; if it strays from that foundational task it evaporates into airy mist and empty phantasms. Thought exists to express and articulate experience, but fundamental or primordial experience for Dilthey is *lived experience* [*Erlebnis*, from *Leben*, life], a reality of consciousness that is ultimate and prior to reflection, "behind which" one cannot go. Such experience contrasts with the notion of *Erfahrung*, or experience that entails taking an attitude toward an object and evaluating it, a kind of "secondhand" experience described and dealt with in associationist psychology. It is not the immediate, inner, and preconscious "lived experience" of life.

Life is full of paradox. It is at once what is closest to us, what we inwardly experience, what our existence consists of, and also an unfathomable mystery: opaque, inscrutable, strange, a "riddle" (VIII:140). As Misch points out, Dilthey uses expressions about "life" or "reality" (synonyms for him), which are "exactly those predicates which appear in original metaphysics as determinations of the All-One" (V:liv). He calls it the unfathomable and the infinite, the ineffable, and so forth. It is Dilthey's absolute, the universal that encompasses all that there is for us. By no means is it just life in the biological or vegetative sense. H. A. Hodges describes life in Dilthey's usage of the term as "not a biological, but a psychological and quasi-metaphysical term referring to all mental states, processes, and activities, conscious or unconscious, and especially those creative and expressive activities which are the substance of history and the object of the human studies."[11] (I would put "metaphysical" in place of Hodges's "quasi-metaphysical" for reasons to be explained later.) Life is Dilthey's touchstone of reality, of truth and knowledge, and of experience for us, yet Dilthey speaks of it in a paradoxical manner. Although Dilthey denies that there is some kind of *Ding an sich* "behind" or "beyond" life as a kind of substratum or ultimate basis for life, of which we see only the appearances, nevertheless life is unfathomable for us. "Nothing exists beyond it for us" (V:1vii). "Knowledge cannot penetrate beyond life" (VIII:180). There is no separate or independent "carrier" of life; to assume such is to slip into the morass of metaphysical notions like substance, nature, essence, and other ontological chimeras. "We know nothing except events [*Geschehen*], and we have no right to suppose a subject [*Träger*] of those events, since that would involve transferring the concept of substance into the world of lived experience" (VII:334). We experience events and change in our own psychological states; whether any "thing" changes is something beyond our capacity for knowing. If one customarily describes *change* as "a succession of states within a unity," Dilthey would insist that we cannot know what such a unity might be "in itself." We know neither the world nor even our personal selves: "In the most intense immersion of the self into itself, it does not encounter itself as substance, being, or the given, but rather as life, activity, and energy" (VII:157). "We cannot grasp the 'essence of our self' in inner experience" (V:1x). Much of Dilthey's language seems to imply that there is some objective status of "things in themselves" that we cannot know, but he explicitly denies this. "Life" is all there is; there is nothing behind it.

Dilthey does offer a beginning toward establishing "objectivity" in his essay of 1890, "Contributions toward Solving the Question of the Origin of Our Belief in the Reality of the External World, and Its Justification." His basic idea is that objectivity is not in some universal logical scheme that is apodictic in character, but is in the experience of the will when it encounters *resistance* or hindrance in carrying out its decisions. "It seems to me that it is on the basis of personal life—of the instincts, feelings, and volitions which make it up and of which our body is merely the exterior side [*Aussenseite*]—that the distinction between self and object and between inner and outer arises among our perceptions" (V:96). The section titled "Impulse and Resistance" (V:98–105) argues that we know the objective existence of the physical world only because the impulses of our will experience resistance from somewhere "outside" us. On the face of it, it appears that this argument does not really deal with the possibility that this "resistance" might also come from another part of the subject's experience. One thinks, for example, of Plato's argument for the three basic powers of the soul in the *Republic* (IV:439ff.) in which reason, passion, and spirit are distinguished from one another partially on the grounds that one part of the soul opposes or is at war with another part, for example, reason versus appetite, and therefore must be *different from it yet part of the same soul*.

Ortega y Gasset says that "the new great Idea in which man is beginning to abide is the idea of life. Dilthey was among its first discoverers."[12] He believed that life was Dilthey's great central idea, but that Dilthey did not realize its full implications. Certainly Dilthey was not alone in the nineteenth and early twentieth centuries in his insistence on a "philosophy of life" or in the strong vitalistic strain in his thought; one need only recall Schopenhauer, Nietzsche, Hans Driesch, and Bergson, not to mention any number of Romantic philosophers or those caught up in the Darwinian revolution. But Dilthey was no mere *Lebensschwärmer*. His special and peculiar contribution in this context, as Otto Bollnow points out, is first of all to the effect that Dilthey defines the conception of life as external flux more precisely as an historical process and secondly . . . to the effect that he does not conclude that, just because the rigid concept of being is incommensurate with life, it follows that thought *per se* is incommensurate with life. . . . We speak more precisely in his case of a *historical* philosophy of life. This *combination of a philosophy of life with the problem of history* is Dilthey's specific and decisive accomplishment.[13]

Historicity of Life

At this point we make the transition from Dilthey's formula of a "philosophy of life" as his worldview to a further facet of it: the *historicity of life*. Dilthey's writings, especially volume VII, are full of pronouncements that "man is a historical being" (VII:291, 278), that "man knows himself only in history, never through introspection" (VII:279), that "only history tells a man what he is" (VIII:226), that *"the totality of human nature exists only in history"* (VIII:204; Dilthey's italics), and so on.[14] In saying that "man is a historical being," Dilthey is not simply reciting the obvious truism that man *has* a history, or that historical records help us study man, but that man is an *essentially* evolutionary, developmental being (if that is not too paradoxical a formulation). Ortega y Gasset articulates Dilthey's idea quite forcefully: "But a mere elimination of this residue of rationalism will at once disclose that 'the substance' of man is precisely his mutable and historical consistency. Man has no 'nature'; he has history. His being is not one but many and manifold, different in each time and place."[15]

Dilthey supporters generally insist that he was not a historicist, especially if one reads that as meaning a complete relativist, and they are right (even if it were only on the grounds that no one can be a *complete* relativist). But there is no denying that he took the force of history in human life extremely seriously. The historicist view says, in effect, that traditional philosophical approaches to the study of man have been altogether faulty in that they try to identify and define man's "essence" or "nature" or the "natural law" that governs him. But man's "nature" seems to change and develop through the historical process, and we must relate what we say about him to a specific historical and cultural context. Dilthey does not go that far, but he comes close at times:

> The nature of man is always the same. But only history brings to light what the possibilities of existence are which that nature contains. Not until a change has transpired in the entire status of human life and consciousness can historical analysis understand, subsequently, what has happened on the grounds of human nature and the conditions under which it has emerged. [Historical analysis] can predict only the consequences of an already attained stage of life and consciousness. (V:425)

He recognizes the finiteness and relativity of every kind of historical phenomenon, be it a religion, an ideal, or a philosophical system as "the last word of the historical worldview," but he also recognizes the effort of thinking and of philosophy to achieve universally valid knowledge. He has dedicated his life to reconciling the two, and he feels confident that it will be done (V:9).

Dilthey was steeped in the work and the spirit of the great German Historical School and personally knew and worked with some of its most renowned members, who influenced him greatly: "To these great impressions I owe the direction my mind has taken" (V:7–9). He went beyond most of them in taking the historicist view that man, individually and as a race, is only the sum total of *what he has become,* and that this in turn will evolve continuously into new configurations. At least to the extent that we know him, man is his history, the residue or precipitate of the historical process that has brought him to his current state. In that sense, man is not a nature; man is a history. Therefore, Dilthey's "philosophy of life" necessarily had to be a *history of life.* Every topic Dilthey deals with in the human sciences is accompanied by its appropriate history, that is, its tie-in with "reality." Philosophical speculation treats the data of history.

Dilthey regarded his own philosophical originality as focused precisely on this alliance of philosophy with history in his thought: "The idea of approaching the constitution of the universe by taking the connection between the spiritual and historical as one's point of departure stands in contrast with all previous philosophical development" (V:xliii). Georg Misch comments on this point and cites Dilthey himself:

> And from this awareness the certainty sprang up in [Dilthey] to do philosophical work as a historian, which he then expressed in 1874: The sum total of such "historical research with a philosophical purpose"—understood as "a total experiential-scientific sphere"—will "provide the key for theoretically understanding the world and life." "Out of my persistent preoccupation with historical phenomena this enterprise of my life took shape. I thought at first I could resolve it as a historian, then as a philosopher: in my way of working these are two names for the same preoccupation with historical facts. (V:xliii)

The intimate inner connection between life and philosophy and history comes out clearly in one of Dilthey's statements from the year he died (1911). Commenting on his dissatisfaction with the positions taken by natural scientists on the one hand and their neotheological opponents on the other with respect to understanding human life, he says:

> Out of this situation arose the dominant impulse behind my philosophical thought, namely, to seek to understand life in its own terms. I was anxious to probe ever more deeply into the historical world to seize its soul, as it were. And my philosophical impulse to gain entry into this reality, to establish its validity and to assure objective knowledge of it: this longing was for me only the other side of my desire to penetrate ever more deeply into the historical world. There were, so to speak, but the two different sides of my life's work which thus came into being. (V:4)

Gerhard Masur describes "the mutual penetration of history and philosophy" as "the principal issue of Dilthey's life" and comments: "It was a grandiose and somehow tragic enterprise he had selected, this effort to solve the conflict between the relative and the absolute."[16] It was because Dilthey was totally consumed with that most universal of beings in the universe, man himself, and indeed in all his manifestations, that Dilthey's pursuit of man took him into all the directions that man himself has taken. It is man himself who "jumped on his horse and rode off in all directions." Dilthey merely tried to follow him. He refused to deal with man as a conceptual abstraction concocted in some form of "logicism" [*Logismus*], such as Aristotle's "rational man," a sort of being one could never meet on the street. He insisted that we study man as history and experience have delivered him to us, man as he *is,* not as some timeless and abstract definition describes him. "The new element in my method lies in linking the study of man with history" (V:xlix).

Immanentism

Another complex of ideas and attitude that help elucidate what Dilthey means by his central idea of "life" centers on his rejection of transcendence and his insistence on a this-worldly conception of reality.

We have already noted that although Dilthey was a pastor's son and studied theology in preparation for the ministry, he soon shifted his major interest and focus from theology to philosophy. This was not an unusual phenomenon; quite a few noted German philosophers came out of theology schools, especially the Tübinger *Stift,* and even Nietzsche was a pastor's son. Dilthey's shift was symptomatic of his gradually maturing alienation from religious concerns and orientation toward more exclusively secular and "modern" pursuits. In his lengthy and insightful introduction to volume V of Dilthey's *Gesammelte Schriften* his son-in-law Georg Misch describes how Dilthey began with theology, moved on to the history of theology and Christianity in the spirit of Baur, Strauss, and Schwegler, and in the process conceived a great distaste for medieval Christianity in particular and for anything having to do with "the beyond" in general. Misch cites Dilthey's own words:

> In fact the historian of Christianity has to endure the tortures of Tantalus. . . . I struggle in vain to wring any inner life from this alien material. . . . This mistrust of human nature in its wholesome serenity [*Ruhe*]—that nature which has always been an object of highest admiration to me; this haste towards the beyond and towards transsensual knowledge, which I hate so thoroughly; this sectarianism [*Sektenleben*], which I find simply incomprehensible. (V:xxiv)

More than one critic has commented on Dilthey's difficulties with religion. Thus Ortega y Gasset remarks: "But as [Dilthey] has no true religious belief, study of religion turns for him into study of history."[17] H. A. Hodges notes this not merely as a personal foible on Dilthey's part, but as a possible question mark about his whole enterprise:

> Dilthey confesses that there are things in Christianity which stretch his power of understanding to the breaking-point. That is indeed obvious from what he writes about it. . . . This points to the first deep cleavage in Europe. Those whose reading of history jumps gaily over from Hadrian to the Medici, as if nothing had happened between, may manage not to see it; but in fact the Christian *Weltanschauung,* taken seriously in its own terms, puts a question mark against all the achievements of civilization, ancient or modern. Catholicism has never quite let the world forget this, and Protestantism wakes up to it from time to time with a start.[18]

Despite his Calvinistic background and training, Dilthey's treatment of religion is as though it were all a foreign substance to him; he seems an outsider to it. In fact, Dilthey was totally committed to "the great doctrine of immanence" (V:xxii). His philosophy was to be "broad, clear, and bright. It has nothing to do with the haze of muggy Christianity [*Dunst dumpfer Christlichkeit*]" (V:liv). In his later years Dilthey was to hold that "all dogmas must be reduced to their universal life-value for each living human being [*für jede menschliche Lebendigkeit*]." "Dogmas of first rank, such as are contained in the symbols Son of God, satisfaction, sacrifice, etc. are untenable if one limits them to the facts of Christian history, but in their universal meaning they designate the highest living content of history," the "absolutely incomprehensible nature of historicity" (V:xxvi–xxvii). Because Dilthey regards early Christianity as a mere trivialization of Greek philosophical monotheism, it is no wonder that for him "[Christianity's] development and the mainsprings of its power constitute the most profound and the most difficult problem in the history of humanity" (IX:90–91). He took it for granted—or rather as historically demonstrated—that religion in the traditional Judeo-Christian sense was no longer possible, any more than any metaphysical system was possible in the modern world.

Even though Dilthey rejected Comte's "crude naturalistic metaphysics" (I:107), his accounts of the development of thought and culture in the West show some parallels with Comte's law of the three stages of man,[19] by which man begins with religion, advances to metaphysical philosophy, and reaches the modern high point of (positivistic) natural science. Dilthey generally makes it clear that one cannot go back to the prescientific and precritical stages. To the extent that he allows religion a quasi-serious role in life today, it is associated with poetry and metaphysics as pursuits that try to grapple with the mystery of human life as a whole. Such activities are all right so long as one does not invent new worlds that exist only in imagination. Dilthey assumes as axiomatic that religion cannot refer to anything "real" outside the mind:

> To know what religion is, is so difficult because all its modes of predication and the permanent products in which it presents itself to study as dogma, faith, superstition, religious art, or religious world view *first require interpretation of the movements of the soul which are behind them.*
>   1. Everything which life and its correlative, the world, objectively contain can be an object of religious valuation.
>   2. But religious valuation is never something primordial [*Ursprüngliches*]. Religious value is not, like life-value, etc., a completely independent core of value [*Wertinbegriff*]. On the contrary, it presupposes experiences within the valuation of life. (VII:267; my italics)

Religious reflection and experience is basically an attempt to grapple seriously with the contents of "life," and safeguards us from superficiality about life (VII:266). Perhaps Dilthey would agree with the view that "religion is what one does with one's spare time." It is absolutely de rigueur for Dilthey, however, that true religion cannot refer to anything transcendent. "Life" in immanent terms is all there is.

Bollnow remarks on Dilthey's formula for understanding life in its own terms: "He feels first of all that with this formula he is associated with the *process of secularization* of all spiritual life which began with the Renaissance and the Reformation," and he notes Dilthey's elective affinity with the Enlightenment by recalling Dilthey's statement: "Out of this situation arose the dominant impulse in my philosophical thought: in the spirit of the great Enlightenment to hold to experiential reality as the one world of our knowledge" (V:418).[20] For Dilthey the Enlightenment was "a happy time" (III:192), to which he devoted much of his historical reflection and writing. He was determined to "interpret life in its own terms, excluding transcendent ideas" (V:xxxix).

Another aspect of Dilthey's immanentist orientation to life and reality is his adoption of the critical method and the epistemological approach as the heart of philosophy. As a young man making his inaugural address for his first chair of philosophy, at Basel in 1867, he declared his standpoint:

> For it seems to me that the fundamental problem of philosophy has been established for all time by Kant. The highest and most universal issue in all human inquiry is this: In what form

is the world, which after all exists for us only in our intuitions and ideas, given to us? Through what processes does our image of the external world in which we live take shape out of the scattered stimuli which intrude on our senses from all directions? And then our image of the spiritual world through inner intuitions? . . . And just as unassailable in its broad outlines, though in need of reform in some particulars, does Kant's result seem to me. He says there is no rigorous knowledge except on the basis of what is given in experience. And in fact the object of this rigorous knowledge is the lawfully ordered system of appearances. Therefore the transsensual world is not accessible to any scientific inquiry; it is based on man's mental disposition [*Gesinnung*]. This critical foundation-laying is the universal task of philosophy. (V:12)

Toward the end of the same address Dilthey professes that his own task and challenge "is clearly pointed out: to pursue Kant's critical path in establishing an experiential science of the human mind in cooperation with scholars working in other fields" (V:27). H. A. Hodges points out that "the 'critical' philosophy of Kant is not, at least ostensibly, a psychological study, such as Hume undertook; but it had a like effect in reducing philosophy to a study of the human mind, its activities and forms of experience."[21] Dilthey stresses throughout his work that philosophy is essentially a study of the human mind and its contents; its heart is logic and epistemology. This orientation is of a piece with the broad trend of modern philosophy since the Cartesian revolution centering on his principle of *cogito, ergo sum,* but it contrasts sharply with ancient and medieval approaches to philosophy that made logic a propaedeutic of philosophy, a handmaiden or instrument that served to safeguard philosophers from committing formal errors in reasoning, and regarded epistemology as a philosophical discipline that dealt with a *part* of reality, that is, the possibility of, and the conditions for, knowledge. Dilthey was always a Kantian to the extent that he held that we cannot go "beyond experience" in our knowledge and that any brand of reasoned metaphysics is disqualified as knowledge or experience from the outset.

There are also substantial differences between Dilthey and Kant. One cannot simply call Dilthey a Kantian or a neo-Kantian. The crux of the differences between them lies in their respective views of experience. Kant's view made human experience consist of a hylomorphic combination of abstract a priori categories of understanding and forms of sensibility as the "form" of experience with the "matter" supplied by sensation, as understood in the associationist psychology of the seventeenth and eighteenth centuries. Central Kantian concepts such as his view of the a priori form of time as purely phenomenal, his idea of a "transcendental unity of apperception," his differentiation of what amounted to "logical subjects" from "logical objects," his assumption of a *Ding an sich* existing "behind" phenomena, his purely formal notion of objectivity as mere conformity with the conditions necessary for experience, are but a few of the ideas Dilthey rejected. After calling Dilthey a Kantian "in some sense," H. A. Hodges notes some huge reservations:

Imagine a Kantian who does not believe in an *a priori,* and who thinks that the categories of substance and cause are not forms of the understanding, but projections into the outer world of the inner experiences of the will. Imagine a Kantian who rejects the doctrine of the phenomenality of the empirical self, and believes that in introspection we perceive our own mind as it truly is. Imagine a Kantian who says that philosophy must learn from psychology, and who boasts that his ethic is more empirical than utilitarianism. That is the kind of Kantian whom we meet in Dilthey.[22]

Georg Misch presents Dilthey's summary statement on the question of epistemology from his unpublished "Berlin Draft" of the 1890s:

> Elementary logical operations, as the forms in which we elevate our consciousness of facts to clarity and distinctness, are the presupposition and condition of our thinking. But it is by means of them that we know about them, that they themselves are modes of experience and therefore possess the same certainty as all inner perception. Hence the relation between form and content of thought which Kant establishes and the presupposition of a preestablished harmony between logicism [*Logismus*] and the object, and, going still further back, the entire metaphysical foundational hypothesis of the unity of both in World Reason are dissolved by the analytical knowledge that logicism can be reduced to these fundamental operations as modes of experience. This dissolution acquires an absolute certitude through the great principle that it is a matter of indifference whether these operations are really an ultimate [*ein letztes*], or whether logicism follows from them: we can reduce logicism to those operations and them in turn to experience, and so it is all the same *for the logical structure of thought grounded on* [*experience*] what the genetic connection is. (V:1xiii; Dilthey's italics)

From these and other statements from Dilthey it is clear that he and Kant may have agreed in rejecting metaphysics in favor of epistemology in philosophy and in making *experience* the touchstone of truth and objectivity for man, but it is also clear that their view of experience and reality was very different. Dilthey found Kant's view of experience far too abstract and purely logical in character. He viewed Kant as seriously deficient in historical understanding and as reducing the infinite wealth of human life and experience to the dry bones of arid speculation. Kant lacked a sense of history, and for Dilthey that meant that he lacked a basic sense of man, because history contains the fullness of what man has done and been and therefore of what he is now.

Despite these serious and extensive differences between himself and Kant, however, Dilthey always honored and recognized the basic soundness of the transcendental approach to philosophy: How is experience possible? is still the basic philosophical question. He saw the *Critique of Pure Reason* as "the greatest philosophical work ever produced by the German mind."[23] Kant's philosophy was on the right track but needs completion. What Kant's *Critique of Pure Reason* did to lay the foundation for valid natural-scientific knowledge, what the *Critique of Practical Reason* did to ground the field of ethics, and what the *Critique of Judgment* did to provide a foundational theory for esthetics, Dilthey now wanted to supplement with his own "Critique of Historical Reason." Such a project was indeed synonymous with what Dilthey thought was his special philosophical calling. His goal was to establish a basis for scientific and objective historical understanding of man, a "logic of history" that did not reduce life itself to logicism, but took account of the fullness of historical experience.

Kant had argued in his *Critiques* that we can *know* only the appearances of things, although we do widely employ "regulative" ideas of reason to order our experience of morality and art and to establish the overall architectonic of the mind's functions. We can never *know* the "thing-in-itself" [*Ding an sich*], because it lies beyond the bounds of experience. We know only phenomena; we cannot know noumena. Dilthey's position on this issue is different. He agrees that we can never know "things in themselves" in some kind of "essence," or "nature," or "substance," and that we are fundamentally restricted by the conditions of our experience from being able to answer metaphysical questions generally, such as those dealing with the meaning of the entire historical process. But Dilthey does not posit a *Ding an sich* at all. There is no "second world" lurking somehow "behind appearances" or "beyond" them. There is no noumenon. There is *only* the world of our experience: human life as we experience it is all there is for us. The facts of our consciousness are coterminous with reality. If anything else exists at all, we have no knowledge of it, and it has no meaning for us. "Of course we know nothing about any real world which lies *outside* of our consciousness. We know of reality (i.e., an external world) only insofar as our will and our positing of goals are determined, since our impulses experience resistance" (V:6).

German Classicism, British Empiricism, French Positivism

Dilthey's acceptance of the critical method of Kant's transcendental philosophy, then, was seriously modified by his own commitment to a radically historical approach to reality and experience and by the strong influence of the historical school on him. At least three other major background influences on Dilthey's thought need to be more explicitly mentioned: the German "classical period," British empiricism, and French positivism.[24]

In his inaugural address at Basel in 1867, "The Poetic and Philosophical Movement in Germany 1770–1800" (V:12–27), Dilthey surveys "three generations" of outstanding poets, philosophers, and other literary and artistic figures in the period when the German states were renowned as "the land of poets and thinkers." The sixty-year period centered on 1800 constituted Germany's "classical period,"[25] comprising German idealistic philosophy, romanticism, and the rise of the Historical School among its most powerful components. Born at the end of this period, Dilthey found many of his intellectual and cultural heroes or at least serious thinkers to be reckoned with from that time, among them Novalis and Lessing, Kant, Fichte, Schelling, Hegel, Schiller, Goethe, and Schleiermacher. The general influence of the poets and the romantics on Dilthey was in highlighting the central role of will and feeling in life; in celebrating personal individuality; in appreciating life in all its myriad expressions and ramifications; in inclining strongly toward an historical-genetic approach to man; in extolling diversity against rationalistic uniformity; in feeling a powerful communion with nature, often with pantheistic overtones; in perceiving the tremendous creative potential of poetry as a key to understanding life;[26] in feeling on his very pulse the expansive freedom and endless mystery of human life. Dilthey's generation stood in awe of the tremendous outpouring of genius in the half century immediately preceding it. The giants of that period lived on in Dilthey's mind and feelings all his life and contributed much to forming his "philosophy of life."

Dilthey was much affected also by the general thrust of the "three revolutionary changes" proclaimed by British seventeenth- and eighteenth-century philosophy: the new experimental method in natural science, announced by Bacon; the ousting of metaphysics from philosophy in favor of experience alone, initiated by Locke; and Hume's call for an application of empirical methods used in natural sciences to human sciences.[27] Dilthey insisted that scientific methods employed in studying nature must be complemented by different scientific methods appropriate to the human sciences. More of that later. One thing is abundantly clear in Locke's and Hume's philosophy, and Dilthey agrees on the point: the study of the human mind, psychology, is the pivotal discipline in dealing not only with epistemology, but also with religion, art, politics, law, or any human sciences whatsoever. They are all sufficiently impressed with the egocentric predicament—the fact that literally everything we can know or experience can be known or experienced only in the mind and in its terms—that the study of the mind and its contents becomes the centerpiece of all philosophizing.

Paradoxically, the empiricist position seems to become an idealist one, not only for a self-professed idealist-empiricist of the stamp of George Berkeley, but even for a Locke and a Hume. They escape that conclusion by insisting that psychology functions like other physical sciences in a physical world and works with physical realities. For his part Dilthey accepts the challenge, which he regards as the most difficult in all philosophy, of establishing the reality of the external world in his essay of 1890, "Contributions toward Solving the Question of the Origin of Our Belief in the Reality of the External World, and Its Justification" (V:90–138). His answer, as we have seen,[28] centers on the experience we have that our impulses encounter resistance in their activity, and this experience is as original with us as the experience of our own mental states. In other words "the world" is not something we have to establish independently, because it is as immediate to us as ourselves. Dilthey did not subscribe to Locke's and Hume's philosophies entirely, especially not to their crude associationist psychology, but he agreed with them that the analysis of the mind and its contents was the heart of the philosophical enterprise. References to their work as well as to that of their nineteenth-century successors John Stuart Mill and Herbert Spencer are numerous in Dilthey's work.

French positivism's foundational work, Auguste Comte's *Cours de la philosophie positive,* began being published in the year Dilthey was born and was completed nine years later in 1842. It held a scientistic position that consisted of a philosophy based on a natural-scientific model that recognized only natural phenomena and laws governing them as real. In effect, natural science explains everything. To believe otherwise is simply to have failed to keep pace with human progress to its current "positive" state. Comte held that history shows a process of development of the human mind from its earliest *theological* stage, in which it tried to answer ultimate questions about the universe and human life by recourse to gods or spirits, to a *metaphysical* stage, in which it addressed similar issues but tried to answer them by abstract reasoning, and finally has arrived at Comte's own stage of *scientific* or *positivistic* explanation, which analyzes all phenomena in their order of simultaneity or succession in time and space. Comte was resolved to establish a science of "sociology" on the positivistic model to replace current moral, political, psychological, and historical theories, which were all still tainted with vestiges of religion or metaphysics. Dilthey explicitly repudiates Comte's version of sociology (I:86ff.; see p. 128ff. of this volume), regarding it, like speculative philosophy of history, as a crude modern version of metaphysics. Dilthey was not a Comtean, but he grew up in a generation dominated by the positivist-materialist approach to man, and he had to contend with that fact in elaborating his own theory of the human sciences. But he was also in broad agreement with Comte's law of the three stages of man, his basically historical approach to understanding man today, and his commitment to solving the social problems and crises of his age through his philosophy.

Toward a "Critique of Historical Reason"

We have noted that Dilthey saw his life's work as establishing a "Critique of Historical Reason," that is, a theoretical basis for understanding human life historically, a kind of "logic of history." What kinds of tools or instruments did he develop for this undertaking?

To begin with, we must recognize the distinction in modes of consciousness indicated by the terms *Erlebnis* and *Vorstellung*.[29] *Erlebnis* ("lived experience," from *Leben,* life) indicates an immediate and prereflective experience of something, an experience in which there is virtual identity between the conscious person and that of which he is conscious, a kind of "unconscious consciousness." Writing in 1908 Dilthey formulates his thoughts on the subject again:

> *Erleben* ["living experience"] is a variously characterized way in which reality is present to me. For an *Erlebnis* does not confront me as something perceived or something represented; it is not given [to me]. On the contrary, the reality which is lived experience is present to me by the fact that I am inwardly aware [*innewerden*] of it, that I immediately possess it as something belonging to me in some sense. Only in thought does it become an object. (VI:313)

He goes on to describe *Erlebnis* as a kind of primordial experience behind which we cannot go (like life itself); one that is neither "given" nor "thought" but immediate. "The expression *Erlebnis* designates a part of this process of life itself. As such it is a reality appearing immediately as such, of which we are aware without subtraction [*ohne Abzug*], not given and not thought" (VI:314). It is incorrect to think of an *Erlebnis* as a given or datum of consciousness because that implies that one is making a distinction between subject and object, between the person who "has" the experience and the contents of the experience itself. The concept of *Erlebnis* is absolutely crucial to Dilthey in formulating his key distinction between natural sciences and human sciences.

Vorstellung ("representation"), on the other hand, implies the subject-object distinction: the "subject" adopts an attitude toward the content of his consciousness and treats it as an object to know, judge, evaluate, and so forth. The natural-scientific approach to reality builds on this idea and this approach. But the basic stuff of life and experience at the primary level consists of *Erlebnisse,* which consist of cognitive, affective, and volitional elements, which, taken together, make up our "psychic structural complex" [*psychischer Strukturzuhammenhang*]. At the level of "lived experiences," the mind has not yet "come to self-consciousness," or to reflective consideration of what the lived experiences mean.

How does one come to know these experiences and "bring them to consciousness"? How does one think about them? The crucial process by which this happens is one in which life *expresses* itself in certain ways, and the expressions of life or "objectifications of life" are known through an inner process of *Verstehen,*[30] or "understanding," through which life comes to know itself. When we "understand" something, we see it in its proper interrelationship of whole and part in the general swirl of mental life and experience. Dilthey uses the term technically to apply to understanding of mental realities exclusively, never physical ones, and he tended to focus more and more on apprehension of the meaning of "objectifications" of experience through *Verstehen*. Thus a kind of paradigmatic pattern emerges: an *Erlebnis* produces an *Ausdruck* ("expression") which is known through *Verstehen*. This means that we come to know life only *indirectly,* or through its expressions. Dilthey makes this clear in the following statement:

> What we once were and how we have developed in such wise as to become what we are now is something we learn from how we have acted, what life-plans we once conceived, how we were active in an occupation, from old lost correspondence, from judgments about us which were expressed long ago. In short, it is the process of understanding [*Verstehens*] whereby life

in its depths achieves illumination about itself. On the other side, we understand [*verstehen*] ourselves and others only because we introduce our own lived experience of life [*unser erlebtes Leben*] into every kind of expression of our own life and that of others. Thus the combination of lived experience, expression, and understanding [*Erleben, Ausdruck, und Verstehen*] is the specific process whereby mankind exists for us as an object of the human sciences. Hence the human sciences are grounded in this connection of life, expression, and understanding. (VII:87)

It is easy to see how central history is in this schema. Borrowing a formulation based on Hegel's doctrine of "objective spirit," Dilthey identifies the "objectifications of life" as the central body of *facts* (literally = "things made"), which tell us about life and about ourselves. Not through introspection, but through examination of the products of human life and activity in the form of such "objectifications" of thought as law, religions, buildings, cultural systems, etc., do we understand life and the mind. It is not merely external realities we come thus to know: "Even the psychophysical living unity [= man] is known to himself through the same double relationship between *Erleben* and *Verstehen*" (VII:86). "Only his actions, his fixed expressions of life and their effects on others teach man about himself; thus he comes to know himself only by the detour of *Verstehen*" (VII:87). "In short, it is the process of *Verstehen* whereby life receives illumination about itself in its own depths" (Ibid.). As the old formulation adopted by Giambattista Vico put it: *scimus quod facimus,* we know what we have made.[31] Dilthey's idea is the same: "The human sciences possess as their comprehensive given the objectifications of life. . . . Spirit understands only what it has created. . . . Everything on which man has put his stamp in the course of his activity constitutes the object of the human sciences. . . . And now we can say that *everything in which spirit has objectified itself* falls within the sphere of the *human sciences*" (VII:148; Dilthey's italics).

Verstehen in Dilthey's usage refers to understanding spiritual or mental reality, that is, understanding other people first, then indirectly ourselves,[32] but also the great cultural manifestations of spirit in society and its institutions. It is the cement that makes the world of human affairs cohere: "*Verstehen* is a rediscovery of the I in the thou. Spirit rediscovers itself at ever higher plateaus of organization. This selfsameness [*Selbigkeit*] of spirit in myself, in you, in every subject of a community, in every system of culture, finally in the totality of spirit and of universal history makes the cooperation of the different accomplishments of the human sciences possible" (VII:191). *Verstehen* is thus the mode of understanding all things human, both on the individual or interpersonal levels and on the level of societal bodies. "Mutual *Verstehen* assures us of the *community* which exists between individuals. . . . The community of living individuals is the point of departure for all relationships of the particular and the universal in the human sciences" (VII:141).

Psychology, Phenomenology, Hermeneutics

As we shall see in more detail, the great task of Dilthey's life—understanding life through history—took the form of providing a scientific epistemological foundation for the human sciences, a foundation intended to put them on as solid a basis as the natural sciences. This is a task Dilthey never finished, though he wrote many sketches and essays that were meant to lead to that goal. During the course of elaborating ideas to this end, he settled on three main stopping points in his search for a foundational science: psychology, phenomenalism, and hermeneutics. It is not as though he believed that there was one single science at the basis of all scientific pursuits, nor even that he believed that there was one such science for nature and another for the human sciences. But he did believe that both the natural and the human sciences need a foundational science to clarify the correct relationships among the special sciences and provide a systematic overview of them. The foundational science would not dictate to the special sciences; instead there would be a continual process of interaction between them. Dilthey never seemed to be totally satisfied that psychology or phenomenalism or hermeneutics provided him fully with the answer he looked for. In the progress of his speculation on the subject he did not totally discard his previously won but temporary stopping points, but tried to incorporate all his gains in a final synthesis which never came to be. One recalls the view that Dilthey's program was one that "no mortal . . . could hope to bring to completion."

For a long time both before and after the *Einleitung* (1883), *psychology* seemed to offer the most promise as a foundational science for the human sciences. The psychological approach to philosophy, with its classic champions in the British empirical tradition of Locke, Berkeley, and Hume, appealed strongly to Dilthey: he, too, saw philosophy as a study dealing with the mind and its contents; saw human nature as the key to human thought and reality; found the "plain historical method" congenial; rejected all obfuscations of metaphysics; and regarded "experience" as the bedrock of knowledge and truth. On the other hand, Dilthey found the opposed rationalist tradition, with its view that purely empirical science resting on merely contingent facts could never achieve the universal and apodictic certitude which an a priori foundation can supply for philosophy, less congenial. He protested against rationalist formalism and a priorism all his life, not only in Kant and in such neo-kantians as Windelband and Rickert, but in the whole history of metaphysics.

Dilthey's own brand of epistemology insisted that we need not establish knowledge or its validity, nor our own existence nor that of the external world, since life and experience provide such knowledge immediately. Psychology need only scrutinize closely what consciousness itself contains and analyze what the psychological foundations are for our use of basic terms like "real," "exist," "truth," and "value" to provide us with a foundational science for the human sciences (see V:149ff.).

A true psychology did not exist as yet. Dilthey complained that traditional psychology was seriously flawed in being excessively formalistic, excessively mechanistic, and excessively superficial. It had virtually nothing meaningful to say about the higher reaches of human experience in art, religion, poetry, and creativity generally, as well as also being deficient in ethical theory. Existing explanatory [*erklärende*] psychology also had the serious defect that its results were purely hypothetical and open to controversy so that a "war of all against all rages in its sphere no less savagely than in the field of metaphysics" (V:142). Hume's ideal of building a psychology on physical laws in the tradition of such naturalists as Lucretius or Hobbes was false to Dilthey's understanding of human nature.

Dilthey hoped to remain in the sphere of psychology for his foundational science, but he wanted a psychology free of hypotheses based on a physical model. In his 1894 essay, "Ideas Concerning a Descriptive and Analytical Psychology" (V:139–240), he calls for a purely descriptive and empirical account of consciousness that rejects any attempts at causal explanation. We do not experience substances or causes as such—they are merely artificial mental constructs or hypostases, which are purely metaphysical—but we do experience the fullness of life. All psychology needs to do is to *describe* and *analyze* what we experience, especially in all the great productions of the human mind, historically. We need an organization of *types* of human behavior for classificatory purposes, but we must not add extraneous elements from metaphysical theory.

In 1894 the psychologist Hermann Ebbinghaus delivered a powerful attack on Dilthey's descriptive psychology at its very heart, the supposed self-givenness of psychic organization of data. He insisted that description and experience do not speak for themselves as purely as Dilthey had maintained; on the contrary, we really *superimpose* patterns and hypotheses on mental contents just as we do with physical contents. Dilthey wrote a rejoinder, but the dispute was never really resolved. The discussion became more and more involved, and Dilthey began to despair of ever reaching agreement about even the fundamentals of psychology.

About the same time, Dilthey was also seriously engaged in controversy with the neo-Kantians, led by Windelband and Rickert, who insisted against Dilthey that a purely descriptive psychological approach to reality can do nothing more than merely register facts; it cannot supply values or go beyond mere facticity without an a priori transcendental foundation. In their eyes Dilthey was guilty of "psychologism," historicism, and the chief corollary of historicism, relativism. For his part he charged the neo-Kantians with extreme formalism, which inevitably leads to total subjectivism and skepticism, and dissolves the richness of experience into thin mists of ideas. The effect of these continuing and inconclusive controversies led Dilthey to withdraw for a time from active theorizing about such matters in favor of writing some purely historical essays.

What brought him back to the barricades of epistemological controversy was the publication of Edmund Husserl's *Logische Untersuchungen* (1900), which provided in Dilthey's view " 'a rigorously descriptive foundation' of the theory of knowledge as a 'phenomenology of knowledge' and thereby created a new philosophical discipline" (VII:10). This "epoch-making" book was one to which he owed a great deal "in utilizing description in theory of knowledge" (VII:14). Despite the close association of the label "phenomenalism" with Husserl's name—a term that might imply we do not know things outside us in an "objective" manner but only in their "appearances" (phenomena)—Dilthey was most struck with his doctrine of the *intentionality* of consciousness and of our ideas. An idea "intends" its object; it does not just toy with ideas for their own sake. Husserl laid heavy stress on the *objectivity* of knowledge, on the claim that our ideas deal with what *is* in fact, and not just with the conditions of our own way of knowing. We do not simply perceive *sensations* bearing certain characteristics; we sense *objects* with those characteristics. Knowledge is not about the knower, but about the known. Although Husserl insisted in his first volume on the validity of formal principles of thought and of objective content, he went on in his second volume to stress the correlative importance of empirical data and descriptive psychology. Husserl's thought made a powerful impression on Dilthey for a reason Michael Ermarth puts succinctly: "Of all existing philosophies, Husserl's phenomenology came closest to a viable, broad-ranging synthesis of transcendental and empirical standpoints. Its appeal for Dilthey must have derived in considerable measure from its roots in the tradition of *Idealrealismus* of which he felt a part."[33]

Dilthey believed that Husserl had gone very far indeed to span the difference between a purely subjectivist psychologism on the one hand and a purely rationalist and a priori formalism on the other hand. His ideas could aid Dilthey substantially in providing a solid scientific and logical component to infuse into Dilthey's philosophy of life and to fend off charges of psychologism. Ermarth sums up again: "After reading Husserl, Dilthey asserted with new assurance that the relations which characterize mental life are not causal relations among psychic acts but structural relations among the contents of those acts. Perhaps most significantly, Husserl provided a new kind of critical test for the validity of cognition, which avoided the strictly formalistic logical coherence of the Kantians."[34]

But Husserl did not give Dilthey completely what he wanted. Useful as he judged the phenomenological method to be, Dilthey was convinced that it did not go far enough or deep enough to serve as the foundational science for the human sciences generally. He eventually came to feel that Husserl had lost his earlier balance and had lapsed into a position strongly verging on the ontological/metaphysical and creating a new kind of *Ding an sich,* in effect, by allowing some measure of what is "intended" in knowledge to remain forever and in principle "beyond" the pale of possible experience. For his part, Husserl published an article in *Logos* in the year Dilthey died (1911), which contained "a searing indictment of all forms of relativism, historicism, psychologism, and 'world-view philosophy.' "[35] The article seemed to be aimed in part at Dilthey, but Dilthey denied that such charges applied to his philosophy.

In Dilthey's later years, even after Husserl's great impact on him, he began to have less and less confidence that psychology and epistemology could ever develop into the kind of foundational science he had hoped they would. In these later years he turned more toward various kinds of "structural coherences" (*Strukturzusammenhänge*), "dynamic coherences" (*Wirkungszusammenhänge*), and other kinds of *Zusammenhänge* to identify nodal units of experience in clusters that could serve to classify experience, identify typical patterns in it, and recognize its salient uniformities better. It was in his later years also that Dilthey turned his most serious attention to his doctrine of *Verstehen,* of objectifications of experience, and of hermeneutics as the science that develops the laws of interpretation we need to understand man by the objectified creations of his spirit in history.

Dilthey gradually came to look upon hermeneutics as the key to understanding as a result of his long-standing reflection on the nature of *Verstehen.*[36] He set down his main thoughts on the subject in his essay "The Rise of Hermeneutics" in 1900 (V:317ff.). As usual in his work, Dilthey pairs a systematic-theoretical section with a historical review of the topic. The paradigmatic sense of hermeneutics in its conventional sense is its use as a theological tool that provides the rules and procedures to be followed in interpreting biblical texts correctly. Dilthey takes hermeneutics in a broader sense in extending it back to the ancient Greeks. He recognizes Schleiermacher as the father of scientific hermeneutics. Dilthey uses a hermeneutic approach in interpreting the objectifications of life produced by man. As we have seen, he believes we know ourselves only indirectly, through the things we have made, the objectified or fixed residues of our thoughts in physical things like buildings or tools and especially in cultural achievements. He obviously assumes an analogy between traditional interpretation of a written text and the broader interpretation of life's objectifications. Dilthey ends his article:

> Let us summarize. *Verstehen,* compared to mere linguistic monuments, becomes an interpretation which attains universal validity. If philological interpretation in hermeneutics becomes conscious of its process and its justification, then Fr. A. Wolf might justifiably assess the

practical use of such a discipline, compared with its living practice, as not very high. But beyond this practical usefulness it seems to me that a second, indeed *principal, task* for the business of interpretation consists in this: in the face of the constant inroads of romantic arbitrariness and skeptical subjectivity into the realm of history, it should establish theoretically the universal validity of interpretation on which all certitude in history rests. Adopted into the framework of the epistemology, logic, and methodology of the human sciences, this doctrine of interpretation will be an important connecting link between philosophy and the historical sciences, a major component of the foundation-laying of the human sciences. (V:331)

The reason why a new measure of objectivity would be available in Dilthey's hermeneutic scheme to combat the romantics and the subjectivists is its focus on completed, existing objects, the existence of which, at least, no one can dispute: "Even the most stringent attention can become an artistically sound procedure [*zu einem kunstmässigen Vorgang*], which has attained a controllable degree of objectivity, only if the expression of life is fixed, so that we can return to it over and over again. Such *artistically sound Verstehen of permanently fixed expressions of life we call exegesis or interpretation*" (V:319). *Verstehen* exhibits different degrees, but it "attains its highest perfection . . . in exegesis or interpretation. By this expression we mean the artistically sound *Verstehen* of permanently fixed expressions of life" (VII:309). Most prominent and most important among such fixed expressions of life is language and literature: "The immense significance of literature for our understanding of spiritual life and history lies in the fact that the inner life of man finds its complete, exhaustive, and objectively comprehensible expression only in language. Hence the art of *Verstehen* centers on the exegesis or *interpretation of the remains of human existence contained in writing*" (V:319).

In his last years, then, Dilthey seems to have modified his earlier central interest in psychology substantially, first under the influence of attacks on it by Ebbinghaus and the neo-Kantians, then under the powerful influence of Husserl's phenomenological approach and his theory of intentionality, and finally under the influence of his hermeneutical approach to understanding not only individual men but also cultural systems and organizations that have acquired an "objectified" form in history. He never departed from his lifelong goal of producing a "critique of historical understanding" as a foundation for the human sciences, but he did pass through substantially different phases in his search for a foundational discipline. Full success eluded his grasp, but he was hopeful even in his later years, concluding his address on his seventieth birthday with the words: "I see the goal. And if I fall by the wayside—my young fellow travelers, my students, I trust, will travel the path to the end" (V:9).

Worldviews

One further major piece of Dilthey's general philosophy needs to be briefly addressed: his theory and typology of worldviews.

Despite Dilthey's belief in truth and in scientific method, in objectivity and understanding, he also often speaks of life as essentially puzzling and mysterious, full of uncanny, dark, and menacing forces. Life is unfathomable, immeasurably deep, inscrutable, ineffable. He uses such expressions not only to describe the attitudes of primitive peoples toward life, but also to describe his own attitude. Thus, for example: "In lived experience we could not comprehend our own self, either in the form of what it discharges [*seines Abflusses*] or in the depth of what it comprises. For the tiny circle of conscious life rises like an island out of unfathomable depths" (VII:220). Dilthey has a strong sense for existentialist concerns such as

> the mystery of life and death, generation and development, chance and relativity. . . . Hegel constructed metaphysically; we analyze the given. And today's analysis of human existence fills us all with the feeling of frailty; the power of dark instinct; suffering from opaqueness and illusions; finitude in everything that is life, even where the highest structures of community life arise from it. Thus we cannot understand objective spirit from reason; on the contrary, we must go back to the structural organization of living persons [*Lebenseinheiten*]. (VII:150)

In short, we are immersed in a sea of the unknown, of mystery, which Dilthey refers to as "the puzzling character [*Rätselhaftigkeit*] of life." The immensity and unfathomability of life plus the ever present element of *chance* in all our doings leaves us with a great challenge to find a focus of stability and integrity for our experience.

From man's overwhelming need to put together a pattern of *meaning* for his life as a whole emerges a *Weltanschauung,* or "worldview," in Dilthey's terminology.[37] Its main purpose is to make sense out of life as a whole: "It is the task of the theory of worldviews [*Weltanschauungslehre*], by analyzing the historical course of religiosity, poetry, and metaphysics in opposition to relativity, systematically to present the relationship of the human mind to the riddle of the world and of life" (V:406). A worldview is not a scientific conclusion or a rational system, but a general sense or feeling about how life as a whole hangs together. Like all things human, worldviews must be studied historically first of all. History shows us that worldviews have arisen from religion, from poetry, and from a metaphysical type of philosophizing. "When a worldview has been raised to a level at which it is grasped and grounded conceptually and thus claims universal validity, we call it metaphysics" (V:401). Dilthey insists that a worldview is only a relative and partial view of reality and that metaphysics is impossible in a systematic philosophical sense. But people do formulate worldviews nevertheless, and Dilthey recognized that activity as something basic to man. He undertook to develop a typology of worldviews on the basis of a comparative-descriptive historical review and analysis.

Although he recognizes that there are many forms of worldview in many hybrid and nuanced combinations, Dilthey finds that history has three principal forms of worldview to show us:

> From the motley manifold of such nuances of worldview, their coherent, pure, effective types stand out significantly. From Democritus, Lucretius, and Epicurus to Hobbes, and from him to the Encyclopedists and to modern materialism as well as to Comte and Avenarius, despite great differences in the systems one can still trace a connectedness which binds these groups of systems into a unitary type whose first form we can designate as *materialistic* or *naturalistic* and whose further development under the conditions of critical consciousness logically leads to *positivism* in Comte's sense. Heraclitus, rigorous Stoicism, Spinoza, Leibniz, Shaftesbury, Goethe, Schelling, Schleiermacher, and Hegel mark the stages of *objective idealism.* Plato, Hellenistic-Roman philosophy of the concepts of life represented by Cicero, Christian speculation, Kant, Fichte, Maine de Biran and kindred French thinkers, and Carlyle make up the developmental steps of the *idealism of freedom.* (V:402)

Hence naturalism, objective idealism, and the idealism of freedom are the three main forms of worldview historically.

Dilthey's doctrine of worldviews holds that these views do not merely reflect a concept or idea of the world, but also encompass the whole range of feelings, attitudes, and evaluations of reality, which make up one's *Lebensstimmung,* one's mood or sense or feeling of life as a whole. The major components of a worldview are a "world picture" (cognitive in character and based on thought), "ideals of life" (based on will and activity), and "experience of life" (based on feeling and values). All these elements are present in every person, but the relative weight given to each one varies, hence his association with one of the worldviews that best reflects his dominant element. A *naturalist* sees man primarily as a part of nature and subject to its laws; his orientation in life is mainly cognitive, and he explains all suggestions of a spiritual order of reality in an ultimately physical way. The *objective idealist* takes a pantheistic view in which mind and body are coalesced into an overarching unity; everything and everyone is part of the same universal reality. He tends to see life largely from the standpoint of feeling and art or esthetics, poetry, and music, and the contemplation of beauty. The *subjective idealist* or *idealist of freedom* puts intellect and freedom and the marks of personality generally at the summit of reality and as at least ontologically prior to any form of matter; he sees man as an *acting* being in pursuit of ideals and moral norms, which transcend physical nature. There is a general correspondence here between the three major worldviews and Kant's three *Critiques* by which the naturalist would be placed with the *Critique of Pure Reason,* the idealist of freedom with the *Critique of Practical Reason,* and the objective idealist with the *Critique of Judgment.*

Dilthey does not set one of the worldviews above either of the others, nor does he say that any one of them derives from another one. As we have seen, no one type is hermetically sealed off from the others, and all sorts of combinations of worldview are possible in individual persons. Nevertheless, each person tries to make his view of the world a coherent meaningful whole that enables him to live around that core of meaning and to arrange all the elements of his experience with reference to it. Elements of other views will be there, but a person will favor one of the three main worldviews and subordinate the others to his main view: "Every great impression shows a man a special side of life; then the world receives a new illumination: if such experiences are repeated and combined, new moods about life come into being. . . . Universal attitudes arise. They change, as life shows man ever new sides (of itself): but certain life moods [*Lebensstimmungen*] are dominant in various individuals, depending on their own peculiar makeup" (VIII:81).

Dilthey was profoundly disturbed by "the anarchy of worldviews," just as he was by the anarchy of metaphysical systems, each of which seemed to contradict and eliminate its competitors in terms of the requirements of reason, none of which, however, could establish itself as the whole and all-sufficient truth in contention with those competitors. Because of Dilthey's view of this seemingly irresolvable conflict among worldviews, as well as because of his pronouncedly historical (if not historicist) method and his affinity with some kinds of vitalism, many analysts regard Dilthey ultimately as a skeptic unable to deal with the destructive implications of wholesale *relativism.* It was certainly not his intention to affiliate himself with the views of skeptics, relativists, or historicists; on the contrary, he believed in and strove for objectivity in his philosophy and validity in his science. Thus in discussing the problems of the history of religion he writes that they "are soluble only in a general scientific system, which depends on philosophical investigations. This system, however, must be objectively valid knowledge which *stands above all unprovable Weltanschauungen,* and is therefore not metaphysical in the old sense" (VI:303). If the charges of relativism, skepticism, and historicism are to be laid at Dilthey's door, one must show that they belong there implicitly in virtue of his own principles despite his explicit rejection of them in his life and thought.[38]

The question which one of the three main worldviews Dilthey belonged to personally is difficult to answer. He never assigned himself to any one of them, and he has prominent aspects of all of them in his thought. The same is doubtless true of the many thinkers Dilthey "assigns roles" to in his typology. Some have seen him as predominantly an objective idealist and as having a worldview that has much in common with Goethe. In any case, Ermarth reminds us of "Dilthey's insistence that all types are only 'provisory' and heuristic," and states that Dilthey "can only be regarded as representing a combination of all three [views]—with the major constituents being objective and subjective idealism, but with a considerable dose of naturalism." Better still, Dilthey is "beyond" any one of the views or, perhaps best of all, "he is both immanent and transcendent to them."[39] Has he perhaps become like God, with a kind of "absolute viewpoint" (with apologies for the paradoxical expression)? Not really, but every worldview tries in effect to "square the circle" of the infinity of being and life in a perspective or combination of perspectives.

Introduction to the Human Sciences

The point is frequently made that Dilthey's lifework was to produce a "Critique of Historical Reason"; one could also describe it by the title of the book here translated: *Introduction to the Human Sciences.* The book he wrote in 1883 contains the theory that "serves as a framework for understanding Dilthey's conception of philosophy, psychology, literary criticism, and history, as well as his analysis of the relations among them and associated disciplines."[40] His whole life was focused on the enterprise of distinguishing the human sciences from the natural sciences and developing a firm theoretical foundation for the human sciences that would establish them as solidly and incontestably as the natural sciences. The sciences of nature needed to be distinguished from, and complemented by, the sciences of man; as mathematics and mechanics are foundational sciences for the study of nature, so too a foundational science must be found for the human sciences. Dilthey spent his life trying to supply one.

Human Sciences

The expression "human sciences" [*Geisteswissenschaften*] poses some problems,[41] not only in English but in German. Dilthey addresses the basic problem:

> The sum of intellectual facts which fall under the notion of science is usually divided into two groups, one marked by the name "natural science"; for the other, oddly enough, there is no generally accepted designation. I subscribe to the linguistic usage of thinkers who call this other half of the intellectual world the "sciences of the mind."[42] In the first place this description has become common and generally understood. . . . It also appears to be the least

inappropriate term, compared with all the other unsuitable labels we have to choose from. It expresses the object of this study extremely imperfectly, for in this study we do not separate data of intellectual life from the psychophysical living unity of human nature. . . . But the expression shares this drawback with every other one which has been current. Science of society (sociology), moral, historical, cultural sciences: all these descriptions suffer from the deficiency of being too narrow with respect to the object they are supposed to be expressing. And the name we have chosen here has at least this merit: it rightly identifies the central core of facts from which one sees the unity of these sciences in reality, maps out their extent, and draws up their boundaries vis-à-vis natural sciences, although imperfectly. (I:5–6)

So Dilthey had to choose between such designations as "cultural," "historical," "moral," "social," "sociological," and the like to describe his subject matter. The problem is compounded further in English by *our* having to render Dilthey's choice of *Geisteswissenschaften,* a hybrid word that has no exact and univocal English equivalent for either the *Geist* part or the *Wissenschaft* part. The modifier "human" seems most appropriate to Dilthey's meaning, because he intended to indicate the entire range of human experience by it, not just the mind's or the spirit's. "Sciences" is better than "studies" even though "science" in English commonly designates the natural or exact sciences, because Dilthey's whole intention in this enterprise was to develop a systematic epistemological and psychological foundation for a "science of man": English usage might well be expanded to advantage in adopting a more generic sense of "science" that reflects German and French usage. Thus the term "human sciences" indicates a group of systematic and methodical scholarly investigations, encompassing the entire range of humanistic and socio-scientific disciplines, which inquire into man as an individual as well as a member of society, particularly with respect to aspects of human life that set it apart from purely natural-scientific inquiry. Each such discipline examines a particular dimension or facet of human life; together they make up our scientific knowledge of man as man. Dilthey's project was first of all to establish the distinction between natural sciences and human sciences as fundamental, and then to discover or develop a foundational science for the human sciences as a group, a "grounding" for them that would put them on a par with the natural sciences.

Among the supplementary materials to the *Einleitung* is one in which Dilthey comments on the organization of the *Einleitung:*

> The starting point of my work is the sum total of research which probes into man, history, and society. I am not beginning with an object, that is, human-social-historical reality, and the relationship of knowledge to this object. These are conceptual abstractions, necessary in their place; indeed, this reality is only an ideal concept that indicates a goal of knowledge we can never fully reach. The factual element given as the foundation of every theory consists of intellectual efforts which have issued from the purpose of knowing man or history or society or mutual relations among these moments.
>
> Each of these efforts is defined by the relation of a knowing subject and its historical horizon to a specific group of facts likewise limited in its range by a fixed horizon. For each of them the object exists only from some point of view. Each is thus a definite relative way of seeing and knowing its object. To one who enters into these labors they confront him as a chaos of relativities. *Subjectivity* [is] *the modern way of viewing things.* (I:412; Dilthey's italics)

This passage makes it clear that Dilthey was acutely aware of the limits of what he could hope to achieve in his undertaking: the goal of knowing man is only an ideal we can never fully attain; our efforts are partial, limited, and subjective. Though he hopes to establish a foundational science for the human sciences that will enable us to classify them properly and define their interrelationships, the unfathomable depth of human life will never give us an absolute and comprehensive verdict about itself.

In his enterprise Dilthey is resolved to remain within the parameters of *Empirie,* or experience in all its dimensions, and not give way to the attractions of transexperiential metaphysical schemes; but he will not limit experience to *Empirismus* in the narrowly positivistic sense of experience that has become a new metaphysics in its own right. So he maintains that the opposition between eighteenth-century natural law systems and the nineteenth-century Historical School can be reconciled "only by laying a foundation for human sciences which maintains the standpoint of experience, of full-blown experiential knowledge [*der unbefangenen Empirie*], even in the face of empiricism [*Empirismus*] itself" (I:81). This insistence on the full range of experience is crucial to Dilthey's approach to the human sciences and to all his efforts to understand man: "*The basic idea of my philosophy* is that thus far no one has ever made total, entire, unmutilated experience— therefore total and full reality—the foundation of philosophizing" (VIII:171; Dilthey's italics).

Natural Sciences and Human Sciences

Why did Dilthey write the *Introduction?* His reason was that natural scientists since Bacon's time have written treatises on the foundation and method of natural sciences, and "it seems necessary to perform a similar service for those who work in history, politics, jurisprudence, or political economy, theology, literature, or art" (I:3). "My hope is that this introduction will lighten the task of politician and jurist, theologian and teacher: to know the role of the principles and rules which guide him in relation to the comprehensive reality of human society" (I:3). Dilthey also notes the critical importance of understanding the forces at work in modern revolutionary society and ways to deal with them, and "that is why the significance of sciences of society has been growing in comparison with natural sciences" (I:4). Thus there were both theoretical and practical motivations behind the enterprise.

After dealing with the reasons for his choice of the term *Geisteswissenschaften* to stand as his counterpart to *Naturwissenschaften,* Dilthey sums up the justification for that fundamental distinction on which the entire project of the *Introduction* and of his life's work depends:

> The motivation behind the habit of seeing these sciences as a unity in contrast with those of nature derives from the depth and fullness of human self-consciousness. Even when unaffected by investigations into the origins of the mind, a man finds in this self-consciousness a sovereignty of will, a responsibility for actions, a capacity for subordinating everything to thought and for resisting any foreign element in the citadel of freedom in his person: by these things he distinguishes himself from all of nature. He finds himself with respect to nature an *imperium in imperio,* to use Spinoza's expression. (I:6)

Dilthey goes on to note how man's life comprises values and goals and how, in contrast with the objective necessity that governs nature, "freedom flashes forth at innumerable points" in the life of man; how the actions of man's mind and will produce true development in human life; how man is capable of self-sacrifice in the cause of achieving his goals. "And all this means something above and beyond the tedious and empty repetition of the process of nature in the mind."

Dilthey takes time at the outset to note the far-reaching aberrational effects of man's tendency to plunge into unwarranted metaphysics by making a gratuitous leap from subjective bases of explanation into objective differences in the structure of reality itself. Especially harmful has been the distinction metaphysicians have made between the world of minds or spirits and that of bodies and between the concepts of essence and existence. A result of these distinctions has been a fundamental dualism in the concept of man's understanding of himself and of reality that has plagued him to the present day. This dualism is shot through with insoluble antinomies that have had the effect of a "constantly irritating spur toward dissolving the metaphysical standpoint altogether" and eventually led man to the realization that concepts like substance arise when self-consciousness accommodates its experience to external experiences, based on the principle of sufficient reason. A result is that we have abandoned the doctrine of material and spiritual substances in favor of a more modest distinction between an outer world we perceive through the senses and an inner world we conceive by reflecting on our immediate experience of psychic events. We can deal with this latter distinction empirically.

All one needs to establish the human sciences as a separate class of sciences, says Dilthey, is simply to distinguish events that the mind links together on the basis of sense impressions from events given primarily in inner experience and without intervention of the senses. Natural sciences will deal with sense-based facts, and human sciences will deal with inner experience. After all, no one can explain the essence of the emotion, the poetic creativity, and the rational reflection that went into the making of a Goethe by physical explanation alone (I:9). Dilthey's full argument for the distinction between natural and human sciences, however, is coextensive with the entire *Introduction*, an enterprise that "combines an historical methodology with a systematic one" (I:xv). As in Hegel's *Phenomenology*, so here too, "the truth is in the whole." But at the outset Dilthey wishes to stress simply the asymmetry and disproportion between material and intellectual processes as a basis for recognizing two different kinds of sciences: "The fundamental problem consequently is establishing the precise kind of incommensurability between relations of intellectual processes and uniformities of material processes which would preclude reducing the former to mere characteristics or facets of matter" (I:12). Dilthey makes the usual arguments based on the unity of consciousness and the spontaneity of will to show the impossibility of reducing mental phenomena to purely physical causes. He concludes the section by citing Du Bois-Reymond to the effect that a "will" in the component elements of matter, which "should will whether it wants to or not, and this in a relation of direct proportionality of the masses involved and in inverse proportion to the square of the distances," is a contradiction in terms (I:14).

Dilthey does not deny the influence of physical nature on man's world: "In reality . . . an individual comes to be, continues to be, and develops on the basis of functions of the animal organism and their relations with surrounding processes of nature." Man's life is a "psychophysical unity." Depending on which point of departure one chooses to adopt in an effort to reconcile the opposing elements, one could arrive at two different and mutually irreducible views: (1) Start from inner experience, and you will find that all nature is subject to the conditions of consciousness: this is the approach of German "transcendental philosophy." (2) Start with the world of nature, just as it is in time and space, and recognize that nature has a constant effect on man's nervous system and his entire body in countless ways, and you will find that consciousness is subject to conditions of nature: this is the approach of the positivists. You have to do justice to both points of view; each has some justification. In general one can say that "mental facts are the highest boundary of facts of nature; facts of nature constitute the lower conditions of mental life" (I:17).

Nature conditions man in two respects. On the one hand the physical structure of the universe affects socio-historical reality in varying ways and degrees; on the other hand man's purposeful activity has its own effect on nature and the earth, but the instruments man uses in his activity are also subject to conditions of natural law. Thus man's purposeful activity in the world is not a case of "mind over matter," but of mind using matter. In the hands of Copernicus a few pages of ancient Greek manuscript became the impetus behind a whole new world picture for man. The relationship between mind and nature is reciprocal. Thus wars are fought for political purposes, but they are fought with instruments of physical force to coerce an enemy to adopt a different attitude, often with regard to physical real estate boundaries and so forth. Physical laws of both organic and inorganic nature come into play: not only laws governing our nervous systems and bodily characteristics, but also laws of geography, climate, raw materials, and so forth. And if man seems to be acquiring ever greater control over nature, this comes about only by following the principle *natura enim non nisi parendo vincitur* (For nature is not overcome except by obeying her; I:20). As for understanding nature as it is "in itself," Dilthey's view is that this is a matter of indifference in his context: "It is enough that the mind can count on nature's lawfulness for the mind's activities in whatever way it encounters nature, enough that the mind can enjoy the beautiful appearance of nature's existence" (I:21).

Dilthey then moves on to provide a provisional survey of "this other half of the *globus intellectualis*," the special human sciences. These sciences still need an overarching organizing principle, because they have come into being haphazardly from the practical requirements of life itself. Examples include the development of Roman law and Greek political theory. Philosophers have tried to provide a general systematic foundation in the past, but they have foundered in the mire of metaphysics. Some—like Bacon, Comenius, Mill, and Spencer—have had the merit of trying to deal with the whole range of the human sciences, but they have been seriously defective in historical knowledge and have succumbed to the modern rage for scientific constructionism, which has had the paradoxical result of making positivism itself the latest form of metaphysics. Others' attempts have been one-sided. Dilthey renders the following verdict about how the problem must be met: "Human sciences do not constitute a whole because of a logical constitution which would be analogous to organization of the knowledge of nature; their structure has developed differently and has to be considered henceforth as it has evolved historically" (I:24).

The content of these sciences consists of "historico-social reality insofar as the consciousness of humanity has preserved it as historical information and insofar as it has been made accessible to science in the form of social information encompassing the present state of affairs" (I:24). But this stock of information, enormous though it is, is spotty and randomly assembled. We have satisfactory materials only in the history of ideas and, in a few isolated instances, in statistics. Much collecting, classifying, and interpreting of materials needs to be done.

Psychology, Anthropology, Ethnology

Dilthey distinguishes three main types of assertion made in those materials: observable *facts*; *theories* created to explain facts; and *value judgments,* often combined with rules of conduct. How they relate to one another requires sound epistemological analysis to decide, but one thing is certain: "Statements about reality in value judgments and imperatives remain radically distinct; hence two kinds of propositions emerge, which are fundamentally different from each other" (I:26–27).

"The goals of the human sciences—to lay hold of the singular and the individual in historico-social reality; to recognize uniformities operative in shaping the singular; to establish goals and rules for its continued development—can be attained only by the devices of reason: analysis and abstraction" (I:27). One needs good abstraction in history, just as one needs good historical data in abstraction if one is to achieve good results. It is vital to recognize that "every special science of the mind consciously lays hold of and knows socio-historical reality only relatively, in its relationship to other sciences of the mind" (I:28). We need a general science that will classify and analyze these special sciences in their mutual relationships.

Individual man himself is the basic element in society and in history, hence in the human sciences; Dilthey is guilty of no "fallacy of misplaced concreteness" here. The human sciences have an advantage in this area of inquiry, because while natural scientists have had to struggle to achieve a tenable view regarding matter, "intelligence finds unity immediately given in its own makeup, a unity which is the basic element in the intricate pattern of society" (I:28). Whereas natural science must proceed hypothetically in taking matter apart conceptually, human sciences have a veritable "inside track" through inner experience, which is direct and immediate, not hypothetical.

The pivotal studies of human beings are *anthropology* and *psychology*,[43] because "the whole of history and life experience makes up their content" (I:29). Although it is true that we have absolutely no intellectual facts apart from individual psyches, individual psychology represents only a fraction of the content of the human sciences. The reason is that man is not just an individual; he is also a member of society, "an individual who is selected from the living structure of historico-social reality" (I:30). No human being is a subject of psychological analysis *alone,* apart from social relationships. One has to avoid the extremes represented by two opposite historical errors, one of which tries to define a "human nature" apart from the historical family of society, and the other of which subsumes every individual under some sort of general idea, such as Aristotle's view of the individual's relationship to the state as that of a part to a whole, or the organic concept, or the notion of a "folk soul." Dilthey rejects all forms of "constructionism" of this kind, that is, synthesized or hypostasized notions that are metaphysical, but he does recognize that "the man whom sound analytical science studies is the individual as a component of society." (I:31–32). Psychology must analyze his social characteristics, and in that capacity anthropology-psychology is the basis of all knowledge of historical life. Anthropology-psychology must analyze empirical data to develop a correct *typology* of man because: "Some type of human nature always stands between the historian and the sources out of which he hopes to awaken figures to pulsating life; some type of human nature stands just as truly between the political thinker who wishes to outline rules for society's development and the reality of society itself. Science will concede correctness and fruitfulness only to this subjective type" (I:32). To accomplish this task, psychology and anthropology must widen their horizons beyond merely recognizing uniformities into recognizing the variety of types of human life and expression that history shows us. In the process they must confine themselves severely to describing *facts* without indulging themselves in hypothesizing. At this point in his career Dilthey has reached a conclusion about the central role of psychology among the special human sciences: "The simplest finding which analysis of socio-historical reality can come up with lies in psychology; accordingly, it is the first and most basic special science of the mind. Correspondingly, its truths are the basis for further construction. But its truths contain only a partial content culled from this reality" (I:33). Because psychology is partial and limited in character, Dilthey states that an *epistemological foundation* is required to relate psychology to other human sciences and to reality itself.

The importance of a full and complete study of the individual comes out clearly in Dilthey's treatment of the function of *biography*. Dilthey himself wrote a first volume for a biography of Schleiermacher and *Hegel's Jugendgeschichte* as well as many biographical essays about great German historical figures.[44] He has an exalted view of the worth of biographical writing: "Understanding the totality of an individual's existence and describing its nature in its historical milieu is a high point of historical writing, fully as valuable in the profundity of its undertaking as any historical description which uses more wide-ranging materials. Here one appreciates the will of a person in the course of his life and destiny in its dignity as an end in itself. The biographer ought to look at a person *sub specie aeterni*" (I:33). To know history and to know human nature one has to know human individuals in the context of the generations and the whole of history.

Analysis that deals with the whole of historico-social reality differs from that which deals with individuals. The French and English have developed *sociology* to deal with this topic, which is much more complex and intricate than the study of individuals is. However, in comparison with the study of nature, which is mute, alien, and external to us, the study of society is far more congenial. "Society is our world" (I:36); we can know it inwardly and intuitively. Although we can establish far more mathematical and formal uniformities in the sphere of nature than we can in sciences of society, where the variables and imponderables seem endless, "nevertheless, all this is more than outweighed by the fact that I myself, who inwardly experience and know myself, am a member of this social body and that the other members are like me in kind and therefore likewise comprehensible to me in their inner being. I understand [*verstehe*] the life of society" (I:37). The common nature we share with other men gives us a unique capacity for understanding them. How do we do that? "The organ of understanding which functions in human sciences is the whole man; great achievements in those sciences do not proceed from mere power of intelligence but from strength of personal life" (I:38). In studying the flow of history men have tried to understand not only their individual places in their own cultural settings; they have also tried to understand what the whole of society, contemporary and historical, means. In their efforts to achieve that broader understanding they have developed many special human sciences.

The art of historical writing holds an especially vital place among the human sciences, because in its descriptive presentation of the past it shows us the universal in the particular; it recognizes types in human history and allows us to make generalizations about man's life and experience. History provides the materials for *anthropology* of the human individual and for *ethnology,* or comparative anthropology, which differentiates varied groups of human beings and examines "how the human race is naturally articulated" into races and peoples as relatively independent cultural and social units. In the process notions such as "nation," "folk soul," "folk spirit," and "organism" are formed, which Dilthey considers to be "as useless for history as the concept of 'living force' is for physiology" (I:141). But not all is dross in such study, for "between the individual and the intricate process of history, science finds three great classes of objects to study: *external organization of society, systems of culture* in it, and *individual peoples*" (I:41–42). All three are interconnected and interdependent.

External Organization of Society, Cultural Systems, Individual Peoples

Dilthey feels a strong urge to dispel abstract notions such as art, science, state, society, and religion from people's minds to lead them more directly to the realities of historico-social life in more concrete and real terms. One has to deal with permanent individual relationships, on the one hand, and with permanent social structures on the other. Family and tribal ties create homogeneous communities, but historical life regularly leads people also to form complexes of common purposes or associations of will that go beyond such communities. Dilthey distinguishes between *cultural systems* in society, which embrace such pursuits as religion and art, language and science, in which people freely engage and cooperate for commonly felt purposes, and *external organizations* of society, which include the state or other powerful entities that embody a collective will and are based on relations of mastery, dependence, property, and community.

Dilthey calls a complex of purposes working toward a common end a *system,* and claims that systems are of many kinds, not just logical ones. There can be economic or artistic or religious systems, for example. Logic, after all, is only one aspect of the fullness of human life and interest. Concepts that deal specifically with systems of culture, as opposed to concepts used in individual psychology, are referred to as *second rank concepts* in the formation of the human sciences, and the principles one establishes with their help are *second rank truths* in the order of the human sciences. Study of the systems of culture uses concepts derived from psychological analysis, but "this relationship is so complicated that only a coherent epistemological and logical foundation, that starts from the special position of knowledge in relation to historical and social reality, can fill the gap which still exists even today between special sciences of psychophysical individuals and those of political economy, law, religion, and so on. Every researcher in the special sciences feels this gap" (I:46). Dilthey's life work was closely linked to the task of establishing such a foundational science. He found that the efforts of French and English scholars to perform this task were inadequate and ineffective, often centering on tiresome debates over the relative merits of deduction versus induction. Dilthey was not looking for some sort of "absolute science," which he would have rejected as simply a metaphysical version of a worldview. The foundational science must instead be built up from the findings of the whole complex of special sciences in an empirical way; it must in turn recognize the uniformities and principles operative in them to be able to classify and interrelate them correctly.

Dilthey holds that human cooperation in the systems of culture does not proceed in a purely mechanical or rational way. Human interactions require other permanent associations, the most obvious of which is "the state." Human passions and sense of community lead to the *external organization* of humanity besides the systems of culture. Its foundations are as deep as those of the cultural systems. In external organization, too, one feels the urgent need to fill the missing gap in the human sciences, namely the foundational science that holds the special sciences together. What is needed is a *single* foundational science which embraces *both* cultural sciences and external organization of humanity, and clarifies the basis for the constant interaction and complementariness between them.

Systems of culture are based ultimately on the richness of the single individual's life in society, a richness not only of ideas, but also of acts of will and of feelings. Thus there is a great variety and complexity in such systems. The systems are permanent; individuals come and go. Each generation contributes more to the existing accumulated fund of experience, which is grounded in and reflects the dominant component of human nature peculiar to each of the systems of culture. Hence systems like law, art, and religion can acquire a permanence and massive objectivity about them, which make them stand out quite independently of the individuals they embrace. Individuals participate commonly in many cultural systems simultaneously, as Dilthey well illustrates with an example that might apply to him personally:

> If a scholar writes a book, this event can be one more link in the chain of truths which comprise science; it is also the most important part of an economic process transacted through the manufacture and sale of copies; moreover it has its legal aspect as the fulfillment of a contract, and it can be a part of the scholar's professional functions, which is fitted into the general administrative picture. Writing down each syllable of this work is thus a part of all these systems. (I:51)

In addition, all of these systems constantly relate to and interact with the external organizations of society.

Dilthey uses the example of *law* as a clear instance of interaction between cultural systems and external organization of society:

> Thus the relations which govern systems of culture and external organization of society with respect to each other in the living complex of purposes of the historico-social world refer to a fact which is the condition for all consistent activity of individuals, a fact in which both systems of culture and external organization of society are bound together as one. This fact is *law*. In it there exists in undivided unity what then goes its separate ways into systems of culture and external organization of society. (I:54)

Law precedes any separation of cultural systems from external organization of society. Law is "a system of purposes grounded in consciousness of justice as a permanently operative psychological fact" (I:54). The consciousness of justice noted here as the basic human component in the legal cultural system is not so much a theoretical matter as it is a matter of the *will* to coordinate wills under one standard of conduct. Law is always a correlative to external organization of society: their mutually dependent reciprocal relationship is something that only an epistemological and logical foundation of the human sciences can clarify. Law presupposes the *general will* or collective will and authority of the community in a specific sphere. Law appears only in the form of imperatives, behind which stands a will that intends to push those imperatives through. It expresses the will of some part of the external organization of society, such as the city, the state, or the church. These bodies maintain their imperatives and seek to punish any infractions of them, even when they lack the power to do so. Law depends on individuals' notions of justice, but law also depends on a will-endowed social organization. It combines aspects of cultural systems and external organization of society, therefore, and acts counter to the general pattern by which individuals tend to split off more and more from creations of the general will.

In the sphere of *morality,* inner culture breaks off from external organization of society in practical matters. Language and religion, art and science, tend to go their own ways, regardless of pressure from external organizations of society. Although these and other cultural systems loom before us as great, massive objective facts, we must study them and their functions in the context of their historical origins and development *before* considering them scientifically. History shows us that the reciprocal relation between law and external organizations of society does not obtain between morality and those external organizations. A system of morality exists, but it does not rest on custom, nor on the record of past human behavior, nor on expedience. It exerts a pressure called moral obligation on a person, a kind of "internal compulsion," which contrasts with the external compulsion associated with law. A particularly difficult point in considering morality is moral motivation, "for only the connection between motive and action is clearly apparent to us; motives themselves appear in a way quite mysterious to us. Hence man's character is a mystery for him, which only his mode of behavior partially unveils to him" (I:62). In general, Dilthey holds, moral motivation consists of a combination of the imperatives of *conscience* and *public opinion*; together they enable morality to function as one of the great cultural systems in society.

Though cultural systems depend primarily on psychical elements in individuals united for a specific purpose, the *external organization* of society is based on relations of community, external association, and domination and subordination of wills in society. *Subjectively* speaking, everyone discovers his will in a nexus of external connections and in relations of dominance and dependence. "The same undivided person is at once member of a family, director of a project, member of the community, citizen, member of a church organization, and at the same time, perhaps, associate in a mutual association or political society" (I:65). *Objectively* speaking, everyone is united by a nexus of community relations and obligations into which he is born, such as the family, the state, and the church. Associations of this kind are "one of the most powerful devices of historical progress," because they unite the generations of man in abiding structures of great influence over the ages. Dilthey is particularly impressed with the historically abiding structure of the Roman Catholic church through many generations.

Consciousness of community and *relations of dominance and dependence* between wills are two psychological facts of second rank, which Dilthey identifies as underlying external organizations of society. Both are merely relative and limited in their effectiveness. Both are also intricate and complex. One must face the difficult problem of the extent to which one can derive facts of the second order (those of the external organization of society) from psychological facts of the first order (those of the cultural sciences) and the even more difficult question of establishing an adequate psychological-epistemological-logical foundation for the human sciences as a whole. But *all relations of association* are composed of the facts of community and dominance/dependence. These two sets of facts "course through the external organization of society like lifeblood in the most delicate system of arteries" (I:68). They also fill human life even apart from any existing association. Thus community and organization exist through sharing common soil and common labor; a sense of national community may long outlast the political form of a state, or precede it for that matter, as the example of the ancient Greek city-states shows. "These two basic psychological relations constitute the entire framework of external organization of humanity. The will-relationship reflected in dominance and dependence finds its limit in the sphere of external freedom; community-relationship finds its limit in the extent to which an individual exists only for himself" (I:70).

An *association* is a permanently established union of wills among people for a specific purpose. One of the things that the human sciences must do is develop an appropriate terminology for their specific material and avoid confusing their language with that of the natural sciences. There is no univocal definition of the boundary between an association and other kinds of cooperation in society. Contractual arrangements differ from associations in that they are *per se* permanent. The work of artists may lead them to form an association, but it does not necessarily do so. The Roman distinction between *societas* and *universitas* might illustrate when a contract becomes an association in a Roman setting but not in a German one. One has to beware of applying constructionist models, especially of the natural law variety, to historically shaped realities of human experience in varying contexts and cultures. Everything associative starts with the family, but it goes in many directions and in many combinations from there.

"The family is the fruitful womb of all human order, of all group life: a community of sacrifice, an economic unit, a protective association, grounded in the powerful natural bond of love and reverence. . . . But even this most concentrated form of unity of will among individuals in the world is only relative. Individuals who make it up do not enter into it totally; *the individual exists in his ultimate depths for himself alone*" (I:74; my italics). Families also make up tribal associations, but the state always embraces the broadest form of social alliance. External social organizations develop beyond the family at an early stage, and the sheer abundance of forms of external organization is immense: from insurance and stock companies, to family life, to despotic states.

As noted above, the role of law and the state is especially important in the life of society. The issue of the existence and force of *natural law* and its relation to positive law is another point of great relevance to the law's complex of purposes. Unfortunately, natural law theories have been ridden with unjustified metaphysical abstractions in place of realities, and one needs to purge them of such excesses. Indeed, the problem that natural law tried to address "is soluble only in cooperation with positive sciences of law," and for their part the latter need to be grounded solidly in epistemology and psychology. In any case, history never shows us an instance of a true law that is not also involved in the external organization of society.

One should note that sciences dealing with external organization of society are abstract; like any other theory they lay hold of only a part of the content of concrete reality. No association swallows up a person entirely. Even the power of the modern state has only a relative and partial sway over the individuals who compose it: "There is something in them which is only in the hand of God" (I:82), in a turn of phrase reminiscent of Ranke's "every individual is immediate to God."

After a brief historical excursus into the history of theorizing in political science, Dilthey concludes this part of his discussion with what has now become a virtual refrain: "Even at this point we see the necessity of laying an epistemological and logical foundation that will clarify the relation of abstract concepts to socio-historical reality" (I:86). He rejects the tendency of political scientists to treat society as a reality existing in its own right.

Philosophy of History and Sociology

The next several sections of the *Introduction* Dilthey devotes to rejecting the pretensions that both philosophy of history and sociology have of being true sciences.

When man examines the extremely diverse and complex data and patterns of purposeful human behavior that constantly shape and reshape cultural systems and external organizations of society, he also entertains a wish to know reality *as a whole:* "We are unceasingly thrown up against the most general and ultimate problem of human science: Is there *knowledge of this whole* of historico-social reality?" (I:87). Each of the special sciences leads us in a different direction; nothing is there to interrelate their work. At a minimum the paths of scientific, moral, and esthetic inquiry are irreducible to one another, so Dilthey reformulates his question: "Is there a science which comprehends this threefold system which transcends special sciences and grasps relations between historical fact, law, and the rule which guides judgment?" (I:89).

German philosophy of history and British-French sociology claim to be such a science. Philosophy of history is really just a secularized development of the Christian notion of a theology of history under divine providence as advanced by Clement and Augustine in antiquity and Vico, Lessing, Herder, Humboldt and Hegel in modern times. Sociology, on the other hand, was spawned by the revolutionary natural-scientific attitude marking the close of the eighteenth century. It began with mathematics and worked toward a comprehensive science of society at the hands of Condorcet and Saint-Simon, Comte, Mill, and Spencer. Both theories are fatally flawed, because they impose abstract schemata of reason or faith on the facts of history and reality. "History no more has any such final and simple word to divulge that would express its true meaning than nature does. . . . If one speaks of philosophy of history, that can only mean historical research with a philosophical purpose and with philosophical means" (I:92). "Therefore those theories of sociology and philosophy of history are false which see in presentation of the particular mere raw material for their abstractions" (I:91).

Both philosophy of history and sociology try to do the impossible, the first by wanting to reduce history to a unity, the second by claiming a total knowledge of society.

The growth of special sciences over the centuries has given us a wealth of information about man. What we need now is a foundational science, which would enable us to integrate our knowledge into a whole. But though special sciences are the sole means we have for understanding history, the science of history itself is moving constantly forward. To know history we must know all the facts and their interrelationships. We need to be able to fit fact, law, and rule into a single unity and provenance, and this is manifestly impossible. All the formulas meant to explain the whole of history are nothing but metaphysics, each form of which centers on a different abstract idea.

The philosophy of history claims to formulate the essence of world history as well as the meaning of the historical process, that is, its value and its purpose (I:96). It may be naturalistic or teleological; it is always universal in its claim; it hypostasizes values and purposes in the world even though "an arrangement of reality can never have value in itself but only in its relation to a system of energies" (I:97). Dilthey insists that the meaning of history must be an extraordinary composite of historical data; it cannot be something imposed on history from the outside. But philosophy of history does not use historical analysis; it persists in its own universal metaphysical ideas.

The root of philosophy of history is actually in religion:[45] "It can be shown with more lucid clarity for philosophy of history than for any other branch of metaphysics that its roots lie in religious experience and that it dries up and withers away if torn away from this matrix. The idea of a unitary plan of human history, of a divine idea of education through history, has been created by *theology*" (I:98). Theology "knows" the beginning and end of history as revealed in the Bible. Augustine's *City of God* traces this world from a metaphysical beginning to a metaphysical end in a philosophy of history that "constitutes the middle point of medieval metaphysics of the spirit" (I:98–99). Bossuet's *Discours sur l'histoire universelle* carried forward the same idea, and Turgot secularized it. Vico leaves the theological parameters of history untouched, but he works like a true historian within them. The eighteenth and nineteenth centuries produced other secular versions of the meaning of the historical process in such forms as Lessing's "education of the human race," Hegel's "absolute spirit," and Comte's positivism. In each case, metaphysical substances such as universal reason, or the world spirit, or society supply the God-substitutes needed in the theories that regard history as the development of these forms of absolute. The upshot of these and other attempts Dilthey surveys is always the same: the mists of metaphysics, shadows without reality.

The *methods* used in philosophy of history and in sociology are fundamentally wrong. The German movement began with men immersed in historical factuality, such as Winckelmann, Herder, the Schlegels, and Humboldt, but it ended with men who cut themselves off from that living root and ended with pure abstractions like Hegel's "spirit" or Schleiermacher's "reason." French sociology, on the other hand, claimed to have vanquished metaphysics with positivism, but Comte simply created a naturalistic metaphysics of history to replace older speculations. John Stuart Mill did not break completely away from Comte's errors, insisting with him to the end that intellectual facts can and must all be reduced to natural-scientific laws. Comte regarded biology as the basic science that would explain all there is to know about the foundations of sociology. Dilthey exclaims: "Crude naturalistic metaphysics—that is the real foundation of his sociology" (I:107). Comte's errors lay ultimately in linking sociology with science of nature, and failing to recognize the truths of historical reflection and the role of other human sciences as well. And although Mill was not as overtly metaphysical as Comte, he still viewed all sciences of man as physical sciences and had no other cognitive resources for dealing with human reality than induction and deduction, the same ones he used for nature. In the face of this kind of situation Dilthey sounds his clarion call: "In contrast with methods of Mill and Buckle . . . we must meet the challenge to establish human sciences through epistemology, to justify and support their independent formation, and to do away definitively with subordinating their principles and their methods to those of natural sciences" (I:109).

Dilthey's final salvo against philosophy of history and sociology is that these sciences fail to recognize the position of historical science in relation to special sciences of society. There is no scientific basis for the vast generalization involved in the theory of historical progress. If we wish to proceed in the only correct way, the way of experience, we must break up the structures of historico-social life into individual structures that are clear and simple, just as natural science has approached its general problem through individual specific sciences of nature. Only by using anthropology—which embraces three major classes of sciences of society: ethnology, sciences of systems of culture, and sciences of external organization of society—can we manage to connect successive states of society. Studying relations between simultaneous facts and changes in society requires a similar analysis of the affairs of society.

Special sciences are mastering ever new bodies of facts and approaching the status of general theories. Their work is valid, yet relative to the kinds of inquiry they have pursued. If that connection is broken, all sorts of pernicious metaphysical ideas ensue, such as the natural law systems of the seventeenth and eighteenth centuries. As long as the special sciences maintain their epistemological limitations with reference to their special fields, they preserve a measure of reality. In contrast, an isolated human science is a dead abstraction. Real progress is being made in impartial analysis, comparative and descriptive procedures, and relating one human science to another. The human sciences are coming to grips not only with permanent objective structures in history, but also with passing historical phenomena like revolutions, movements, and epochs. A theory of the human sciences is becoming more necessary and more possible.

Conclusion to Book I

The last section of Book I of the *Introduction* sums things up for Dilthey. It begins thus:

> All the threads of our previous considerations come together in the following insight. We achieve knowledge of historico-social reality in special human sciences. But these require awareness of the relation of their truths to reality, whose partial contents they make up, and to other truths that, like them, have been abstracted from this reality. Only such consciousness can impart full clarity to their concepts and full evidence to their propositions.
>
> Out of these premises emerges the task of developing an *epistemological foundation of human sciences*. (I:116)

Dilthey says one could well designate solving this task as a "critique of historical reason, that is, of man's capacity for knowing himself and the society and history he has fashioned" (I:116). This undertaking must link epistemology and logic in providing a synopsis of its field, but that field is restricted to the special human sciences.

In former days, when positive sciences coincided with formal logic, it was enough to proceed with formal rules of evidence in logic, but now one must satisfy a *critical* standard of evidence while using materials provided by the special sciences. We must know and critically test the source of all ideas or information we have. "Hence demands which logic makes on concepts and propositions lead us back to the chief problem of all epistemology: the nature of immediate knowledge of facts of consciousness and relation of this knowledge to knowledge which builds on the principle of sufficient reason" (I:118). We need an epistemology not only of individuals, but also of systems of culture and external organization of society to attain a true methodology of the human sciences. "Thus logic emerges as the connecting link between epistemological foundation-laying and special sciences; with that arises the *inner structure of modern science* which must replace the old metaphysical structure of our knowledge" (I:119).

Dilthey cautions that the foundation to be laid is restricted in its use to the *human sciences alone,* for if the same foundation used by natural sciences could also serve for the human sciences—or vice versa—the human sciences would have no special characteristics and could be reduced to the natural sciences. It is time for the human sciences, which have lagged behind the natural sciences in this regard, to emerge in their own right with their own distinctive foundation and methods.

Book II

Dilthey's *Introduction* in its final, unfinished form consists of two books. The first, or introductory, book is summarized in its full title: "Synopsis of the Special Human Sciences, in Which the Necessity of an Underlying Science Is Demonstrated." The second, and final, book (the main corpus or positive part of the *Introduction* was never written) bears the title: "Metaphysics as the Foundation of the Human Sciences. Its Hegemony and Decline." Here, too, the title tells all. Book II is a wide-ranging history and critique of metaphysical thought in the history of Europe (and Arab and Jewish thought in the Medieval period), something Dilthey felt on principle was necessary to provide to shed light on both the positive and the negative aspects of what European man (and medieval Arabs) have already done in philosophy. In this, as in all areas of life, we must not begin without a sense of where we are now in the light of where we have been. As Ortega y Gasset puts it: "We think *with* our past and *from* the level to which our past has taken us. It is therefore the philosopher's first concern to clarify the historical situation in which he finds himself. But this historical situation is itself the consequence of previous historical situations."[46] Masur declares: "To analyze the growth of this 'European metaphysics' Dilthey dedicated his great book, *Die Einleitung in die Geisteswissenschaften*,"[47] in effect ignoring the first or systematic part of the book in favor of the historical review. This view is of a piece with Bernhard Groethuysen's remark in his Foreword to the *Einleitung:* "Dilthey regarded this second book as so important in the general framework of his ideas that he once compared it to the position of the *Phenomenology* in Hegel's system" (I:vi).

Section 1 of Book II covers "Mythical Thought and the Rise of Science in Europe"; Section 2 moves on to the "Metaphysical Stage in the Development of the Ancient Peoples"; Section 3 deals with the "Metaphysical Stage of Modern European Peoples"; and Section 4 concludes the survey with the "Dissolution of the Metaphysical Attitude of Men toward Reality." About thirty percent of the *Introduction* is devoted to Dilthey's synopsis of the special human sciences and his argument for their need of a foundational science, in other words the section just summarized in the foregoing pages. Seventy percent of the *Introduction* is given over to the history and critique of European metaphysics just noted, to show that metaphysics can never serve as a foundational science for the human sciences, for both history and philosophy show that metaphysics is dead, at least in principle and soon in fact also.

What this means is that the *Introduction* as a whole has merely *stated* Dilthey's problem and project in declaring the need for a foundational science and has "cleared the ground" for that foundational science of the future by disqualifying the great historical attempts to supply that science in the past, that is, metaphysics. So the *Introduction* is but an overture to Dilthey's thought and work and an appropriate symbol as well: though stating his lifetime project, it is but an introduction and, as such, was never finished. But though Dilthey never produced the full "critique of historical reason" or the complete "introduction to the human sciences" to which he dedicated his life, he did do much preparatory work toward that end in later studies, most of them contained in volumes V, VI, VII, and VIII of the *Gesammelte Schriften*.

Later Studies

Volume V is titled by its editors "The Spiritual World. Introduction to the Philosophy of Life. First Half. Essays toward Laying a Foundation for the Human Sciences." It contains an important anticipation of the *Introduction* in Dilthey's 1875 essay "On the Study of the History of the Sciences of Man, Society, and the State" (31–73). Major essays that deal with specific problems relating to the foundational science called for by the

Introduction include (1) "Contributions toward Solving the Question of the Origin of Our Belief in the Reality of the External World, and Its Justification" (1890: 90–138); (2) "Ideas Concerning Descriptive and Analytical Psychology" (1894: 139–240); (3) "(On Comparative Psychology.) Contributions toward the Study of Individuality (1895–96)" (241–316; manuscripts incomplete); (4) "The Rise of Hermeneutics" (1900: 317–338); and (5) "The Essence of Philosophy" (1907:339–416).

Volume VI is titled "The Spiritual World. Introduction to the Philosophy of Life. Second Half. Essays on Poetics, Ethics, and Pedagogy." Its most important contents include (1) "The Imagination of the Poet. Building Stones for a Poetics" (1887:103–241) and (2) "The Three Epochs of Modern Esthetics and Its Current Task" (1892:242–287). Rudolf Makkreel's study *Dilthey: Philosopher of the Human Studies,* which highlights the central importance of Dilthey's aesthetic writings, uses these materials extensively.

Volume VII is titled "Establishing the Historical World in the Human Sciences," which is the heading for the second large block of material in the volume, after "Studies toward Laying a Foundation of the Human Sciences" and before "Plan for Continuation of Establishing the Historical World in the Human Studies." This volume contains Dilthey's most mature thoughts about history and his nearest approximation to his life goal of "a critique of historical reason." It centers on clarifying and interrelating virtually all his key concepts regarding the understanding of history, for example, "human sciences," "understanding," "expression," "objectifications of life," "the categories of life," and "biography."

Volume VIII is titled "Theory of Worldviews. Essays toward the Philosophy of Philosophy." Here Dilthey discusses the conflict between man's efforts to achieve a universally valid concept of life and the world, and the relativizing of all such attempts in the historical process. Specifically, *art, religion,* and *philosophy* regularly develop worldviews that aspire to be final and ultimate declarations about life and the world, but history shows us that there is an apparently irresolvable conflict among the varieties of positions taken. Dilthey also describes the typology of worldviews that history has produced: naturalism, idealism of freedom, and objective idealism and names their chief representatives.

It is clear from the foregoing brief description of the contents of volumes V through VIII of Dilthey's writings that although their contents are not the promised positive elaboration of the program proposed and begun in the *Introduction,* they do give us a clear indication of the general direction Dilthey took in trying to carry his life's work to completion.

Evaluation of Dilthey's Work

Positive Contributions

Dilthey's work has won the admiration of many serious readers and has been a powerful stimulus to philosophical speculation in the twentieth century. Perhaps not everyone would wish to go as far as Ortega y Gasset in calling Dilthey "the most important philosopher in the second half of the nineteenth century,"[48] but most would agree that the fragmentariness and inconclusiveness of his work have not prevented

Dilthey from identifying a large complex of critical issues for humanistic and social-scientific studies and from taking some imaginative and thought-provoking initiatives in dealing with those issues in our technology-dominated century.

The key distinction Dilthey made and developed between the natural sciences and the human sciences has become virtually axiomatic for most historians, humanistic scholars, curricula designers, and for many social scientists as well. He has been a powerful voice in preventing the wholesale reduction of the human sciences—with their fundamental distinctiveness in subject matter, methods, and type of experience—to the more univocal naturalistic-positivistic pressures of the modern era. In that role he has been a champion of the uniqueness of persons in the physical world. His deep appreciation of the role of history, not only pragmatically but also theoretically, as man's premier instrument for understanding his life and experience, both individual and social, has been enlightening for a prevailing Western tradition of predominantly reasoned and natural-law approaches to man. H. S. Hughes thought that "one may state Dilthey's significance in most general fashion by characterizing his work as the first thoroughgoing and sophisticated confrontation of history with positivism and natural science."[49]

Because of his approach to psychology and experience as a whole, both for individuals and for society, Dilthey has been styled "the German William James." He has had a strong influence on leading thinkers such as Ernst Troeltsch, Martin Heidegger, Max Weber, Max Scheler, Karl Jaspers, Ortega y Gasset, and many others. Hughes says "the contemporary tradition of intellectual history . . . grew naturally out of Dilthey's teaching," as did Hughes's own study.[50] Masur's opinion is that Dilthey's literary legacy "presents, beyond question, one of the most impressive achievements in the whole field of human studies."[51] After discussing Dilthey's fine biographical books and essays, he says of some shorter essays on Kant and others that "they all confirm the impression that no one has ever disclosed the history of the German mind in its most outstanding representatives more revealingly than Dilthey in these studies."[52] Masur sums up Dilthey's "main contributions to the history of ideas" as "his application of the idea of world vision on [sic] the course of occidental civilization, his concept of European metaphysics, his penetration into the great Enlightenment movement, and finally his sympathetic understanding of German culture."[53] Ortega y Gasset concurs regarding Dilthey's splendid historical essays: "Dilthey's historical studies are perhaps the best work ever done in history—in the eyes of those who are in on the secret of his thinking."[54] Hajo Holborn regards Dilthey highly as a philosopher, but also says "he was both a great and original historical thinker and a master of historical presentation."[55] Otto Bollnow's assessment of Dilthey's achievement is summarized in these words: "Dilthey's significance lies above all in establishing a historical philosophy of life. He combines philosophy of life's general thrust toward letting life in all its fullness, instead of understanding alone, penetrate into philosophizing, with methodical disciplining through concrete historical research."[56]

Herbert Deissler credits Dilthey's *Einleitung* with being the decisive influence behind bringing the methods of the human sciences and the distinctive character of their truths to serious discussion. He notes that Dilthey's works on hermeneutics and historical typologies, plus his descriptive/understanding (*beschreibende und verstehende*) method have been very fruitful in the human sciences, especially among the ranks of phenomenologists and existentialists.[57]

Stephen and William Emery speak of Dilthey as "the great German humanist" who "has made noteworthy contributions to the history and fields of philosophy: metaphysics, epistemology, ethics, and aesthetics. He is distinguished also in such allied areas as psychology, sociology, history, literature, music, religion, and education."[58] Rudolf Makkreel and Michael Ermarth, the authors of the two most significant recent studies of Dilthey in English,[59] are sparing of overt encomiums in their assessments, but they are clearly friendly critics. They frequently defend Dilthey against the many misunderstandings of him one can find in the literature, and they make it clear that they regard Dilthey as much more of a seminal philosopher in his own right than a merely transitional figure.

It is not difficult to extend the list of favorable readings of Dilthey on variants of the grounds mentioned in these pages. There is indeed ample reason to regard Dilthey as a major contributor to the theory and practice of history and the human sciences generally.

Common Reservations

The most frequent negative charges laid at Dilthey's door are that he is a historicist (in the pejorative sense) or a vitalist in his philosophizing, the upshot of which is that his thought inevitably leads one into a morass of relativism and skepticism without escape. Such charges are bolstered by his doctrine of a plurality of irreducible worldviews (the *Weltanschauungslehre*) that define our basic postures toward reality, but cannot be reduced to noncontradictory unity. His philosophical approach, which centers on epistemology and psychology with their strongly subjective features, and his insistence on the "unfathomable" character of life contribute also to those assessments.

It seems certain that Dilthey was at least not a professed or avowed relativist or skeptic. The question is, then, whether those powerful elements in his thought that bear one so strongly toward a position where, in Yeats's words, "the center cannot hold," are sufficiently counterbalanced by islands of stability based somehow on "life" or "reality." The incompleteness of Dilthey's work of providing a "critique of historical reason" has made it harder for his defenders to establish a truly firm center for his thought with distinctness and clarity, while making it easier, even for critics who find many good ideas and initiatives in Dilthey, to see him primarily as a transitional figure in philosophy. Makkreel's and especially Ermarth's studies provide extensive apologetic discussions in defense of Dilthey against his main critics. I refer the reader to those discussions; I address myself here to some other basic philosophical considerations regarding Dilthey's work about which the critics have had relatively little to say.

Dilthey and Metaphysics

Most of the *Introduction to the Human Sciences* and considerable sections of Dilthey's other works are devoted to the paradoxical enterprise of burying a corpse over and over again. The corpse is metaphysics, and the gravedigger is Dilthey, who seems never to tire of his task. Perhaps he believed that although the idea that "metaphysics is dead" has been established in principle, there were still some people who had not yet absorbed the idea, just as some people had not yet absorbed the idea behind Nietzsche's pronouncement that "God is dead" so that it required some repetition. The ideas are related.

For all Dilthey's historical erudition and philosophical innovativeness, his work suffers from a serious measure of confusion that centers on such fundamental philosophical concepts as metaphysics, reality, objectivity, life, and experience. These are, of course, "ideas that everyone knows," but also terms that engender endless interpretation and variety of emphasis. I focus mainly on the term *metaphysics* in Dilthey's thought, but the discussion will also directly affect the other key terms as well.

At the outset, note that Dilthey uses the term *metaphysics* in two main, different senses: one of them designates a legitimate activity with roots in human nature itself, and the other indicates an illegitimate activity that is merely "a historically bounded phenomenon," though it has been active for more than two millennia. (Dilthey reviews the principal historical forms of this illegitimate activity on pages 151–57 of the *Introduction*.)

Legitimate metaphysics is really just a general feeling we have about life and experience as a whole. It is basically our worldview. Thus Dilthey, like Kant before him, was moved by the starry heavens above and by the depths of the soul and was convinced that "wherever a man by his will breaks through the structure of perception, desire, impulse, and pleasure, and is no longer self-interested, here we have the meta-physical [*sic*] element, which the history of metaphysics we have described has merely reflected in countless images. *For metaphysical science is a historically limited phenomenon, but the meta-physical* [*sic*] *consciousness of the person is eternal*" (I:385–86; my italics). Metaphysical consciousness of this kind, like worldviews generally, arises out of feelings of art, poetry, and especially religion. It expresses a persistent and fundamental human impulse toward metaphysics in the sense of a constant need to interpret the meaning of the world and of life as a whole. True metaphysics must adopt "the standpoint of life" in reflecting on the whole of life. Thus "the metaphysical consciousness" or a metaphysical frame of mind or feeling is not only legitimate but is a part of our nature. After hammering away at metaphysical speculation and systems throughout most of the *Introduction*, Dilthey makes it clear that he does not believe that man's basic metaphysical feeling is dead just because metaphysical systems are dead:

> From this point on, the *metaphysical argument* . . . was destroyed as such. . . . What remains is the *metaphysical mind-set*, the basic metaphysical feeling of man which has accompanied him through the long period of his history. . . . This fundamental metaphysical feeling was everywhere intertwined in the human mind with the psychological origin of belief in God. It rests on the immensity of space, which is a symbol of infinity, and on the pure light of the stars, which appears to point to a higher world, but above all on the harmonious order. . . . All this is tied together in *one* frame of mind. . . . One cannot break this feeling down into some sort of demonstration. Metaphysics remains mute. But when the stillness of night comes, even we can still hear the harmony of the spheres sounding from the stars, about which the Pythagoreans said that only the noise of the world drowned it out. This is an inextinguishable metaphysical disposition which underlies all arguments and will outlive them all. (I:364)

"Inner metaphysical consciousness is immortal" (II:498), because man always wants to know "the complete picture" of life and reality.

The historically conditioned phenomenon of metaphysics, which bears the brunt of the attacks in the *Introduction*, is an illegitimate attempt to reduce life and reality to some conceptual system or construction that transcends the bounds of our experience, has lost its roots in life, and is nothing more than a mist or a chimera. In this sense "metaphysics is precisely the natural system which emerges from subordinating reality to the law of knowing. Thus metaphysics in general is the conception of science under whose hegemony study of man and society has developed and under whose influence they remain even today, although in diminished scope and degree" (I:125). Dilthey rejects metaphysics as "the form of philosophy that deals scientifically with the world structure as conceived in its relationship to life as though that structure were an objectivity independent of life" (VIII:51). It is this kind of metaphysics that is "a historically bounded phenomenon" (I:133). The critical failing consists in the attempt to conceptualize or systematize the fullness of life in some sense: "When a worldview is thus elevated into a conceptual system, and when that system is scientifically grounded and therefore emerges with a claim to universal validity, metaphysics comes into being" (VIII:94; see V:401). *Metaphysics is, in effect, a reasoned worldview.*

Dilthey observes that, in contrast with the special sciences with their clearly demarcated areas of inquiry, philosophy has always tried to produce a comprehensive system of reality based on reasoned grounds. Thus Dilthey writes "with respect to metaphysical systems" (Georg Misch's phrase):

> The philosophical mind that concentrates its activity in a narrower sphere does not share such overwhelming magic, but also does not share such dangers; its influence is positive, its results more permanent. Philosophy or, better said, metaphysics in this sense is comprehensive consciousness, or reflection on life and the world. It has always been its peculiar feature, in contrast with the special sciences, that it was always directed toward this 'higher consciousness' as such. (V:429–30)

In other words, philosophy should restrict its activity and thereby achieve positive and more permanent results. One needs to exercise restraint here because "The system-building mind never rests; for it is after all grounded in the metaphysical need to solve the riddle of the world and of life in universally valid, scientific knowledge" (II:347). Of course philosophy can never provide a complete solution to the mystery of the world (VIII:82), but it does enable us to interpret and deal with our experience of life and the world.

Dilthey is saying then: (1) We have a profound and inextinguishable need for metaphysics, that is, for universally valid knowledge about life and the world, but (2) such knowledge is beyond our cognitive capacity. It is virtually the same situation Kant describes in the opening words of the preface to the first edition of the *Critique of Pure Reason:* "Human reason has this peculiar fate that in one species of its knowledge it is burdened by questions which, as prescribed by the very nature of reason itself, it is not able to ignore, but which, as transcending all its powers, it is also not able to answer."[60] We face a kind of "epistemological original sin" here: Everyone is born with the desire to practice metaphysics, but no one should do so because it is against the laws of possible experience. The situation is also like a "broken hermeneutical circle." In a sound one, one needs to know the whole before one can understand the part, but one must know the part(s) before one can understand the whole. Here we have metaphysical systems that ultimately derive from our natural metaphysical urge, and the metaphysical urge, in turn, calls for conceptualization and systematization. But the system breaks down, because the "natural urge" to build metaphysics is in fact an "unnatural urge," for it is urging something impossible to achieve for that being for whom it is supposed to be natural.

How do we know that the urge to construct a metaphysical system is misplaced or impossible to carry out? The main argument for Kant and for Dilthey is that all such attempts lead to *antinomies,* that is, to mutually contradictory and exclusive yet necessary propositions, for example, "The world is eternal" and "The world is created in time." Other antinomies include ascribing personal qualities to an infinite God; maintaining divine omnipotence and human freedom; proving the existence of God and human immortality, and their opposites, and so forth. The *Introduction* provides an exposition of them, along with a running commentary, in the historical survey of Book II.

There are some serious problems with Dilthey's handling of the subject of metaphysics and worldviews, and of antinomies and their resolutions.

The Ontological/Epistemological Problem

Dilthey takes it as historically demonstrated, especially through the work of Kant and the British empiricists, that epistemology and psychology, which deal solely with data of consciousness, constitute the only proper subject matter of philosophical knowledge. We can know only "what is on our mind," as it were; we must avoid, at all costs, any ventures into ontology, which aims at saying what something is in itself, and not necessarily just in reference to data of consciousness. The guiding Kantian *critical* perspective in Dilthey's thought, though he does not recognize Kant's *Ding an sich,* allows him to recognize things only as they appear to consciousness. This is all that "life" gives us; we cannot go beyond or behind it. It is obvious to Dilthey that our life begins and ends in the totality of our life of consciousness:

> Only in inner experience, in facts of consciousness, did I find a firm anchorage for my thinking, and I am confident that no reader will evade the proof of this point. All science is a science of experience, but all experience has its original constitution and its validity in the conditions of our consciousness, in which experience takes place—in the totality of our nature. We call this standpoint—which logically sees the impossibility of going beyond these conditions, which would be like seeing without an eye or directing the knowing look behind the eye itself—the *epistemological standpoint; modern science can recognize no other.* (I:xvii; my italics)

Unfortunately for this point of view, it seems impossible to construct an epistemology without an ontology. No matter what position we state, we are *always* trying to "tell it like it is," to state an objective state of affairs that is not merely true in relation to our minds or our moods but simply true or not true. If one adopts a rigorously epistemological approach, one's ontological statement is restricted to what that approach will allow, but *positing that approach is itself an ontological statement.* And an ontological statement is a metaphysical statement. Thus, for example, Kant's distinction between "the transcendental," as purporting to show the presuppositions for experience and "the transcendent," indicating something beyond all possible experience, requires an ontological/metaphysical position regarding exactly what can or cannot be an object of experience. Even when Kant deals with the merely regulative use of ideas of pure reason in the "Appendix to the Transcendental Dialectic," he certainly does not allow one to use or not to use these ideas arbitrarily. For example, he writes: "The law of reason which requires us to seek for this unity is a necessary law, since without it we should have no reason at all, and without reason no coherent employment of the understanding, and in the absence of this no sufficient criterion of empirical truth. In order, therefore, to secure an empirical criterion we have no option save to presuppose the systematic unity of nature as objectively valid and necessary."[61]

One cannot proceed as though adoption of an epistemological *method* as the sole valid method is somehow "ontology free." Erich Rothacker points out: "Quite universally speaking, one can recognize philosophical oppositions as the background to all controversies about methods" and again: "All methodological measures, all value judgments in a particular scientific work are determined by a perspective which is ultimately a worldview. Nothing is a matter of course [*selbstverständlich*]; everything is filled with assumptions and consequences."[62] Ortega y Gasset chides Dilthey with a "strange inconsistency" in reducing the facts of consciousness, "the only reality there is" (in the estimation of both of them), to mere cognitive efforts and concludes that he is "hampered . . . by the epistemological mania, that Kantian and positivist *ontophobia*."[63] The ontophobia in question is a matter of degree and placement. Both Ortega y Gasset and Dilthey restrict being to facts of consciousness, but Ortega y Gasset accuses Dilthey of narrowing even that range of being to the merely cognitive (which, by the way, does not reflect Dilthey's view accurately). The point, however, is that every thinker must necessarily place reality *somewhere* in an ontological sense. Where that place is reflects each thinker's worldview. How he puts things together systematically—even epistemologically—is his metaphysics.

Many modern thinkers' terror over the very words *metaphysics* or *ontology* makes it seem as though they were trying to find a way to say something without being caught in the act of saying it. The situation is suggestive of the novelist's problem of how to deal with the narrator in his story. The ideal would seem to be to have the story tell itself. But this is impossible. The novelist may come forward bluntly and announce himself as the narrator, or he may invent a fictitious narrator, or he may let the characters "speak for themselves" in interior monologues, etc. But if a story is told, there is always a narrator somewhere. So also in every philosophical position there is not only a worldview represented but also a conceptualization of that worldview: "When a worldview is thus elevated into a conceptual system, and that system is scientifically grounded and therefore emerges with a claim to universal validity, metaphysics comes into being" (VIII:94). How does this statement apply to Dilthey's own philosophy? Even if he adopted a "philosophy of 'as if,' " like Hans Vaihinger—saying that we really do not know things as they are, but the situation is 'as if' this or that were true—he would still be saying how things *are* with respect to our ability to know.

What misleads people at times is a philosopher's announcement that his position is not metaphysical but "only epistemological" or "only phenomenological" or "merely analyzes language." But there is no thought without metaphysics, and therefore no epistemology without metaphysics. For the thought or statement has to be about *something*. If a man is not saying anything about objective reality at *some* level, he is not saying anything at all. The only way we can talk or think is in saying that something is so, or is not so, or might be so, or we do not know about it, or some other formulation that always ultimately entails a declaration about objective reality in intention. And if one rejoins that a man might *intend* to say something real, but he cannot or will not or might not, that too requires a metaphysical stance. Thought is about *things* at some point, and so is every true philosophy, even if it says the only things are ideas. It takes a metaphysics to refute a metaphysics; it takes an ontology to oust an ontology, and the reason is that every philosophical position must claim to express reality at some point.

Dilthey's equation of reality with facts of consciousness is built on the egocentric predicament that we have experience only with our minds, so that all that exists for us is facts of consciousness. The principle is true as far as it goes, but the fact that our mental apparatus *conditions* all our thoughts does not prove that we know *only* our thoughts and nothing *through* our thoughts. That is pure solipsism, and if it were true it would make it impossible to pursue philosophy or anything else in community or to put forth such views to "others."

Dilthey is not a solipsist, but in adopting the epistemological point of view as the only possible one, he finds it necessary to go about establishing the existence of the external world (even though he also calls it immediately given to us) and of our knowledge of other minds. It is no wonder that, given his premises, he calls the question about the reality of the external world "the most stubborn of all puzzles connected with this task of laying a foundation. From the cognitive standpoint alone, the outer world always remains just a phenomenon" (I:xviii–xix). The whole man "feels" the outer world when his will encounters resistance from something "outside" him. It is not altogether clear why such resistance could not come from the "inside" instead. Thus Plato in the *Republic* found a conflict or resistance in internal states of mind that led him to conclude to the existence of mind, appetite, and spirit in the same soul (IV:436ff.). Dilthey's entire treatment of the question of an external world and of other persons in it is a "belief" or "faith" [*Glaube*] we have in those things, though he offers arguments justifying that belief. Thus we have a cognitive awareness of the resistance the will encounters and a cognitive awareness of a moral sort for the existence of other persons and our ability to understand them sympathetically and talk to them meaningfully. But the ultimate conclusion is the same: One must assume that thought deals with something outside the mind itself. One does, in the end, balance the scholastic axiom *quidquid recipitur, recipitur per modum recipientis* with a correlative axiom that a recipient will in turn be affected by the nature of the objective contents he receives. (Dilthey himself credits Kant with avoiding the one-sided Fichtean epistemology because he assumes the existence of an affecting factor just as much as he does the existence of conditions of consciousness.) Every philosophy, even one restricted to epistemology, will necessarily purport to make objective statements about reality that are independent of merely mental states, even if our access to reality is always mediated by mind. Anytime we draw a distinction between "reality" and "appearance"—and what philosopher does not? what person does not?—we are simply talking metaphysics.

Uses of the Term Metaphysics

We have seen that Dilthey uses the term *metaphysics* to describe a basic feeling man has about the meaning of all reality (natural, legitimate use) and a system of concepts purporting to explain the world (historical, illegitimate use). In fact, the term has many different meanings.[64] For example, in a review of some eight meanings of the word, Roger Hancock writes:

> In modern philosophical usage "metaphysics" refers generally to the field of philosophy dealing with questions about the kinds of things there are and their modes of being. . . . In the eighteenth and nineteenth centuries "metaphysics" was used broadly to include questions about the reality of the external world, the existence of other minds, the possibility of a priori

knowledge, and the nature of sensation, memory, abstraction, and so on. In present usage these questions are included in the study of epistemology.[65]

My contention is that Dilthey is a metaphysician in the first sense as well as the second; the second sense covers but a subset of issues embraced by the first sense. Recognition of this would have made it possible for Dilthey to write with less confusion in this area.

One of the great perennial philosophical questions is about the nature of philosophy itself. Philosophers differ from one another ultimately because they have different worldviews or pictures of reality, and consequently different ideas about what philosophy is, which is supposed to interpret reality systematically, as well as different ideas about philosophical method, which is supposed to guide philosophers to their goal. Given Dilthey's theory of worldviews and his strong historical approach to philosophy, he seems to be guilty of a most unlikely shortcoming, namely his assumption that the philosophical problems of his day, and particularly the Kantian critical/epistemological approach in philosophy, were set down for all time. To be sure, Dilthey found fault with Kant's unhistorical approach to reality and to philosophy, for example in Kant's assumption that Wolff's brand of metaphysics was held by all earlier metaphysicians (I:308)— namely as a science of pure reason, even though Aristotle, for example, was not a metaphysician in this sense (I:132). But in his own treatment of metaphysics, especially the metaphysics of the Middle Ages, even though he recognizes many times that the metaphysics of the Middle Ages was basically rooted in religion or "theological metaphysics," his critique of it persistently deals with it as though it were a metaphysics in the Wolffian mold. More of this later.

Kant thought that he could cure the fundamental metaphysical fallacy, which has taken many forms ("the battlefield of endless controversies"), by settling critically, once and for all, what the mind can do and what it cannot do in the realm of experience. Despite its difficulty and complexity, the project seemed almost modest in comparison with the wild speculative flights of fancy the metaphysicians have engaged in. But the apparent modesty of the project was deceptive, just as was the very modest-sounding intention of Ranke not to indulge in speculative theories in writing history but simply to describe events "as they actually happened," or just as the modest-sounding intention of some philosophers to limit their activity solely to analyzing language. Despite Kant's great contributions to philosophy, the anarchy of philosophical systems has continued, just as many forms of historiography have succeeded Ranke, and many uses of language persist in our sciences. Dilthey, too, was dismayed by the anarchy and apparent relativity of every religious and philosophical position ever taken, but the anarchy continues unabated. One might object that this is being unfair to Dilthey, because he was not able to provide the complete epistemological foundation he sought for the human sciences. But does anyone really expect that he would have settled the basic issues respecting the nature and method of how one must proceed to study the totality of human life scientifically? It hardly seems possible, for Dilthey himself speaks often of the "riddle of life" and its "unfathomable" character in terms that suggest that no one will ever "solve" it. It is ironic, however, that he could hope to overcome the anarchy of metaphysical views by plunging into the maze of views centered on issues of epistemology—"the epistemological bunghole," as someone has styled it, that can stop up the flow of philosophical thought as readily as any other kind of metaphysics. Who has not thought himself into giddiness by trying to unravel this mystery? Has anyone ever squared this circle to everyone else's satisfaction? In writing of the "deep and irreconcilable conflicts in actual life," Hodges notes that if they are due to misunderstanding, that misunderstanding must be so profound as to make us wonder whether we can understand anything historical with objectivity. And he continues: "Nor can [such misunderstanding] be resolved by a mere epistemological analysis. . . . for our *Weltanschauungen* affect our theory of knowledge, as well as being affected by it, and the enquiry which Dilthey calls *Selbstbesinnung* and Collingwood calls 'metaphysics' is the sport of our disagreements, rather than their conqueror."[66]

Terminological Naïveté

Dilthey's use of a whole list of common yet critical words—such as life, reality, objectivity, and experience—leaves much to be desired. He almost seems to take it for granted that each such word has only one meaning, and each person agrees on what that meaning is. Thus he speaks of "life" as though there is only one sense and meaning for the word that is to be the absolute, the touchstone of all truth, and as though the "standpoint of life" will somehow resolve all difficulties. Metaphysical theories are airy mists, phantoms, and delusions, because they transcend all possible "experience." One must stay firmly on the ground of "reality" and "objectivity" and "scientific validity."

The difficulty is that people have fought over the meaning of these terms since the beginning and continue to do so now. One man's "reality" is another man's "illusion." People have differing worldviews, which they express in essentially metaphysical ideas and systems on the strength of a basic human urge to formulate a coherent meaning for their lives and experience; it is not an idle sport. As we have seen, Dilthey recognizes this metaphysical consciousness, but protests against the unwarranted attempt to formulate theories or systems about that totality, because that is foolish metaphysics. One must stay with "reality," "experience," and so on.

Surely it is clear that these words mean all sorts of things to different people. Why is it impossible for "experience" to suggest the transcendent, as it did for Plato, Aristotle, Augustine, Aquinas, and many others, in their attempts to *interpret* life in its universal dimensions? Why is it impossible that "life" should have the "other dimension" Louis Dupré writes about, or that "life" should give "signals of transcendence" to the sociologist Peter Berger?[67] How is it that Dilthey finds Comte's positivism illegitimate and metaphysical, except ultimately on the grounds that it conflicts with his notion of "reality," "experience," and so on? Ermarth notes: "It is true that life is Dilthey's 'a priori,' just as 'experience' is the a priori of all empiricism. Dilthey would point out that the argument is circular. He insisted that *Erlebnis* cannot be fully defined or grasped logically."[68] Thus when Dilthey rejects the narrow physicalistic associationist psychology of the seventeenth and eighteenth centuries as inadequate to the demands of the full range of "experience," the naturalist philosopher's view of reality would not go along with him. Likewise the people who wrestle with metaphysics and religion all their lives in an effort to grapple with life's meaning are not likely to see a great light if Dilthey points them toward "life" and "experience" as the key. How does Dilthey know that religious dogmas or beliefs can have no direct truth-content in their common acceptance, but must be reinterpreted only as comments on "life" in his sense, unless he has made "life" as he understands it an absolute, an a priori, a court of final instance which he alone can interpret correctly? Is it enough for him to justify his religious reductionism on the grounds that "I am not a religious nature,"[69] or that religion is foreign to his view of ultimate reality? How does he know, except through his own view of reality, that Plato's Idea of the Good or Aquinas's God as the *ens realissimum* must be replaced in that capacity by man and his life?

These common terms, that "everybody knows and understands," require some serious clarification as to their source and the basis of their claim to validity. Dilthey goes a long way in that direction in his theory of worldviews, but he does not seem to accept the inclusion of himself and his own worldview within the scope of application of that theory. Others may be assigned a specific niche in the schema of worldviews; Dilthey does not assign himself such a niche.

Antinomies, Anarchies, Analogies

As noted, both Kant and Dilthey were disturbed by the anarchy of metaphysical views and presumably intended to remedy the situation. In his *Critique of Pure Reason* Kant tries to show the illusionistic character of metaphysics because of the antinomies that accompany it in such areas as "proofs" for God, freedom, and immortality. In Dilthey's historical/critical survey in the *Introduction,* he also shows a series of antinomies involved in metaphysical positions. Have they proven their point?

One could argue this variously with respect to individual philosophers, but their main argument, that is, that metaphysics exceeds experience and is therefore impossible, is a metaphysics in its own right. They reject all traditional forms of metaphysics in favor of their own unacknowledged versions. They reject older metaphysics as "false," in that it "transcends experience," but their own metaphysics is "true," in that it reflects "experience" as it is. Though they do not label their own epistemologies as metaphysics, they are metaphysics because they are talking about the real structure of the mind in them. Not that Kant's and Dilthey's metaphysics coincide. Dilthey argues that "we must leave the pure and fine air of Kant's critique of reason to do justice to the completely different nature of the historical object," because Kant's approach is one of those that left one with "the same insoluble problem as the possibility of knowledge prior to or independently of knowledge itself" (VII:277–78). Hence, even for Dilthey, Kant's whole enterprise is, if not explicitly antinomical, at least impossible and ridden with contradiction. For his own part, Dilthey acknowledges antinomies to be inherent in the mystery of life itself (not to mention the self-contradictory attempt to destroy all metaphysics with a metaphysics of one's own). Surely Dilthey must have felt the heavy pressure of antinomies weighing against his own system that, on the one hand, said that all reality for us is mental, but, on the other hand, that a "feeling of resistance" our will encounters is sufficient to develop a view of the reality of the external world, other people, the entire field of pragmatic history, the philosophical tradition, etc. Was that not what was behind his great attraction to Husserl's ideas?

Dilthey's long history and critique of metaphysical speculation in the West seems also to be inconsistent and misleading. What Dilthey gives with one hand, he often takes back with the other. Over and over he shows that he knows what a given thinker is trying to do philosophically, but then passes judgment on that thinker in terms of totally different criteria. Let us note a few examples.

Dilthey concedes that Kant's view of metaphysics as rooted in pure reason is not true for Aristotle's metaphysics (I:132), but he insists on other occasions (e.g., I:303, 308, 323, 390–97) that true metaphysics is a science of reason, that the principle of sufficient reason has guided metaphysics from the start, and that all metaphysics must be rationalistic to be consistent; and he proceeds to dispatch Aristotle as a rationalist. He concedes that Plato's "system" is not a closed, exhaustive, and complete picture of reality—noting particularly his use of myths and his speculation about a Highest Good implied by lower levels of reality but transcending all categories of ordinary experience—but he evaluates Plato's "system" as though it were pure rational metaphysics, not an "open-ended" system.

But the worst confusion occurs in his treatment of the Middle Ages. Even though he says many times that the medieval worldview was essentially religious—i.e., based on faith in divine revelation as its absolute—he persists over and over again in demanding that medieval thinkers logically *prove* their faith positions completely. And if they cannot do so—even by their own admission and from the nature of the case—Dilthey concludes that their entire philosophical speculation was essentially antinomical. But that conclusion would be valid only if the medievals were saying that they had an airtight logical scheme of pure reason that would exhaustively explain such things as the meaning of world history, the precise relationship between rationality and freedom, whether the world is eternal or not, etc. In fact, the great task of medieval philosophy/theology was to do as much justice as possible *by reason,* to the contents of what they believed *by faith.* They believed that both the contents of faith and the requirements of reason were from God, and their main speculative task was to try to reconcile the two as much as possible. They did not believe that they could fuse the two into one, such that faith would no longer be necessary once reason had supplied all answers to the meaning of life in compelling fashion. What Dilthey calls the "intrinsically contradictory character of medieval metaphysics" (I:327) would perhaps be true in a purely immanentist frame of reference such as Dilthey's, but is not necessarily so in a medieval frame of reference which said that not all being is being in space and time, that the term "being" is not univocal, but analogical (Dilthey charges the Middle Ages with failing to be univocal in their meanings, as though they did not admit it themselves), that there *really* is a transcendent God apart from us and the world, that God *really* has revealed himself in history, etc. Dilthey not only does not believe these things himself, but will also not allow the medievals to believe them, in the sense that he attacks their positions in the same way as he would attack the philosophy of Christian Wolff. If Dilthey can concede that Aristotle's metaphysics was not based on pure reason, surely he must have seen that medieval metaphysics was far less so. And surely he must have seen that religious faith, not reason, held the primary position in the medieval worldview and that despite the large role given to reason and logic in the age, none of the major medieval thinkers was anything other than primarily a religious thinker. It is apparently due to the profound difference between the medieval worldview and Dilthey's worldview that he not only felt a strong disgust in dealing with the Middle Ages, but also could never really deal with it in its own terms.

Following are a few examples of the point in question. Dilthey concedes that the best medieval thinkers rejected the ontological argument for God's existence (I:310),[70] but he deals with all medieval arguments for God's existence in much the same way Kant did: as variations on the ontological argument. (Nor does he even consider the fact that medieval arguments for God's existence merely argue for an unmoved mover for things moved, for a primary efficient cause in a series of essentially subordinated causes, for a necessary cause in a series of contingent causes, for a highest perfection implied by lesser degrees of perfection, and for a highest, intelligent purpose governing lower purposes; but they do not argue for God in the full sense in which medievals believed in God through revelation.

Thus no one claimed a "proof" for the "Credo in unum deum" of faith.) Dilthey quotes Augustine's profound awareness that God's attributes cannot be expressed adequately by reason ("great without quantitative determination, omnipresent without occupying a place, cause of changes without any change in himself . . ." [I:288]) and takes that as a proof that the idea of God is "antinomical." If that means that reason, univocal and immanent categories, etc., cannot deal with the mystery of God, this is something that medievals conceded virtually unanimously. Dilthey charges that the medievals failed to come up with a univocal metaphysical system (I:397), even though the medievals themselves argued that being is not univocal but analogical and even though a substantial part of medieval theology was "negative theology," that is, a theology which stressed that we have no *positive* knowledge of God by reason, but only an idea of what God is *not*. If Aquinas argues that he *believes* in creation from nothing by God because his religion holds that view, and if he explains that "from nothing" means *ex nihilo sui et subjecti*, that is, by God's power alone, and not from pre-existing material or a "part" of God, but also not "from nothing pure and simple," Dilthey reads this not as a tenet of faith but as another instance of medieval irrationality. If Aristotle and Averroës argue that the world is eternal while Aquinas, accepting the world's origin in time on faith, argues that one cannot *prove* either that the world is eternal or arises in time, Dilthey reads this as another irresolvable antinomy. Again, Dilthey explicitly admits that Augustine's *City of God* has religious roots and is "a theological philosophy of history" (I:98ff.), but proceeds to judge it as a pure construct of reason on a par with other philosophies of history that have claimed to discover the meaning of the historical process. The list could go on and on. It seems clear that Dilthey is "talking right past" the Middle Ages in the sense that he is making of the philosophical Middle Ages nothing more than a series of purely logical constructs of reason and judging them accordingly, but the Middle Ages are not accurately reflected in such a picture. For all of Dilthey's hammering home the idea of epistemology as the necessary, crucial foundation for all true philosophizing, he fails to see that medieval notions such as religious faith, divine revelation, negative theology, analogical nature of being, insistence on mystery, and the like, are essentially shot through with *epistemological* consequences of which the Medievals were intensely aware. It was the *status quaestionis* of their whole problematic in philosophy.

Obviously the foregoing remarks represent but a few of the ways both Kant and Dilthey offer partial and misleading ideas regarding forms of past metaphysical thought. While much more could be said on this score, the game is not worth the candle unless one recognizes that both of them are really attempting to replace earlier forms of metaphysics (or faith) by their own versions of metaphysics, which happen to fly the flags of "epistemology" or "experience" or "life" or "reality." As for the bugbear of antinomies, besides noting that they often do not apply where Kant and Dilthey would have them apply, it is not difficult to assemble a mass of them to apply to Kant's or Dilthey's own philosophy. These antinomies, as we have noted, would focus especially on the self-contradictory attempts to describe an objective and universally valid epistemological structure for man and at the same time to profess either to say nothing about a *Ding an sich*, even of the mind (Kant), or to describe merely facts of consciousness but also to claim their validity for the external world, for other minds, and for the whole world of pragmatic history. Dilthey admits that life is ineffable and that there are "*immanent antinomies* in the field of reality given in experience itself" (V:175). He develops an elaborate schema of irreducible worldviews, such that each person views the world only from a particular vantage point and with a particular "feeling" that amounts to a kind of faith about how things ultimately hang together. He rejects the possibility of reducing the historical process to the "unity of a single formula or principle" (I:96ff.) or to any kind of metaphysical system. But he somehow knows ultimate reality well enough to be able to pronounce on what the final rules governing knowledge and experience and life are. And of course those rules apply not just to himself but to everyone.

Worldviews and Metaphysics, Faith and Reason

What are we to conclude from all this? Is reason bankrupt? Must we declare not only Dilthey but everyone else consigned to limitless relativity and therefore absurdity? Is Dilthey's doctrine of worldviews his closest approach to the truth despite its relativistic implications? What about our inescapable need to pronounce objectively and, as it were, "absolutely" about reality, combined with our limited, incomplete, and partial hold on reality? Is skepticism the last word in philosophy?

These questions are more than enough to exercise one's mind for a lifetime. We seem to have a finite grasp on an infinite (indefinite?) reality, and Dilthey has rendered a fine service in analyzing worldviews as some of the ultimate, seemingly irreducible ways man can "view the whole." His own *Weltanschauung* was his "philosophy of life." "Life" was his absolute, his a priori, his *Ding an sich*. Does this make him a relativist? Yes and no. Yes, because his worldview or his grasp of reality is finite and partial and perspectival; no, because he plotted out his *Sitz im Leben* in the universe in absolute terms. The great paradox of human life is that each of us absolutizes the relative and relativizes the absolute; each of us objectifies the subjective and subjectifies the objective. Unless we maintain total silence (but even deliberate silence is meaningful), we will at some point and in some fashion assert something which we will not admit is *merely* relative or subjective. Dilthey said that life is unfathomable and ineffable, to be sure, but he also insisted that it has certain characteristics regarding which he will fight anyone who disagrees with him.

Certainly there is much in Dilthey's work with which most of us will agree. He is expressing something relative in an absolute way. It appears that we must *express* the ultimate as an absolute, and *believe* it as a faith. We have faith in our absolute. Michael Ermarth remarks on Dilthey's rejection of Kant's formalism in favor of common sense and "belief," citing Dilthey's conclusion that "all scientific knowledge begins in belief, that is, with the acceptance of presuppositions." Ermarth is quick to add that this does not involve any sort of smuggling of religious faith into the theory of knowledge but rather, as William James later held, "Dilthey was simply calling attention to the fact that all knowledge contains a fiduciary element which can never be proven on purely rational or logical grounds. . . . Ultimately one has simply to suppose the validity of knowledge without any exhaustive prior demonstration of absolute criteria."[71]

It appears, then, that a worldview of this kind is really secular nomenclature for *faith,* and if one wishes to deny that religious faith is involved, the faith in question neverthe-less functions much like religious faith. It is faith in an absolute, which as faith cannot be proven. It is like a universal speculative philosophy of history, which, as Dilthey saw, was really a secularized religious view. As Heidegger remarks, "metaphysics in itself is theology." Or, as the title of Book II, Section I, chapter 3 of Dilthey's *Introduction* has it: "Religious Life as the Basis of Metaphysics." Philosophizing about this faith is metaphysics: no philosopher can avoid some version of it, any more than any thinking person can exist without some brand of faith, some reference to an absolute. If this is true, we are "believers," but because our grasp of reality is finite and piecemeal, we are believers in different kinds of things. We have many "truths," but no one has *the truth*. Expressed thus, it appears that faith is prior to reason, or that reasoning is about the contents of our basic faith regarding reality. The final test of a metaphysics or reasoned worldview is how adequately it does justice to all the dimensions of life and experience. Dilthey doubtless had a similar view of things, but would disagree with many people about exactly what will do justice to all the demands of life.

This is not to say that reason is dead or ineffective or necessarily deludes us. It is our most powerful instrument for attaining a hold on truth, and its exercise and validity is assumed even by those who would deny it. If one will not concede such first principles of knowledge as the principle of identity, or the principle of (non-) contradiction, or some form of the principle of sufficient reason (related to the principle that "nothing comes from nothing"), or that the whole is greater than a part and other tautologies, it is impossible even to discuss this or any other matter with him. If we had no reason or knowledge to lead us to truth, then we have no philosophy either, or this discussion. Exactly how our reason relates to what Dilthey calls "the riddle of life" is another matter.

If one's faith is that reason is omnicompetent, this can lead to endless antinomies. Many leading members of the existentialist movement, such as Nietzsche, Sartre, and Camus, have made the paradoxical argument that everything is absurd, meaningless, and without purpose on the grounds that in a purely immanentist frame of reference reason is totally inadequate to explain life; on the other hand, they also refuse a "cheap and dishonest" or "unauthentic" solution of having recourse to an absolute, God or other. Christian and Jewish existentialists, such as Kierkegaard, Marcel, and Buber, agree with the atheistic camp that the world in its own terms is absurd and irrational, but accept the "leap of faith" into a transcendent realm wherein they find meaning and value. Dilthey tried, in effect, to combine the opposite views by a straightforward placement of his absolute, *life,* in an immanentist setting (or does the immanentist/transcendent distinction lapse?), ascribes all truth and reality to it, says it is ineffable and our knowledge of it is limited, anathematizes all the nay-sayers, and insists that this is *the truth* for all of us. He also believed in a scientific perspective that "must be objectively valid knowledge that stands above all unprovable worldviews, and is therefore not metaphysical in the old sense" (VI:303). This suggests that science will supersede worldviews in ultimacy, but Dilthey does not explain how this will come about. It remains a mere velleity for him, a kind of optative metaphysics he coupled with his declared view of life as an unfathomable riddle. Perhaps it might have been useful for Dilthey to have revisited the great Scholastic thinkers who—despite their shortcomings and those of their systems—at least recognized that they held a faith and developed a metaphysics in wrestling with the unfathomable riddle of life.

Notes

1. H. Stuart Hughes, *Consciousness and Society* (New York: Vintage Books, 1961), 199.
2. Cited by Dilthey's student, Hermann Nohl. "Wilhelm Dilthey 1833–1911" in *Die Grossen Deutschen,* vol. 4 (Berlin: Propyläen Verlag, 1957).

3. Bernhard Groethuysen, "Wilhelm Dilthey," *Deutsche Rundschau* (Jan.–June 1913), 154–55:69.

4. Ibid.

5. Michael Ermarth, *Wilhelm Dilthey: The Critique of Historical Reason* (Chicago and London: University of Chicago Press, 1978), 5.

6. José Ortega y Gasset, *Concord and Liberty* (New York: W. W. Norton & Co., 1946), 140.

7. Franz von Baader, *Sämtliche Werke* (Aalen: Scientia Verlag, 1963), 2:137ff.

8. See Ermarth, *Wilhelm Dilthey,* 360 n.15.

9. For further comments on the difficulty of Dilthey's style, see Ermarth, *Wilhelm Dilthey,* 4–5, and H. P. Rickman, ed., *Wilhelm Dilthey: Pattern and Meaning in History—Thoughts on History and Society* (New York: Harper & Row, 1961), 20.

10. Otto Bollnow, *Dilthey: Eine Einführung in seine Philosophie,* 3d ed. (Stuttgart: Kohlhammer Verlag, 1955), 31.

11. Herbert A. Hodges, *Wilhelm Dilthey, An Introduction* (New York: Howard Fertig Publisher, 1969), 157.

12. Ortega y Gasset, *Concord and Liberty,* 132.

13. Bollnow, *Dilthey,* 35 (Bollnow's italics).

14. Ibid., 218ff.

15. Ortega y Gasset, *Concord and Liberty,* 148.

16. Gerhard Masur, "Wilhelm Dilthey and the History of Ideas," *Journal of the History of Ideas* 13 (1952): 96.

17. Ortega y Gasset, *Concord and Liberty,* 143. It is interesting to note in conjunction with these remarks on Dilthey's poor understanding of religion that in his lengthy list of representatives of the types of worldview (over sixty names), Dilthey does not mention anyone who is primarily a religious thinker (though he does mention "the Christian tradition"), not even in the ranks of idealists of freedom. For all his extremely numerous and far-ranging historical essays, notes, and sketches—including his strong youthful interest in "the history of Christianity"—he has said virtually nothing about Christ or Moses, the patriarchs, prophets, apostles, or evangelists. Even his interest in Schleiermacher seems obliquely and tangentially connected with any religious dimension. It is ironic that one whose life was dedicated to historical studies, especially *Geistesgeschichte,* should leave this giant lacuna in his survey of significant worldviews.

18. Herbert A. Hodges, *The Philosophy of Wilhelm Dilthey* (1952; reprint, Westport, Conn.: Greenwood Press, 1974), 358.

19. For assessments of Dilthey's treatment of the history of the stages of European intellectual history, see Ortega y Gasset, *Concord and Liberty,* 172ff. and Masur, "Wilhelm Dilthey," 99ff.

20. Bollnow, *Dilthey,* 14.

21. Hodges, *Wilhelm Dilthey,* 5.

22. Hodges, *Philosophy,* 1–2.

23. Cited by Ermarth, *Wilhelm Dilthey,* 149.

24. See ibid., 15–93, for a good overview of the major intellectual and cultural currents in Europe in the nineteenth century.

25. See Groethuysen, "Wilhelm Dilthey," 71ff.

26. See Rudolf Makkreel, *Dilthey: Philosopher of the Human Studies* (Princeton: Princeton University Press, 1975) for a study that argues for "the centrality of Dilthey's aesthetic writings" (p. ix), and pays particular attention to Dilthey's theory of poetry as the key to his thought.

27. See Hodges, *Philosophy,* 16.

28. See page 14 of this introduction.

29. See Hodges, *Philosophy,* 38ff.

30. *Verstehen* is one of Dilthey's major concepts bearing on how we come to know things in the human sciences. There is extensive coverage of the term in all the Dilthey literature. Note Karl-Otto Apel, "Das Verstehen," *Archiv für Begriffsgeschichte* 1 (1955):142–99; Theodore Abel, "The Operation Called Verstehen," *American Journal of Sociology* 54 (1948): 211–18; and especially Joachim Wach, *Das Verstehen: Grundzüge einer Geschichte der Hermeneutischen Theorie im 19. Jahrhundert,* 3 vols. (Tübingen: J. C. B. Mohr Verlag, 1926–33).

31. Cp. Josef Ratzinger, *Einführung in das Christentum* (Munich: Kosel Verlag, 1968), 37: "In the midst of the ocean of doubt which threatens mankind since the collapse of the old metaphysics at the beginning of the modern era, solid ground has been found here once again in *fact,* on the

basis of which man can attempt to build himself a new existence. The rule of fact begins, i.e., the radical turning of man to his own work as the only thing he is certain about."

32. Note the similarity in idea to the Master-Slave section of the introduction to Hegel's *Phenomenology of the Spirit.*

33. Ermarth, *Wilhelm Dilthey,* 201.

34. Ibid., 204.

35. Ibid., 206. For the relations between Dilthey and Husserl throughout their exchange of views, see 197ff.

36. See pp. 23–24 of this introduction.

37. For Dilthey's main treatments of the subject of worldviews, see the entirety of vol. 8; vol. 5, 378ff., and vol. 7, passim.

38. See Ermarth, *Wilhelm Dilthey,* 334ff., for a defense of Dilthey against such charges.

39. Ibid., 334.

40. Makkreel, *Dilthey,* 35.

41. See Ermarth, *Wilhelm Dilthey,* 359–60, for an explanation of his translation of *Geisteswissenschaften* as "human sciences."

42. *Geisteswissenschaften* has been translated throughout the book as "human sciences." An exception is made here because Dilthey is clearly commenting on the contrast between *Geist* and *Natur* here.

43. One should note that "anthropology" in German usage refers to a philosophical study of the nature of man, not the English social-scientific sense of a natural history of man.

44. See, for example, the lengthy essays "Leibniz and His Age" and "Frederick the Great and the German Enlightenment" in vol. 3, or the numerous short biographical sketches and portraits in vol. 15, or the essays on Stein, Humboldt, Hardenberg, Gneisenau, and Scharnhorst in vol. 12 of the *Gesammelte Schriften.*

45. On the notion of modern philosophies of history in a speculative sense as secularized religions, see, for example, Karl Löwith, *Meaning in History* (Chicago: University of Chicago Press, 1949) or Eric Voegelin, *The New Science of Politics* (Chicago: University of Chicago Press, 1952).

46. Ortega y Gasset, *Concord and Liberty,* 172.

47. Masur, "Wilhelm Dilthey," 99.

48. Ortega y Gasset, *Concord and Liberty,* 131.

49. Hughes, *Consciousness and Society,* 194.

50. Ibid., 200.

51. Masur, "Wilhelm Dilthey," 94.

52. Ibid., 105.

53. Ibid., 106.

54. Ortega y Gasset, *Concord and Liberty,* 138.

55. Hajo Holborn, "Wilhelm Dilthey and the Critique of Historical Reason," *Journal of the History of Ideas* 11 (Jan. 1950), 114.

56. *Neue Deutsche Biographie,* vol. 3 (Berlin: Duncker & Humblot Verlag, 1957), 724.

57. *Staatslexikon,* publication of the Görresgesellschaft, 6th ed., vol. 2, (Freiburg: Herder Verlag, 1958), col. 913.

58. Wilhelm Dilthey, *The Essence of Philosophy,* trans. Stephen A. Emery and William T. Emery (New York: Ams Press), ix.

59. See notes 5 and 26 above.

60. *Critique of Pure Reason,* trans. Norman Kemp Smith (London: Macmillan & Co., 1963), 7.

61. Ibid., 538.

62. Erich Rothacker, *Logik und Systematik der Geisteswissenschaften* (1927; reprint, R. Olden-bourg Verlag, 1965), 31–52.

63. Ortega y Gasset, *Concord and Liberty,* 181.

64. See *Historisches Wörterbuch der Philosophie,* ed. Joachim Ritter and Karlfried Gründer, vol. 5 (Darmstadt: Wissenschaftliche Buchgesellschaft, 1980) for ninety-three closely packed columns on the term *Metaphysik,* followed by variants thereof in articles such as "Inductive Metaphysics" and "Critique of Metaphysics." Copious bibliographies.

65. In *The Encyclopedia of Philosophy,* vol. 5 (New York: The Macmillan Company and The Free Press, 1967), 289–90.

66. Hodges, *Philosophy*, 359.

67. See Louis Dupré, *The Other Dimension: A Search for the Meaning of Religious Attitudes* (Garden City, N.Y.: Doubleday & Company, Inc., 1972) and Peter Berger, *A Rumor of Angels* (Garden City, N.Y.: Doubleday Anchor, 1970).

68. Ermarth, *Wilhelm Dilthey*, 366.

69. Ibid., 22.

70. The expression "ontological argument" first appeared in the eighteenth century, and is perhaps best known through Kant's attack on it in the Transcendental Dialectic section of his *Critique of Pure Reason*. It is, in essence, an a priori argument that the existence of the idea of God as the most perfect being necessarily involves the objective existence of God. St. Anselm of Canterbury (c. 1033–1109) first formulated the argument in his *Proslogion* (chapter 2ff.) and was promptly criticized for it by his fellow Benedictine, Gaunilo. Thomas Aquinas rejects the argument in the *Summa Theologiae* (I q. 2 a. 1), but it was revived by Descartes in his *Meditations* (3 and 5) and in his *Discourse on Method* (Part IV). Few critics accept its validity as an argument.

71. Ermarth, *Wilhelm Dilthey*, 154.

Introduction to the *HUMAN SCIENCES*

An Attempt to Lay a
Foundation for the Study
of Society and History

Contents

Preface

The book whose first half I am publishing here combines a historical methodology with a systematic one, in order to solve the question of the philosophical foundations of the human sciences with the highest degree of certitude I can attain. The historical method follows the path of development which philosophy has pursued up to now in struggling toward such foundations. It seeks to identify the historical setting of individual theories in this development and to supply an orientation to the historically conditioned value of those theories. Indeed, by penetrating the interrelationships of that previous development, it seeks to reach a judgment on the most basic motive power behind the current scientific movement. In this way the historical description paves the way for the epistemological foundation, which will be the subject of the other half of this undertaking.

Because the historical and the systematic presentations should thus complement each other, the historical section will be easier to understand if I give some indication here of the basic systematic rationale.

The emancipation of the special sciences began at the end of the Middle Ages. But disciplines dealing with society and history remained in the traditional service of metaphysics until well into the eighteenth century. In fact, the growing power of natural science meant a new relationship of servility for those disciplines, one no less oppressive than the old one. The historical school—taken in a very broad sense—was the first to bring about the emancipation of historical consciousness and historical science from metaphysics. The system of social ideas in France in the seventeenth and eighteenth centuries—ideas such as natural law, natural religion, abstract political theory, and abstract political economy—bore its practical fruit in the French Revolution. And, at the same time, when the armies of this Revolution occupied and destroyed the old, oddly ramshackle structure of the German empire, weather-beaten by the ravages of a thousand years' history, there had developed in our homeland an insight into historical growth as the process in which all spiritual realities take their origin. And this insight brought to light the falsity of that whole system of social ideas. The historical school reached from Winckelmann and Herder through the romanticist school and on to Niebuhr, Jacob Grimm, Savigny, and Böckh. It was strengthened by the counterrevolution, expanding in England through Burke and in France through Guizot and Tocqueville. It took part in struggles of European society as the enemy of the ideas of the eighteenth century, whether they had to do with law, the state, or religion. A purely empirical way of looking at things animated this school: a loving immersion into the individual character of the historical process; a universal spirit of historical insight which seeks to determine the value of a state of affairs only in the context of its general development; and an historical spirit in social science which seeks to illumine and guide the present in its study of the past; finally, a spirit which sees the life of the spirit in every instance as historical life.

From that school a stream of new ideas has flowed into all the special sciences through countless channels.

But until now the historical school has not broken through the inner barriers which were bound to limit its theoretical development as well as its effect on life. What was missing from its study and evaluation of historical phenomena was a link with the analysis of facts of consciousness. Hence a foundation built on what is ultimately the only certain knowledge there is, in short, a philosophical foundation, was missing: There was just no sound connection established with epistemology and psychology. As a result, it never achieved a method of explanation either. But historical insight and comparative methods by themselves are incapable of establishing an independent system of human sciences or of exercising any practical influence on life. This is how things stood when Comte, John Stuart Mill, and Buckle then attempted to solve the riddle of the historical world anew by applying the principles and methods of natural science—accompanied by the ineffective protest of a livelier and profounder [historical] insight that could, however, neither establish its foundations nor develop in the face of the feebler, lower-level idea which, however, was based on analysis. The opposition of Carlyle and other spirited minds to exact science—both in the intensity of their hatred and in the constraint of their language and speech—was an indication of what the situation was like. And in the face of such uncertainty about the foundations of the human sciences special scientists soon either retreated to a position of mere description or came to be satisfied with subjective and clever views, or simply threw themselves back into the arms of a metaphysics which promised its adherents principles with the power to reshape practical living.

It was out of concern for this condition of the human sciences that I decided to try to provide a philosophical foundation for the principle behind the historical school and for the work of the special sciences which are presently so thoroughly dominated by it. I hoped thereby to smooth over the conflict between this historical school and the abstract theories. In my work I was tortured by the same questions which trouble every thinking historian, jurist, or politician. So there spontaneously arose in me the desire and the plan of laying the foundation of the human sciences. What is the complex of principles which underlies, at one and the same time, the judgment of the historian, the conclusions of the national economist, and the concepts of the jurist, and gives them their certitude? Is their system ultimately a metaphysical one? Is there perhaps a philosophy of history or a natural law based on metaphysical concepts? Or, if one refutes that suggestion, then where is the solid basis for the system of principles which ties together and guarantees the special sciences?

The answers of Comte and the positivists as well as John Stuart Mill and the empiricists to these questions seemed to me to mutilate historical reality to accommodate it to concepts and methods of the natural sciences. Reaction against such procedures, represented ingeniously by Lotze's *Microcosm,* seemed to me to sacrifice the justified independence of the special sciences, the productive power of their experiential methods, and the solidity of their foundations, to a sentimental disposition which longs to revive through science a satisfaction of mind which is gone forever. Only in inner experience, in facts of consciousness, did I find a firm anchorage for my thinking, and I am confident that no reader will evade the proof of this point. All science is a science of experience, but all experience has its original constitution and its validity in the conditions of our consciousness, in which experience takes place—in the totality of our nature. We call this standpoint—which logically sees the impossibility of going beyond these conditions, which would be like seeing without an eye or directing the knowing look behind the eye itself—the epistemological standpoint; modern science can recognize no other. Furthermore, it seemed to me that precisely from this standpoint the independence of human sciences finds a foundation of the sort that the historical school needs. For on the basis of that standpoint the idea we have of the whole of nature proves to be a mere shadow cast by a reality which remains hidden from us. By contrast, we lay hold of reality as it is only through facts of consciousness given in our inner experience. Analysis of these facts is the core of the human sciences. And so, in a fashion consonant with the spirit of the historical school, knowledge of principles of the mental world remains in the sphere of the mental world, and the human sciences constitute a system which is independent in its own right.

If it is true that on such matters I found myself to be in agreement on many counts with the epistemological views of Locke, Hume, and Kant, nevertheless I was compelled to conceive of this relationship of the facts of consciousness, in which all of us agree to recognize the whole basis of philosophy, in a different way than they did. If one sets aside some impulses, few in number and never developed scientifically (such as those of Herder and Wilhelm von Humboldt), earlier epistemology, both empirical and Kantian, explains experience and knowledge on the basis of a framework which is purely ideational. There is no real blood flowing in the veins of the knowing subject fabricated by Locke, Hume, and Kant, but only the diluted juice of reason as mere mental activity. But dealing with the whole man in history and psychology led me to take the whole man—in the multiplicity of his powers: this willing-feeling-perceiving being—as the basis for explaining knowledge and its concepts (such as outer world, time, substance, cause), even though, to be sure, knowledge appears to weave these concepts solely out of raw material it gets from perceiving, imagining, and thinking. The method of the following undertaking is therefore this: I compare every element of current abstract scientific thinking with the whole of human nature presented by experience, the study of language, and the study of history, and I look for their interrelationship. And the result is: The most important elements of our image and knowledge of reality—such as the unity of life in the person, the outer world, individuals apart from us, their life in time, and their influence on each other—are all things we can explain from this totality of human nature, whose real life process [*Lebensprozess*] manifests itself in its various aspects through willing, feeling, and imagining. It is not the assumption of a rigid a priori of our cognitive capacity, but only the history of development alone, proceeding from the totality of our being, which can answer the questions we all have to address to philosophy.

At this point we appear to have a solution to the most stubborn of all puzzles connected with this task of laying a foundation: the question about the origin and validity of our conviction about the reality of the external world. From the cognitive standpoint alone, the outer world always remains just a phenomenon; but from the standpoint of our total willing-feeling-perceiving being, external reality (that is, an "other" which is independent of us—leaving aside completely its spatial characteristics) is something we encounter simultaneously with our very selves and just as certainly. Consequently, it is given to us as life, not merely as idea. We do not know about this outer world by some sort of cause-and-effect reasoning procedure or anything like that; in fact, these ideas about cause and effect are themselves nothing but abstractions arising from the activity of our wills. In this way the horizon of experience expands, though it seemed at first as though experience gave us information only about our own internal states. The external world is as original with us as the unity of our life itself, and so is the presence of other living individuals. But the extent to which I can show this and the degree to which it will be further possible to establish a solid structure for knowledge of society and history on the basis of the standpoint outlined above must be left to the later judgment of the reader concerning the foundation-laying itself.

I have not shied away from a certain degree of detail in setting out the main idea and the leading principles for this epistemological basis of the human sciences in their relationship to the various aspects of the scholarly thinking of the present time; and this has solidified that idea and those principles in various ways. So this undertaking starts from an overview of the special human sciences, for the mass of material and the subject of this entire enterprise lie in them, and it will reason backward from them (first book). The first volume will then take the history of philosophical thought, which is in search of a solid basis for knowledge, through the historical period which saw the fate of the metaphysical foundation-laying decided (second book). I will try to show that a commonly recognized metaphysics was conditioned by a state of the sciences which we have since superseded, and that consequently the time of a metaphysical foundation for the human sciences is completely past. The second volume will first follow the historical progression to the stage of the special sciences and of epistemology, and it will survey and evaluate epistemological works done up to the present time (third book). It will then try its own epistemological foundation-laying for the human sciences (fourth and fifth books). The fullness of detail in the historical part has arisen not only out of the practical requirements of an introduction but also out of my conviction about the value of historical personal reflection paralleling epistemological reflection. The same conviction finds expression in the preference given for several generations now to the history of philosophy as well as in Hegel's, the later Schelling's, and Comte's efforts to establish their systems on a historical basis. The justification for this conviction is even more evident from the standpoint of historical development. For the history of intellectual development shows the growth of the same tree in the bright light of the sun, whose roots in the soil it is the task of a fundamental epistemological inquiry to search out.

My task has taken me through very different fields of knowledge; one will thus have to forgive me an occasional error. I hope the work will be commensurate, even if only to a degree, to its task of bringing together the essence of the historical and systematic insights which the jurist and the statesman, the theologian and the historian need as a basis for fruitful study of their disciplines.

This work is appearing before I have paid off an old obligation of finishing the biography of Schleiermacher. After finishing the preliminary work for the second half of the biography, I became aware while working through the materials that the exposition and critique of Schleiermacher's system everywhere presupposed discussions about the ultimate questions of philosophy. So the biography was delayed until the appearance of the present book, which will thus spare me such discussions there.

Easter, 1883   WILHELM DILTHEY
Berlin

Synopsis of the Organization of the Special Human Sciences, in Which the Necessity of an Underlying Science is Demonstrated

> Moreover, to this point reality has always revealed herself more nobly and beautifully to a science which investigates her in accord with her own laws than the most extreme efforts of mythical imagination and metaphysical speculation have been able to depict her.
>
> Hermann Helmholtz

1. Purpose of This Introduction to the Human Sciences

Since Bacon's famous work, treatises which discuss the foundation and method of the natural sciences and thus serve as introductions to their study have been written for the most part by natural scientists. The most famous of those treatises is by Sir John Herschel. It seems necessary to perform a similar service for those who work in history, politics, jurisprudence, or political economy, theology, literature, or art. Those who dedicate themselves to these sciences usually get involved in them because of practical requirements of society, which wants to supply occupational training to equip leaders of society with knowledge necessary to do their work. But this occupational training will enable an individual to achieve outstanding success only to the extent that it goes beyond merely technical training. One can compare society to a great machine workshop kept in operation by the services of countless persons. One who is trained in the isolated technology of a single occupation among those activities, no matter how thoroughly he has mastered his trade, is in the position of a laborer who works away his entire life in one solitary phase of this industry: he has no idea of the forces which set the industry in motion, no conception of its other parts or their contributions to the purpose of the whole enterprise. He is a servile instrument of society, not its consciously cooperative organ. My hope is that this introduction will lighten the task of politician and jurist, theologian and teacher: to know the role of the principles and rules which guide him in relation to the comprehensive reality of human society, to which, after all, his life's work is ultimately dedicated at that point at which he actively participates in it.

Insights we need to accomplish this task go back essentially to truths we must assume as the foundation for knowledge both of nature and of the historico-social world. Looked at in this way, this undertaking, which is based on the necessities of practical life, coincides with a problem which the purely theoretical situation poses.

Sciences which deal with historico-social reality are searching more intensely than ever before for their foundation and mutual relationships. Causes which operate in the special positive sciences are cooperating in this enterprise with more powerful impulses which have sprung from the social convulsions occurring since the French Revolution. Knowledge of the forces which prevail in society, of the causes of its convulsions, of the resources needed for sound progress and available in society, has become vital for our civilization. That is why the significance of sciences of society has been growing in comparison with natural sciences. In the large format of our modern life a transformation of scientific interests is being effected which is like the one which occurred in the small Greek polities of the fifth and fourth centuries B.C., when upheavals in this society of city-states produced the negative theories of Sophistic natural law and, in opposition to them, the work of the Socratic schools on the state.

2. Human Sciences as an Independent Whole alongside Natural Sciences

In this work we will group together the entire range of sciences which deal with historico-social reality under the name of "the human sciences" [*Geisteswissenschaften*]. The concept of these sciences by which they constitute a whole, and the demarcation of this whole as against natural science can ultimately be explained and established only in this work itself. Here at its beginning we are simply declaring the meaning we will give to the term when we use it and giving a provisional exposition of the essentials for establishing a distinction between natural sciences and this whole which comprises human sciences.

By "science" linguistic usage understands a sum total of propositions whose elements are concepts, that is, fully defined, univocal, and universally valid throughout the cognitive system; whose connecting links have an established basis; whose parts, finally, are bound together as a unit for communication, either because one can conceptualize a constituent element of reality in its totality through this chain of propositions or because one can regulate a branch of human activity by it. Under the expression "science," then, we are here designating every embodiment of intellectual data in which we find the characteristic notes just listed and to which as a result the name of science is generally applied. Accordingly, we are provisionally outlining the extent of our field of work. These intellectual data which have developed historically among men and to which general linguistic usage has applied the designation of sciences of man, of history, and of society constitute the reality which we wish not so much to master as mainly to comprehend. Empirical method demands that we draw from this stock of sciences themselves to analyze historically and critically the value of the individual procedures which thinking uses in solving its problems in this area; it demands further that we clarify, through observation of that great development whose subject is humanity itself, what the nature of knowledge and understanding is in this field. Such a method stands in contrast with one used recently all too often, precisely by the so-called positivists. They derive the content of the concept "science" from a definition of knowledge developed for the most part in the pursuit of natural science, and they decide on the basis of that kind of content what sorts of intellectual activities merit the name and rank of "science." And so some of them, acting on an arbitrary notion of knowledge, have shortsightedly and arrogantly refused the status of science to historical writing as produced by its great masters; others have maintained that sciences based on imperatives are in no way judgments about reality and must be transformed into knowledge of reality.

The sum of intellectual facts which fall under the notion of science is usually divided into two groups, one marked by the name "natural science"; for the other, oddly enough, there is no generally accepted designation. I subscribe to the linguistic usage of thinkers who call this other half of the intellectual world the "sciences of the mind" [*Geisteswissenschaften,* see note 42, page 62]. In the first place this description has become common and generally understood, not least because of the wide dissemination of John Stuart Mill's *Logic.* It also appears to be the least inappropriate term, compared with all the other unsuitable labels we have to choose from. It expresses the object of this study extremely imperfectly, for in this study we do not separate data of intellectual life from the psychophysical living unity of human nature. A theory which aims at describing and analyzing socio-historical facts cannot prescind from this totality of human nature and restrict itself to the intellectual. But the expression shares this drawback with every other one which has been current. Science of society (sociology), moral, historical, cultural sciences: all these descriptions suffer from the deficiency of being too narrow with respect to the object they are supposed to be expressing. And the name we have chosen here has at least this merit: it rightly identifies the central core of facts from which one sees the unity of these sciences in reality, maps out their extent, and draws up their boundaries vis-à-vis natural sciences, although imperfectly.

The motivation behind the habit of seeing these sciences as a unity in contrast with those of nature derives from the depth and fullness of human self-consciousness. Even when unaffected by investigations into the origins of the mind, a man finds in this self-consciousness a sovereignty of will, a responsibility for actions, a capacity for subordinating everything to thought and for resisting any foreign element in the citadel of freedom in his person: by these things he distinguishes himself from all of nature. He finds himself with respect to nature an *imperium in imperio*,[1] to use Spinoza's expression. And because for him only data of his own consciousness exist, a result is that every value and every goal in life has its locus in this independently functioning intellectual world within him, and every goal of his activities consists in producing intellectual results. And so he distinguishes nature from history, in which, surrounded though it is by that structure of objective necessity which nature consists of, freedom flashes forth at innumerable points in the whole. Here the actions of the will—in contrast with the mechanical process of changes in nature (which already contains from the start everything which ensues later)—really produce something and achieve true development both in the individual and in humanity as a whole. This is accomplished through expenditure of energy and through sacrifices, whose meaning the individual is constantly aware of in his experience. And all this means something above and beyond the tedious and empty repetition of the process of nature in the mind—a notion which idol worshipers of intellectual development luxuriate in as an ideal of historical progress.

Of course the metaphysical epoch—in whose view this difference in bases of explanation was immediately turned into a substantial difference in objective organization of the world's structure itself—struggled in vain to identify and establish formulas for the objective foundation of the differences between the facts of intellectual life and those of the processes of nature. Among all the changes which the metaphysics of the ancients experienced at the hands of medieval thinkers, none has been more important than the fact that, in the context of the dominant religious and theological movements in which these thinkers stood, the definition of the difference between the world of minds and that of bodies (together with the relation of both of these worlds to the deity) came to occupy the central focus in the system. The principal metaphysical work of the Middle Ages, *Summa de Veritate Catholicae Fidei* of Thomas, beginning with the second book, outlines an organization of the created world in which essence (*essentia, quidditas*) is distinguished from existence (*esse*), although they are identical in God himself.[2] In the hierarchy of created beings this *Summa* identifies, as a necessary highest member, spiritual substances not composed of matter and form but essentially incorporeal: these are the angels. It distinguishes them from intellectual substances or incorporeal subsisting forms which require bodies for perfecting their species (i.e., the species of man). In a polemic against the Arab philosophers the book develops over this point a metaphysics of the human spirit whose influence we can trace to the most recent metaphysical writers of our time.[3] From this world of imperishable substances it then distinguishes that part of created being essentially composed of matter and form. Other outstanding metaphysicians then related Thomas's metaphysics of the mind (rational psychology) to the new mechanistic view of the universe and the corpuscular theory, which were becoming dominant. But every attempt failed which tried to use the new concept of nature to construct a tenable conception of the relation between mind and body on the basis of this doctrine of substance. If Descartes developed his conception of nature as a huge machine on the basis of clear, distinct characteristics of bodies as spatial magnitudes, and if he regarded the quantity of motion found in this whole as something constant, nonetheless a contradiction entered his system as soon as one assumed that even a single soul introduced a motion into this material system from the outside. And the inconceivability of an influence by nonspatial substances on this extended system was not in the least diminished by the fact that Descartes reduced the spatial extent of this reciprocal effect to a single point—as if he could make the difficulty disappear by doing that. The rashness of the view that the deity maintained this play of reciprocal influences by constantly intervening himself as well as of the other view that, on the contrary, the deity (as the most skillful craftsman) has so set the two clocks of the material system and of the spiritual world from the beginning that a process of nature would seem to call forth a perception, and an act of the will would seem to effect a change in the outer world—these views demonstrated as clearly as possible the incompatibility of the new metaphysics of nature with the traditional metaphysics of spiritual substances. Thus this problem acted like a constantly irritating spur toward dissolving the metaphysical standpoint altogether. This dissolution was to reach its full term in the knowledge, which was to develop later, that experience of self-consciousness is the starting point for the concept of substance and that this concept of substance arises from accommodating the experience of self-consciousness to external experiences achieved by knowledge built on the principle of sufficient reason. And so this doctrine of spiritual substances is nothing but a transferral of the concept developed in that sort of metamorphosis back to the experience in which its first impulse was given.

In place of the contrast between material and spiritual substances there emerged the contrast between outer world, as something given in external perception (sensation) through the senses, and inner world, as something given primarily through the inner conception of psychic events and actions (reflection). In this way the problem assumes a more modest form, but one which includes the possibility of empirical treatment. And the same kinds of experiences which had resulted in scientifically untenable expression in the doctrine of substance in rational psychology are now asserting themselves in the context of the new and better methods.

To begin with, it suffices for independently establishing the human sciences that, critically speaking, those events the mind links together out of material supplied exclusively by the senses be separated as a special class from facts given primarily in inner experience (i.e., without any cooperation of the senses) and are then formed out of the original stuff of inner experience on the occasion of external natural processes in such a way that they seem to be attributed to these processes through a procedure amounting to analogical inference. Thus a special realm of experiences emerges, which has its independent origin and its content in inner experience and accordingly is naturally the object of a special science of experience. And so long as no one maintains that he can derive and better explain the essence of the emotion, poetic creativity, and rational reflection, which we call Goethe's life, out of the design of his brain or the characteristics of his body, then no one will challenge the independent position of such a science. Because what exists for us exists in virtue of this inner experience, and because we thus encounter what has value or is an end for us only in the experience of our feeling and our will, it follows that it is in such a science that principles of our knowledge exist which determine the extent to which nature can exist for us; and it is in this science that principles of our conduct exist which explain the presence of the purposes, goods, and values which are the basis for all practical commerce with nature.

The deeper roots of the independent status of human sciences alongside natural sciences (which status constitutes the focal point of the construction [*Konstruktion*] of the human sciences in this book) will be established gradually in this work. This is because I will carry out the analysis of the total experience of the intellectual world, in its incommensurability with all sense experience of nature, throughout the book. I am only clarifying this problem here to the extent of referring to the double sense in which the asymmetrical nature of these two sets of facts can be maintained; correspondingly, the concept of the boundaries of knowledge of nature also takes on a double significance.[4]

One of our foremost natural scientists has undertaken to determine these boundaries in a much discussed treatise and has just recently explained more fully the delineations of his science.[5] If we were to imagine all modifications in the physical world to be reduced to movements of atoms caused by their constant central forces, we would know the universe in natural-scientific terms. "A mind"—he starts off with this image from Laplace—"which at a given moment knew all the forces operating in nature and the mutual relationship of the beings which make up nature, if it were also comprehensive enough to subject these data to analysis, would grasp the motions of the greatest celestial bodies as well as of the lightest atom in one and the same formula."[6] Because human understanding of the science of astronomy is "a faint likeness of such a mind," Du Bois-Reymond calls the knowledge of a material system imagined by Laplace an astronomical one. From this conception one arrives in fact at a very clear idea of the limits which circumscribe the tendency of the natural scientific mind.

Allow me to introduce into our reflection a distinction which bears on the concept of limits to knowledge of nature. Because we encounter reality, as the correlative of experience, through the cooperation of our senses with inner experience,[7] the difference in the provenance of the elements which comprise our experience results in an incommensurability in the elements of our scientific calculation. And this incommensurability does not permit us to derive the reality of either particular source from the other. Thus we attain a conception of matter on the basis of spatial characteristics, but only by way of the facticity [*Faktizität*] of the sense of touch, in which we encounter resistance. Each one of the senses is imprisoned inside a range of sense qualities peculiar to it, and we have to make a transition from sensation to awareness of an internal state of affairs if we are to grasp a mental state at a given moment. Consequently, all we can do is accept data in the dissimilarity in which they appear because of their difference in origin; their factual character is unfathomable for us. All our knowledge is limited to establishing uniformities of sequence and simultaneity, which relate data to one another in our experience. These limits are situated in the very conditions of our experience itself, limits existing at every point in natural science; they are not external constraints our knowledge of nature clashes with, but conditions of knowledge immanent in experience itself. But the presence of these immanent barriers of knowledge in no way constitutes a hindrance to knowing. If one understands by the term "conceiving" a full clarity in comprehending a state of affairs, then we are dealing here with limits which conceiving itself encounters. But regardless whether science subsumes either [sense] qualities or facts of consciousness in the calculation it makes in deducing changes in reality from movements of atoms: even if it is possible to subsume those qualities or facts in that way, the fact that one could not make such a deduction does not hinder the operation of those changes. I can no more find a transition from mere mathematical determination or quantity of motion to a color or a sound than I can to a process of consciousness. I can no better explain blue light by the appropriate oscillation frequency than I can a negative judgment in a cerebral process. Because physics leaves it to physiology to explain the sense-quality "blue," and physiology in turn (since it also cannot conjure up "blue" from the motion of material parts) turns it over to psychology, it ends up, as in a Chinese puzzle, stuck with psychology. In itself, however, the hypothesis that postulates that sense-qualities arise in the process of sensation is first of all just an expedient supporting the calculation that changes I experience in reality are rooted in a certain class of changes which make up part of the content of my experience. This is done to reduce them to one level, as far as possible, for easier understanding. If it were possible to substitute constantly and solidly established facts of consciousness for definitely determined facts which have a solid place in the system of the mechanistic view of nature, and then, in accordance with the system of uniformities in which the latter facts are located, to establish the onset of processes of consciousness as being in complete harmony with experience, then these facts of consciousness would be as well fitted into the structure of knowledge of nature as any sound or color is.

But precisely at this point the dissimilarity of material and intellectual processes asserts itself in a completely different sense and sets down totally different limits for knowledge of nature. Impossibility of deriving intellectual facts from those of the mechanistic order of nature (an impossibility grounded in the difference of their provenience) does not prevent one from adapting the former into the system of the latter. Only when relations between facts of the intellectual world prove to be so different in kind from uniformities of the course of nature that subordination of intellectual facts to those established by mechanistic knowledge of nature is out of the question—only then can we demonstrate, not immanent limits for experiential knowledge, but limits at which knowledge of nature stops and independent science of the mind begins which is organized around its own central focus. The fundamental problem consequently is establishing the precise kind of incommensurability between relations of intellectual processes and uniformities of material processes which would preclude reducing the former to mere characteristics or facets of matter. That dissimilarity must accordingly be of a sort completely different from the dissimilarity between individual spheres of material laws of the kind that mathematics, physics, chemistry, and physiology manifest in an ever more logically developed order of subordination among themselves. Excluding facts of the mind from the framework of matter with its characteristic laws always assumes that contradiction will ensue if one attempts to subordinate facts from one sphere to those of the other. Indeed, this is what we mean when we say that the facts of self-consciousness and the unity of consciousness connected with it, as well as freedom and the facts of moral life linked to it, demonstrate the incommensurability of intellectual life with matter. Contrast that with spatial organization and divisibility of matter and with mechanical necessity which controls the activity of individual particles of matter. Efforts to formulate this kind of difference between mind and nature based on unity of consciousness and spontaneity of will are almost as old as more rigorous reflection on the relation between mind and nature in general.

Because the famous natural scientist has introduced into his exposition this differentiation between immanent boundaries of experience on the one hand and limits to subordinating facts under the system of knowledge of nature on the other hand, concepts of boundaries and inexplicability acquire a precisely definable meaning; in consequence, difficulties disappear which had become prominent in the controversy over boundaries of the knowledge of nature occasioned by his treatise. Existence of immanent boundaries of experience in no way decides the question of subordinating intellectual facts under the system of knowledge of matter. If one makes an attempt, as Häckel and other scholars have done, to assume psychic life in the elements of an organisim and thus produce such a subordination of intellectual events to the system of nature, such an experiment by no means excludes knowledge of the immanent boundaries of all experience; only the second kind of investigation of the limits of knowledge of nature renders a verdict on that attempt. That is why Du Bois-Reymond himself pressed on to this second investigation and used not only the argument of unity of consciousness but also the other one of spontaneity of will in his demonstration. His demonstration "that the processes of the mind are never to be understood from their material conditions"[8] is carried out in the following fashion. Even if we had a complete knowledge of all the parts of the material system and their mutual relations and movements, it still remains completely incomprehensible how it should not be a matter of indifference to a quantity of carbon, hydrogen, nitrogen, or oxygen atoms what positions they occupy or how they move. This inexplicability of the spiritual similarly persists if one outfits these elements like monads, each with its own isolated consciousness; on the basis of this assumption, moreover, one cannot explain unitary consciousness of the individual.[9] The thesis he has to prove contains in the expression "never to be understood" a double meaning which, in the proof itself, results in the appearance of two arguments of totally different importance. He maintains first that the attempt to derive intellectual facts from material changes (this attempt is now regarded as crude materialism and has died out, except in the form of assuming psychic characteristics in the elements) cannot remove the immanent boundary of all experience—which is certainly so, but proves nothing against subordinating mind to knowledge of nature. And he then goes on to maintain that this attempt must founder on the contradiction between our conception of matter and the attribute of unity which characterizes our consciousness. In his later polemic against Häckel he adds another argument, that under such an assumption a further contradiction arises between how a material element in the system of nature is mechanically determined and how spontaneity of will is experienced: a "will" (in the components of matter) which "should will whether it wants to or not, and this in a relation of direct proportionality of the masses involved and in inverse proportion to the square of the distances" is a contradiction in terms.[10]

3. Relationship of This Whole to That of the Natural Sciences

Nevertheless, to a great extent the human sciences include facts of nature and are founded on knowledge of nature.

If one were to imagine purely intellectual beings in a realm of persons consisting solely of such beings, then their emergence, preservation, and development, as well as their disappearance (regardless of what notion one might entertain about the background from which they would emerge and into which they would return) would be bound to conditions of an intellectual kind; their well-being would be based on their relation to the intellectual world; their interconnections with one another and their actions on one another would be effected through purely intellectual means, and the permanent effects of their actions would be of a purely intellectual kind; even their withdrawal from the realm of persons would have its basis in the intellectual. The system governing such individuals would be known by sciences of the mind alone. In reality, however, an individual comes to be, continues to be, and develops on the basis of functions of the animal organism and their relations with the surrounding process of nature; his feeling of life is at least partially grounded in these functions; his impressions are conditioned by his sense organs and their modifications from the side of the external world; we find that the abundance and flexibility of his ideas and the intensity as well as the direction of his acts of will depend in many ways on changes in his nervous system. An impulse of the will shortens his muscle fibers, and an outward activity is similarly linked with changes in the relative positions of the molecules of his organism; lasting effects of his acts of will exist only as changes in the material world. Thus a man's intellectual life is part of the psychophysical unity of life as his human existence and life manifests it, separable from that unity only through abstraction. The system comprising these living individuals is the reality which constitutes the object of the historico-social sciences.

In fact, the human being as a living unity, in virtue of the double standpoint of our conception (regardless of the metaphysical state of the case), is present to us as a grouping of intellectual facts as far as inner awareness is concerned and conversely as a corporeal whole insofar as we perceive through the senses. Inner awareness and external perception never occur in the same act, and therefore we never encounter the fact of intellectual life simultaneously with the fact of bodily existence.[11] Hence two different and mutually irreducible standpoints necessarily result for the scientific approach, which seeks to grasp intellectual facts and the physical world in their mutual relationship (whose expression is the psychophysical unity of life). If I start from inner experience, I find the entire outer world given to me in my consciousness, the laws of this totality of nature being subject to conditions of my consciousness, hence dependent on them. This is the standpoint which German philosophy at the turning point between the eighteenth century and our own called transcendental philosophy. If, however, I take the system of nature just as it stands before me as a reality for my natural mode of apprehension and I perceive in the temporal process of this outer world and its spatial divisions the psychic events included in it; and if I find that changes in intellectual life depend on the intervention which nature or experiment makes and consists in material changes which exert pressure on the nervous system; and if observation of living development and of pathological states expands these experiences into a comprehensive picture of how the corporeal conditions the intellectual: then there emerges the conception of the natural scientist who presses from the outside inward, from material change to intellectual change. Thus the antagonism between the philosopher and the natural scientist is determined by the opposition between their points of departure.

Let us now take the viewpoint of natural science as our point of departure. As long as this viewpoint remains conscious of its limitations, its results are indisputable. They acquire a more precise determination of their epistemological value only from the standpoint of inner experience. Natural science analyzes causal connections of the process of nature. Where this analysis has reached the points at which a material state of affairs or a material change is regularly connected with a psychic state of affairs or a psychic change (without there being any further connecting link discernible between them), then precisely this regular relationship alone is all that can be established; one cannot, however, describe the relation as one of cause and effect. We find uniformities of life in the one sphere regularly linked with those in the other, and the mathematical concept of function is the expression of this relationship. A conception of this relation by which intellectual changes alongside corporeal changes would be comparable to the running of two synchronized clocks is as much in accord with experience as a conception which assumes only one clock mechanism as the basis of explanation or, nonfiguratively, which regards both spheres of experience as different manifestations of a single ground. Dependence of the intellectual on the structure of nature is therefore the relationship by which the general system of nature causally determines those material states and changes regularly connected for us with intellectual states and changes with no further recognizable mediation between them. Thus knowledge of nature observes the concatenation of causes working up to the level of psychophysical life itself. But here a change takes place in which the relation of the material and the psychical eludes causal conceptualization, and this change retroactively evokes a change in the material world. In this connection the importance of the structure of the nervous system reveals itself to the physiologist's research. The confusing phenomena of life are analyzed into a clear conception of dependencies whose effect is to lead the process of nature to introduce changes which touch man himself. Those changes impinge on the nervous system through the gates of the sense organs: sensation, imagination, feeling, and desire arise and react on the course of nature. The unity of life itself, which fills us with an immediate feeling of our undivided existence, is dissolved into a system of relationships we can establish empirically between facts of consciousness and the structure and functions of the nervous system. For we know only by means of the nervous system that every mental act is accompanied by a change in our bodies; conversely, we know only by means of its effect on the nervous system that every bodily change is accompanied by a change in our psychic condition.

From this analysis of the psychophysical unities of life a clearer concept now emerges of their dependence on the whole system of nature in which they appear and act, and out of which they withdraw again; hence the dependence of the study of socio-historical reality on knowledge of nature as well. On this basis one can assess the degree of justification appropriate to the theories of Auguste Comte and Herbert Spencer on the position of these sciences in the general hierarchy of science they have drawn up. Just as this treatise will try to establish the relative independence of human sciences, it must also develop the other side of the position of those sciences in the picture of science as a whole. And this other side is the system of dependencies by which human sciences are conditioned by knowledge of nature and consequently make up the last and highest member in a structure which begins with a foundation in mathematics. Mental facts are the highest boundary of facts of nature; facts of nature constitute the lower conditions of mental life. Precisely because the realm of persons (i.e., of human society and history) is the highest phenomenon in the earthly sphere of experience, knowledge of it requires at countless points that we know the system of presuppositions laid down for its development in the world of nature.

And in fact man, in line with his position in the causal order of nature as just outlined, is conditioned by nature in a *double respect*.

As we have seen, the psychophysical individual constantly receives impulses from the general course of nature by way of the nervous system and in turn reacts on nature's course. But it is in the very nature of that individual that the actions it generates are principally of a purposeful kind. For this psychophysical individual it may happen, on the one hand, that the process of nature and its makeup might take the lead in shaping the purposes themselves; on the other hand, nature's process might cooperate with that individual as a means for attaining these goals. And so, even when we *exercise volition*, when we influence nature, simply because we are not blind forces but wills which determine their ends through deliberation, we are dependent on the order of nature. Accordingly, psychophysical individuals are doubly dependent on the course of nature. On the one hand, the process of nature (from the standpoint of the position of the earth in the cosmic whole as a system of causes) affects socio-historical reality, and the great problem of the relationship of the course of nature and of freedom in this reality resolves itself for the empirical scientist into countless special questions bearing on the relation between facts of mind and influences of nature. On the other hand, however, there are counteractive forces arising out of the purposes of this realm of persons which react back on nature and on the earth (which man regards in this sense as his home, where he tries to make himself comfortable), and even these reactive forces are dependent on his use of the system of natural laws. All goals exist for man exclusively in the mental process itself, for after all it is only there that anything at all exists for him; but a purpose seeks out its instruments within the order of nature. How surprising the change is, often, that the creative power of the mind has wrought in the external world; and yet it is in the latter alone that the agency exists by which the value so fashioned is also available for others. Such, for example, are the few pages which came into the hands of Copernicus as a material residue of the profoundest mental labor of the ancients, suggesting that he assume motion of the earth; those pages became the starting point for revolutionizing our world picture.

At this point one can see how relative the boundary is which separates these two classes of sciences from each other. Disputes such as those carried on over the position of general philology are fruitless. At both of the transition points which lead from study of nature to that of mind, that is, at those points at which the system of nature influences development of the mind and at those other points at which mind influences nature or acts as a transit point for influencing another mind, knowledge of both types is thoroughly mixed together. Knowledge of natural sciences blends with that of human sciences. As a matter of fact, in accord with the double manner in which the process of nature conditions the life of the mind, knowledge of the formative influence of nature is frequently intertwined with establishing the influence nature exercises as the material content of activity. Thus from knowledge of natural laws of formation of sounds we derive an important part·of grammar and of music theory; conversely, the genius of language or music is bound up with these natural laws, and understanding of this dependency therefore affects the study of achievements of that genius.

Further, we can see at this point that knowledge of conditions existing in nature and developed by natural science in large measure constitutes the foundation for studying mental facts. The entire cosmic structure conditions not only development of an individual man but also expansion of the human race over the entire earth and shaping of its historical destiny. Wars, for example, constitute a principal component of all history, for history, as political, is mainly concerned with the will of states, which in turn expresses itself in weapons with which it tries to have its way. But theory of war depends in the first place on knowledge of the physical, which affords a foundation and a means for disputing wills. For it is only by physical force that war pursues its goal of imposing our will on the enemy. This also implies that we should force the enemy on the battlefield to a level of defenselessness (which constitutes the theoretical goal of the violence known as war), to a point at which his position is more disadvantageous than the sacrifice we demand of him and can be exchanged only for one still worse. In this grand calculation, therefore, the most important and most preoccupying figures for science to consider are physical conditions and means, while there is very little to say about psychic factors.

Indeed, sciences of man, society, and history are founded on those of nature in the first place insofar as we can study psychophysical units only with the aid of biology, but also insofar as the means by which their development and purposeful activity take place (and toward whose mastery they are largely oriented) is nature. With regard to the first aspect, sciences of the organism make up their foundation; with regard to the second, sciences are mainly those of inorganic nature. Of course the structure one must explain consists first of all in the fact that these natural conditions determine development and distribution of intellectual life on the face of the earth, and in the fact that man's purposeful activity is tied to laws of nature and is thus conditioned by knowledge and exploitation of nature. So the first relation manifests only man's dependence on nature, but the second includes this dependence only as the other side of the history of his increasing mastery over the universe. Ritter has done a comparative analysis of the part of the first relationship which encompasses the relations of man to his natural milieu. Brilliant insights— especially his comparative assessment of the continents of the earth based on the articulation of their contours—give an inkling of a kind of predestination implicit in spatial relationships of the world. Subsequent work, however, has not substantiated this view, which Ritter regarded as a teleology of universal history and which Buckle adopted into the service of naturalism. In place of the idea of uniform dependency of man on natural conditions the more cautious view emerges that the struggle of intellectual-moral forces with the conditions of lifeless space has steadily lessened the dependency relationship in the case of historical peoples (in contrast with ahistorical ones). So even here an independent science of historico-spatial reality has asserted itself, a science which uses natural conditions in its explanations. The other relationship shows, however, that along with dependence which is implicit in adapting to natural conditions, we see a mastery of space so bound up with scientific thought and technology that mankind historically achieves mastery precisely by means of its subordination. *Natura enim non nisi parendo vincitur.*[12]

Nevertheless, we cannot consider the problem of the relation of human sciences to knowledge of nature as solved until we resolve that contradiction with which we set out—between the transcendental standpoint (for which nature is subject to the conditions of consciousness) and the objective empirical standpoint (for which the development of the intellectual is subject to the conditions of the universe). This task makes up one side of the problem of knowledge. If one restricts this problem to the human sciences, it appears that a solution which will satisfy everyone is not impossible. Conditions of such a solution would be: demonstrating the objective reality of inner experience and verifying the existence of an outer world. One would thus have intellectual events and intellectual beings existing in this outer world in virtue of a process of communication of our inner being into that outer world. Just as the blinded eye which has gazed into the sun multiplies its image in the most varied colors and at the most varied spatial locations, so does our conception multiply the image of our inner life and translate it into manifold modifications at various locations in the universe around us. But we can logically describe and justify this process as an analogical conclusion which begins with this inner life originally given to us alone, proceeds by way of ideas formed from expressions linked to that inner life, and ends in a cognate being and ground corresponding to related phenomena of the outer world. Whatever nature might be in itself, we may satisfy study of the causes of mental reality if we can in any case conceive of their appearances and use them as signs of the real and if we can conceive of uniformities in their simultaneity and succession and use them as a sign of such uniformities in the real. But if one enters into the realm of the mind and investigates nature insofar as it is the object of intelligence or insofar as it is interwoven with the will as end or means, it remains for the mind only what it is in the mind; whatever it might be in itself is entirely a matter of indifference here. It is enough that the mind can count on nature's lawfulness for the mind's activities in whatever way it encounters nature, enough that the mind can enjoy the beautiful appearance of nature's existence.

4. Synopses of the Human Sciences

For the person who ventures into this work on the human sciences we must try to provide a provisional survey of this other half of the intellectual world and thereby define the task of the work.

The sciences of the mind are not yet constituted as a whole [*als ein Ganzes*]. They still cannot erect a structure which would organize their individual truths according to their relationships of dependence on other truths and on experience.

These sciences have arisen out of the practical activity of life itself and have been developed through the demands of vocational training; classification of the faculties which serve this vocational training is thus the organic [*naturgewachsene*] form of their structure. Indeed, their first concepts and rules were discovered for the most part in the exercise of social functions themselves. Ihering has shown how juridical reflection has created the basic concepts of Roman law through deliberate intellectual effort carried out in the practice of law. Similarly, analysis of the older Greek constitutions also shows the results in them of a remarkable power of conscious political thought based on clear concepts and principles. The basic idea that freedom of the individual is focused in his participation in political power, but that the state government regulates this participation in proportion to the individual's accomplishments for the common good, was first a leading idea for the art of politics itself and was subsequently only developed by the great theoreticians of the Socratic school in a scientific connection. At that time progress toward comprehensive scientific theories depended mainly on the need to give vocational training to the leading social classes. Thus as early as the period of the Sophists in Greece, rhetoric and politics arose from the requirements of higher political instruction, and the history of most of the human sciences among modern peoples shows the dominant influences of the same basic relationship. Literature of the Romans about their public affairs received its most ancient articulation through the fact that it developed out of instructions for priests and individual magistrates.[13] Hence, finally, organization [*Systematik*] of the human sciences which include the basis of vocational training for the leading organs of society as well as the description of this organization in encyclopedias arose from the need for an overview of the requisites for such preparatory instruction. The most natural form of these encyclopedias, as Schleiermacher has masterfully shown with theology, will always be one which organizes from the standpoint of this purpose.

Within these restrictions, the person involved in the human sciences will find in such encyclopedic works an overview of specific prominent groupings of these sciences.[14]

Attempts which go beyond such efforts and seek to discover the general organization of sciences dealing with historic-social reality have come out of philosophy. To the extent that they have sought to deduce this organization from metaphysical principles, they have succumbed to the fate of all metaphysics. Bacon has used a better method inasmuch as he related available sciences of the mind to the problem of knowledge of reality based on experience and measured their accomplishments and their deficiencies by the task to be done. In his *Pansophia* Comenius sought to derive the correct order of steps to be followed in imparting instruction from the relationship of inner dependence which truths bore to one another. And just as, in contrast with the false concept of formal education, he thus discovered the basic idea of a future educational program (unfortunately still in the future even today), he paved the way for a correct classification of the sciences through the principle of dependence of truths in one another. Inasmuch as Comte brought under investigation the connection between this logical order of dependence between truths and the historical relationship of their order of appearance, he created the foundation for a true philosophy of the sciences. He regarded the constitution of the science of historico-social realities as the goal of his great work, and in fact his work did produce a strong movement in this direction: Mill, Littré, and Herbert Spencer have picked up the problem of the structure of the historico-social sciences.[15] These labors afford the person venturing into the human sciences a completely different kind of survey than does the classification of vocational studies. They fit the human sciences into the general framework of knowledge; they attack the problem of these sciences in its full extent; and they set about a solution with a scientific construction which embraces the whole of historico-social reality. Nevertheless, filled with the currently dominant rage for bold scientific construction among the English and the French—without an intimate feeling for historical reality built up only over many years of work in special research—these positivists have failed to discover precisely the point of departure for their efforts which would have corresponded to their principle of unifying the individual sciences. They ought to have begun their work by establishing the architectonic of the immense edifice of positive human sciences—an edifice constantly broadened by additions, altered time and time again from within, taking shape gradually over thousands of years. They ought to have made themselves understood through fuller penetration into its general structural plan and in this way, with a sound eye for the logic of history, have done justice to the many-sidedness in which these sciences have actually developed. They have set up a temporary structure, which is no more tenable than the wild speculations of Schelling and Oken about nature. And so it has happened that German philosophies of mind developed on a metaphysical principle—by Hegel, Schleiermacher, and the later Schelling—use advances made by positive human sciences more incisively than works of these positive philosophers do.

Other attempts at comprehensive organization in the sphere of human sciences have come about in Germany out of preoccupation with problems of political science, which involves, of course, an inherent one-sidedness of viewpoint.[16]

Human sciences do not constitute a whole because of a logical constitution which would be analogous to organization of the knowledge of nature; their structure has developed differently and has to be considered henceforth as it has evolved historically.

5. Their Material

The content of these sciences consists of historico-social reality insofar as the consciousness of humanity has preserved it as historical information and insofar as it has been made accessible to science in the form of social information encompassing the present state of affairs. As immense as this material is, nevertheless its incompleteness is obvious. Interests which in no way correspond to the needs of science and conditions of transmission totally unrelated to those needs have determined the state of our historical information. From that time on in which kinfolk and comrades-in-arms gathered around the campfire told stories about the deeds of their heroes and the divine origin of their tribe, the strong interest of people living together has selected and preserved facts from out of the murky flow of routine human existence. The interest of a later period along with historical dispensation have decided what portion of these facts should come down to us. Historical writing, as a liberal art of representation, summarizes from this immeasurable whole one part worthy of attention from some viewpoint or other. Furthermore, today's society lives so to speak on top of the layers and rubble of the past. Residues of cultural labors in language and superstition, in custom and in law, but also in material changes which transcend mere records, contain a tradition which supports written records in an invaluable way. In fact, the hand of historical dispensation has decided even about their preservation. Only in two particulars does a state of materials exist which answers to the requirements of science. The course of intellectual movements in modern Europe has been preserved in an adequate state of completeness in the treatises which are its components. And the work done in statistics allows—for the brief period and the narrow range of countries in which they have been used—a mathematically based insight into the facts of society which they comprise; they make it possible to lay a precise foundation for studying the present condition of society.

Lack of clarity in organizing this immense material also figures into this fragmentariness; indeed, it has contributed considerably to increase it. When human intelligence began to bring reality under the control of thought, moved by wonder it first directed its attention toward the heavens; this vault over us, which seems to rest on the arc of the horizon, engaged its interest: a self-contained spatial universe which encompasses man always and everywhere. So it was that orientation in the structure of the world was the starting point for scientific research in the eastern countries and in Europe. The universe of intellectual facts in all its immensity is not visible to the eye but only to the unifying intelligence of the researcher; it makes its appearance in some isolated part or other where a scholar links facts together, tests them, and establishes their validity; then it builds itself up in the inner realm of the mind. Critical sifting of traditions and establishing and assembling facts thus make up a first comprehensive accomplishment of the human sciences. Now that philology has developed an exemplary technique for the most difficult and most beautiful material in history—classical antiquity—this work is carried on in part in countless monographs and in part as an ingredient of more far-reaching investigations. Organization of this pure description of historico-social reality—given that this organization has the goal of describing types and variations of intellectual reality around the world in space and time on the basis of terrestrial physics and with the help of geography—can maintain its clarity only by constantly falling back on clear spatial measure, numerical relationships, and chronology, and with the help of graphic depiction.

Mere collecting and sifting of material gradually crosses over here into conceptual reworking and organizing.

6. Three kinds of Assertion in Them

The human sciences—as they exist and function in virtue of the logic of the concern which has been operative in their history (and not as those bold architects wish who want to construct them anew)—combine three different classes of assertion. One of them expresses reality which is given in observation: it contains the historical component of knowledge. A second class develops the uniform behavior of parts of this reality which we isolate by abstraction: this class contains the theoretical component of knowledge. The third class expresses value judgments and prescribes rules: it contains the practical component of the human sciences. Facts, theorems, value judgments and rules: the human sciences comprise these three classes of propositions. And the relation between the historical, the abstract-theoretical, and practical tendencies pervades the human sciences as a universal fundamental relationship. Because they are a standing refutation of Spinoza's principle *omnis determinatio est negatio*,[17] the idea of the singular or the individual is as much of a final goal in them as development of abstract uniformities is. From its first root in consciousness to its highest point, the system of value judgments and imperatives is independent of the first two classes. The relationship of these three functions to one another in thinking consciousness can be developed only in the course of epistemological analysis (more comprehensively: of personal reflection). In any case, statements about reality in value judgments and imperatives remain radically distinct; hence two kinds of propositions emerge, which are fundamentally different from each other. We must also recognize that this difference in human sciences results in a double structural basis for them. Given how they have developed, human sciences embrace not only knowledge of what exists but also awareness of the system of value judgments and imperatives as one in which values, ideals, rules, and an orientation toward shaping the future are linked together. A political judgment which rejects an institution is not true or false but right or wrong, depending on how one evaluates the tendency and purpose of that judgment; but a political judgment which discusses the relations of this institution to other institutions can be true or false. Only when this insight guides the theory of proposition, assertion, and judgment [*Satz, Aussage, Urteil*] will we have an epistemological foundation which does not compress the state of the human sciences into the confines of a knowledge of uniformities analogous to those in the natural sciences and thereby mutilate them, but one which comprehends and establishes them in accord with how they have developed.

7. Separating Out the Special Sciences from Historico-Social Reality

The goals of the human sciences—to lay hold of the singular and the individual in historico-social reality; to recognize uniformities operative in shaping the singular; to establish goals and rules for its continued development—can be attained only by the devices of reason: analysis and abstraction. Abstract expression, in which one ignores some aspects of a state of affairs and develops others, is not the exclusive final goal of these sciences, but it is their indispensable means. Just as abstract thinking may not dissolve the independence of other goals of these sciences, neither can historical or theoretical knowledge nor development of rules which in fact guide society dispense with abstract thinking. The dispute between the historical and abstract schools arose because the abstract school committed the first mistake and the historical school the other. Every special science originates only by the device of selecting a portion of historico-social reality. Even history ignores the features of the lives of individual men and of society which, in the period to be described, are the same as those of all other periods; its eye is directed toward the distinctive and the singular. The individual historian may deceive himself in such matters, because directing his attention in a certain way causes the selection of features to arise immediately with his sources; but whoever compares his real accomplishment with the whole range of facts of socio-historical reality must recognize this. From this comes the important thesis that every individual science of the mind consciously lays hold of and knows socio-historical reality only relatively, in its relationship to other sciences of the mind. The organization of these sciences and their healthy growth in their separated state are consequently bound up with insight into the relation of each of their truths to the whole of reality of which they are a part; their organization and growth are bound up also with constant awareness of the abstraction by which these truths exist and of their limited cognitive value because of their abstract character.

We are now in a position to introduce the basic analyses by which special sciences of the mind have sought to master their enormous subject matter.

8. Sciences of Individual Human Beings as Elements of This Reality

Analysis finds in living unities (the psychophysical individuals) the elements out of which society and history are constructed, and study of these living unities makes up the most fundamental group of sciences of the mind. For natural sciences the physical appearance of bodies of varying size—which move about in space, now extending themselves and expanding their range, now drawing back and reducing it, bodies in which changes of characteristics occur—is given as the starting point of their investigations. They have only gradually come closer to more tenable views about the constitution of matter. In this particular, a much more favorable relationship exists between historico-social reality and intelligence. Intelligence finds unity immediately given in its own makeup, a unity which is the basic element in the intricate pattern of society; but the natural sciences have to discover that element. The subjects to which thought, in accordance with its unfailing law, attaches predicates (through which all knowledge takes place) are elements which the natural sciences arrive at only hypothetically by breaking up external reality, rupturing and taking things apart, whereas the human sciences encounter them as real unities given as facts in inner experience. Natural science constructs matter out of small elementary particles no longer capable of existing independently and conceivable only as components of molecules; unities which mutually interact in the marvelously intertwined whole of history and society are individuals, psychophysical wholes, each of which is different from every other, each of which is a world in itself. After all, the world exists nowhere else but precisely in the mind of such an individual. We can elucidate this immensity of a psychophysical whole—which ultimately simply contains the immensity of nature itself—by analyzing the world of ideas. For it is there that a particular view first takes form out of perceptions and conceptions, and then, no matter what abundance of elements that view consists of, it enters as an element into the conscious combination and separation of ideas. And this uniqueness of each such individual, who acts at some point in the immense intellectual universe, can be tracked down to its individual components in accordance with the principle *individuum est ineffabile,*[18] by which we will recognize that uniqueness for the first time in its full range of meaning.

Anthropology and psychology contain the theory of these psychophysical units of life. The whole of history and life experience makes up their content, and it is especially conclusions from the study of psychological mass movements which will attain ever-increasing importance in that theory. Utilization of the entire wealth of facts which make up the general content of the human sciences is something true psychology has in common not only with theories to be discussed shortly, but also with history. But we must insist on this point: except for psychic individuals which make up the object of psychology, we have absolutely no intellectual fact in our experience. But since psychology in no way comprises all the facts which are objects of the human sciences or (what amounts to the same thing) which experience permits us to grasp in psychic unities, it follows that psychology deals with only a part of the content of what goes on in every individual. We can therefore isolate psychology from the total science of historico-social reality only by abstraction, and we can develop it only in constant reference to that total science. It is true that the psychophysical unity is locked up in itself by the fact that only what is posited in its own will can be a purpose for it, only what it encounters in its own feeling can be worthwhile, only what the bar of its own consciousness verifies as certain and evident can be real and true for it. But on the other hand this whole, thus sealed off and certain of its unity in self-consciousness, appears only in the context of social reality; its organization shows it receives outside influences and responds to them; its entire content is only one transitory configuration which has appeared among the general contents of mind in history and society; indeed, the highest characteristic of its being is that it lives in something other than itself. The subject matter of psychology, accordingly, is always simply an individual selected from the living structure of historico-social reality; the task of psychology is to establish, through abstraction, the general characteristics which individual psychical beings develop in that structure. Psychology does not experientially encounter a man as if he did not interact with society and as if he existed *before* society, nor can it reveal such a man. If it could, construction of the human sciences would have taken shape incomparably more simply than it has. Even the very narrow range of vaguely expressible characteristics we incline to ascribe to man as such is subject to the unresolved strife of seriously conflicting hypotheses.

At this point, therefore, we can immediately dismiss a procedure which makes the edifice of human sciences unsafe inasmuch as it inserts hypotheses into their foundation walls. People have handled the relationship of individuals to society in constructionist fashion [*konstruktiv*] on the basis of two opposite hypotheses.[19] Since Plato's idea of the state as man writ large appeared in opposition to the natural law of the Sophists, these two theories have been at war with each other, just as the atomistic and the dynamic theories have been, in relation to constructing society. Of course in their further development they have come closer to each other, but one cannot resolve their opposition until one abandons the constructionist method which produced it, until one sees the special sciences of social reality as parts of a comprehensive analytical method, and until one regards individual truths as declarations about part of the contents of this reality. In this analytical process of investigation one cannot develop psychology the way one does in the first of these hypotheses: as the description of the original endowment of an individual wrested away from the historical family of society. After all, fundamental relationships of the will, for example, have their arena of activity in individuals, but not their basis of explanation. This kind of isolating, plus mechanistically joining individuals as a method for constructing society, was the root error of the old natural-law school. The one-sidedness of this view has been countered again and again by an opposite one-sidedness. In opposition to mechanistic structuring of society, this latter view has drafted formulas which express the unity of the social body and thus were supposed to do justice to the other half of the case. A formula of this type is to subsume the individual's relationship to the state under the relationship of the part to the whole (which has priority over the part), as in Aristotle's political science; another is to work out the conception of the state as a well-ordered animal organism, as political writers of the Middle Ages did (a view which important contemporary writers defend and expand); still another is the concept of a folk soul or a folk spirit. Only in the context of historical opposition do these attempts to subordinate the unity of individuals to an idea have a transitory justification. "Folk soul" lacks the unity of self-consciousness and activity which we express in the concept of soul. The concept of organism substitutes another problem for a given one, and it is indeed possible—as John Stuart Mill has remarked—that we might solve the problem of society earlier and more satisfactorily than we do the problem of the animal organism. But even now we can show the extraordinary difference between these two types of systems in which mutually conditioning functions work together toward a common result. Hence we must not subject the relation that psychical entities bear to society to any sort of construction whatsoever. Categories like unity and multiplicity or whole and part are not applicable to such constructions. Even when we cannot do without them in a description, we must never forget that they have had their living origin in the experience the individual has had of himself; consequently we cannot explain more by referring back to the lived experience [*Erlebnis*] which the individual represents for himself in society than experience [*Erfahrung*] is capable of telling us in its own right.

The human being as a fact which precedes history and society is a fiction of genetic explanation. The man whom sound analytical science studies is the individual as a component of society. The difficult problem which psychology has to solve is this: analytical knowledge of the universal characteristics of this man.

Seen in this way, anthropology and psychology are the foundation of all knowledge of historical life and of all rules for the direction and continued development of society. They are not simply a man's deeper penetration into the study of himself. Some type of human nature always stands between the historian and the sources out of which he hopes to awaken figures to pulsating life; some type of human nature stands just as truly between the political thinker who wishes to outline rules for society's development and the reality of society itself. Science will concede correctness and fruitfulness only to this subjective type. It seeks to develop general principles whose subject is this individual unity, whose predicates are all declarations about it which can be fruitful for understanding society and history. However, this task of psychology and anthropology implies an extension of the scope of science. Above and beyond previous research into uniformities of intellectual life, science must recognize typical differences in that life; it must describe and analyze the imagination of the artist and the temperament of the man of action; it must expand the study of forms of intellectual life by describing its actual development and its content. By this means we will fill the gap in previous systems of socio-historical reality between psychology on the one side and esthetics, ethics, sciences of political bodies, and history on the other side. Until now this position has been occupied only by vague generalizations of experience of life, creations of poets, descriptions of characters and destinies by men of the world, and by indefinite general truths which the historian weaves into his narrative.

Psychology can solve the problems of such a fundamental science only to the extent that it stays within the boundaries of a descriptive science which tests facts and uniformities by facts and sharply distinguishes itself from the interpretive brand of psychology which wants to make the whole structure of intellectual life deducible on the basis of certain assumptions. Only by this process can we acquire an exact, unprejudiced, established content for psychology, a content which allows us to verify psychological hypotheses. But above all: only thus can special human sciences finally acquire a solid foundation, whereas now even the best presentations of psychology just pile hypotheses on hypotheses.

We now summarize the result for the general plan of this presentation. The simplest finding which analysis of socio-historical reality can come up with lies in psychology; accordingly, it is the first and most basic special science of the mind. Correspondingly, its truths are the basis for further construction. But its truths contain only a partial content culled from this reality and thus presuppose a relationship to that whole. Hence we can explain the relationship of psychological science to other human sciences and to reality itself (whose partial contents they compose) only if we lay down an epistemological foundation. For psychology, however, a result of its position in the organization of the human sciences is that it must distinguish itself as a descriptive science (a concept to be developed more fully in the foundation-laying process) from the interpretive science which, because it is by its nature hypothetical, undertakes to subject facts of intellectual life to simple assumptions.

Description of the individual psychophysical living unit is biography. The memory of the race has found very many individual lives interesting and worthy of preserving. Carlyle once said of history: "Wise remembrance and wise forgetfulness—this is the key to everything."[20] From the point of view of the power with which the individual attracts the attention and love of other individuals to himself, it is the unique human existence which affects a person more strongly than any other object or any generalization. The place of biography in general historiography corresponds to the place of anthropology in theoretical sciences of historico-social reality. Hence the progress of anthropology and the growing recognition of its fundamental role will also further the view that understanding the totality of an individual's existence and describing its nature in its historical milieu is a high point of historical writing, fully as valuable in the profundity of its undertaking as any historical description which uses more wide-ranging materials. Here one appreciates the will of a person in the course of his life and destiny in its dignity as an end in itself. The biographer ought to look at a person *sub specie aeterni,* just as he himself feels in those moments when between himself and the deity everything else is covering, garment, and means [*Hülle, Gewand, und Mittel*] and he feels as close to the starry heavens as he does to any part of earth. Biography thus presents the fundamental historical fact in its purity, fullness, and actuality. And only the historian who constructs history, so to speak, out of these living individuals; who through the concept of type and representation tries to get closer to understanding social classes, social associations in general, and historical periods; who links individual careers together through the concept of the generations— only he will grasp the reality of a historical whole, in contrast with the dead abstractions usually culled from the archives.

If biography is an important resource for further developing true scientific psychology [*Realpsychologie*], it is also true that it has its foundation in the current state of the latter science. One can describe the true method of the biographer as applying the sciences of anthropology and psychology to the problem of making a living individual, his development and his destiny, alive and understandable.

Rules for personal conduct of life have always made up a further branch of literature; some of the most beautiful and most profound writings of all literature are dedicated to this theme. But if we are to make them scientific, the effort to do so will take us back to considering personally the connection between our knowledge of the reality of the individual [*der Lebenseinheit*] and our consciousness of the mutual value-relations our will and our feeling encounter in life.

At the boundary between natural sciences and psychology an area of investigation has been charted which its first highly gifted elaborator has designated as psychophysics and which the colloraboration of outstanding scientists has expanded into a sketch of a physiological psychology. This science began with the position that, disregarding metaphysical argument about body and soul, it wished to establish as precisely as possible the actual relations existing between these two phenomenal areas. Fechner made the neutral concept of function in its mathematical sense (which remains as extremely abstract as one can imagine) its basis and seized on the establishment of the existing dependencies, describable in two opposite directions, as the goal of this science. The functional relationship between stimulus and sensation constituted the focal point of his investigations. Nevertheless, if this science wishes completely to fill the gap which exists between physiology and psychology and if it wishes to include all the points of contact between corporeal and psychical life and make the bond between physiology and psychology as complete and as effective as possible, then it will find itself obliged to work this relationship into the comprehensive conception of the causal structure of all reality. In fact, the one-sided dependence of psychical events and changes on physiological ones makes up the principal subject matter of such physiological psychology. It develops the dependence of intellectual life on its corporeal basis; it investigates boundaries within which such dependence is demonstrable; then it also describes the reactions which go from intellectual changes to corporeal ones. Thus it traces intellectual life from relations which prevail between the physiological functioning of sense organs and the psychical process of perceiving and observing; to relations between the appearance, disappearance, and combination of ideas, on the one hand, and to the structure and functions of the brain, on the other hand; finally, on to relations between the reflex mechanism and motor system and, correspondingly, articulation, speech, and controlled movement.

9. Relationship of Knowledge to the Structure of Historico-Scientific Reality

This analysis of particular psycho-physical individuals is different from analysis concerned with the whole of historico-social reality. Frenchmen and Englishmen have outlined the concept of a general science which develops the theory of this whole and have labeled it sociology. In fact, one cannot separate knowledge of the development of society from knowledge of its present status. Both kinds of facts make up a system. The present situation in which society finds itself is the result of the earlier one and is at the same time the precondition for the next one. Its determinate status at the present moment is already part of history in the next moment. Thus we must consider every cross section which depicts the status of society at a given moment as a historical situation as soon as one rises above that moment. We can therefore use the concept of society to designate this self-developing whole.[21]

This society, that is, the total historico-social reality, confronts the individual as an object of consideration much more intricate and puzzling than our own organism or any of its most mysterious parts, such as the brain. The stream of development flows on unceasingly in it as particular individuals which constitute it make their entries onto the stage of life and then their departures from it. So the individual finds himself in society as an element interacting with other elements. He has not fashioned the whole into which he is born. Of the laws within whose limits individuals here affect one another he knows only a few, and those vaguely. It is true that the same processes of which he is totally conscious in himself by inner perception have constructed this whole outside him. But their complexities are so great and the conditions of nature under which they appear are so manifold, and the means of measuring and testing them are so narrowly constricted, that difficulties which appear almost insuperable hinder knowledge of this structure of society. Out of this situation arises the difference between our relation to society and our relation to nature. We know the state of society inwardly; we can reproduce it in ourselves up to a point by observing our own condition, and we intuitively follow the depiction of the historical world with love and hate, with passionate joy, with full involvement of our emotions. But nature is mute for us. Only the power of our imagination sheds a glimmer of light and inwardness over it. For insofar as we are a complex of corporeal elements in reciprocal relation with it, there is no inner perception accompanying the play of this mutual influence. And that is why even nature can wear an expression of noble repose for us. This expression would disappear if we were to perceive or were forced to imagine essentially the same varied play of inner life which society presents to us. Nature is alien to us. After all, it is for us only an outer thing, not an inner one. Society is our world. The play of mutual influences in it is something we coexperience with the full force of our entire being, because we inwardly feel the turbulent bustle of those conditions and forces which make up the social system. We are obliged to correct our image of its condition in constantly fluctuating value judgments and to refashion it, at least conceptually, by an untiring effort of will.

All this impresses some characteristic notes on the study of society which distinguish it decisively from that of nature. Uniformities we can establish in the sphere of society are far inferior in number, significance, and formal precision to laws we can determine about nature on the solid foundation of spatial relationships and characteristics of motion. We can show that motions of heavenly bodies—not just of our planetary system but even of stars which are light-years away from us—are subject to such a simple law as gravitation, and we can calculate them for long stretches of time in advance. Sciences of society cannot offer this sort of satisfaction to our understanding. The difficulties in knowing a single psychical entity are multiplied by the great varieties and uniqueness of these entities, by the way they work together in society, by the complexity of natural conditions which bind them together, and by the sum total of mutual influences brought to bear in the succession of many generations, which does not allow us to deduce directly from human nature as we now know it the state of affairs of earlier times or to infer present states of affairs from a general type of human nature. Nevertheless, all this is more than outweighed by the fact that I myself, who inwardly experience and know myself, am a member of this social body and that the other members are like me in kind and therefore likewise comprehensible to me in their inner being. I understand [*verstehe*] the life of society.[22] The individual is an element in interactions of society, a point of intersection for different systems of these interactions, reacting to their impulses with deliberate direction of will and action; but the individual is also the intelligence which sees and investigates all this. The play of what are for us soulless active causes is cut off here from the play of concepts, feelings, and motives. And the uniqueness and wealth of reciprocal influences disclosed here are limitless. A waterfall is composed of homogeneous falling water droplets; but a single declaration—which is after all only a breath of air from the mouth—shocks the entire living population of a continent through a play of motives in purely individual human beings: so different is the mutual effect appearing here, namely, motivation arising out of thought, and from every other kind of cause! Other distinctive characteristics flow from this. The organ of understanding which functions in human sciences is the whole man; great achievements in those sciences do not proceed from mere power of intelligence but from strength of personal life. Without any ulterior aim of acquiring knowledge of the entire system, this spiritual activity finds itself attracted and satisfied by the unique and the actual in this spiritual world, and with intellectual understanding we find that practical direction in judgment, an ideal, and a rule are bound up as well.

These basic relationships occasion two kinds of reflection by the individual about his relation to society. On the one hand, he acts in this (societal) whole with deliberation, establishes rules for his activity, and looks for conditions thereof in the structure of the intellectual world. On the other hand, the individual functions as a perceptive intelligence and would like to acquire knowledge of this (societal) whole. From one point of view sciences of society have thus grown out of the individual's consciousness about his own activity and the conditions for it; this is the way that grammar, rhetoric, logic, esthetics, ethics, and jurisprudence first came into being. And this is the reason why their position in the structure of human sciences has remained in a shaky middle ground between analysis and rule-making aimed at the particular activity of the individual and analysis and rule-making aimed at the entire social system. If it is true that politics also, especially in the beginning at least, had this same interest, that interest was nevertheless already linked with another interest—that of supervising political bodies. It was exclusively out of such a need for a free, contemplative overview inwardly motivated by interest in the human that historical writing came into being. But because the kinds of occupations in society branched out in ever more varied ways, technical training for these trades developed and embraced an ever increasing amount of theory. The ensuing technical theories, impelled by practical necessity, continually pressed more deeply into the essence of society. Concern for knowledge gradually transformed them into true sciences, which, besides their practical aim, collaborated on the problem of knowing historico-social reality.

Differentiation of special sciences of society accordingly did not take place through some device of theoretical understanding which might have undertaken to solve the problem of the fact of the socio-historical world by methodically analyzing its object of investigation; life itself produced that differentiation. As often as a distinct sphere of social activity came about which produced an ordering of facts affecting the activity of the individual, conditions were present for a theory to emerge. So the great process of differentiation of society by which its marvelously intertwined edifice has come about carried in itself conditions and needs by which the reflection of every relatively independently developed sphere of life took the form of a theory. And so, finally, society—in which, like the most powerful of all machines, each one of its wheels and rollers functions in its particular way and yet also has a function to perform in the whole as well—is represented in full measure, to some degree, in the juxtaposition and interaction of such manifold theories.

Likewise, positive sciences of the mind at first asserted no need to establish relations of these single theories to one another and to the general structure of historico-social reality, whose partial contents they separately considered. Only late and one by one did philosophy of mind, of history, and of society step in to fill the gap, and we shall show the reasons why they did not achieve the status of constantly and securely developing sciences. So the real and developed sciences emerge singly and loosely bound from the broad background of the great fact of socio-historical reality. Their relation to this living fact and descriptive presentation of it, not their relation to a comprehensive science, is all that defines their position.

10. Scientific Study of the Natural Classification of Humanity in General as Well as of Individual Peoples

This descriptive presentation—which one can designate historical and social science in the broadest sense—comprises the complex facts of the intellectual world in their general structure, as the contemporary art of historical writing and statistics understand it. We saw earlier (pp. 90–91) how mere collecting and sifting of materials in a motley multiplicity of studies gradually passes over into science through ever more intense, thoughtful elaboration. We especially stressed the independent significance of the place of historical writing in this entire picture—between collecting facts and setting apart uniform elements from them in a single theory. We saw it as an art because in it, as in the fantasy of the artist, we see the universal in the particular, yet we do not separate it from that particular through abstraction and present it for its own sake—a process which first takes place in theory. Here, only the idea in the historian's mind fills and shapes the particular, and if he makes a generalization, it sheds light on the facts only as in a lightning flash and releases abstract thinking only for a moment. Indeed, generalization serves the poet also in this way, inasmuch as for a moment it elevates the soul of his listener out of the turmoil, sufferings, and passions he is describing and into the world of untrammeled thought.

From the historian's insightful overview of the manifold life of humanity, however, a first descriptive organization of homogenous material now splits off. It attaches itself quite naturally to anthropology of the individual person. If this anthropology has identified the general human type, general laws of life of psychological beings, and differences of individual types built into these laws, then *ethnology,* or comparative anthropology, goes on from there. Uniformities of lesser extent make up its subject matter, the kind of uniformities which distinguish groups within the whole from one another and appear as individual branches of humanity: the natural articulation of the human race and, based on that and subject to conditions generally prevalent in the world, the ensuing distribution of intellectual life and its variations on the face of the earth. Ethnology investigates, therefore, how on the basis of the family unit and of kinship, in the form of concentric circles formed by degrees of descent, the human race is naturally articulated, that is, how in every narrower circle (based on closer relationship) new common characteristics appear. From questions about unity of descent and genus [*Art*], about the oldest domicile, about the age and common characteristics of the human race, this science then turns its attention to defining individual races and determining their characteristics and to the groups which each of these races encompasses. On the basis of geography it develops the distribution of intellectual life and its variations on the surface of the earth: we see the flood of population spread out, following the line of least resistance, just as a network of water adapts itself to conditions of the ground.

Historical activity and historical destiny intertwine with this genealogical articulation, and this way *peoples* [*Völker*] establish themselves as living and relatively independent centers of culture in the social framework of a period and as bearers of historical development. Of course a people has its foundation in the genealogical structure of nature, one evident even physically. But though related peoples show an affinity of bodily type which maintains itself with amazing permanence, their historical intellectual physiognomy shapes itself into ever more subtly ramified differences in all the various spheres of a people's life.

This individual living unity in a people—which manifests itself in the mutual affinity of all its expressions of life, such as its law, its language, and its religious core—is expressed mystically through concepts like "folk soul," "nation," "folk spirit," and "organism." These concepts are as useless for history as the concept of "living force" is for physiology. We can explain what the expression "people" means only analytically (within limits), with the help of investigations which we can designate as theories of second rank in the methodological system of human sciences. These presuppose the truths of anthropology; they apply these truths to mutual interactions of individuals subject to conditions of the order of nature. Thus arise sciences of systems of culture in their various forms, of external organization of society, and of individual groups in it. Between the individual and the intricate process of history, science finds three great classes of objects to study: external organization of society, systems of culture in it, and individual peoples. These are permanent sets of facts, among which the one dealing with peoples as wholes is the most complex and the most difficult. Because all three are only parts of the content of real life, we cannot grasp any of them historically or reflect on them theoretically without referring to scientific study of the others. However, corresponding to the complexity of the situation, scholars have worked on the fact of a particular people only with the help of analysis of the other two facts. What is meant by the expression "folk soul" or "folk spirit," "nation," and "national culture" can be graphically described and analyzed only to the extent that one first grasps the different aspects of a people's life, for example, its language, religion, and art, in their mutual interactions. This requires us to move on to the next step in analyzing historico-social reality.

11. Distinction between Two Further Classes of Special Sciences

Whoever studies phenomena of history and society is confronted at every point by abstract entities such as art, science, state, society, and religion. They are like clouds of mist which prevent us from seeing reality and do not admit of being understood themselves. Just as substantial forms, heavenly spirits, and essences once stood between the eye of the researcher and laws which govern atoms and molecules, so these entities disguise both the reality of historico-social life and the interaction of living psychophysical individuals in accordance with laws of the universe and of those individuals' innate genealogical structuring. I would like to teach people how to see this reality—an art that has long wanted to be practiced in the same way as we see spatial figures—and to chase away these mists and phantoms.

In the immense manifold of tiny, apparently disappearing effects which radiate from individual to individual through the medium of material processes, not one effect is lost, any more than a ray of sunshine is lost in the physical world. But who could follow the development of the effects of this ray of sunshine? Only when homogeneous results coalesce in the social world do situations arise which speak a loud and clear language to us. Some of these situations arise out of a homogeneous but transitory marshaling of forces in a particular direction or perhaps through the unique force of a single mighty willpower (which, however, can produce great results only in the direction in which such forces are concentrated in history and society). Thus sudden powerful convulsions such as revolutions and wars break out and pass away in history. They leave lasting effects only to the extent that they modify an already existing permanent social structure. In this way the epoch of Storm and Stress, prompted by the powerful personality of Rousseau, affected the pent-up vigor of our national life and gave a different shape to our poetry. Precisely these permanent structures are the other strongly prominent factor in social reality, but they arise out of permanent individual relationships, and they alone have so far found a truly scientific theoretical elaboration.

As we saw, the natural foundation of social organization—which reaches back into the deepest metaphysical mystery and from that point binds us together in sexual love, filial love, and love for mother earth with strong dark bonds of powerful natural feelings—brings about in the basic relationships of genealogical organization and settlement a homogeneity of smaller and larger groups and community among them. Historical life develops this homogeneity, in virtue of which individual peoples in particular lend themselves to study as determinate entities. Over and above this, there now emerge permanent structures, objects of social analysis, either when a purpose based on a component element of human nature (hence permanent in character) relates psychical acts of particular individuals to one another and thus organizes them into a complex of purposes or when permanent causes unite wills into an association as a whole—whether these causes be situated in the order of nature or in the order of human purposes. Insofar as we consider that first state of affairs, we distinguish systems of culture in society; insofar as we look at the latter state of affairs, we see the external organization which humanity has set up for itself: states, associations, and—if one probes further—the web of permanent alliances of wills corresponding to basic relations of mastery, dependence, property, and community: something recently designated in a narrower sense as "society" in contrast with "the state."

Individuals are busily engaged in the interplay of historico-social life to the extent that in the spontaneity of their energies they seek to realize a multiplicity of purposes. Because of the limited character of human existence, needs of human nature are not satisfied by isolated activity of the individual person but rather by division of labor and succession of generations. This becomes possible through the homogeneity of human nature and its supervisory reason which serves these purposes. These characteristics adapt our activity to the results of the work of our ancestors and to cooperation with activity of our contemporaries. In this way the basic goals of human life permeate both history and society.

In line with the principle of sufficient reason underlying all knowledge, science now undertakes to establish the dependencies within such a complex of purposes (based on a component element of human nature and transcending the individual) between the individual psychical or psychophysical elements which comprise that complex and also to establish dependencies between their properties. Science determines how one element conditions another in this complex of purposes and how, upon the appearance of one characteristic in that structure, the appearance of another is shown to be dependent on it. Because we know these elements we can (within limits) express them in words. Thus this complex is reflected as a totality consisting of propositions. Still, these propositions are very different from one another in character: depending on whether psychical elements linked together in the complex of purpose belong predominantly to thought or to feeling or to will, we find that truths, expressions of feeling, and rules will go their separate ways. And to this difference in their nature corresponds one in their association and consequently in dependencies which science discerns between them. One can already see at this point that it was one of the greatest errors of the abstract school to conceive all these connections univocally as logical ones and thus in the last analysis to reduce all these spiritual-purposeful activities to reason and thought alone. I choose for such a complex of purposes the expression *system*.

Dependencies which thus exist in relation to the complex of purposes made up of psychical or psychophysical elements in a single system exist in the first place in reference to those basic relationships of that system which are uniformly proper to it at all points. Such dependencies make up the *general theory of a system*. Schleiermacher has identified dependencies of this most general type in the system of religion between the fact of religious feeling and facts of dogmatic theology and philosophical worldview, between the fact of this feeling and facts of worship and of religious fellowship. Thünen's law expresses the relationship by which distance from a market conditions the intensity of agriculture carried on, for it influences the sale of agricultural products.[23] People find and describe such dependencies as a matter of course by combining analysis of the system with inferences based on the kind of interaction of psychical or psychophyical elements in that system as well as conditions of nature and society affecting that interaction. Then there exist dependencies of a lesser extent between modifications of these general properties of a system—which make up a *special configuration* [*Einzelgestalt*] of it. Thus a dogma in a particular religious system is not independent of other dogmas linked with it in the same system. Indeed, the main problem of the history of dogma and of dogmatic theology—as Schleiermacher's profound analysis of religion clearly demonstrated—consists in showing in both sciences how dependence of dogmas on one another is grounded in the nature of religion, especially of Christianity, rather than in an interpolated logical relationship of dependence (which can only deliver a doctrinal system).

And indeed these sciences of systems of culture are based on psychic or psychophysical contents, to which correspond concepts specifically different from those used in individual psychology. In comparison with the latter they can be designated as *second rank concepts* in constructing the human sciences. Because their material content [*Inhaltlichkeit*] is located in that element of human nature on which the purpose-complex of a system is based, that content produces an historically cumulative composite of facts from the interaction of individuals subject to conditions of nature. And these facts are distinct from the basic material content developed in psychology: they constitute the foundation for analyzing the system. Thus the concept of scientific certitude in its various guises—as conviction about reality in perception, as evidence in thought, as consciousness of necessity in accordance with the principle of sufficient reason in knowledge—dominates the whole theory of science. So the psychophysical concepts of need, economy, work, value, and the like constitute the necessary foundation for the analysis to be carried out by political economy. And, as with the concepts, so here (according to the relationship which links concepts with principles) there likewise exists a relationship among the fundamental principles of these sciences and findings of anthropology which permits us to designate those principles as *second rank truths* in the ascending order of human sciences.

We can insert one further piece into the structure of argumentation to which this analysis of special sciences is devoted. One can study facts which constitute systems of culture only by using facts which psychological analysis recognizes. Concepts and principles which make up the foundation of knowledge of these systems depend on the concepts and principles which psychology develops. But this relationship is so complicated that only a coherent epistemological and logical foundation, that starts from the special position of knowledge in relation to historical and social reality, can fill the gap which still exists even today between special sciences of psychophysical individuals and those of political economy, law, religion, and so on. Every researcher in the special sciences feels this gap. Because English-French theory of knowledge recognizes even here a mere question of deductive versus inductive method and therefore believes that one can solve this difficult question along purely logical lines by investigating the range of these two operations, it has demonstrated its uselessness nowhere more clearly than in its lengthy debates over this point. The methodological presuppositions of these debates are false. The question is not, as these researchers put it, whether these sciences are capable of deductive development, which would in turn be subject to inductive verification and application to the complex relations of actual life, nor is it whether they are to be developed inductively and then to be confirmed by deduction from human nature. The very formulation of the question is based on an abstract schema introduced from the physical sciences. Only studying the work of knowing, which is subject to conditions of the special task of human sciences, can solve the problem of the system at issue here.

One could imagine that beings existed whose interaction proceeded only in such an interpenetration of psychical acts in one or more systems. One would then think that all activities of such beings were capable of intervening in such a complex of purposes and one would reduce their entire relationship to one another to this ability: to adapt their purposeful activity to one or several of such complexes. Even if each one of these beings were to adapt its activity to the activity of those in front of, or alongside, it to steer that activity appropriately, every one of them would remain isolated; only the intellect would establish a connection between them. They would take one another into account rationally, but there would be no living feeling of community among them. They would accomplish the tasks of their purpose-complexes so punctiliously and completely, like conscious atoms, that no coercion or association would be necessary among them.

Man is not a being of this sort. There are other characteristics of his nature which in the interplay of these psychical atoms with the ones described add other permanent relations; we call the most obvious ones "the state." Consequently there is another theoretical consideration of social life which finds its focal point in political science. The unbridled power of his passions and his inner need and feeling for community thus make a man (as a component in the structure of these systems) into a member of the *external organization* of humanity. From the structure which a complex of psychic elements manifests in the purpose-complex of a system and from the analysis of the elements which investigate relations in that system, we distinguish the structure which arises out of an association of wills and the analysis of the features of external organization of society, of communities, of associations, and of the framework which arises out of relationships of domination and external constraint of will.

The foundation on which this other form of lasting mutual relationships rests is as profound as the foundation which produces the fact of the systems. In the first place it lies in the characteristic of the human being by which he is a social being. Permanent feelings of belonging together, and not simply cold calculation of relationships, are linked to the natural framework in which the human being exists, uniformities which arise thereby, and lasting relations of psychical acts in one human being to those in another human being. Other forces more violent in character coerce wills into associations: interest and compulsion. If both forces work side by side, then the ancient controversy as to what share each of them has in the origin of the social compact or the state can be resolved only on a case-by-case basis through historical analysis.

The nature and extent of the sciences which thus arise will be made evident in more detail only later through discussion of the cultural systems and their sciences. Before we proceed to these, let us draw two further conclusions in the context of the demonstration which permeates this analysis of human sciences.

Obviously, the same relationship by which concepts and principles of sciences of culture were dependent on those of anthropology exists also in this area of sciences of external organization of society. We will discuss facts of second rank, which are the foundation here, at a later point because we can see them with sufficient clarity only after we analyze the systems of culture more thoroughly. But no matter how we shall define them, they must include that same problem whose presence proves the necessity of a science which, subject to the general conditions of human knowledge, investigates the formation of a process of knowledge aimed at historical and social reality and describes its boundaries, its resources, and the order of truths which humanity's will to knowledge is bound to pursue in this area. The gap in the structure of scientific thought has made itself as strongly felt in political science as in sciences of religion or political economy.

If the logician focuses his attention on the relation of these two classes of sciences to each other, he confronts a demand for methodical awareness of the system of the process of knowledge in which these special sciences have arisen; and this demand leads to still more. In accordance with the nature of the analytical process by which they were distinguished from one another, one can develop sciences of each of these two classes only by constantly referring truths of one class to those of the other class. And in each of these classes the same relation exists; otherwise how could truths of the science of esthetics be developed independently of any relationship to those of morality and those of religion, because after all the origin of art—the fact of an ideal—points back to this living connection? We also have knowledge here, inasmuch as we analyze and abstractly develop a partial content; but awareness and use of this structure are the great methodological demand which emerges from this situation. One must never forget the relation of the partial content (to a degree already specially prepared) to the organism of reality in which alone life itself pulsates; on the contrary, knowledge can give exact form to concepts and principles and assign them their appropriate cognitive value only from this standpoint. It was the fundamental error of the abstract school to ignore the relation of the abstracted partial content to the living whole and ultimately to treat these abstractions as realities. It was the complementary but no less disastrous error of the historical school—in its profound feeling for living, irrationally powerful reality which transcends all knowledge based on the principle of sufficient reason—to flee from the world of abstraction.

12. Sciences of Systems of Culture

The point of departure for understanding the *concept of systems* of societal life consists of the richness of life of the individual himself, who as a component of society is the subject matter of the first group of sciences. Let us just imagine for a moment this richness of life in a given individual as something totally unlike that in another individual and not communicable to him. In such a case those individuals might be able to overpower and subjugate each other through physical force, but they would really possess nothing in common; each would be sealed up in himself against all others. As a matter of fact there is in every individual a point at which he simply does not fit into such coordination of his activities with others. Whatever part of the fullness of life of the individual is determined by this factor does not enter into any of the systems of social life. Similarity of individuals is a precondition for a communality in the content of their lives. Next, let us imagine the life of each of these individuals as comparable and communicable, though simple and indivisible: social activity would then constitute one system. Let us clarify the simplest characteristics of such a basic system. It rests in the first place on the interaction of individuals in society insofar as that interaction, based on a component of human nature common to those individuals, results in meshing together activities in which this component of human nature is satisfied. Such a basic system thereby differentiates itself from every arrangement which comprises only a system of means for the needs of society. If one begins with the interplay between individuals, then direct interplay—in which individual A extends his influence to B, C, and D and is influenced by them in turn—is distinguished from indirect interplay, which rests on the further extension of change in B to R and Z. Through the first, a horizon of direct interactions of particular individuals comes about, a very different horizon for each of them. Indirect interactions in society are limited only by the mediating conditions of the external world. A system like this, resting as it does on direct and indirect interactions of individuals in society, necessarily exhibits properties of increase and development. For to the laws of the psychical living individual which affect increase and development one must add the corresponding basic law of their interactions by which perceptions, feelings, and concepts, in their transmission from A to B, retain their former strength in individual A even as they go over to B. If there were just one such system alone, it would comprise the total life of society; the process of communication in it and its content would be one and simple. In reality the richness of an individual's life is broken up into perceptions and thoughts, feelings and acts of the will. Regardless, then, what divisions and combinations might otherwise occur in it, by this fact alone (in virtue of the natural organization of psychical life) this living content makes possible a variety of systems in the life of society.

These systems are permanent; but particular individuals themselves make their entry onto the stage of life and then pass on. For each of these systems is grounded on a definite component of the person, which keeps recurring through all its modifications. Religion, art, and law are imperishable; but individuals in whom they live change. Thus the fullness and richness of human nature flow anew into the system founded on them in every generation, insofar as they exist in a component of that human nature or are connected with it. And even if, for example, art is grounded in the power of imagination as one component of human nature, nevertheless the whole richness of human nature exists in its creations. But the system receives its full reality and objectivity only through the fact that the external world has the power to store up and pass on influences of individuals, who live so briefly, in a more permanent or self-regenerative way. This combination of elements of the external world, so usefully arranged for purposes of such a system, together with the living, though transitory, activity of persons, generates an external permanence independent of individuals themselves and the character of massive objectivity of those systems. And so each of these systems takes shape as a mode of activity founded on a component of the nature of persons and developed from it in all sorts of ways. This mode of activity satisfies one of the purposes of the societal whole and is equipped with the means, either established and permanent in the external world or self-renewing through activity itself, which serve the purpose of this activity.

A single individual is a point of intersection of a plurality of systems which continue to become ever more subtly specialized as a culture moves forward. Indeed, one and the same living act of an individual can demonstrate this many-sidedness. If a scholar writes a book, this event can be one more link in the chain of truths which comprise science; it is also the most important part of an economic process transacted through the manufacture and sale of copies; moreover it has its legal aspect as the fulfillment of a contract, and it can be a part of the scholar's professional functions, which is fitted into the general administrative picture. Writing down each syllable of this work is thus a part of all these systems.

Abstract science places these systems, thus interwoven, into historico-social reality alongside one another. After all, the individual is born into those systems and thus encounters them as an objective situation which existed before him, remains after him, and influences him through his arrangements. They thus present themselves to scientific imagination as independently existing objective facts. Not just the economic order, or religion, but even science itself graphically confronts us as such a reality. The comprehensive deduction that argues from the phenomenon of the firmament, the daily and yearly movements of the sun, and the sometimes so intricate movements of the stars about it, to the actual positions, masses, forms of movement, and velocities of spatial bodies, is part of the very makeup of the human being of today as an objective state of affairs. It is part of a still more comprehensive state of affairs in natural science, irrespective of the persons who make that deduction: it is a state of affairs which confronts the individual as an intellectual reality.

Because these systems are thus analyzed side by side, one can carry on investigations of this kind only with constant reference to the other class of investigations that deal with communities and associations of the historico-social world. With regard to this relationship there is a difference between individual systems which is important for the constitution of these sciences.

Each of them develops in the whole of historico-social reality. For each of them is the product of an element of human nature, of an activity rooted in that element and more fully determined through the complex of purposes operative in social life. It is present in this common basis of society in every age, even though it does not attain a separate and interiorly rich development until it reaches a higher cultural level. To a greater or lesser degree these systems are related to the external organization of society, and this relationship conditions their further development. In particular one cannot separate systems into which the practical activity of society has split up from study of the body politic, for its will influences all the external actions of individuals subject to it.

Relations between Systems of Culture and External Organization of Society; Law

The previous chapter [*Kapitel*] was devoted to describing the difference between systems of culture and external organization of society. The present chapter [*Kapitel*], which deals with the sciences of systems of culture, has first of all developed this concept of system of culture on the basis of that earlier description. From the notion of the difference between systems of culture and external organization of society we now turn to the conception of the *relations* between them.

In this mature period, when he first expanded his natural-scientific viewpoint into a worldview through the progress he had made in analyzing the historical world—after the death of his friend, Karl August—Goethe expressed his view of the historical world from the solitude at Dornburg as follows (July, 1828). His point of departure is the view of the castle and the region below it; from there a vivid image for this abstract truth comes to him: "From generation to generation the world of reason is decisively directed toward logical activity." The view of socio-historical reality which follows from this he summarizes in the "lofty word of a wise man": "The world of reason should be seen as a great immortal individual who unceasingly accomplishes what is necessary and thereby makes himself the master even of the contingent." This sentence sums up in a formula what the survey we are here attempting of historico-social reality and its sciences has gleaned—and will continue to glean—in the course of a gradual analysis which takes individuals, as the elements of historico-social reality, for its point of departure. Interaction of individuals seems accidental and haphazard. Birth and death and the whole contingent character of fate; the emotions, and the narrow egoism which strut so in the forefront of life's stage: all this seems to confirm the view of observers of human nature who see in social life only the play and counterplay of interests of individuals influenced by chance; it also seems to confirm the view of the pragmatic historian for whom the course of history likewise comes down to a matter of the play of personal forces. But actually it is precisely *by means of this interaction of particular individuals*—their emotions, their vanities, and their interests—that the *necessary complex of purposes in the history of humanity* is realized. The pragmatic historian and Hegel misunderstand each other because they speak to each other as the solid earth might to the airy heights. Yet each has hold of part of the truth. For everything which man accomplishes in this historico-social world happens through the compression-spring [*Sprungfeder*] of his will: it is purpose, however, which functions as the motive power in that will. It is his nature, it is the universally valid and the supraindividual in him, no matter what formula one uses to grasp it, on which the complex of purposes which permeates wills rests. In this complex of purposes the usual activity of men, which is concerned only with itself, nevertheless accomplishes what it must. And even from among the deeds of its heroes history permits everything to vanish without a trace which does not fit into this complex of purposes. But this great purpose-system has mainly *two means* at its disposal. The first is the logical interplay between particular actions of different individuals, out of which systems of culture arise. The other is the power of the great will-directed agencies [*Willenseinheiten*] in history which produce consistent activity in society through the individual wills subject to them. Both these means produce a system of purposes; in fact both of them are a living system of purposes. But this system is accomplished in one case through action of independent individuals whose activity is harmonized with one another in the nature of things, in another case through power which a will-directed agency exercises on the individuals it controls. Free activity and regulated activity, self-seeking and community, confront one another as opposites here. But both of these great sets of facts are *related* to one another, just as everything is in living history. The independent deliberate activity of individuals soon forms associations to further its goals; it soon looks for and finds footholds in existing organization of society, or it is forced to obey this organization even against its will. In every case, however, it is always subject to the general control of the external organization of society, which both assures a margin of free play to independent and reasonable activity of individuals and sets limits to it.

Thus the relations which govern systems of culture and external organization of society with respect to each other in the living complex of purposes of the historico-social world refer to a fact which is the condition for all consistent activity of individuals, a fact in which both systems of culture and external organization of society are bound together as one. This fact is *law*. In it there exists in undivided unity what then goes its separate ways into systems of culture and external organization of society. Thus the fact of law clarifies the nature of the separation which occurs here and of the manifold relationships existing in what is separated.

In the fact of law, as the root of social-communal life for men, systems of culture are not yet separated from external organization of society. The special feature of this situation is that every concept of law includes in it the moment of external organization of society. At this point we can explain part of the difficulties which confront the person who intends to derive a general concept of law from the reality of existing law. We can also explain how the inclination of one camp of positivist researchers to emphasize one of the two halves of the fact of law is always opposed by the inclination of the other camp to insist on the half neglected by the other side.

Law is a system of purposes grounded in consciousness of justice as a permanently operative psychological fact. Whoever disputes this runs into conflict with the actual findings of history of law, in which faith in a higher order, consciousness of justice, and positive law are intrinsically linked to one another. He runs into conflict with actual findings of the living power of consciousness of justice which overlaps positive law, indeed opposes it. He mutilates the reality of law (as it appears, for example, in the historical position of customary law) so that he can accommodate it in his conceptual scheme. So in this case the systematic spirit, which is so seldom conscious of the limitations of its function in human sciences, sacrifices fullness of reality to the abstract demand for simplicity of conceptualization.

But this legal complex of purposes aims at externally coordinating wills under a fixed and universal standard which enables one to define individuals' spheres of influence on each other and on the world of things as well as on wills in general [*auf die Gesamtwillen*]. Law exists only in this function. Even the consciousness of justice is not a theoretical position but rather a matter of the will.

Even viewed externally, the complex of purposes in law is correlative to the fact of external organization of society: the two things always simply exist side by side and together. But they are not related as cause and effect; on the contrary, each requires the other as a condition for its existence. This relationship is one of the most difficult and most important forms of causal relationship; it can be explained only in the context of an epistemological and logical grounding of the human sciences. Thus once again we add a link here to the chain of our argument which shows how positive sciences of the mind lead us back to a basic underlying science precisely at those points decisive for their more rigorous scientific development. Exact scientists in search of clarity, though not at the price of shallowness, constantly find themselves referred back to such a fundamental science. Insofar as this correlative relation exists between the purpose-complex of law and external organization of society, then law—as a system of purposes in which the idea of justice is operative—presupposes the general will, that is, the united will of the community and its authority over a specific area of affairs. The theoretical proposition that the purpose-complex of law—if one imagines it hypothetically as existing in the absence of any sort of general will—would have to result in the emergence of such a general will is an idea without useful content. It merely states that there are forces at work in human nature connected with the system of purposes which arises out of consciousness of justice, and that this purpose-complex would then also be able to lay hold of those forces to create for itself a basis for its effectiveness. Because these forces are available and because they function in effect as the mainsprings of one's mental life, that is exactly why wherever human nature exists there is also external organization of society: there is no need to wait for the requirements of legal order. And just as this principle is true, so also—in accordance with the declared duality of sense in law which extends to every last legal concept—would the corresponding principle be true, which sets out from the opposite side of the fact of law. If one were to imagine an external organization of society, say the family group or the state, as functioning all alone, that unit would immediately avail itself of components in human nature which are operative in the idea of justice; it would proceed to develop its own legal structure, and it would use fixed and universally valid norms of justice to organize the spheres of influence of its subordinates with regard to one another and to things [*die Sachen*], and in relation to itself.

And so the two facts of system of purposes in law and of external organization of society are correlative. But even this insight does not exhaust the true nature of their relationship.

Law appears only in the form of imperatives, behind which there is a will which intends to push these imperatives through. Now this will is a general will, that is, the unitary will of a community which has its locus in the external organization of society, for example, in the municipality, the state, or the church. That is to say, the more we go back to the oldest conditions of society and get close to its genealogical articulation, the more distinctly do we find this situation: the spheres of power of individuals in relation to one another and to things [*Sachen*] are measured in relation to functions of these individuals in society and consequently in relation to external organization of this society. The process by which private law acquired independent status in relation to functions of individuals and their property in society indicates a late stage in which growing individualism determines the development of law, and the process always remains purely relative. Because in this way the general will assesses the rights of individuals with regard to their function in the organization it governs, development of law has its locus in this general will too. Accordingly, it is also this general will which maintains the imperatives it issues and of course includes an incentive to punish any violations thereof. And in fact this incentive exists and fights to have its way regardless of whether the general will has or does not have at its disposal specific ordinary organs for formulating, promulgating, and executing its commands. Indeed, for example, in the one direction they are not available in customary law, in the other direction in international law, while they are lacking in constitutional law with respect to principles affecting the sovereign himself.

Consequently in forming law the general will, which is the bearer of the law, cooperates with the sense of justice in individuals. These individuals are and remain living lawmaking forces. On the one hand, formation of law depends on their idea of justice; on the other hand, it depends on the will-endowed social institution [*Willenseinheit*] which has emerged in external social organization. Law, therefore, is characterized neither by total dominance of a function of the general will nor by total dominance of a system of culture. It combines within itself essential characteristics of both classes of social facts.

Apart from the law, interrelated *activities of individuals* (in which a cultural system is formed) and *creations of the general will* (which are organs of external organization of society) separate from one another to an *increasing degree*.

To be sure, the system which *political economy* analyzes has not been arranged by the will of the state, but it is strongly influenced by the entire organization of the historicosocial totality and is considerably affected as well by dispositions made by the will of the state in individual political bodies. Thus from one point of view it appears to be the subject matter of a general theory of economy; from another point of view it appears to be the embodiment of individual entities, that is, economic units, each of which is conditioned not only by everything which affects fellow countrymen in general but also by the will of the state and the legal system. Study of the general characteristics of the system—which stem from the component of man's nature in which it is grounded as well as from general laws of nature and society which govern its functioning—expands at this point through studying the influence which national organization and regulatory effect of the state exercise.

In the sphere of *morality* inner culture breaks away from the external organization of society in the matter of practical activity. If we leave behind the systems into which practical activity of society has been subdivided, we find this separation everywhere. *Language* and *religion* have developed into several separate entities under the effect of diverse organization of mankind, of historical currents, and of natural conditions.

Among these entities, the component and purpose of spiritual activity, which uniformly permeate both systems, unfold into a multiplicity of remarkable configurations. *Art* and *science* are world facts free from all hindrance of barriers of states or peoples or religions, no matter how strongly these spheres of the social cosmos have influenced them and continue to do so to a high degree even today. One can develop the system of art and of science in their basic outlines without any need to introduce external organization of society into the investigation for developing these basic outlines. Neither the foundations of esthetics nor of epistemology include the influence of national character on art and science or the effect of the state and of associations on them.

From the discussion of the relation in which systems of culture (the knowledge of which concerns us here) stand to external organization of society, we now turn to general characteristics of sciences of the systems of culture and to questions about defining the extent of these sciences.

Knowledge of Systems of Culture; Ethics Is a Science of a System of Culture

Knowledge of a particular system is achieved in a web of methodical operations; it is knowledge conditioned by the position of that system in the context of historico-social reality. The resources of that knowledge are manifold: analysis of the system; comparison of individual forms comprised by the system; utilization of the relations which link this area of investigation on the one hand to psychological knowledge of living individuals (which are the elements of interactions which make up the system) and on the other hand to the historico-social system from which it has been isolated for purposes of research. But the *process of knowledge itself is only one.* We can prove the untenability of separating philosophical from positivist investigation simply by the fact that we can adequately establish concepts which this knowledge uses (for example, will and sound judgment in law; imagination and the ideal in art) as well as elementary principles it arrives at or sets out from (for example, the principle of good management in political economy; the principle of the transformation of ideas under the influence of one's inner life in esthetics; the laws of thought in epistemology) only with the help of psychology. Indeed, one can resolve even the great antitheses which divide exact scientists with respect to defining these systems only with the help of truly descriptive psychology, because these disputes are partially due to differences in the typical model of human nature which those scientists entertain. I will illustrate this important point with one striking example. Derivation of speech, of customs, and of law from rational invention has long dominated even positive sciences of those systems. This psychological theory was superseded by the marvelous intuition of a *Volksgeist* creating unconsciously in the manner of artistic genius and of organic development of its principal living expressions. This theory, borne along by the metaphysical formula of an unconsciously creative world spirit, failed, however (with the same psychological one-sidedness as the older version), to see the difference between creations based on heightened capacity of intuition and those produced by the hard work of understanding and calculation. Intuition functions unconsciously in the orderly unfolding of its images, as one can study in the elementary processes first uncovered by Johannes Müller: psychological investigations in this direction also affect understanding of forms in the system of art.[24] Understanding that works with concepts, formulas, and institutions is of another kind. Thus Ihering has undertaken to prove that the concepts and formulas of ancient Roman law are products of deliberate, rationally schooled juristic science, of the hard work of juristic thought—which process has of course not been preserved in its original fluid character but rather "objectified and compressed into the smallest possible space, that is, into the form of legal concepts." Ihering illustrates juridical method—as the method of analytical understanding in contrast with its material (the actual relationships of life)—first in the structure of ancient Roman legal process and business of law and then in the structure of material legal concepts of this ancient Roman jurisprudence. If one takes this problem in a general and comparative sense for the system of law, then cooperation of psychology is indispensable. Ihering himself, inasmuch as he pressed on from his *Spirit of Roman Law* to his study on *Purpose in Law* and attempted to prove that "purpose is the foundation of the whole legal system," had to make the decision "to do some philosophizing in his field," that is, to look for a psychological foundation.[25]

One can locate these systems and their appropriate place in social life only in the context of the very investigations in whose early stages we find ourselves now. In the meantime they loom before us as great, manifest, objective facts. The human mind has shaped them in such wise before going on to consider them scientifically. There is a stage in the development of these systems in which theoretical reflection has not yet been distinguished from practical acting and shaping. Hence the same understanding which later turned its attention to purely theoretical establishment and explanation of law and of economic life had previously been occupied with formation of these systems. Some of these mighty realities (or so they seem, at least, to scientific imagination), such as religion and law, have developed into extensive scientific complexes.

As far as I can see, it seems that only consideration of the areas of law and morality could pose difficulties if one applied the conception of basic societal systems described here to the situation of positive sciences of the mind. These difficulties are completely different with respect to law than they are with respect to morality, and we have tried to unravel them in the foregoing. According to what we have set forth, we can distinguish sciences of law from those of external organization of society only in an imperfect way. For in law the character of a system of culture is not distinct from that of a component of external organization of society and it combines within itself essential characteristics of both classes of social facts. We face a problem of a completely different kind if we conceive of morality as a kind of system which also has a function in social life and if we conceive of ethics as a science of such a system of culture. Some very profound scholars regard it not as such an objectivity but as an imperative of personal life. Even a philosopher of the tendency of Herbert Spencer, in the design of his massive work, has separated ethics of "the theory of the righteous life," as its concluding portion, from sociology. It is thus unavoidable that we keep in mind this instance of opposition to the conception at hand.

In fact a *system of morality* does exist—richly graduated, maturing through a long historical process, in many ways determined by peculiarities of locale, expressed in a multiplicity of forms: a reality no less mighty and true than religion or law. Custom—as the rule, the recurrent, the form of the abiding and the universal in behavior—constitutes only the neutral foundation which embraces not only the advantage [*Erwerb*] of discovering the most expeditious behavior needed for reaching a goal with the least possible resistance, but also the accumulated wealth of maxims of morality, which are themselves an aspect of customary law. In this respect customary law includes the essence of general convictions about law insofar as they prove themselves in practice to be the dominant power over particular ones. In this sense Ulpian defines mores as *tacitus consensus populi, longa consuetudine inveteratus.*[26] Custom is sharply delineated according to peoples and states. By contrast, morality makes a single ideal system merely modified by difference in structures, communities, and associations. Investigation of this ideal system is carried out by combining personal psychological considerations with comparison of its variations among different peoples; Jacob Burckhardt, among all historians, has shown the deepest insight into this kind of investigation.

This system of morality does not consist in actions of men; indeed, one cannot even study it primarily through them. Rather it consists in a definite group of facts of consciousness and in that segment of human activity which they produce. We shall first try to grasp these facts of consciousness in their fullness. We encounter the ethical in a double form, and the two forms in which it appears have become points of departure for two one-sided schools of morality. It is present as judgment of behavior by an observer and as an element in motivation, which gives it a content independent of the success of that behavior in the external forum (consequently also independent of its expedience as well). The ethical is the same in both forms. In one it appears as living power behind motivation; in the other as power which responds externally to behavior of other individuals in nonpartisan approval or disapproval. One can prove this important thesis by the following. Whenever I find myself acting under pressure of moral obligation, I can express that obligation in the same principle which underlies my judgment as a neutral observer. Because ethics has until now always taken one or the other form as its basis—Kant and Fichte taking the ethical as living power in motivation and the principal English moralists along with Herbart taking it as a power responding to actions of others from the outside—they lost sight of a comprehensive and completely fundamental insight into the matter. For an observer's approval and disapproval indeed contain the ethical in undifferentiated form (a priceless advantage), but one which is feeble as well. In particular, the inner connection of motive with the entire contents of the mind, which is revealed so clearly and powerfully in the ethical struggles an acting person wages, is very watered down here. But where one makes the ethical in motivation the object of investigation, analysis is very difficult. For only the connection between motive and action is clearly apparent to us; motives themselves appear in a way quite mysterious to us. Hence man's character is a mystery for him, which only his mode of behavior partially unveils to him. Transparency in the complex of character, motive, and action is appropriate to figures fashioned by a poet but not to intuition into real life. Hence even the esthetic element in the phenomenon of an existing person lies in the fact that reflection of his creative soul still shines more luminously in his own activities than it does in those of others.

In this double guise, ethical consciousness interweaves its way in an endlessly ramified play of actions and reactions through the whole of human society. In line with what we have seen above, we can analyze its motive power into two kinds of forces. It functions in the first place in direct fashion as cultivation of moral consciousness and, under its impact, as regulator of activity. Everything which makes life worthwhile for a person rests on the foundation of conscience: for anyone who has a feeling for his own dignity and consequently looks with composure at whatever else might change nevertheless requires this foundation not only in himself but also in those whom he loves, to be able to live. The other form of psychological power through which ethical consciousness works in society is indirect. Moral consciousness which develops in society exerts pressure on the individual. It is precisely because of this that morality as a system dominates the broadest spectrum of society and governs the most diverse sorts of motives in it. Even lowest-level motives, like slaves, are forced to serve this power of the moral system. Public opinion, judgment of other people, and honor: these are the powerful bonds which hold society together where compulsion wielded by law fails. And even if a person were completely convinced that the majority of those who condemn him would behave precisely as he has done if only they could escape the judgment of the world in doing so—even this does not invalidate the jurisdiction to which his soul is subject. He is like a beast of prey under the spell of the eyes of a brave man or like a criminal under the sway of the hundred eyes of the law. If he really wants to escape this overwhelming mass of public moral opinion, then he can withstand the impetus of its momentum only if he finds himself in the company of others, that is, in another atmosphere of public opinion which sustains him. But for those who are at the beginning of personal development, for those who do not feel morally independent, yes, in individual cases, finally, even for those who are on the highest plateau morally speaking, this regulatory power of public moral conscience transmits the total effect of moral culture. And no one would be able to produce that effect completely and independently for himself at every moment of his active life in all its manifold ramifications.

Hence an independent system of morality takes shape in society. Along with that of the law, which is oriented toward external compulsion, it regulates behavior with a kind of internal compulsion. Morality, therefore, does not have its place in human sciences as a mere sum total of imperatives which regulate the life of the individual; on the contrary, its subject matter is one of the great systems which function in the life of society.

In conjunction with the organization of these systems which directly accomplish purposes based on components of human nature, there are systems of instruments which serve the direct purposes of social life. Education is an instrumental system of this sort. In response to needs of society individual instructional bodies have sprung up—the achievements of private individuals as well as of groups—from very unpretentious beginnings. They have differentiated themselves from one another and have entered into relations with one another; only gradually and partially has the system of education been subsumed into the organization of the state administration itself.

In virtue of constant adaptation of one activity to another in these systems and in virtue of common purposes of the groups composing them, these systems achieve a general accommodation of their functions and accomplishments to one another in society, which gives their inner relations some of the characteristics of an organism. Human life goals are formative forces of society, and as systems split off from one another by reason of their differing places in the whole, so these systems in their mutual relationships make up a corresponding organization of a higher order. The ultimate regulator of this rational purposeful activity in society is the state.

13. Sciences of External Organization of Society

Psychological Foundations

In contrast with these sciences which treat of systems of culture and their content and investigate those systems historically, theoretically, and legally, a universally and uniformly applied method of abstraction has distinguished other sciences which deal with external organization of society. In sciences of systems of culture, one thinks of psychological elements in various individuals, chiefly, only with respect to their role in a system of purposes. There is a way of looking at things different from this, one which considers external organization of society, that is, relations of community, of external association, of domination, and of subordination of wills in society. The same tendency of abstraction is operative whenever one distinguishes political history from cultural history. In particular, permanent groupings which appear in the life of humanity on the basis of its articulation into peoples and are the chief bearers of its progress come under this double viewpoint in this way: as relations of psychical elements in different individuals in a system of purposes, they come under a cultural system; as a union of wills based on fundamental relationships of community and dependence, they come under external organization of society.

Let us explain this concept of external organization. Seen from the *standpoint of the subject, one's experience* is that one discovers one's will in a nexus of external connections, in relations of dominance and dependence with regard to persons and things, and in relations of community. The same undivided person is at once member of a family, director of a project, member of the community, citizen, member of a church organization, and at the same time, perhaps, associate in a mutual association or political society. A person's will can thus be intertwined in an exceedingly complex web, and it will function in each of its strands only by means of the social group of which it is a part. This state of affairs, composed as it is, results in a mixture of a feeling of power and pressure, of community feeling and of self-interest, of external obligation and of freedom—all of which makes up a substantial part of our feeling of self. *Seen objectively,* we find individuals in society related to one another not just through mutual correspondence of their activities, not as merely self-sufficient individuals or even as individuals committed to one another in the depths of their moral freedom; on the contrary, this society constitutes a nexus of relationships of community and of obligation into which wills of individuals are fitted or tied, so to speak. And, indeed, a look at society shows us first of all an immense number of infinitesimally small, rapidly vanishing relations in which wills appear to be united and in binding relationship. Lasting relationships of this kind also arise out of economic life and other cultural systems. But above all: in family, state, church, in corporate bodies and in institutions, wills are brought together into associations which establish partial unity among them. These are abiding structures, though admittedly very different in duration: they perdure, while individuals enter and leave them, as an organism perdures despite the access and egress of molecules and atoms which make it up. How many generations of people, how many configurations of society has the mightiest organization this world has ever seen, the Roman Catholic church, seen come and go— from the time when slaves crept alongside their masters into underground crypts of martyrs to the time when, in their mighty cathedrals, the aristocratic landowner and the vassal, with a peasant freeman between them, the guild member from the city and the monk, were united, even to our own day, in which this motley arrangement has been largely superseded in the modern state! Hence historically associations of the most varied duration have been interwoven with one another. Because associative life of men unites one generation with another in a structure which outlasts them, acquisitions which have piled up through the work of the human race in cultural systems accumulate in the more durable form, which thus comes into being, with more security and cover, as though under a protective blanket. Thus association is one of the most powerful devices of historical progress. Because it unites those now living with those before and after them, strong-willed entities [*willensmächtige Einheiten*] spring up whose actions and interactions fill the grand theater of world history. The fruitfulness of this principle in future formation of society defies imagination. Indeed, even Kant's observation of man was unable to chase away the fantasy from his soul, which—to the feeling of kinship which embraces humanity, to coordination of our activities and our purposes, and to local associations we establish on this earth as our common dwelling place—added an external connection as well, an association embracing the entire human race.

Two psychological facts everywhere underlie this external organization of humanity. Consequently, they belong to psychological facts of second rank, which lay the foundation for these theoretical special sciences of society.

One of these facts is present in every kind of *community* and *consciousness of community*. If we designate it "sense of community" or "instinct for sociability," then—as in the distinction of powers with regard to psychical facts of the first order—we must insist that this is only a shorthand expression for the X which underlies this fact; this X might just as well contain a plurality of factors as a single foundation. The fact itself, however, is this: Provided that some contrary psychical influence does not cancel it out, a feeling of community is connected to some degree in cases of very different psychological relations between individuals; with the consciousness of common ancestry; with a common locale for living together; with the homogeneity of individuals grounded on such relations (for dissimilarity as such is not a bond of community, but only insofar as it makes possible cooperation of unlike persons for a specific task, whether it be just that of a stimulating conversation or a refreshing impression in the routine of daily life); with the many-faceted common organization occasioned by problems and goals of psychic life; or with the fact of association. Thus if A has a goal to achieve and the motivation needed for it, and if these things depend on a corresponding cooperative effort on the part of B and C, then A is involved in a feeling of togetherness and community: a solidarity of interests. We can clearly separate two psychological facts from each other: the underlying relationship, and the feeling of community whereby it is reflected in some degree in one's affective life. Every art of analysis is mocked by the extraordinary complexity and subtlety of shading with which this feeling, which is so important for historico-social life, vibrates through the external organization of humanity and enlivens it with its warmth. Analysis of this feeling is thus one of the basic problems of these special theories of society. Even at this point there lurks the obfuscating mist of an abstraction (an instinct or a sense which usually passes itself off as a substantive entity in political science and in history) between the observer and the complexity of the phenomenon. It calls for individual analysis. How extraordinary was the effect on theology of that particular analysis in which Schleiermacher's famous fourth *Discourse on Religion* undertook, on the basis of religious feeling, to derive the need for religious fellowship and characteristics of a sense of congregation [*Gemeindebewusstsein*] in their specific difference from other forms of this general feeling of community and in this way sought to show the relationships between the most important cultural system and the external organization arising out of it. His experiment shows with particular clarity that to begin with we have here a penetration into lived experience itself, which corresponds to self-observation in individual psychology and can appear separately from comparative investigation of historical phenomena as well as from psychological analysis, even though this naturally produces one-sided results.

The relation of *dominance* and *dependence* between wills constitutes the other one of these two psychological and psychophysical facts so fundamental for understanding external organization of society. This relation, too, like that of community, is only relative; accordingly every association is only relative. Even the highest degree of intensification of external relationship of power is limited and can in some circumstances be defeated by a contrary force. It is possible to move a resisting person from one place to another; but to compel him to move himself to this place is something we can do only by activating a motive in him which works more powerfully than motives which are influencing him to remain. The quantitative element in this scale of intensities, whose outcome is external coercion of will through intensification to the point that no contrary-acting motive has any prospect of success, that is, external compulsion, and connection of these quantitative relations with the concept of mechanics of society make this series of concepts one of the most fruitful in the class we have called concepts of second rank. To the extent that a will is not externally compelled, we call its condition freedom.

At this point we again pick up the inferences which lead to insight into the nature of the foundation-laying process of the human sciences. One might have guessed that concepts of psychological or psychophysical facts and principles regarding them would underlie sciences of external organization of society—facts and principles which correspond to those on which sciences of culture are grounded. A feeling of solidarity, a feeling of self-interest (a condition for which we have no proper word), domination, dependence, freedom, compulsion: these are the kinds of psychological and psychophysical facts of second rank, knowledge of which (in concepts and principles) lies at the basis of the study of the external organization of society. Here the first question is what the relationship of these facts to one another is. For example, can we not resolve the feeling of community into one of mutual dependence? A further question is about the extent to which analysis of these facts and their derivation from psychological facts of the first order is possible. So now we conclude: for both classes of theoretical sciences of society the fundamental facts are such that we can analyze them only by using psychological concepts and principles. The focus of all problems of such foundation-laying is therefore: the possibility of knowledge of living psychical individuals and the boundaries of such knowledge. It is thus a question of the relation of psychological knowledge to facts of second rank, by which we can decide about the nature of these theoretical sciences of society.

The psychological facts described—of community on the one hand and of dominance/dependence (mutual dependence is naturally included here) on the other hand—course through the external organization of society like lifeblood in the most delicate system of arteries. Viewed psychologically, *all relations of association are composed of them*. And indeed the existence of these feelings is by no means always linked to the presence of an association; rather, these psychological and psychophysical elements of all associative life extend much further in society than associative life itself. And so we find in the organic growth pattern of society, which is determined in the first place by genealogical structure, that in accordance with basic relations of descent and kinship, with larger groups always encompassing smaller ones and these latter in turn arranged in order according to their kinship bonds: the thoroughgoing modification of human nature discernible in the larger group is always more precisely defined within the circle of the smaller group by new marks of still closer uniformity. And on this natural foundation a more intimate mutuality and a certain degree of awareness of belonging together in terms of similarity as well as of recollection of common ancestry and kinship now unites each such group into a relative totality. Even where no association is connected with them, these communities persist. Whenever a colonial settlement [*Niederlassung*] is made, a new organization comes into being which differs from the genealogical one, a new feeling of community marked by a sense of being at home by common soil and common labor; and this community, too, is independent of the formation of any sort of association. The historical power of great personalities or historical intervention in the form of great actions taken by peoples change, demolish, or combine things differently and in closer detail than interlocking circles of communities held together solely by general genealogical organization or by common soil would do. Above all, the nations [*Völker*] have formed themselves through world-historical action which breaks through the natural order. But even if they have acquired a full sense of belonging together as a rule (not always, as the example of the Greek polities held together by national feeling shows) by galvanizing themselves into the unity of a state, this national community—which is reflected as national feeling in the emotional life of the individuals belonging to the group—is capable of long outlasting the existence of the state, and so, in this case too, community does not depend on the duration of an association. Mutualities and dependency relationships of a permanent kind which arise on the basis of cultural systems of mankind now intersect still further with the spheres of community established through genealogical structure and settlement. Community of speech follows on genealogical ordering and national life; affinity of rank by birth or of property or occupation produces class consciousness; equality of relations of economic ownership and of social level and breeding conditioned by them binds individuals into a class which feels that it belongs together and contrasts its own interests with those of other classes. Similarity of conviction and activity establishes political and ecclesiastical parties. These are common elements of which not one, in and of itself, makes up an association. On the other hand, out of the complex of purposes in the systems, relations of dependence emerge which the state likewise does not directly produce but which, arising from cultural systems, assert themselves in the state. Their relation to the force of compulsion coming from the state itself constitutes one of the main problems of mechanics of society. The two most effective kinds of dependence of this type are those arising from economic life and from church life.

Thus these two basic psychological relations constitute the entire framework of external organization of humanity. The will-relationship reflected in dominance and dependence finds its limit in the sphere of external freedom; community-relationship finds its limit in the extent to which an individual exists only for himself. For the sake of clarity let us expressly stress this point: totally different from all these external relationships of will is action arising out of the depths of human freedom whereby a will sacrifices itself either partially or totally; it does not unite itself as one will with another, but partially sacrifices itself as a will. This aspect in an action or a relationship makes it a moral one.

External Organization of Society as a Historical State of Affairs

By an *association* [*Verband*] we understand a permanently established union of wills among a number of people for a specific purpose. No matter how variously forms of association have taken shape, they all have one characteristic in common: their union goes beyond a mere amorphous sense of belonging together and community and beyond the closer sort of interaction in a group which is left to individual choice. This kind of voluntary union has a structure; the wills involved are bound together in a definite form of cooperation. Between these characteristics of every association, however, there exists a very simple relation. We can even call it tautological that the union of wills among several persons is established for a particular purpose. For regardless of what influence even violence might have on forming such a union of wills, nevertheless violence is only a form and manner in which one can coordinate the structure. Will sets the arm of force into motion, and that will is guided by some purpose: it lays hold of and subdues a subject because he is a means for realizing a purpose-complex that will wants to achieve. Therefore Aristotle is right when he says in this spirit at the beginning of his *Politics: pasa koinonia agathou tinos heneka sunestēken.*[27] Even historically viewed, force has brought people into subjection only to make its subjects conform to the general purpose of its own activity. A permanent complex of purposes, however, introduces structure into the organization of individuals subject to it as well as of the goods it needs. Hence the character of the purposive system determines the character of a given structure; the purpose complex functions as a law of formation in shaping the association. What a remarkable fact! The relation of purpose to function and structure—which in the realm of organic beings serves as a guide to investigation only as a hypothetically introduced device of knowledge—is here a lived, historically demonstrable fact accessible to experience in society. And what a reversal of relationships, then, to wish to use the concept of organism as we can establish it in facts of organic nature (in which it is unclear and hypothetical) as the guide for social situations arising from this relation (which are experienced and clear).

Therefore it is much more natural that natural science now gladly uses the analogy with social facts whenever it speaks of the animal organism. It is just that in this way the danger arises that a new game in natural philosophy, involving life in matter, will little by little creep into the picture on account of this imagery. In any case, for political science the problem is clearly sketched out in this regard. Since natural sciences, with their sensible subject matter, have graphic material to work with and since they have developed a graphic, even penetrating, terminology (with which one is strongly tempted to fill in gaps in the terminology of the social sciences), the problem is to establish clear and appropriate expressions in the human sciences, which would fill the present gaps and so construct a pure and coherent terminology. This would protect human sciences from confusing their language with that of natural sciences and would promote, even terminologically, the development of solid and universally valid concepts in the sphere of intellectual data.

One cannot conceptually establish the *boundary* which separates an association from other forms of cooperation in society in a manner univocal yet uniformly valid for all legal systems.

The note of permanence distinguishes an association from transitional relations of wills in a complex of purposes, particularly in a contract, only to the extent that it is not in the nature of a contract *per se* to produce permanent relations. Moreover this characteristic is indefinite in itself, and even if it is related to a purpose-complex which by nature tends toward a permanent connection, nevertheless this relation does not make it possible clearly to demarcate the association as against more transitional forms of voluntary association. For, to begin with, not every purpose leads to an association. Many of our expressions of life, even though they may be purposeful, do not involve purposeful activity of other persons. And where such activity *is* involved, often the purpose can be achieved by coordinating individual activities of persons working successively or simultaneously. Thus it is in the nature of artistic creativity that its forms arise from the lonely depths of the soul and yet, at a particular point, they go on to enter into the realm of shadows which fill the imagination of the human race, and in this silent realm occupy a place in a purpose-complex which transcends the artist. Finally, where such a purpose-complex involves other people, then a contract generally suffices inasmuch as it effects a union with respect to a particular business matter or a series of them. From this·point the path to an association involves a further development, in which it is impossible to apply the concept in a uniformly valid way for the complexities of life and legal ordinances of the most varied levels of culture. For this distinction between a contract related to one business matter (or a series of them) and establishment of an association is something fixed by law; consequently, by its very nature it can be expressed clearly only in legal terms. And because systems of law are different, so also, for example, a construction which uses the Roman contrast between *societas* and *universitas* to determine the point at which contractual relations pass over into associative relations is clearly useless for defining the point in German law at which some form of association emerges.

One can no more establish the boundary line for associations in a conceptual form valid for all legal systems than one can establish a *classification* of associations of that kind.

As a legal idea, the concept which draws these boundaries necessarily belongs to some particular legal system. Therefore, one can compare the function such a concept has in a particular legal system only with one which corresponds to a like concept in another legal system. Thus one can compare the function which corresponds to concepts of *municipium, collegium,* and *societas publicanorum* in the Roman legal system with the function which concepts of community, guild, and cooperative society have in German law. As the epistemological foundation-laying will show us, however, we simply cannot subject entities like the family and the state to real conceptual construction. Every method which sets itself this task is assembling a mechanical construct. Over and over again we find repeated in other forms the basic error of natural law theory which, setting out from the correct viewpoint that law is something grounded in a basic element of human nature and is thus not just an arbitrary system arising from the whim of the state, then proceeds in its turn to construct the state out of law. This is fatally mistaking the other side of the situation, the mighty primordial character of human associative life. The method of synthetic construction is very fruitful in deducing legal relationships in a legal system defined in its essentials; but it has its limits there. We can understand this great historical reality only as such, that is, we can understand it only in its historical context, the fundamental law of which is this: associative life of man has not been shaped synthetically but instead has differentiated and developed itself out of the unity of the family group. All that our knowledge can do is this: working back from the organization of this associative life such as we find it accessible to us at the levels of external organization of society which are the closest possible to primitive conditions, to interpret evidence which sheds light on the great *historical process* in which *external organization of society has set itself apart* from the life-and-power-filled *unity of the family group* and to subject associative life and development of associations by various peoples and families of peoples to comparative analysis. The extraordinary significance of the development of Germanic association for such comparative investigation consists in the fact that sufficient historical data[28] are available for a relatively very early stage in the development of an association, one which was destined to experience a marvelously rich unfolding of cooperative existence. In the sphere of external organization of humanity the comprehensive basic law of historical life is still clearly perceptible in its power: the law, as I shall show, by which even the totality of inner purposeful life has differentiated itself only gradually into particular cultural systems and by which these cultural systems have attained only gradually to their full independence and individual development.

The family is the fruitful womb of all human order, of all group life: a community of sacrifice, an economic unit, a protective association, grounded in the powerful natural bond of love and reverence. It contains its permanent function intertwined in still undifferentiated unity with law, government, and religious community. But even this most concentrated form of unity of will among individuals in the world is only relative. Individuals who make it up do not enter into it totally; the individual exists in his ultimate depths for himself alone. If the view which submerges human freedom and action in the natural life of the organism regards the family as a "social fabric cell,"[29] then such a concept destroys the free independence of the individual in the family group right at the outset of the science of society. Whoever begins with a family life made up of "cells" can end up only with a socialistic organization of society.

Insofar as families also constitute tribal associations [*Verbände der Geschlechterordnung*] and these enter into associations of differing kinds (such as those in a colonial settlement) or are included in broader associative structures, the function of the state—in accordance with the basic function of the state: to be a power which makes sovereignty its specific characteristic—must always have its locus in the broadest social alliance. Thus family-association and state-association part company. Where the Germans enter the historical picture we find this separation long since completed and German home-association already formed in its own right; from the time in which the kinship group [*Sippe*] might have once united families into an independent union, we find only remnants and folk groups surviving as independent state communities. The stages which transpired here, unseen by any observer—before Caesar or Tacitus compiled their records on what happened in the northern wilderness—are only partially accessible in travelers' reports about associative life of primitives. But while remains of the oldest Germanic community life point to the fact that patriarchal power (*mundium*) which prevailed in the family group was not decisive for tribal association generally, we encounter here among many tribes a governmental system headed by chiefs which developed out of patriarchal home arrangement. Thus the process of differentiation which led to external social organization among the various families of peoples and races was different from the very beginning. This imposes severe limits on comparative analysis which uses conditions prevailing among primitives to illuminate the ancient situation of modern European nations.

But external organization of society—in the family, in tribal arrangements, in associations based on locale, in all manorial relationships, in the church and other religious communities, in manifold modifications of these forms—unfolds with a mighty natural originality and incommensurability, a suppleness and an adaptability, such that each of these groups fosters within it an indefinite and variable multiplicity of purposes, abandons this purpose-complex and takes up that one—indeed even lets this purpose go for today to take it up again tomorrow—and, by the way, has a tendency to satisfy every general community need. Thus there exists in associative life of humanity the most uniformly thoroughgoing difference between these social groupings and others which have been set up by a definite act of a conscious union of wills for a deliberately determined and defined purpose, and which consequently naturally belong to a later stage of associative life for each people.

If one surveys the whole of the external organization which humanity has thus fashioned for itself, one finds that the sheer abundance of forms is immense. In all these forms the relation between purpose, function, and structure gives us the law of development and thus the points of departure for comparative analysis. And in any historical cross section, study of the associative life of humanity finds practically every degree of extent of purpose-system behind any association, from community life of the family to the mutual insurance company against hail damage; it finds virtually every form of structure, from despotic states in the heart of Africa to the modern joint-stock company, in which each stockholder fully maintains his individual personality and merely contractually commits a precisely defined part of his wealth to the common endeavor.

Task of Describing Theoretically the External Organization of Society

The previous discussion has determined the fundamental psychological facts which underlie the entire fabric of the external organization of society in a way which is everywhere uniform and everywhere somehow interconnected. It has outlined the associative life of humanity built on those facts in an historical overview, while rejecting a merely conceptual definition and classification of them. From this standpoint one can now at least identify the problem which speculation poses in this historical totality. Two questions are especially important for the position and development of the special sciences into which this theory of external organization of society is divided. One has to do with the relation of external organization, especially the state, to law; the other has to do with the relation of state to society.

Because the question about the relation of law to *external organization of society* is the first to be dealt with, our next task is to tie in the results of our previous discussion about law[30] with the concept of external organization of society just now developed.

Not every purpose, as we saw,[31] produces an association; many of our activities in life simply do not become engaged with those of other persons in such a way as to form a system of purposes. If such a system is formed, it can often be achieved by merely coordinating individual activities without the support of any kind of association. But there are goals which an association can achieve better or only an association can achieve. Hence arises the relationship which exists between living activity of individuals, systems of culture, and external organization of society. Some of these expressions of life lead to no permanent connection between psychophysical living individuals; others do result in such a purpose-complex and accordingly take the form of a system. Indeed, it happens that the task they are busy about is accomplished in some cases by mere cooperation of persons in a system of purposes, and in other cases is accomplished by unity of wills in an association.

Systems and external organization are so intertwined in the roots of human existence and social order that only a difference in point of view distinguishes them. The most vital interests of man are the control of his will over means or goods which satisfy his needs and their adaptation to these needs, but they also include security for his person and the property he thus acquires. This is the focal point of the relation between law and the state. A man's body might be able to withstand the ravages of nature for a long time; but his life and livelihood are menaced every hour by his fellows. That is why reflection on the connection between psychic elements among several people in a systematic purpose-complex was an abstraction. The unbridled violence of the passions does not allow a man to enter into the order of such a purpose complex with clear self-control. A strong hand holds each person in check; the social body which accomplishes this must be superior to any other force in the sphere governed by its strong hand and must therefore be endowed with the attribute of sovereignty. And that power is a "state," regardless of whether it is still confined to the family unit or a tribal union or a municipality, or whether its functions have already become differentiated from those of these groups. It is not as though the state, through its union of wills, performed a task which would otherwise be taken care of, though not as well, by the combined efforts of individuals; rather, the state is the sine qua non of all such cooperation. This protective function is directed outwardly in protecting subjects; it is directed inwardly in erecting and forcibly maintaining rules of law.

Consequently, *law is a function of the external organization of society*. In this organization its locus is in the general will. It judges individuals' spheres of influence by the task they perform in this external organization in accordance with their positions in it. It is a prerequisite for all rational activity of individuals in the systems of culture.[32]

Yet law has another side as well, one which makes it akin to systems of culture.[33] It is a complex of purposes. Every will produces such a complex, and thus the will of the state also does in every one of its manifestations, whether it be building roads, organizing armies, or creating laws. This will of the state is also dependent on the cooperation of its subjects in all its expressions, not just in law. But the complex of purposes of the law has special characteristics, which flow from the relation of consciousness of justice to the order of law.

The state does not create this system through its own naked will, either in the abstract (the way the system recurs uniformly in all systems of law) or in the concrete system of a specific legal order. In this respect law is not made but discovered. As paradoxical as it sounds, this is the profound *idea of natural law*. The oldest belief, according to which the legal system of the individual state was derived from the gods, transformed itself in the course of Greek thought into the principle that divine universal law was the creative ground of every state and legal system.[34] This was the oldest form of the assumption of a natural law in Europe. It was a view which regarded that law as the foundation of every single piece of positive legislation. The first theorists who posited natural law in contrast with positive laws of the particular state, and so hypostatized natural law, were Archelaus and Hippias, who made their appearance among the ruins of the older Greek natural law. Hippias's historical significance was that—evidently in connection with his archaeological studies—he distinguished unwritten laws (which are found constantly among the most disparate peoples, separated from one another by their languages and thus not in communication with one another) as natural law in contrast with positive law and denied any binding power to the latter.[35] The tragedies of Sophocles constitute a telling monument of this phase of natural law. Sophocles doubtless adopted this contrast between unwritten norms of law and positive legislation from the debates of his period, but he gave them classical expression. If natural law thus fashioned the concept of a purpose-complex in law which makes it into a system—whether it viewed this complex as divine or natural—nevertheless it naturally distinguished from it the element which the will of the community had added to it. Hence medieval natural law theorists contrasted the natural system with positive law which sprang from the power of an association.[36]

It is on the basis of the state of affairs which natural law wished to express in this way that one side of the relationship between sciences of law and of the state rests: the relative independence of sciences of law. Law is an end in itself. Consciousness of justice functions in cooperation with organized general will in the course of the emergence and maintenance of legal order. For it is the content of will whose power is rooted in the depths of personality and of religious experience.

The idea of natural law became erroneous because people treated this purpose-complex in law as cut off from its relationships, especially those to economic life and to external organization of society, and shifted it into a sphere outside of historical development. Hence abstractions usurped the place of realities; most creations of the legal system remained inexplicable.

The core of these abstract theories can be scientifically elaborated only by the method common to all sciences of society, that is, a combination of historical and psychological analysis. At this point we can draw a further conclusion in the chain of ideas which lead back to the position of individual human sciences in relation to their foundation. *This problem which natural law posed* for itself is *soluble only in cooperation with the positive sciences of law.* For their part these latter can achieve clear awareness of the role of the abstractions they use in relation to reality only through a fundamental epistemological science, that is, through establishing how the concepts and principles these sciences use are related to psychological and psychophysical concepts and principles. It follows that there is no special philosophy of law as such; rather, its task must fall to the philosophically grounded system of positive sciences of the mind. This does not exclude the possibility that division of labor and school administration [*Schulbetrieb*] might make it seem useful that the task of general science of law should also be carried on as natural law from time to time; but it defines the methodical structure in which the solution of such a task simply must take place.

How could this general science of law know the law except in its living connection with the general will in the organization of society? The importance of the facts of convictions about law, of elementary psychological impulses linked to them, of customary law, and of international law can extend only far enough to show the existence of a component of human nature on which the character of law as an end in itself rests. We will expand this demonstration significantly in historically considering the relations of legal concepts and legal institutions to religious ideas which we see at the perceptible beginnings of our culture. But—and this is the other side of this relationship of law to the state—no argumentation can have the range necessary to prove the existence of an actual law independent of external organization of society. The legal order is the order of purposes of society, an order its external organization upholds through force. And indeed (p. 123) force wielded by the state (in the general sense of the word developed on pp. 122–23) constitutes the decisive mainstay of the legal order. But we saw an external binding together of wills pervading all of organized society (p. 117ff.); thus it becomes clear how in society other general wills besides the state make law and uphold it. Every legal concept therefore includes a moment of external organization of society. On the other hand, every association can be established only through legal concepts. This is just as true as the fact that associative life of humanity has not grown out of the need for legal order and that the will of the state did not first invent consciousness of justice through its legal enactments.

In this way the other side of the relation of legal sciences to political sciences becomes clear: every concept in the former can be developed only in virtue of concepts in the latter, and vice versa.

Investigation of both sides of law in general jurisprudence leads to a still more general problem which transcends law. The purpose-complex which embraces law has developed through individual general wills, in the work of individual nations; that is, it has developed historically. The contrast between the eighteenth century, which dissolved historico-social reality into an aggregate of natural systems which underlie the influences of historical pragmatism, and the historical school of the nineteenth century, which opposed this abstraction, but—despite its higher standpoint and because of its lack of truly empirical philosophy—failed to attain knowledge of historico-social reality which was clear (thus usable) in its concepts and principles, is a contrast we can overcome only by laying a foundation for human sciences which maintains the standpoint of experience and of fullblown experiential knowledge [*Empirie*] even in the face of empiricism [*Empirismus*] itself. On the basis of such a foundation, problems which arise in law can approach solution: questions which have grown up along with mankind itself, which exercised thinkers as early as the fifth century before Christ and still divide jurisprudence into different camps today, and other questions which hover today between the spirit of the eighteenth and that of the nineteenth century.

Beyond these roots of human existence and social communal life, *systems and associations* [*Systeme und Verbände*] are more clearly differentiated. *Religion,* as a system of belief, is separable from the association in which it resides to such a degree that an outstanding and devout theologian of the last generation could question the appropriateness of church associations to our present-day Christian life. In *science* and *art,* however, coordination of independent special activities reaches such a degree of cultivation that the significance of associations formed to achieve artistic and scientific purposes recedes completely by comparison; accordingly, esthetics and philosophy, the sciences which formally study these systems, develop their objects of study without ever giving thought to such associations.

In this fashion an unself-conscious art of abstraction has distinguished these two kinds of science from each other with increasing clarity. It did this even though basic training of the individual and his activity in groups naturally connected the study of the system with that of association.

From these statements about the relation of association to system there arises finally a methodologically important consequence relating to the *nature of the sciences* which deal with *external organization* of humanity.

Sciences of the external organization of society do not treat of concrete reality itself, any more than sciences of culture do. Every theory gets hold of only part of the content of the complexity of reality. Theories of historico-social life divide up the immensely complicated realm of actuality they approach to penetrate it. And so, science also selects association out of the reality of life as an object of consideration. A group of individuals joined in an association is never completely swallowed up by the latter. In modern life it is common for a person to belong to several associations not subsumed under one another in any simple way. But even if a person belonged only to *one* association, his entire essence still does not go into it. If one thinks of the oldest family association, one is looking at the elementary social body, the most concentrated form of unity of will conceivable among men. Yet even here the union of wills in it is only relative: individuals who make it up are not swallowed up in it entirely, as if it were their essential unity. What our observation spontaneously demarcates in spatial terms as a country, people, and state and thus imagines as a total reality when we use the name of Germany or France, is not the state and is not the object of political science. No matter how deeply the strong hand of the state reaches into the living unity of the individual and lays hold of him, still the state obligates and subjects individuals only partially, only relatively; there is something in them which is only in the hand of God. And no matter how much political science comprehends about conditions governing this general will [*Willenseinheit*], it still deals directly merely with a partial fact accessible only through abstraction. As for the reality which people living in a territory constitute, political science leaves untouched a residue of very considerable importance. State power itself comprises only a determinate quantum, subject to the state's purposes, of the entire power of the people. This power must of course be greater than any other power in its territory, but the necessary preponderance of power comes only through its organization and through the cooperation of psychological motives with it.[37]

Within external organization, *society* (taken in a narrower sense) has recently been distinguished from *the state*.

Since it first appeared in Europe, study of external organization of society has had its focal point in *political science*. In the twilight of life of the Greek city-states appeared the two great political theorists who set down the foundations for this discipline. It is true that at that time there still existed *phylae* and *phratriae* on the one hand and *demes*[38] on the other as remnants of old orders of tribes and communities. They possessed corporate personality and power, and alongside them were also free associations. But in the positive law of Athens there appears[39] to have been no distinction between a resolution establishing a corporation and an agreement for a common commercial enterprise. The general concept of *koinōnia* covered all corporative life [*Verbandsleben*], and a distinction like the Roman one between *universitas* and *societas* had not been developed. Aristotle therefore merely formulates the result of Greek development of associations when he uses the concept of *koinōnia* as his point of departure in his *Politics* and traces the genetic relation which leads from family association to village association (*kōme*) and from this to city-state (*polis*), but then lets village association disappear as a stage of merely historical interest in his own political theory and allots no place in his state to free guilds. In fact, in Greek life every form of communal association perished in the hegemony of the city-state. Further elements of a theory of external organization of society then developed in jurisprudence and in ecclesiastical science. In the broad daylight of history we see the greatest association Europe has produced, the Catholic church, grow up, express its nature in theoretical formulas, and create a legal order for itself based on that nature.

European society after the French Revolution exhibited a completely new phenomenon as the restraining mechanisms, so to speak, which in its earlier organization had stood between the strong passions of the working classes and state power supporting the economic and legal order, had now fallen away for the most part. Rapid growth of industry and of communication links confronted state power with a daily increasing mass of workers bound together through community of interests transcending individual state boundaries and ever more clearly conscious of their interests through the progress of Enlightenment. In consideration of this new situation people attempted to develop a new theory, *science of society*. In France sociology meant carrying out the gigantic dream of deducing knowledge of the true nature of society from a combination of all the truths discovered by science; of outlining, on the basis of this knowledge, a new external organization of society corresponding to prevailing facts of science and industry; and of directing the new society with this knowledge. In this spirit Count Saint-Simon developed the concept of sociology during the violent crises at the turn of the century. His student Comte devoted the intense labor of an entire lifetime to systematic development of this science with consistent tenacity.

The idea and experiment of sociology arose in Germany in reaction to this work and under the impact of the same societal situation.[40] In a healthy, scientifically positive sense it did not attempt to substitute for political sciences through a single totality of enormous dimensions; rather, it sought to supplement them. Ever since Schlözer began to examine the abstract concept of the state, its inadequacy had become steadily more obvious through the historical school, which in its research had penetrated to a whole new depth of understanding the phenomenon of a people [*des Volkes*]. Hegel, Herbart, and Krause labored in the same direction. It is undeniable that one who moves from the particular life of individuals toward the fact of state power encounters between the two a broad sphere of facts which contain permanent relationships of these individuals to one another as well as to the world of property. Individuals do not exist as isolated atoms vis-à-vis the state power but as an organization [*ein Zusammenhang*]. In line with our previous exposition one must further acknowledge that, based on the natural organization of the family and of settlement and in the interaction of activities of cultural life in their relation to properties, an organization comes into being which the state supports and makes possible from its very beginning but which, as it is, is not totally subsumed under the power of the state. The expressions "people" [*Volk*] and "society" obviously reflect this fact.

The question concerning the justification for the existence of a special science of society is not a question about the existence of this fact, but about the appropriateness of making it the object of a special science. On the whole, the question whether a certain partial content of reality is suited to develop proven and fruitful principles from that content is like the question whether a knife lying before me is sharp or not. One has to cut. One establishes a new science by discovering important truths, not just by marking off a terrain as yet unoccupied in the wide world of facts. That must arouse some doubts about *Robert von Mohl's* project. This man sets out from the position that between the individual person, the family, the tribe, and the community,[41] on the one hand, and the state, on the other, there are homogeneous relations and accordingly permanent formations of individual elements of the population. These groups are formed through community of ancestry of privileged families, community of personal prominence, community of relations of property and acquisition, and community of religion. Whether on the grounds of this outline of a situation "general sociology, that is, establishing the concept and general laws"[42] of society, is necessary could be demonstrated only by discovering these laws. Any other kind of consideration promises no results. Throughout many years of work Lorenz von Stein has been trying to develop such a system of truths. What he is striving for is an actual explanatory theory which should fit in between theory of property[43] (in its final wording: between knowledge of economic activity, of the function of consciousness of God, and of the work of knowledge),[44] on the one hand, and political science on the other. If we were to translate that into the frame of reference developed here, then this science would be the connecting link between sciences of systems of culture and political science. Society is for him, accordingly, a permanent and universal aspect of all conditions of human community and an essential and powerful element in the whole of world history.[45] Not until we subject his deeply pondered theory to logical testing later can we decide the question whether the truths he developed justify staking out a science of sociology.

Even at this point we see the necessity of laying an epistemological and logical foundation that will clarify the relation of abstract concepts to socio-historical reality, part of whose contents they make up. For there is an obvious tendency by political scientists to treat society as a reality existing in its own right. Indeed, Mohl claims to understand society directly as "a real life, an organism existing apart from the state,"[46] as if any one of its spheres of life, in the absence of all-sustaining state power and the legal order of the state, could have the permanence which by his own admission belongs to its essential character. Stein constructs social arrangements and associations and then has unity in the state assert itself above them in absolute self-determination to the highest form of corporate personality. If one sees in his account that society and the state confront each other as opposite powers, still the empiricist can ascribe this situation only to the distinction made between state power at a given time and the free forces found in its sphere of influence (which are not bound by the state, but are in their own system of relations). In a theoretical consideration of power relationships in political life one can focus on the power relationship between state authority and these free forces just as readily as one can focus on power relationships between units of the state. But society in this sense also encompasses remains of older state arrangements; it is not composed, as Stein's society is, of relations based on a specific origin.

14. Philosophy of History and Sociology Are Not True Sciences

We are at the boundary of the special sciences of historico-social reality developed so far. These have mainly investigated the structure and functions of the most important permanent facts regarding psychophysical interactions between individuals in the universe. It takes continuous practice to think of these narrower systems of interaction—layered over one another, mutually intersecting, and crossing one another in their bearers, the individuals—at the same time as parts of reality and not as abstractions. There are different people in each one of us: a family member, a citizen, a colleague. We find ourselves in a complex of moral obligations, in a legal order, in a purpose-complex of life directed toward gratification. Only in personal reflection do we find the unity and continuity of life in us which supports and holds together all these relations. Even human society in general lives by the production, formation, separation, and combination of these permanent states of affairs, without society or one of the individuals who contribute to carrying them on thereby being conscious of their organization. What a process of differentiation it was in which Roman law set apart a sphere of private law or the medieval church helped the religious sphere to full independence! From arrangements which serve the domination of man over nature to the highest creations of religion and art the human mind works constantly in this way on defining and shaping these systems and on developing the external organization of society. This is a picture every bit as sublime as any which natural science can depict with respect to the origin and structure of the cosmos: though individuals come and go, every one of them is nevertheless a bearer and cobuilder of this enormous structure of historico-social reality.

If a special science wrests these permanent conditions away from the incessant whirling play of alterations which fills the historico-social world, they still take their origin and their sustenance only from the common ground of this reality. Their life runs its course in relation to the whole out of which they have been extracted, to individuals who are its carriers and shapers, and to other permanent organizations which society embraces. The problem of the mutual relationship of functions of these systems in the economy of social reality emerges. We would like to know this reality itself, as a living whole. And so we are unceasingly thrown up against the most general and ultimate problem of human studies: Is there a *knowledge of this whole* of historico-social reality?

Scientific elaboration of facts which one or other of the special sciences achieves in fact leads the scholar into several connections whose ends he appears unable to discover or tie together. I will illustrate this by the example of the study of poetic works. One can understand the manifold world of poetry, in the succession of its appearances, only in and from the comprehensive reality of the cultural system. For the plot, motive, and characters of a great poetic work are determined by the ideal of life, world picture, and social reality of the time in which it appeared and retrospectively through the world-historical tradition and development of poetic materials, motives, and characters. On the other hand, analysis of a poetic work and its effect points back to general laws which underlie this part of the system of culture represented in art. For the most important concepts we use in recognizing a poetic work and the laws which operate in its formation are grounded in the imagination of the poet and its relation to the world of experience, and we can glean them only by analyzing them. Imagination, however, which we seem at first to encounter as a miracle and as a phenomenon totally different from the everyday life of man, is something analysis finds to be only the more powerful organization of some men, which is grounded in the extraordinary strength of certain processes. Consequently, intellectual life, in accordance with its general laws, grows in these mighty organizations to a totality of form and achievement which completely departs from the level of the average person and nevertheless is grounded only in the same laws. We are thus led back into anthropology. Esthetic sensibility makes up the correlative fact of imagination. They are related to one another as moral judgment is to motive forces behind behavior. This fact too—which explains the effect of poems, the technique built on calculating these effects, and the transmission of esthetic sentiments to an age—is a corollary of general laws of intellectual life. Thus study of the history of poetic works and national literatures is conditioned at two points by study of intellectual life in general. In the first place, we found that it depends on knowledge of the whole of historico-social reality. The concrete causal system is woven into that of human culture in general. But in the second place we also found that the nature of the intellectual activity which has produced these creations functions according to laws which govern intellectual life in general. Therefore true poetics, which should be the foundation for the study of literature and its history, must take its concepts and principles from a combination of historical research and this general study of human nature. Not to be despised, finally, is the ancient task of such poetics: sketching out rules for producing and evaluating poetic works. Two classical works of Lessing have shown how to derive clear rules from conditions which govern our esthetic sensibility in virtue of the universal nature of a particular artistic task. Of course Lessing, pursuing a strategy unique to him of dividing questions and selecting individual problems he could solve at a given time, deliberately left in obscurity the background of a general method of evaluating what determines the impression made by poetical works.

But it is clear that treatment of such a universally conceived problem through analysis of esthetic effects would have taken one back to the most universal characteristics of human nature. So we cannot free esthetic judgment from our conception of this part of history; for this judgment is after all at the root of the interest which selects one work for consideration from the stream of what is indifferent to us. We cannot produce exact causal knowledge which would exclude judgment. We cannot separate judgment from historical knowledge by any kind of spiritual chemistry as long as the knower is a whole person. But on the other hand, judgment and rule, as they are woven into the structure of this knowledge, make up a third independent class of principles which one cannot derive from the other two. This is something we encountered at the beginning of this survey. Such a system could hold together only psychologically; but only a self-reflection which transcends the special sciences takes us that deep.

One can demonstrate this threefold connection of every individual investigation and every individual science with the whole of historico-social reality and its knowledge at every other point: connection with the concrete causal complex of all the facts and modifications of this reality, with general laws governing this reality, and with the system of values and imperatives bound up with the relationship of a person to the complex of his tasks. And so now we ask more precisely: Is there a science which comprehends this *threefold system which transcends special sciences* and grasps relations between historical fact, law, and the rule which guides judgment?

Two sciences bearing proud titles, the *philosophy of history* in Germany and *sociology* in England and France, claim to be knowledge of this kind.

The origin of one of these sciences lay in the Christian idea of the inner connectedness of progressive education in the history of mankind. Clement and Augustine paved the way for it; Vico, Lessing, Herder, Humboldt, and Hegel carried it out. Under the mighty impetus it received from the Christian idea of a general education of all nations by providence and of a kingdom of God realized through it, it still exists. The origin of the other lay in the convulsions of European society since the last third of the eighteenth century; a new organization of society was supposed to take place under the direction of the scientific spirit which increased so powerfully in the eighteenth century. Out of this need the structure of the entire system of scientific truths from mathematics upward was supposed to be established and as their last member the new redemptive science of society was to be founded. Condorcet and Saint-Simon were its forerunners, Comte was the founder of this comprehensive science of society, and John Stuart Mill was its logician; in Herbert Spencer's detailed presentation it is beginning to lay aside the fantasies which beset its tempestuous youth.[47]

It would certainly be a wretched thing if we were to believe that the way the historian's art (as we saw) sees universal organization of human affairs in the particular were the only and exclusive form in which the organization of this immense historico-social world exists for us. A great *task of historical writing* will always consist in this *artistic presentation,* something which the rage for generalization exhibited by some recent English and French scholars cannot nullify. For we want to perceive reality, and the course of episte-mological investigation will show that it exists for us as it is, in its own factuality unchanged by any medium, only in this world of the mind. And in fact in our knowledge of all human affairs we have an interest not merely in representation alone, but in spirit, in sympathy, and in enthusiasm (in which Goethe rightly discerned the most beautiful fruit of historical reflection). Commitment transforms the soul of the true sympathetic [*kongenialen*] historian into a universe which reflects the entire historical world. In this universe of moral forces the unique and the singular has a completely different significance than it does in physical nature. Comprehending it is not a means but an end in itself, for the need on which it rests is ineradicable and is given us along with the highest element in our nature. That is why the eye of the historian is drawn by natural predilection to the extraordinary. Without wishing to, indeed often without knowing it, even he is constantly making abstractions. For his eye loses its fresh sensitivity to aspects of those situations which recur in all historical phenomena, just as the effect of an impression is deadened if it constantly strikes a particular spot on the retina. It required the philanthropic motives of the eighteenth century to make truly visible again—alongside the extraordinary, such as actions of kings and fortunes of states—the everyday or what is common to all in a period, the "mores" as Voltaire put it, as well as changes which take place with respect to that everyday element. And the substratum of what is always the same in human nature and in world affairs never appears at all in the artistic depiction of history. Hence it also rests on an abstraction. But it is an involuntary one, and because it springs from the strongest motive forces in human nature, we are usually not aware of it at all. Inasmuch as we coexperience something in the past through the art of historical representation, we are taught as though by the drama of life itself. Indeed, our being is expanded, and psychic forces stronger than our own intensify our existence.

Therefore those theories of sociology and philosophy of history are false which see in the presentation of the particular mere raw material for their abstractions. This superstition, which subjects the labors of historians to an arcane process to transform alchemistically the singular materials they discover into pure gold of abstraction and to force history to betray its ultimate secret, is just as foolhardy as ever a dream of an alchemist natural philosopher who purported to entice the great [magical] word of nature from her. History has no more any such final and simple word to divulge that would express its true meaning than nature does. And every bit as mistaken as this superstition is the procedure usually linked with it. This procedure seeks to unite views already formed by historians. But the thinker who deals with the historical world must be master of history and all its methods in his direct contact with immediate raw material. He must submit himself to the same law of hard work on the raw materials which the historian obeys. To make a coherent whole out of material which the historian has already tied together into an artistic whole through his insight and labor, whether one does this with psychological or with metaphysical principles, is an operation which will forever be condemned to unfruitfulness. If one speaks of philosophy of history, that can only mean historical research with a philosophical purpose and with philosophical means.

But now this is the other side of the matter. The *bond between the particular and the general,* which lies in the original intuition of the historian, is torn apart by *analysis,* which subjects a particular component of this whole to theoretical consideration. Every theory which springs up in this fashion among the special sciences of society we have discussed is a further step in divorcing a general explanatory system from the *web of facts.* And nothing stops this process; the *general system* which historico-social reality comprises must become the object of theoretical reflection aimed at what is explainable in this system.

But is philosophy of history or is sociology this theoretical reflection? The structure of this entire presentation contains premises which force us to give a negative reply to this question.

15. Their Task Is Unrealizable

Determination of the Province of Historical Science within the Structure of Human Sciences

There is an irresolvable contradiction between the task which both of these sciences have set for themselves and the resources at their disposal for its execution.

By *philosophy of history* I understand a theory which undertakes to discern the system of historical reality through a corresponding system of unified principles. This feature of unity of thought is inseparable from theory, which has its distinctive task precisely in recognizing the system of the whole. And so philosophy of history locates this unity now in a blueprint of historical process, now in a basic concept (an idea), now in a formula or a set of formulas which express the law of development. *Sociology* (I speak here only of the French school) escalates this claim to knowledge even further inasmuch as it aspires to introduce scientific direction of society by the knowledge it has of this system.

Because of our immersion in the organization of special human sciences, the following insight has dawned on us. In these sciences the wisdom of many centuries has been able to break down the general problem of historico-social reality into special problems. These sciences have subjected these special problems to rigorous scientific treatment; the core of real knowledge built up in them through this continuous labor is in a process of slow but steady growth. Of course it is necessary for these sciences to become conscious of the relation of their truths to the reality about which, after all, they offer only a partial material description, and consequently to become conscious of the relationships in which they stand to other sciences which abstraction has separated from that same reality. Precisely this is what we need, that out of the nature of the task which this reality poses for human knowledge and recognition, we might understand the devices that knowledge uses to penetrate this reality, break it up, and take it apart. We have to know what knowledge can master with its instruments and what resists it and remains an irreducible fact; in short, we need an epistemology of human sciences or, more profoundly, we need self-reflection [*Selbstbesinnung*], which would secure to concepts and principles of those sciences their relation to reality, their evidence, and their relations to one another. This theory would achieve for the first time a genuine scientific direction for these positive efforts toward clear-cut and solid truths. It would lay the foundations at last for coopera-tion of special sciences toward knowledge of the whole. But just as in this way these special sciences—rendered more conscious of themselves through such epistemology, sure of their value and their limits, taking their relationships into account—march on-ward in all directions, *so it is they are the sole instruments for explaining history,* and there is no conceivable sense in imagining a solution to the problem of the plan of history apart from them. For to understand this plan means to dissolve it—an immensely complex thing—into its components, to look for uniformities in what is relatively simple and in virtue of them to move on then to the more complex. Hence *applying* the special sciences thus far described to clarifying the structure of history takes place in the *advancing science of history* itself in an ever higher degree. Understanding each part of history demands commitment of the united forces of the various special human sciences, from anthropology upward. When Ranke once said that he would like to efface himself to see things as they were, this was but a beautiful and powerful expression of the true historian's profound desire for objective reality. But this desire must equip itself with scientific knowledge of the psychic individuals who compose this reality and of the permanent configurations which develop through their interactions and are the bearers of historical progress; otherwise it will not conquer this reality, which, after all, one does not comprehend in a mere glance or perception but only through analysis and dissection. If there is anything hidden away as a kernel of truth behind this hope of philosophy of history, it is this: historical research based on the most comprehensive possible mastery of the special human sciences. Just as physics and chemistry are resources for studying organic life, so also anthropology, jurisprudence, and political science are resources for studying history.

One can express this clear state of affairs [*Zusammenhang*] methodically in this way: we can know the exceedingly complex reality of history only through sciences which investigate uniformities among the more simple facts into which we can break down this reality. And so we answer the question posed above first of all by saying: knowledge of the whole of historico-social reality, toward which we found ourselves driven as to the most universal and ultimate problem of the human sciences, actualizes itself successively in a system of truths resting on epistemological self-reflection. In this system special theories of historical reality build up toward a theory of man; but these special theories are used in a true progressive science of history to explain ever more of the factual historical reality which is bound up with the interactions of individuals. In this complex of truths we recognize the relation between fact, law, and rule through self-reflection. In that complex, too, we find out how far removed we are still from any foreseeable possibility of a general theory of the historical process and in what a modest sense we can speak of such a theory at all. Universal history, insofar as it is not something superhuman, would be the finishing touch to this totality of the human sciences.[48]

Such a procedure cannot, of course, trace the course of history back to the *unity of a formula or a principle,* any more than physiology can do so with life. By analyzing and manipulating most of the grounds of explanation, science can only approach the discovery of simple explanatory principles. Hence philosophy of history would have to give up its claims if it wished to use the procedure with which absolutely all real knowledge of the historical process is bound up. As it is now, it is simply wearing itself out trying to square the circle. And so its trickery is apparent enough to the logician as well. If I keep to the phenomenon of a system of reality, I can link together characteristics which present themselves to my observation in an abstraction which binds them together, one which contains the developmental law of this structure as in a kind of universal idea [*Allgemeinvorstellung*]. No matter how shaky and confused it may be, some kind of universal idea of historical reality surfaces in everyone who has preoccupied himself with it and has then unified this system of reality in an intellectual picture. Abstractions of this kind anticipate the work of analysis in all areas. An entity of this sort was the mysteriously spherical motion which ancient astronomy made its basis, or the living force in which biology of bygone days expressed the cause of the leading characteristics of organic life. And every formula which Hegel, Schleiermacher, or Comte have set up to express the law of history belongs to this natural thinking which always precedes analysis and is nothing other than—metaphysics. These pretentious general concepts of philosophy of history are nothing but the *notiones universales* which Spinoza has depicted so masterfully in their natural origin and their fateful effect on scientific thought.[49] Naturally these abstractions which formulate the process of history always stress only one aspect of this process which stirs the soul with the consciousness of immense riches, and so every philosophy singles out a somewhat different abstraction from this mighty reality.[50] If one wished to derive a principle for philosophy of history from Aristotle's gradation of natural powers leading up to man, it would differ from Comte's in specific content somewhat as a view of the same city from different elevations, and this in turn would differ in like manner from Herder's *Humanität*,[51] or the penetration of nature by reason according to Schleiermacher, or Hegel's progress in the consciousness of freedom. And just as excessively broad definitions are true as propositions [*Sätze*] and false only as definitions, so also what is hidden away in the folded garments of these formulas is not usually wrong, but is merely a wretched and inadequate expression for the mighty reality whose contents it claims to formulate.

Because philosophy of history claims to express in its formula the whole essence of the course of world history, it wishes to formulate not only the causal structure but the *meaning of the historical process as well,* that is, its value and its goal, insofar as it recognizes such meaning alongside causal structure. The extremities of our consciousness—knowledge of reality and consciousness of value and rule—are tied together as one in their general conception: whether it be that the general conception views this unity as set down in the metaphysical ground of the world, actualizing the world's purpose by a system of efficient causes, or that, with Spinoza and the naturalists, it views purposes which man sets for himself and values he ascribes to facts of reality as an ephemeral form of inner life in certain products of nature which do not derive from the blind power of nature. Thus philosophy of history may be teleological or naturalistic; its further characteristic is that its formula for the world's course also represents the meaning, purpose, and value it sees realized in the world. Negatively expressed, philosophy of history is not satisfied with investigating accessible causal structure by allowing the feeling of the value of the world's course to prevail as it appears in our consciousness as a fact, neither truncating that feeling nor introducing it impertinently into research. This is what the true special-science researcher does. Nor does philosophy of history proceed from values and rules to the point in self-reflection at which they are linked to conception and thought. That is what the critical thinker does. Otherwise it would recognize that value and rule exist only with reference to our system of energies and that without reference to such a system they no longer have a conceivable meaning. An arrangement of reality can never have value in itself but only in its relation to a system of energies. From this it further follows that we naturally discover that what we sense in the system of our energies as a value and what we conceive of as a rule for our will is, it turns out, the value-and-meaning content of the world's historical process. Every formula in which we express the meaning of history is only a reflection of our own active internal self. Even the power which the concept of progress possesses resides less in the idea of a goal than in personal experience of our struggling will, of our life's work, and of happy awareness of the energy in that life's work. This personal experience would project itself into the picture of universal progress even if such progress could in no way be demonstrated entirely and clearly in the reality of the world's historical process. So it is that the ineradicable feeling of the value and meaning of the historical world process rests on this state of affairs. And a writer like Herder, with his universal idea of *Humanität*, never got beyond confused consciousness of this richness of human existence and this abundance of its happy evolution. But from this standpoint the philosophy of history, advancing still further in self-reflection, would have to infer the following: The meaning of historical reality is built up from an immense manifold of individual values, just as its causal structure is built up from the same manifold of interactions. The meaning of history is thus an extraordinary composite. So the same task would have arisen here as well: self-reflection which investigates the origin of value and rule in psychic life and their relation to being and reality, and gradual, lengthy analysis which dissects this side of the intricate historical totality. For only the help of historical research can enable us to investigate, with any prospect of having a universally valid context, what is of value to man and what rules should guide the activity of society. And so we stand once again before the same basic situation: philosophy of history, rather than using methods of historical analysis and self-examination (which is also analytic in its nature), persists in universal ideas which either represent the general effect of the historical world process in some short-hand formula like an essence [*Wesenheit*] or sketch out this composite picture from a universal metaphysical principle.

It can be shown with more lucid clarity for philosophy of history than for any other branch of metaphysics that its roots lie in religious experience and that it dries up and withers away if torn away from this matrix. The idea of a unitary plan of human history, of a divine idea of education through history, has been created by *theology*. For theology there were fixed points available for such construction at the beginning and end of all history; thus arose a truly feasible task of pulling together connecting threads through the course of history between the fall of man and the last judgment. In his mighty work *De Civitate Dei* Augustine had the course of history on this earth originate from the metaphysical world and he then dissolved it once again into this metaphysical world. For according to him the battle between the heavenly and the earthly city already begins in regions of the world of spirits: demons confront the angels; Cain, as the *civis hujus seculi,* confronts Abel, as the *peregrinus in seculo;* the world monarchy of Babylon, and Rome (which replaces it in world hegemony), as the second Babylon, confront the city of God which develops among the Jewish people, has its middle point in history in the appear-ance of Christ, and since then develops itself as a kind a metaphysical entity, a mystical body, on this earth. Then finally the struggle of demons and of the earthly *civitas* in their service against the city of God on this earth ends in the last judgment and everything reverts again to the metaphysical world. This philosophy of history constitutes the mid-dle point of medieval metaphysics of the spirit. Through the theory of spiritual sub-stances which the general metaphysics of the Middle Ages developed, it acquired a foundation of rigorous metaphysical stability. In the development of the papal church and its struggle with the empire it maintained a powerful actuality and a manifest timeliness. In the canonical theory of the legal nature of this mystical body it attained to the most decisive consequences for conceiving the external organization of society. The hard realities with which it operates, as long as they have validity, leave no one any room for doubts, which otherwise burden every attempt to express the meaning of history in a systematic formula. No one may ask why the laborious upward climb of mankind was necessary, because original sin is before one's eyes. No one may ask why the blessing of history benefits only a minority, because the counsel of God or [man's] perverse will contain the answer in one form or other. Likewise, no one may question the structure of this history by which the world's course has a single meaning and humanity is a real unity, because—according to the massive conception of traditionalism, bolstered by the notion of procreation as an act of evil lust—the corrupt blood of Adam flows through every element of this whole and tinges it with its dark taint and because, on the other side, one can find in the mystical body of the church a corresponding real guidance of grace from heaven. The literature, which continues within the parameters set down by Augustine, reaches to Bossuet's *Discours sur l'histoire universelle,* and because the bishop of Meaux inserts a more rigorous conception of causal structure as well as a concept of a general national spirit, he constitutes the connecting link between this theological philosophy of history and efforts of the eighteenth century. Turgot's *Plan of Universal History* evolved from the idea of giving a rational solution to the task addressed by Bossuet; it secularized the philosophy of history. Vico's *Principi di scienza nuova* leaves the external outlines of theological philosophy of history standing; within this enormous edifice, however, his positive work—truly historical research with a philosophical purpose—settled down in traditional history of the nations and traced the problem of the developmental history of the nations [*Völker*] and of the epochs common to all the nations of this history of development.

The idea of a single plan for the historical course of the world underwent a change, inasmuch as it is maintained in the eighteenth century despite being separated from the solid premises of its theological system: out of the massive reality of that plan a metaphysical shadow play emerges. Out of the darkness of an unknown beginning, mysteriously intricate processes of the historical world course now make their appearance, only to lose themselves in the same darkness in a forward direction. Why this laborious upward climb of humanity? Why the misery of the world? Why the restriction of progress to a minority? From the standpoint of Augustine all this could easily be explained; from the standpoint of the eighteenth century it was a riddle for whose solution there was no clear point of leverage. That is why every eighteenth century attempt to show the plan and meaning of human history is but a transformation of the old system: Lessing's education of the human race, Hegel's self-unfolding of God, Comte's transformation of hierarchical organization are nothing other than this. Because the mystical body (which in the Middle Ages comprised the structure of world history within it) is dissolved into atoms [*Individuen*] in the thought pattern of the eighteenth century, one has to find a substitute in an idea which preserves this unity of humanity. *Two developments* appear, both of which call metaphysics to their aid for this purpose and exclude any truly scientific handling of the problem.

One of them substitutes *metaphysical substances,* such as *universal reason* or the world spirit, and regards history as the development of these. To be sure, it is once again the case here that such formulas contain a truth. The link between the individual and humanity is a reality. Indeed, precisely this is the profoundest psychological problem history presents to us: how the instrument of progress in history is ultimately the self-sacrificing devotion of the individual to persons whom he loves, to the purposive complex of a system of culture to which his inner calling is ordered, to the general life of associations he feels himself a member of, even to a future unknown to him and toward which he is working—in short, morality, for this has no other characteristic note than self-sacrifice. But formulas for connecting the individual with the historical whole, true in what they express about the personal feeling involved in this connection, come into conflict with all healthy sensibility because they sink all the values of life into a metaphysical unity which unfolds in history. What a person experiences in his innermost soul, struggling with destiny, in the depth of his conscience, is something which exists *for him,* not for the world process and not for some sort of organism of human society. But to such metaphysics, the gripping reality of life is visible only in silhouette.

Nor is anything changed here if—in a further sublimation, as it were—one substitutes *society* as a unity for this universal reason. The bond which makes it into a unity is transformed from living experience into a formula and is something metaphysical. When Comte proceeded from his *philosophie positive* and its method to a kind of religion as the basis of future society, it was not due to an arbitrary quirk in his mind which might have issued from events of his life or, say, from deterioration of his intelligence; it was rather a fate which was inherent in the original contradiction between his formula of the unitary system of history (plus the tendency based on it toward organizing society through spiritual power) and his positivist method. The split this occasioned among his adherents simply illustrates this contradiction in a system which set out to derive an imperative for society from laws of the system of nature.

German individualism was forced to try to give another twist to the idea, one which led it also to metaphysics. For it, unlimited development of the individual in his relation to development of the human race became the means for solving the problem of philosophy of history. But metaphysics is already locked in struggle at this point with critical consciousness of the limits of historical knowledge, and this struggle wends its way through all the intellectual elaborations of this position.

Kant himself found the structure of history in the plan of providence. For "the means which nature uses to effect the development of all its potentialities [*Anlagen*] is their antagonism in society"—man's "unsociable sociability."[52] His hypothesis is limited to investigating how the problem of establishing a general society of citizens ruling by law is resolved in history.

> In any case it always remains strange in this connection that older generations appear to transact their laborious business only for the sake of later generations, that is, to prepare a step for the latter, from which they can raise still higher the edifice which nature has in mind; strange also that only the very latest ones have the good fortune to dwell in that edifice on which a long series of their ancestors (unwittingly, to be sure) had worked without being able, nonetheless, to participate in the happiness which they had prepared. But as mysterious as this is, it is nevertheless also necessary, once one assumes that one class of animals should have reason and, as a class of reasoning beings who all die off but whose species is immortal, should nevertheless complete the development of these endowments.[53]

Lessing had solved this difficulty through the idea of a transmigration of souls: "What? Now what if it were as good as settled that the great slowly turning wheel which brings the race closer to perfection should be set in motion only through smaller and faster wheels, of which each should sacrifice its own particularity to that purpose? There is no other way! The same path on which the race attains to its perfection is the one which every single man must first have trod upon."[54]

Herder behaves more realistically and more critically than either of these men. Although he called his work *Ideas toward a Philosophy of History,* he nevertheless used the expression, which Voltaire had already used, in a different sense and he did not establish a formula for the meaning of history. His great and lasting accomplishment arose from combining positive sciences in a philosophical, that is, comprehensive, spirit. With the touch of genius he combined natural history of that time with the idea of universal history, an idea which had hovered before the mind of Turgot, and Voltaire had grasped, but which Schlözer had adopted in Germany in his remarkable *Idea of Universal History*. By way of this connection there now emerged from the observations already treasured in antiquity about the connection of natural conditions with historical life those leading ideas on which Ritter's universal geography is based. Herder also linked ideas about the ascending series of organizations up to man (notions he shared with Goethe and which have had their impact on natural philosophy) with an analogical argument for higher levels of the intellectual world and, based on these, for immortality. Kant criticized this argument to the effect that Herder could conclude at most to the existence of other higher beings. But from this point on, his work is essentially that of a universal historian. Combining the two factors of conditions of nature and of human nature, he wants to develop human history in a strictly causal system. For he is after all a student of Leibniz and is disposed still more firmly by Spinoza against external teleology.[55] He sees the purposiveness which prevails in world history as well as in nature as accomplished only in the form of the causal system. To this wise reservation on his part corresponds the fact that he indeed recognized Lessing's problem—but he abandoned it as a transcendent one. "If anyone should say that it is not individual man but the race which is educated, he would make no sense at all to me, because race and species are only general concepts, except insofar as they exist in particular beings—as if I were to speak of animality or stoniness in general." He expressly rejects this as medieval metaphysics and thus remains with Lessing on the solid ground of realism, which recognized only individuals and consequently also only development of individuals as the meaning of the world's history. But for every notion of the kind of development taking place in individuals he observes, with clear reference to Lessing: "As to the way this would take place—what philosophy on earth could there be which could give us certainty about that?"

I am not going to deal with how closely *Lotze's* concept of philosophy of history touches on that of Herder, both with respect to the connection between causal and teleological reflection and with respect to the realism which recognizes only individuals and what is conducive to their development. On this point, however, Lotze believed that he must go beyond Herder. He does that, inasmuch as he, so to speak, applies the method by which Kant justified belief in God and immortality to the systematic structure of history and thus tries to demonstrate participation of the deceased in the progress of history as a *condition* of that systematic structure. "No education of humanity is thinkable unless its results will someday be the common property of those who have been left behind at various points of this earthly career; no development of an idea has meaning unless it will be manifest to everyone at the end what he previously suffered unknowingly as the bearer of this development."[56] Feeling versus feeling (for it is into this that reflection on the plan of history finally melts away here—a consideration which began once with such hard realities in Augustine and appears to dissolve of itself into a fine mist): this elegiac conception of a contemplative share of the dead in that which we struggle through here—reminiscent of the old pictures showing angels' heads gazing down from the clouds of heaven on the martyrs and the suffering they still had to bear— seems to us too much when we are soberly critical but as too little when we are dreaming, because we can possess the result of the development of mankind only in lived experience and not in idle musing.

16. Their Methods Are Wrong

If the task which these sciences have set themselves is consequently an inherently unrealizable one, it is also true that their methods are useful for deceiving through generalizations, to be sure, but not for producing permanent expansion of knowledge.

The method of German *philosophy of history* grew out of a movement which, in contrast with the natural system of human sciences created in the eighteenth century, immersed itself in the factuality of the historical. The carriers of this movement were Winckelmann, Herder, the Schlegels, and Wilhelm von Humboldt. They used a procedure which I call that of original intuition [*der genialen Anschauung*]. This procedure was not any sort of special method, but rather the process of fruitful fermentation itself, in which special sciences of the mind interact with one another: a world of becoming. The metaphysical school reduced this original intuition to a principle. Indeed, through such concentration of content, the original intuition produced an unusually energetic impact for a short time. But this concentration came about only because the *notiones universales* then spread their gray net over the historical world. Hegel's "Spirit," which comes to consciousness of its freedom in history, or Schleiermacher's "Reason," which permeates and shapes nature, is an abstract substance which condenses the historical world process in a color-less abstraction, a subject outside space and time, like the Mothers to whom Faust descends. Hegel's world-historical epochs are thus universal concepts abstracted from intuition; in fact a metaphysical principle guides the abstraction which fashions them. For world history according to him is "a series of determinations of freedom which emanate from the concept of freedom." The basic figures serving as agents of Reason in Schleiermacher's conception are also universal concepts abstracted from intuition, figures in whom Reason's activity is regarded "as a manifold apart from determinations of space and time and distinguished by conceptual determinations." Hegel, who sets out from history, arranges these universal ideas in chronological series; Schleiermacher, who sets out from experience of contemporary society, spreads them out next to one another, like another realm of nature.

The methods *sociology* has used of course come forward with the claim that because of sociology the epoch of metaphysics is finished and that of positive philosophy has begun. But the founder of this philosophy, Comte, has only created a naturalistic metaphysics of history, which as such was much less suited to facts of the historical process than Hegel's or Schleiermacher's was. Hence his universal concepts are also much less fruitful. And while John Stuart Mill broke with the grosser errors of Comte, the subtler ones continue to work in him. In the spirit of French philosophy of the eighteenth century, Comte's sociology arose from subordinating the historical world to the system of knowledge of nature; Stuart Mill maintained and defended at least the subordination of the method of study of intellectual facts to methods of natural science.

Comte's view regards the study of the human mind as dependent on the science of biology and sees whatever uniformities one can observe in the succession of intellectual states as the outcome of uniformities in the body's states; and so he denies that one can study lawfulness in psychic states by itself. According to Comte, therefore, the historical order of succession which assigns a historical place to sciences of society corresponds to this logical relation of dependence among the sciences. Because sociology presupposes truths of all the natural sciences, it is only after all of them that it attains its state of maturity, that is, establishes principles which combine particular truths discovered into a scientific whole. Chemistry reached this stage in the second half of the last century with Lavoisier; physiology did not do so until the beginning of our century with Bichat's histology; and so it seemed to Comte that establishing the social sciences, as the highest class of scientific endeavor, fell to himself.[57] To be sure, he acknowledges (despite his penchant for uniform regimentation of science) that between sociology and the sciences preceding it—especially biology, which also comprises our meager knowledge of psychological states—a relation exists other than the one between any of the earlier sciences and truths which condition them. At this highest point of the sciences the relation between deduction and induction is reversed: generalization from material given by history is the crucial point of the procedure of science of society, and deduction from results of biology only verifies the laws thus established. Two assumptions underlie this ordering of intellectual phenomena under the system of the knowledge of nature; one of them is indemonstrable and the other is patently false. To assume an exclusive determination of psychic states through physiological ones is a premature conclusion from data which, according to the judgment of unprejudiced physiological researchers themselves, permit absolutely no decision.[58] The assertion that inner perception is intrinsically impossible and unfruitful, "an undertaking which our posterity will one day see brought to the stage for their amusement," has been erroneously deduced by distorting the process of perception and will be refuted in detail.

In this context of the hierarchy of sciences Comte unfolds "the necessary direction of the general structure of human development,"[59] which then serves him as the principle for guiding society, from an intuition of the historical course of the world, and he verifies it through biology. In this biological verification we manifestly touch on the living pulse [*Lebensknoten*] of his sociology. What, then, is the biological basis whose appearance first made the creation of sociology possible? Comte declares that the method which sociology uses had to be developed first in the sphere of research into nature. One had first to recognize the setting (*milieu*) in which a man finds himself in sciences of inorganic nature. Be that as it may, we nevertheless require a connection which reaches into the heart of sociology itself. It is hard to keep from smiling; this connection consists in the fact that stability of external biological organization proves stability of a certain basic psychic structure; and then—but let us look at his own words: "We have seen that the general direction of human evolution consists chiefly in reducing more and more the inevitable preponderance (necessarily always fundamental and yet excessive from the start) of emotional life over intellectual life, or, using the anatomical formula, of the posterior region of the brain over the anterior region."[60] Crude naturalistic metaphysics—that is the real foundation of his sociology! But the "general direction of human evolution," as he gleans it from intuition of the historical course of the world, is once again nothing more than a *notio universalis,* a confused and indeterminate universal idea he has abstracted from a mere overview of the structure of history. It is an unscientific abstraction under whose broad mantle the growing mastery of man over nature and the increasing influence of higher faculties over lower, of intelligence over emotions, and of our social over our egoistic inclinations come together.[61] These abstract images of philosophers of history merely portray the process of world history in constantly varied abridgments.

If one moves on to the matter of execution, by which this student of de Maistre establishes his papacy of natural-scientific understanding, it constitutes a remarkable confirmation of our position. The law which Comte has really discovered, which expresses relations of logical dependence of truths on one another to their historical succession (though he formulates that law only imperfectly), belongs to a special science of the mind, and he discovered it by dint of persistent and incisive preoccupation with this sphere of social reality. Turgot established the generalization about the three epochs in its true essential features, and Comte's application of it failed because he was ignorant of the particulars of the history of theology and metaphysics. Hence his sociology cannot shake the position which positive study of historico-social life has always maintained: as one half of the universe of the sciences, resting on its own special and independent epistemological basis, progressing primarily through its own instruments of knowledge even while it was also conditioned by the progress of sciences of the physical world and by conditions and forms of life in it.

If Comte thus brought his sociology into a dazzling, though false, relationship with natural sciences, he also failed, on the other side, to recognize and exploit the true and fruitful relation of every historical reflection to the special sciences of man and society. In contradiction with his principle of positive philosophy he deduced his impetuous generalizations (except for his theory of the context of development of intelligence) apart from any connection with methodical use of positive sciences of the mind.

One must regard the kind of subordination which *Stuart Mill* sets forth in his chapter on logic of the human sciences as weakening this principle of subordination of historical phenomena to natural sciences as we find it in Comte. Though he turns his back on the metaphysical in Comte (and thereby could have worked toward a more healthy tendency in reflecting on history), nevertheless his subordination of the human sciences to those of nature continues to work in fatal fashion in his method. He distinguishes himself from Comte as one distinguishes the natural system of social functions and spheres of life based on psychology, which Englishmen had established in the eighteenth century, from the system founded on natural sciences, which French materialists of the eighteenth century had defended. He completely acknowledges the independence of explanatory grounds of the human sciences. But he subordinates their methods too fully to the schema he has developed from his study of natural sciences. As he says in this connection:

> If there are some subjects on which the results obtained have finally received the unanimous assent of all who have attended to the proof, and others on which mankind have not yet been equally successful; on which the most sagacious minds have occupied themselves from the earliest date, and have never succeeded in establishing any considerable body of truths, so as to be beyond denial or doubt; it is by generalizing the methods successfully followed in the former inquiries, and adapting them to the latter, that we may hope to remove this blot on the face of science.[62]

As contestable as this argument is, "accommodation" of the methods of human sciences established by it has been just as unfruitful. Particularly with Mill, one perceives the monotonous and tiresome prattling of the words *induction* and *deduction* currently resounding in our direction from all the countries around us. The entire history of the human sciences is a counterproof against the idea of such an "accommodation." These sciences have a basis and structure completely different from those of nature. Their object consists of given, not inferred, units which we understand from within; we know and understand here first, in order gradually to comprehend [*wir wissen, verstehen hier zuerst, um allmählich zu erkennen*]. Progressive analysis of a totality we possessed from the beginning in immediate consciousness and understanding: this is, then, the character of the history of these sciences. Theory of states or of poetry, such as the Greeks of Alexander's time possessed, compares with our political science or esthetics completely differently than natural-scientific notions of that epoch do with ours. And there is a special kind of experience which takes place here: its object first gradually takes shape before the eyes of advancing science; individuals and actions are the elements of this experience, an immersion of all powers of the soul into its object is its nature. These hints suffice to show that, in contrast with methods of Mill and Buckle, which to some extent approach human sciences from the outside, we must meet the challenge to establish human sciences through epistemology, to justify and support their independent formation, and to do away definitively with subordinating their principles and their methods to those of natural sciences.

17. They Do Not Recognize the Position of Historical Science in Relation to Special Sciences of Society

Intimately linked with these errors regarding problematic and method is the false relationship these fantasies of sciences bear to actually existing special sciences. From their tumultuous efforts they expect something which can only be the product of persistent labor of many generations. And so all these isolated schemes are like brick structures which use a veneer to imitate the granite blocks, columns, and embellishments which come into being only through patient and tedious work on refractory material.

In the countless gradations of variation among individual units and the endlessly diffuse and variable play of causes, effects, and interactions among them (as the reality of the historico-social world), science, in seeking to understand this reality, seizes on the typical among facts and uniformities among relations, on the one side in the *succession* of factual situations and changes, on the other side in their *simultaneity*.

One aspect of the problem of the general structure of this reality consists of the extremely complex totality of the progress of society from its life situation [*Lebensstande*] (*status societatis*) in one particular cross section to that in another particular one, and finally from its first life situation which we can identify to one which makes up the present situation in society (a status whose idea shaped the earlier concept of statistics). This side of the problem has been the core of philosophy of history from the beginning as the *theory of historical progress;* Comte labeled it the dynamics of society. Philosophy of history has never been able directly to deduce a sufficiently definite general law of this progress from socio-historical reality. Such a theory would have to include either the relation between formulas of which each, individually, would express the essence of a particular *status societatis,* so that comparison between such states would give us the law of general progress; or such a theory would have to express in a formula the essence of all causal relations which produce changes in the general complex of society. Needless to say, derivation of a formula of either type from a general intuition of historico-social reality totally surpasses human capacity for intuition.

If the structure of historico-social life, considered from the aspect of the succession of conditions it embraces, should be tested by the method of experience, then the entirety of that structure must be *broken up into individual structures* which are clearer and simpler. One must employ the same procedure natural sciences have used to break down their comprehensive problem regarding organization of external nature and to build up special systems of natural laws such as the theory of equilibrium and movement of bodies, of sound, light, heat, magnetism, and electricity, as well as the chemical behavior of bodies; this is their approach to solving their general problem. But there are special sciences which have used this procedure. The only possible path for investigating historical totality, that is, breaking it down into individual structures, has been taken long ago in special theories of systems of culture and external organization of society. Study of the individual as the living unit in society's composition is the condition for researching states of affairs which we can abstract from the interaction of these living units in society. Only on this foundation of the results of anthropology—by means of theoretical sciences of society in their three major classes (ethnology, sciences of systems of culture, and sciences of external organization of society)—can we gradually bring the problem of the connection between successive states of society closer to solution. And, as a matter of fact, all the exact and fruitful laws which human sciences have until now arrived at have been discovered in this way. Examples include Grimm's law in linguistics, Thünen's law in political economy, generalizations concerning structure, developmental history, and disturbances in the life of the state since Aristotle, principles which Winckelmann, Heyne, and the Schlegels have discovered concerning developmental history of the arts, and Comte's law of the relation between logical dependence of sciences on one another and their historical sequence.

The other side of this problem of the general structure of historico-social reality, study of the *relations* between *simultaneous facts* and *changes,* likewise demands analysis of the complex state of affairs of such a *status societatis.* One can compare relations of dependence and affinity—such as occur among phenomena of an age and manifest themselves in disturbance which appears in other conditions of society when changes occur in one of the components of the general social condition—with the relation which obtains between components or between functions of an organism. They underlie the concept of the culture of an age or epoch, and every cultural-historical description begins with them. Hegel grasped them with a maximum of energy; his tactic was to use literary products of an age to shed light on its intellectual makeup, and on that foundation he grounded his erroneous theory of the representative character of philosophical systems for the whole spirit of a period. French and English sociologists summarize these relations in the concept of consensus between contemporary social phenomena. But a precise expression for the affinity between the different components and for the dependence of one on another obviously presupposes distinguishing here too the individual members and systems which make up the *status societatis.* Indeed, an overview of the character of the culture of an epoch must show how similar basic relationships express themselves as affinity amid the disparity of members and systems of the society.

To this relationship, which the methodology of human sciences will have to develop more fully, corresponds the actual condition of *general truths* in philosophy of history and in sociology. Vico, Turgot, Condorcet, and Herder were, first and foremost, universal historians with a philosophical purpose. The sweeping vision with which they linked sciences with one another—such as Vico did with jurisprudence and philology, Herder with natural history and history, and Turgot with political economy, natural sciences, and history—first paved the way for modern science of history. The term *philosophy of history*—indeed not infrequently its work, including efforts which have achieved fruitful combinations on the path toward true universal history—comprises at the same time, however, theories of a completely different kind which owe the largest part of their prestige to their connection with those efforts. From these formulas which claim to express the meaning of history no fruitful truth has issued. There is nothing here but metaphysical mist. Nowhere is it thicker than in Comte, who transformed de Maistre's Catholicism into the phantom of hierarchical guidance of society through the sciences.[63] And if now and then clearer thoughts do emerge from these mists, they are propositions about the function, structure, and history of development of individual peoples, religions, states, sciences, and arts, or about relations between these in the context of the historical world. Every relatively exact picture which enables any philosophy of history to clothe its shadowy basic idea with flesh and blood is composed of these statements about the life of the members and systems of humanity.[64]

18. Increasing Expansion and Perfection of Special Sciences

Meanwhile the special sciences of mind are mastering ever new bodies of facts; by adopting a comparative method and a psychological foundation they are more and more acquiring the character of general theories. And if they are becoming ever more clearly conscious of their relations to one another in reality, then it must be clear that in their context the problems of sociology, of philosophy of spirit, or of history which can be resolved at all are gradually coming closer to solution.

We have seen how these special sciences were separated from the universal system through analysis and abstraction. Their truth lies only in relation to the reality in which their abstract propositions are contained. Only to the extent that this relation is included in those propositions do they have any validity with respect to this reality. It was by rupturing this connection that disastrous errors have come about, which, as abstract natural law, abstract political economy, the system of natural religion—in short, the natural system of the seventeenth and eighteenth centuries—have ruined the sciences and injured society. Because special sciences, for epistemological reasons, continue to relate their propositions to the reality from which they have been abstracted, these propositions, no matter how abstract they are, preserve the measure of their validity with regard to reality. But we saw further that we have no knowledge of the concrete total structure of historico-social reality except for knowledge we attain by breaking down that total structure into individual structures, that is, into those we arrive at through these special sciences. Ultimately, our knowledge of this structure is only a matter of making perfectly clear and conscious to ourselves the logical connection through which the special sciences grasp it or allow us to recognize it. In contrast, isolated special sciences of the mind must fall subject to a dead abstraction; isolated philosophy of spirit is a phantom; separation of the philosophical way of viewing historico-social reality from the positive way is the destructive legacy of metaphysics.

Development of special human sciences shows progress in harmony with this. Impartial analyses (free from abstractions of bygone days) of specific structures from the sphere of external organization of society or of systems of culture, of which we have had a multitude since Tocqueville's splendid work, lay bare the inner organization of historical creations. Comparative method has passed its test in linguistics and has expanded successfully into mythology; it promises to impart the character of genuine theories gradually to all special sciences. No exact scientist neglects the link with anthropology anymore.

But sciences of systems of culture and of external organization of society are principally linked to anthropology through the psychic and psychophysical facts I have labeled those of second rank. Analysis of these facts, which come about through interaction of individuals in society and are by no means fully subsumable under those of anthropology, determines to a considerable degree the theoretical rigor of the special sciences whose foundation they are. Facts of need, work, mastery, and satisfaction are psychophysical; they are components of the foundations of political economy and political and legal science, and their analysis allows us to penetrate into the mechanics of society, so to speak. One could imagine a universal standpoint, a kind of psycho-physics of society: one which would deal with relations between the distribution of the changing total mass of psychological life on earth and with distribution of the forces available in nature, forces which are brought into the service of this total mass, and, finally, make it possible for this mass to satisfy its needs. Other important psychological facts underlie the systems of higher intellectual culture, such as the fact of communication and the transformation which takes place in it. In communication a condition remains in A while it also passes over to B; on this basis quantitative relations in every system of intellectual movement are grounded. If one begins by assuming that in science there is total communicability of concepts and propositions from the thinker who has discovered them to one intellectually capable of understanding him, then the interesting problem arises of investigating the causes of disturbances which have hindered a regular advance of this sort in the history of knowledge.

In the historical world, which like the sea is always agitated by waves, we encounter permanent states of affairs which, as partial contents of psycho-physical interactions such as religions, states, and arts, present us with lasting structures and as such are researched by special human sciences; we also encounter extensive and internally coherent processes of more transitory nature; they appear in historical interaction, develop, expand, and then disappear again soon. Revolutions, epochs, movements: these are names of such historical phenomena, which are much harder to grasp than the permanent structures which external organization of society or systems of culture produce. Aristotle himself already devoted an incisive investigation to revolutions. But it is especially intellectual movements which must become more accessible, in time, to very exact treatment, for they permit quantitative determinations. From that epoch in history on, in which printing appeared and attained a sufficient level of activity, applying statistical method to the stock of libraries enables us to measure the intensity of intellectual activity and pattern of interest at a particular moment of society. We can thus describe the entire process beginning with the situation of a cultural circle and its degree of excitement and interest, through its first fumbling attempts, right on to brilliant creation. Description of results of such statistics will gain much in vividness through graphic presentation.

Hence positive science will exert itself to bring even the more transitory connections among general mutual relations of individuals in society under theoretical consideration. But we have arrived at the frontier at which what has been achieved leads on to future challenges—from which frontier we look across to distant shores.

19. Necessity of an Epistemological Foundation for Special Human Sciences

All the threads of our previous considerations come together in the following insight. We achieve knowledge of historico-social reality in special human sciences. But these require awareness of the relation of their truths to reality, whose partial contents they make up, and to other truths that, like them, have been abstracted from this reality. Only such consciousness can impart full clarity to their concepts and full evidence to their propositions.

Out of these premises emerges the task of developing an *epistemological foundation of human sciences* and of then using the instrument developed in that foundation to determine the inner connection between special human sciences, the limits in which knowledge is possible in them, and the relation of these truths to one another. One could designate the solution of this task as a critique of historical reason, that is, of man's capacity for knowing himself and the society and history he has fashioned.

If it wishes to reach its goal, such foundation-laying of human sciences must differentiate itself from previous work of this kind in two respects. It connects *epistemology* and *logic* with each other and thus prepares a solution for the task which academic life describes as synopsis [*Enzyklopädie*] and methodology. But, on the other side, it restricts its *problem* to the *sphere of human sciences*.

To fashion logic as *theory of method* is the general tendency of all leading logical works of our century. But the problem of methodology acquires a special form through the setting in which it appears in modern German philosophy. This form of undertaking is objectively inherent in the entire system of our philosophy and must distinguish every methodology which appears among us in contrast with the works of Stuart Mill, Whewell, or Jevons.

Analysis of conditions of consciousness has dissolved immediate certainty of the external world, objective truth of perception, and principles which express characteristics of the spatial; it has done the same to concepts of substance and cause which express the nature of the real. And in fact the results of physics and physiology have partially carried and partially confirmed this analysis. Thus the obligation arises of infusing this critical consciousness into the special sciences. When positive sciences of an earlier age coincided with the formal logic of those days, it was enough to satisfy demands of evidence if one brought facts and propositions which appeared immediately certain into line with laws of discursive thinking. Now, however, from the critical standpoint, there are other demands to make on forming a thought-structure fully conscious of its trustworthiness in the special sciences. Hence logic faces the challenge of developing these demands which the critical standpoint must make on fashioning a thought-structure clearly conscious of its trustworthiness in the special sciences.

Logic which fulfills these demands forms the connecting link between the standpoint which critical philosophy has attained and the fundamental concepts and principles of the special sciences. For the rules which this logic outlines seek to guarantee the trustworthiness of the principles of special sciences through a system grounded in elements to which analysis of the consciousness of that trustworthiness leads us back. We see here also the inexorable movement in the science of our century to tear down the boundaries which narrow specialization has erected between philosophy and special sciences.

But logic can meet the demands of critical consciousness only if it expands its sphere beyond analysis of discursive thought. Formal logic restricts itself to laws of discursive reason which we have been able to abstract from the feeling of conviction which accompanies judgments and inferences taking place in our consciousness. This logic, on the contrary, which draws the consequences of the critical standpoint, incorporates investigations identified by Kant as transcendental esthetic and analytic, that is, the complex of processes which underlie discursive thought. Thus it searches backward into the nature and epistemological value of processes whose results our earliest recollection finds already at hand. Indeed, this logic can provide a fundamental correlative principle [*Prinzip der Äquivalenz*] for the thus emergent structure which encompasses both inner and outer perception as well as discursive reason. According to that correlative principle, the act by which the process of perception goes beyond what is given it is of equal value with discursive thought. *Helmholtz's* profoundly conceived idea of unconscious inferences[65] lies in the direction of such expansion of logic. This expansion must then work in turn on formulas which describe elements and norms of discursive thought. The logical ideal itself changes. *Sigwart* has altered formulas of logic from this standpoint and thus has established a methodology based on a critical standpoint.[66] Once we have critical consciousness, it is impossible to have evidence of a first and second class or knowers of a first and second rank: now only that concept is logically perfect which contains in it consciousness of its provenance; only that proposition is trustworthy whose grounding reaches back to unimpeachable knowledge. Critically speaking, logical demands put on the concept are not satisfied until, in the context of knowledge in which the concept appears, awareness of the epistemological formative process of that concept is present as well and until this awareness also univocally determines the place of that concept in the system of symbols which relate the system to reality. Logical demands put on judgment are not satisfied until consciousness of its logical ground in the context of knowledge in which it appears includes epistemological clarity regarding the validity and range of the entire structure of psychic acts which make up this ground. Hence the demands which logic makes on concepts and propositions lead us back to the chief problem of all epistemology: the nature of immediate knowledge of facts of consciousness and relation of this knowledge to knowledge which builds on the principle of sufficient reason.

This extension of the field of vision of logic coincides with the direction of positive sciences themselves. Because natural-scientific thinking goes beyond natural relations of our sensations to individual things in space and time, it finds itself led back at every point to exactly defining these perceptions themselves and accordingly to determining their sequence in a universally valid temporal framework, to universally valid determinations of place and magnitude, and to eliminating errors of observation—in short, to methods which enable us to bring formation of judgments of perception itself to logical perfection. Concerning human sciences, however, it has become clear to us that psychic and psychophysical facts constitute the foundation of a theory not only of individuals but likewise of systems of culture as well as of external organization of society and that these facts underlie historical intuition and analysis in every one of their stages. Hence only epistemological investigation of how we encounter them and evidence appropriate to them can establish the true methodology of human sciences.

Thus logic emerges as the connecting link between epistemological foundation-laying and special sciences; with that arises the *inner structure of modern science* which must replace the old metaphysical structure of our knowledge.

The second peculiarity in defining the task of this introduction lies in *restricting it to foundation-laying of the human sciences*.[67] If conditions which govern knowledge of nature were fundamental in the same sense for the edifice of human sciences, then all types of procedure one used to acquire natural knowledge under these conditions would also apply to study of the mind, and in fact *only* such procedures. Ultimately, the kind of dependence of truths on one another and the kind of relation of sciences to one another would be the same here as there; and then separating foundation-laying of human sciences from that of natural sciences would be pointless. In reality, precisely the most controversial of those conditions governing natural-scientific knowledge, namely, spatial arrangement and motion in the external world, are without influence on the evidence of human sciences, because the mere fact that such phenomena exist and are signs of something real suffices for constructing their propositions.[68] If we enter into this narrower foundation, we see the possibility of achieving a certitude about the system of truths in sciences of man, society, and history which natural sciences, insofar as they seek to do more than merely describe phenomena, can never attain. In reality, moreover, modes of procedure of the human sciences (as those in which one understands their object even before one knows it,[69] and indeed in the totality of the soul)[70] are very different from those of natural sciences.[71] And one needs only to weigh the position which the idea of a fact as such has here,[72] and then its progress through various degrees of elaboration under the effect of analysis,[73] to recognize the completely different structure of organization in these sciences. Finally, fact, law, feeling of value, and rule come together here in an inner connection not present in that way in natural sciences. We can know this organization only in self-reflection,[74] hence self-reflection has to solve a special problem of human sciences here as well, one which, as we saw, did not find a solution from the metaphysical standpoint of philosophy of history.

Consequently, separate treatment of this kind permits the true nature of human sciences to emerge in their own right and thus perhaps contributes to breaking fetters in which the older and stronger sister has bound this younger one, from the time when Descartes, Spinoza, and Hobbes transferred methods they had matured in mathematics and natural sciences to these sciences which had lagged behind.

Metaphysics as the Foundation of the Human Sciences. Its Hegemony and Decline

---

Goddesses reign in majestic isolation,
About them no place, nor less a time;
To speak of them is most difficult.

Faust: Where is the path?

There is no path! Where no one has trod,
One must not tread.

Goethe[1]

Section 1. Mythical Thought and the Rise of Science in Europe

1. Task Arising from the Results of Book One

The first, or introductory, book mainly described the object of this work in synoptic fashion: historico-social reality in the structured form in which it builds itself up from individual units in the natural ordering of the human race; sciences of this reality also, that is, human sciences, separately and in the inner relations in which they have emerged from the struggle of knowledge with this reality. The intent was so that one embarking on this introduction could immediately become aware of the object itself in its reality.

The leading scientific idea of this work afforded that opportunity. For according to that idea all knowledge which deviates from previous results of philosophical reflection emanates from one basic idea that philosophy is first of all instruction on how to grasp reality or actuality in pure experience and how to classify it within limits prescribed by the critique of knowledge. For the person engaging in human sciences this work consequently seeks to create the organs, as it were, for experiencing the historico-social world. For this is the mighty soul of contemporary science: an insatiable longing for reality which, now that it has transformed the natural sciences, wishes to gain mastery of the historico-social world in order to comprehend the totality of the world if possible and to acquire the means to intervene in the march of human society.

So far, however, no one has ever made this total, complete, uncurtailed experience the basis for philosophizing; on the contrary, empiricism is no less abstract than speculation. The man whom influential empiricist schools fabricate out of sensations and perceptions, as though out of atoms, contradicts inner experience (from whose elements, after all, we derive the conception of man); such a machine would be unable to survive in the world for a single day. The structure of society, as deduced from this empiricist conception, is just as much a construction designed with abstract elements as the structure which the speculative schools have erected. Real society is neither a mechanism nor, as others more nobly conceive it, an organism. Analysis of reality which satisfies the rigid demands of science and acknowledgment of actual reality which goes beyond this analysis are only two different sides of the same standpoint of experience. "In contemplation and in action," remarks Goethe, "one must distinguish the accessible from the inaccessible; otherwise one can accomplish little in life as well as in science."

In opposition to currently dominant empiricism and speculation, it was first of all necessary to make historico-social reality visible in its full actuality; all subsequent investigations refer to this reality. In opposition to schemata of one science spanning the entire structure of this reality, it was necessary to demonstrate the interplay of the accomplishments of historically developed and fruitful special sciences; in them the great process of a relative, yet progressive, knowledge of social life is accomplished. And if we encountered the reader occupied with special sciences or active in the technology of occupational life linked with them, then, in contrast with this isolation, it was necessary to demonstrate the need for a fundamental science which develops the relations of special sciences to the progressive march of knowledge. All the human sciences take us back to such a foundation-laying.

Let us turn our attention to this foundation-laying itself. To construct it we need take from the foregoing only the proof of the necessity of a general science which provides a basis for the human sciences. However, it must now begin to present the rigorous grounding for the intuition of historico-social reality developed in the first book and for the process in which knowledge of it takes place, insofar as this intuition is more than mere classification of facts.

In the literature of the human sciences we find *two* different *forms of such foundation-laying*. Although people have tried to ground human sciences in *self-reflection* [*Selbstbesinnung*], hence in epistemology and psychology, in a few works first prompted through the critical philosophy of the eighteenth century, their grounding in *metaphysics* has occurred for more than two thousand years now. For this long a time people traced knowledge of the intellectual world to knowledge of God as its creator and to science of the universal inner structure of reality as the ground of nature as well as spirit. Especially until the fifteenth century (except for the period from the establishment of Alexandrian science to the building up of Christian metaphysics) metaphysics ruled the special sciences like a queen. For, as its own concept necessarily requires, if metaphysics is recognized at all it subordinates all special sciences to itself. But such recognition was taken for granted for as long a time as the mind was certain it knew the universal inner system of reality. For metaphysics is precisely the natural system which emerges from subordinating reality to the law of knowing. Thus metaphysics in general is the conception of science under whose hegemony study of man and society has developed and under whose influence they remain even today, although in diminished scope and degree.

At the gateway to the human sciences, therefore, we are confronted by metaphysics—along with skepticism, which accompanies it like its shadow. Proof of its untenability constitutes the negative part of the foundation-laying of the special sciences, something we recognized as necessary in the first book. And indeed we are trying to expand the abstract demonstration of the eighteenth century through historical knowledge of this great phenomenon. It is true that the eighteenth century has refuted metaphysics. But the German spirit, as opposed to the English and the French, lives in historical consciousness of continuity whose threads did not rupture for us in the sixteenth and seventeenth centuries; on this rests its historical depth, in which the past makes up a moment of current historical consciousness. Thus, on the one side, love of the greatness of antiquity won support for discredited metaphysics in our country even in the nineteenth century among noble minds; but, on the other side, precisely the same thoroughgoing immersion into the spirit of the past and into investigation of the history of thought has made it possible for us to recognize metaphysics historically in its origin, its power, and its downfall. For mankind will be fully able to overcome this great historical fact—like any other which has had its day, but which still drags its tradition along behind it—only if it comprehends it.

If the reader follows this presentation, he will be prepared historically for the epistemological foundation-laying. As the following description will establish, metaphysics, as the natural system, was a *necessary stage* in the intellectual development of the European nations. Therefore one who embarks on the sciences cannot by any means push aside the standpoint of metaphysics through arguments alone; no, he must, if not live through it, at least think it through completely and dissolve it in this way. Its influences stretch through the entire complex of modern concepts; literature of religion and of the state, of law and of history, has come about for the most part under its direction, and the remainder itself usually finds itself influenced by it, even against its will. Only one who has clarified this standpoint for himself in its full force, that is, the need for it which is rooted in man's unchanging nature, one who has understood it historically and known the causes of its long-lasting strength, one who has unfolded its consequences for himself—only such a one can free his way of thinking completely from this metaphysical ground and recognize and eliminate influences of metaphysics in the literature of human sciences available to him. After all, mankind itself has taken this path. So only one who has known the simple and hard form of *prima philosophia* in its history will see through the untenability of metaphysics which is currently dominant and is connected with empirical sciences or accommodated to them, that is, the philosophy of monists of natural philosophy, of Schopenhauer, and of his followers and Lotze's. Finally, only one who has recognized the grounds for separating philosophical from empirical human sciences (grounds located precisely within this metaphysics) and has pursued the consequences of this separation in the history of metaphysics will recognize the permanent housing of the metaphysical spirit in this division into rational and empirical sciences and decisively do away with it, in order to clear the ground for sound understanding of the system of human sciences.

2. Concept of Metaphysics; Problem of Its Relationship to Those Phenomena Most Nearly Related to It

Consideration of the historical world posed a difficult question for us. The interplay of individuals, their freedom, indeed their arbitrariness (taking these words in the sense of names for the experience and not for a theory), the variety of national characters and individualities, finally destinies which arise out of the system of nature in which all this takes place; this entire pragmatism of history produces a *composite world-historical nexus of purposes* through the uniformity of human nature as well as through other characteristics in it which make it possible for an individual to cooperate with something which transcends him. Such cooperation takes place in the great systems rooted in free interaction of forces as well as in external organizations of humanity: in the state and law, economic life, speech and religion, art and science. In this way unity, necessity, and law arise in the history of our human race. The pragmatic historian might revel in the play of individual forces, in deeds of nature and destiny or perhaps of some "higher hand," and the metaphysician might substitute his abstract formulas for these active forces as if they—like the astral spirits of astrology, which is also fed by metaphysical notions—prescribed its path to the human race: neither one of these even makes contact with this question itself. The secret of history and of humanity is more profound than either the one or the other. Its veil is lifted where one sees the will of man busied with itself yet contributing, even in opposition to his own intent, to some complex of purposes which transcends him, or when one sees his limited intelligence accomplish something in this complex which the latter requires, but which his individual intelligence neither intended nor foresaw. The blind Faust, in the final illusory labor of his life, is the symbol of all heroes of history, just as much as the Faust who shapes nature and history with a ruler's eye and hand.

In this living complex, which is grounded in the totality of human nature, the human race's *intellectual development* gradually set itself apart in science. Science constitutes a rational system which transcends the individual. Purposeful activity of individual persons, which Schleiermacher calls "will to knowledge" and others call "instinct for knowledge" (names for a fact of consciousness, not an explanation of this fact), has to take account of corresponding purposeful activity of other persons, to accept it, and to reach out to it. And, indeed, it is precisely ideas, concepts and propositions which are simply communicable. Hence one finds so constant an advance taking place in this structure or system that it is unmatched in any other field of human activity. However, a general will does not direct this purposeful complex of scientific endeavor; on the contrary, it is realized in the free activity of specific individuals. The general theory of this system is epistemology and logic. It deals with the mutual relation of elements to one another in this rational system of the process of knowledge which takes place in the human race— insofar as that relation is capable of general formulation.[2] Thus it looks for necessity, uniformity, and law in an epistemological structure which transcends the individual. Its content is the history of human knowledge as a fact and its terminal point consists of the composite law of formation [*das zusammengesetzte Bildungsgesetz*] in this history of knowledge. For although very powerful and sometimes extremely self-willed individuals create part of the history of science, and although various talents of nations influence this history, while the milieu of society in which this process of knowledge takes place always codetermines that process: nevertheless, the history of the scientific mind manifests a coherent unity which goes beyond such pragmatism. Pascal regards the human race as a single individual who always continues to learn. Goethe compares history of the sciences to a vast fugue in which the voices of nations make their appearance one after another.

Metaphysics appeared among the European peoples in this nexus of purposes in the history of the sciences at a specific point, the fifth century B.C.; it dominated the scientific spirit of Europe in two great time periods, and for several centuries now has been in a gradual process of dissolution.

The expression metaphysics is used in so many senses that we must first historically determine, to a degree, the sum total of facts which the term designates here.

It is well known that the expression originally designated merely Aristotle's placing of "first philosophy" after his natural-scientific writings, but then, in conformity with the tendency of the period, people interpreted it as referring to science which goes beyond nature.[3]

What Aristotle understood by first philosophy is most appropriately made the basis of definition for this concept, because through Aristotle this science acquired its own independent form, clearly distinct from special sciences, and because the concept of metaphysics, as Aristotle coined it in that connection, was inherent in the logical course of the process of knowledge. We can prove that what occurred here historically was at the same time something which had been determined within the nexus of purposes in the history of the sciences. According to Aristotle, we distinguish science from experience by the fact that science knows the ground, which is located in an efficient cause. We distinguish wisdom—in which desire for knowledge finds the locus of its satisfaction in itself (the word *wisdom* is taken here in its narrowest and loftiest sense, hence as "first wisdom")—from special science by the fact that it knows first causes, which in a universal sense are the basis of the whole of reality. It contains the causes for special spheres of experience and uses these causes to control all activity. This first perfect wisdom is precisely first philosophy. While special sciences, for example, mathematics, deal with specific spheres of being, this first philosophy deals with totality of being, or being as being, that is, universal determinations of being. And while every special science, in line with its task of knowing a specific area of being, goes back only to a point in establishing causes (which point is in turn conditioned in a backward direction in the system of knowledge), first philosophy deals with the grounds of all being, grounds not conditioned any further in the process of knowing.[4]

This definition of first philosophy, or metaphysics, which Aristotle devised is maintained by the most outstanding metaphysicians of the Middle Ages.[5] In modern philosophy the most abstract of Aristotle's formulas prevails more and more, one which defines metaphysics as the science of causes which are not further conditioned within the process of knowledge. Thus Baumgarten defines metaphysics as the science of the first causes of knowledge. And Kant also was in full agreement with Aristotle in defining the concept of that science he calls dogmatic metaphysics and whose dissolution he undertook to accomplish. In this critique of reason he fastened precisely on Aristotle's concept of unconditioned causes. Every general proposition (says Kant), insofar as it can serve as the major premise in a syllogism, is a principle by which something is known if it is subsumed under the condition of that principle. These general propositions as such are only comparative principles. But reason subjects all the rules of understanding to its own unity; in place of conditioned knowledge of the understanding it seeks unconditioned. In this it is guided by its synthetic principle: if the conditioned is given, then the entire series of mutually subordinate conditions (which series is thus itself unconditioned) is also given. According to Kant, this principle is the principle of dogmatic metaphysics, and he sees metaphysics as a necessary stage in the development of human intelligence.[6] Subsequently, most philosophical writers of the last generation have agreed with Aristotle's definition.[7] In this sense materialism or natural-scientific monism is just as truly metaphysics as Plato's theory of ideas, for in them also the universal, necessary determinations of being are the question at issue.

From Aristotle's definition of metaphysics, by way of the sure insights of critical philosophy, we find a characteristic note of metaphysics which likewise admits of no dispute. Kant has rightly stressed this characteristic. All metaphysics goes beyond experience. *It expands what is given in experience through an objective and universal inner structure* which arises only in elaborating experience under the conditions of consciousness. Herbart has masterfully described this true character of all metaphysics, as it reveals itself to us historically, from the standpoint of critical thought. Every theory of atoms which does not regard the atom as merely a methodological device widens experience through concepts which have sprung up in elaborating this experience under the conditions of consciousness. Natural-scientific monism adds to our experience a relation between material and psychic processes which exists in no experience; on the contrary, it expands experience. According to that relation, either psychic life is diffused everywhere throughout the elements of matter or the causes of the appearance of psychic life lie in the general characteristics of these elements.

Some writers use the expression metaphysics in a sense which deviates from this dominant usage because they pursue *individual relations* into which, naturally, the thus historically conceived fact of metaphysics enters.

In its elementary terms *Kant's concept* of dogmatic metaphysics seemed merely to adopt Aristotle's concept and think it through further. This is based on the following: from its natural standpoint, knowledge moves essentially in the direction from discovered conditioned truths to their ultimate unconditioned basis. From this tendency of knowing, Aristotle's metaphysics emerged as an historical fact, and so did the concept of retroactively unconditioned causes, through which, as it were, one reveals the compression spring behind the purposive nexus of thought which sets this metaphysical tendency of mind into motion. And Kant's profound insight seized on the same necessity in the ground of the conditions of consciousness as well. From his critical standpoint, as we saw further, he also saw through the epistemological assumption this dogmatic metaphysics contained. But here begins his deviation from Aristotle. In accordance with his epistemological principle he wants to sketch out the concept of metaphysics from its origin in knowledge. But now he is thinking on the basis of the unprovable assumption that universal and necessary truths would have a kind of a priori knowledge as their condition. And so for him metaphysics, as the science which strives to bring the highest rational unity possible to us into our knowledge,[8] accordingly acquires the distinction of being the *system of pure reason,* that is, "philosophical knowledge in systematic organization on the basis of pure reason."[9] And so he defines metaphysics on the basis of its origin in pure reason, which alone makes possible philosophical or apodictic knowledge. As opposed to *dogmatic* metaphysics he distinguishes his own as *critical* metaphysics; but he bends expressions of the old school into an epistemological sense in other cases as well. His conception of metaphysics passed on to his school.[10] But this deviation from historical linguistic usage embroiled Kant in contradictions, for even Aristotle's metaphysics is not such a pure science of reason, and it introduces an obscurity into Kant's terminology which is remarked even by his admirers.

A different use of the term highlights an aspect of metaphysics most evident in the general conception of educated people, and this usage is thus very widespread in life. It is true that monistic systems of natural philosophy are metaphysics too. But the focal point of the great historical mass of metaphysics lies closer to the mighty speculations which not only go beyond experience but also assume a realm of intellectual substances distinct from anything physical. These speculations therefore look into *what is hidden and essential beyond the world of the senses:* a second world. Thus when the term *metaphysics* is used, one finds the idea most strongly associated with the conceptual world of a Plato or an Aristotle, a Thomas Aquinas or a Leibniz. And this notion of metaphysics is supported by the name itself, which Kant, too, referred to as an object located *trans physicam.*[11] In this instance also a single aspect of metaphysics is one-sidedly emphasized; some of the deepest roots of the class of metaphysical systems we are speaking of reach into the world of faith, and from these roots those systems draw part of their power to dominate the mind of entire ages.

Finally, writers designate as metaphysics *every state of conviction* concerning the universal objective structure of reality or, more narrowly, concerning that which transcends reality, and so they speak of a natural, or folk, metaphysics. They correctly express an affinity between these convictions and metaphysics as a science, but consciousness of this affinity is more suitably described by a figurative application of the expressions noted rather than by such an extension of the literal sense of metaphysics, which annuls the historical restriction of its meaning to science.

So we use the expression metaphysics in the developed sense stamped on it by Aristotle. Although science in general can perish again only if humanity does, in its system this *metaphysics is a historically bounded phenomenon*. Other facts of intellectual life precede it in the nexus of purposes in our intellectual development; still others accompany it, and they will replace it in its hegemony. The historical process shows us as examples of such other facts: religion, myth, theology, special sciences of nature and of historico-social reality, and finally self-reflection and the epistemology which arises within it. And so the problem which concerns us also takes on this form: What are the relations of metaphysics to the nexus of purposes of intellectual development and to the other great facts of intellectual life which make up this nexus?

Comte tried to express these relations in a simple law which said that in man's intellectual development a stage of theology was replaced by one of metaphysics, and this by a stage of positive sciences. Hence for him and his widespread school metaphysics is a passing phenomenon in the history of the progressive scientific spirit, just as it is for Kant and his school in Germany and for John Stuart Mill in England.

Kant, too, finally came to terms with metaphysics, and this profoundest mind produced by the modern European peoples already recognized that in the history of intelligence a necessary structure exists which is grounded in the nature of the human cognitive capacity itself. The human mind has gone through three stages: "the first was the stage of dogmatism" (translated into common usage=of metaphysics); "the second was that of skepticism, the third that of the critique of pure reason; this chronological sequence is founded on the nature of man's cognitive capacity."[12] The difficulty in this drama of the process of knowledge lies, according to Kant, in the nature of reason developed above.[13] Reason gives rise to a natural and unavoidable illusion, and so the human mind becomes implicated in the dialectical contradiction between dogmatism (metaphysics) and skepticism; but the epistemological solution to this contradiction is criticism.[14]

Both Kant's theory and Comte's contain a one-sided view of the situation. Comte has not examined at all the historical relations of metaphysics to the important part of the intellectual movement which consists of skepticism, self-reflection, and epistemology; he has treated the relations of metaphysics to religion, myth, and theology without analysis, necessary at this point, of the composite facts of the case, and so his theory comes into conflict with facts of history and society. Indeed, his very conception of metaphysics lacks historical insight into the true foundations of its power. For his part Kant presents us with a construction, not a historical presentation, and this construction is one-sidedly determined by his epistemological standpoint and, within that standpoint, by his derivation of all apodictic knowledge from conditions of consciousness. The following presentation analyzes only the historical state of the question; later the results of analysis of consciousness can serve as a corroboration of it.

3. Religious Life as the Basis of Metaphysics; Period of Mythical Thought

No one can doubt that a period preceded the rise of the sciences in Europe in which intellectual development was carried on in language, poetry, and mythical conception, and the progress of experiences in practical life, whereas metaphysics or science did not yet exist.[15] Six hundred years before Christ we encounter the Europeans (unseparated from the Greeks of Asia Minor) in close communication with civilizations surrounding them and in transition to the stage of physical science and metaphysics. Thus natural science and metaphysics arose in Europe at an ascertainable time, one accessible in its basic character to research; this was after mythical thought had been dominant for an incalculably long period, which is lost in total darkness. This long and dark epoch receives direct light only in its last stage through extant poetic works and traditions which allow partial reconstruction of lost ones. What preceded these monuments in this epoch is accessible only to comparative cultural history. And, indeed, for the Indo-Germanic peoples, comparative history can use the tool of language to discover the stages of their external condition, their advancing external civilization, and indeed perhaps the development of their ideas; it can use the tool of comparative mythology to trace the transformations of basic Indo-Germanic myths and divine the basic outlines of the external organization [of society] and of its law. But the inner life of man escapes historical restoration in the period which one might call (in contrast with the prehistoric) the preliterary one, that is, a period in which poetic works have not come down to us. When Lubbock tries to argue that all peoples have gone through a stage of atheism, that is, of complete absence of any kind of religious idea,[16] or Herbert Spencer that all religion has arisen out of ideas about the dead,[17] these are but the orgies of an empiricism which disregards the limits of knowledge. At the boundary points of history one can in fact only invent, just as at every other boundary point of experience. Hence we limit ourselves in the first place to the period in which literary documents give us a picture of man's inner life.

Because we are observing these limits of historical knowledge, first of all we find that within those limits a *distinction between myth and religion* pervades the condition of simultaneity and succession among the great facts of intellectual life. The lack of such a distinction is the first reason for the mistakenness of Comte's law. Religious experience is linked to myth and to theology, to metaphysics and to self-reflection, in a much more complicated relationship than Comte assumed. We are convinced of this through reflection on the present intellectual situation. After all, with his own system in the nineteenth century, Comte must have discovered that it did not get beyond the second stage (that of metaphysics) in the human sciences; in fact, through a kind of scientific atavism, it even sank back finally into the first, or theological, stage. But history speaks even more clearly against Comte. The age of exclusive hegemony of mythical thought passed by for the Greek tribes; but religious life remained and continued to have influence. Science awakened gradually; mythical thought continued alongside it, and where religious life constituted the dominant focus of interest, it used some of the propositions developed by science. Indeed, it now happened that religious life in natures deeply moved by it—such as Xenophanes, Heraclitus, and Parmenides were—found a new language in metaphysical thought. But it also outlived this kind of expression. For metaphysics is transitory too, and self-reflection, which dissolves metaphysics, finds in its own depths once again—religious experience.

So the empirical relation of simultaneity and succession of the great facts woven into the history of intelligence demonstrates this: *religious life* is a state of affairs *bound up not only with mythical thought,* but *with metaphysics, and with self-reflection.* Regardless of how close the character of its connection with these last phenomena might be, we must distinguish religious life from them as a fact of much more comprehensive scope than them. In fact, not only in the same period but even in the same mind one can find united—without contradiction—religious life, mythical conceptions, and metaphysical thought. This was so with many Greek thinkers; with marvelous seriousness Heraclitus, Parmenides, and Plato struggled to formulate mythical language commensurate with their conceptual universe. In the same mind religious experience and theology are also linked with metaphysics, as was so with many medieval thinkers. But one cannot conceive the same fact mythically and explain it rationally at the same time. These relationships separate religious life from mythical conceptions even more clearly.

For the purpose at hand—a presentation in conformity with experience—defining the concept of religious life would easily expose us to the suspicion of making a construction;[18] it suffices if we *pass on the available facts regarding religious life and describe them.* The presence of lived experience [*Erlebnis*[19]] or of inner experience [*innerer Erfahrung*] in general is something we cannot deny. For this immediate knowledge is the content of experience, analysis of which then becomes knowledge and science of the intellectual world. This science would not exist if inner *Erlebnis* or inner experience were not present. Experiences of such a kind include human freedom, conscience and guilt, also the contrast running through all spheres of inner life between the perfect and the imperfect, between the transitory and the eternal, as well as man's yearning for the latter. And, indeed, these inner experiences are ingredients of religious life. But religious life also embraces, at the same time, consciousness of an absolute dependence of the subject. Schleiermacher has shown the origin of this consciousness in lived experience [*Erlebnis*]. Recently Max Müller has tried to provide a more solid empirical foundation for this theory. "If it sounds too rash for us to say that a person really sees the invisible, then let us say that he feels the pressure of the invisible, and this invisible something is in fact just a special name for the infinite with which primitive man thus acquires his first feeling."[20] And so consideration of religious states of mind everywhere leads us back to interweaving the experience of dependence with experience of a higher life independent of nature.

The *characteristic feature of religious life* is that it makes assertions in virtue of a different kind of conviction than scientific evidence is. In the face of all attacks religious faith points to inner experience, to that which the soul can experience interiorly even now and to that which it has encountered historically. That faith is neither carried by reasoning nor can it be refuted by it. It is born from the fullness of all powers of the soul, and even after the process of differentiating intellectual life has distinguished poetry, metaphysics, and sciences as relatively independent forms of this intellectual life, religious experience continues in the depth of the soul and influences these forms. For knowledge which operates in the sciences will never become master of the original experience which is present to the soul in immediate knowledge. Knowledge works on this experience, as it were, from the outside inward. But no matter if knowledge continuously reduces new facts to thought and necessity—and that is its function; with tenacious power of opposition, free will, responsibility, the ideal, and the will of God maintain their position against it in consciousness. Those things will remain, even if they contradict the necessary structure of knowledge. It is true that knowledge must govern its object with necessity in accordance with its own inner law. But must or can knowledge therefore make everything its object? Must it or can it know everything?

This insight that *religious life is the permanent substratum of intellectual development* and not a passing phase in man's mental life is one we shall round out later through psychological analysis. We can demonstrate this relation historically for only a limited period of time in the development which has taken place thus far. One cannot show historically that religious life has made up a part of human nature in every period in the way that we can establish it as the substratum of the historical life of Europe. We can only conclude this much from what has developed thus far: if at any point in the line of historical development stretching backward from us, the facts were to force us to acknowledge an *areligious condition* (religion in the sense of primordial religious experience in which it already contains the awareness of good and evil and its relation to a structure on which man is dependent)—which, however, is not the case—then this point would immediately be a *boundary point of historical understanding*. We might, to be sure, have some historical information about such a period, but the period would lie beyond the boundaries of our historical understanding. For we understand only by transmitting our inner experience to an external actuality which is dead in itself. If we were to imagine that elements of inner experience, whose origin we cannot trace but which first make possible the structure of such experience in our consciousness, were absent from a historical situation, then we would have arrived at the boundary of historical understanding itself. This does not exclude the possibility that such a state has existed. It might be possible that elements of inner experience, even though we could not trace them to their origin, would neverthe-less not be primary, and epistemology has to test such a possibility. But it is out of the question that we should understand such a state and should use it to explain a situation in which this untraceable element then appears; it is out of the question, therefore, that we should have historical understanding of a nonreligious state and of the emergence of a religious state from it. In England as well as here, outstanding recent empiricist writers on the origins of culture fall prey to the following contradiction. Thus far they have discovered no nontraceable facts of inner experience in the primordial condition of mankind, but they are not willing to forgo understanding this state historically nor to forgo deducing the succeeding state from it.

Insofar as linking together bare facts extends to social experience at all, therefore, there has never been a time in which the individual, as he was, would not have found himself to be merely existing, determined by his history, and consequently absolutely dependent, and thus have found the horizon of the world itself—viewed in physical terms and conceived causally—to be dissolving into infinity in all directions.[21] There has never been a time when man's free spontaneity would not have struggled with "the other" whose pressure enveloped him; and even mythical ideas have their powerful roots in the will. There has never been a time when man did not entertain images of something purer and more perfect to contrast with his wretched life. And everything man has discovered through his activity showed his mind, which experiences pleasure and pain, hopes and fears, and his will, which loves and hates, a double aspect. All this is life, not inferential knowledge. As soon as these untraceable elements of my own life and my inner experi-ence fail to coincide with historical facts (and, indeed, with facts guaranteed by solid arguments), that is, fail to come together as historical understanding, then I have arrived at the boundary of historical method. At this point the realm of the historically transcen-dent begins. For the historical method also has an inner boundary in the process of consciousness, and therefore immovable, just as truly as natural-scientific knowledge has such a boundary. Because this method allows the shadows of the past to appear to our present consciousness as historical facts, it can impart reality to them only from the life and reality of this consciousness.

Thus far, before the psychological analysis, we have established the important thesis that religious life is the solid substratum of the intellectual development known to us in history. Now, we find *religious life connected with mythical ideas in a definite way* from the period of the extant epic poetry of the Greeks to the rise of science. From what we can still ascertain about the nature of this connection we take a few very general characteristics necessary for insight into the complex of purposes of intellectual history.

Mythical thought forms a real and living organization of phenomena especially significant to men of those times. It thereby accomplishes something which perception, imagination, and activity, which are in daily traffic with objects, do not accomplish; nor does language. It is true that perception and imagination constantly connect sense impressions with objects to which one can ascribe characteristics, conditions, and activities. They posit relationships between these things, especially that of cause and effect. One must guard as emphatically as possible against notions which portray these characteristic features of our way of seeing things (which features arise out of our daily minor trafficking with objects) as though, in the period of formation of myths, such features were swallowed up in a general animation of the cosmic system. In fact, language expresses an early awareness of relations arising in that way. Relation of roots, division into parts of speech, cases, tenses, organization of syntax, classification of facts under general names, and so forth: all this reflects relations which people grasped and differentiated in reality. Later philosophical thought links up at many points with language; mythical ideas are profoundly intertwined with it. However, what is accomplished here is totally different from the establishment by mythical thoughts of the real and universal structure linking together phenomena which were significant for men of those days. The function of mythical thought in this period is thus analogous to one which metaphysics has for a later period. It is neither religion nor the consciousness of God it includes which marks such a first stage, and so it is not the idea of the supernatural either; on the contrary, these things constitute an abiding precondition for the intellectual life of humanity. Comte's theorem about the first stage of intellectual development, which he labels the theological one, is therefore untenable, because it fails to separate the function of mythical thought from the position of religion in the context of intellectual development. And his assumption about the influence of religious ideas on European society—that it has steadily decreased in history and is gradually disappearing in the face of science—has not been confirmed by history.

As a matter of fact, *mythical thought demonstrates relative independence with respect to religious life*. To be sure, the real structure of phenomena described by mythical thought rests on religious life: this is the living power in that structure which transcends everything visible. But this structure is not grounded in religious experience alone. It is likewise determined by the way people of those days experienced reality. Reality was life to them and it remains life to them; it does not become an object of understanding by knowledge. Therefore it is will, factuality, and history at every point, that is, living, primordial reality. Because it is present to the entire living person and has not yet been subordinated to any kind of cognitive analysis and abstraction (hence dilution), it is accordingly itself life. And just as the structure which mythical thought builds up in this way does not spring from religious life alone, neither can a mythical form of thought totally exhaust the content of the latter. Life is never exhausted by thought. Religious experience, on the contrary, remains the eternally inward thing; hence it never finds adequate expression in any myth or any idea of God. It is the same sort of relationship which exists on a higher level between religion and metaphysics.

So, for the prescientific period of the Greek tribes, for example, the language of myth has a *significance which transcends the expression of religious life*. The basic myths of the Indo-Germanic peoples, as comparative mythology struggles to establish them, are like the roots of their languages in this respect, that they are relatively independent means of expression which maintain themselves as permanent vehicles of description amid change in religious circumstances. They persist through constantly new transformations (whose laws derive from those of imagination), no matter what change images of the gods and the religious consciousness underlying them undergo. They hold sway so independently in the imagination of these peoples that they do not die out among them even when the faith which expressed itself in them is extinguished.

In relative independence they serve a need which goes beyond religious consciousness, that of linking together phenomena of nature and of society and of providing a first kind of explanation of them. Here we encounter the oldest form of the general relationship which links the religious substratum of Europe's intellectual development to Europe's effective tendency to devise a coherent connection between, and explanation of, phenomena. The type of explanation is imperfect in the highest degree; people experienced and regarded the structure of phenomena as a system based on will, an interaction of living stimuli and behavior. It was therefore able to contain the intellectual development of these vigorous tribes within it for only a limited time; then the thrust toward explanation burst its imperfect shell.

4. Rise of Science in Europe

We have only a very imperfect knowledge of the causal structure of the historical process in which this event took place in which scientific explanation of the cosmos arose out of mythical thought. According to estimates of the most renowned scholars of the Alexandrian period, at least three centuries separate the Homeric poems from the birth of the first man who, according to tradition, attempted to explain the world scientifically: Thales. A contemporary of Solon, he lived in the second half of the seventh century and in the first part of the sixth century B.C. In this long and dark period from the Homeric poems to Thales, *the development of enlightening intelligence advanced in two directions,* as far as we can judge.

Experience which arose out of the tasks of life, particularly in industry and trade, brought an *ever increasing territorial expanse* in the world and in that expanse an *ever increasing array of facts* under its control, that is, its ability to influence, to predict, and to understand the necessity of the system. And in the process experience used gains made by peoples of more ancient culture with whom the Greeks were in communication. It is an open question whether there ever was a time in which separation of a sphere of experience from a sphere of mythical thought did not occur to any extent or in any form at all. But the progress manifest in further evolution of mythical thought is a verifiable fact; that progress paved the way for science, but it also essentially transformed the mythical world itself.

Living forces which man, driven by his feelings, sensed as the hand of the infinite laid upon him, forces which he feared and loved, were being continually pushed back to the horizon of the expanding zone of natural events, and from that point on they were lost in darkness.

In Homer's poetry we find the mythical world already in retreat. The divine powers constitute an order unto themselves, a divine family organization with a political framework governing their voluntary relationships [*Willensverhältnisse*]; their proper domiciles are separated from the sphere of the ordinary work of a Greek of that time in agriculture, industry, and trade; they sojourn only for a time in this sphere, notably for a passing visit in their temples, and their influence on the area subject to experience and thought becomes a supernatural intervention. Likewise, no more marriages between Olympian gods and men are reported from the period of the Trojan and post-Trojan events in Homer's poems. In fact, we find in these poems a definite awareness of decreasing traffic between gods and men. Thus the progress of enlightenment continually extended the sphere dominated by natural explanation and made minds ever more skeptical about assuming supernatural intervention.

Of course this progress is linked to a change in feeling about life. The pattern of life of heroic kingship decayed; epic poetry, which had been its expression, ossified. A feeling about life which corresponded to changed political and social conditions proclaimed itself openly in elegy and iambic poetry; personal, turbulent, inner life became the focal point of interest. In lyric poetry, at least from the time of Thales, there are even signs which portray reliance on the gods as retreating behind this independent feeling for life.[22] Along with this blossoming of a poetry of feeling went a view of morals in which the mind assumed mastery over the area of moral experience.

The *other direction* in which the spirit of enlightenment proceeded is still evident in the remains of literature about *theogonies*. Hesiod's extant theogony, the most important among them, was indeed available to the first philosophers, at least in its essentials. Out of material from the sphere of mythic thought the movement of enlightenment fashioned in these theogonies an inner organization of the world-process advancing through a series of generations. And in fact this world-process does not transpire either as a mere relationship of freely acting powers nor as a system bound together by universal ideas of nature. Night, heaven, earth, and eros are ideas located in a twilight zone between facts of nature and of personal power. General ideas of an order of nature worked themselves free from the personal element.

These two directions taken by the mind *destroyed the system of the world* which *mythical thought* had mapped out. The "other" (which, as nature, we contrast with our self) receives its living character from the self-awareness in which it is present. Mythical thought grasps this character with a full sense of life, but its truth does not withstand the test of reason. Experience of regularity in transformation of material elements, in succession of conditions in the world, and in play of changes in it demands another explanation; a system of nature different from one which centers on relations of personal wills becomes necessary. And so the task begins of devising this system rationally, in a way that corresponds to reality. Things linked together in active and passive roles, changes locked into other changes, movement in space: all this is given over to observation and should now be known as part of a system.

A long and laborious path begins for experiential and experimental thought, and when we come to its end we shall say: we can no more break up this "other" which is nature into cognitive elements and thereby know it thoroughly than mythical thought was able to penetrate it. It remains impenetrable because it is an actuality given us in the totality of the powers of our soul. There is no metaphysical knowledge of nature.

All this was yet to come. But first of all we are tracing how, in a manner gradually prepared for by the two movements of the mind noted above, the *great fact of scientific explanation of the cosmos now emerged*. This fact emerged in the sixth century B.C. when in the Ionian and Italian Greek colonies of the time basic mathematical and astronomical insights and methods were applied to the problem which had also preoccupied mythical thought: the origin of the cosmos. The colonial cities of Ionia had rapidly advanced toward developing democratic constitutions and toward unleashing all their powers. The organization of their laws of worship made the intellectual movement among them less dependent on the priesthood than it was in the ancient oriental cultural states surrounding them. And now the riches accumulated in those cities gave independent men leisure and means for research. For independent development of individual purpose-complexes in human society was tied to their realization by a particular class of persons. But now growth of wealth created for the first time a precondition for individuals to devote themselves fully and in historical continuity to knowledge of nature. At the same time, through a world-historical dispensation of the rarest kind, the extremely ancient sites of culture in the Orient (and, particularly during the second half of the seventh century B.C., in Egypt) were opened up to these independent, experienced men of the world. They now used geometry, such as it had been developed as a practical art and as a collection of individual propositions in Egypt, and the tradition of long astronomical observation and recording, such as they existed in observatories of the East, for orientation in the universe whose image mythical thought had handed down to them.

With that the Greeks embarked on an intellectual voyage whose larger context, reaching back into the Orient, we still know insufficiently. But it is a voyage determined by the nexus of purposes linked to knowledge. We can subject reality to thought only by separating individual parts of its content and by knowing these parts in isolation. For thought cannot comprehend reality in its complex form. The first science which came into being through this method was *mathematics*. Space and number were separated from reality early, and they are completely amenable to rational treatment. One can easily abstract consideration of bounded surfaces and bodies by observing real things, and from such self-contained structures geometrical investigation began. Corresponding to the nature of their object, geometry and arithmetic were the first sciences to arrive at clear truths. People had already taken this path in analyzing reality before the Greeks became involved with the system of knowledge, but now the peculiarity of the Greek mind met it halfway. Power of observation and sense of form were the characteristics of this mind; this is most strikingly evident in the manifestly clear and coherent image of the universe which the Homeric epics already contain. Then incipient Greek science, especially in the Pythagorean school, completely separated investigation of spatial and numerical relationships from the field of practical tasks and examined them without reference to applicability. Similarly, inchoate *astronomy* started by constructing a globe and beginning to draw lines on it. Mathematics, particularly geometry and descriptive astronomy, and in a later period logic also—as theories which to an extent remain contemplatively within the sphere of pure and applied forms—constitute the highest intellectual achievements of the Greek mind.

5. Character of the Oldest Greek Science

One hundred years of this progressive development of Greek science passed before these physicists subjected the nature of the first causes from which they derived the cosmos to more rigid general reflection. And yet this was a precondition for the emergence of a separate science of metaphysics. If we find Thales at the peak of his activity in the first third of the sixth century B.C., the life and activity of Heraclitus and Parmenides, who took this step forward, reach well into the fifth century.

Throughout these one hundred years, advancing orientation in the universe through the resources of mathematics and astronomy stand in the foreground of interest; it is with them that attempts to establish the original condition and essential ground of the universe link up. The surveying eye of man, especially where the sea affords it a vast perspective, finds itself on a plane surface bounded by the arc of the horizon, above which is the hemispheric vault of the heavens. Geographical knowledge determines the extent of this globe and the distribution of water and land on it. A view that seafaring Greeks held as early as the Homeric period now regarded water or the ocean as the birthplace of everything. This is where *Thales* came in. Homer's ocean, which flowed around the disc of the earth, expanded in his view: this world-disc floats on water and everything has emanated from it. Most importantly, Thales advanced the task of orientation in this cosmic space, and here lay the essential core of what was taking place. *Anaximander* continued this work, drew a map of the universe [*Erdtafel*], and introduced the use of the gnomon, which was at that time the most important instrument used in astronomy. From the state of a universal flood—in assuming which he agreed with Thales—he went back to an unbounded being which temporally preceded this condition. This is a being from which everything definite and bounded has separated itself, an imperishable being which spatially embraces and governs everything else. And, in fact, reliable witness testifies that he designated this unbounded, all-living, immortal being as a principle[23] and thus introduced this term (though, to be sure, mainly in the sense of beginning and cause), which is so important for metaphysical thought. This expression indicated that now knowing was conscious of its task and therefore set aside science for its province.

Phenomena of atmospheric disturbance also provided an explanatory tool for further *cosmological investigations* by Ionian physicists. Just as in the atmosphere moist precipitation, warmth, and turbulent air are connected together, for these primitive attempts at explanation it appears that everything comes now from air, now from fire, and now from water.

The science of the south Italian colonies, which the *association of the Pythagoreans* pursued, also had its starting point, its essential interest, and its importance for intellectual development in increasing orientation within the universe, with the help of mathematics and astronomy. In this school a nonutilitarian reflection on the relationship of numbers and spatial forms developed, in other words, pure mathematical science. Indeed, its investigations had already dealt with relations between numbers and spatial magnitudes, and so the idea of the irrational surfaced among them in mathematics. In addition, their schema of the cosmos was astronomical: in the center of the world was the limiting and formative being which was to them, in the loveliest Greek spirit, the divine being; because it attracts the unbounded to itself, numerical order of the cosmos comes into being.

All these explanations of the universe, even though as explanations they worked toward gradually dissolving mythical thinking, were still *combined with a very considerable element of mythical faith*. The principle from which these first researchers drew conclusions still contained many features of a mythical setting. It included formative power within it akin to mythical forces, capacity for metamorphosis, purposefulness, and, as it were, footprints of the gods in its operation. Thus it was also intertwined with a mythical polytheism these physicists held whose roots are scarcely visible to us. We should not reinterpret Thales's conviction that the world was full of gods as if it were modern pantheism. Anaximander's mythical belief was that all things, as they perish, are doing penance and suffering for the injustice of their separate existence in accordance with the temporal order.[24] We can ascribe no other teaching to Pythagoras with as much certainty as we can the one about transmigration of souls, and the association he founded clung to the cult of Apollo and to religious rites with conservative tenacity. Notions of a perfect being define the cosmic idea of the south Italian schools. Indeed, the idea so characteristic of the Greek mind makes its appearance here, that the limited is the divine—against which one might hold Spinoza's position: *omnis determinatio est negatio*.[25] And so one should by no means simply trace this ancient worldview to a primitive form of pantheism, such as has often happened since Schleiermacher.

So it was slowly and gradually, even after explanatory science had struggled to independence, that it broke the force of mythical grounds of explanation and of the mythical system. It was through such hard work that, out of the initial compactness [*Gebundenheit*] of the general life of the mind, in which reality is given to man and always remains given, the nexus of purposes of scientific knowledge worked its way toward independence. Replacing primitive ideas by ideas more suited to their object was that difficult for this science. For it is the totality of the powers of the mind which originally produces the structure of things; it is only step by step that knowledge draws the purely cognitive elements out of that whole. Life is the first and ever present being; abstractions of knowing are the second thing, and they merely relate to life. This is how important basic characteristics of ancient thought emerged. It did not begin with the relative but with the absolute, and it grasped the absolute with those determinations which stem from religious experience. Reality for ancient thought was something living: the structure of phenomena was for it something psychical or at any rate something analogous to the psychical.

Still, human intelligence has never made greater progress than in the century that had just transpired when Heraclitus and then Parmenides appeared. Science was now available. Phenomena, in their regularity and organization, were derived predominantly from natural causes. The corollary to the independence which had now emerged in Greek science was the expression *cosmos*. The ancients traced it to Pythagoras: "Pythagoras was the first to call the universe a cosmos because of the order which rules it."[26] This word is like a mirror of Greek intelligence itself, steeped in rational regularity and harmonious organization of relationships and movements of the universe. In it the esthetic character of the Greek mind expresses itself as originally and profoundly as in the bodies which Phidias and Praxiteles formed. No longer did one now pursue the trail of an arbitrary and intervening god in nature; the gods govern in the beautiful and regular system of forms which make up the cosmos. In the same spirit, a society rationally arranged into regularly functioning forms transferred the expressions *law* and *rational speech* to states in the physical universe.[27]

But the *whole manner of inferring phenomena*, as it existed in the science of the universe, *could not satisfy growing demands of knowledge*. If one ascribes life to any element of nature or the power to transform itself into other elements or to expand and contract, then it is a matter of indifference from which of these elements the explanation proceeds, for in this way one can infer everything from everything. And had not these physicists, alternately but with equal facility, explained other parts of the system of nature through a transformation from water, or fire, or air? In Heraclitus speculation developed this view of an inner capacity for change as the universal feature of every condition in the universe; in Parmenides it opposed the demands of thought to this endless change. Thus arose metaphysics in the narrow sense.

Section 2. Metaphysical Stage in the Development of the Ancient Peoples

1. Various Metaphysical Standpoints are Investigated and Prove Themselves Incapable of Further Development at the Time

We have reached a new stage in the purpose-nexus of knowledge: In the generation of Heraclitus and Parmenides progressive intelligence is trying to define the general character of the system of the cosmos and of a principle governing this system. It is developing the characteristics of a principle which make it usable for explaining natural phenomena. This supposes that it is now making its previous attempts to infer the phenomena of the cosmos *objective*.

For a hundred years the new science had sought to connect and explain phenomena of the external world by observing change and motion. It had also developed the concept of principle, that is, of a first thing which is the temporal starting point and first cause of phenomena and from which one can deduce the latter. This concept expressed the will to knowledge itself. Many causes now pushed toward reflection about the *most general characteristics of such a principle* and in general of the structure of the world—causes such as change in principles; impossibility of proving one of these principles; difficulties in observing change which underlay the previous method; no less great difficulties in individual ideas which such explanation had at its disposal. We call reflection which presupposes individual explanations in this way and deduces general characteristics of every imaginable world system *metaphysical reflection*.

This metaphysical reflection analyzed the structure of reality in the external world. To be sure, this structure was grounded ultimately in consciousness and only together with the historical world constituted the whole of reality; but the metaphysical thinking of the Greeks nevertheless *conceived this structure in study of the external world*. The result of this was that metaphysical concepts remained bound to spatial intuition. The rational formative principle was already a limiting being among the Pythagoreans; it had an analogous character for the Eleatics and Plato. Explanation of the cosmos resolved everything—even to the highest concept to which the Greek mind attained, that of the unmoved mover—into motions and phenomena in space.

Can we now express the inner law which guided analysis of the structure of reality at this stage of knowledge? To begin with, the world presented to incipient scientific thought a manifold of particular things linked to one another in changing patterns of acting and being acted on, moving in space, increasing and decreasing, even coming into existence and passing out of it. The Hellenes, as one of the newly emerging metaphysicians observed, spoke erroneously of coming to be and passing away. In fact, language itself proves that these ideas dominated the simple conception of nature. Clouds appear to gather and to dissipate in the air, and so do particular things. Even the gods of Greek myth had come to be in time. Using the idea of an original, powerfully formative material substance and its transformations, the century of Greek science which had just run its course had now, in southern Italy, reduced to a system these views based on the contrast between limiting formative power and unlimited being. It is very difficult for us to appreciate the intellectual outlook of an educated Greek of those days who began to doubt the gods and then saw himself in this vortex of material transformations. For religion and exact science provide a man of our time with firm reference points for his worldview. The Greek of that time, however, now had no fixed point among the play of phenomena. Mythical religion could not give him one, nor did positive science exist which could offer him a foothold. But man is always aware that his activities and condition are grounded in his own person. He cannot imagine that his ego is a state or an activity belonging to something lying beyond him. This is his feeling of life. And the "other," the external something he discovers over against his will, is to him amid all changes likewise a condition and an expression of a foundation not in turn itself a state or activity of something beyond it. It is all the same if this independent foundation exists in the particular thing or in the one Spinozistic substance or in atoms: the external something given us in self-awareness inescapably has this character. If we define *substance* as that which is the subject for all predicate determinations or the underlying basis for all states of being and activities, then a man looks, so to speak, through the vortex and the play of colors among phenomena into the substantial which lies beyond them; he cannot do otherwise. He subordinates even the idea of activity or the concept of causality to this substantial entity. And in himself—in the play of his motives, stimuli, and purposes—he must likewise look for a *solid point which would regulate his behavior*. Thus in himself and in what he encounters opposed to his person outside himself are the two fixed points which make up the natural goals of his reflection: a substantial foundation for external reality and, in his activity, an end which is not a means, the highest good of his will.

This state of affairs explains why *true being and the highest good* were the *two central questions* for the philosophy of the ancients. These questions are not derivative. It is not subjective tenacity of assertion but necessity of thought which human knowledge seeks first of all. This tenacity of assertion is, so to speak, the subjective logical side of the objective soundness of purpose within us and substance outside us. One can see this historically in the fact that it was first of all insecurity and doubt, which disturbed certainty of thought, which stirred up the question about the logical connection between cause and effect or about a cause which is secure in itself.

In fact, in the process which we have to describe now, *knowledge* of the world's substance *has still not fought itself free of the context* which formerly held knowledge bound up, as it were, in the *totality of the powers of the human mind*. The gods had still found a place in the world of the Ionian physicists as well as of the Pythagoreans. Now that the structure of the cosmos was defined in its most universal characteristics there was in principle no more place for them in it. Xenophanes, Heraclitus, Parmenides, and Anaxagoras—the leading minds of the new period—developed a world structure which, through the clear consciousness of its universal character and of its range which embraced all phenomena, virtually occupied the entire terrain of reality. That had not yet been so in the world of Anaximander or Pythagoras. And it made no difference for the change coming about that the gods still continued to hold a position of personal need for one or other of these men, as was obviously so with Xenophanes, for example. But what was the consequence of this change now for the metaphysical conception of the world order? The whole essence of higher feelings, religious life, ethical consciousness, the feeling of beauty and of the infinite value of the world were now inherent in this world system itself. All the characteristics which religious and ethical life had ascribed to the gods now fell into this cosmic ordering. The highest good itself and the end which is no longer means were referred back to it. Thus in this being which unified phenomena were located the perfect, good, and beautiful being; complete being as opposed to the inadequate in reality; solid and inwardly blessed being as opposed to the incompleteness of reality.

Xenophanes defines the one being, which this structure is to him, in theological terms. The law which Heraclitus says rules in the flux of appearances is defined not only by contradictories or the way upward and downward; it has a profound religious background. The beginning of Parmenides' didactic poem announces in ancient grandeur a truth which clings closely to religious faith. The Pythagoreans show the same character.

So it corresponds to the structure of intellectual development and to the mind of this period in antiquity that profounder reflection on the principle of the cosmos came out of *religious life* and accordingly asserted itself as a claim on the idea of the deity. The Pythagorean school had prepared the way for separating what was given in perception from metaphysical world order. The cosmos was broken up into two explanatory causes with regard to its origin. In contrast with the unbounded came that which is shape and gives shape, the principle of form; the Pythagoreans conceived of this mathematically and described it in relationships between number and spatial magnitude, and they pursued it into the real world of sounds as well as into the harmonic relationships of the cosmic masses. *Xenophanes* demonstrated the principle of one being from religious awareness. The notion of the death of the gods is impious, but what has temporal origin is also transitory; therefore we ascribe an *eternal* and unchangeable condition to the deity. Likewise, a plurality of gods is not compatible with consciousness of the power and perfection of the deity; the eternal deity is therefore *one*. Thus in Xenophanes we find linked with reflection on the characteristics of the principle of the universe the beginning of an incisive polemic against the mythical notion which assumes a multiplicity of gods who are born and die; he already perceives the anthropomorphic element in belief in the gods and its untenability.

The more rigorous development of this principle of the all-one seems to have been furthered by the fact that *Heraclitus*, finally, deduced the formula of universal flux as the basis of the view of nature held by the Ionian physicists. Awareness of the difference between the metaphysical consciousness surfacing in him and all previous research filled him with acerbic pride and devastating criticism. According to the profound insight of Heraclitus this metaphysical consciousness refers precisely to that which constantly surrounds man, what he continually hears and sees: while the usual condition of man is to exist in a place and yet not be mentally there, this metaphysical reflection grasps precisely what is recurrent in wakeful consciousness and expresses it. And so metaphysics is in opposition to vulgar vegetative existence, which is like sleep; to empiricism which ranges across the cosmos with its specialized information and orientation but does not teach the meaning of it; and to false art whose representatives [*Typen*] among his contemporaries and predecessors he saw in Pythagoras, Xenophanes, and Hecateus. The cosmic law of change now dawns on this metaphysical consciousness, a law uniformly operative at every point of the universe. The self-modifying all-one is not only present as itself in opposites; its opposite is contained in every single phenomenon itself; in our life is death, in our death is life. In these ideas which dissolve all being, then, lay the reason why Heraclitus turned away from positive science of his time. Heraclitus also subjected his physics to the basic idea of change and he included even the sun in his rhythm of transformation: every day it should rise anew.

This idea that constancy exists only in the law of changes without a doubt contains an important point of departure for true insights; but in the state of the sciences at that time Heraclitus had to do violence to ideas and to facts, and his school (the society of "the fluxists") naturally succumbed to skepticism. For if only the flux of things exists, that is, conversion of one state of matter into another, then constancy occurs only in the law of this conversion; and we could not identify a principle which would be the carrier of this conversion movement. Thus when Heraclitus designated fire as such a principle, even if just symbolically, his system lapsed into an internal contradiction. Moreover, he subjected the regular and constant circular movements of the stars also to an explanation based on the principle of change, and the result of this had to be that the constant unchanging cause which those movements demand contradicts the rhythm of changes. So Heraclitus necessarily came into conflict with the astronomical ideas of his time; he thus arrived at his own peculiar paradoxical astronomical assertions, which can only be interpreted as a step backward.

Parmenides was probably the man who brought the idea of Xenophanes to full metaphysical clarity in opposition to formulas of Heraclitus. Like Heraclitus he strove to become more profoundly conscious of the content of the idea of the world. He too was no longer seeking primarily to orient himself in the universe or to establish factual relations between movements of its large bodies. To be sure, Parmenides was the first person who, as a writer, supported the great discovery of the global shape of the earth, even if he cannot be labeled its discoverer; for it is not out of the question that he might have found this epoch-making astronomical insight already present among the Pythagoreans in his south Italian homeland. But the beginning of his didactic poem shows that metaphysical reflection on the most universal characteristics of the structure of the world seemed to him also to be the great task of his life. The same beginning also makes it evident that this world structure included for him all the religious depth of the mythical age, just as was the case with Heraclitus. All the luster of the mythical world, the home of the gods, and their radiant figures now passed into this metaphysical world. Hence it is also a divine voice which at the beginning of his poem summarizes the whole contrast between truth and error in the following assertions: the existing is, the nonexisting is not; error is grounded in the contrary assumption that the nonexistent has existence and that being does not exist.

The fragments do not suffice to establish the exact meaning which his explanation and grounding of this major proposition had.[1] There is no doubt that he based this proposition on the fact that being cannot be separated from thought; what does not exist can be neither known nor expressed. This demonstration obviously implies that the act of conceiving in which reality is present no longer remains if one removes the reality given in it. But of course this sort of modern expression runs the danger of failing to comprehend the simple and total meaning of this ancient thought. Somewhat more simply and closer to Parmenides' usage we say: if *being* is not present (an abstract designation for the "is" which the objectivity given in ideation expresses), then of course no thinking can take place either. Thus since nothing else exists apart from being, then thinking also is not something distinct from being. For outside of being is absolutely nothing; it is, so to speak, the locus in which even the statement takes place. Thinking and being are therefore the same. A nonexisting thing is thus a nonthought, a piece of nonsense in the strictest sense.[2]

These propositions contain, at any rate, the kernel of a metaphysical expression of the cognitive law of contradiction; but they extend farther than this. They express, in compact profundity, the discovery of the structure of consciousness, in which an object is inseparably connected with a subject and the object possesses the character of substantial solidity.

And so on the one hand these propositions are the *sufficient basis for truths* which Greek thought now first added to mathematics and which made possible the transition from the latter to scientific reflection on the cosmos; on the other hand, in the darkness in which they first appear to consciousness, they are the *starting point for extravagant demands of thought* regarding the most general characteristics of the world system.

These *truths* implicitly contained in the above-cited propositions of Parmenides are simple. The first one lies in the idea of the peculiarity of structure of our consciousness, which Aristotle put into a more precisely defined, hence tenable, form in his formula of the *principle of contradiction*. The second one lies in the physical principle: *there is no coming to be and no passing away.*[3] One must exclude any coming to be and passing away from true being. For being cannot come from the nonexistent because the latter is precisely that which is not, but being would generate nothing other than itself. This proposition too did not receive a more precisely restricted and tenable form until later, especially through Anaxagoras and Democritus. The two propositions, freed from their indefiniteness and the exaggerations which clung to them in Parmenides' formulation, were added to the truths of mathematics and thus made possible a solid beginning for knowledge of nature.

Parmenides, however, because of the imperfect and indefinite way he conceived these truths, arrived at conclusions which made this worldview too a *useless one for exact research* and so ultimately allowed it a usefulness only for the demonstrations of skepticism. Modern natural science, inasmuch as it proceeds from preservation of matter and energy, transfers the entire changeability and multiplicity of predicates into relations. Parmenides exaggerates the range of the valid basic principle of knowledge of nature which says *ex nihilo nihil fit* and constructs an eternal being, extended continuously in space and excluding all change and motion, one into which all the perfection of the divine world order is merged for him. On its basis he denies the actual, changeable, manifold world and thus cannot explain even its appearance.

Thus *Parmenides, Zeno,* and *Melissus* revolutionized the entire explanation of the world which physical science before them had fashioned. This older physics had explained the cosmos on the basis of a formative principle which included indeterminate change and, with the help of ideas about the motion of matter in space, qualitative change, and emergence of the many from the one. Now *all the constructive principles which this physics used were called into question*. Whatever has magnitude is divisible; in this way I will never arrive at the simple, out of which the composite is made, unless I leave behind the sphere of the spatial. But if I do leave it behind, then I can never put together the spatial out of nonspatial simple being. Likewise, every space between two spatial magnitudes is infinitely divisible. However, every spatial magnitude is contained by another one. The path that a body in motion traverses is infinitely divisible.

In fact, within metaphysics itself it is impossible to resolve the difficulties these thinkers thus demonstrated about space, motion, and multiplicity; only an epistemological standpoint which goes back to the origin of concepts can resolve these contradictions. It recognizes how we encounter reality in observation and how unlimited freedom of the will can arbitrarily divide and combine this reality, how it can use abstraction to reconstruct the real continuum and motion through points or analysis to reconstruct the path of motion into such points, without thereby ever reaching the reality of the fact itself which is observed.

Consciousness of the dark residue of facts not deducible from it pursues every metaphysical theorem like its shadow. Heraclitus's Becoming contradicted his conception of fire as the living substratum to which Becoming clings; the changing world contradicted the Being of Parmenides. The progress of metaphysics tends naturally toward ever more complicated assumptions which, in the same degree, are more apt to explain facts, yet on the other side contain a growing number of inner difficulties.

2. Anaxagoras and the Rise of Monotheistic Metaphysics in Europe

Besides Zeno and Melissus, who thus directed their devastating dialectic against all devices of physical explanation of the world on the basis of the newly won standpoint, there now appeared *Leucippus, Empedocles,* and *Anaxagoras,* who transformed explanation of the physical world on this foundation. That skeptical and this progressive movement exist side by side in the same generation. Even at that time it proved true that in science a useful result accrues to those who do not so much possess the truth, as opposed to error, but who, impelled onward by their faith in knowledge, make a new effort to come closer to it, even if in the process they use assumptions which, given the understanding of the period, they cannot develop free from objections. Thus at that time people used motion and empty space in their explanations, even though doubtless none of the researchers who used these notions was able to get rid of the difficulties they entailed. For this is the purpose complex of human science: one makes attempt after attempt to come closer to reality and make its condition understandable; sound attempts outlast unsound ones. And so the new basic metaphysical concept of an *element* emerged at that time, and the more precisely articulated one of an *atom.* The consequences for the concept of being which the Eleatic school drew from both the principles mentioned had gone beyond what was inherent in these principles. At first, negative consequences emerged as predominant: the world picture of the all-one being destroyed the manifold cosmos. Therefore the will to knowledge now moved beyond it: Leucippus, Empedocles, and Democritus tried to accommodate the principle of being to the task of explaining the changing manifold world.

Their basic theorem began accordingly with Parmenides. There is neither coming to be nor passing away, but—so they continue—*only connection and separation of material particles by means of motion in space.* This theorem appeared among them in completely identical form. We can prove that it derived from the Eleatic school.[4] Of course we can no longer demonstrate the historical relations in which these men evidently stood with respect to one another. Likewise, we unfortunately do not know the kind of argumentation Leucippus, Empedocles, Anaxagoras, and Democritus used to justify their theory of unchanging particles in relation to the one Eleatic Being. However that may be, in the development of European metaphysics from the concept of Being people developed one of several possibilities available, indeed the one closest to hand: breaking up reality into elements which satisfied the demands of thought for unchanging fixed points for its calculation but did not exclude explanation of change, multiplicity, and motion. With that, significant progress was made. In place of force which functioned in indefinite self-transformation or the relation of such force to unbounded matter (Pythagoreans), homogeneous and unchanging elements now appeared. By that force one could explain everything; these elements made possible clear and distinct calculation in explaining the world.

With that *a new class of concepts* appeared in explaining the cosmos. Such were Leucippus' atom, Anaxagoras' seeds of things, Empedocles' elements, and the mathematical figures from which Plato constructed the physical world. The first cause as a ground of explanation (*arkhē*) was a metaphysical category which, as a partial content given uniformly throughout reality, one could make the basis of all reality. People developed the concept of element or particle (atom) from external nature and because of its characteristic of rigid unchangeableness it has validity only for external nature. It is also not an *ingredient* of the reality of nature, that is, a simple concept contained in nature, such as that of motion, speed, force, and mass. Rather, it is a constructive creation for explaining natural phenomena, exactly like the concept of the Platonic idea.

Because the concept of element appeared as a metaphysical reality and was treated as such, *difficulties arose which under these conditions were insuperable*. An example of such a difficulty lay in the assumption already ascribed to Leucippus that one could impute existence not only to being but also to nonbeing, that is, to empty space. And yet, without this assumption motion was impossible. Anaxagoras denies, indeed fights against, empty space,[5] but then of course he cannot explain the deflection of his particles. A further difficulty lay in assuming indivisibility of small bodies, such as the atomists did. It was against this, it appears, that Anaxagoras directed his profound doctrine of the relativity of magnitude.[6] Finally, a difficulty lay in the inexplicability of qualitative change from atoms; Anaxagoras developed a very complex theory in opposition to it, and here one notes what importance the appearance of Protagoras had for the further development of atomic theory. For Protagoras stands between Leucippus and Anaxagoras on the one side and completion of the atomistic system on the other. His theory of sense perception first made possible the scientifically grounded separation of notions of the qualitative from atoms, and that Democritus had an exchange of views with Protagoras, perhaps in a special treatise, has been expressly reported.[7] The atomic theory of Democritus, surrounded by so many difficulties and linked with skepticism through Protagoras, acquired a still more skeptical stance through Metrodorus and Nausiphanes. And thus it came down to Epicurus through Nausiphanes.[8] It maintained itself in defiance of all difficulties because it is a valid part of explanation of nature, as subsequent development will show.

If the concept of particles was a constructionist metaphysical concept, these theoreticians of particles now faced the constructionist problem of whether one could explain the cosmos on their basis alone.

At this stage of development—it was Athens's most beautiful period—in the context of the state of the sciences that the construction of the cosmos in its first grandly conceived projection emerged, which created for European metaphysics its long-lasting power over the mind in our part of the world. This is the doctrine of a world reason, distinct from the cosmos itself, which as the prime mover is the cause of the regular, even purposeful, system in the cosmos.

Monotheism, that is, the idea of one God, who is totally distinct from nature not only in concept but also in actuality and governs the world as a purely spiritual power, arose in the West in connection with astronomical investigations; it was carried in that sphere for two millennia by a rationale which had its support in the conception of the structure of the world. It is with reverence that I approach the man who first thought out this simple connection between regular motions of the stars and a first mover. His person seemed to antiquity to be representative of the direction of the mind toward what was worth knowing [*das Wissenswerte*], ignoring anything which cleverness seeks for its own advantage. "Anaxagoras is supposed to have given the following answer to a person who asked him why after all anyone would prefer being to nonbeing: because of the contemplation of the heavens and the order which prevails throughout the entire cosmos."[9] This passage clarifies the context in which the ancients saw the spirit of his astronomical research as linked with his monotheistic metaphysics. That was the source which suffused his whole being with the character of composed dignity, yes nobility, which, as trustworthy reporters tell us, he communicated to his friend Pericles.[10]

The fragments of his work on nature breathe the same simple majesty. One automatically compares its beginning with the great Israelite document of monotheism, the account of creation. "All things existed together, immense in number and smallness; for even the small was an immense thing. And since all things existed together, nothing stood out distinctly from the rest, on account of the smallness of things."[11] But Anaxagoras analyzes the original state of matter with the means provided by south Italian metaphysics. The oldest idea of matter conceived of as caught up in spontaneous transformation—an idea which permitted one to deduce everything and therefore ultimately nothing—had been put aside in this south Italian metaphysics. In union with it and in agreement with Empedocles and Democritus on this point, Anaxagoras made the following principle the basis of his thought: "The Hellenes speak mistakenly of coming to be and perishing. For nothing comes to be or perishes."[12] Connection and separation, and consequently motion, of substances in space took the place of coming to be and passing away. These particles which Anaxagoras, Leucippus, and Democritus made their foundation have remained the basis of every theory of the system of nature which demands a solid beginning accessible to reason. Anaxagoras's "seeds of things,"[13] or simply "things" (things in miniature, as it were) were distinct from Democritus's atoms in several particulars. Given the state of science at his time, Anaxagoras developed the austerest conceivable realism. In his particles we find every gradation of quality which sense perception encounters anywhere. And because he had no conception of chemical process, he had to resort to two auxiliary principles whose paradoxical character tradition has no longer understood in context. All the seeds of things are contained in every natural object. But the capacity our senses have for sensation is confined within narrow limits, and on this basis he explains the deceptive appearance of qualitative changes.[14] But then we already find in Anaxagoras the theorem concerning the relativity of magnitude, which the sophistic period exploited in a negative sense and whose importance Hobbes later developed independently. It appears that Anaxagoras assumed in this connection that we should also regard every smallest part we can conceive as a system which contains a multiplicity of parts. He has passed down various experiments through which he undertook to establish fundamental concepts in physics. Tradition looked on him as a physicist in an eminent degree.

By means of a daring induction he now translated the physics of earth to the heavenly firmament.

A huge meteorite fell near Aegospotami once in broad daylight. Anaxagoras assumed that it came from the sphere of the stars, and he thus concluded from the fall of this meteorite to the physical homogeneity of the entire structure of the world.[15] Because he estimated the orbit of the moon around the earth to be closer than the orbit of the sun and accordingly derived solar eclipses from the interposition of the moon between the earth and the sun, he must have also concluded from solar eclipses that the moon must be a large and dense mass.[16] We can no longer clearly reproduce the arguments he used in going on to determine positions, magnitudes, and causes of illumination of individual stars. He explained lunar eclipses partially through the earth's shadow and partially through dark bodies located between the earth and the moon. Because the moon describes the path nearest the earth among the planets known to us, it is obvious that it comes between the earth and the sun in solar eclipses. Anaxagoras proposed a theory of phases of the moon; and—we find Plato calling attention to this as Anaxagoras's sensation-making assertion[17]—he deduced the light of the moon (at least partially) from its illumination by the sun; "because the sun goes around it in a circle, it is constantly shedding new light on it (the moon)."[18] In this connection he regards the moon with its depressions and mountains as inhabited. It is reminiscent of the meteorite when he interprets the fable that the Nemean lion has fallen from the sky to mean that it might well have fallen from the moon.[19] He thought of the sun as a burning mass of stone whirling through a more distant region of the sky. And when comparing its size with that of the moon, he declared the sun to be much larger than the Peloponnesus, to which he likened the moon in size. To him stars were also burning masses whose warmth we do not feel only because of distance.

This knowledge of physical homogeneity in the constitution of all bodies served him as a general principle, so that on the basis of the fact of the revolution of the stars (which served him as a minor premise) he could draw his great metaphysical conclusion. For the theorem about the physical homogeneity of all bodies in the world also contains the insight that gravity operates in all of them. This made it necessary to assume an extraordinarily powerful force counteracting gravity, a force which has produced and now maintains the circular motion of these ponderous and mighty bodies. In the case of the great meteorite mentioned, Anaxagoras appended this explanation: the entire world of stars consists of stones; if the mighty rotation were to let up, then they would have to fall down.[20] Without ascribing this comparison to Anaxagoras, the sources liken this relationship underlying the rotation of the stars—between gravity which pulls the heavenly bodies downward and the force producing the rotation which prevents their falling—to the relationship by which the stone does not fall out of the sling and water is not spilled out of a rotating basin if the rotation is faster than the downward motion of the water.[21]

At the point we have reached with this conclusion we now find a second, allied conclusion, whose parts we can perhaps still supply convincingly. Anaxagoras used it to identify the force which produces revolutions of the stars in space as a continually and purposefully working one which, though separated altogether from earth's matter, provokes and maintains the revolution of the stars from the outside. Thus the world-principle of reason (*nous*) makes its way into history through the vehicle of astronomical reasoning.

The revolution Anaxagoras traces to the force opposing gravity is one he expressly identifies with the revolution (*perikhōrēsis*) "in which the stars, sun and moon, air and ether presently turn."[22] This revolution is naturally the apparent one in which the entire heaven with all its stars moves once every day from east to west around our earth. Anaxagoras knew of the turning of the entire earth on its axis, even though he did not yet grasp this concept of axis in its mathematical rigor. If he now followed the parallel orbits in which some of the stars revolve in part over the horizon and others do so completely, even to the smallest orbits of the Bear or of the star β of the Little Bear, which then stood closest to the pole, then he must have constructed an idea for himself, no matter how imperfect, of the northern terminus of this axis.[23] At this point a combination of reports appears unavoidable, one which enables us for the first time to establish their relationship to one another and to the state of astronomy at that time.[24] *This position,* which would form the northern terminus of a spindle around which we would imagine the revolution as taking place, *is the cosmic point from which* nous (world reason) *started the rotating motion in matter* and from which it is still currently operated. *Nous* began with the small, and the point at which this happened was the pole. The pole was accordingly the place at which rotation began; then from there the rotation expanded more and more and will continue to expand; and, from that rotation, separation of particles of matter was achieved along with the rotation. Reconstruction of Anaxagoras's basic view in this way is only a clearer idea of what the following propositions contain: the revolution produced by *nous* is identical with the present revolution of the earth; *nous,* however, has effected this revolution from a small initial point and has expanded the revolution more and more from there. For these propositions take us to a starting point at which the smallest orbit of the globe is described.

If one begins with this basic conception, one perceives how Anaxagoras decided on his monotheism. If he had begun with distribution of the effect of gravity in all the heavenly bodies and postulated a counteractive force, so now he concluded further on the basis of universal rotation of all locations on the earth (while he reserved a special mechanical ground for explaining special movements of the sun, moon, and planets) to a *power independent of the matter of these bodies, purposeful, and therefore operating intelligently.* "The other has joined a part of everything to itself. But *nous* is an immense and tyrannical being and is not mixed together with anything[25] but rather rests alone for itself and on itself."[26] Above all: *nous* must be distinguished from matter, for if it were mixed with "the other," the element mixed in with it would hinder its ability to dominate things as it now does, because it is based on itself alone.[27] Indeed, on the whole it was simplest to think of such an independent power producing the universal revolution as spatially separated from the earth and as producing the rotation and formation of the world from a point of leverage outside it. For Anaxagoras, to whom *nous* was the "lightest" and "purest" of all "things" and consequently a type of refined matter or rather something located *on the fringes of* materiality, this conception was unavoidable. Furthermore, knowledge of the universal motions of the entire celestial sphere completed this argument to the effect that this force operating from the outside was one. Finally, consideration of the inner purposefulness of the world structure and of individual organizations of the earth showed this first mover to be a *nous,* which acted according to an inner purposefulness. This teleology of the universe does not consist, however, in its orientation to human purposes but rather is an immanent teleology whose expression is beauty and whose corollary for understanding is a unified system, which thus points back to an ordering, but, so to speak, impersonal intelligence.[28]

So in the most beautiful epoch of Greek history, out of the science of the cosmos (especially research in astronomy), Greek monotheism sprang up, that is, the idea of conscious purpose as director of the unified and purposeful sum total of motion in the cosmos and of reason as the independently and purposefully acting mover. The Athenian population of those days—partly from a sense of an alien sort of sublimity they sensed in him, partly as a joke—called the man who devised that idea *"nous."* This great teaching enveloped the circle of Anaxagoras, Pericles, and Phidias with a strangeness which people of traditional belief felt strongly, and this made it unpopular. Phidias gave this idea its artistic expression in his statue of Zeus.[29]

This is not the place to show specifically how Anaxagoras overcame the difficulties attendant on carrying through his great idea. An imagined difficulty forced him to the first step in his more precise construction of the origin of the world. The affair is very indicative of the preponderance of ideas of geometrical regularity in the Greek mind. The oblique position of the pole and of the parallel orbits of the stars relative to the horizon led him to assume that originally revolution of the stars took place parallel to the horizon from east to west and that consequently the rotational axis of the earth stood perpendicular to the upper surface of the earth (to which he imputed the form of a flat cylinder [*Walze*]). The terminus of this axis touched the cupola which thus arose above the horizon in the middle (at the zenith). Then, because the surface of the earth inclined toward the south, the pole acquired its present position; and in fact this happened right after the emergence of organic life on earth. The reporters relate this to the emergence of varying climates and inhabited versus uninhabitable zones of the earth.[30]

Anaxagoras's conception of how the stars and their paths came to be through the rotation which *nous* introduced into the world's matter is very imperfect. One sees here also, just as in atomic theory: from particular premises which conform to modern science there are still no corresponding results, because other necessary premises are lacking and false physical ideas abstracted from sense appearance are put in their place. What is bound together in Anaxagoras's primordial state is torn apart through rotation and, as its nature dictates, the warm-shining-fiery substance Anaxagoras calls ether now rises upward. From the atmosphere the watery element is precipitated downward and from it the solid element which, in accordance with a further basic idea, strives toward a state of rest. From this sinking mass the revolving motion tears off parts which now rotate as stars.

But at this point the vital question of this cosmogony first appears. Anaxagoras above all had to answer the challenge of explaining heavenly motions known to him which do *not* admit of being subordinated to the daily universal rotation: for example, the annual motion of the sun, the path of the moon, and the apparently irregular movements of the other planets known to him. He explained these movements mechanically by introducing a third cosmic cause[31] in the counterpressure of air squeezed together by the revolution of these stars.

Here was the point which made this grandly conceived cosmogony of Anaxagoras appear no longer possible by Plato's time. More exact knowledge of the apparent paths of the five planets visible to the naked eye—whose number was already determined by Plato's time—made the explanation based on counterpressure of the air appear totally inadequate. So Anaxagoras's monotheistic metaphysics underwent a remarkable transformation.

From the special motion of the planets one side eliminated the common daily motion of the entire heavens on the plane of the equator as fictitious and traced it to a daily movement of the earth. Consequently, it did not need to adapt these special movements of the planets to a common rotation. The other side conceived of an enormous mechanism which would produce the complex motion of the planets in the general movement of the heavens. It accordingly abandoned the assumption of a single simple force to explain this system of movements. The first option is one first adopted by the Pythagoreans; we find this cosmic view in the fragments of *Philolaus*. The astronomical school, joined by Aristotle, tried the second one, and then the dominant metaphysics of the Middle Ages based itself partially on this view and partially on the new attempt of *Hipparchus* and *Ptolemy*. Hence this dominant European metaphysics was led further in elaborating its notion of the force which moved the celestial world by analyzing the more complicated paths of the planets. This analysis took place according to the rule of astronomical research Plato formulated: if one sets out from paths which planets describe in the heavens, then one should look for uniform and regular movements which explain the given paths without doing violence to the facts.[32] This formula for the task embraces a correct conception of problem and method but also includes that arbitrary presupposition about the movements which pinned down ancient astronomy to the task of tracing things to orbital movements. Because this formula was used, Anaxagoras's doctrine of the world-moving *nous* was transformed into Aristotle's doctrine of a realm of spirits in which, under the first, unmoved mover who immediately effects the perfect motion of the sphere of the fixed stars, the revolution of other numerous spheres with just as many eternal and incorporeal beings is produced.

3. Mechanistic Worldview Established by Leucippus and Democritus; Causes of Its Temporary Powerlessness against Monotheistic Metaphysics

At the time, it was in vain that this great teaching about reason's purposeful direction of the world was opposed by the atomistic worldview which Leucippus and Democritus established and through Epicurus and Lucretius stretched to Gassendi and to modern theories of a pure mechanics of particles. Among the reasons which stood in the way of Democritus's influence in his time was in the first place certainly the fact that, based on his premises, a more exact explanation of the motions of the heavenly bodies was totally impossible at that time.

We have already described how, along with the general state of Greek science after the emergence of Parmenidean metaphysics, the theory of material particles also appeared; its representatives were Empedocles, Anaxagoras, Leucippus, and Democritus.[33] And it is still possible to show how the atomistic theory of the last two thinkers named was chiefly grounded in metaphysical considerations. For Leucippus and Democritus, assuming the reality of movement and of division, proved their theory from the Eleatic concept of being as an indivisible unity and from its concomitant denial of coming to be and passing away:[34] in this way they deduced the atom and empty space.

We are trying to clarify the significance of atomistic theory in the form invented at that time by Leucippus and Democritus. In the process we are prescinding entirely from its metaphysical grounding we have just spoken of and we are separating consideration of its general scientific value from that of its usefulness in the state of science at that time. As established now by Leucippus and Democritus, this atomistic theory—measured by *its scientific usefulness*—is the *most significant metaphysical theory of all antiquity.* It is the simple expression of the demand made by knowledge on its object, that it have solid and constant foundations for the play of changes, of coming to be and passing away. The atomistic theory achieves this by using natural understanding to trace the processes of division and composition of things and the apparent disappearance of a thing together with its reappearance in the alteration of its compositional form [*Aggregatzustandes*[35]]. In this way it arrives at small things or substances which, because they continuously fill space, are indivisible wholes. For if tearing something into pieces is regarded as possible because this thing consists of discrete parts, then the limits of such tearing up consist in parts not further divisible because they are no longer composed of discrete parts. Atomistic theory can then designate the indivisible units as unchangeable, just as the true Parmenidean substances are; for atomistic theory holds that change can be explained only by a displacement of parts. Finally—and this is the true meaning of all genuine atomistic theory—it can *transfer this graphic picture of movements in space,* distances, extensions, and masses *to this world of the tiny which is hidden from sight.* Empty space also belongs among the components of this vivid picture. For before we develop adequate concepts of the atmosphere, we believe we see things withdraw into empty space, and even after correcting this idea we can think of motion only with the help of this auxiliary concept of an empty something into which objects withdraw. This simple intuition [*Anschaulichkeit*] is supplemented by two further theorems. We trace every action which takes place in the cosmos to touch, pressure, and impulse; accordingly, we reduce every change to the motion of persistently homogeneous atoms in space. Hence all impressions of qualities apart from density, hardness, and weight are ascribed to sensation and removed from the objects themselves.[36] This type of consideration must have been agreeable to an understanding occupied with sensible objects, even if at first it had only the validity of metaphysics, as long as it provided even a meager applicability to problems of natural science. And that is why, once this kind of thinking occurred, it was never again lost to Greek thought.

But this atomistic theory was unable to attain hegemony at the time of Leucippus and Democritus because *conditions were lacking for its use in explaining phenomena.* Movements of masses in space constituted the chief problem of natural science in those days, and since the appearance of Anaxagoras, investigation of the planets had come more and more to the fore. Nevertheless, in decisive aspects of his astronomical construction, Democritus still leaned on Anaxagoras, even though the latter's theory was bound to prove inadequate. In fact, Democritus's assumptions afforded him no means at all for astronomical explanations.

If one assumes[37] that he considered the fall of atoms in empty space from up above downward because of their weight and that he considered the ratio of velocity of this falling motion to their mass as presuppositions for explaining the cosmos and that consequently he devised a coherent mechanical viewpoint, then the grounds of explanation he used appear to be totally inadequate. The misproportion between this theory and explanation of the rationally ordered cosmos in this case could scarcely provoke anything other than a smile in Plato's mathematical school. For even the path of a thrown body could demonstrate how transitory the effect of individual impulses of atoms striking one another is when compared with constant downward pressure of gravity.

Nevertheless this view of reports concerning Democritus is hardly tenable. Democritus clung to his position that eternal motion of atoms in empty space was determined by their relation to empty space. He conceived the original state of motion as a circular movement of all atoms, as *dinos*. In this *dinos* atoms strike against one another and combine, and out of their aggregation a cosmos takes shape, which is then finally pulverized by a cosmos composed of mightier masses. Wherever a particular linkage of atoms occurs, there exists in it a definite quantitative proportion of atomic mass to empty space contained in the connection. This determines difference in weights among [masses of] equal magnitude and ascension of some atomic connections and descension of other ones, with correspondingly different velocity. The vagueness and erroneousness of these basic conceptions must have made such movement of atoms appear entirely worthless for explaining the world.

The same situation obtains in biology, in which we can still recognize in the sources the original advance Democritus made in knowledge of nature; in fact, in this area Democritus is clearly the only notable predecessor of Aristotle. Insofar as still largely unclassified fragments and reports shed light on the matter, Democritus's merit consisted in constructing a painstaking descriptive science; indeed in this regard he does not even disdain to clarify a state of affairs by using the idea of a teleological relationship between the organs of the animal body and the tasks of its life.

This enables us to understand what happened next. Europe's monotheistic metaphysics pushed aside, as unsatisfactory constructions, not only pantheistic elements of the older period (which continued to have influence through Diogenes of Apollonia) but also the mechanical explanation of the world. But it was unable to destroy them utterly. *The mechanical worldview* expressed a possibility conformable to reason and continued to stand, with strong consciousness of its power rooted in its reckoning with sensible facts; its day of victory did not come of course until experimental methods gained mastery over those facts. *The pantheistic worldview* corresponded to a disposition of mind which soon effected its renewal in the Stoical school. But stronger than these two basic metaphysical views was the *skeptical spirit*. In the Eleatic school it had uncovered contradictions in basic conceptions of physics of the cosmos which no metaphysics could resolve. Using the contradiction involved in Becoming, it made a playground of skepticism out of the school of Heraclitus. This skeptical spirit had grown with every new metaphysical attempt, and it now deluged the whole of Greek science. It was favored by changes in the social and political life of Athens which, since Anaxagoras, centralized Greek science. It was assisted by a change in scientific interests which pushed preoccupation with intellectual facts, with language, rhetoric, and the state into the foreground. Under these circumstances the beginning of epistemology emerged in contrast with science of the cosmos.

Let us look ahead for a moment. Under these circumstances, what will be *the fate of the monotheistic worldview?* Not even the skeptical movement disturbed monotheistic metaphysics; intuition of the rational structure of the cosmos gave it a ground independent of particular metaphysical positions; in addition, an inner development of religious life carried it; and that is how Plato and Aristotle will complete it on the new foundation laid down by the Sophists and Socrates. The highest expression which the Greek mind discovered for the structure of the world came into being, an expression which appears to intuition as the beautiful and to knowledge as the rational.

This will happen because the fundamental idea of monotheism links up with a *new determination* of the essential element in which the *structure of the cosmos* can be discovered. If one looks for what truly exists, one has a choice of two paths. One can analyze the changing world into constant components whose relations change; or one can seek constancy in the uniformity which thought grasps within change itself. And we can find this uniformity first of all in the recurring contents of reality. Long periods will transpire during which human intelligence will persist mainly at this level of knowledge. And then, in consequence of a profoundly probing analysis of phenomena, it will find the rule of changes in the law; with that the possibility arises of finding approaches to this law in the constant components.

But something else also happens. Every form of European thought is followed by a skeptical awareness of difficulties and contradictions in its basic assumptions. Over and over again metaphysics tirelessly begins anew the labor of construction at a profounder level of abstraction. Will not the difficulties and contradictions which accompany metaphysics always return, only in a more complicated way?

4. Period of Socrates and the Sophists; Method of Establishing the Basis of Knowledge Is Introduced

Since about the middle of the fifth century B.C. a new intellectual revolution took place in Greece which moved minds more profoundly than any other change of ideas had done since the event of the rise of science itself.

The skeptical spirit grew with every new metaphysical scheme and now asserted itself with sovereign self-consciousness. Social and political changes strengthened the feeling of independence in individuals. They brought about a change in the direction of interests, by which technology in activity connected with the life of the state moved to the foreground of social reality. They created a brilliant occupational class, the *Sophists,* who as though by magic attracted the attention of all Greece and responded to the newly emergent demand by offering higher instruction in political affairs. Besides nature, the world of mind began to open up for the Greeks.

At the beginning of this convulsion of all scientific concepts Protagoras, the leading mind of this new professional class before Gorgias, expressed the formula of the period. The relativism to which this formula gave expression contains the initial impulse of a theory of knowledge.

Man is "the measure of all things, of things that are, how they are, and of things that are not, how they are not"; this was the statement in the famous beginning of his chief philosophical treatise. Whatever appears to be so for each person *is* so for him. But we must understand these theses of Protagoras exactly in relation to the limits in which we can prove them with certainty from the meager fragments. They are not the expression of a general theory of consciousness which commanded every given fact of consciousness. Hence they do not contain our current critical standpoint. Instead, they are only the formula for his ingenious theory of perception which had obviously developed under the influence of medical ideas of his time, and they are limited in that context to predicative determinations about the external world; but they do not call the reality of that external world into question. Let us elucidate this further. The major premise of the argument which led to his formula was: knowledge is external perception. We can no longer establish whether this major premise was a presupposition of his standpoint not expressly brought to consciousness or whether he laid it down with deliberate clarity. The minor premise indicated about perception that it could not be separated from its object nor could the object be separated from it, that is, the perceived object cannot be separated from the perceiving subject for whom it is there. Thus Protagoras is the founder of the theory of relativism, which was later developed further by the skeptics.[38] But this relativism of his asserted that the qualities of things existed only in relationship; still he did not assert this about objectivity [*Dinglichkeit*] itself. If one mentally sets aside the subject which tastes sweetness, then "sweet" no longer exists; it exists only in relation to sensation. But his more detailed theory of perception shows that he did not think that the object itself disappeared with the sensation of the sweet. If an object comes into contact with a sense organ so that the object is active and the organ is passive, then seeing, hearing, or the particular sense perception takes place in this sense organ; but the object now appears as colored, sounding—in short, in various sensible qualities. This explanation of the event first made possible a theory of perception for Protagoras's relativism. One can clearly see that he could not at one and the same time posit reality of movement outside the subject as that which caused perception to occur for that subject, and also do away with reality of movement by calling into question all objectivity itself.[39] Then he unfolded different states of the perceiving subject and thus showed the dependence of qualities of the phenomenal object on these states. So his theory of perception produced the paradox that perceptions contradict one another, yet they are all equally true.[40]

This *relativism,* along with the skepticism of the Eleatic and Heraclitean philosophers, led Plato to look for knowledge beyond changing phenomena. Relativism could be spiritedly driven off by Aristotle, but not refuted. It held on to its followers and appears after Aristotle in the armor of the skeptical school, an armor impenetrable to Greek metaphysics of the cosmos.

Sophist writings drawing skeptical consequences from the negative wing of the Eleatic school were far less important. One of them was the nihilistic inflammatory essay by *Gorgias* "On the Nonexistent, or Nature." It marks the extremest point to which content-empty skepticism proceeded. But it is important to establish that, even at this point, the assumptions of the metaphysics of the ancients were not infringed on. We have no indication that Gorgias might have maintained the phenomenalism of the external world. *No Greek* did that; for that would have meant that he would have *crossed over* the line from objective standpoint to *that of self-consciousness.* Instead, Gorgias's controversial thesis in fact presupposes that *another being apart from that of the external world does not exist.* In genuine Greek fashion he cancels out being by showing that one cannot think the external world through concepts contained in it. He does this by means of an assumption about being which shows that he is still completely caught up in objective science of the cosmos. For he destroys the possibility that being should be thought of as without a beginning and as one, a position the Eleatics had handed down, through arguments based on the spatiality of being. Thus this spatiality of being appears as a presupposition of his thinking.[41] Of a piece with this is that he attributes to all being that it be either moved or at rest, but then thinks of movement in the sense that it includes division. He has no conception of the idea that, once he has destroyed the concepts which make it possible to think of the external world, the subject which perceives and thinks might still remain behind as reality. So we see skepticism knocking up against the limits of Greek thought in his mind; but it does not break through.

For before self-reflection discovered in the subject itself a reality not susceptible to any doubt, people sought out reality only by way of immersion into the system of nature. Hence when reality was denied in antiquity, this denial was linked either with a tragic consciousness of separation of knowledge from its object or with a frivolous consciousness which played with appearance and delighted in it.[42]

Socrates' mighty intelligence was the arena where a profound and persistent mental labor took place, which led to the attainment of a new stage in the purpose complex of knowledge. In sophistry he encountered a doubting, testing subject before which current metaphysics could not hold its own. He sought for anchorage among the enormous convulsions besetting all ideas; this positive element in his great truth-thirsty nature set him apart from the Sophists. He first persistently applied the method of *going back from current knowledge and belief of his time to the justification* [Rechtsgrund] *for every proposition.*[43] In other words, in place of a method which derives from original ideas he posited a method which traces every idea to its logical ground.[44] And indeed, just as even scientific life among this Greek people was a public life, the simplest and most readily available form of investigation of the ground for the swirl of opinions had to be the *question* concerning this logical ground which would not let go of the person interrogated until he had said all that could be said: *Socratic discourse.*[45] It unleashed analytic method in the history of intelligence, a method which traced things to the final epistemological basis for a scientific state of affairs and finally for scientific conviction in general. Hence this discourse, once the tireless questioner had been reduced to silence by his judges, became the technical form of his school's philosophy. Inasmuch as he thus tested current science and current convictions with respect to their legitimacy, he proved that *there was still no science in existence,* indeed in any area at all.[46] From the entire science of the cosmos the only thing which stood up to his method was tracing the purposeful structure in the cosmos to a world-shaping reason. But he also found no clear consciousness of scientific necessity in the sphere of moral or social life. He saw the activity of the statesman and the method of the poet as lacking all clarity concerning their logical ground and therefore as incapable of justifying themselves before thought. At the same time, however, he discovered that *just* and *unjust, good* and *bad, beautiful* and *ugly,* have unchangeable *meaning,* free from the strife of opinions.

Here, in the area of behavior, the power of self-reflection he introduced into history achieved positive results. The epistemological ground for propositions and principles in this area lies first of all in ethical consciousness. Although Socrates set out from prevalent notions and dominant principles of his time, he tested them in particular cases and by the attitude of ethical consciousness toward them, and in this way, making his way through contrary instances, he developed ethical concepts. He defined his method more precisely by questioning moral consciousness so that, using general concepts involving it as the ground of knowledge, he could develop and justify concepts which could provide a clear standard for behavior.[47]

But has Socrates gone beyond the limits we have designated as those for Greek man in general? It does not dawn even on Socrates' self-reflection that the external world is a phenomenon of self-consciousness, but that in that self-consciousness being and reality is given to us, the knowledge of which for the very first time discloses for us an unassailable reality. To be sure, this self-reflection is the deepest point which Greek man reached on the way back to true positivism, just as Gorgias' frivolous "nothing" indicates the extreme limit to which his skeptical attitude attained. But it was only the way back to the epistemological basis of knowledge; hence out of it sprang logic as theory of knowledge, which Plato saw as a possibility and Aristotle carried out. The search for the epistemological basis for ethical principles in consciousness took place in this context, then; and out of that search comes Platonic-Aristotelian ethics. Hence this self-reflection is logical and ethical; it draws up rules for the relation of thought to external being in knowledge of the external world and, for the relation of will to external being, in activity. But there is still no inkling in it that in self-consciousness a mighty reality is surfacing, indeed the only one of which we are immediately conscious; still less is there an inkling that all reality is given to us only in our experience. For this reality will not be available for metaphysical reflection until the will steps into its purview.

5. Plato

Using the new method of Socrates, Plato further developed the science of the cosmos, of its rational structure, and of its reasonable unitary first cause. Thus, reflecting the scientific result produced by Socrates, *metaphysics as the science of reason* came into being. Out of his writings we select only this progress in the structure of knowledge; at this point we resist the magic of those writings which arises from the fusion of such principles with the sensibilities of a genius who was saturated with the beauty of the Greek world.

Progress of Metaphysical Method.

The progress mentioned was achieved in the Socratic school. Science (at that time one called it philosophy) now no longer consists of inferring phenomena from a principle, but is a conceptual system in which a *proposition* is guaranteed by its *epistemological basis*. To Plato's logical mind all thinkers before Socrates appeared to be tellers of fairy tales.

> Everyone, it appears, has told us his little story as though we were children. One says that being is threefold in nature; at one time there was strife among its parts, but then peace was made, there were marriages and procreations and rearing of children. Another holds that being is dual in character—moist and dry, or warm and cold; he makes a common bed for its two parts and has them marry. But our Eleatic folk, going back to Xenophanes and even earlier, tells its story as though what we call everything were only one thing.[48]

In contrast with all this, for Socrates' pupil the mark of true knowledge is the connection between the proposition and its epistemological ground and the *conceptual necessity* determined by that connection.[49] This system of knowledge based on cause and effect thus appears to consciousness as that which constitutes science. In fact, Plato's organizing mind directs the Socratic question about the connection of principles people assert with what is established in consciousness, not to those whom he finds in the marketplace—as Socrates did—but rather to tellers of fairy tales of former days in general, "as if they were present themselves."[50] He uses the Socratic method in questioning: dialogue is thus his technical style; dialectic is his method; Socrates, whom his enemies killed in order to silence his questions, is the leader of the discussion; it is on his behalf that Plato now takes revenge on these enemies.

Indeed, because Plato's organizing mind encompassed the mathematics of the period in his school and made this school a focal point of mathematical thought, especially by testing mathematical science of nature (particularly astronomy) with respect to its theoretical value and its evidence, the idea of bringing our knowledge to an accounting produced the *first insight* into the coherent *organization of sciences* of the cosmos. Philosophy now acquired the task of going back from presuppositions introduced in those sciences without accounting for their validity to ultimate cognitive grounds which contain this accounting.[51] And so there arose in Plato a clear consciousness of the problem whose solution on the formal side was Greek epistemology and on the material side Greek metaphysics. These two fundamental philosophical sciences were unseparated in Plato's mind, and even for Aristotle they were only two sides of the same cognitive system. Plato labeled this cognitive system dialectic.

Hence rendering an account of knowledge was added to previous investigation, which had been directed to first causes. Knowledge looks for the *actual conditions* we must assume to enable us to think of being, knowledge, the cosmos, and ethical willing. For Plato these conditions lie in the *Ideas* and their mutual relations. The Ideas are not subject to the relativity of sense perception and are not affected by difficulties attending knowledge of the changing world; on the contrary, they take their place alongside knowledge of the static, always homogeneous and typical *spatial figures* and their *relations,* as well as of *numbers* and their *proportions.* Like them the Ideas are never regarded as particular external objects in the unstable condition of the world; in their typical state, however, they are conditions, presentable to understanding and accessible to rigorous scientific treatment, which make existence [*Dasein*] as well as knowledge of the world possible.[52]

The revolutionary convulsion of European science thus led to a *higher stage of methodical thought;* let us sketch the relation of this stage to the older attempts we are now leaving behind us.

As the development since Thales shows, the means of previous intellectual advances consisted in expanding experience and adapting explanations to its condition. The cognitive method which history of the sciences discloses in this connection consisted in positing assumptions (substitution) and then tentatively using them: many imperfect explanations constantly fall by the wayside as we watch this cruelty of the nexus of purposes continually wrought around us against the painstaking labor of individuals and are ourselves threatened by that cruelty; but explanations fit to survive accommodate themselves step by step to the demands of knowledge of reality and so develop further. This is how the atomistic theory and the theory of substantial forms gradually developed. And mathematics, though still to a modest degree, was already used as the foundation of this ordering of experiences under viable explanations. Explanations of science up to the revolution brought about by Plato consist only in an unmethodical etiological argument to a cosmic causal structure. From Plato on, explanation consists in *methodically working back to conditions* which make a science of the cosmos possible. This method proceeds from the correspondence of the structure of knowledge with the real structure of the cosmos. Therefore, based on a natural point of view, it regards these conditions as in some way causes (hence presuppositions, principles). Just as this form of scientific procedure is described for its own sake, so logic sets itself apart from the metaphysical system itself, even though both remain in inner contact with each other, through the assumption of their mutual correspondence. Aristotle was to be the first to take this step, and he thereby created full methodological clarity for this metaphysics erected on the basis of the natural worldview. Accordingly, his logic is nothing but an exposition of the more perfect method of metaphysics that we have just described.

Doctrine of Substantial Forms of the Cosmos Enters into Monotheistic Metaphysics

What are, then, the principles that provide this justification of our knowledge and whose development is the final goal of Plato's science?

European metaphysics now takes a further decisive step with respect to its content as well. The state of science was such that notions like those of the origin and perfection of orbital motions in the heavens or of the striving of every earthly body set in motion for its state of rest had not yet been improved through a persistent, experimentally supported effort to break down complex structures into individual relations of dependence. Under such scientific conditions it was really impossible to conduct a cognitively useful search for constant conditions of the changeable world among *atoms* and their characteristics. For between these atoms and the structure of forms of the cosmos there was no connection whatever. It was in the *system of forms* themselves and in *psychical causes* corresponding to that system that the European mind had to see the world's metaphysical system which contained its ultimate ground of explanation.

Who would not feel in the captivating brilliance of Plato's most beautiful works that the Ideas were valid not merely as conditions for the given in his rich, poetic, morally powerful soul! His starting points are the moral person, enthusiasm, love, the beautiful, rational, harmonious world; his ideal is the truly existing, which encompasses all perfection in it which his sublime spiritual orientation demanded. He *saw* the Ideas in these facts; he did not merely think them as conditions for them. At this point, however, we must exclude any discussion which deals with the origin of this great teaching. We are concerned with the organization of his thoughts insofar as it enters into argumentation and in this systematic form influences further development of European metaphysics.

The *movement of the metaphysical mind* which sets out *from Plato* finds Being, which is inferred from Becoming and Passing Away, in the background of phenomena that appear in time and space, a background which our *universal ideas* express or to which they lead up. Metaphysics thus merely continues what language has begun. Language has already set apart substances from individual appearances in the words for general ideas, especially for genera and species. Our usage of words inevitably entails that we feel this constantly recurring element which conceptualization brings to things as a type is a power over them which forces these things to realize a law. The general idea, which receives a finished expression in the verbal sign, already contains a *knowledge of what is permanently uniform* in the coming and going of impressions insofar as we can produce this knowledge *without analysis of appearances,* hence from mere intuition of them alone. However, we accomplish this process in speech without awareness of the value of its products for knowing the structure of appearances. But because we *become aware of this* and consequently determine, correct, and define these general notions in their relationship to facts they represent and to other general notions ordered next to, above, or below them, the *concept* and system of concepts comes into being. And because philosophy undertakes to determine the content and structure of the world in the system of these concepts, the form of metaphysics emerges which we can label "a philosophy of the concept." It has dominated European thought until, so to speak, the curtain was drawn away from the deeper-lying uniformity of the world system.

This *metaphysics of substantial forms* expressed what the unaided eye of knowledge sees. What the play of forces in the cosmos constantly produces anew constitutes a cognizable, always selfsame content of the world. And what constantly recurs amid changes of locations, conditions, and times—no, rather is always there and never disappears—makes up an imperishable system of *ideas.* Though the individual person appears and disappears at a specific point in space and time, what the concept of man expresses nevertheless abides. Likewise, this is all we think of, for the most part, when we struggle to conceive of the content of the world. We think of genera and species and characteristics and activities which make up letters of the text of this world. Looked at in their relations to one another and as natural knowledge sees them, these things are the constant condition of the world which natural knowledge *discovers in a finished state,* on which it *can change nothing at all,* and which thus confronts it as an objective and timeless condition. And once we then coined those letters and text as scientific concepts, they contained our knowledge of the world's makeup for as long a time as we were unable to take phenomena apart and trace them analytically to interaction of laws. During this whole period metaphysics of substantial forms was the last word in European knowledge. And even later, metaphysical thought encountered a new problem in relating the mechanism of nature to this ideally and teleologically conceived content of the world process.

However, from the standpoint of the natural system of our ideas—one that metaphysics adopts—we cannot appropriately define the *relationship of these ideas,* constituting as they do the fixed content of the world process, to that world process, that is, to *reality.* By distinguishing what we find in thought as a ground of explanation (with respect to its origin and the validity conditioned by that origin) from what we find as reality in perception, theory of knowledge, for the first time, was able to express correctly the relation of object to idea. That is why we see every metaphysical theory of this relationship destroyed through its contradictions; each one foundered on the impossibility of expressing conceptually the content of the relationship of ideas to objects. But positive science, which looked for the universal in the law of the changeable, established for the first time the truly scientific foundation which established limits of validity and the basis of stability for these types of reality.

This was in general the historical position of the metaphysics of substantial forms created by Plato in the pattern of intellectual development.

Within this metaphysics of substantial forms, however, Plato developed only *one of the possibilities* for expressing the relation of these *Ideas* to reality and to *individual things* and therefore for bringing the real being of the Ideas and the real being of individual things into an inner objective unity. *Plato's Idea* is the object of conceptual thought. Just as conceptual thinking extracts the Idea from things as archetypical, as graspable only in thought, and as perfect, so the Idea subsists as an independent substance apart from the particular things that participate in it, to be sure, but remain behind it. The realm of these eternal, imperishable, invisible Ideas appears to be connected in the Greek mind, as though by golden threads, with mythical faith. We are preparing to present the demonstration of the theory of Ideas by stressing a few simple components of its structure to which the writings which lie open before us constantly refer us.

The critique of sense perception and of the reality it reveals had led to undeniable results; hence Plato found himself steered toward thought and truth given in thought. In this context he now separated the object of thought from that of sensation. For he fully acknowledged the subjectivity of sense impressions, but did not press on to the insight that the fact of Being itself is also included in these impressions, that is, in experience. Hence in this reality given through experience he does not grasp the object of thought at the same time; he does not consider thinking in its natural relationship to perceiving. On the contrary, *thinking* for him meant *grasping a special reality,* that is, Being itself. To be sure, he thereby avoided the inner contradiction into which the objectivism of Aristotle ran later through his assumption of a *universal real entity in the particular,* but of course he fell into difficulties of a different nature. With the passage of years a tendency grew in Plato to develop a rigorous science out of relations of these Ideas. To the Greek of that time the process by which mathematics had freed itself from practical affairs as a science and had brought its principles into relationship with one another was still recent; in his school Plato now wished to establish alongside, indeed above, mathematics the *science of relations of concepts* as well. But as important as these theoretical motives for the doctrine of Ideas were, for Plato that doctrine had support at a deeper level in other motives which go beyond knowledge. Even after the mythical system had given way to scientific thought, we encounter something which stems from the fullness of the life of the soul as the inextinguishable background behind all rational discoveries: in Heraclitus' World Law as well as in the Eternal Being of the Eleatics; it is the background behind the Numbers of the Pythagoreans and the Love and Hate of Empedocles and Anaxagoras' Reason, yes even behind Democritus' Soul diffused throughout the world. Socrates and Plato now brought what had been lived through or experienced to philosophical consciousness in a still wider sense. Methodical self-reflection led to emergence of the great *ethical facts,* which had existed before as well, but which had remained to some extent below the horizon of philosophical consciousness. One can raise the question whether the doctrine of Ideas in its first conception, such as we have it in the *Phaedrus,* was not still restricted to moral ideas. Regardless of how we answer this question, the typical and archetypical in the Ideas proves what role the elevated disposition of Plato's mind, the moral and esthetic elements, played in building up his world of Ideas.

It was this, therefore, that the young Plato, with the eye of genius, read out of the conceptual definitions of his teacher. We can describe the true, eternal Being in the system of concepts which grasp the abiding element in change. These components that we can describe in concepts—the Ideas, and their relations to one another—make up the conceptually necessary conditions of the given. In this connection Plato flatly designates the doctrine of Ideas a "sure hypothesis."[53] As has been rightly observed, the science of these Ideas, his science, is therefore ontological, not genetic, in character.

However, what the concept does not grasp in reality and what one consequently cannot make comprehensible from the Idea is *matter*. It is an amorphous, undefined essence, the cause and ground of explanation (insofar as it explains anything at all) of change and imperfection in phenomena, the obscure residue which Plato's science leaves behind from reality as something apart from thought and ultimately incomprehensible, a term for a nonconcept, that is, for X, closer consideration of which would later destroy this whole doctrine of Forms.

Foundation of This Metaphysics of Substantial Forms; Its Monotheistic Conclusion

What are, then, the *parts of the demonstration* Plato used to show that the Ideas which he saw in man's morally powerful spirit and in the cosmos filled with beauty and rationality were conditions for the given? Or which he used to derive their definitions and draft the science of their relations?

It was in conformity with the structure of the great movement he brought into being that he put the demand to demonstrate the *possibility of knowing* in the forefront. He saw this possibility disputed all around by the Sophists; Socrates, in an expansion of philosophical reflection, had defended it; intellectual interest was turned toward it.

Plato's *demonstration* from knowledge is *indirect*. It excludes the possibility that knowledge should spring from external perception and thus argued that it belongs to a cognitive power different from and independent of perception. His demonstration corresponds to the other demonstration that the highest good does not consist in pleasure and that justice does not arise out of the struggle for the interests of material beings and consequently we must ascribe behavior of the individual and of the state to a motive independent of our physical being. At the basis of both demonstrations, as the major premise, lies a disjunction whose defectiveness makes Plato's argument inadequate. Together they distinguish a higher faculty of reason from sensibility. Then from this higher faculty Plato demonstrates the existence of the Ideas as independent essences in the following manner.

According to Plato, the human being bears the *ideal world* within himself, independently of external sense experience. Socrates' self-reflection was expanded and intensified in Plato's powerful personality. In the artistic description which Plato gives of Socrates in his writings—the highest creation of the poetic power of the Athenians—this self-reflection has become, so to speak, personified. Plato then shows analytically the content of human nature in the poet, in religious experience, and in enthusiasm. Finally, he takes a rigorous proof for the *presence of knowledge-content in man* that is *independent of experience* from the science of his time and his school, namely mathematics, and in this particular as well he is a forerunner of Kant. The dialogue *Meno* shows in drastic terms how mathematical truth is not acquired but how only an already existing inner intuition is developed in it.[54] For Plato the *condition* of this state of affairs is *transcendent contact of the soul with the Ideas,* and this doctrine of Plato—as an attempt to explain the content of our spiritual life, and here particularly of our intelligence, as something independent of external sensation—takes its place alongside Kant's theory.

Kant traces the state of affairs we are concerned with here to a *form* of the mind, of intelligence as well as will. At root this is something simply inconceivable. It is impossible for a content-filled determination to emerge from a mere form of thinking; but cause and the good are evidently such *content-filled* determinations. And if the notion of the relation of causality or of substance were grounded in a form of our intelligence, as, for example, that of equality or difference is, then it would likewise have to be as univocally defined and transparent to intelligence as they are. Hence, to begin with, Plato's doctrine contains a tenable truth even as against Kant.

However, the limitation of the Greek mind asserts itself at this point. The true nature of inner experience was not yet in its field of vision. For the Greek mind all *knowing* is a *kind of seeing;* for it, theoretical and practical behavior relate to a being that exists apart from intuition and presuppose that being; consequently, the Greek mind views knowledge, as well as behavior, as a contact of intelligence with something outside it, and in fact views knowledge as assimilation of this thing confronting it.

In this connection it is all the same whether the subject's position is skeptical or dogmatic: the Greek mind understands knowing and acting as types of relationship of this subject to an existing being. Skepticism merely maintains the inability of the cognitive faculty to comprehend the object as it is; accordingly, it teaches only the theoretical and practical withdrawal of the subject within himself; it teaches renunciation, or the subject's isolation amid being. In contrast with that, the dogmatic position of Greek thinkers proceeds from the sure feeling of affinity with the universe; thus it is ultimately grounded in Greek natural religion; hence it expresses itself in the principle which underlies older dogmatic theories of perception and of thought: like is known by like. Plato's argument springs from this Greek way of thinking: content that the soul discovers in itself, but that it has not acquired in experience during this life, must have been acquired before it. Our knowledge is recollection; ideas we find within us are ones we have seen before. According to Plato even our moral ideas are present to us in virtue of such intuition. If one begins with the earlier origin of the *Phaedrus*, one finds here the fundamental basis of the doctrine of the transcendence of the Ideas.[55]

All the other more or less rigorous arguments of Plato proceeding from knowledge to the doctrine of Ideas as its basis rest on the same foundations. *Knowledge cannot be derived from sensation and representation;* on the contrary, it is separate from them and *independent* of them. Furthermore, an *independently existing* object must correspond to that separate knowledge. Hence Plato argues: in accordance with its difference from changeable sensation, unchangeable knowledge must have an unchangeable object corresponding to it. After all, if the concept of a thing remains in the soul while the thing itself perishes, then a permanent object must correspond to that concept. Or he uses Eleatic principles to argue: something nonexistent is unknowable, and because a representation refers to something that combines being and nonbeing within it, that representation is only partially knowledge; but because true knowledge is present in the concept, the concept must have an object which is distinct from the object of a representation. The same connection between knowledge and being is then also developed from the concept of being: the thing does not cleanly represent what is contained in its concept; on the contrary its predicates are relative and variable. Therefore it has no complete reality; the latter belongs only to what the concept expresses—but we cannot abstract this from any sense perception of things.

Thus within the sphere of self-reflection which entered into metaphysics with the Socratic school and expanded its horizon, it is precisely reflection about knowledge which stands in the forefront, for the argument proceeded from knowledge to its presupposition, the Ideas. Nevertheless, linked to this argument is the argument *from the ethical*. For the entire contents of human nature, as this tremendously realistic mind experienced it in himself, was for him a proof for their connection with a higher world because one could not derive them from materiality.

Accordingly, the second component of the disjunctive inference fundamental to Plato's system (the inference to the independence of reason) has for its major premise the disjunction: the purpose of activity for the individual is traceable either to pleasure or to some *independent ground of the ethical* set apart from the ephemeral character of pleasure; the purpose of the state's will has arisen either out of internecine self-seeking pleasure-oriented interests or else it is grounded in a substantial foundation independent of them. Plato's polemic against sophistry excludes the first term of the disjunction, and this exclusion makes up the minor premise of his argument. His discussions of this matter unravel the content of our moral consciousness in a truly profound fashion; and thus a new sphere of most important experiences (prepared for by the Socratic school) surfaces above the horizon of philosophical reflection and remains thenceforth in the consciousness of mankind. But as we did with Socrates, once again we stumble at this point on the peculiar limits of Greek mentality in Plato. Even where self-reflection emerges for this mind so attuned to the cosmos, it does not find the reality of realities given in immediate consciousness or the will-filled self in which the entire world is first present. No, intuition which exists only in devotion to what it intuits, and formative power which shapes what is intuited in the stuff of reality—that is the schema governing how this self-reflection regards the intellectual and its content. And where the skeptical mind denies itself this relationship to an object, there remains for it only "renunciation," [*"Enthaltung"*]. Therefore Plato conceives the independent ground of the ethical only as an *intuition of the archetypes of the beautiful and the good*. Thus inference from moral consciousness on the basis of the disjunction mentioned is subordinated ultimately to inference from knowledge. This argument first deduced the existence of the pleasure-independent, essentially ethical, and on this basis it then proves that the fact of the ethical presupposes the archetypes of the beautiful and the good that we contemplate when we act.[56]

Plato describes this connection in an impressive image. The *Idea of the Good* is queen of the intelligible world as the sun is of the visible world. The sense of sight *per se* does not make it possible for us to see the real; rather, light which radiates from the sun must reveal it. Hence the bond of light links sense of sight and perceptible object with each other for vision; the same sun grants the visible world its generation and its growth as well. So the Idea of the Good is the mysterious but real bond of the cosmos. This image expresses the system in which metaphysics connects the ultimate ground of knowledge with the ultimate cause of reality.

At this point we again pick up the thread of the history of metaphysical argumentation from *astronomical* facts. In Plato's system this method of argument is mediated by a notion of the influence of the world of Ideas, which of course only has the validity of a myth. To Plato, mathematics and astronomy are still the only sciences of the cosmos, and he too concludes in the first place on the basis of *rational ordering of the heavenly bodies,* whose expression is their beauty, to the *rational cause* of them. "But to say that reason has ordered all things is appropriate for one who beholds the world and the sun, the moon and the stars, and their whole heavenly circle."[57] He supports his more detailed conclusions by the following theory. Every motion imparted by an impulse changes to a state of rest. At the time this was an erroneous abstraction based on experience of motions of collided bodies: people observed that every terrestrial body reverted to a state of rest after being pushed once, and they had no notion yet of friction and air resistance. So they ascribed the capacity for moving from within, and therefore permanently, only to the soul; they regarded motion of mere bodies as imparted motion and every imparted motion as transitory. These are assumptions which the *Phaedrus* had already developed, and this psychism [*Psychismus*] was in agreement with mythical ideas. From this, then, stems the inference from regular and constant motions of the stars to constantly operative psychic entities as causes of these motions. But such intelligent causes must be deduced from the harmonious mathematical relationships of the revolutions of the spheres into which the paths of the planets can be analyzed. For the relations of the revolutions to extent, direction and velocity—which at that time were completely removed from mechanical consideration—were conceived of and made intelligible as relations between psychic substances. But over and above this, in general the reflection of the Ideas hovers over the entire cosmos.

The transcendence of this Platonic ordering of Ideas coalesced later with the transcendence of the invisible world of Christianity. In their innermost character they are thoroughly different from each other. To be sure, Plato felt the terrestrial world as something foreign to him; but only insofar as it is not the pure expression of substantial Forms. He flees into the realm of these perfect Forms, and so the highest upward impetus of his soul remains bound to the cosmos. In his view relations of these transcendent substances to one another are only conceptual; in fact, he recognizes them, like relations of geometrical figures, by comparing, establishing differences and partial commonality. And though he tries to explain the actual cosmos by them by means of the Idea of the Good, despite all the mythical luster which surrounds his presentation, it is through a schema derived from external cosmic relationships of motion that he conceives the action of the deity itself: a world-shaper who gives form to matter.

6. Aristotle and Establishment of a Separate Metaphysical Science

Aristotle completed the metaphysics of substantial forms. In it science looked for what stays uniform in alteration and change, but discovered this permanent and thus cognitively accessible element chiefly in what the general idea or concept contains. This metaphysics corresponded to natural science, which in its analysis went back by preference to intelligible and rational natural forms; hence explanation of such natural forms was connected with psychical causes which were thought of as guided by ideas; an element of mythical thought persisted in thus assuming psychical causes for the course of nature. And, indeed, in Aristotle this metaphysics of substantial forms became a means of subjecting reality to knowledge, whereas Plato saw in actual objects only gigantic shadows cast by Ideas. Aristotle transformed Plato's vision of an unchanging order of Ideas into a vision of a *primordial, eternal, actual world in which the Forms maintain themselves in unchanging self-identity,* even amid change in *heredity, development,* and *degeneration* in this world. Hence Aristotle marks an important point in the historical concatenation of thoughts which makes up the development of European thought.

Scientific Conditions

Aristotle thinks under the *assumption that the intellectual event takes hold of existing being outside of us;*[58] one can label this standpoint dogmatism or objectivism. Indeed, Aristotle develops the idea of knowledge of like through like—which is the form this assumption took in the Greek mind influenced by its natural religion and mythology—into a positive theorem, which has also guided an influential school of modern metaphysics.

Aristotle emphasized[59] the importance that the principle "like is known only by like" had for the speculation of older Greek philosophers. According to Heraclitus, something moved is known by something moved. In this connection Aristotle cites the following verse from Empedocles:

> We always see earth through earth and water through water,
> Divine ether through ether, consuming fire through fire,
> Love through love, and strife through sad strife.

In like manner Parmenides started with the fact that a thing senses what is akin to it;[60] Philolaus develops the idea that number joins things harmoniously to the soul. Finally, Aristotle finds the same principle that like is known by like again in his teacher, Plato.[61]

Aristotle terminates this development with the following theorem. *Nous,* or *divine* Reason, is the principle and goal which conditions the *rational in things* at every point, at least indirectly, and so *human* reason, which is akin to the divine, enables us to know the cosmos, insofar as it is rational.[62] In virtue of this correspondence, metaphysics, or the science of reason, is possible.

If Plato inclined to trace the process by which we read the ideal content of the cosmos from it, as it were, to our innate possession of this content, and if, relative to that innate possession, he allowed the other factor in the process, experience, to play a secondary role (indeed, he nowhere clearly defines its role), nevertheless for Aristotle external perception and experience hold a prominent and externally solid position. For him, the theorem of correspondence extends also to the relation of perception to what is perceivable. Consequently, he had to try to solve the difficulty which now arose: human reason carries in itself the ground of its knowledge of the rationality of the cosmos, but it acquires this knowledge only through experience. He insists that we cannot have knowledge of the Ideas without having consciousness of this knowledge,[63] and he tries to solve the problem thus emerging in his metaphysical system through the concept of development. In human thought there is, prior to the process of knowledge, a potentiality (*dynamis*) for immediate knowledge of highest principles, and it is actualized in the process of knowledge itself.[64] Carrying out this fundamental epistemological intuition, despite the profound insights it contains, cannot shed light on the point Plato had left in the dark: the relation of the condition of knowledge given in human reason (*nous*) to the other condition located in experience. The individual sense organ corresponds to objects of a particular class; something that has the capacity for perceiving (according to the general method of solution mentioned above) is constituted the same potentially as the object of perception is actually;[65] hence in its own sphere of objects the healthy sense organ perceives something true. Indeed, Aristotle shows that in general we possess all the possible senses,[66] so that we consequently also grasp the whole of reality through the senses, and this conviction may be regarded as the keystone of his objective realism. As the sense organ is related to what we can sense, just so is reason, or *nous,* related to what we can think. Accordingly, reason, too, grasps principles through immediate intuition which excludes all error;[67] a principle of this kind is the cognitive principle of contradiction. But neither the range of principles of knowledge located in *nous* nor the relation of the inductive process working back from perceptions to concepts and axioms originally located in *nous* ultimately attains clarity.

This objective standpoint of Aristotle represents the natural attitude of human intelligence toward the cosmos. And, secondly, in fact, it was conditioned *by the stage science found itself in* at the time of Aristotle, that is, what human intelligence *knew* about the cosmos at that time.

To be sure, science of the cosmos had freed from objects the consideration of general relations which prevail among numbers and spatial figures;[68] but there still existed no study—abstracting from objects, set apart, existing in its own right—of the other characteristics of those objects, such as motion, gravity, or light. The schools of Anaxagoras, Leucippus, and Democritus inclined toward a partially or totally mechanistic point of view, but even they applied only extremely indefinite, incoherent, and in part erroneous notions of motion, pressure, gravity, and the like in explaining the cosmos. We recognized in this the reason why the mechanistic point of view was defeated in its struggle with the view which related forms to psychical entities.[69] After all, it is only with

Archimedes that we encounter some appropriate and definite ideas about mechanics. Under such conditions observation of movements of the stars was still predominant in Greek natural science. Because of their great distance from us these stars presented themselves to the human mind as automatically freed from their other physical character-istics. After the study of the stars, comparative study of the more interesting objects on the earth prevailed, among which organic bodies naturally attracted the most attention.

For this stage of the positive sciences the most appropriate metaphysics was one that described forms of reality as they express themselves in universal ideas; described the relations between these forms in *concepts;* and based explanation of reality on them as *metaphysical entities.* But atomistic theory was less suited to this stage. After all, at that time it, too, was only a metaphysical theorem, not an instrument of experiment and calculation. Its material particles were conceptually established subjects of the system of nature, and in fact they proved unfruitful in explaining the cosmos. For the connecting links between them and forms of nature were missing: suitable and definite ideas about motion, gravity, pressure, and so on, as well as coherent development of such ideas in abstract sciences.

Aristotle's authoritative mind, which made him master of two millennia, focused on how he connected these scientific conditions we have described and on how he then *reduced the natural attitude of intelligence toward the cosmos to a system* which satisfied every demand one could make at this *stage of the sciences.* He mastered all the positive sciences of his time (we know least about mathematics); in most of them he was a pioneer. As a consequence he did not curtail any of their assumptions at any point which might have made it necessary to step beyond his metaphysical foundation. He gave sensation its due; he recognized in becoming, in motion, in change, and in the manifold a reality which must not be denied by idle ratiocination but must be explained. For him the individual thing, the particular substance, possessed the fullest reality given to us. So it happened that while some particular formulations of his ideas were superseded in the discussions of subsequent centuries, the foundations of his system stood fast as long as the indicated stage of the sciences continued. During this entire period people expanded his metaphys-ics, to be sure, but they kept intact its existing assumptions.

Separation of Logic from Metaphysics and Its Relationship to It

Under these presuppositions metaphysics, the queen of the sciences, emerged as a separate discipline. The achievement of Aristotle which chiefly made this possible was the separate treatment of logic. Aristotle subjected the conceptually necessary structure formed by knowledge to theoretical examination. He established the first theory of the forms and laws of scientific demonstration.

We now link up with our exposition of the two classes of *immediate truths:* percep-tions and principles. Between the two moves all other knowledge as *mediate knowledge.* For premises of every scientific argument lead ultimately to something immediately certain, which can be either perception, as something first for us, or immediate rational intuition, as something first in itself. Aristotle's *Analytic*[70] closes with a reference to the latter as the deepest ground of mediate thought or ratiocination.

The world-historical *importance of Aristotelian logic* consists in the fact that it investi-gated and analyzed the forms of this mediating thought with logical thoroughness for the first time, and it did this with logical understanding of the highest rank. Thus emerged the doctrine of the syllogism.[71] For that time this logic offered first of all a key for resolving propositions disputed by the Sophists and thus ended the long revolutionary movement which had comprised the period of the Sophists, Socrates, Antisthenes, and the Megarians. In addition, this logic contained the means to improve the special sciences formally. As mathematics was bound to offer Aristotle the most significant example of logical developments in that time, so his book of laws of logic in its turn supplied the means to give geometry as a science the simple, rigorous, paradigmatic form which Euclid's *Book of Elements* demonstrates; and this form then became the model for mathematical developments ever since then.[72]

The *limitations* of Aristotle's logic were determined by the excessively close connection it had with metaphysics. With respect to the simple, truth is grasping it in ideas, a kind of touching (*thigganein*)—and such touching is the ultimate assumption of this Greek objectivism; with respect to the composite, truth is that mental combination which corresponds to existing reality, and error is another combination which contradicts it.[73] Consequently, we have to extend the relationship of *correspondence* even to the area of *mediating thought:* forms of this thought and relations among existing things correspond to one another. Hence the concept expresses essence; hence true affirmative judgment connects what is connected among things, and the matching negative one separates what is separate among things; hence the middle term in the perfect pattern of syllogistic argument corresponds to cause in the pattern of reality. Finally, however one conceives the relation of the kinds of assertion about being (*genē tōn kategoriōn*)—the categories—to Aristotle's conceptual system: these categories likewise correspond to forms of being.[74]

Moreover, this conception of the relationship as we find it in Aristotle maintains its justification and its power so long as the logical forms which discursive thinking offers are not dissolved and relations between thought and its object are not pursued beyond the finished object. In this point as well, Aristotle shows himself to be a metaphysician who clings to forms of reality. His analysis of science does not go beyond dissolving forms into forms, hence it shows the same limitation as astronomical analysis of the world structure by the ancients did. What speech and discursive thought offer as a system dissolves into a mutual relationship of forms, and the latter are related to forms of reality in their capacity for reflecting them. Schleiermacher (with his theory of correspondence), Trendelenburg, and Überweg have held fast to this objectivistic standpoint, regardless of their individual points of difference from Aristotle.

The *concept of correspondence,* that is, of the correspondence between perception and thought on the one hand and of reality and being on the other hand—to which henceforth the entire foundation of this natural system leads back—is *completely obscure*. No one can imagine how something we think could correspond to something actually existing outside us. We can define what similarity means in mathematical terms; but here a similarity is maintained which is completely indefinite. Indeed, one can say that if the phenomena of mirroring did not exist in nature and by imitation in human art, such an idea could scarcely have arisen at all.

The more detailed system of logical thought, as developed in Aristotle's doctrine of argument and proof, is a counterpart of the metaphysical system he adopts. This follows from the notion of correspondence we have spoken about. Sigwart says, quite to the point:

> Because Aristotle assumes an objective system of concepts which is actualized in the real world in such a way that the concept always appears as something which constitutes the

essence of things and as the cause of their particular determinations, all judgments containing true knowledge present themselves to him as an expression of necessary conceptual relationships, and the syllogism exists to reveal the full power and range of every single concept of knowledge inasmuch as it connects individual judgments with one another and makes them dependent on one another through their conceptual unity. And the linguistic expression of these conceptual relations follows from the fact that they always appear at the same time as the essence of the particular existing thing so that the latter, in its conceptual determination, is the proper subject of judgment and the relation of concepts thus comes to light in the universal or particular, the affirmative or the negative judgment.[75]

From this follow the position of the categorical judgment, the significance of the first figure along with derivation of the other figures from it, the position of the middle term, which is supposed to correspond to the cause: in short, the principal characteristic notes of Aristotle's Analytic.

Consequently, Aristotle's teaching on the syllogism stood unshaken as long as the assumption of an objective system of concepts realized in the cosmos was maintained. From the time that logic surrendered this assumption, it needed a new foundation. And if it nevertheless strove to hold on to Aristotle's logical doctrine of forms, it was trying to protect the shadow of something whose substance was gone.[76]

Establishment of an Independent Science of Metaphysics

Thus Aristotle first considered the logical organizations of the thinker in his own right apart from, though in relation to, the real organization of actual existence. Accordingly, he made a clearer distinction between the concept of ground and that of cause: [77] he *separated metaphysics from logic*. This separation was an important step forward in the natural system, hence in the confines of objectivism, compared with the earlier unity of metaphysics and logic. Nor is the significance of this separation for the stage we are describing diminished by the fact that this independence of metaphysics would be called into question from the critical standpoint, because the real structure is after all available to us only in and through our consciousness and every component of this structure which metaphysics analyzes—such as substance, quantity, and time—is only a fact of consciousness.

And just as Aristotle distinguished his First Philosophy from logic, he also separated it *from mathematics and physics*. Special sciences, such as mathematics, deal with special provinces of existing being, but First Philosophy deals with the universal determinations of existing being. In establishing their grounds special sciences go back only to a certain point, but metaphysics goes back to grounds that are unconditioned within the cognitive process. It is the science of universal and unchanging *principles*.[78] Indeed, Aristotle proceeds from what is given in the cosmos *backward* to principles. And even if the references to the physical writings prove nothing, nevertheless this connection becomes clear, that metaphysics acquires its demonstration of first causes from physics and in turn confirms the integrity of the principles of physics mainly only through historical-critical examination.[79] This connection argues primarily from the recognition and consideration of motion. "However, for us the basic principle stands fast that things existing by nature, either all of them or at least some of them, are in motion; indeed, this is evidently so by inference from experience."[80] Accordingly, Eleatic denial of motion is for Aristotle, who lived for the challenge of explaining nature, nothing but barren denial of all science of the cosmos. From the constant and perfect motions of the stars, from the play of changes beneath the moon, knowledge goes back to first causes, which at the same time contain the first grounds of explanation. Thus we know the real structure of the cosmos, which is the object of rigorous science, through an analysis which reasons from that cosmos (as the composite reality given to us) back to principles, which are the true subjects of the structure of nature.[81]

So long as no epistemological foundation had been laid down, one half of the possibility of bringing the positive sciences toward formal completion rested on the independent science of metaphysics, just as the other half was grounded on logical self-reflection. Thus metaphysics became the necessary foundation of the sciences of the cosmos, and it endowed them for the first time with rationally prepared basic concepts. At the heart of this metaphysics the critical standpoint was then in its preparatory stage. For rational analysis of the universal components of reality first made it possible to grasp facts of consciousness among them. In its womb something else was being prepared which can perhaps take epistemology beyond Kant. For if the impossibility of giving these particles of reality a logically clear form should become clear, then our historical and psychological consideration would acquire insight into an origin which could not lie in abstract understanding.

Metaphysical System of the World

This metaphysical analysis achieves, as its first great accomplishment, the discovery and rational description of the general components of reality as they disclosed themselves to Aristotle's investigation. Such elements or principles, which are to be found everywhere in the real system of the cosmos, offer themselves to everyday perception in reality, in an object and its characteristics, in activity and passivity. Aristotle first isolated these general components, which are intertwined in the cosmos, and attempted to describe them as simple bodies. There is no need for us here to examine the very obscure and difficult relationship between the categories he discovered and his metaphysical principles; for us the clarity of his results is enough.

The tragic fate of this great and constantly ongoing work of metaphysics, which unceasingly tries to unravel universal components of reality in such a way that a real and objective knowledge of the world system might be possible, now begins to reveal itself to us scene by scene! Sense qualities, space, time, motion and rest, substance and accidents, cause and effect, form and matter—all these are general components we encounter at every point in the external world and therefore are contained in our *consciousness of external reality* in general. Regardless of difference of philosophical standpoints, the question now arises from all this: Will it be possible to achieve *clarity about these elements apart from investigation of consciousness* and the general conditions of all reality given in it? Let the course of the history of metaphysics itself gradually give us the answer to this question. First the simple concepts of being and substance present themselves for such consideration.

1. Aristotle's metaphysical analysis everywhere detects *substances* and their states, which are related to each other[82]; here we are at the core of Aristotle's metaphysical writings.

"A science exists which investigates *being* as being [*to on hei on*] and attributes which essentially belong to its nature. This science is not identical with any of the special sciences; for none of these other sciences proceeds with universal investigations of being as being. On the contrary, they cut off a part of being and investigate its peculiar constitution."[83] Mathematics treats of being as number, line, or surface; physics deals with being as motion and element. But First Philosophy considers it insofar as it is everywhere identical: being as such.

This concept of being (the object of metaphysics) is used in various senses; this word can designate substance (*ousia*) as well as one of its qualities. But the concept of being is always related to that of substance.[84] For if we say that something exists apart from substance, this can be only because it belongs to a substance, indeed to a particular one. Consequently, the first sense in which we speak of being is that of the being of a particular substance: we designate everything else as existing only because it is the quantity, the quality, the property, and so on of such a being.[85]

Metaphysics is therefore first of all the *science of substances* and, as we shall see, the highest point it attains is knowledge of the divine substance. Only in an improper sense may one say that it deals with *being in its broader senses,* whether that being appear as something qualitative, quantitative, or some other predicative determination.[86] The following simple components of speech and the reality corresponding to it are more precisely distinguished in this way: substance is a measurable quantity with a characteristic definition, hence bearing a relation to other things, namely relations of time and place, activity and passivity.[87] Thus substance constitutes the central point of Aristotle's metaphysics just as it had been the focal point in the metaphysics of the Atomists and Plato. Only with the emergence of the special empirical sciences does the concept of causality, which is related to the concept of law, move into the foreground. Can Aristotle's metaphysics bring this basic concept of substance to comprehensible clarity?

A definition mentioned in Plato's *Sophist*[88] delineates the *truly existing* [*ontōs on*] as that which has the *power to act and to be acted on,* and, after others had anticipated him, Leibniz adopted this definition once again.[89] This definition takes the concept of substance back to that of power or causal relation and dissolves it in the latter. At the later stage, when Leibniz appeared, this sort of conceptual definition could prove useful in substituting for the notion of substance a concept with greater applicability for natural scientific thought. But it does not express what we think regarding the state of an object nor, consequently, what the knowledge-serving distinction between substance and what inheres in it is trying to demarcate. Aristotle's realistic mind took pains to designate this directly.

On the one hand, Aristotle defines what we understand by substance in the *actual structure* of reality. It is that which is *not an accidental property* of another but rather something *of which something else is an accident.* When Aristotle speaks of a particular substance and its substratum, he expresses himself through a graphic and spatial idea. On the other hand, he establishes what we understand by substance in the *structure of thought.* In this structure substance is a *subject;* it designates that which is the carrier of predicative determinations in a judgment, hence all other forms of expression (categories) are predicated of substance.[90]

If one connects this last determination with the earlier one, then Aristotle is searching metaphysics for the subject or subjects for all characteristics and changes we encounter in the cosmos. This is the nature of every metaphysical tendency of mind: it is not directed toward the system in which states and alterations are linked to one another but rather goes directly to the subject or subjects which lie beyond them.

But insofar as it seeks to know the objective relationship between substance and accident as it exists in these subjects, Aristotle's metaphysics is working with relations it cannot elucidate. What does it mean to exist in oneself or to exist in another? Spinoza still expressed substance, as opposed to accident, through the characteristic of existing in oneself; the accident exists in the substance. This spatial representation is only an image. What the image means is not transparent to the understanding, such as equality or difference are, and one cannot demonstrate it by any external experience. In reality this existing-in-oneself is given in the experience of independence or self-consciousness, and we understand that because we experience it. And without going beyond the logical form of connection between subject and predicate, is it at all possible to clarify further the relationship of this metaphysical thing to the logical expression of the relation inhering in substance?

In the context at hand the specific different senses in which Aristotle goes on to use the expression substance is of no interest at all. They arise from the fact that Aristotle speaks of the most varied subjects to which his metaphysics goes back: of matter as foundation [*hupokeimenon*], of essence which corresponds to concept (*hē kata ton logon ousia*), of particular object [*tode ti*]. In particular, determinations so imperfectly developed that we leave them out of consideration depend on the particular object as the First Substance.[91]

Among other class concepts of predication (the categories), *action and passion* have the greatest importance for metaphysics. The concept of causality appears in modern metaphysics alongside that of substance; indeed, there is a tendency to dissolve substance into power. It is characteristic of metaphysics of the ancients that investigation of the problems inherent in this concept is still insignificant; substances, their motions in space, and forms make up the mental horizon of their physics and consequently of their metaphysics. In this context action and passion are subordinate to the obviously manifest perception of *motion*.[92] In fact, in the context of world explanation the fact of motion in substances leads back to the ultimate explanatory concepts of the Aristotelian system, which in that system must take the place of a fundamental notion of cause and knowledge of the laws of motion and of change; we shall later encounter the concept of power [*dunamis*], which terminates the analysis of reality but is untenable. In particular cases Aristotle was well aware of the difficulty of holding on to the difference between action and passion without exception. Thus a sensation is a passion, yet the sense of sight realizes its nature actively in seeing.[93] He also notes the other difficulty of describing the influence of the agent on the patient, but how unsatisfactory is the solution he contrives that things that are different influence one another on the basis of what they have in common, and that an agent makes a patient like itself![94]

2. Thus Aristotle struggles in vain to make concepts like substance and cause really understandable; but the difficulties are compounded because he also uses the Platonic doctrine of *substantial forms* to elucidate the world system. It is true that he victoriously refutes Plato's doctrine of the separate existence of the Ideas; but will he be able to clarify some other objective relationship of the Ideas to objects?

Aristotle attributes reality in the strict sense only to an individual substance. But this insight, which corresponds to the natural scientist and the sound empiricist in him, is incompatible with what he holds on to in the doctrine of Ideas from the standpoint of the natural system of metaphysics. He too finds *knowledge* only where one knows through a *universal concept*; only to the extent that the torch of universal ideas illuminates individual substance can one clarify the latter. The universal concept makes the essential definition, or *form*, of the object visible; and that form constitutes its *substance in a secondary sense*, that is, as it is present to the mind [*hē kata ton logon ousia*]. The ground for these propositions about knowledge lies in the assumption which is the root of all metaphysical abstraction: immediate knowledge and experience in which the particular object is given to us is regarded as paltrier and less perfect than the universal concept or proposition. In line with this presupposition is the metaphysical assumption: what is worthwhile in particular substances and what connects them with the deity is the conceptual element in them. In the *contradiction between these presuppositions* and Aristotle's healthy insight into *individual substance* we see once again the impossibility of defining, from the standpoint of metaphysics, the relationship of the individual object to what universal concepts express as the content of the world. According to Aristotle, the individual object alone has full reality, but we have knowledge only of the universal essential definition in which it participates. From this two difficulties result. It contradicts the basic idea of the knowability of the cosmos that what is truly real in it remains unknowable. Then, according to the general assumptions of the theory of Ideas (corresponding to knowledge of universal determinations of substance), a reality of forms is assumed, and this assumption now leads to the paltry and unfortunate concept of a substance which after all does not have the reality that a particular substance has. Can this confusion inherent in the double sense of being and of substance be resolved before epistemology develops the simple truth that the way in which thinking posits the universal bears no comparison with the way in which perception experiences the reality of the particular? (Consequently, before the false, metaphysical relation is replaced by a tenable, epistemological one?)[95]

This metaphysics of substantial forms has even more striking consequences among the special sciences. Science connected with it renounces any *knowledge of the changeable* in its object, for it apprehends only permanent forms. It gives up knowledge of the *contingent,* for it is directed solely toward determinations of essence. Kepler's calculation of Mars [*sic*] deviated from observation by only a few minutes, but those few minutes gave him no rest and were the impulse behind his great discovery. But this metaphysics, by contrast, pushed into the sphere of matter the entire residue it could not explain and had left behind in the area of changing appearances. Thus Aristotle expressly explained that particular differences in a species, such as color of eyes or pitch of voice, were indifferent matters as far as teleological explanation was concerned: they were relegated to effects of matter.[96] Not until people took account of deviations from a type, of connecting links between one type and another, and of changes, did science break through these limitations of Aristotelian metaphysics, and knowledge based on the law of the changeable and on history of development made its appearance.

3. Because Aristotle thus shifted the reality of the Ideas into the real world, resolution of this reality into four principles took place: matter, form, purpose, and efficient cause; and, as the final concepts of his system which completed the resolution of reality, the principles of dynamis (power) and energy appeared.

Thought stresses *form,* the daughter of Plato's Idea, as the unchanging element in the cosmos. This comprises the essence of particular substances. Because unchanging forms are included in generation and corruption, but their alteration requires a bearer, we distinguish *matter* in the cosmos as its second constitutive principle. In the course of nature, then, form is both the *end* (whose realization nature's course strives for) and the *efficient cause* which—like an object's soul,[97] so to speak, working from the inside out—sets that object in motion or effects its motion from the outside. Consequently, this way of looking at things does not deduce what occurs in the course of nature from its conditions in nature which work together according to laws; on the contrary, in place of a cooperative action of laws the concept of *dynamis,* or power, appears, to which corresponds the concept of purposive reality, or *energy.*

Aristotle's system of science is contained in these concepts; they are already developed in the first books of the metaphysics as the means for comprehending nature, and they lead one on through the cosmic system of motion to the unmoved mover. For this is the soul of Aristotle's conception of nature: not the distinction between efficient cause, purpose, and form—that is only an analytical device—but identification of purpose, which is form, with efficient cause and separation of this triune real factor from the real factor of matter (even though it does not appear in isolation in the cosmos). And here also is where the character of his natural science is decided. In modern thought, study of motions is separated from the idea of purpose; motion is determined by elements proper to it alone. And so a result of the modern view of nature is that, if it does not wish to desist from metaphysical evaluation of the Ideas, it does keep that distinct from the mechanical way of looking at things, such as Leibniz has done. For Aristotle, on the contrary, the concept of motion remains bound to forms of the cosmos; it is not really freed from them, any more than analysis of thinking in Aristotle's logic goes beyond forms of thought. Thus arises his distinction between perfect circular motion which turns back on itself and straight motion which ends at a point. For this viewpoint the rational aspect in circular motion is something pristine, indeed immediately stipulated in the deity. This conception established the fateful contrast between forms of nature beneath the moon and those beyond the moon, and as long as it ruled the minds of men there was no possibility for a mechanics of the heavens. The characteristic feature of precisely those tendencies in Greek study of nature that proved successful is this: that study remains bound to the intuition of mathematical beauty and inner purposiveness in cosmic forms. To be sure, it breaks up composite forms of motion into simpler ones, but in these simpler ones the teleological and esthetic character of form is preserved.

Hence Aristotle wishes indeed to trace motion in the universe to its causes (under motion, in a genuinely Greek spirit, he classifies even qualitative change). But because in his view all motive power is purposeful action which actualizes form (for him the cause of motion lies in the form), so it is always exclusively power contained in the form and producing development which is the cause of another form like it. Hence this explanation is confined to a magic circle in which the forms are always already present whose explanation is at issue: they are forces which produce life in the universe; they lead logically back to a first motive force.

Metaphysics and Natural Science

The accomplishments of such an explanation of nature are determined by this character it has. Just as the Platonic school was a center for mathematical research, so now the Aristotelian school became a center for *descriptive and comparative sciences.* Precisely because the importance of this Aristotelian school was so immense for the progress of the sciences and the spirit of scientific inquiry and empirical research was so highly developed, a lively interest has been aroused by the question why even this school was satisfied with indefinite, isolated, and in part erroneous notions about motion, pressure, gravity, and so on, and why it did not progress to sounder mechanical and physical ideas. One asks about the reasons why *successful* Greek special research was restricted to formal disciplines of mathematics and logic and to descriptive and comparative sciences for such a long time. This question is obviously linked to another one which determined the hegemony of the metaphysics of substantial forms. *Formal and descriptive character of the sciences* and *metaphysics of forms* are *correlative historical facts.* One is going in circles if one considers metaphysics as the cause which has prevented progress of the scientific mind beyond these limits of the period, for then one must explain the power of this metaphysics. This suggests that both the character of the sciences at this stage and the hegemony of metaphysics are grounded in common and deeper-lying causes.

The ancients were not deficient in understanding facts and in observation; indeed, they used experimentation to a greater extent than people usually assume, even though social conditions were a hindrance in this area: the opposition of a ruling citizenry, which also cultivated science, to the slave class on which the burden of manual labor fell, and, connected with that, disdain for physical labor. Aristotle's genius for *observation* and its extension over an enormous area have aroused the wonder of exact scientists in the modern period to an ever increasing degree. If Aristotle not infrequently confuses what observations brought him and what he deduced from them by argument, especially by analogy, certainly the predominance of reasoning in the Greek mind asserted itself disadvantageously in this instance. Moreover, one finds many experiments mentioned in the writings of Aristotle, some of which others had carried out before him and some of which he carried out himself. But here once notices inexactness in their reporting, lack of every kind of quantitative determination, but especially the barrenness of experimentation by Aristotle and his contemporaries in actually solving theoretical problems. There was no antipathy toward experiment but an inability to make a correct use of it. Nor can this have been due to a lack of instruments which would make quantitative determinations possible. Not until questions put to nature demand such instruments are they invented, and even the lack of an industry managed by scientifically trained people would only have made the appearance of such inventions more difficult.

In particular one cannot dispute that the *contemplative* disposition of the *Greek* mind which grasped the conceptual and esthetic character of forms kept scientific reflection at the level of contemplation and made verification of ideas in nature more difficult. The human race does not begin with assumption-free, methodical investigations of nature but rather with content-filled intuition, at first religious, then with contemplative meditation on the cosmos, in which the purpose-nexus of nature was held fast for a long time. Orientation, comprehension of forms, and numerical proportions in the universe are the first thing; men regard the order of the heavens with religious awe and contemplative bliss because of its perfection; classes of organisms exhibit an ascending purposefulness filled with physical life and make possible descriptive science based on them. And so reflection which older faith had directed immediately toward the heavens shifts toward special investigation of natural bodies on the earth, but is held up a longer time at this level on account of a pious fear (based on primitive religion) of dissecting a living creature. This magic circle of intuition of *an ideal system* is a self-enclosed one; it nowhere appears to show a gap, and it is the triumph of metaphysics to find a place in it for all facts which experience has to offer. There is no question about this historical situation; one can only ask what importance it has as a ground of explanation. Nevertheless, one may allow us to introduce a *second,* more hypothetical, *ground of explanation.* Separate consideration of a sphere of related partial contents—such as mechanics, optics, and acoustics offer—presupposes a high degree of *abstraction* in the scientist, which is only a *result of long technical development of the isolated science.* In mathematics, psychological conditions we shall discuss later paved the way for such abstraction from the beginning. In astronomy, because of the distance of the stars, consideration of their motions was separated from that of their other characteristics. Before the Alexandrian school, however, no other area saw a quantity of related, kindred partial contents of natural phenomena subjected to a definite explanatory idea appropriate to them. Original insights such as that of the Pythagorean school into tonal relationships had no decisive consequences. Descriptive and comparative natural science had no need of such abstraction; it had a guiding thread in the idea of purpose and for the time being went back to psychic causes. And so we have an explanation why the splendid accomplishments of the Aristotelian school in this area were accompanied by a total lack of sound mechanical and physical ideas in that school.

The Deity as Ultimate and Highest Object of Metaphysics

The terminus of Aristotle's metaphysics is his theology. In it we have for the first time a complete bonding of Anaxagoras's monotheism with the doctrine of substantial forms.

Since Anaxagoras, dominant European metaphysics has meant establishing the doctrine of an ultimate, intelligent cause, independent of the world. But here this doctrine encounters changed conditions in metaphysical concepts and the general scientific situation. Thus it experiences a series of transformations during the two-thousand-year life of metaphysics after Anaxagoras. The transformations are evident enough in the writings of Plato, Aristotle, and medieval philosophers and therefore require no detailed discussion. The structure of this history demands only proof that metaphysics continuously possessed a positive scientific *anchor in astronomical arguments,* which gave it unshakeable certainty. These arguments, supported by such as those from the teleology of organisms, contributed substantially to the fact that metaphysics maintained the character of a world power for two thousand years: a royal authority, not merely in the narrow circle of scholars but over the minds of all educated people, by which uneducated masses also remained under its sway.

Religious experience, which contains the most profound and indestructible foundation for faith in God, is something only a minority of men understand with the self-composure of a believing heart undisturbed by the swirl of selfish interests. The authority of the church was often disputed in the Middle Ages. External instruments of ecclesiastical obedience and the ecclesiastical system of penalties were unable to hold back constantly seething movements and the ultimate fragmentation of the church. But for these two thousand years the metaphysics of an intelligent world-cause, grounded on the state of European science, stood unshaken.

In this particular as well, Aristotle essentially determined the form of European metaphysics by the way he summarized the most important facts and arguments. The deity is the mover who ultimately conditions all movements in the cosmos (though in an indirect way); indeed, the motions of the stars in their harmoniousness express the motive power inherent in purpose; astronomy is the mathematical science most akin to philosophy.[98] These thoughts marched forward in the path first trodden by Anaxagoras, and a train of ideas continues to work on from them right to Kepler's investigations, which were inspired by the rational and harmonious character of the world—investigations which saw the perfection of God mirrored in measurements and numbers.

Aristotle's theology is found in the *treatise* inserted as the twelfth book of the collection of metaphysical writings. It contains their high point, for it proves the existence of the individual substance that is immaterial and immutable, and Aristotle designated it from the start as the proper object of First Philosophy.[99] The treatise is related on the one hand to the argument of the Physics and the writing on the heavens, and on the other hand to the basic outlines of the metaphysical writings.

This Aristotelian theology dominates the entire Middle Ages. Nevertheless, in later philosophical development, the first-created intelligence took over the role of mover of the heaven of the fixed stars, and the divine substances that Aristotle used to produce the composite motions of the other world bodies became a fantastic realm of spirits of heavenly bodies. The contrast between the ethereal world and orbital motion on one side and the world of the four elements and straight-line motions on the other, that is, between the province of the eternal and that of generation and corruption, now became the spatial framework for a contrast deriving from the internal world. Thus arose the representation which Dante's timeless poem has immortalized.

Aristotle's argument for the unmoved mover has two aspects.

The first aspect of this demonstration shows with especial clarity how there is no place for spontaneous will in this metaphysics, so that the kind of transcendence whose essence is to proceed from nature back to will does not yet exist for it. Aristotle therefore teaches the following. *Motion* is eternal; it is impossible to conceive of a temporal beginning of it. We cannot think of the system of motions in the cosmos as though every motion had a further cause of motion behind it and this chain of causes of motion went on to infinity; for then we would never arrive at a truly efficient first cause, without which, however, all effects would remain ultimately unexplained. Therefore we must assume a final *stopping point*. And we must designate this first cause as *unmoved*. If it moves itself, then we must distinguish that which is moved in it from that which effects the moving, to which accordingly we cannot impute being-moved. Because motion is continuous, we cannot trace it back to a changing will after the manner of wills in animate beings; we must instead go back to a first unmoved cause. Thus we arrive at the unmoved mover as pure activity or pure act and to the metaphysical construction of the first movement as a circular motion.[100]

The other aspect of the proof reflects on the *conceptual forms* realized in movements of the cosmos. Motion appears in this connection as determination of matter through form. Because motion in the heavens is unalterably homogeneous and turns back on itself, so we must think of the energy which produces it as incorporeal form, or *pure energy*. In the latter the final purpose and the motive power of the world coincide.[101] "To attain this highest purpose is the best for everyone"; it "moves like something which is loved."[102] To this side of the demonstration of monotheism belongs the noble presentation one finds in Cicero. Aristotle here develops Anaxagoras' idea into the comprehensive proof of the existence of God from the teleology of the world, and Aristotle's whole system can ultimately be subsumed under such a proof.

Let us imagine people who have always lived under the earth in good and bright houses embellished with statues and paintings and provided with all things, of which they have an abundance, and who are considered happy. But suppose they had never come up to the surface of the earth, and they had only heard through an obscure saga that there was such a thing as a deity and the power of the gods. If the earth were ever to open up for these people and if they were then able to climb out of their hidden domiciles to the places we live in and then go outside; if they were then suddenly to see the earth, the seas, and the sky, were to perceive masses of clouds and the power of the wind; if they were to look up at the sun and were to know its greatness and beauty as well as its effect, that it is the sun which creates the day by pouring out its light over the whole of the heavens; if, after night had shadowed the earth, they saw the whole of the heavens studded and decorated with stars and observed the changing light of the moon in its waxing and waning, the rising and setting of all these heavenly bodies and their eternal, unchanging paths: then they would certainly be convinced that gods existed and that these mighty works came from the gods.[103]

Even this poetic description looks for support for monotheism in the beauty and orderliness of the paths of the heavenly bodies.

But in Aristotle, as in Plato, the basic monotheistic idea includes assuming various causes which do not come from God.

The astronomical problem had become much more complex, the chief question being the paths of the planets. The attempt was made to trace their apparent paths to *revolutions of spheres,* differing in duration, direction, and extent, and Aristotle now made the revolution of such spheres (to which the stars were attached) his foundation as well. Hence the assumptions of this astronomical theory lay in intermingling these different revolutions. Neither Aristotle nor any other thinker of the millennium after him reduced these assumptions to the system of a *mechanical* conception. And so Aristotle conceived the relation of these motions to one another mythically as an inner *relation of psychical forces* or of starry spirits to one another. Each of these psychic forces realizes, so to speak, a specific idea of circular motion; fifty-five spheres (he prefers this hypothesis as the more likely one[104]) outside the firmament of the fixed stars are interlaced in their revolutions. Accordingly, alongside the highest reason are these fifty-five starry spirits, eternal and immutable, who produce the turning of the spheres; then the forms of reality and finally immortal spirits linked with human souls, which spirits are likewise designated as reason. And matter is also an ultimate, independent fact.

According to Aristotle, the deity is related psychically with these principles; they make up a complex of purposes which finds its capstone in the deity. So the deity rules like a commander-in-chief in an army, that is, through the power by which one soul determines another. Only on this basis can we explain the harmonious structure of the universe under the deity as its head, even though that deity is not the creative cause of it. Pure mind, the thought of thought [*das Denken des Denkens*], thinks only itself in its immutable and blessed life and, as the highest goal, causes motion by attracting, not by trying to accomplish what is inherent in the goal itself; thus it works like one soul on other, lesser souls. So the final word of Greek metaphysics is the relation existing between psychical entities as a ground of explanation of the cosmos, just as Homer had already envisaged it in his polity of the gods.

7. Metaphysics of the Greeks and Socio-Historical Reality

The connection intelligence has with socio-historical reality has proven to be completely different from the relation it has to nature. Not only do interests, strife of factions, and social feelings and passions influence theory to a much higher degree here. Not only is the actual effect of theory determined here by its relation to these interests and emotional agitations in society. Even if one considers the system which the development of the human sciences constitutes insofar as interests and passions of the society in which it is located do not affect it, it manifests a relation to its object different from that which prevails in the scientific knowledge of nature.

We have discussed this in the first book. In consequence of this basic relationship the history of the human sciences makes up a relatively independent totality which has developed in coordination with progress of the natural sciences; this development is subject to its own conditions, regarding which one may consult the first book. And those conditions now chiefly determine the relation which Greek metaphysics bears to study of intellectual facts.

Limits of Greek Humanistic Science [*Geisteswissenschaft*]

The range of experience of socio-historical reality has been built up first among the generations which have reflected on it. The school of Miletus regarded nature virtually as a self-contained whole, just as does a scientist of our day: it was a matter of simply gaining knowledge of the given. But not until the period in which Greek science appeared did the more comprehensive socio-historical sphere of experience dealt with by the human sciences emerge. Conditions of surrounding ancient cultural states were too unfamiliar and too alien to the Greek tribes for them to have been able to become the object of truly fruitful investigation. In fact, here we once again run up against a limitation of the Greek mind grounded in the Greek's deepest feeling for life. The Greek demonstrates an energetic interest in understanding only with respect to another Greek and, secondarily, a related Italic. The cycle of legends which surrounds the head of Solon as the great representative of the moderate Greek art of living and governing proves, it is true, their eager sympathy in the great catastrophes of those cultural lands. Herodotus' history shows the active curiosity of Greek scholars about foreign lands and peoples. The *Cyropaedia* shows how efficiency of monarchical institutions preoccupied citizens of these free, but politically and militarily inadequately protected, city-states. But the Greek scholar demonstrates no need to delve into the literature of foreign peoples in their own language to get closer to the wellsprings of their intellectual life. He perceives the basic expressions of life of these people as something foreign to him. For him their real culture lies on the border of what makes up his own historico-social reality. On the other hand the culture of his own people and their political life, insofar as historical knowledge deals with them, first developed only gradually in the period when Greek science began. Consequently, insofar as the historico-social world comprises the human race and its organization, it still remained below the horizon for the Greek mind.

Linked with this narrow limitation we discover a positive error which sprang from it. Greek theories achieved their full development at a time when precisely the highest ranking polities of purely Greek origin had already passed their zenith. Regardless of the respect even Plato still had for the political life of the Spartans and what great hopes he still wanted to pin on a constitution which would emulate the taut, unified force of their state system in a nobler direction, for Aristotle an example of a genuinely Greek state which might have escaped the fate of decay no longer existed. Thus the idea of a cycle of human affairs or of social as well as political conditions, or the still more gloomy idea of their gradual disappearance, grew out of experience itself. And this total lack of any notion of progress and development is connected with limiting the spirit of inquiry to Greek man, as noted above. Thus the Greek investigator of social and historical reality still had no historical awareness of an inner progressive development, and he approached a feeling for his real connection with the entire human race only late and gradually through mediation of the Macedonian kingdom and the Roman Empire and through the influence of the Orient.

To this limitation of the Greek mind, which is linked to the range of its historical purview, there corresponds another one which has to do with the relation of the person to society. And this limitation, too, is rooted in the innermost soul of Greek man. Dedication to the world's rationality is linked to lack of penetration into the mysteries of the life of the soul, a lack of understanding of the free person in contrast with everything which is nature. Only at a later period shall the will—which regards itself as an infinitely valuable end in itself—when it attains to metaphysical reflection, change the attitude of man toward nature and society. But for the Greek of that time the particular will still makes no claim in its own right to a sphere of sovereign authority which the state is obligated to protect and may not rob him of. Law does not yet have the task of securing for the individual this sphere of liberty within which he may function. Freedom does not yet have the meaning of unrestrained development and movement of the will in this sphere. On the contrary, the state is an institution of domination; freedom consists in participating in this domination. The Greek soul does not yet feel a need for a sphere of life which lies beyond all social order. Slavery, killing crippled or feeble newly born children, and ostracism characterize this imperfect evaluation of man. Incessant struggle for a share in political power characterizes the effect of that evaluation on society.

Within these boundaries the picture the peoples of the Mediterranean had of socio-historical reality went through the same stages which the picture of modern peoples has also traversed, though on a greater scale and modified by changed circumstances.

Stage of Deriving Social Order from a Divine Origin

In the first of these stages, during the *hegemony of mythical thought, the order of society was traced to divine ordinance.* The Greeks shared this idea of the origin of social order with the adjacent great Asiatic states, despite how different details of the idea among the Greeks were as compared with the Orientals. It maintained its leading position as long as the heroic period lasted. In this period all power was personal. The heroic king had no physical means of force to compel the obedience of a perpetually refractory nobility; there was no written constitution which might have established a legal claim. Hence all ideas and feelings in those days were immersed in the element of the personal. Poetry was a song about heroes; to connect the heroic element of the present to a higher element from the past and to trace the latter all the way to personal powers of the gods; to perceive and enjoy in images of the political state of the gods the motives of one's own life in mightier pulsation: this was a fundamental mark of social feelings and ideas of that period.

The notion of connection between social order and personal powers of a higher world then remained a living ingredient in Greek convictions.[105] Isolated to the north as though by broad crossbars of mountain from the continent, central Greece is divided by the ramification of the mountains into a number of cantons protected in their independence by mountains with high and narrow accesses; at the same time it is open to the sea, which protects and connects. Across the mild sea are isles like piers of a bridge. In many of these cantons the power of mythical ideas maintained itself for a long time with tenacious force. For the roots of mythical faith for these self-enclosed communities lay in the local cults, as one can still see from the late report of Pausanias.

At the same time these geographical conditions also worked toward developing small polities in which political freedom unfolded in a setting of active intellectual development. Hence political freedom first found a lasting, artistically powerful and scientifically grounded expression in the writings of the Greeks. And that is how it first became an imperishable acquisition for European political development. This signficance of the political literature of the Greeks is indestructible. However, it is much diminished by a one-sidedness of their political conception, which we shall soon discuss, and which has likewise communicated itself to modern political life.

We detect the first beginnings of this literature in the large coastal cities whose political, social, and intellectual development took place very rapidly. Here the need arose to replace mythical faith in the social order through a *metaphysical foundation*. Indeed, a first theoretical reflection on society of this kind began when the social order as such was related to the metaphysical structure of the universe. Heraclitus is the most powerful representative of this metaphysical grounding of social order; but remnants of Pythagorean ideas also point to such a grounding, although it was obviously thoroughly shot through with mythical elements.

Natural Law of the Sophists as an Atomistic Metaphysics of Society and Reasons for Its Unfruitfulness

The Greek conception of social order entered a new phase in the period of the *Sophists*. The appearance of Protagoras and Gorgias is the starting point of this great intellectual upheaval. Nevertheless, it would be erroneous to make the class of the Sophists responsible for the change in political ideas which now took place. (The Sophists' name designated first of all a changed system of instruction in Greece, not an alteration in philosophy.) The theories of the Sophists merely follow a complete change in social feelings and are its expression. This change was provoked by the gradual destruction of the old tribal constitution in which the individual had still felt himself to be an element of the ordering of society and by which he had been embraced in his essential living relationships. The tragedy of *Aeschylus* continued to shape the myths of a bygone day so profoundly because it still sensed the relations and feelings underlying them. Now an individualistic tendency in interests, feelings, and ideas became dominant. Athens became the focal point of this change in social feelings. Moreover, the revolution which thus took place was powerfully furthered by the centralization of the intellectual movement in this city and the skeptical spirit that was gaining ground in it. Anaxagoras created in fifth-century Athens a dominant power of intellectual enlightenment; one may assume that Zeno appeared there at that time and gained influence through his skeptical turn of mind; the appearance of Protagoras and Gorgias further advanced the same spirit of skeptical enlightenment in the city. If the Sophists were not originators of the transformation which took place in the life and thought of Greek society at that time, nevertheless it received extraordinary support when this new order of representatives of higher instruction attracted Athenian youth by answering to the need of a time in which speech had become the most powerful means for gaining influence and wealth. An ideal of personal training arose, in the spirit of which Cicero later saw the life-ideal of a Roman man in the orator. In a later period humanism renewed not only the culture of the ancients but also this educational ideal of theirs and thereby introduced the unhappy dominance of formal education among us. The root of all this can be found in the teaching activity of the Sophists; from it went forth the spirit of the rhetorical schools which spread across the ancient world. In vain did Plato and Aristotle, in contrast with the poor rhetorician Isocrates, fight this sickness of Greek life in their battle against the Sophists; it was in vain because only the Sophists, in the private instructional system of the Greek polities in which school fell to free competition, were offering precisely what answered to the dominant inclinations. A system of private instruction, after all, can never be better than the average mentality of the time. Thus in countless channels the individualistic and skeptical spirit, such as it had developed since the middle of the fifth century, flowed downward toward the level of the masses, there to divide itself by way of popular assemblies, theater, and the new sophistical instruction, first in Athens and then, from this center, all over Greece.

The *first generation of Sophists,* however, still displayed no decided and clear negative attitude about the prevailing social order. The premises of such a negative posture lay in the relativism of Protagoras. Nor was Protagoras's the kind of mind which would fail to see its importance.[106] But if he had already actually developed the consequences of this relativism, then the myth which Plato recounts in his name in the dialogue named after him would be unintelligible. Gorgias—a linguistic genius, judicious in his attitude to life, a neutral professional type unmoved by any strong emotion with respect to moral and social problems—left undisturbed the moral ideals of life in their manifold actuality;[107] for him they constitute the presupposition for his technique, which was concerned only with the power and the art of engendering credibility.

Nevertheless, implicit in the movement which the first-generation Sophists produced was the point of departure for a negative philosophy of society. The enormous transformation of intellectual interests which took place in this period and is the great work of the Sophists (joined by Socrates in this respect) now emphasized intellectual facts, language, thought, rhetoric, political life, and morality as objects of scientific investigation. A picture of what goes on in the mind first emerged through reflection on these intellectual facts in contrast with material conceptions of the soul. The same transformation of intellectual development, on the other hand, relativized every phenomenon. And so the wise moderation of the first generation of Sophists with respect to the social order of Greece and its religious foundations gradually had to give way to a more radical attitude.

Between the first and the second generation of Sophists stands *Hippias.* In his person, too, one senses, in a modification different from that of Protagoras or Gorgias, the atmosphere of a completely altered period. A masterly many-sidedness whose intellectual ambition transcended the small city-states basked in the spendor of a time in which art became secular and an expression of a beautiful requirement of life and every scientific problem became the subject of radical debates, a time in which one could acquire riches and fame on a hitherto unprecedented scale in the wide theater of Greek-speaking peoples. I have shown that the contrast between divine unwritten law and human statutes, which Sophocles expressed with incisive poetical power, acquired scientific formulation at the hands of Archelaus and Hippias.[108] Hippias put cosmic divine law, which in Heraclitus' metaphysics had been the creative reason for the entire social order of individual states, in opposition to these individual orders. The law of nature and the statute of the particular state were slogans of the time, and from then on one looked for this contrast among totally different phenomena of intellectual life.

But a much more radical relationship to social order was inherent in Protagoras' relativism, and the *second generation of Sophists* developed it. Now one derived social order from the play of individuals' egoism, just as the school of Leucippus derived the order of the cosmos from the play of atoms. A metaphysical cosmogony of moral and social order comes into being. We find that this cosmogony of society already used the entire metaphysical machinery of this radical natural law, such as we find it again in Hobbes and Spinoza: the lawless *struggle* for existence and power among strong, animal-like individuals; the *compact* in which a legal order arises which then protects order from the worst instance of violation, to be sure, but at the same time bars the way to the highest happiness of absolute rule; the *emergence of morality and religion as an expansion of the laws of the state* in the interests of the many or the strong; finally the *persistence of egoistic interest* among individuals as the true lever of social movements.[109] *Euripides* is the representative poet of these new individualistic times, and in his plays he has made such radical theorems the basis for the behavior of certain persons with an energy which betrays his own personal interest. Aristophanes, in a famous dialogue, ridiculed the proposition that there is no independently grounded law in the face of force as a controversial issue of his times. And so this radical natural law made itself heard in political assemblies, just as it did in the theater; or at least we can conclude as much from speeches in Thucydides, regardless what the degree of their authenticity might be in each case.[110]

The limitations of Greek man and Greek society described above determine the *boundaries of this natural law*. In no case does Greek natural law have to do with subjective spheres of justice of individuals working together in society; in no case is freedom in that kind of sense the goal of this natural law. Striving of the individual, according to these radical writings, is directed only toward participation of social atoms in the power and advantage of the social order which thus arises. Hence here they support tyrants and there the idea of democratic equality of these social atoms in the political order; in either case the slavery of every lofty and ideal will is their last word. But the moderate school which Hippias represents directs this natural-law metaphysics only toward separating objective order of nature from the positive law of a particular state. The political science of the Cynics and the Stoics collides with these limits, but it does not break through them. In this area it is related to our modern view of law exactly as sophistical and skeptical relativism is related to modern epistemology.

Thus, inherent in this movement were *germs for various tendencies* of that theory of society designated as *natural law*. Once natural law had been developed, it was handed down from the ancient peoples to modern ones in relatively unbroken succession. It was also cultivated in the Middle Ages in an extensive literature. But its hegemony and its practical effectiveness depended even for modern peoples on the emergence of the stage of social development in which it arose among the ancient peoples. Not until the destruction of the feudal orders among this second generation of European peoples did their natural law rise to a leading position in the history of society. It now accomplished its negative work, as the termination of which one must regard the influence of Rousseau on the Revolution and Pufendorf, Kant, and Fichte on the German work of reform. For its starting point is precisely the isolated individual, abstract man, characterized by features uniformly proper to him at all times, in abstract relationships which flow from these features and on a similarly abstract foundation. From such premises natural law deduces the general features of every social order. These general features become for it the norm for the critique of old European society and for the new order of a future one. Thus this conceptual fiction attained a frightful reality in the Revolution and its attempt to construct society on the foundation of abstract human atoms.

Natural law can be labeled a *metaphysics of society,* if the expression metaphysics be allowed in this narrower sense, in which it would express a science which presents the entire objective inner structure of societal facts as a theory. Natural law is distinguished from metaphysics in the full sense precisely because its intent is directed only to construction of the inner organization of society; hence in its most perfect form it does not posit an objective inner structure of all phenomena as the basis of study of society but treats this topic independently. Within these limits it has the features of metaphysics. It does not analyze reality but synthesizes it out of abstract partial contents of individuals as though from its true causes, and it regards the structure which so arises as the real cause of the social order.[111]

Has this social atomism in the scientific context of the time proven *more fruitful* for *detailed explanation* [*Spezialerklärung*] *of historical phenomena* than natural-scientific atomism did for phenomena of the cosmos? Extant remains of the natural law of the period permit us no fully satisfactory judgment. Yet even here we are still able to establish a relationship analogous to the one we observed in the natural science of the same period.[112] Natural law began with psychical individuals and sought to explain civic society as embraced by a single *polis;* for this concrete political body is the object of Greek political science. The basic psychological concepts of interest, satisfaction, and advantage which sophistic natural law uses are very imperfect. Between basic psychological ideas and the complex fact of this political totality lie connecting links such as division of labor, national wealth, levels of scientific life, forms of family law and property regulation, and religious faith and its independent power, and so forth, the scientific elaboration of which is first determined by exact scientific study of the complex political totality. But, as we have shown in the first book, only abstract sciences, which coordinate the related partial contents of psychical life contained in society, can elaborate these facts. Although corresponding abstract sciences in natural science first started to take shape in very isolated beginnings during the Alexandrian period, technical theories of grammar, logic, rhetoric, poetry, national economy, and juristic technique already existed quite early; the needs of society had produced them, as the first book has also shown. Despite that, Greek ideas about division of labor, about factors of national wealth, and about money never attained an appreciably higher level than their ideas of pressure, motion, and gravity, and, as far as we can tell, the Greeks never used exact juristic concepts in these speculations. As a result their natural-law construction of society was condemned to the same relative sterility that their atomistic construction of the cosmos was. In this sphere as well, for many centuries to come victory fell to the Socratic school with its metaphysics of substantial forms as opposed to metaphysics of social atoms.

Political Science of the Socratic School; Ideal State of Plato; Comparative Political Science of Aristotle

The *Socratic school* arose out of the need to discover a solid anchorage in the midst of the relative truths which the Sophists had left behind. In the Greek cognitive schema one can seek such anchorage either by mirroring objective being in thought or by determining being through activity. It is given as substance in reality or as highest good in the world of willing and acting, whether that of individuals or of communities. Socrates left aside the possibility of a solid anchorage for knowledge of the world; but he found one for action: in *ethical concepts*. This separation of theoretical and practical philosophy indicates a boundary which stems from the limitation of Greek thought in general. The solid starting point of all knowledge, even of the objective world, lies in the interior or in consciousness: this thought lies beyond even the purview of Socrates. Not until this clear insight is present does the moral world, the solid anchor-point of all activity in it, enter into the comprehensive structure of human science. Not until that insight arrives is the false separation of theoretical from practical sciences overcome; not until then can one ground the true separation of natural sciences from human sciences.

Inasmuch as Socrates discovers an unchangeable element in his ethical concepts, *political science* also acquires a *clear purpose*. The goal of the state does not arise now out of the play of atoms which compose it; on the contrary, for Socrates there is in knowledge an unshakeably solid point around which individuals gravitate: the Good. The Good is not relatively but absolutely certain. Thus this goal, as the idea which dominates the organization of the state, subordinates individuals to itself. This political conception of Socrates came into conflict with the prevalent democracy and with the equal right of each social atom with respect to leadership of the state, a right this democracy expressed most bluntly in distributing state offices by lot. Knowledge makes one a ruler; it is the precondition for a share in the leadership of the state.

Plato's great organizing mind constructs the *ideal state* out of this idea as a counterpart to the external cosmos: the state as a work of art. He found Athenian society dissolved into social atoms; so he conceived the idea that, instead of incorporating the relation between political knowledge and power as well as participation in state leadership into the existing political structure, he would construct the state on the basis of this abstract relation. Among modern peoples this notion has subsequently had continuing influence on the current reality of state organizations, and so Plato appears as a prophetic genius with respect to essential features of the modern bureaucratic state. Surrounded as he was by struggles of the city-states for power and by the war of interests, he also found it necessary to have the highest concentration of all particular interests and particular forces in the judicious, unified state will which he devised. Accordingly, he equipped his ideal state with the most extreme means available in the scope of the Greek city-state—which, by the way, regulated property and freedom in an artistically plenipotentiary way—in order to produce this subordination of particular wills and interests to the leadership of reason. So an arrangement comes about in which the insightful rule, the strong support them, and the masses, preoccupied with earning a living, obey: an image of the psyche. The virtues of the parts of the soul are those of the classes in the state. Just as striving for the Good is grounded in the psyche's relation to the world of Ideas, so that same striving (again in connection with that world of Ideas) fashions the ideal of a social cosmos, the state, as a unity which has indeed come into being, but is an indestructibly fused unity because of the (mutual) accommodation of powers in the souls. The art of politics shapes the social cosmos according to ideas of justice and other virtues from the raw material of souls, just as the good God has formed the external world. Thus arises macro-man: a real unity just as individual man is.

The intrinsic untenability of this kind of metaphysics of society is obvious. The analogy of man writ large only shifts the problem of how a general will, that is, a system of wills which works as a unity, arises out of particular wills. Plato has accomplished his task neither for the individual soul nor for the state. On the contrary, his parts of souls can no more constitute a real psychical unity than his three classes can make up a unified society.

Because Plato's starting point was not the interests of individuals or the reality of human nature as it actually is,[113] the structure of a community of interests which makes up the foundation of the actual state did not emerge for him; on the contrary, he despised it as something lowly and made no investigation into labor, industry, or trade. The false aristocratic tendency underlying this is related to the tendency the Greeks demonstrated everywhere in the knowledge of nature. Thus the idea and physical power are left to hold the state together; meanwhile, the interests of classes in the state go their separate ways and must tear it apart. With a kind of conceptual absolutism Plato treats the real interests of individuals simply as refractory material for the political virtuoso, instead of recognizing the framework of dependence and community (which manifests itself as the will of the state) as a result of the combination of interests. So he constructs a state in the air here. The upshot is a most concentrated unity, but one which is at the same time powerless with regard to the play of interests. This man writ large is a trope; the real unity of the state asserted in this trope is not only incomprehensible—it remains such always and everywhere, because it is nothing but metaphysics—but the attempt is not even made to explain the trope through concepts. Hence grave material flaws are combined with a more general error of a methodical kind. One is supposed to understand the state before analyzing the interests and purpose-nexuses which make up its reality in man and in virtue of which it lives and has power. A result of this error is that in place of a system of facts (purpose-nexuses, interests) the metaphysical phantasm of man writ large emerges.[114]

Aristotle tried to replace this trope by a formula. He seeks to sketch the concept of the real unity which the state is. His political science is so instructive here also because it shows how this fundamental concept of social metaphysics shares with other principal metaphysical concepts the characteristic of resisting complete resolution into simply clear conceptual elements.

It has been shown that the given subjects for declarations about social reality are individuals. The subjects for declarations about nature are inaccessible to us, whereas those of social life—acting and being acted upon, and conditions in social life—are contained in inner experience.[115] Aristotle has defined *rational individual beings as substances*. But in the context of his metaphysics he looked on the state made up of these single individual beings as a unity that is not a subsequent combination of them. Indeed, he did not assimilate his concept of the state into his metaphysics, because the latter ends short of the practical world and accordingly just before the great problem of the will, and in his system the sphere of practical reason is separated from that of theoretical science. But the premises for his conception of the unity of the state are the following. The *teleological system* demonstrates an increase of functions in the realm of organic beings that corresponds to a heightening of the psychical element. The race of men is thus the highest substantial form in the ladder of organic beings. Particular individuals in this human race are linked together in still another way than just by realizing a substantial form. Individual human beings find themselves in *social wholes,* in which individuals are related as parts. Bees and other gregarious animals also make up such totalities, but man, endowed by nature with speech and understanding for this purpose and possessing power to distinguish right from wrong, does so in much closer association. This community (*koinōnie*), as a *family,* is inseparable from human existence in general, and as the family expands into the *village community* and then on into the *polis,* the innate striving for community attains in the polis the ultimate goal of autarchy, that is, of complete self-sufficiency; the *polis* is the *goal* of more elementary forms of community, a goal that is already effectual even in less composite forms. In this context appears Aristotle's formula that the *state is a totality* which is *prior to families and individuals as its parts.*[116] This formula expresses the idea that the state is not a construct of human volition but a system grounded in nature. In nature, in which purpose is operative, there is a system of determining factors which actualize themselves only through and in particular individuals but which lead these individuals to communal organization (*taxis*) in a polity, because it is only in the latter that the goal of eudaemonism is achieved in a self-sufficient way. Such determining factors are, for example, inequality between individuals, opposition between rulers and ruled, and the proportion between performance and political power. They possess necessity of purpose. And indeed the system (*sustēma*) into which polity's goal orders the multitude (*plēthos*) is made up of dissimilar components. Nor is the individual completely swallowed up by this purpose either. One can compare cooperation of dissimilar individuals as parts in a whole with that of parts in an organism. The individual person is related to the whole state as a foot or hand is to a body.

Thus Aristotle paved the way for the notion of the *state as an organism,* which has played so fateful a role in the history of political sciences. The concept of the organism is in its way the final word of this metaphysics of the state. And like every concept of the unity of the state which does not in some measure explain that unity analytically by the actuality of the state's life, that concept is a conceptual fabrication of metaphysics. Analysis can break down what we experience in social life within certain limits, but it can never express the richness of life in a formula.[117] Hence one cannot describe the reality of the state by a specific number of conceptual elements. This is already evident in Aristotle's case in the obscurity of the idea he forms of the state as an organic whole, and this obscurity, because it lies in the nature of the case itself, has never been overcome.[118]

Nevertheless, Aristotle's way of thinking, which regarded the state as a real nexus of purposes, has proven most fruitful for *comparative study of the state.* In the sphere of the mind it has performed almost as radical a task for study of the state as Aristotle's teleological reflection accomplished in the study of nature for biological sciences. To be sure, one cannot conceive of the state as the realization of a unified idea or purpose; even Aristotle's so soundly developed teleological idea of eudaemonism[119] is only an abstract formula. But in reality, will, interests, and purposes make up the framework of the state, hence one may regard the tendency toward realization of eudaemonism, which Aristotle assumes is present in society, as at least an imperfect shorthand formulation of the facts of the case. Hence Aristotle's teleological point of view in this case attains the level of factuality. So his viewpoint could employ comparative analysis of states to establish basic outlines of their structure and to define the principal forms of political life. And it carried out this task so completely that the concepts so fashioned have maintained their value even till today. This work of Aristotle and his school was a precondition for explanatory methods in the political sciences just as it has been in biology.

Hence here too metaphysics of substantial forms has proven fruitful at a *stage* of science in which *means for analyzing* the structure of processes according to laws were *not yet available.*

All associational relationships, as our special theoretical discussion showed,[120] and therefore the state too, are, psychologically speaking, composed of relations of dependence and community. From this system of passive and active determinations of will arises the psychological relation of command and obedience, ruler and subject, on which the state's unity of will is grounded. But this system of dependencies and communalities is only the facade of real relations of interests to one another. Material factors of the state's life are focused particularly in purposes and interests that the free interaction of the activities of individuals does not satisfy. Here we perceive the real side of something which, considered as mere relations of will alone, appears to be the mechanics of society and of the life of the state and culminates in the existence of the sovereign will of the state. We can designate this condition of external relations of will in a state as the form of the state or also as a constitution.

Corresponding to this situation is the fact that Aristotle's political science defined external forms or constitutions chiefly by using the comparative method. The real life of the state is so extraordinarily complex that even modern, truly analytical science is still at the beginning of its scientific treatment. But antiquity did not yet possess conditions for such truly analytical method at all. It lacked a developed psychology, as well as the special sciences placed between it and politics. With regard to ordering real purposes in the state's life, it was hindered from fruitful analysis of the sort which sciences such as political economy and writers such as Niebuhr and Tocqueville began to achieve only much later.

Consequently, Greek *political science* was at its apex, by preference, with Aristotle's analysis of *constitutions*. As a result of this narrowness in angle of vision, the state loses its identity for Aristotle if its constitution is changed. The state (*polis*) is a community (*koinōnia*) and the essence of this community (*koinōnia politōn*) is designated by the constitution (*politeia*); consequently, if the constitution changes, so does the state. In the process the people remain the same, just as the same persons make up the tragic chorus and go from that into the comic chorus. Behind the change in the form of the state Aristotle fails to perceive the people's permanent community of interests, which is what constitutes the political structure; on the contrary, for him the state constitution is the essential element which makes up the state.[121] Of a piece with that is that for him the politician is related to citizens as an artist is to his material. The masses are the material for constructing the state.[122] So Aristotle substitutes a false opposition between matter and form for the real structure of society, and this opposition was just as disastrous for him in political science as it was in natural sciences. In actuality, there exist in the state a ubiquitously formative force, a nexus of purposes, relationships of interests, and a ubiquitous content: for *the person* exists everywhere in it. In the life goals of the people who compose it is grounded the life of the state as well. But here, as happens to a degree for the Greeks in general, historical awareness of natural growth disappears altogether behind the feeling of power of the politician, who demands to knead the state as a plastic artist does his material. And at the same time awareness of the continuity of law also recedes; thus Aristotle, in the context mentioned above, raises the further question about the extent to which, when a change is made in the state constitution, obligations the earlier state incurred are still valid or likewise cease.

And so the *law* we have established regarding *development of European science is corroborated* in a surprising way even *in the human sciences*. European science seeks first of all to know reality in its extreme complexity directly; it describes, compares, and traces it to supposed or metaphysically putative causes. In a gradual way at first, it isolates individual spheres of partial contents of reality from one another and subjects them to persistent and abstract causal examination. Phenomena of motion, for example, make up such a sphere, those of economic life another one. In abstract sciences the march of knowledge now reveals the basic characteristics of the partial contents belonging to individual spheres and replaces, say, teleological notions such as Aristotle used in his explanation by appropriate concepts. In its dominant position among the sciences, *metaphysics was a fact corresponding to the first state of reflection.*

External organization of society in *states* has most forcefully attracted the attention of investigators who made socio-historical reality their field of study. For here we encounter the remarkable phenomenon of a unity of will which transcended particular wills. This phenomenon must have seemed much more astounding to the Greeks than to the monarchical peoples of the East. For the latter their kings represented unity of will in a personal way, and by contrast it was, so to speak, incorporeal in these Greek polities. This problem of unity of will in the state preoccupied the writers known as Sophists. States struggling with one another make up the subject matter of the great Greek historians. The average man and how he lives, works, enjoys, and suffers at a given time was as little visible to history as was humanity itself. The same problem preoccupied the Socratic school most of all, and it became the subject of a theory of society which corresponded to the metaphysical standpoint of European thought. Correspondence between a very successful descriptive study of political forms and metaphysics comes about in the now established comparative science of the structure and forms of states.

This comparative political science, according to what we have presented, proceeds from considering the *relation of sovereignty* as expressed in the constitution. For Aristotle a *constitution* is the ordering of the state with respect to the government of the official authorities, especially of the sovereign power above them all.[123] He sees the *citizen,* accordingly, as one who participates in functions of state administration and dispensation of justice.[124] Indeed, Aristotle makes the concept developed by the Socratic school regarding the *relation between political performance* and *share in power and property* into the basis of his analysis of the constitution into its formal elements (to be distinguished from knowledge based on factors of the state as a reality) and of the search for the principal forms of state constitution. Aristotle expands this concept of performance with an unprejudiced, realistic, fact-comparing mind. Performance is related to the *goal of the political totality* whose life and activity is at stake. He defines this goal in his system through the rising series of distinctive functions of living beings: it consists in *eudaemonism* of the totality and its parts, the individual citizens. The state is thus comparable to a living, purposefully operating entity. Difference in the *kind of eudaemonism* which the living political totality seeks in accordance with its own *conditions of life* determines difference in assessing achievements, and this has an effect on calculating the proportion between performances and shares in power and profit. These relations constitute the *structure of a political totality.* Aristotle completes the image of this structure of a living being when he traces back relations between performance and the living relations and conditions which are its foundation. Thus emerge the foundations for a morphological, comparative study of states and for the brilliant theory of disturbances of equilibrium and the genesis of revolutions.

Aristotle's comparative political science is limited by its inability to use causal concepts taken from developed antecedent sciences in its analysis but instead is referred in the main to imperfect teleological ideas. Aristotle thus rashly concluded to the natural necessity of slavery because he assumed natural inequality among men, without considering its origin in historical conditions and the possibility of overcoming those conditions suggested thereby. Thus he took the distinction between the naturally perfect (i.e., corresponding to the nexus of purposes) and its deviations, a distinction which caused so much havoc in his physics, and introduced it into his politics as well; one must reject his distinction between perfect constitutions and imperfect ones as an arbitrary construction of a reality which shows only differences of degree. But the most harmful thing was the one-sided way he identified the state with its constitution. Aristotle's political formalism has hindered realistic consideration of the state to a high degree.

Aristotle and the Aristotelian school, however, are also the focal point for an incomparable activity of collecting, historical writing, and theory which goes beyond political science. Alongside theories of poetry, rhetoric, scientific thought, and moral life we find historical writing in the sciences, artwork, and religious ideas in the Aristotelian school. Indeed, in his *Bios Hellados* Dicaearchus moves on to a cultural-historical mode of treatment; he distinguishes the legendary golden age of a moderate and peaceful state of nature, the emergence of nomadic life, and, as a further historical stage, the sedentary life which agriculture produces; with the natural conditions of Greece he links a picture of Greek life in which customs, enjoyment of life, festivals, and constitutions are seen together in inner unity. Hence the accomplishments of the Aristotelian school for the human sciences are in no respect inferior to those for the natural sciences.

Finally, let us indicate the *position of the study of human society in the structure of science* in the period covered. Just as special theories about the systems of culture and about the external organization of society had grown out of the requirements of technical assistance for occupational life, so they have preserved this practical character, which also gave politics its direction toward the best constitution. Theoretical science in the strict sense ends as a whole for these philosophers where the will begins to erect its own realm. From this standpoint it is already clear that this period did not yet see how *freedom of the will* was compatible with subordinating all appearances to the law of causality. But more permanent than such limitation of metaphysics, which was to be only transitory, was the effect in this direction of the general and permanent *relation of the entire metaphysics of substantial forms to the problem of freedom*. This metaphysics reduced only universal forms of reality to the structure of knowledge; but freedom of the individual was not affected by them. With an enviable assurance of the consciousness of freedom given in inner experience and still undisturbed by the question of the relation of that consciousness to the causal system which establishes science, Aristotle declares that action as well as omission, virtue as well as vice lie within our control.[125]

8. Dissolution of Metaphysics in Skepticism; Ancients Enter the Stage of Special Sciences

The position Aristotle ascribes to knowledge with respect to reality is one which metaphysics itself ascribes to it. The explanatory history of metaphysics has therefore now accomplished its main work; only further development of metaphysics still lies before it.

Meanwhile, skepticism continued to exist since the period of the Sophists. Pyrrho, founder of the skeptical school, appeared immediately after Aristotle. The debates of this school, but especially those of the more recent, skeptically oriented Academy, filled the third and second centuries B.C. and culminated in Sextus Empiricus' summary of the arguments against all sciences. In comparison with the relativism of Protagoras they show progress in skeptical thought inasmuch as, based on the now established logic and metaphysics, they use the distinctions between sensation and thought, phenomenon and objective substratum for the phenomenon, syllogism and induction, and so forth in elaborating their fundamental skeptical idea. In the process the boundary line which the Greek mind set down for skepticism stood out still more clearly. Within the presuppositions of the ancient peoples, however, this skepticism proved to be completely invincible. It remained victorious on the broad battleground of Greek metaphysics.

Skepticism

What are the *limitations of the reasoning* of the skeptical schools of antiquity? If one reads what has survived from them it seems only reasonable if we come to the aid of the skeptics from our higher standpoint, if we raise up, in effect, what from their angle of vision lay below their horizon. Thus it is clear that they disputed and *dissolved* only what lay in their purview: *antiquity's objective knowledge of the world*. It is also clear that their critique did not see other things at all—and thus missed them. Socrates' ignorance was akin to the feeling for truth of a future time. Turned in on himself, Pyrrho stood at the boundary line of the Greek world. He calmly established that all metaphysics and all positive knowledge which the Greek mind had been able to catch sight of is not objective truth. The time was still to come when from a higher standpoint one saw other things which the skeptics from Pyrrho to Sextus Empiricus could not perceive. Their final judgment on the whole position of the metaphysician has remained valid: they destroyed metaphysics. But, in fact, metaphysics is not the same as the truth.

Accordingly, we shall expand things through our own insight in order to understand the skeptics thoroughly. They speak of a condition of sense perception which man passively experiences,[126] and distinguish this from knowing.[127] But they have no inkling that awareness of such a state, which they do not dispute, is itself a kind of knowledge; in fact it is the most certain knowledge, from which all knowledge must hold its certainty in fee. Instead, in conformity with the metaphysical standpoint, they seek truth exclusively in something which thinking posits as the objective foundation for the phenomenon given us in external perception.[128] Thus they indeed acknowledge seeing and thinking as undeniable facts; but for them these facts do not contain worthwhile knowledge, namely, knowledge of the facts of consciousness. As a consequence, they do not clearly develop the notion that the external world is only a phenomenon for consciousness and so they fail to arrive at a coherent view of the external world in this sense.[129] On the contrary, they merely ask whether one can use the sense impression given in consciousness as a symbol of the objective basis of such phenomena. And they rightly deny that one can. They correctly deny any kind of knowledge of this objective basis of phenomena: the Kantian thing-in-itself.[130] Hence they are in error only insofar as they use this reason to dispute the possibility of all knowledge.

Thus Sextus Empiricus expressly declares: the skeptic does not destroy the phenomenon; he acknowledges the passive condition in which he finds himself in sensation and merely doubts any assertion concerning an objective substratum for this condition.[131] In agreement with this view we find the limits of skepticism given in Diogenes Laertius, insofar as the skeptics establish these limits in confronting the distortions of metaphysicians. Conditions we experience, that is, phenomena (*ta phainomena*), are not called into question; but what is called into question is any knowledge of something that is true, that is, of something which underlies those phenomena in the external world.[132] These express declarations show that the skeptics completely failed to use rightly the phenomena of consciousness, which they recognized, for the problem of knowledge. Therefore they deny all knowledge of anything truly existing, even though they have basically refuted only knowledge of the external world. This limitation of their thought is manifested most clearly through a remarkable dispute. If the skeptics say: everything is false, the metaphysicians assert: therefore so is your declaration, and so it cancels itself out. The soundest response of the skeptics to that is this: in using such words the skeptic is only expressing what his own state is, without expressing any opinion, without saying anything at all about an underlying foundation for phenomena outside himself.[133] At this point the epistemologist must intervene to settle the quarrel and must say: precisely in this situation is true knowledge given, and in it lies the starting point of all philosophy.

Now that we have clarified these limitations of skepticism for ourselves, if anyone thinks knowledge of the objective basis of what appears to us in our sensations is possible, we emphatically refer him to the definitive repudiation of every such effort in the extant remains of the admirable skeptical school. Insofar as it refers to proof of the impossibility of all metaphysics, the *relativism* of modern philosophers is not distinct from that of Sextus Empiricus in any point at all. Modern relativism does go beyond him, however, with respect to developing a theory of the structure of phenomena within the confines of insight into their relativity. However, the theory of probability of the most famous of all skeptics, Carneades, already develops the idea that even after one renounces claims to the truth, it is possible to develop a coherent structure of phenomena for the purpose of establishing the value of a single impression.

The relativism of the skeptics proves the *impossibility* of knowing the objective makeup of the *external world* through the criticism of *sensation* as well as *thought*. Thus it paves the way for the great demonstration which the seventeenth and eighteenth centuries have given us, when the empirical school since Locke analyzed sensation to find the possibility of objective knowledge in it, and simultaneously the rational school analyzed thinking with the same purpose in mind. The undeniable result of the process was that neither the one nor the other could discover a source of metaphysical knowledge of the objective structure of phenomena.

Consequently, the first question is: What is the cognitive value of *what is given in sense perception?* Images of phenomena are determined first of all by the *sense organs*. Protagorean grounding of relativism through observations about the senses is now deepened by advanced biological study. Instruments of sight in *living beings* are extremely varied and force us to infer a difference in the visual images they mediate. This school applies here the method of observing subjective phenomena of the senses and of using the conditions under which they appear as analogies to form an idea of how visual images of animals deviate from normal human visual impressions. The same method is followed also with respect to the other sense organs. If fever makes our tongue dry, we experience taste sensations different from those in normal conditions, and so we can assume that corresponding differences in an animal's organization are also accompanied by variation in sensations of taste. The result is summed up in the following beautiful image: Just as pressure of the same hand on a lyre evokes now a deep tone and now a high one, so also the play of the same objects in action produces completely different phenomena as a result of subtle and varied tuning of sensations built into the makeup of living beings. One can also show the same difference in *the human sphere;* hallucinatory visual phenomena and great differences in reaction to impressions through pleasure and displeasure are evidence of this. But in addition objects are given to us in *five kinds of sense perceptions.* So the same apple is present to us as smooth, good-smelling, sweet, and yellow. Now, who can say whether it has just one inner constitution but appears different in accordance with the differing disposition of the sense organs? The image mentioned before about pressure of the same hand on the lyre can illustrate this possibility. And is it not just as possible for the apple to have five different characteristics, or even more, unknown to us? One who is born both blind and dumb assumes that only three classes of characteristics of objects exist. But we are not justified in responding to such reflections by invoking the help of nature to make our sense organs correspond to their objects. Indeed, even impressions in a single sense organ are dependent on *change in its states.* If poured on inflamed members, the same water appears boiling to us which we perceive as lukewarm when our skin temperature is normal. Thus the skeptical position closely approximates the theory of sense energies developed by Johannes Müller.[134]

Insight into relativity of sense images broadens when we perceive how *variable external circumstances* surrounding an object given to us effect a difference of impressions. The same objective cause of a sound produces a different impression in thinner air than it does in heavier air; if one scrapes a goat's horn, which looks black in its general setting, one's sense impression changes to white; a single grain of sand seems hard, a heap of sand soft.[135]

In this fashion the skeptic extracts the *general formula* of the *relativity of every perceptual image* or sense impression. All the tropes he posits ultimately prove to be modifications of one comprehensive theorem of the relativity of impressions.[136] These impressions are conditioned by the subject and by external conditions affecting the objective thing that emerges. And so, in opposition to all metaphysics which pretends to penetrate to the essential, one can assert that sensations can express only relations of the objective.

What about *understanding?* And what about *thought?* The skeptics' refutation of objective knowledge of nature is much more imperfect on this point than it is in investigating the cognitive value of sense perception. Plato's and Aristotle's science of reason had been discredited. Carneades starts by assuming that understanding must derive its content from sensation. Let us therefore first of all abide by this presupposition. The problem here acquires its most universal scope through the concept of the *criterion.* It is clear that sense perceptions do not contain a criterion which would separate true perceptions from false ones. We cannot distinguish the former from the latter by any internal characteristic proper to them. Thus we must look for the criterion in thought or in understanding. But thought is now in the same situation as someone who sees the portrait of a person whom he does not know and is asked to judge how good a likeness the portrait is by looking at it alone. Our understanding cannot decide on the basis of sense images about the unknown element which lies at their root. If, however, we assume with Plato and Aristotle that thinking has its own proper content, then we cannot establish its relationship to reality. *Understanding in man's inner life* contains no datum by which to establish what exists *outside* it. Nor can syllogistic reasoning help us out of such difficulties. Skeptics acknowledge this fully: If the the major premise of a syllogism were certain, without being merely derived from other syllogisms, then it must be demonstrated through a complete inductive procedure, and then what is apparently gained in the conclusion is already contained in the major premise; thus no new truth emerges in the conclusion. Hence every mode of reasoning already presupposes a truth of final instance, which is, however, available to man neither in sensation nor in understanding.

These proofs of the impossibility of objective knowledge are completely *victorious against every metaphysics,* because metaphysics claims to prove an objective structure of the world outside us. But they do not refute knowledge in general. For they overlook the fact that a reality is given in ourselves which cannot be driven away. The disjunction—either external sensation or thinking—has a gap in it. The skeptics failed to see this, and even Kant did not see it.

But skepticism also uncovers *difficulties in the real concepts* which are the bonds of every metaphysical construction of the world, and these difficulties are in part insuperable. Thus it rightly sees that the concept of *cause* does not express a reality but a mere relation; as such a relation, however, a cause has no real existence but is merely thought as a kind of supplement to the real.[137] It observes that a cause can be thought of neither as preceding its effect nor as simultaneous with it. Skepticism shows that every attempt to clarify the relationship between cause and effect in its individual components is unrealizable. Accordingly, the skeptics used arguments, against which there is no defense, to attack the relationship between cause and effect. Carneades called the concept of *God as cause of the world* into question in a very superficial attack on the superficial teleology which sees the goal of nature in man, but also by discovering the antinomy between properties of a personal being and the nature of perfect and infinite being.[138] He also demonstrated recognized difficulties in analytically understanding the basic mathematical and physical concepts of *body, extension, motion,* and *mixture.*

Opposition of skeptical schools to the *practical philosophy* of the metaphysicians focuses on the assault on the fundamental theory of the *highest good.* And this polemic also shows the weak point in the skeptical position very clearly. The skeptics' most penetrating argument is this one. The will's striving for the good as its object presupposes that the good does not already consist in this striving itself, because we of course wish to escape the condition of striving, but rather in its goal. However, this goal cannot be a condition outside ourself, but must be our own condition, our own mental disposition; even a bodily state is present to us as a good only insofar as we comprehend it mentally. Thus far the presentation is excellent. But now the constantly operative confusion of immediate with abstract knowledge enters the picture. We cannot know which frame of mind is the good for us because we do not even know whether and what the soul is, whose disposition is the point in question. A crude fallacy of skepticism!

Post-Aristotelian Metaphysics and Its Subjective Character

Philosophy had been the organizing power which had still guided the entire aggregate of scientific investigations at the close of the Aristotelian school, just as the mathematical and astronomical had been in the Platonic school. The history of the skeptical mind, as we have depicted it, shows, however, that even the perfecting of metaphysics in Aristotle could not overcome the negative epistemological standpoint which, as represented by the Sophists, had confronted what was at first a more imperfect metaphysics. But preparations were underway for a change because *natural and human sciences had made progress* under the organizational influence of metaphysical philosophy. Thus a further *separation* was made in the great *process of differentiation* of the European mind. To a degree the special sciences now broke loose from metaphysics, natural philosophy, and practical philosophy. Still, this separation did not yet take place as conclusively as it has in the modern period. Many of the most important exact scientists remained in an academic alliance with, or even in intimate relationship to, one of the metaphysical schools. It was of a piece with this development that at the same time new metaphysical sects arose that devoted themselves to the cause of personal spiritual satisfaction.

Thus a metaphysics which surrendered its role as leader of the scientific movement parted company with special sciences which developed positivistically, that is, empirically and comparatively. Stoical, Epicurean, and eclectic metaphysics were cultural forces at work in the great educated society; special science, however, rested its case exclusively on experience and served the civilization which strove for domination of the world.

The *metaphysical systems* mentioned summarized results in simpler fashion and made them communicable. They removed those results as much as possible from attacks of the skeptics by less stringent demands on rigor of methods of reasoning and they moved closer to the growing empirical spirit. Thus their goal lay in a disposition of mind, their context in the general culture, their manner of presentation in simplification. The Epicureans did not make *atomism* more fruitful in explaining the complex of nature than it had been in the system of Democritus. For the assumption of the Epicureans that atoms fall from upper to lower regions in empty space because of their weight, with the same velocity and with some deviation from the vertical, was so manifestly unsuited for explaining the cosmos that only the frivolity of the school and its outmoded views in astronomy make this part of the system understandable. Even though the Stoics pushed *monotheism* toward empiricism or gave it a pantheistic hue, it did not overcome the opposition between a motive, form-encompassing force and matter.

History has only to record that, from the appearance of Leucippus on, *opposition between a mechanistic-atomistic* explanation of nature and a *theistic-teleological* one persisted for as long as the ancient peoples lived. Atomistic intellectual effort never ceased for a single day. The atomistic view was that the cosmos is a mere aggregate in which each individual part stands by itself, as though no other parts existed. The primordial state of the world, the state out of which it unfolds, may be compared with the first state of society which the natural-right theorists imagined. These theorists held that individuals are thrown into the world and think only of themselves; they are now bumping up against one another because of the smallness of that world. Indeed, this standpoint develops with ever clearer one-sidedness so that it eliminates the entire problem: How can individual objects be subject to common laws and influence one another? Thus generation after generation propagates the battle between clarity, which recognizes only what the senses can perceive, and depth, which would like to express the incomprehensible and yet factual element of a system, one that cannot reside in any single material element. Goethe once called this the struggle between belief and unbelief and declared this opposition to be the profoundest one in all history. In the ancient world neither mechanistic philosophy nor skeptical philosophy took any part in tracing the order of nature, observed particularly in the stars, to an intelligent cause. In virtue of its sterile, purely negative attitude toward phenomena, skepticism rejected the possibility of knowing existing being at all. The philosophy of the atomists at least kept alive the problem whose scientific treatment by modern peoples later called into question the metaphysics of an intelligent cause: the problem of a mechanical explanation of the cosmos.

At one point a change took place which stretched from metaphysics to the great questions of the special sciences and is extraordinarily important for later intellectual development. The conditions which had governed *Greek-national political science no longer* existed. In the period of its hegemony the thing to do was to form an athletic individual state; freedom in these states consisted of a share in government, and a modern person would have believed that the condition of an Athenian citizen in the time of Cleon was in many respects the same as slavery. To be sure, even amid the period of national development there was opposition to this situation. The political writings of Antisthenes (who is still not sufficiently appreciated) and of Diogenes, one of them lacking full citizenship and the other proscribed, asserted the interior freedom of the wise man against the pressure of the state and a feeling of the alienation of interior life against the whole uproarious bustle of the external political apparatus. As Greek-national development ended, as the campaigns of Alexander opened up the East, and as later the Roman Empire set about its world-historical mission of unifying all civilized nations under one law and one head, a gradual change in perception of life occurred for the person who day in and day out compared the Greek and the Italic with the dark-skinned inhabitants of eastern lands and sensed the universally human element in them. The bond that forged a connection to the state for the oriental who lived and taught in Greece, or for the Greek national who was under a Macedonian prince, or later under Roman aristocrats, was of a totally different kind than that which had bound Socrates to the laws of his native city. Thus a completely transformed political philosophy came about.

Literature about the *state* was in a process of constant growth. Cicero speaks with wonder about the great number and the intellectual importance of political works from the school of Plato and Aristotle. We know the titles of political treatises of Speusippus of Athens, Xenocrates of Chalcedon, Heraclides from Pontic Heraclea, and those of Theophrastus of Eresus (many), Demetrius of Phalerum, and Dicaearchus of Messana. Besides the apparently few Epicurean political writings (or rather antipolitical writings), there was a rich Stoic political literature—the writings of Zeno of Citium, Cleanthes of Assus, Herill of Carthage, Perseus of Citium, Chrysippus of Soli, Sphaerus of the Bosphorus, Diogenes of Seleucia, and Panaetius of Rhodes. One notices that in the Stoic school there is a significant preponderance of origin from barbarian lands. Zeno is designated a Phoenician; Persaeus was supposed to have been at first a slave of Zeno. Because the Stoa attracted barbarian peoples, and because the transmission to the Romans of Greek speculations on the state and on law took place, a link was formed between political science, especially Stoic, and the successor monarchies to Alexander with their life requirements, as well as with Roman political life. The Stoic school *combines a simplified teleological metaphysics* with the idea of the *law of nature,* and in this context (which was adapted to practical need) lay a major aspect of its influence. Then through the *Romans* the epoch-making combination of *speculations about natural law and positive jurisprudence* was accomplished.

And in this literature a *change in the social feeling* of man in the last centuries before Christ then worked its way through. It is already noticeable in the way the selfish quietism of the Epicureans transformed the natural law of the older national period. According to this school, the state is grounded on a security pact dictated by advantage; thus the private individual and his interests are the measure of his value. The altered social mood found a nobler expression, however, in the political science of the Stoic school. Monotheistic metaphysics drew conclusions here which Greek national spirit and its institutions had previously held in check. The totality of all rational beings is now regarded as a state which contains particular states as a city contains houses. This state lives under a law that is superior to all particular legal ordinances because it is the universal law of nature. Citizens of this state are endowed with certain rights that rest on that universal law. The wise man's radius of action is this world state.

Independence of Special Sciences

At the same time, as mentioned before, ancient peoples entered into the stage of the special sciences. Intellectual changes of such a thoroughgoing sort are usually accompanied by changes in the attitude of persons who are their agents and also by the establishment of scientific institutions. Alongside the philosophical schools scientific institutions founded by princes and governments now made their appearance. Through the creations of a generous and wise political program Alexandria became the hub of the new intellectual movement; intellectual leadership thereby passed from Athens over to it. For from this time on there was a need for observatories with an ever richer inventory of instruments, for zoological and botanical gardens, for anatomical institutes and enormous libraries, in order to stay at the peak of these positive sciences. What now took place is not inferior to what the metaphysical movement had thus far accomplished. If the entry of modern European peoples into the stage of positive sciences from the fifteenth century on is a Renaissance, it is also true that in the Renaissance positive research was resumed at the point at which the special sciences of the ancients were forced to let go of the thread of their work. Let no one believe that the episode of Italian Platonism or the renewal of pure Aristotelianism in Italy and Germany represented the core of the European Renaissance as an intellectual development.

Nevertheless, the *harvest of the metaphysical stage* of the ancient peoples constituted the foundation for the accomplishments of this subsequent period, in which the center of gravity of intellectual progress lay in the special sciences. The *concepts* acquired were the first condition of this progress. Thus Greek metaphysics had produced the concepts of substance and of the atom, distinguished those of cause and condition or ground, and carried through the concept of form in special areas. It had demonstrated basic relationships such as the relation between structure, function, and purpose in an organism or between performance and sharing of power and wealth in a political unit. The second condition lay in in the development of *fundamental principles* (which were not equally supported by evidence, however). Examples of such included the following: there is no transition from nonbeing to being or from being back into nothingness; the same thing, understood in the same sense, cannot be both asserted and denied; spatial motion presupposes empty space. Finally, an important condition lay in *logical consciousness*. The task of subjecting reality to knowledge had brought Greek minds during the Sophist epoch into revolutionary movement, in the maelstrom of which all Greek science at one time was on the verge of perishing. The "scientific legislation" of Aristotelian logic defeated this revolution and made calm progress in positive sciences possible for the first time. In it lay a precondition for establishing the mathematical sciences, such as Euclid demonstrates. We must give credit to its assistance alone that at the same time as metaphysicians and physicists were quarreling over the possibility of a criterion of truth, Euclid's *Elements* could come into being. In the unassailable progression of its proofs, that work seemed to defy the contradictions of the whole world and became the classical model of evidence.

The limitations of this metaphysics logically also asserted themselves in this stage of the special sciences; new paths which the special sciences, in part, had set out upon were not uniformly maintained. In mathematics the instrument for exact science was developed which was to enable the Arabs and the Germanic-Romanic people to discover nature. Likewise, there was a steady increase in the use of measuring instruments and in experimentation that not merely observes phenomena but deliberately produces them under altered conditions. Ptolemy's investigations of refraction of light rays in their passage through fields of unequal density constitute an outstanding example of methodical experimental treatment of a problem. Here the rays are directed from the air into water and glass, and from water into glass at varying angles of incidence. The most fundamental ideas which sciences of nature now attained are contained in Archimedes' work in statics. Working in a predominantly mathematical way and starting with the principle that bodies of equal weight and operating at an equal distance are in equilibrium with one another, he developed the general principle of leverage and laid the foundation for hydrostatics. But dynamics remained completely foreign to Archimedes, and he found no successors in antiquity.[139] No less characteristic is the total absence of chemistry at this stage of the special sciences among the ancients. The *Aristotelian* theory of the four so-called elements is derived from the more basic theory of four fundamental characteristics, even though the four elements themselves were a legacy from an older period. Thus only predicative determinations and their combinations were the object of this theory; it did not break things up into subject-units, that is, substances. So it had no direct effect on experiments which might have tried to break down given objects. *Atomic theory* had effected only an ideal dissolution of matter, and its notion of units qualitatively like one another must at first have had a somewhat counterproductive effect on the rise of fundamental ideas in chemistry. Requirements of the art of *medicine* prompted the attempt of Asclepiades of Bithynia to bring the idea of corpuscles closer to reflection about organisms[140] and the recipe we find in Dioscorides for producing certain chemical preparations which physicians used. In contrast with such scattered beginnings, natural sciences guided by geometrical constructions or teleological notions—such as astronomy, geography, and biology—made regular progress.

Thus there emerged even among the ancients of this epoch of the special sciences an *image of a cosmos* of immense extension and yet of scientific exactitude, and that image constituted the framework for their study of human sciences. Eratosthenes, Hipparchus, and Ptolemy encompass the circling masses of the stars and the earth. A first attempt at measuring degrees sought to determine the approximate circumference of the earth; Eratosthenes founded geography as a science. Surveying of the plant cover of the earth and of its animal population, such as Aristotle and Theophrastus had done, was now supplemented by advances in dissecting animal and human bodies, which probed especially deeply into knowledge of the vascular system [*der Gefässe*].

Alexander's campaign of conquest and the expansion of the Roman Empire then extraordinarily expanded knowledge of the distribution of the human race on the earth together with its differences. Thereupon men brought influence of soil and climate on intellectual and moral differences among men into the sphere of investigation. Material of the human sciences was now critically collected and investigated within the confines of Greek life, which had now come within the scope of history. Individual systems of culture, especially language, were analyzed. Comparative study of states became an established acquisition of science. With its support, *Polybius* undertook to explain the great world-historical phenomenon which filled the horizon of his time, the rise of Rome to world power. In his work he tries to make *political science,* as we have described it in its strength and limitations in the case of Aristotle, the *foundation of an explanatory science of history.* His comparative analysis of constitutions (as contained in the fragments of the sixth book) finds actualized in the mixed Roman constitution an equilibrium of powers in which each power is controlled by the others and is thus kept from excesses. Besides this, he sees as reasons for Rome's development of power a happy organization of the state with respect to material resources (which Rome used to achieve what Sparta, for example, despite its similarly mixed constitution, could not achieve) and a sense of law founded on reverence for the gods. One can regard *Pliny's* description of the world—at least with regard to its conception, despite its great superficiality in execution—as the capstone of the great work of the ancients of Europe, which consisted in embracing the cosmos, from the movement of bodies in space to the propagation of and intellectual life of, the human race on earth. Indeed, he has a special predilection for tracing the influence of the system of nature on human culture. The concept of the cosmos had arisen at the dawn of Greek intellectual life; now in the great works of Eratosthenes, Hipparchus, and Ptolemy—of whose wide-ranging intelligence we still feel a trace in Pliny's plan—the youthful dreams of these peoples were fulfilled in their old age.

Nevertheless, the culture of the ancient world disintegrated without the special sciences having been united into a whole which might have really replaced metaphysics. There was skepticism, indeed, but there was no theory of knowledge which could organize the system of the special sciences anew when the great illusion of the metaphysical foundation of the sciences had dissolved. What the mind had not been able to achieve in its campaign of conquest through the whole world, namely, a solid foundation for thought and for conduct, it now finds, by reversing its course, within itself.

Section 3. Metaphysical Stage of Modern European Peoples

---

1. Christianity, Epistemology, and Metaphysics

Imagine a man from the earliest period of our race as—sheltered by a cave, enveloped by night and by danger—he awaited the morning. When daybreak arrived and the first rays of the rising sun sought him out, how he must have felt at the approach of this saving power! Such is the way people of the ancient world felt as as the rays of the rising light from a pure world fell on them in Christianity. But that they felt so was not simply because Christian faith communicated a firm conviction of blessed immortality and that it offered them a new community, indeed a new civil society amid the ruins of the ancient states.[1] Both things were important ingredients in the strength of the new religion. However, both were also only a result of more profound change in the life of the soul.

In the present context we can touch on only this change and even that only insofar as it refers to development of the purposive structure of knowledge. A sharp critique of Christian consciousness permeates Spinoza's *Ethics*. At the root of it is Spinoza's personal view that perfection is simply power, and the joy of life expresses this growing perfection; on the other hand, all pain expresses nothing but imperfection and powerlessness. The deep Christian life of the soul severed the connection between ideas of perfection and those of the splendor, the power, and the happiness of life. Indeed, the connection between consciousness of God and harmonious beauty of the universe takes second place behind the connection of this space-transcending, sublimest of human feelings with the experiences of the poorest human heart, restlessly agitated within narrow limits by the nature of its existence. The view which Greek science had of the cosmos and the artistic construction of a counterpart to this cosmos in the ethical-social world as the political science of the ancients mapped it out rested above all on that former connection. Now one is called on to think of the perfection of the deity itself as conjoined to servitude and suffering; or, rather, one is not so much called on to think this conjunction: in religious experience they are one. The perfect being has no need to radiate in the splendor of the starry heavens and bask in happiness and power. God's kingdom is not of this world. So the will is no longer satisfied with producing an objective state of affairs, in the visible ethical artwork of politics or of the accomplished statesman and orator. On the contrary, the will goes beyond all this (which is a mere figure of the world) and back into itself. The will which shapes objective states of affairs in the world remains in the sphere of consciousness of the world where its goals belong. But in Christianity the will experiences its own proper metaphysical character. With that we reach the boundary line of our consideration, that is here devoted to the human and the historical alone.

This profound change in the life of man's soul includes the conditions under which the *limitations of ancient science could be broken through* and gradually were broken through.

For the Greek mind, knowing was mirroring an objective thing in the intelligence. Now experience becomes the focal point of all the interests of the new communities; but this is just simple awareness of what is given in personality and in consciousness of the self. This awareness is filled with a certitude which excludes every doubt. With the enormous interest they generate, experiences of the will and of the heart swallow up every other object of knowledge; in their *self-assurance* they prove all-powerful compared with any result gained from observing the cosmos or with any doubt which might stem from considering the relation of intelligence to objects to be mirrored in it. If this community faith had immediately developed a science perfectly appropriate to it, that science would have had to rest on a foundation ultimately resting on inner experience.

But this inner structure which, with respect to scientific grounding, occupies a place between Christianity and *knowledge* that grows *out of inner experience,* did not produce a corresponding scientific grounding in the Middle Ages. The reason for this was the preponderant power of ancient culture, within which Christianity now began to assert itself gradually. Moreover, the relation of religious experience to knowledge worked in the same direction from within. For after all even the most inward religious life of the soul finds expression only in a framework of ideas. Schleiermacher said once: "The development of Christianity in the West has a great mass of objective consciousness for its support; in a more precise sense, however, we can regard this mass of objective consciousness only as a means of understanding."[2]

Personal certitude of inner experiences of will and heart as well as the content of these experiences, hence change occurring in the profoundest depth of the soul—all this not only included the demand for a foundation based on inner experience; it also had an *effect* in another direction on *later intellectual development,* both on *knowledge of nature* and on *human sciences.*

On the one hand people turned away from mere intellectual harmony in the universe. It was not in this uniform beauty one can describe in universal concepts that the purpose of the universe lay for the Christian; it was not in meditating on it that he experienced the affinity human reason enjoys with divine reason. The relation of man to nature was transformed for him, and the notion of creation out of nothing and the opposition between spirit and flesh gave one an idea of the extent of this change. On the other hand the altered condition of the life of the soul produced a completely *new relation of metaphysical consciousness to the world of the spirit.* In the most sublime idea ever conceived about the structure of this spiritual world were conjoined the simply great ideas of the kingdom of God and of the brotherhood of man as well as their independence, at their highest level, from all natural conditions of existence. This idea now began its victorious march forward. It was actualized in the social order of the Christian community, which was founded on sacrifice and in which the individual Christian felt himself well protected, as though by a sheltering boat on the stormy sea of life. To be sure, this consciousness of the inner freedom of man and the elimination of inequalities and national limitations between these citizens [*Freien*] existed also in the later development of ancient philosophy, especially among the Stoics. But this inner freedom was attainable only by the wise, whereas here on the contrary it was accessible to anyone through faith. Corresponding to all this were the notions of a genealogical structure in the history of the human race and of a metaphysical bond which unites human society.

All this lay in the experience of Christianity. The *first scientific descriptions* of it appeared in an epoch of struggle between the old religions and Christian communities in the first centuries after Christ. Revelation, religion, and the struggle of the religions: these were the great affair of humanity in these centuries. The philosophy of Hellenistic Judaism as developed by Philo, Gnosticism, Neoplatonism (as the philosophical restoration of polytheism), and the philosophy of the Fathers of the church have in common the basic features of a *world formula* to which Spinoza's and Schopenhauer's systems likewise owe the simple compactness of their constructions. In this formula *nature* and *history* are already intertwined. The formula derives the emergence of the finite, as something imperfect and subject to change, from the deity, and then shows the return of this finite being to God. Thus the starting point of this metaphysics is the deity grasped in religious experience; its problem is the emergence of finite being in its given character. This emergence appears as a living psychical process in which the poor frailty of human life then also arises, until, in a kind of inverse process, return to the deity takes place.

The philosophy of Judaism developed first, that of paganism followed; the *philosophy of Christianity* victoriously superseded them both. For it bore within it a powerful *historical reality,* a reality which made contact in the life of the soul with the innermost core of every reality which had existed historically before it and experienced it in its inner harmony with itself. In the face of this historical reality, ecstasies and visions disappeared like gossamer in the wind. While Christianity was fighting for its victory, dogma in this struggle of religions developed the conclusive formulation that God—in contrast with all the partial revelations the Jews and the pagans claimed—had entered essentially, totally, and without reservation into the revelation through Christ. Consequently, all earlier revelations were subordinated to this one as its *preparatory stages.* Thus God's essence, in contrast with its setting in the self-contained concept of substance which antiquity held, was now caught up in historical life. And so *historical consciousness,* taking the expression in its highest sense, first came into being.

We understand to the extent that, out of the depth of our own lives, we can restore life and breath to the dust of the past. It requires, so to speak, a removal of our self from one site to another if we are to understand the progress of historical development from within and in its central context. The general psychological condition for this is always present in our imagination; but it is not until imagination has relived the historical process at the deepest points at which forward movement occurs that thorough understanding of historical development emerges. When Jewish Law, pagan consciousness of the world, and Christian faith clashed with one another in Saint Paul's struggles of conscience; when in his experience faith in the Law and faith in Christ were juxtaposed as two living experiences in his innermost understanding, both based on experience of the living God, coexisting in his consciousness were a great historical past and a great historical present, both in their deepest, that is, religious, foundations; and he experienced an interior transition by which the total consciousness of a historical development of the entire life of the soul awakened in him. For we understand only the facts of history which we relive in the richness of our souls. And our experience mediates this understanding to us to the extent that it reaches down into the deep and central basis of culture, although all of us, to be sure, only partially understand what is past. The most intense liveliness of imagination and the greatest vital richness of one's interior life are not enough if the life of the soul itself is not historical in this sense. Thus there is a line which goes from here to the idea of the education of the human race in Clement, from this to Augustine's *City of God,* and from this book to every modern attempt to grasp the inner structure of human history. The struggle of religions with one another in the Christian life of the soul filled with historical reality has produced historical awareness of a development of the entire life of the soul. For it was impossible to describe perfect moral life conceptually to the Christian community in the formula of the moral law or of the highest good; that community experienced it as an unfathomable living entity in the life of Christ and in the struggle of one's own will. Hence the life of Christ did not come into relationship with other propositions but with other figures of ethical-religious life who existed before it and among whom it now appeared. And this historical consciousness found a solid external framework in the genealogical structure of the history of humanity created in Judaism.

Thus completely altered conditions had arisen for the intellectual development of European man. Characteristics of the will had emerged from the stillness of individual life and moved into the foreground of world history, movements which set the will apart from the entire system of nature: movements such as self-sacrifice, recognition of the divine in pain and in lowliness, and sincere renunciation of whatever the will is obliged *per se* to reject. The relation of persons to one another in this, their essential core that decides the question of their entire worth, constituted a kingdom of God in which every distinction of peoples, cults, and education was annulled, hence a kingdom which stood apart from any sort of political association. And if the metaphysics which Greek antiquity had created was to survive, it had to acquire a relationship to this new world of will and of history. Also inherent in the intellectual formation of the declining ancient peoples as well as in the destiny of the religious process were conditions which determined the direction in which this took place.[3]

2. Augustine

Christian communities were the agents of the most effective among a plurality of related movements which gave their distinctive stamp to the spiritual life of the declining peoples of the period of the Roman emperors.

The literature of the first centuries after Christ reflects an altered spiritual condition. We saw it prepared for in Greco-Roman society. First among the Greeks and then among the Romans, interests of the private individual predominated more and more, so that in Alexandrine literature and its Roman imitations the description of the life of the soul freed itself from the context of the moral and political order of society. The inwardness of Christianity found the focal point of its conception and treatment of all of reality, indeed entry into the mysterious metaphysical world as well, in the life of the soul. Psychological portraits attracted the attention of readers to a pronounced degree in the first centuries after Christ; discussions of religious experiences and states of mind covered a broad spectrum; the novel, meditation describing interior states, the legend which in many ways falls back on novelistic motives and satisfies the needs of imagination in Christian circles, the sermon, the epistle, and discussion of questions which touch on the nature of man and his destiny are all things which stood in the forefront of literature. In addition, philosophy put the knowledge of the cosmos already attained in the service of forming character and establishing an internally harmonized state of mind. Epicurus had already identified the value of the natural sciences chiefly in liberating the mind from false ideas, and the Stoics held that the goal of philosophy consisted in forming character; now, in the centuries from the period of Christ to the collapse of ancient culture, tasks of philosophical science were completely intertwined with requirements of religious-moral life. Living together under the common roof of the Roman Empire, Greeks accommodated their ideas about life to oriental notions and symbols; Egyptians, Jews, and others transformed the Greek image of the world still more forcefully. In the society of that time, dissatisfied and threatened in so many ways, orientation toward the beyond won out. As Jacob Burckhardt puts it: "The essential power of such new directions usually derives from unfathomable depths; one cannot simply deduce them as consequences issuing from previous conditions." Everywhere we find revealed faith interwoven with religious life in which, in the inner recesses of one's will, one experiences God as will, person to person. We cannot even touch on the difficult task of analyzing the content of monotheistic religion at this point. But the deep secret of this religion lies in the relation between experience of one's own states and God's activity in the soul and in destiny; it is here that religious life has its own proper realm, removed from knowledge of the common sort, indeed from every kind of conceptualization. Now in this period, as though coming out of invisible depths or from the underground of religious life, revealed faith penetrated the science of metaphysics, where it always remains an intruder and is bound to create confusion. Thus a thesis now appeared in metaphysics which would have contained a completely new metaphysical principle if that thesis had not lain altogether beyond the limits of scientific thought. This thesis maintained that immediate communication from God to the human soul takes place, that is, that the soul receives God's revelation immediately. Thus at the time of Christ, Philo, supported by arguments of the skeptics,[4] denied the possibility of scientific knowledge of the cosmos. At the same time he asserted in opposition to inner experience (in a manner like that of later positivists): the eye, to be sure, perceives objects outside itself, but it does not perceive itself; similarly, neither can reason conceive itself.[5] Hence he concluded to the necessity of illumination through divine revelation. In pagan circles, so brilliant and influential a writer as Plutarch defended communications from a world of higher powers. And Plotinus combined faith in an ecstatic state in which the soul finds itself to be one with God with the stability of a rigorous metaphysics. A foreign element flooded the barriers of universally valid science, for experiences which anyone can verify occur only in perceptions about the world and in facts of consciousness. Now emanationist metaphysics arose as well, once imagination, spurred by oriental tales of fabulous beings, struggled to master the mystery of proximity or distance of God and yet was able to express it only in pictorial symbols of knowledge of nature. This was a sterile hybrid construct born from the marriage of religion and philosophy, imagination and thought, Orient and Occident. There was no semblance of an idea with which a history of metaphysics would have to reckon seriously, even though its aftereffects carry through the entire Middle Ages and on into the modern period.

The Fathers

In the midst of these spiritual movements the ancient church strove to bring the content of Christian experience to full consciousness and to comprehensive description in formulas, as well as to offer proof of the universal validity of Christianity, which was the correlative to Christianity's claim to world dominion. Execution of the task described, through *writings of the Fathers* and declarations of the councils, fills the centuries from the close of the apostolic age to Gregory the Great and the end of the sixth century. This period still belonged to the culture of the ancient peoples who, in the beginning, even after the fall of the western Roman Empire, alone produced scientific writers. In fact, the Fathers could undertake the execution of their task in a double direction. If one was to establish the meaning of Christian experience and its content, this took them back into analysis of the facts of consciousness. For in the state of Christian consciousness we encounter for the first time a state of mind which made possible an epistemological foundation that had the positive goal of establishing the reality of the inner world. And the objective of effectively defending Christianity made this kind of foundation necessary. How profoundly the intellectual effort of the Fathers went in this direction we shall establish in the case of the greatest of them. But the other direction was the predominant one. It was the tragic destiny of Christianity to extract the holiest experiences of the human heart from the quiet of the individual's life and introduce them among the motive forces of world-historical mass movements, and to evoke mechanistic morality and hierarchical hypocrisy in the process. In the sphere of theory it succumbed to a fate which weighed no less heavily on its further development. If Christianity wished to bring the content of its experience to full consciousness, it had to take that content into the conceptual framework of the external world, which governed it with respect to relations of space, time, substance, and causality. Thus to develop this content in dogma was at the same time to alienate it. For even in revealed faith it was inherently possible to develop dogma as an authoritative system emanating from the will of God, and such a system reflected the Roman spirit, which introduced its legal formulas right into the heart of the doctrine of the Christian faith. Greek genius spawned a different kind of alienation. In the cosmic concepts of logos, emanation from God, and attainment of participation in his being and immortality, a grand, though myth-related, symbolism emerged as the language of Christian faith. Thus only too many factors worked to cause the content of Christianity to present itself as an objective system deriving from God. A counterpart to ancient metaphysics came into being. We are going to describe the structure which thus took shape and reached from the depths of personal consciousness up into the transcendent world by using the example of the writer who represents the extreme limits of what was accomplished in this period.

Augustine

We begin, therefore, with the following question. In this period of the Fathers of the church, to what extent was the right of the new self-assurance of faith and of the heart scientifically maintained against ancient philosophy, especially against skepticism as its last word? The profoundest thinker of this new era of metaphysics and the mightiest personage among writers of the entire ancient Christian world was *Augustine,* and it seemed that he would succeed in laying a foundation of Christian knowledge which would correspond to the great reality of Christianity. What the gentle soul of Origen, not to mention other scientifically less important Greek Fathers, had tried, the passionate soul of Augustine accomplished for many centuries to come: he drove off and superseded the worldview of the ancients with a comprehensive doctrinal framework of Christian science. How far did Augustine succeed?

To this man steeped in religious experience *problems of the cosmos became completely indifferent.* "What do you wish to know, then?" In the *Soliloquies* reason addressed the soul in those words. "I wish to know God and the soul." "And nothing more?" "Nothing at all." *Self-reflection* is thus the focal point of Augustine's first writings, which gushed forth from his inward self in a powerful stream (and thus had an inner coherence about them) from A.D. 386 on.

But self-reflection discovers complete certainty only concerning the *interior life*. It is also certain about the world, to be sure, but as that which appears to the self, as its phenomenon. Thus in Augustine's view every doubt advanced by the Academy is directed only against the point that what seems to be such to the self is in fact what it seems. But there can be no doubt that something does appear to the self. He continues: I call this totality before my eyes the world.[6] Hence the expression *world* signifies for him a *phenomenon of consciousness*. And the progress in knowledge of the phenomenality of the world we find in Augustine is determined by the fact that he is interested in the entire external world only insofar as it has meaning for the life of the soul.

The refutation of the Academy was written primarily from the standpoint of this self-certainty of the ego. So the *Soliloquies* probe into the depths of the interior life and there discover the immortality of the soul and the existence of God: one of those meditations whose very form allows one to perceive the self-preoccupied life of the soul. Then, in that same interior life, the dialogue on free will seeks a resolution of one of the greatest controversies of the period. And in the tract on true religion he develops the content of faith from the self-certainty of the subject, which achieves self-awareness through doubting, thinking, and living. The starting point is always the same here: it lies in *discovering the reality in one's own interior life*. "You who wish to know yourself, do you know that you exist?" "I know it." "How so?" "I don't know." "Do you feel yourself to be simple or complex?" "I don't know." "Do you know that you move yourself?" "I don't know that." "Do you know that you think?" "I know that." "Then it's true that you think?" "Yes, it is true." In fact, Augustine, like Descartes later on, connects his self-certainty with doubt itself. For in doubting I am aware that I think, that I am aware of myself. This awareness comprises not merely thinking alone but the totality of my person. Using an expression both profound and true, he designates the object of self-certainty as *life*. Augustine's most mature treatise, *The City of God,* also expresses the same idea perfectly. That we are, that we know, that we love ourselves and our knowledge, is certain to us:

> For we do not touch this through some sense organ of our body as we do external objects, such as colors through our sight, sounds through our hearing, etc. On the contrary, independently of the deceptive contents of imagination or hallucination, I am certain that I exist, that I know that, and that I embrace it with a feeling of love. Likewise, I am not afraid of the reasons given by academic skeptics concerning these truths, to the effect that I might be mistaken. For if I am mistaken, then I exist. One who does not exist cannot be mistaken.[7]

The self-awareness which surfaces here in Augustine, after related initiatives by the Neoplatonists, is completely different from that of Socrates and the Socratics. For here at last an immense reality appears in self-consciousness, and this knowledge swallows up all interest in studying the cosmos. Hence this self-consciousness is not merely a return to the epistemological ground of knowledge, and what emerges from it is not merely theory of knowledge.[8] In this reflection a man becomes aware of the essence of *his very self,* and his conviction of the reality of the *world* is at least assigned its own proper place; but above all he grasps the essence of *God* in that reflection, indeed he seems to half uncover even the mystery of the triune God through it. The three questions posed by ancient logic, physics, and ethics—what is the ground of certitude in thought? what is the cause of the world? and what does the Highest Good consist in?[9]—lead back to a common condition which governs knowledge, nature, and practical living, and that is the idea of God.[10] But two of these questions arise in self-reflection and are answered in it. Indeed, this self-reflection does not attain its fullest achievement until the religious-moral process of faith has disclosed all the depths of the soul. The famous *crede ut intelligas* says first of all that the full range of experience must be present to analysis if the latter is to be exhaustive. The distinctive element in the content of this Christian experience lies above all in humility, which is grounded in the seriousness of conscience when it passes judgment.[11]

Augustine's self-reflection, as distinct in these basic features from any earlier related scientific investigation, first of all subjects knowledge itself to analysis. One of the three basic questions asked about the ground of certitude in thought. And yet this self-reflection does not result in an epistemological foundation either. Christian science planned from this point of departure did not execute its task appropriately. Why did it not do so? During the years when the idea of such foundation-laying preoccupied Augustine, his thoughts were still fixed in the direction set down for him by the Neoplatonists; later, when he had left that behind him too, the objective authorities of the Catholic church and of Catholic dogma became too predominant in his mind; in addition, the interests of great ecclesiastical and dogmatic struggles occupied his attention day in and day out; but the decisive element was, in our view, the limitation inherent in his nature.

Thus out of his self-reflection, chiefly *through the Platonic concept of the veritates aeternae, metaphysics* surfaced once again.

At that point (cited above) in *The City of God* he says further: "I who was mistaken would still exist, however, even if I were mistaken. Therefore, without a doubt I am free from error in holding that I know that I exist. From this it follows that I am also not mistaken in holding that I know that I know. For just as fully as I know that I exist, I also know that I know."[12] In Augustine's system the doctrine of truths which are certain in themselves is immediately attached to this idea of knowledge, in a manner very like that in Descartes' system later. As a matter of fact this *progression from self-certitude to truths which are in se certain* is presented in detail in his first fundamental writings. To begin with, we will develop the first premise of the line of reasoning we find there. In my doubt itself I find a standard by which I distinguish the true from the false. The clearest case for applying such a standard is reason's law of contradiction. In fact this law is a member taken from a system of laws of truth. This system, which we can designate "truth," is unalterable. To it belong numbers and their relationships as well as equality and similarity, and above all unity. For we cannot find unity in any sense perception; we do not find it in bodies; on the contrary, it is something which our thought denies to bodies, hence it is proper to thought. Although this first premise of argument proceeds from the experience of reality in us, it nevertheless also shows the power of inherited (especially Neoplatonic) masses of ideas over the passionate and uneven genius of Augustine. For that premise uses the psychical reality of living experience only as the point of departure for arriving at the a priori abstract notions which the metaphysical science of reason had developed. The fateful distortion of the true state of affairs, a distortion which assigns the first place in the mind to this abstract element, continues on; consequently, it is inevitable that it will also hold the first place in the objective structure to be erected. From this first premise we arrive at the second one in the chain of reasoning. Augustine continues to think with the Platonists. This system of truths is comprehended by the activity of reason, which is a purely intellectual insight. The soul sees truth through its own self, not by means of the body and its sense organs. There exists "a connection between the intuiting mind and the truth which it sees." We are right back in the middle of Plato's metaphysics again, which we thought we had left behind us. All knowledge is reflection of an object which lies outside the mirror. And the object of this knowledge is the unchanging order of truths which transcends the coming and going of individuals, their errors, and their transitoriness: it is in God. Even in his later writings Augustine accepts the intelligible world of Plato with the Neoplatonic school's supplement that God is the metaphysical subject which contains the world of ideas.[13] This entire argument includes, though with a new shift in emphasis, the inference from human thought to divine thought as its precondition, and it arrives only at the concept of a logical world order, not of God. The argument for God based on the character of the world, with its purposeful beauty and its changeableness, leans on that same reasoning.

On the other hand there are *elements* in Augustine's inner experience which *transcend this Platonizing connection* between man's intellect, the world, and God—namely, in the *veritates aeternae*. But even these elements push Augustine outside self-reflection into objective metaphysics. Consequently, in conjunction with the component of new theological metaphysics we have just described, which derives from antiquity, particularly Neoplatonism, they constitute a second component of that metaphysics, one going beyond the thought of antiquity. The progression from the principle of self-certitude to an objective metaphysics of those elements is as follows.

In interior experience I am directly aware of myself; all else is something absent from my mind or alien to it. Therefore Augustine demands that the mind should not seek to know itself through a cognitive process which uses the imagination's images of external objects, such as elements of the order of nature. On the contrary, "the mind should not search for itself as though it were an object foreign to it, but rather direct the will's intent, which has led that will to stray about among external things, to itself." "And the mind should not know itself as if it were something it was ignorant of, but rather it should distinguish itself only from that which it knows as 'the other.' " The mind possesses and knows itself completely, and even inasmuch as it seeks to know itself, it already knows itself completely. This knowledge it has of itself answers more adequately to the demands of scientific truth than does its knowledge of external nature. Augustine uses the profound epistemological truth contained in these statements for the following conclusion. We become aware of ourselves because we comprehend thinking, remembering, and willing as our acts, and in becoming aware of them we have true knowledge of ourselves. But to have true knowledge of something means to know its substance. Therefore we know the substance of the soul.[14] If introducing the concept of substance involves an untenable and, in this context, an unnecessary use of metaphysics, Augustine nevertheless uses correct method in demonstrating that we cannot regard this life of the soul as something produced by matter. He deduces from analysis of the life of the soul that one may not trace its properties to corporeal elements.[15] The problem is that here too the dogmatic concept of the substance of the soul injects itself immediately. The final result of linking together these conclusions is this: We cannot trace the soul back to the material order of nature, but inasmuch as it changes it must have an unchanging ground. Therefore *God is the cause of the soul,* as he is of the changing world in general. The soul is created by God, for whatever does not participate in his immutable character cannot be a part of the substance of God.[16]

But Augustine inferred his metaphysical order particularly from his self-reflection on the facts of willing. Man's cognitive behavior receded more and more for him behind these experiences of the will. In emphasizing the element of the will's approval in judgment, he subordinates knowing itself to willing,[17] so that knowing in this sense is believing. Through this sort of faith we are in the first place certain of the external world, insofar as we engage in practical activity.[18] Then, in the same context of practical behavior, we find ourselves referred to a Highest Good, a Good accessible to us only in faith, because it is invisible, and in hope, because it is not present to us.[19] If in our previously developed context *God* was certain as the locus of the *veritates aeternae,* so he is certain here as *the Highest Good*.[20] Therefore, in this faith we are certain of the reality of the world as well as of God.

Hence Augustine's *self-reflection* is only the *starting point for a new metaphysics.* And at the core of this metaphysics there is a *struggle between the veritates aeternae:* between the intellect, which holds fast to the world's rationality, and the *will of God,* of which man is certain in his practical conduct. For where will exists, we have also a series of changes determined by a purpose. Augustine would like to establish the living relationship of God to humanity and his plan in history,[21] and yet at the same time preserve the immutability of God—imbued as he is with the ancient idea that all change implies transitoriness.

Historical circumstance and the nature of his personal genius thus determined the *position of Augustine between epistemology and metaphysics.* If they denied logical consistency to the philosopher, they compensated the writer for that though his world-historical influence. For inasmuch as he knew the full and exclusive reality of facts of consciousness but did not subject these facts to coherent ordering (succumbing to them instead in his imagination and in the web of the richest powers of his soul), this made him, to be sure, a fragmented philosopher, but also one of the greatest writers of all time.

Greek science had sought after knowledge of the cosmos and ended in skepticism, with the insight that any knowledge of the objective substratum of phenomena was impossible. On this basis the skeptics had prematurely concluded the impossibility of all knowledge. It is true that they did not deny the truth of states of mind we find existing in us; but they neglected them as something of no value for us. From the change in the direction of interests which Christianity had brought about, Augustine drew the epistemological consequence. Neither Tertullian's inspirations nor Clement's nor Origen's syncretism devoted to creating a Neoplatonic age were able to accomplish that. As a consequence Augustine constitutes an independent member in the gradual and difficult progression from objective metaphysics to epistemology.

But the position which he thus claims is due not to his analytical power but to the genius of his personal feeling for life. And this fact made itself felt in a twofold direction.

Augustine is entirely free of the metaphysician's inclination to substitute the necessity of thought for reality or the cognitive component of a complete psychical fact for the whole of it. He abides in the feeling and imagination of life as a whole. Thus he designates what remains impervious to doubt not exclusively as thought but also as life. And in this the difference between his nature and that of Descartes expresses itself. Augustine would like to express what the living drive which motivates his passionate nature contains. He was the first to have the need and the audacity to describe his own history as it grew out of this living drive and reflected its inner destiny. He passed through the world as an unfettered and powerful natural force, uninhibited by conventional restraints, a mighty man: he had always lived out what he had thought. His *Confessions* stamped his image on the Middle Ages: a burning heart which finds its rest in God alone. On the other hand, in a general psychological description he also struggled to express the dark impulse toward happiness in its essential features; he pursued that impulse through the twilight of consciousness in which it hovers and into the realm of illusions which spring up there, until this drive loses itself in the beautiful world of God's creations, but always accompanied by the awareness that the alteration of states which arise in the process is not the attainment of the Highest Good.[22] Finally, his writings come back again and again at particular points to review and to brood over the states of his soul. In a profound way these writings traced the connection of psychical facts with the will and the whole person, whereas those facts had until then been explained predominantly as cognitive life. One might compare his sensitive discussions on the senses,[23] on the obscure life of the will in a child,[24] and his observations and speculations on the pervasive importance of rhythm in the spiritual life.[25] Likewise, his writings also traced concepts which metaphysics had previously handled abstractly and had analyzed into perceptual elements to their foundations in the totality of the life of the soul; in this respect his investigations on time, for example, will always remain exemplary.[26]

But his ability to analyze was not equal to his brilliant capacity for living representation. Can this surprise anyone? This naturally powerful soul whom nothing but God could satisfy was not one to get used to dedicating his life to analyzing concepts. Of course Augustine, like no one else in the centuries since Paul, was able to evaluate the intellectual forces around him on the grand scale and in consequence of that, surrounded as he was by the ruins of ancient speculation, he rightly understood the truth of Greek skepticism as compared with the objective worldview. He was then able to discover the decisive point at which Christian experience cancelled out ancient skepticism and so was able to grasp a standpoint akin to the critical one. But he was unable to carry it through. He lacked the analytical power needed to subject the science of external reality to that standpoint and to erect the science of inner reality on its basis as well as to dissolve the false concepts that claim to hold intellectual and natural facts together in an objective whole. What emerged from this was no system. One will not recognize Augustine's true greatness as a writer until one develops the psychological structure which he has, and does without the systematic structure which he does not have.

And no medieval man saw further than Augustine. Hence instead of an epistemologically grounded exposition of religious experience and its expression in concepts, an objective systematic structure came into being. There emerged in *theology a second type of metaphysics,* profounder in its point of departure but, with respect to its relation to the practical tasks of life, impurely mixed with positive elements based on authority: *a metaphysics of the will* uncritical in every respect. Sometimes in conflict, sometimes in external harmony, Augustine, the representative of the metaphysics of the will, and Aristotle, the chief of the metaphysicians of the cosmos, now made their way through the Middle Ages. Indeed, Augustine (as well as Plato and Aristotle) not only lives on in *Scholasticism,* but, insofar as he refuses to subordinate what is given in immediate knowledge to concepts discovered earlier concerning the external world, finds successors among the *mystics.* Even the literary forms in which mysticism expressed itself show this connection with Augustine.[27] Mysticism likewise did not go a single step beyond Augustine in epistemological grounding for its opposition to metaphysics; it merely shut itself up more thoroughly within the element of inner experience. Thus it survived not by reason of its scientific foundation; on the contrary, its inner life sustained it. It thus preserved the independence of personal life of faith through the flowering and the demise of medieval metaphysics, until this independence received a scientific foundation in Kant and Schleiermacher.

3. New Generation of Peoples and Their Metaphysical Stage

More than a millennium separates Augustine from the age of Copernicus, Luther, Galileo, Descartes, and Grotius. The metaphysics thus far described had developed in the Mediterranean states of antiquity. Metaphysics as the foundation for the sciences was now also handed down to the new generation of peoples which received the heritage of the older generation.

Augustine experienced the event of the Germans ruling as masters in the city of Rome; they took over hegemony of the West while the Arabs rose to power in the East. Because the content of these peoples' intellectual life had previously consisted predominantly of religious ideas, it was natural that theological and metaphysical problems stirred them deeply. A *parallel development* took place among the *peoples of Islam* and in *Christendom*; striking analogies of this development appear during the long era of theological metaphysics. And yet a profound contrast manifested itself in the process: the Arabs adopted the mathematical and natural-scientific works of the Greeks along with their metaphysics; the metaphysics of the West elaborated a more profound conception of the human-historical world in conjunction with the independent activity of the Germanic-Romanic peoples in political life.

The intellectual labor of the *Arabs* began in the theological movement, which made up the first epoch of their intellectual life. Mutazalites, the Arab rationalists, dealt with problems which arise apart from any study of the external world, where the experiences of moral-religious life seek for clearly defined expression in definite concepts. As often as such an expression is posited in a monotheistic faith, antinomies appear which are inescapably inherent in religious thought—such as those between free will and predestination, and between the unity of God and his attributes. Thus the same questions arose here in the Orient which stirred the Christian West previously and simultaneously. Indeed, in both places, the impulse lay in religious life itself, and acquaintance with ancient thought merely provided sustenance to the movement. The attempt by the Brethren of Purity, that remarkable secret society in the service of free inquiry, to join Aristotle, Neoplatonism, and Islam in an encyclopedic unity makes up a further stage in this development of thought. This attempt misfired also. "They tire one out," declared Sheik Sagastani, "but they do not satisfy; they roam about, but they never arrive; they sing, but they bring no cheer; they weave, but with thin threads; they comb, but they ruffle the hair; they imagine what does not and cannot exist."[28] Apart from theology, this nation—intellectually active, acute in observation, but lacking in depth and in moral independence, assisted by the natural endowment of the peoples subject to it—carried forward the mathematical/natural-scientific work of the Greeks. And the metaphysics of the Arabs, a restoration of Aristotle with Neoplatonic interpolations, assigned the will a secondary place as compared with the one, necessary, rationally universal system. Indeed, in some of its most important representatives, such as Ibn Badja [Avempace] and Ibn Roschd [Averroës], it proceeded from such assumptions to deny personal immortality. The results of the natural-scientific and metaphysical research of the Arabs were transmitted to the West; in contrast, the victory of the orthodox school of the Asharites over the philosophers, which was decided in the twelfth century, combined with the dead despotism of the political constitution, caused all interior life in Islam itself to dry up.

In the course of development of the *Romanic-Germanic peoples* who shaped the structure of European Christianity, metaphysics died out much more slowly: it was the long dream of youth of these nations. For when those nations came into their metaphysical inheritance, they were still in their heroic period. They were under the guidance of the church and of theology. Notions of psychical forces pervading the universe were for them, as they once were for the Greeks, the natural expression of their mentality, which had scarcely outgrown the mythical epoch of thought. Within the limits of the theology handed down to them, they used the residue of their mythical feeling and thinking, plus related elements they found among the ancients, to construct a rich and fantastic world, filled with saints, miracle stories, black magic, and all sorts of spirits. With difficulty they became comfortable with available metaphysics, such as it had been perfected in Aristotle. With the passage of time their knowledge of Aristotle grew; gradually capacity for abstract thought increased among them. Thus there sprang up a complete system which held sway over their minds with sovereign authority. Never has the power of metaphysics been as great as in these centuries in which it was linked with theology and the church. And in this development Aristotelian metaphysics underwent an essential transformation. Elements appeared in the new metaphysics which maintained their hegemony among modern peoples for a long time, and still maintain it today in many particulars and among broad sectors of the European population. For the historical position of these new peoples afforded them not only many disadvantages when compared with the ancients, but also great advantages. European man now had behind him a past which was concluded. Entire peoples and states have lived out their time on territory where a new world has been erected. They spoke in the very same Roman tongue which still prevails, and in the literature of this tongue the most important part of Greek development has also been preserved. However, these young Germanic-Romanic peoples also found themselves engaged in struggle with an Orient powerfully stirred up by Islam. Political and military opposition between them was at the same time felt as a struggle of the two great world religions fighting for mastery, and continued right into the sphere of metaphysics. The metaphysicians of Christendom found themselves confronted by penetrating systems which had emerged from Islam and were intrinsically hostile to Christianity. All this afforded the metaphysics of the newer European peoples a preponderance over that of the ancients in two respects.

The altered situation made it possible for the metaphysicians, on the one hand, to proceed to an abstraction not possible to the Greeks in their natural and national growth. They arrived at *abstractions of the most extreme degree*. For they now subjected the metaphysics, religious truths, legal principles, and political theories of the past to reflection which, despite the severest shortcomings in knowledge and comprehension of the historical, nevertheless had the remains of this past available as material. And in fact, with respect to the question which proofs could stand up to reason and which concepts one could resolve into rational components, ecclesiastical authority did not at first restrict metaphysical reflection. Despite how disastrous for philosophy, which can thrive only in independence, the influence of ecclesiastical ideas and authority on the minds of medieval men was, the church still left open this question about what part of the given contents of traditional metaphysics and the prevalent faith corresponded to reason and was accessible to it.

On the other hand, the altered situation made it possible for metaphysicians to extend their system, which had arisen out of scientific investigation of nature, to the *historical world*. The latter now spread itself out as a vast reality before their eyes. Christian science united it inwardly with the deepest principles of the metaphysical world, and it used these principles to constitute a coherent totality in its own right. At the same time the Christian dualism of spirit and flesh separated this realm of the spirit, as a structure grounded in the transcendent, more sharply from the whole of nature. Medieval metaphysics thus experienced an expansion by which, for the first time, it classified spiritual facts and historico-social reality under itself as a member on a par with nature and knowledge of nature.

Thus the intellectual labor of metaphysics began for a second time. The will to knowledge continued to strive to permeate with intellectual content those subjects whose activity and properties manifest themselves in nature, self-experience, and history; meanwhile the life which this will to knowledge was to study now reached depths inaccessible to the metaphysical consciousness of antiquity. It lies outside the ambit of our discussion to consider how metaphysical speculation tried to resolve the Trinity and the Incarnation into clear and demonstrable components and finally had to recognize the insolubility of Christian dogma for the understanding. But the human mind also experienced for the second time that a natural metaphysical system is simply impossible. Metaphysics melted away before rational criticism like snow before the increasing warmth of the sun. And so the second metaphysical stage ended the same as the first in this respect, despite how much richer in content the residue was which it left behind it.

This process allows us to peer still more deeply into the *essence of metaphysics* and into the *impossibility* of its permanent *duration*. For only history tells us what the great material facts of the mind essentially contain. Medieval metaphysics comprised an expansion of worldview which, within limits, persists today. It contained a more profound spiritual life than that of antiquity had been. And the more strenuously it took pains to clarify what the horizon of metaphysical speculation comprised, the clearer became the impossibility of doing so. Much of the blame rests with the faulty intellectual training of the writers who created metaphysics. They had only an external conception of the task of reconciling the great realities of Christianity with the concepts which Greek, especially Aristotelian, metaphysics used to express them, because they had no access to the deeper scientific motives of Greek metaphysics. Just as these motives had grown out of the labor of real science, so only such persons as were occupied with the same type of work could understand them and the concepts and principles which arose from them. The concepts of substantial form, the eternity of the world, and the unmoved mover had arisen in response to demands of knowledge which sought to explain the cosmos, just as had the concept of the atom or that of empty space. Other concepts were determined by exact natural-scientific research. Hence the concepts of the ancients in the hands of the Scholastics are like plants whose natural habitat and environment are unknown and which have been torn out of their own soil and placed in a greenhouse. These concepts were then linked with totally incompatible ones without any noticeable resistance. Thus one finds creation out of nothing and the living act and personality of God bound up with concepts which issued from the immutability of the first substance or from the Aristotelian concept of motion. But no matter how much this lack of a really scientific spirit must have aggravated the solution of the tasks mentioned, that is, systematically uniting Christian life with science of the cosmos, nevertheless that lack does not explain the total collapse of this metaphysics as a science, a collapse which marks the close of the metaphysical stage of the modern peoples and their entry into that of the real sciences; on the contrary, the intrinsic impossibility of the task is made manifest. Because this metaphysics is prompted first of all by interest in experiences of the will and the heart, it becomes clearer than before that we cannot use our understanding to resolve what we possess in life into a system of fully transparent concepts. Inasmuch as the conditions of nature are supposed to be linked with those of the historical world in an objective system, the profound *contradiction* between the *necessity* appropriate to reason and the *freedom* experienced by will penetrates the core of metaphysics and tears its framework apart.

Nevertheless, at the same time this second epoch of metaphysics accomplished a *permanent positive step forward* in the intellectual development of Europe, which has been preserved for modern man and for the free combination of epistemology, special science, and religious faith. The following must be added to what has already been mentioned. In antiquity science had set itself apart as an independent complex of purposes and it had attained autonomous standing. In the great institutes of Alexandria and in the other scientific foci of later antiquity, science also preserved an external organization which made continuity in positive achievements possible. Thus science, as a system which embraced peoples, stood in contrast with the changing and fragmented life of the state. The power and sovereignty of Christian consciousness then embodied itself during the Middle Ages in the autonomous edifice of the Catholic church, which received the legacy of many political fruits of the Roman Empire. If that church entailed the sacrifice of individual freedom of Christian consciousness for a time, nevertheless the great corporative ordinances [*Ordnungen*] of faith and knowledge paved the way for a future in which it was possible to differentiate and externally organize particular purpose-nexuses while maintaining inner freedom of the life of the soul. This is a future which even today we see only in uncertain outlines. In the meantime religious life and mystical schools maintained the consciousness that the meta-physical [*sic*] essence of man is expressed in inner experience, as life, in an individual way which excludes universally valid scientific formulation. To the conceptual structure developed from the external world, metaphysics added one derived from religious life: creation from nothing, the inner activity and, as it were, historicity of God, and the destiny of the will. And though medieval metaphysics perished on account of the inner contradiction which thus arose, personal consciousness of our meta-physical [*sic*] nature, one incapable of any universally valid scientific grounding, existed and persisted as the heart of European society. Its pulsation was felt among the mystics, in the Reformation, and in that mighty Puritanism which lives on as truly in Kant or Fichte as in Milton or Carlyle, and which embraces a part of the future within it.

4. The First Period of Medieval Thought

The problems of the three monotheistic religions constituted the starting point of the intellectual work of the Middle Ages. We will begin with the simplest one. Judaism,

Christianity, and Islam have their focal point in a relationship of the will of man to God. Hence they comprise a series of elements which belong to inner experience. But because our cognition is tied to images of external experience, we can *perceive* what belongs to *lived experience* only in the context of our *picture* of the external world. The simplest proof of this is the failure of every attempt to distinguish God from one's own self without the aid of any image of a spatially distinct externality, or to conceive of him in relation to this self without an element of spatial position and influence, or, say, to effect the concept of creation without any images of spatial appearance and temporal formation, no matter how swiftly fleeting they might be. Therefore religious experience in the monotheistic religions likewise presents itself in a world of images which is only an outer garment and shell or an *illustration of inner experience,* so to speak, as was the case in the Indo-Germanic religions from whose mythical conception of the world we saw Greek metaphysics arise.[29] And *thought* necessarily strives to elucidate these notions which illustrate religious experience, to *analyze* them, and to *connect* them to one another *without contradiction.*

Theology and Its Instrument of Dialectics

In the process, dogmatic thought constantly runs into components of thought which belong to the picture of the external world. And because Christianity, paganism, and Islam had the elaboration of these elements available to them through the interpretive science of the cosmos, concepts from this explanatory science were mixed into their theology. Hence the development of formulas which were supposed to define religious experience in a grouping of ideas and justify them against other formulas in the same religion as well as against other religions has not been effected logically on the basis of the self-certainty of inner experience given in Christianity.[30] On the contrary, the powerful and fresh stream of these inner experiences discharged into the broad and muddy river of western metaphysics, which carried elements of the most diverse sorts along with it. Metaphysical syncretism—the denouement of the long development of Greco-Roman thought—seemed to offer religious thought the means of forming itself into a system and of maintaining itself as such. Thus arose Christian *theology*; Jewish and Mohammedan theology took shape similarly.

In fact the work of theology was the focus of all systematic thought among modern peoples only for a limited time. In the Christian West this time lasted longer than among the peoples of Islam; from Alcuin and the eighth century it stretched to the end of the twelfth century here.

During these four centuries the possible *relations between the content of faith and understanding* asserted themselves in forms that have persisted until today. The party dominant in the hierarchy regarded the content of faith as a reality inaccessible to reason and given to our corrupt nature authoritatively in revelation. In accordance with the relation we have described between faith based on revelation and inner experience, this standpoint joined a second one which developed Christianity's knowledge that one cannot present inner religious experiences in a comprehensible system.[31] But this second position in relation to content of faith also appeared more independently of the principle of authority, particularly in the mystical schools. A third party's most important representative during this period was Anselm. That party also based its assumptions on Augustine. It combined the two sides of medieval thought in an abstrusely profound notion: There is a rational dimension to every mystery of faith, even the most profound, and we would be able to think it through just as divine reason does if our thinking capacity were as powerful as God's; but this dimension is visible only from the standpoint of faith.[32] The last of these parties regarded human understanding as the norm for the content of faith, and the degree of self-confidence this understanding had in asserting itself was what mainly determined the party's differences. Hence it can be labeled rationalism. It did not acquire its power merely from the drive for knowledge which became the rage, particularly in the twelfth century; Abelard could also exploit the battle of authorities about the mysteries of faith boldly and skillfully in his treatise *Yes and No* in favor of deciding questions of faith through the understanding; at the same time the dispute among most monotheistic religions made their final validity dependent on the judgment of thought. Conversations between representatives of the various religions—such as the *Book of the Khazar* and Abelard's dialogue between a philosopher, a Jew, and a Christian—demonstrate the power of this actual relationship. That is how it could happen that a dialectical movement whose negative results shocked many contemporaries could follow on completion of material for the knowledge of Aristotelian logic.[33] The content of faith was already seen as an anticipation of rational knowledge,[34] and the question was raised: If the dogmas of Christianity are accessible to rational treatment, why was revelation necessary?

Grasping the content of faith through reason, which was the focus of so much struggle during these centuries, employs *dialectics* (logic) as its *instrument*. It has been convincingly demonstrated how the meager original transmission of the materials of logic and the slow expansion of knowledge of genuine Aristotelian logic[35] affected the efficacy of this instrument. But the dialectics of these centuries appears in a more favorable light if one grasps the other side of the history of that time, its relation to tasks of theology, and the dependence of its most important features on this task. Just as Aristotle's logic was affected by the role and task of metaphysics of the cosmos, so the dialectics of the Middle Ages was affected by the role and task of theology, as its theory of knowledge. Corresponding to this relationship, medieval logic was involved in very lively discussions about the relation of the forms of thought to the rationality of reality as rooted in God. The principles of Platonic-Aristotelian philosophy on this point, as developed by the Neoplatonists, constituted the basis for the theology of most of the church Fathers, especially Augustine. At the same time there was in the material handed down on logic a scanty communication which, as though through a narrow opening, afforded a look into disputes of antiquity otherwise unknown in that period.[36] Among the multitude of parties which tried a solution to this now passionately discussed problem, one can distinguish three classes—if one focuses attention on the metaphysical significance of the problem which exclusively concerns us. What generally determined the formation of these parties was that the metaphysical stage of science possessed a comprehensible system of phenomena only as a system of forms which presented themselves in universal concepts. Some assumed a real process of logical specification in the substance of things, whether they thought of this according to the formula of an emanation, such as Scotus Erigena did, or that of creation. Thus, according to William of Champeaux, at first forms of the highest genera approach as yet undifferentiated matter and in each of these genera such forms arise as differentiate the genus into species and so on down until individuals emerge.[37] Others rejected such a real process of logical specification and contented themselves with assuming a real relationship between divine understanding in which the forms reside, reality into which God's understanding informs them, and human under-standing by which one can abstract them from objects.[38] Nominalism made up the common character of a third class of dialecticians. Their relation to the task of theology essentially determined the fate of these three factions. The first of them, as Abelard's perspicuity demonstrated to it, must logically lead to essential unity of one and the same substance, thus to pantheism.[39] The last of them, the nominalistic theory, proved itself totally incapable of serving as a basis for theology until it was related to inner experience at a later stage. That was the ground apart from which it could not sustain itself in this first period of medieval thought. After all, Roscelin's nominalism denied all objective validity not only to the relation of an individual thing to its class but also of the part to the whole. But on this latter relationship rested the entire structure of the divine plan of salvation on which the church was founded. Adam's sin, redemption in Christ, and the connection of the individual with the church were unthinkable without this structure of parts in a whole. Likewise, the doctrine of the Trinity appeared to assume a real relation of the individual to the overrarching concept. Thus the middle position, as Abelard had first successfully represented it, won the victory: It corresponded best with the task of medieval metaphysics, that is until nominalism earned a deeper right through the theory of inner experience and of the will it manifested.

If a dialectical foundation was a prime desideratum in this struggle of understanding with the content of faith during the four centuries in question, nevertheless that was only a *preparation for theology*. Indeed, the immediate task consisted in further developing the *demonstration of the existence of a transcendent world*; however, the accomplishments of these centuries make up part of the history of the grounding of the transcendent world on rational proof, which we are not interested in considering in isolation. Moreover, understanding sought to orient itself in the transcendent world and to *develop conceptually the structure of the content of faith*. In the process the fate of the understanding preoccupied with this task in this period was decided, which affords us an incisive look into the living conditions of metaphysical thought. In the most important points, instead of fixing a formula which would permanently satisfy understanding, contradictions piled on contradictions ensued. And this situation occurred not only in specific dogmas of particular monotheistic religions but also became evident in propositions common to them, and accordingly are closely related to one another metaphysically.

A contradiction occurs in two propositions of which the one excludes the other. It consists therefore in a relationship of predicates of the same subject, in virtue of which they mutually exclude or cancel themselves out in relation to that subject. Such a contradiction of two propositions is an antinomy if the two propositions are unavoidable, hence antinomies are propositions which express something contradictory with equal necessity about the same subject. Antiquity first developed the antinomies contained in our conception of the external world; they have their root in the relation of our knowledge to external sensations. The second half of all antinomies arises inasmuch as inner experiences are related to external structure of perception, and knowledge tries to subject them to its law. In this class, the first antinomies to appear historically were those of religious understanding, theology, and metaphysics which assimilated religious experience. Their battleground was the theology and metaphysics of the Middle Ages, and they functioned just as destructively in old Protestant dogma. Among these antinomies the first ones to attain to classical development in the era of the church Fathers and in the early Middle Ages were those which did not yet presuppose science of the cosmos, but rather issued out of the relation of religious experience to understanding and logical reflection.

Because religious life is forced to express itself in a cognitive system and because antinomies are inherent in the heart of this kind of system, they appear in parallel forms alongside each other in the theology of Christianity, of Judaism, and of Islam. Indeed, awareness of these antinomies in no way appears for the first time in a period of dogmatic dissolution; on the contrary, religious perception and thought struggle with them from the very start; they constitute a major factor in the development of dogma itself and they perpetuate factions and strife in individual religions. But religion is not science; indeed, what is even more important to say, it is also not something conceptual [*Vorstellen*]. Antinomies of religious conceptualization do not dissolve religious experience. Just as antinomies in our conception of space fail to force us to forgo spatial observation, neither do contradictions inherent in religious concepts diminish religious life in us or degrade it in its importance for our life in general. The painter is not bothered by antinomies in the concept of space, for they do not confuse his spatial images. In precisely this way, religious antinomies do not hinder the free movement of religious life itself. But they certainly do render impossible the logical development of religious understanding, its analysis, and the connection of concepts which thus arise into a systematic unity such as Schleiermacher was still searching for.

Antinomy between the Conception of an Omnipotent and Omniscient God and the Conception of the Freedom of Man

The first and most fundamental antinomy of religious consciousness is grounded in the fact that the subject discovers itself at every given moment to be *absolutely determined* and dependent on its past, but at the same time knows that it is *free*. This double relationship, as the description of religious life shows, is, so to speak, the spring which powers the continual labor of the religious mind, in which the idea of God first attains its full development. Thus in the life of religious knowledge an antinomy appears which no formula has been able to overcome. God is at one moment the subject of the predicates of goodness, omnipotence, and omniscience, but all these predicates of his seem to be limited by man's freedom of will and responsibility, and their limitation is their annulment. Perhaps no question has engaged the reflection of more men on earth and none has worked in more powerful natures than this one, which has convulsed the conceptual world of Islam and has stirred up a Paul, Augustine, Luther, Calvin, and Cromwell. If we traverse the broad field of ruins of the sects and treatises which this problem has provoked, we feel more powerfully than otherwise how completely over and done with dogma lies behind us. For today none of these controversies or distinctions still moves the hearts of men. Their time is past. And the stillness of death rests today on the broad expanse of these ruins.

The Christian West, just to touch on what is only too well known, struggled in vain from the time of the Church Fathers on with the antinomies between the immutability of God and the reciprocity between human behavior and the divine will, between God's foreknowledge of actions and man's freedom to perform them or omit them, and between God's omnipotence and human will.[40] The turmoil of the Pelagian dispute had long since died away in the West, and the freedom of the will, man's responsibility, and with it his autonomy, had (except for a negligible residue) fallen victim to the tendency of the Catholic church to conceive of all good in the human world as coming down from God through the organs of the church, when the *same controversy broke out in the Islamic countries*. The Islamic rationalists, the Mutazilites,[41] started from the inner problems of religion, even though they then enlisted the assistance of Greek science for their solution; indeed, they might have been influenced also by the theology and sects of the Christians.[42] Throughout the *Koran* courses the contradiction between a rigid doctrine of predestination, according to which God Himself has created for hell a number of men incapable of receiving his truth, and practical faith in freedom of the will, on which human responsibility rests. The *Mutazilites* assert first one side of the antinomy, that is, the personal certainty of *freedom* we have through inner experience. According to them we experience the human will as an autonomous principle which activates the body, as its instrument, to movement, and its freedom includes the idea that judgment regarding good and evil accompanies it.[43] From this point they develop theses which, given the doctrine of God's omnipotence and omniscience, cancel each other out, hence exclude coherent understanding. We cannot trace evil to God as its cause, for evil is an essential attribute of the evil being (in contrast with the view which says that this attribute vanishes in the total system of the world order); for if God were the cause of evil, that would annul his goodness.[44] One cannot deny freedom; by doing so one would deny responsibility and consequently the exercise of God's justice with respect to reward and punishment. While the Mutazilites thus defended freedom at the cost of God's omnipotence, on the other side those sects which logically developed the stronger impulse in Islam defended *predestination* at the cost of freedom. The *Jabarites* simply denied that man's actions are his own, and traced them to God. They were divided only on the point that some of them absolutely and totally denied man the capacity of acting; others simply ascribed no influence whatsoever to this created capacity.[45] Among the freethinkers, Amr al Gahiz maintained the necessity of human actions, and he distinguished deliberate decision from instinctual behavior only by the fact that we consciously think in the case of a decision.[46] Between the difficulties which thus arise on either side when one takes the issue of freedom and predestination seriously, *al-Ashari* slides through with a halfway position. On the one hand there is certainly still a difference given in inner experience between involuntary movements and deliberate ones; but the same action, as seen from God's standpoint, is something God produces and accomplishes, though, as seen by man, it is an "appropriation" of something God has performed.[47] For this reason al-Ashari became the basis of later orthodox Scholasticism of Islam, which congealed in dessicated and yet half-formed formulas.

Averroës later expressed the *antinomy* which appears *in this struggle of the theological sects* with conclusive intellectual clarity in the following way. In this question, one of the most difficult of religion, he places proofs in opposition to one another, and "that is why the Moslems have split into two parties: one party believes that man himself is the responsible cause of virtue and vice, and that these result in reward and punishment for him. These are the Mutazilites. The other party believes the contrary, namely, that man is coerced and forced into his behavior." We can describe the "contradiction in proofs taken from reason in this question" in the following two parts, of which each is simultaneously necessary and impossible. *Thesis:* "If we assume that a man produces and fashions his own actions, then it follows necessarily that there are actions which occur apart from the will of God and his free decision, and so there would then be a creator apart from God. But all Moslems are agreed that there is no creator apart from God" (and Averroës proves the uniqueness of God metaphysically in another place from the unity of the world[48]). *Antithesis:* "But if we assume that man does not freely perform his own activities, then it follows necessarily that he is forced to them; for there is no middle road between coercion and personal freedom. And if man is forced into his actions, then responsibility falls into the category of what is impossible to accomplish."[49] Among Christian theologians of the first period of medieval thought Anselm described our antinomy in the following two contradictions. *First contradiction:* "Foreknowledge of God and free will appear to contradict each other. For that which God foresees must necessarily occur in the future; but what occurs through free will occurs without any necessity." *Second contradiction:* "What God predetermines must happen in the future. Therefore, if God predetermines the good and evil which occur, then nothing occurs through free will." Hence free will and predetermination cancel each other.[50]

Regardless of what distinctions theological metaphysics in the East and the West has offered against this antinomy, there is no escaping it in the *conceptual schema* and *understanding's* analysis and synthesis of it. Every free subject appears as an autonomous power alongside the power of God. Thus when the idea of an all-powerful will surfaces in consciousness, then all particular wills disappear before it like stars before the rising sun. At every moment and at every point the omnipotence of God determines the existence and permanence of individual will, and if that omnipotence were withdrawn, then the will would collapse within itself, either totally or in its corresponding condition or part. This appears with particular clarity in the formula of Christian Scholasticism, which says that preservation in being is nothing but continuation of creation.[51] Because God does everything himself in creation, it follows that as the preserver of creation he is also, at every moment and so to speak at every point, the efficient and creative preservative cause for the human will as well.

We leave behind this region where understanding is embroiled in contradictions of knowledge, with its subterfuges and distinctions, when in the realm of *mysticism*—of the Sufis, the Victorines, and their successors—the conceptually clear distinction between opposed wills of God and man is submerged in the abyss of the deity. But even mysticism and pantheistic speculation associated with it discover the same unresolved problem in the murky depth of a living, divine world-ground which encompasses the human will. For if this world-ground embraces the human will in its freely flowing unity, then freedom is preserved as an act in God, to be sure, but responsibility for evil falls so much the more surely on God,[52] and the individual's feeling of autonomy becomes so much the more incomprehensible.

Therefore the only solution which remains possible in the end is from the *epistemological standpoint*. Something which we cannot conceive in an objective system we can perhaps recognize in its inalienable otherness as coming from a different source and we can perhaps bring it into a mutual relationship which is external, to be sure, but is also governed by laws. Thus the antinomy of ancient metaphysics of the cosmos—between the continuous nature of intuition and the discrete nature of intellectual knowledge, and between change in reality and its composition of unchangeable parts in understanding— remained invincible in this natural metaphysical system. Hence epistemological insight and the admittedly external yet lawful relationship of these psychical elements, which come from different sources and thus cannot be traced to one another, will have to satisfy us.

What debris and rubble we would have to wander through if I wished to describe the individual *evasions theological understanding has attempted* in the face of this antinomy. The method is everywhere the same. One brings God's action, as though through space, as closely and in as many ways as possible to those points in the world at which free will appears: it surrounds them and entwines them totally. Further, one uses conceptual determinations to bring the causal activity of God in the actions of men at these points as closely together with the content of free will as one can possibly do. But no matter how tightly God's action entwines freedom in the world's system: at every point at which one thinks of them as cooperating with one another, a contradiction remains. And no matter how much this alchemistic art strives to bring together the characteristics of freedom with those of necessity and finally to transform the latter into the former, they remain obstinately apart.

Following his Arab predecessors closely, Averroës summed up the first of these two methods of at least diminishing the severity of the contradiction as follows. God has created the power of the will, which has the ability to work for opposite things, but he has also created a system of causes through whose mediation alone the will can approach the external things it wishes to attain. At the same time this will is also inwardly bound to the causal system, because positing a goal is conditioned by the objective relationship between our conception and objects.[53] Jewish philosophers use the same method as the Arab ones. They share the formal incisiveness and the material shallowness of this presentation, but they are guided more thoroughly than the Islamic thinkers by the consciousness of freedom.[54] Thus the *Book of the Khazar* [*Kusari*] by the famous Jewish poet Jehuda Halevi starts with the system of causes grounded in God. In this system God produces changes either directly or through intermediary causes, and in this chain of causes appear the deliberate actions of man. Where they appear, the transition from this necessary concatenation to freedom occurs. "A choice has grounds which lead back in a chain to the first cause, but this concatenation is without coercion because the soul finds itself between one decision and its contrary and can do as it wills."[55] And Christian theologians of the Middle Ages have the merit of having postulated a mechanism in the cooperation of God's action with human freedom in every act of will whereby an A and a non-A cooperate with each other in good neighborly fashion as the springs of activity.

The other method of dulling the sharpness of the antinomy consists in using conceptual determinations to bring together the idea of dependence in the causal system grounded in God with that of freedom. Sometimes the attempt is made to weaken causality of God in relation to the actions of men, sometimes to dilute and volatilize freedom of man; such conceptual determinations extend from the teaching of the Asharites to the Protestant dogmaticians. Thus one sees Anselm volatilize the human will to the point of being a wretched residue of a capacity for maintaining a direction imparted to it by God,[56] but this residue nevertheless implies both a limit to the divine will and the creature's absolute power. Thus Thomas traces reality in human activity to God as its cause, whereas defect in that activity, in virtue of which it is evil, he ascribes to the creature.[57] As if the impulse to evil were not something positive! And because things cooperate with God according to their nature, and the nature of the human will is freedom, he finds God's will to be in accord with man's freedom.[58] Other debris from work on these contradictions is evident when Anselm determines God's foreknowledge to be an eternal and immutable knowledge even of what is changeable, hence understanding strives to break through the form of its own way of thinking in time;[59] or when

Introduction to the Human Sciences

others wish to think of God's providence as referring only to the general, and understanding thus destroys the content of faith in the act of laboring to save it.

The upshot of the struggle with this class of antinomies in the Middle Ages was different for the theologians of Islam than it was for those of Christendom. Although Islam inclined toward submerging all individual freedom in divine power and toward the God of despotism and the flat desert, consciousness of personal freedom of the individual became ever more powerful in Christendom. It had its seat in the Franciscan school. Duns Scotus created the first thoroughgoing theory of will in its relation to understanding,[60] and in Occam appeared the epistemological contrast between immediate knowledge and knowledge proceeding under the guidance of the principle of sufficient reason—which was the condition for understanding freedom. "Liberty of the will cannot be proven by reason. Nevertheless, it can obviously be known through experience in the fact of experience that no matter how much reason may dictate something, the will can nonetheless choose this or not choose it."[61]

Antinomies in the Conception of God Based on His Attributes

A second class of antinomies arises out of the fact that religious experiences, insofar as they underlie the idea of God, are expressed in a conceptual framework. The idea of God must enter into the order of ideas in which our self and the world also have their place, and yet no system of understanding composed of formulas can answer to the demands which religious life puts on this idea. Between the idea of God as it is given in *religious experience* and the *conditions of understanding* there is an intrinsic *heterogeneity,* and this causes the antinomy in understanding the supreme being. Proof of this situation lies in the first place in describing the barren intellectual labor people have expended on it since the Middle Ages and can be supplemented later on through psychological consideration.

The entire Middle Ages struggled also with this second class of antinomies, and a comparative study can follow them through the theological metaphysics of Judaism, Christianity, and Islam. In fact there is an antinomy between the *idea of God* and its *description through attributes in formulas of the understanding*. One constructs the thesis through pronouncements about God's attributes, which pronouncements are necessary to the understanding, so that if one were to eliminate them, one would then eliminate the notion of God himself along with them. The antithesis consists of the propositions: because in God subject and predicate are not distinguished, but the attributes of God would be his predicates, then one must deny that God has any attributes; because God is simple, but the difference in attributes would posit a multiplicity in him, then for this reason as well one may not ascribe attributes to God; and because God is perfection, but every attribute would express something limited, then once again the inappropriateness of assuming attributes of God results.[62] A series of other antinomies arises from *relations of content* between *individual components of the idea of God*. Our concept of God in his relation to the world and to us is bound up with spatial and temporal relations which govern the world and ourselves, but the idea of God excludes spatial and temporal determinations. Our religious life experiences God as a will, but we can imagine a will only as a person, and we can imagine a person only as delimited with respect to other persons. Finally, the absolute causality of God, that is, his omnipotence, which is also the cause of evils in the world, contradicts the moral ideal in him, that is, his goodness, and thus arises the insoluble problem of theodicy.[63]

This whole class of antinomies, like the one treated earlier, is also inherent in religious understanding and one immediately feels it if one tries to express that understanding in formulas or to resolve the antinomies. *Augustine* expressed this antinomical element in the idea of God with his characteristic energy: "great without quantitative determination, omnipresent without occupying a place, cause of changes without any change in himself, etc."[64] Awareness of these contradictions appears with great clarity in Islam among the *Mutazilites*; it led them to deny the properties of God.[65] Indeed, according to one member of this school, who admittedly went further in denying God's attributes than the others did, God has no knowledge. For knowledge would either have God for its object, which would result in separating knower and known in God, and accordingly one would be cancelling out his total unity, which Islam so rigorously stresses; or else knowledge would have an object outside God, and then God, with respect to this attribute of his, would be dependent on the existence of this object outside him.[66] Then the Mutazilites questioned God's location in space (which attribute is unavoidable in our understanding) as well as all the physical features inherent in our understanding.[67] And the *Arab philosophers* concluded: Every idea comes into being by distinguishing a subject which is supposed to be understood from predicates one is supposed to use to understand it; but to distinguish between a bearer of attributes and these attributes themselves, that is, between a substance and its attributes, such as would thus emerge, is to destroy the simplicity of God;[68] therefore we cannot know the essence of God. We also find *Christian theologians of the early Middle Ages* in remarkable agreement with the Islamic sects with respect to this antinomy as well. Scotus Erigena and Abelard showed the impossibility of any adequate declaration about God: because such a declaration would consist of concepts, but these are used only to designate relative and finite things; because such a declaration would be subject to categories, but even the category of substance excludes accidents, and thus limits God; because it would be composed of concepts, but God is simple; finally, because by using a verb it would express a motion, but God is beyond the opposition between motion and rest.[69]

Early on, reflection about the origin of our ideas of God's attributes was linked with this critique of his attributes, and this likewise led to negative results. Insight into the *origin of the determinations concerning God* had to give an ultimate decision about what the cognitive value of these determinations was. The theology of the Arabs distinguished relative and negative attributes of God, and Jewish theology, without deviating much from that, at times also distinguished attributes of activity.[70] Christian theology, following a distinction already made in the second century and surfacing often from then on among the Neoplatonists,[71] juxtaposed the "three ways" by which one arrives at the properties of God: the *way of eminence, of causality, and of removal*, or, as this last one is more commonly called, of *negation*.[72] One cannot maintain the last distinction in the face of the dichotomy of methods for ascending to the idea of God; for if restriction is merely an aspect of denial, then one cannot separate the *way of eminence* from the *way of negation*. If, in correcting the distinction, one traces the attributes of God to those in which denial destroys the finite in the religious ideal and those in which one makes God conceivable through his creative activity in the world, then this investigation of the origin of the ideas of God's attributes also leads to knowledge of their inappropriateness. For where is the limit then in the process of sublation [*Aufhebung*]? And where is the justification, then, for arguing from what we perceive in the world to the nature of its cause, since this cause of the world can be totally heterogeneous?

Thus the medieval effort to determine the essence of God through his attributes concludes with the fundamental insight into the unsuitability of this idea of God for the religious ideal. Here too *every subterfuge is in vain*. The task of holding on to the content of the ideal in us and yet of sublating human and finite form and multiplicity is insoluble. Spinoza's harsh expression regarding any such attempt, namely, that the intellect and will of God are no more like ours than the Dog star is to the barking animal, merely develops theological theses of Judaism. Thus Abraham ben David says: "The will of God is specifically different from our own; for our will is grounded on desire, and this consists in the wish to possess something one does not have. But God needs nothing, rather all things need him, and from the viewpoint of purpose his will is precisely the contrary of that which we understand by our will."[73] And Maimonides even raises the question: "Is there, then, any other similarity between our knowledge and God's than that of the name?"[74] When, in reference to another difficulty, the church Fathers and the Scholastics declare that God's attributes are identical to one another,[75] this identity between what is different is a piece of nonsense. When Thomas says that the multiplicity of attributes through which we know God is grounded in the reflection of God in the world and in our intellectual comprehension of them, and then in the context of his theological metaphysics says that the manifold perfection of creatures should be thought of as contained in the simple nature of God, then he acknowledges that every expression is simply *inadequate* and needs amplification through others, yet *he does not relinquish knowledge of God*.[76] Although Thomas penetratingly emphasizes that the content of a declaration is not dependent on the way we make declarations, so that no distinction in God is posited by a distinction we make in a proposition,[77] the upshot of this is to make it all the clearer how impossible it is to understand in a simple way a content we grasp by making distinctions. Thus no distinction made by medieval theological metaphysics takes us beyond a merely symbolical significance of the idea of God. But with that one gives up on knowledge of attributes of God which corresponds with its object, and all finite relative determinations contain merely the sense of a hieroglyphics of the infinite and the absolute.[78]

5. Theology Is Linked with Knowledge of Nature and with Aristotelian Science of the Cosmos

From its inception, *theology* was intertwined with elements of antiquity's science of the cosmos. It used these elements to solve its problems, regardless of whether they stemmed from Platonic, Aristotelian, or Stoic philosophy, just as one fitted marble fragments, wherever one found them, into the churches of those days. Within its range one could find formulas, defenses, attempts at proof, and dialectical treatment. It had its Enlightenment types and freethinkers, both in the East and in the West.[79]

Arabs' Knowledge of Nature and Their Aristotelian Standpoint

But in the continuity of science *knowledge of the cosmos* created by the Greeks maintained and developed itself as the other half of intellectual life, totally different from that of theology. This science of the cosmos, the creation of the Greeks, disputed with theology and complemented it: thus arose the metaphysical worldview of the Middle Ages. And in fact the change by which knowledge of nature gradually fought its way through and became the most pervasive in the intellectual development of the West in the Middle Ages began among the Arabs. Hence we begin with the *Arabs*.

The contrast of the metaphysical thought of the Arabs and the Jews with that of classical peoples is something they became aware of themselves. The survey of metaphysical and theological views of the human race, such as Shahrastani attempted, mentions at its beginning a distinction used by the Arabs, according to which the Greeks (and the Persians) devoted themselves principally to determining the external nature of things and to a preoccupation with physical objects, whereas the Arabs and Jews turned to intellectual things and the inner character of objects.[80] And the *Book of the Khazar* remarks similarly that the Greeks reject what they cannot find on the basis of the physical world, whereas the prophets took as their starting point for certainty in knowledge "that which they have seen with the eye of the spirit," and non-Greek philosophers have accepted these inner intuitions into their sphere of speculation.[81] Regardless of how things stand regarding the original or the constant direction of these various peoples, such passages rightly show the contrast between Greek science of the cosmos and the dominant direction of theological metaphysics among the Arabs and the Jews as it continued until the appearance of natural-scientific research and then Aristotelian metaphysics among the Arabs, and persisted without interruption among the Jews throughout the entire Middle Ages. And the Christian West gradually recognized still more clearly the one-sidedness of the cosmic science of the Greeks.

Thus in the period we have just gone through, *theology* (to an extent a metaphysics of religious experience) chiefly occupied the preponderant interest of the Arabs, Jews, and Western peoples. To be sure, theology depended in many ways on concepts developed by the Greeks, and the Mutazilites as well as Augustine or Scotus Erigena used them to a great extent; this world of theological thought was also disciplined by ancient logic and the doctrine of categories. Nevertheless, the entire conceptual framework during this period shaped itself around the nodal point of religious experiences and concepts; this central interest attracted fragments of Greek knowledge and subordinated them to itself. A change in the intellectual life of the Middle Ages did not come about until the *Arabs*, particularly, discovered a *second center of intellectual activity in Greek knowledge of nature and cosmic speculation* and began to construct a sphere of knowledge of nature around it.

In the Orient Aristotle and some important mathematical, astronomical, and medical writings of the Greeks had never been lost. After the demise of Greek philosophy the schools of the Christian Syrians became the chief seats of knowledge of the Greek language, metaphysics, and knowledge of nature. Syrian translations of Greek writings transmitted knowledge of them and were often used as the basis for translations into Arabic.[82] In fact the Syrian Aristotle, as it came down to the Arabs, was very different from the original; of course in the present condition of our knowledge we cannot yet adequately establish a detailed relationship between the Syrian Aristotle and the theories of Arab philosophers such as they first appeared with Alkindi and Alfarabi.[83] With the transfer of residence of the caliphs to Bagdad, which was located in the middle between two centers of knowledge of nature, that is, India and the schools of Greek science, the Arabs became the carriers of this tradition and its further development. At that time, not much more than one hundred years had passed since these Arab Bedouins had crossed the boundaries of their country and taken control of Palestine and Syria, and history has no comparable example of such a marvelously swift transition out of a relatively low intellectual condition into that of a refined civilization. The art of Syrian physicians, which these Bedouins who were beginning to dominate Asia needed, introduced Hippocrates and Galen, and knowledge of nature as well as theology referred to Aristotle; worship and administration made mathematical and astronomical knowledge necessary—a noble scientific curiosity swept the nation. Under Almamun (813–833) many Greek manuscripts came from Constantinople as a gift from the emperor; a translation project ordered and controlled by the caliphs occupied the ninth century and went on into the tenth: translations of writings of Aristotle, Hippocrates, Galen, Dioscorides, Euclid, Apollonius of Perga, Archimedes, and Ptolemy put the Arabs into a position to take up the work of natural science at the point where the Greeks had left it.

The natural-scientific movement which thus arose in Islam further developed the exact sciences which had existed in Alexandria and maintained the differentiation of science as it had been carried on at that time. Of course we cannot establish the importance of the Arabs in developing this exact knowledge of nature with enough certitude yet,[84] but, given their geographical position and their expansion over such a vast empire, the importance accruing to their *intermediary role* is beyond all doubt. Thus the West owes the Indian system of numerical notation and the expansion of Greek algebra to their mediation.[85]

And they have unquestionably prepared the way for the rise of modern natural science through *independent advances* in two directions.

The Arabs acquired the *art of alchemy* along with other science from Alexandria. Unfortunately, we do not sufficiently know the condition in which it passed to them. This art, which tried to refine metals [*Metallveredlung*], gave chemical experiment an autonomous footing, whereas previously it had sometimes served medicine, sometimes technology. It thus enkindled a great enthusiasm for *real analysis of natural objects,* after the ideational analyses of metaphysical methods had deceived mankind for so long. It nourished this enthusiasm through the secret hope, grounded in the theory of transformation of metals, of offering a preparation which would make it possible to change base metals into silver and ultimately into gold. Thus, in its position on mercury and sulfur, it developed the germ of a theoretical view which was not founded, like the Aristotelian one on the four elements, on intuition and speculation but on real analysis [*Zerspaltung*]. People did not understand these terms to mean simply quicksilver and brimstone, but substances whose behavior under experiment, especially under the impact of fire, arranged them into one or the other of these two classes. It was along this path that the genuine problem first arose of discovering the components of matter in the contents presented in chemical analysis. And regardless of how imperfect the results of this first alchemist epoch were from a theoretical point of view, they still prepared the way for quantitative investigations and a suitable idea of the constitution of matter. At the same time this alchemist art produced a large number of recipes for the first time and led to new chemical procedures.[86]

Communication to the West

The other direction in which the Arabs paved the way for the rise of modern science of nature by their independent progress consisted in developing and using mathematics as an instrument for describing *quantitative determinations* about nature. Inventive use of instruments of measurement; tireless improvement of devices of Greek measurement of degrees, supported by expansion in knowledge of the earth; then the cooperation of richly equipped observatories for improving and completing astronomical data; and the cooperation of many scientists and generously distributed support as part of a grand plan produced a network of quantitative determinations superimposed on the Alexandrian foundation, which was destined to perform priceless services for a creative natural-scientific epoch. Thus in the Alfonsan tables—which summed up the common work of Moorish, Jewish, and Christian astronomers serving king Alfonso of Castile (this also was completely in the style of the caliphs)—the output of Arab astronomy was passed on, and these tables then became the basis for astronomical studies.[87]

Thus knowledge of the natural-scientific heritage of the Greeks and the independent increase of this legacy passed on to the new generation of peoples in living communication with one another, particularly through mediation of the Jews. Knowledge of nature became a second independent focus of intellectual effort and satisfaction alongside inner religious experience and theology. The light was ignited in the realm of Islam, spread out over Spain, and soon enough, as the figure of a man like Gerbert shows, its rays fell on the Christian West as well.

Nevertheless, this *Arabic knowledge of nature was just as incapable as the Alexandrian of replacing the* current *descriptive and theological structure of* knowledge of the cosmos through an attempt, no matter how imperfect, at *causal explanation*. We have recognized the dominant activity of formal and descriptive sciences and the power of metaphysics of psychical forces and substantial forms as correlative historical facts.[88] Formal sciences of mathematics and logic, descriptive astronomy and the part of geography covered by the limits of descriptive science: these made up the knowledge which attained a high degree of development among the Arabs and constituted the focal point of higher intellectual interests. The closest external connection [*Zusammenhang*] of these sciences consisted in the general image of the cosmos which Eratosthenes, Hipparchus, and Ptolemy had striven for earlier. Hence the encyclopedic tendency of Alexandrian science is naturally evident to a still greater degree in the knowledge of the Middle Ages. It manifests itself, linked to a metaphysical and theological grounding, in the *Encyclopedia of the Brethren of Purity* [*der Lauteren Brüder*] and in the Western works of Bede, Isidore, yes even Albert the Great. On the other hand, some other sciences in Arabic knowledge of nature—such as mechanics, optics and acoustics, which treat kindred parts of natural experience as a special class and thus make it possible to derive composite uniformities from the whole of nature—were not yet advanced enough to permit one to try to explain natural phenomena based on natural laws causally. Indeed, the prospect of explaining nature causally, which Democritus' atoms once appeared to offer by way of an arbitrary method in the narrow range of known natural facts,[89] had to give ground at first in face of growing knowledge of how complex nature's structure was; hence we find among the Arabs an extreme example of the atomistic view of nature in the service of the orthodox Mutakalimun. Mechanics, which was the fundamental science for all explanatory knowledge of nature, made no progress among the Arabs. Their ideas on motion, pressure, gravity, and so on were just as unsatisfactory as those of the Alexandrians for replacing metaphysical fictions of psychical entities and substantial forms. Advances beyond Ptolemy in optics, as described in Alhazen's extant work, had no influence at first on the general view of nature. Advances in chemistry did not yet allow one to dissolve matter into its real components and establish their behavior, and so one notes an inclination in Averroës to bring Aristotelian doctrine on matter closer to that of Anaxagoras, but there was still no way to replace Aristotle's view with one grounded in real knowledge of nature. In Arab-Moorish astronomy people raised questions about Ptolemy's complicated epicyclical hypothesis,[90] but their attempts to replace it by a more suitable one were unsuccessful. Finally, paleontology had not recognized, in their transitional character, the organic forms which appear to maintain themselves unchanged amid the comings and goings of individuals on earth, nor had anyone investigated these forms causally; on the contrary, understanding still had to deal with them teleologically.

Hence the condition of the natural sciences in the whole period from their emergence among the Arabs to the demise of Arabic scientific culture did not eliminate the need for metaphysical ideas of psychical causes and their manifestations in the forms of the universe to explain nature.

In fact the peculiar form which this teleological metaphysics of psychical causes had maintained in the system and school of Aristotle corresponded to the state of knowledge of nature for a long time. The Arabs had discovered the peripatetic school in a flourishing state among the Syrian Christians. It is pointless to ask whether this external circumstances was decisive for their study of Aristotle,[91] because, at their level of knowledge of nature, positive causes were already on hand which would lead them to see Aristotle's system as the most appropriate form of science of the cosmos. Of course the positive natural science of the Alexandrians and the Arabs was not everywhere in total agreement with Aristotle's system. And of course the legacy of mathematical science of nature among the Arabs by no means always flowed together in unison with their peripatetic school's development. Thurot proved the permanence of the relative separation of positive natural science from metaphysics, which was the outcome of the development of ancient science, on the basis of one outstanding case. The hydrostatic theorem (which is called after its discoverer "Archimedes' principle") was known to mathematicians both in subsequent Greek and in Arabic history of science and was preserved in their tradition, but it was not known to the metaphysicians.[92] Still, exact science did not yet affect the core of Aristotle's metaphysics either; on the contrary, there was simply agreement between the general outlines of knowledge of nature and those of Aristotle's metaphysics. The telescope had not yet shown changes on other heavenly bodies; there was still no incipient general physics of the universe, and so the Aristotelian doctrine of a double world held its own: the perfect and unchanging order of the stars and the alternation of generation and corruption under the moon. Thus a pantheistically conceived world-reason did not express the rationality of the cosmos; instead, the world of the stars remained the locus of a conscious intelligence which radiated from there and manifested itself in a lower world. Indeed, theological metaphysics, which regarded this contrast in the cosmos as a symbol of a contrast given in inner experience, gave this schema more authoritative power than it could possess in the ancient world. And the system which stretches from the world of the stars to the changing earth with its vegetation and its inhabitants adopted descriptive science of the cosmos as totally in correspondence with that metaphysics.

Thus along with adoption of Greek knowledge of nature went the translation of Aristotle. It began under Almamun, and during the ninth and tenth centuries translations of Aristotle were being continually completed. On this foundation and in interaction with the living study of nature, Arab philosophy attained its full development in Avicenna and Averroës: as an independent continuation of the peripatetic school.

While the Arabs thus cultivated knowledge of nature and Aristotelian science besides theology from the ninth century on, in the *Christian West,* where everything developed on a larger scale, *theology* was almost exclusively *dominant* for a long time. Encyclopedias delivered dead information about nature. In the tenth century Gerbert brought something of the light of Arabic knowledge of nature from Spain; Constantine the African returned from his trips to the Orient with medical treatises, and Adelard of Bath likewise picked up some natural-scientific knowledge from the Arabs; then translations of Aristotle, his commentators, and Arab physicists followed one another in quicker succession.[93] But the darkness which enveloped knowledge of nature lightened only feebly. Until the end of the twelfth century, intellectual life of the West pulsated in theology and in the related metaphysical consideration of human history and society. Nor was anything changed by the fact that Aristotle's logic was used as a powerful instrument in theological dialectics and that Abelard's bold subjectivity asserted the rights of understanding with more insight than ever before. Of course the negative thrust of theological dialecticians of that time destroyed the solidity of traditional dogma. Just as in the corresponding phenomena of Islam, doubt, even despair, of understanding developed irresistibly out of the antinomies of religious understanding. It was in vain that Bernard of Clairvaux and the Victorines sought peace of mind in mysticism. But just then, for the first time, theological metaphysics ceased being the focal point of all of European thought as the natural science and natural philosophy of the ancients and the Arabs now rose above the horizon of Western Christianity and gradually became completely visible. This was the greatest transformation which took place in the course of the intellectual development of Europe during the Middle Ages.

Repeated prohibitions of the natural-scientific and metaphysical writings of Aristotle did not stop this *transformation in the West.* By the first third of the thirteenth century practically the entire corpus of Aristotle's writings was translated. The systems of Avicenna and Averroës were known, and they threatened the Christian faith. Western metaphysics of the Middle Ages arose in defense of this faith, using a combination of Christian theology and the metaphysical philosophy of history which issued from it, plus the Arabic Aristotle and knowledge of nature connected with its study. As the seat of this metaphysics, the University of Paris became the center of Europe's intellectual movement. For a century, beginning with the middle of the thirteenth—when Albert the Great and Thomas Aquinas (his student from the Dominican monastery at Cologne), Duns Scotus, and the boldest and mightiest of the Scholastics, the antipapal William of Occam, taught—the eyes of all Europe were drawn to this new science of reason and its destiny. At the same time material was now made available for Western Christians to make an independent advance in the natural sciences. This work developed slowly, broadly, and deeply. External conditions affecting the sciences in monasteries and at institutes directed by the church supported the preponderance of theological-metaphysical interest, and the preoccupation of the court of Frederick the Second with the natural sciences, as inspired by the example of the caliphs, found no imitators. The political constitution of Europe gave weight to problems of history and the state, as well as to writings on the subject, a weight they did not possess in the despotic realms of Islam. Ideas strongly influenced the course of public affairs in the West even then, and they attracted particular public attention. The independent, indeed brilliant, progress the Christian West made in areas of special knowledge thus lay chiefly in the sphere of the human sciences during the thirteenth and fourteenth centuries. Thus scholars used the expansion of knowledge of nature first of all to establish an encyclopedic unity of knowledge carried forward by metaphysics. The treatise *De Natura Rerum* by Thomas of Cantiprato, the *Speculum Majus* by Vincent of Beauvais, the *Book of Nature* by Conrad von Megenberg, and *The World Picture* by Pierre d'Ailly were all consonant with this intellectual direction, and it determined all Albert the Great's activity. We cannot satisfactorily decide as yet which of the individual results we encounter first in Albert issued from his independent study of nature; but one cannot deny that he promoted the descriptive science of nature in his personal observation and investigation. Then in Roger Bacon awareness of the significance of mathematics as "the alphabet of philosophy" emerged, as well as of experimental science as "the mistress of the speculative sciences." He sensed the power of knowledge of efficient causes grounded in experience in contrast with syllogistic pseudoscience, and his powerful imagination anticipated the results of his work in remarkable previsions of future discoveries. On the other hand, the partially imported and partially independent inventions which paved the way for the age of discoveries gradually surfaced in the West.[94]

6. Second Period of Medieval Thought

The new stage of medieval thought begins with the transmission of Arabic knowledge of nature and of Aristotelian philosophy and lasts until the end of the Middle Ages. The earlier period had created dialectic as the foundation for theology, had further developed the proof designed by the Fathers (especially Augustine) that a transcendent order of immaterial being exists, and had answered the challenge of creating an understandable structuring of the content of faith in a theology which, however, did not yet distinguish methodically between what reason can comprehend and what it cannot. These tasks themselves now acquire a more mature formulation under the new conditions. Comparison of Christianity, Islam, and Judaism sheds its light on the field of theology; comparison of Aristotle's science of reason with the theology of the religions illuminated the boundaries of the demonstrable and of religious mystery; connecting knowledge of nature with theology expanded the horizon of reason. Under these new conditions, how did people perceive the challenges we identified in the former period and how did they attempt to meet them?

Conclusion of Metaphysics of Substantial Forms

Because the science of the cosmos was now linked with the theology of the monotheistic religions, further insoluble difficulties arose, to be sure, which brought about the dissolution of medieval metaphysics, but as long as one could cover them up and could harmonize the good element in the will with the rational element in thought (i.e., the Christian element with the Greek science of reason), the result of all this was recognition of a splendid *formula* which brought previous *metaphysics to completion in a systematic unity*.

First of all, in place of Plato's and Aristotle's analytic results, which contain the ultimate presuppositions of the cosmos, one substituted the constructionist Philonic-Neoplatonic idea. According to that, *ideas are located in God*, and the forces which permeate the universe radiate from this intelligible world. Augustine as well as other Church Fathers adopted this idea into the philosophy of Christianity[95] and linked it with the doctrine of creation. Augustine held that God creates things as an expression of the intelligible world of unchanging ideas existing in him. Thus metaphysics, as the science of reason, now acquired a simpler and more systematic framework for its structure: *it imagines the intelligible world in God as reflected in creation*, and *it inserts* principles corresponding to this objective structure *into the particular mind created by God*.[96]

So, at the height of this development the following theory took shape, which Thomas Aquinas sensitively developed. Aquinas held that Plato erroneously assumed that the object of knowledge must exist in the same way in itself as it does in our knowledge, that is, immaterially and immutably. But actually abstraction can divide what is undivided in the object and consider one component of it for itself, prescinding from the others. The component of the object which our thought stresses in its general concept is thus real, but it is only part of that object's reality. Therefore reality which corresponds to universal concepts is given only in individual objects: "Universals are not things existing in their own right; on the contrary, they have their being in the particular alone." On the other hand, the human intellect nevertheless separates out an essential element in the universals, for the divine intellect contains them and informs objects with them. Thus Thomas can use a formula which apparently puts an end to the dispute about universals. The *universals* exist *before* particular things, *in* them, and *after* them. They exist before them in the divine, archetypical understanding; they exist in things as part of the content which makes up their general being; and they exist after them as concepts produced by abstractive understanding. This formula can then easily be expanded to accommodate modern science, and such an expansion has taken place. The Middle Ages prepared the way for it: in God exist not only universal concepts but universal truths, the laws of change in the world process.[97]

In these propositions metaphysics as the science of reason received the most perfect form it attained during the Middle Ages. This science of reason seeks to make the rationality of the world clear and comprehensible; its problem is the nature of this rationality, its origin in the world, and the origin of our knowledge of it in consciousness. The solution of the problem is also pushed into the realm of the transcendent in this formula. For it contains a relation among three members, in each of which the same X, the unresolved general form of particular things, recurs. Intelligence, the world system, and God are these members. In fact God is not only the efficient and final cause of the world, but also its exemplary cause. Or, as Scotus shows God to be the ultimate condition of the intrinsic and necessary world system: the world system contains a chain of causes, an order of purposes, and a hierarchy of perfection. All three series lead to an initial point that is not conditioned in turn by a previous member of the same series and exists in fact in the same substance. For, just as Spinoza argued later on, to be necessarily from oneself can be true only of a substance. Thus God is the necessary cause in this metaphysical context.[98]

The number of truths which this science of reason believed it could establish constantly diminished during its work until finally, at the time of *Occam*, the *formula* itself, according to which the world is present in God in universal concepts, was *dissolved* and experience of the particular asserted its claims, not only with respect to the external world but, for Roger Bacon as well as Occam, even with respect to the interior world.

Rational Grounding of the Transcendent World

Because the focal point of medieval metaphysics lay in consciousness of God and people looked at the world and man from God's perspective, this science of reason in the second period of Western philosophy, following its impulse to subject everything to rational necessity, first tried to establish the existence of God, then developed God's attributes, and from there extended itself to created spiritual beings. A result of this was that individual proofs for the existence of God came to the fore in metaphysics and similar proofs were established for the existence of a spiritual world, to which man also belonged. The abstract metaphysics of Wolff's school treated rational theology, cosmology, and psychology ontologically on an equal footing as the three parts of metaphysical science, and Kant accordingly undertook to derive ideas in these three areas from the single essence of reason. Historical consideration of the Middle Ages shows that rational theology and psychology—because they reach back into a transcendent world of faith with their conclusions—occupy a totally different position in the human cognitive structure than cosmology, which strives only to perfect concepts of reality.

Inferences Regarding Existence of God

We will consider first the proofs for the existence of God, or *rational theology*.

Christianity had its historical presupposition in the monotheistic result of ancient science of the cosmos,[99] and the church Fathers regarded the argument for God from the character of the world with its purposive beauty combined with change as a compelling one. During the long centuries of the *Middle Ages no serious scholar rejected* the *derivation of the world from God,* and especially the argument from the revolution of the heavens to its first mover, even though they did subject the degree of its evidence to investigation; all other truths of faith, on the other hand, came under discussion to a greater or lesser extent. From the year 1240 on, for a period of several decades, church authority struggled with a party at the University of Paris which propagated the extreme consequences of Averroës' doctrine. Thus the eternity of the world was defended in the university since the "first beginning," as a miracle, broke through the necessary system of nature; creation out of nothing was attacked as incompatible with the demands of science; so were the assumptions of a first parentless man and, consequently, the Last Judgment. The crux of this skeptical movement lay in questioning the survival of the individual soul, because one cannot deduce it from the doctrine of substantial forms. From these assumptions, then, followed the bold utterance "that the pronouncements of the theologians are founded on fables" and another one like it: "that the wise men of the world are the philosophers alone."[100] But among all the theses which circulated among students and teachers at the University of Paris at the time and came under ecclesiastical censure, there is none which would have called the existence of God into question. A second center of the skeptical spirit in the thirteenth century[101] was the court of Frederick II in the South. Superstitious understanding of the common people surrounded the intellectually powerful figure of the great emperor with stories in which the most remarkable thing was his skepticism and his inclination toward experimental answers to such questions as people were accustomed to leaving to syllogistic discussions. People claimed to have knowledge that he had men's bodies opened up to study their digestion; that he had wanted to have children raised apart from society to solve the question of man's original language. An experiment of this kind recalls the philosophical novel of Ibn Tufayl, circulated in the thirteenth century, and dealt with the natural development of man. Documents drafted during the Curia's dispute with the emperor as well as public opinion accused him of denying immortality and ascribed the ultimate motivation of his reign of terror in the Kingdom of Sicily to this materialistic rejection of any notion of an afterlife. Of course the terrible saying about the three deceivers—that is, the founders of the three religions of the West—cannot be laid at the emperor's door; but the idea that the philosophical truth in all three religions was enveloped in fables must be regarded as a commonplace among the enlightened at this motley court that resided sometimes in the East and sometimes in the West among religiously mixed peoples. And yet, among all the witticisms which circulated about Frederick at that time, we have no record of any which might have touched on the argument for God as cause of the world.[102] If one investigates expressions of skepticism from other circles, one finds that the hostile and crass mockeries of God (such as Alberich of Romano reported) absolutely presuppose the existence of God.[103] And the doubts of the nominalists against *every* point of rational religious science went in Occam's case even to the point of subjecting the grounds for the existence of God to sharp criticism—in fact he even boldly expressed the possibility that the *world moves itself*; but even he nevertheless acknowledged the paramount power of proofs for the existence of God.[104]

The reason for this fact that the metaphysical mind of the Middle Ages had an unshakeable strong point in evidence for the existence of God, while no other truth of faith lay untouched by doubt, cannot be discovered in the strength of religious convictions; for, as we just saw, these were shaken in many ways. It did not lay in the tradition of the structure of world history, which was tied to God both at its beginning and at its end; for no matter how important this tradition was for medieval man's sense of life and style of thinking, bold minds nevertheless at least subjected it to doubt, though not yet to examination. Least of all can we find it in the ontological argument, for the force of that argument was disputed by the best orthodox scholars. It lay in the argument which led back to God on the basis of the current state of knowledge of nature concerning the uniform and harmoniously intertwining paths of the stars and the purposiveness which governed the forms of nature. This proof does not appear as a single argument but rather, as in Aristotle, is the framework of the entire view of nature. Of course the Scholastics of this period at first stated a fixed number of individual proofs of the existence of God which were mutually independent, and Scholastic metaphysics continued to maintain at least the distinction between the cosmological and teleological (physico-theological) proofs; but this fragmented academic formulation did not carry the weight of reasoning for the medieval mind that arguments which argued from the world to God contained.[105]

Terrestrial physics had remained fixed in its early beginnings and no one used it to explain phenomena of the starry world; neither devices of calculation nor art of instrumentation bridged the gap between events on earth and those beyond in outer space; one understood gravity as a terrestrial fact, and no one had proved that changes had occurred at any point in space beyond the earth's atmosphere. This separation of the world of heavenly bodies from that beneath the moon was used as a comprehensible graphic representation of the great contrast Christianity discerns in all earthly change and all earthly imperfection in comparison with what is not of this world. Dante's cosmic poem illustrates the significance of this astronomical transcendence for the spirit of the Middle

Ages; its three parts conclude by design, each in its own way, with another look at the starry heavens, the last of those parts with the famous words: "the love which moves the sun and the other stars."[106]

The *argument itself* proceeded from the uniformity of motions in the heavens and their purposefulness, which regulates the entire economy of the earthly world up to man himself, to a perfect and spiritual substance. For most of the Scholastics it rested on the astronomical construction they found in their Aristotle, or, more rarely, on one they took from Ptolemy. Sometimes the argument used the supplementary proposition which Anaxagoras, Plato, and Aristotle used, that every motion of a body in space presupposed a cause of the motion outside that body; sometimes it used the distinction of motions on earth, which are straight and come to rest at a terminus, from those of the heavens, which are circular and continuous, hence point back to an intelligent principle of infinite power. One can find it as well in Albert the Great or Thomas, in Bonaventura or Duns Scotus.[107] Although rigorous evidence was ascribed to the argument, most theologians thought it a probable assumption that the deity effected these motions in the heavens through created spirits of a superhuman sort, and one could determine the number of angels producing the motion by that of the spheres being moved. The doctrine of the angels was linked with the astronomical worldview on the basis of Aristotelian theory, hence here too it was ultimately *psychical relations rather than a mechanical structure of nature* which offered the final basis for interpreting motions in the cosmos. Prevailing European metaphysics continued to hold on to a mythical voluntary system of psychical forces as the final explanatory ground of the external structure of the world.

Organic beings on earth demonstrated a purposiveness which led one back to God. Albert the Great, who stood especially close to Aristotle in this particular as well, outfitted this proof with an enormous amount of evidence. "Through the manner and the measure of its being, through the specific essence which assigns it its determined place in the series of other creatures, through the weight or the order in which it is in harmony with the others according to its use and exercises influence on the realization of the world's purpose, the created being manifestly proves the power of a mighty, wise, and good creator."[108]

Proof for the existence of God from the harmonious system of processes of the universe has been with us from the time of Anaxagoras. As a matter of fact there has been a change in the middle terms people have used to argue from observation of the world to the idea of God. For in every period, concepts which the state of the positive sciences had developed about the system of nature formed those middle terms. The function of this proof in the body of the metaphysics of an epoch depends therefore on the view of nature developed at the time. Kant's unhistorical mind mistook this basic situation, inasmuch as he even bothered to make the useless attempt to extract a metaphysics-in-itself out of the various systems; but as a rule he was satisfied with simply decreeing that Wolff's compendia constituted such a metaphysics-in-itself. Actually every form of proof of a rational world cause which argues from the cosmos to its presuppositions has only a relative epistemological value, that is, in its relation to other concepts of nature of its time. Even the complete grounding which comes about only in the context of the system itself and which connects the cosmological textbook proof (which is totally insufficient by itself) with the physico-theological one has no significance beyond this either. It can only demonstrate that if one assumes the concepts which underlie the interpretation of reality at a given time, then one must go back to a first, purposefully operative cause. The concept of God in that grounding is only one member in the system of conditions which one makes the basis for interpreting phenomena at a particular stage of knowledge, and the indispensability of this member depends on the relation of that assumption to other assumptions already on hand. Thus Newton needed an impetus besides gravitation; he needed a reason for the purposefulness in measurements of relations of the planetary paths; gravitation expressed only part of the conditions, and the God which he said he needed besides it likewise expressed only another part of these conditions which— assuming matter, space, time, cause, and substance—seemed necessary to him to interpret reality. Thus a rigorous *proof of the existence of God based on the cosmos is impossible* so long as one cannot make the *objective validity* of a complete *system of concepts of nature* its basis. We also wish to stress some particular reservations. A proof of this type would presuppose that one can apply the concept of causality to the world system. As medieval philosophers already established, it would not allow us to conclude to a world creator but only, in Kant's expression, "to a world architect who would always be extremely restricted by the possibilities in the matter he works with." It would not lead beyond a cause proportional to known rational unity, and little by little concepts of nature in the modern period have changed so much with respect to this rational unity that compelling force of the argument for an independent personal being distinct from the world has died out.

Different from every such particular proof is the consciousness, underlying them all, of the rationality linked with consideration of the paths and dimensions of the stars and the forms of the organic world; this merely expresses that we see beyond ourselves into something analogous to human thought, something which corresponds to it in the world. It is one aspect of the indestructible human consciousness of God, and though it produces individual proofs, it remains in existence after they have been broken down; but of itself it does not contain the certainty of a personal being distinct from the world.[109]

Besides this form of argumentation there is only *one other one,* which we call the *psychological* one. It starts out from *analysis of inner experience*; here it finds psychological elements fused into living and personal conviction, elements which assure the pious man of God's existence independently of any knowledge of nature. Thus the free *morality* of a being capable of self-sacrifice but incapable of regarding itself as its own creator leads that being beyond all concepts of nature and posits divine will as its cause. The *way we experience transitoriness in ourselves* as well as the *error* and *imperfection* of what we are, viewed psychologically, implies that a standard exists which transcends all this; if this standard were totally unreal, then our feeling of imperfection and guilt would be an empty sentimentality which would measure reality by unreal mental fantasies. Living *consciousness of moral values* demands that they not be considered as a by-product of the natural order in our consciousness, but rather as a powerful reality toward which the ordering of the world is directed and to which victory is assured in the world order. If ancient thought described that aspect of our metaphysical disposition developed in the proof based on the unified harmoniousness of the cosmos, so Christian thought addressed itself principally to this other side of that disposition—traversing the depths of our self and honestly striving to assimilate the experiences of the will within us. To be sure, Christianity has its historical presupposition in the monotheistic outcome of ancient science of the cosmos and a permanent part of its concept of God in consciousness of the rationality of the universe; but the certitude of God, whom that consciousness considers more than just an intelligent cause, consists for it most of all in experiences of the soul and the will. The entire literature of the Fathers and of the Middle Ages is filled with arguments for the existence of God based on these inner experiences, among which the three noted above are especially prominent.[110] And just as so much in the Middle Ages was symbolical, so this structure of the moral order in God was made visible at that time in the hierarchy, in which grace and power flowed downward from God; every sacrifice of the Mass made the presence of God felt in the here and now.

What was certain to the pious person in a subjective and personal way and what church Fathers and medieval writers expressed freely and personally in countless forms, *Christian metaphysics* wished to reduce to an *argument* which was *compelling* for everyone. And in fact this psychological grounding acquired its most abstract conceptual formulation in the ontological proof. Anselm set himself the profound task of discovering a ground for God which did not presuppose the existence and nature of the world. He derived an intuition into the existence of God from the concept of God by way of logical analysis. The untenability of the ontological argument so produced has been demonstrated convincingly from Gaunilo to Thomas Aquinas and from him to Kant: certainty regarding God's existence, a certainty independent of the science of the cosmos, is not grounded in the abstract concept of God but in the living connection of the idea of God with the totality of psychical life. Anselm expressed this living and natural connection more suitably in his earlier proof: here he showed consciousness of a highest good and an absolute perfection to be the foundation of our consciousness of differing degrees of the good and the perfect. Thus one argues to God as the highest good, in contrast with the argument to God as intelligent cause.[111] As is well known, Raymond of Sebond tried to give the moral proof a coercive form.

Nevertheless, all attempts to impart the form of metaphysical argument to the structure of interior, especially moral, experiences of faith in God were just as ephemeral in their significance as the enterprise of arguing from the cosmos to a personal God. For it is *impossible to describe with universal validity the elements of inner experience* which these attempts analyzed in drawing their conclusions. For those elements have to do precisely with practical religion, and this is personal life. In fact this practical faith is so independent of theoretical description that a man is capable of living the life of God, so to speak, even though his intellectual condition has imposed the destiny of doubting God on him. Hence practical faith first discovered the true nature of its certitude in Protestantism, after the metaphysics of the Middle Ages had disintegrated.

Proofs for Immortality of the Soul

From rational theology, which was the center of medieval thought in general, we now turn to *rational psychology*.

It acquired its permanent systematic form from the metaphysicians as early as the period of the struggle between Christianity, Judaism, and Greco-Roman polytheism. We have already noted how experiences of the heart and study of the life of the soul came to the fore in the first centuries after Christ. The predominance of private life already worked in the same direction. Then imperial sovereignty directed all eyes in Roman society with breathless excitement on *one man,* and one can observe in the case of Tacitus what a change historical vision now underwent. His personal portraits of the emperors express the altered interests of society. There were more profound motives at work as well; longing for immortality is the hallmark of senescent antiquity. Tomb inscriptions of that time show that the idea of a powerless dream life in the underworld now completely gave way to expectation of a higher life. "You blessed souls of the just," it says in one such grave inscription, "guide the innocent Magnilla through the Elysian groves and fields into your dwellings." The tale of Amor and Psyche and the depiction of Psyche under the symbol of the butterfly, which was becoming popular, are signs of this yearning. Mystery cults pointed out the ways this ardent desire sought out the heart of God. Boethius' beautiful work *On the Consolation of Philosophy* looked to the last moment with confidence: When the soul endowed with a good conscience and freed from the prison of earth now freely aspires toward heaven, then all earthly activity appears as nothing to it when compared with enjoying the joys of heaven. The core of Christian literature of the first centuries is the feeling of the moral person's infinite worth before God. Establishing the *theory of a realm of immortal individual substantial souls is but the scientific expression of this change in the life of the soul.* Now the world of spirits and its realm rises above the horizon of metaphysical meditation. The literary expression of this fact lies in the stylistic forms of meditations, soliloquies, and monologues, and solitary communion of the mind with itself now became a deep fountainhead of scientific thought.

Plotinus, the purest and noblest defender of a paganism locked in a death struggle with Christianity, shows in his system the disposition of mind of the new period, which was so alien to genuine Greek and Roman life. Ammonius, his teacher, had been raised after all in the new life of the soul of the Christian communities. Just as the uncertain tradition still permits us to know that Ammonius already undertook to prove the immateriality of the soul,[112] so we find that Plotinus developed this proof into a complete metaphysics of the life of the soul directed against the theories of the Epicureans and the Stoics. Origen was in contact with him at several points in his treatise *On Principles*; he performed the same task for Christian communities embroiled in struggles with the Gnostics as Plotinus did for the pagan world.

Plotinus proved through a long series of reasons that the soul exists as an immaterial being. We call attention especially to the following argument. Knowledge is incapable of deriving a spiritual result from mutual relations of corporeal elements; no composition can explain the emergence of consciousness, which was not present in the components; no kind of art can extract reason from the irrational.[113] This argument means only that, so far as our knowledge is concerned, psychical life is a fact that is totally distinct from material realities and can never be derived from them.[114] But Plotinus goes on in this context to the proof which has held the first place in European metaphysics. Plato and Aristotle paved the way for it. With deep insight *Plato* had emphasized: If we are in a position to compare what is given us in the various senses and to pronounce on similarity and dissimilarity, then that can happen only in something distinct from the sense organs, that is, in the soul itself.[115] And then *Aristotle* had recognized that the judgment "sweet is not white" is impossible if these sensations are distributed among different subjects and are not together in one and the same subject.[116] Plotinus undertakes to prove in general: If the soul were material, then neither sensation, nor thought, nor knowledge, nor the moral, nor the beautiful would exist for us. If something is supposed to perceive something else, he argues in this connection, it must be a unity. Because emergent images are a manifold in virtue of the plurality of sense organs—indeed, if they compose a manifold within the sphere of sensation of a *single* sense organ—then they *must be fused together into an object through a self-identical unity;* sense impressions must come together in an indivisible unity. He expresses the idea in a striking image in this way: Sensations must come together from the entire periphery of sense life like the radii of a circle in the indivisible center of the life of the soul. Otherwise, many sensations would interiorly arise next to one another. Then part A of this material and extended soul would possess its impression for itself, and so would B and C. Things would ultimately end as if an individual A acquired perceptions and alongside him an individual B. Further, if we are in a position to *compare two impressions* and to *differentiate* them from each other, then this presupposes they are *held together in a unity* with each other. In this proof and in other more subordinate ones, Plotinus thought through completely the great thesis of the incommensurability of activity of consciousness with what we posit as the basis for the process of changes in the external world. Of course he mistakenly attributed a positive metaphysical probative force to this principle; but people have ascribed the same force to that principle in the entire further development up to Leibniz, Wolff, Mendelssohn, and even Lotze. In reality, however, it has only a *negative value,* that is, with respect to every type of materialistic or so-called monistic metaphysics.[117]

Augustine deepened and strengthened this grounding of the theory of soul-substances through his *epistemological viewpoint.* He explains: "I venture to assert that with regard to immateriality of the soul I not only have faith but knowledge in the strict sense."[118] We saw[119] that his knowledge was based on the fact that all knowledge of the outside world must succumb to skepticism (which has reference to this kind of knowledge), but that self-certainty emerges in inner experience. He recognizes inner experience as knowledge in which the entire life of the soul is already given to us when the intention of knowing its essence arises. He expressed the specific difference of this inner experience from all knowledge of the external course of nature, and he discerned the inferiority of the latter for the structure of knowledge. Indeed, the content of inner experience also showed Augustine the dissimilarity of spiritual life from that of the course of nature and consequently the impossibility of deriving spiritual from material processes. We cannot conceive of intellectual life as a quality of the subject-body, because one cannot trace the achievements of intellectual life to those of a material totality. In particular it is characteristic of mind that it is totally present at every point in the body and can make sense impressions into an object of consciousness, of comparison, and of judgment.[120]

Medieval philosophers then further extended the metaphysics of substantial souls which the Neoplatonists and Augustine, who associated himself with them, founded. They linked up with Neoplatonically tinged sources and with Augustine and deduced from the nature of spiritual processes that one cannot derive them from matter nor can one conceive them in any way as material.[121] In all their more stringent proofs of immortality they start by comparing accomplishments of psychical life with characteristics of spatial and corporeal being, deduce in this way the existence of a substantial soul, and from that conclude to immortality. Even though others, especially the *Arab peripatetics,* develop this line of reasoning more subtly and variously, nevertheless, at the same time, they shift its starting point disadvantageously, as far as its probative force is concerned. They do not start with facts of sensation and comparison but with those of abstract science and general concepts given in it. One can establish this for the most important Arab proofs gathered together in the excellent presentation in *The Destruction of the Destructions* by Averroës. The principal reason is this: Abstract science is an indivisible unity and one can therefore ascribe it only to a subject which is likewise an indivisible unity.[122] In the *West* the same reasons recur: There must be an indivisible substantial soul, and what is indivisible is indestructible.[123] Reasons of another sort also supplemented them.[124] The moral order requires penalties, but these do not always occur with regularity in this world; we discover in ourselves that we naturally strive for happiness, and this must be satisfied; on the basis of the teleological connection of the world with God it follows that creation must return to its principle, and just as creation proceeded from the divine intellect, it attains its completion in intellectual beings.[125]

The demonstrative force of the argument for the existence of immaterial substances remained unshaken during the Middle Ages. For the dogmatic concepts of nature entertained by medieval metaphysicians provided a foundation to argue for a spiritual substance distinct from nature. But medieval thinkers already recognized that the further argument about individual immortality of particular souls was untenable. Just as Averroës questioned individual immortality in the Orient, so in the Christian West Amalrich of Bene and David of Dinant, probably influenced by Arab doctrine, also proceeded to deny personal immortality. In fact they were drawing the consequences of the science of reason when they saw differences of genera, of species, and of individuals as merely etched into being (which corresponds to the highest concept), and so they regarded every individual existence as merely the transitory modification of the selfsame substance. And Duns Scotus uses one of the related viewpoints described above to fend off every kind of materialistic notion, to be sure, but he no longer acknowledges that individual immortality follows from it.[126]

In accordance with its rather slight interest in developing concepts of reality scientifically, the Middle Ages developed the system of *cosmological* theses only to a very imperfect degree, and what it added to the output of antiquity was a problem which stemmed from its interest in a transcendent world. For the antinomies which criticism by the Eleatics, Sophists, and skeptics had shown to exist in the concept of the world, such as spatial finiteness and infinity or the continuity of external reality and its divisibility into discrete parts, were now forgotten or the distinctness of their concepts was blurred. On the other hand, the antinomy did make its appearance which was the pivotal point of all the struggles of the later Middle Ages concerning the rational grounding of the Christian idea of God. This is the antinomy between the theorem of the eternity of the world and that of creation, that is, the origin of the world in time from the will of God alone. Logical consistency of the world order in accordance with relations of motions to one another in the external world—whose representatives were Aristotle and the Arabic Aristotle, Averroës—found itself in contradiction with Christian belief, and this was the most important part of the so-called struggle between belief and unbelief in the Middle Ages.

Inner Contradiction of Medieval Metaphysics, Which Arises from Linking Theology with Science of the Universe

Character of Systems Which Arose in This Way

Medieval metaphysics issued from the confluence of two streams, of which one had arisen in Europe and the other in the East. Because it embraced its task more completely in this stage, the antinomy in it between inner experience and sensation asserted itself much more thoroughly than before for knowledge. This antinomy now appears as a contradiction between the system of nature, whose concept is established through external sensation, and the moral-religious world order, whose certainty arises from inner experiences of man's will and grows continuously and indestructibly from them. From the standpoint of the natural worldview founded by Aristotle and taken over by the Scholastics, which held that both the one and the other world order was an objective system, the antinomy was insoluble. At one moment it developed the thesis and antithesis in the various schools, at another it functioned in particular systems themselves, tearing them to pieces with contradictions. Then it associated itself with contradictions which science of the cosmos and theology already suffered from, and thus the general *character of medieval metaphysics with its characteristic feature of antinomies* emerged ever more clearly. That character expressed itself in the form of its presentation and dissolved every system into questions in which thesis and antithesis fought each other at every point. And the principal contradiction came to light at completely different points of the medieval system, like a hidden blood disease, in the dispute between God's will and his understanding, between the eternity of the world and creation out of nothing, between eternal truths and the economy of salvation. Indeed, it extended its influence finally into constructing the great social dualism of the medieval world.

Antinomy between the Conception of Divine Intellect and That of Divine Will

Metaphysics, or the science of reason, as perfected in Aristotle, described God as "thought of thought" [*Denken des Denkens*]. For the Middle Ages Aristotle embodied the thesis that the world given in external experience constitutes a system which is adapted to thought, a system known as rationality, coherence, and purposefulness, and one that can be traced to a highest intelligence.

As we saw, the *peripatetics of Islam* were connected with the older peripatetic school and were influenced by increasing knowledge of nature. From the way a metaphysical system emerges from study of the external world they drew a conclusion which carried Aristotle's science of reason a step further toward Spinoza and modern intellectualistic pantheism.[127] If one remains in the study of external reality, then "nothing comes from nothing" remains true.[128] On the basis of this assumption Averroës holds fast to Aristotelian eternity of the world. The rational structure of this eternal world is linked to God's understanding and at the same time to the human intellect. This relationship, which is basic to the science of reason, acquires a different formulation among Arab peripatetics, especially Averroës, because he (following the lead of Avempace) does not separate individual human intelligences from one another, but regards them as contained in universal understanding. Thus the first formulation arose of something which appears as infinite intellect of God in Spinoza and as world reason in German speculation.

This *unity of the intellect active in pure knowledge* appears from one point of view as the justified consequence of Aristotelian science of reason.

If one abstracts from experiences of the will, then one finds in the intellect, taken thus in isolation, a structure which transcends the individual, one in which the premises of Aristotle's thought reach back into Plato's thought and beyond into the thought of Parmenides and others, and the universal validity of propositions strives to cancel the individual. This impersonal element in thought contains a greater weight for the metaphysical worldview in proportion as the system of general concepts and truths in the mind achieves autonomy. If the essence of the human mind is found in thought, then there is no principle available which would secure the individual mind its own autonomous center; for such a principle lies only in feeling for life and in the will.

Let us apply these general propositions. The intellectualism of the Arab peripatetics, as it reached its high point in Averroës, discovers the bond which holds the world system together in processes of knowledge, and it viewed even union of the soul with God as taking place in knowledge. Thus, as a logical result of his acceptance of Aristotle's basic idea of science of reason, *Averroës lacks a principle of individuation for the intellectual world,*[129] for matter provides such a principle only for individual physical objects. In fact Averroës was extremely conscious of *characteristics of thought which connect* its acts in different individuals inwardly into a rational system. He concludes from this that because thought has the unchanging as its object, it must itself be eternal.[130] In the framework of science, which transcends all generation and corruption of individuals, the appearance of this or that thinker is merely fortuitous, but understanding itself is eternal.[131] The single understanding corresponds to sameness of the truth of reason in many individuals.[132] Only thus can one explain that the intellect is capable of knowing the universal, without reference to the finite position it occupies in the corporeal world because of matter.[133] Therefore human science as an internally coherent whole is a divinely grounded, necessary, and eternal component of the world order. It is independent of the life of the individual person. It is necessary that a philosopher belong to the human species.[134] In this panlogistic state of his system we encounter once again in Averroës the pantheistic consequence of a science of reason which sees the rationality of the world in the real organization of genera and species. Averroës' theory of the eternal and universal understanding arose more precisely from the Aristotelian view of principles of individuation. The particular being is composed of matter and form; we are not to ascribe matter to minds or souls, but their form or substance is identical; therefore they must be identical themselves.[135] And shifting the starting point of proofs for immortality, which we emphasized in his presentation of them, is of a piece with that. The immortality of the human mind which Averroës recognizes as established in science of reason consists in union with the "active intellect" [*"wirkenden Geiste"*] which radiates from God.

What still distinguishes this theory from Spinoza's infinite divine intellect or from the panlogism of the German philosophy of identity? In natural-scientific thought the astronomical construction of the world separated God spatially from the world and still distinguished the sphere of perfect and unchanging motions from that of change, generation, and corruption. Hence the *emanationist form of panlogism,* which preceded the pantheistic form, emerged among the Arab peripatetics. A schema comes into being which on the one hand posits a system of movement that is graduated downward in the world, and on the other hand posits knowledge. Knowledge radiates from divine science and, like light which shines into a clouded atmosphere, is dissipated and weakened as it spreads from one sphere of motion in the world to another. Thus in Averroës' emanationist conception, intelligences split from one another in a downward direction toward the separate intellect which unites with the soul in human thought. This is the completely ephemeral part of Averroës' famous theory about the separate unitary intellect, which provoked so much written commentary in the Christian West.[136]

Between this *science of the rational structure of the universe* and the doctrine of an actual *will* in God, there exists an *insoluble contradiction.* Averroës' inexorable acuity recognized it and excluded free will in God by the following reasoning.[137] Either the world is possible in the sense that owing to God's choice other characteristics of things could also have been created, or a highest purpose has been actualized in the world through appropriate means and in a system which cannot be conceived otherwise than it is. Only in the latter case does a rational system exist for us which takes us to a first thought [*ein erstes Denken*]. "If one does not see that among created things connecting links exist between their origins and their terminal points, such that the existence of the terminal points is based on that of the connecting links, then there is no order or sequence, and if these do not exist then there is no proof that these beings have a willing and knowing principle of activity [*Agens*]. For the ordering and the sequential arranging and the basing of causes on effects[138] proves that they derive from intelligence and wisdom." According to him, therefore, to recognize rational structure back to its first principle is to know God, and to regard things as contingent is to deny God. Impossibility of freedom of choice in God also results from the fact that it would presuppose a shortcoming, a passive condition, and a change in him. Therefore, will in God signifies that the idea of the most perfect purpose activates a necessary system of causal activity in God. And Averroës calls this the goodness of God!

If Thomas Aquinas achieves only a contrived equilibrium between theses and antitheses in this whole arena of struggle for Scholasticism,[139] *Duns Scotus*[140] on the contrary understood this antinomy quite clearly. He did not try, as Averroës did, to get rid of it by setting the will aside; on the contrary, his system marks the point at which medieval thought recognizes both the rational structure of the world and the sway of freedom unforced by understanding with the same energetic keenness of mind. That is why his system is torn down the middle by this contradiction. The element in the worldview which acknowledges a rational and necessary system and traces it to an intelligent cause is totally separated from another element which establishes a nonderivative actuality, which could just as well be other than it is, and a free will, which can either choose something or not, and it traces both of these to a principle of the will. A precondition for this was that Scotus undertook the first thorough analysis of freedom of the will; and this is something which permeates his entire writing. He adopts an independent position about Aristotle, who did not sufficiently handle the problem of distinguishing between will and thought,[141] and takes a step toward clearly comprehending *self-determining spontaneity*.[142] This is an immediately given actuality.[143] *It cannot be denied*. For the contingency of the course of the world is obvious; anyone who disputes it should be tortured to the point at which he acknowledges that it is also possible for him not to be tortured. But this contingency points to a free cause. However, one *cannot explain* the fact of free will, for it is precisely its hallmark that we cannot break it down in a conceptual system. Therefore God's thought and will are two *ultimate grounds of explanation*, and we cannot reduce either of them to the other.[144] It is true that will depends on intellect, but the will can choose or not choose what the intellect understands in complete independence of that intellect. Thus in Duns Scotus's system dualism expresses the antinomy that affects his system. He has understood this antinomy so well that one needs only to rethink his concepts into psychological and epistemological terms. For, according to him, understanding is a natural power which works by law of necessity, whereas in the will, but only there, we transcend the necessary order of nature; in fact the will is free precisely inasmuch as in it the search for a reason ends.[145] Finally, Duns Scotus pursued the assumption of a divine freedom independent of understanding to the position that he viewed even moral laws as grounded exclusively in the free will act of God.

Thus medieval thought recognized the impossibility of formulating the inner relationship between will and intellect in this highest divine being (a reflection, on a prodigious scale, of the contrast between our scientific thought about the cosmos and the experiences of our will). For it could deny neither will nor intelligence in God, nor could it subordinate one of them to the other, and least of all could it juxtapose them coordinately with each other as ultimate objective and mutually heterogeneous facts as Duns Scotus did.

And just as Averroës one-sidedly developed the one aspect of this antinomial world order, so we find that *Occam* in particular carried the other aspect to its ultimate consequences during the metaphysical development of the Christian West.[146] In their further progress the former antinomy had to end in panlogism, and the latter had to *destroy metaphysics and make room for inner experience and for the will* manifested in it. The former leads to Spinoza and Hegel, and the latter to the mystics and the Reformers. But because the principle of the will and of freedom is asserted inside metaphysics itself, the contradiction between form and content inherent here destroys metaphysics, whose essence is deductive logical coherence. That contradiction appears in Occam and his students as frivolity and as flight into a supernatural haven of ignorance; at the same time Occam expressed a profound seriousness in maintaining the great principle of free personality and its willpower in the face of all authority and all empty abstraction.

Because *Occam* thus developed the antithesis of the antinomy just as one-sidedly as Averroës had developed its thesis, *nominalism now acquired a living content*. With Roscelin nominalism had adopted a barrenly negative approach in denying concepts which express a universal or a totality, and the whole of theological dogmatics, which was the doctrine of the economy of salvation, rested precisely on such concepts. Now the principle of experience, which had previously been only a fruitless rehearsal of antiquity and an inane play of the understanding, functioned positively and constructively. In Roger Bacon it founded the study of the external world and in Occam the independent consideration of inner experience. Occam is the mightiest medieval thinker since Augustine. Just as he proclaimed the independence of will, so he also depicted it in his life through struggle. He was inspired by the modern principle of the independent willpower of the person. Particular things make up the object of knowing; universal concepts are signs; the link between them and divine intellect, which had held together the whole science of reason, was broken; and practical theology itself was destroyed by the contradiction between Scholastic examination of understanding as its form and experience of the will as its content.

When Luther, an enthusiastic reader of Occam, expressed the independence of experiences of the will and separated personal faith from all metaphysics, even formally, a freer form of consciousness succeeded the metaphysics of the Middle Ages. But truth works so slowly in history that old Protestant dogmatics allowed the concepts of medieval theological metaphysics to appear once again, as though in a shadow play. Rationality of the external world is the basic assumption of science, and the system of phenomena in accordance with the principle of sufficient reason is its ideal; but where experiences of the will and the soul begin, this kind of knowledge has no more place.

Antinomy between Eternity of the World and Its Creation in Time

The antinomy which tore the inner core of medieval metaphysics to pieces continues in the idea of the relation of God to the world. To science of the cosmos the world is eternal; to experience of the will it is a creation in time and out of nothing. The Arab peripatetics were the representatives of the first position, and the conviction of the eternity of the world and the independence of matter, like the denial of immortality, made the figure of Averroës the type of metaphysical infidelity to the Western Middle Ages. From Albert on, Western metaphysics fought this conviction with telling reasons. For its part it sought in vain to make creation of the world out of nothing and in time comprehensible and to find a place for it in a science of the cosmos.

The theory of the eternity of the world was necessary in Aristotle's science.[147] In the cosmic view of the system of motions there is no way possible toward the idea of a motionless condition or in fact toward that of an absence of matter; one must conceive of this system as eternal. The principle that nothing comes from nothing demands the eternity of the world and excludes any doctrine of creation.[148]

The Christian *doctrine of creation* conceptually expressed the inner experience of transcendence of the will as against the natural order, just as it had its highest experience in capacity for self-sacrifice. It denied the process of nature as an explanation of the world, whether one views that process as emanationist or naturalistic;[149] it also denied the limitation of God's power through matter. But it could express its positive content only through formulas which are inconceivable to the mind: "out of nothing," "not of the essence of God," and "in time."[150]

An antimony arises out of the *contradiction between these two concepts,* inasmuch as the uncritical standpoint forces religious consciousness to recognize the relation of God to the world in some way. For under the conditions of thought and knowledge we must think of the world as either eternal or begun in time; either it must be formed out of matter or it must be created out of nothing. And in fact one can posit either of these two terms by canceling the other.

The struggle of the Middle Ages with this antimony is manifested in the fact that thesis and antithesis are annihilated on decisive grounds, but attempts at a satisfying positive statement are in vain. This dispute among Arab theologians and philosophers persists from the beginning of the eighth century, but the epoch of Averroës, Albert the Great, and Thomas Aquinas is particularly filled with it. On the one hand *Christian philosophy* refutes the existence of matter and the eternity of the world. The theory of formation of matter had been growing slowly among Arab peripatetics since Avicenna; in Averroës it attained its most stringent form, for he held that forms exist like seeds in matter and are extracted [*extrahuntur*] by the deity, and as these theories penetrated the West Albert took up the struggle against them. Albert proved the impossibility of the eternity of the world on the grounds that an infinite amount of time cannot have preceded the present moment, for otherwise this moment in time could not have come about.[151] And the impossibility of having matter alongside God is shown by the fact that matter would limit God and would thus destroy the idea of God. On the other hand the *Arabs* showed that in the context of the natural view of the world creation is inconceivable. For as Averroës correctly argues, generation in time out of nothing would annul the basic principle of science: nothing comes out of nothing. It is impossible to conceive of a change for which no reason exists outside of it and which does not proceed from within from some other change.[152] If Albert and Thomas defend themselves against this by distinguishing the natural system of motion from a transcendent cause,[153] then we have arrived at a transition from the supersensible to natural processes, which escapes understanding. Hence, after Thomas creation was left to faith and was excluded from metaphysics.

Another antimony is connected with this one, but already leads into the metaphysical treatment of the human sciences. In the mind of God reality exists in eternal truths and in the form of the *universal;* in his will it exists as history, and, in the context of the latter it is precisely the individual person toward whom God's will is related.

These Antinomies Cannot Be Solved by Any Metaphysics

Thus arises the intrinsically contradictory character of medieval metaphysics. The objective and conceptually necessary structure of the world finds itself confronted by free will in God, whose expressions are the historical world, creation out of nothing, and the moral-religious order of society. We encounter here the first, still imperfect, form of a contradiction which was destined to destroy metaphysics from within and to posit an independent human science over against natural science. Indeed, Kant's critique of metaphysics took its direction from this task of "thinking together" the necessary system of causes and the moral world.

Or how could the objective immutability of an ideational system which precedes all particular facts and expresses their meaning outside time permanently abide in a will which is living history, a will whose providence is directed to the individual and whose acts are unique realities? With formal dexterity Albert the Great and Thomas arranged a treaty between these two concepts. Duns Scotus tore it up. He recognized free will in God as well as intellect, and that free will could have produced an altogether different world,[154] and with that the cognitively necessary metaphysical system is abrogated to the extent that this free will extends, for it excludes a rational system. And if our next task is to fit God's understanding and will, these two feuding abstractions, into a psychological framework, then we find that the inappropriate analogy of human consciousness is secretly directing this idea: fantastic mirror images of our own spiritual life, stretched out on a vast scale, rise to greet us. As certainly as the personality of God is a given for us as a reality in our lives, because we are also a given to ourselves, it is just as certain that we can project ourselves into the deity only by a playful transference by which the contradiction between this being we dream up and the creator of heaven and earth is evident. What foolish dreams! Occam leaves no hiding place in God for the rational system.

How was it ever supposed to be possible, once we recognized universal concepts as creations of abstractions, that we could conceive of their existence in God's understanding, apart from his will, as the explanatory ground for particular objects? Such an assumption simply repeats the error of a system of laws and ideas which anticipates reality and imposes its commands on it. Laws are only abstract expressions for regularity among changes; universal concepts are expressions for what abides permanently in the coming and going of objects. But if one shifts the origin of this system of ideas and laws to the action of God, another piece of nonsense ensues, namely, that the will creates truths. In fact there is no metaphysical solution possible here, only an epistemological one. The source of what I call an object or reality is different from the source of what I develop as concepts and laws, hence as truth in thought, for explaining this reality. Inasmuch as I am starting from this difference in psychological origin, I cannot solve the difficulties, to be sure, but I can explain their insolubility and prove that the formulation of the question in which they arose is incorrect.

How could one ever settle the dispute over whether God created the world as it is because it is good or whether it is good because he created it as it is? Every discussion of these questions posits either a God who wills, but in whom the good does not yet exist, or a God in whom the intelligible world of the good exists, but who does not yet will.

Neither the first nor the second is a real God, and so this metaphysics is nothing but a game of abstractions.

7. Medieval Metaphysics of History and Society

In its classical period the metaphysics of the Middle Ages proved that human souls are immaterial, immortal substances. Then as people, starting with Duns Scotus, began to dispute the demonstrability of immortality, discussion of the topic remained an issue among the schools, but failed to influence people's convictions. Denial of individual immortality surfaced only in the narrow circle of the radical enlightenment, which was predominantly under Arab influence. Thus immaterial substances of various kinds were a *metaphysical realm* for medieval man: angels, evil spirits, and men. Under God as their head they constitute a hierarchy of spirits whose order of rank was neatly described and established in a treatise *On the Heavenly Hierarchy,* which appeared before the middle of the sixth century under the name of Dionysius the Areopagite. This hierarchy extends from the throne of God down to the last cottage and constitutes the enormous reality, so palpable to the medieval mind, which was the foundation for all its metaphysical speculations on history and society.

Metaphysical Realm of Immaterial Substances

There was no more hesitation in *extending metaphysical reasoning to this spiritual and social world*. Using reasons first advanced by the Neoplatonists and then more comprehensively from the teleological structure of the world in God, Thomas Aquinas proved that a realm of finite spirits exists and that in it creation returns to its principle; just as it proceeded from divine intellect, so must it attain its completion in spiritual beings.[155] Indeed, using a further metaphysical argument he deduces the organization of the spiritual world, according to which God is separate from the realm of the angels and the latter from that of human souls.[156] Thus medieval philosophy created a complete metaphysics of spiritual substances which maintained its credibility in the minds of European peoples for a long time, even after attacks on it constantly increased in extent and weight from Duns Scotus on.

We were approaching the noble conception of the Middle Ages, which now took its place alongside the metaphysics of nature as the creation of the Greek mind. It consists in the philosophy of history and society grounded in the doctrine of spiritual substances. As dependent as medieval thought was in so many ways on the thought of the ancients, here it was creative, and the most remarkable features of the political activity of medieval man were codetermined by this system of ideas, whether one wishes to consider the theocratic character of medieval society, or the force of the imperial idea in it, or that of the unity of Christianity as it appears most powerfully in the crusades. So we see once again how important a *function metaphysics* had to exercise in European society. At the same time it becomes clear how, as metaphysics pressed forward in its advance, one irresolvable antinomy after another appeared, for after all it did not leave any really resolved behind it. It was like the legendary heroes who, the more they struggled, the more firmly they became entwined in their bonds.

Metaphysics grasps spiritual substances which make up the kingdom of God in their core, as wills, and so it views human and historical life as consisting in *cooperation of the will's activity in these created substances with divine providence,* which uses its power of will to lead them all to their goal. This schema of life is completely different from the viewpoint of the ancients. They had formed their conception of the deity from the cosmos, and even their teleological systems recognized only the rationality of the world order. But now God enters history and moves men's hearts toward fulfilling his purpose. Hence the realization of a plan for the world now replaces the concept of rationality of the world, and that plan regards the world's rationality as but a means or an instrument. It firmly sets down a goal for development, and so the idea of a purpose acquires new meaning.

Because this plan of God is supposed to be rationally compatible with man's freedom, the problem constituted by the *antinomy of freedom* and an objective *world system* determining man enters the core of the Christian metaphysics of history. In the context of the real historical world that problem corresponds to one we saw surface during the Middle Ages in the idea of God due to the antinomy between a rationally necessary system and free will.[157] It has assumed many forms ever since the opposition between the Greek and Latin fathers and the Pelagian controversy. But just as it had been impossible to conceive how the existence of ideas was related to the existence of particular things without contradiction in the past, so now it was just as impossible to interpret meaningfully the intrinsic relationship of creative, preservative, and directive divine will with respect to the freedom, guilt, and unhappiness of human wills by any sort of understandable magical formula. Just as it was then impossible to construct an objective and coherent system from the concept of substance, so now it was impossible to wrest from the concept of causality a real inner relation between components of the system of causes and effects which would leave enough room for the will. The formula to which the metaphysical thought of the Middle Ages arrived at this point was the following. All activity of a finite subject, be it a natural object or a will, receives power for its activity from the first cause at every instant. But the activity of finite substances is not simply related retroactively to that of the first primordial cause or substance like an intermediate link in a chain of causes. Activity which a finite created being, hence a will too, produces is totally determined by its nature and likewise totally determined by the nature of the first cause. In the teleological order finite real being is like an instrument in the hand of God, and God uses that instrument according to the nature of this *real* being, even though also in *his* system of purposes as well. Thus God uses man's will according to its nature, which includes freedom, and in the direction of its final goal, which includes likeness with himself, hence freedom once again.[158] But the formulas Thomas devised tried in vain to maneuver between deism, which claims for God something like the perfection of performance appropriate to a machine builder so that God's world does not constantly need assistance, and pantheism, which says that if one continually preserves a particular being in its entirety, then one must also totally cause all effects which flow from that being too. Contradictions well up everywhere as soon as one seeks to harmonize the irreconcilable by artificial contrivances instead of showing epistemologically the origin of these different components of our conception of life and thus exposing the purely psychological significance of this antinomy. We cannot think of a causal system where we think of freedom. Neither can we demarcate their mutual boundaries externally. And whatever kind of external demarcation we might wish to attempt, it will not be able to make the creation of finite beings by God comprehensible in such a way that God could be acquitted of the charge of authorship of evil; nor can it resolve the contradiction between divine foreknowledge and human freedom.

The changed view of the realm of spirits is reflected in the poetry of the Middle Ages produced by the Christianized Romanic-Germanic peoples and in the epics of chivalry as well as in Dante's *Divine Comedy*. No longer is it merely mutually counterpoised self-contained types alone which are active in this poetry, but rather the history of the life of the soul, especially of the will (as Augustine says, people are always nothing other than wills); hence a conception of this history of the will in its relations with God's providential will. In this conception, however, an unresolved split exists between inner free development and the dark background of forces of all kinds which influence the will.

Establishing a Metaphysical System in That Realm

The *realm of individual spirits creates a metaphysical nexus of purposes which is expressed in revelation*. The entirety of the European Middle Ages agrees on this point, and differences occur only about the question of how much of this content of the whole of history we can know conceptually.

Metaphysics of the course of history and of the organization of society during the Middle Ages had its ultimate grounds in consciousness that the *ideal content* of this course and this organization is *located in God, is proclaimed in His revelation,* and is accomplished according to his plan in the history of mankind and will continue to be so accomplished. With this an advance of great significance was achieved in comparison with antiquity. The purposeful life of man, as it unfolds in systems of culture and functions through external organization of society, was recognized as a unitary system and traced to an explanatory principle. Thus knowledge of the inner structure of processes of human society attained an interest completely independent of any purpose of technical application in practical life.[159] Now one sought for this knowledge at times in the monk's cell through intensified meditation on the idea of the providence of God; and the Curia's publicists and those of the imperial court used it at times in the service of factions.

Aristotle's political science method was already unsatisfactory inasmuch as in its analysis it could not use causal concepts based on well-developed previously existing sciences and thus could not explain particular purpose-complexes such as economic life, law, and religion through analytical knowledge but only through imperfect ideas about a teleology existing in nature.[160] But the Middle Ages were still much less inclined to analyze methodically the structures which presented themselves in particular cultural systems and ultimately underlay external organization of society and to use the partial contents of social reality thus acquired for explanatory purposes. In addition, the social reality available to the Middle Ages still contained the *contents of historical life at a lower level of specialization*. At that time the observer's eye saw a connection with the law of God or opposition to that law in every spiritual content. Medieval thought did not regard religion, scientific truth, morality, and law as relatively independent purpose-complexes; on the contrary, it saw an *ideal content* in them, and only an actualization of that content under the conditions of nature or man's action would effect any differentiation of these forms of life. Thus because God contains the ideal of reason in himself, people saw in him the source of natural law, which they regarded as a binding norm, indeed the highest one, and consequently as actual law.[161] Therefore they analyzed and described the ideational content of historical life not as it actually exists there—as law, morality, art, and so on—but they sought it instead in God in uniform and sublime indeterminateness. They relegated further interpretation to the system of conditions under which this ideational content is actualized in the arena of the world. Thus medieval metaphysics of society posed the problem of the human sciences in a world-embracing spirit, but in place of its methodical resolution it sketched only a grandiose theological schema for organizing historical life.

Hence the Middle Ages possess no other *study of general characteristics of law, morality, and so on, than this metaphysical one.* And just as the foundation of metaphysics is inwardly rent asunder by the *contradiction* between the will of God and the necessary system of the cosmos in his understanding and between the economy of salvation and necessary truths, so that contradiction is also continued in the metaphysics of society. The antinomy which thus ensues joins that between human freedom and divine providence. The command and execution of God's will as well as the institutions and reality they posit are in conflict, sometimes tacitly and sometimes clamorously, with the edifice based on rational necessity. What follows will show that God's will and plan were the more powerful part of this theological metaphysics; indeed, they also had the last word.

From this consciousness which revelation communicated about the ideal content of the world's course and history radiated the *light* which illuminated the *inner structure of world history* for this medieval metaphysics of society.

The unity of world history lies in the plan of God. Augustine writes: "God willed that not only heaven and earth, not only angels and men, but even the inner core of the little, so easily despised animal, the wing of a bird, the tiny blade of grass, and the leaf of a tree should not be deprived of an appropriateness and, so to speak, a peaceful harmony among their parts; it is incredible that he should wish to exclude the realms of men and their relationships of dominance and dependence from the legislation of his providence."[162] Revelation has established this structure of God's providential plan in its beginning, middle, and end. The progenitor of the human race, in whom all have sinned; Christ, in whom all have been redeemed; and the Second Coming, in which everything will be judged, are such fixed points between which interpretation of the facts of history now weaves its threads. This interpretation is exclusively *teleological.* It does not consider elements of the course of history as members of a causal series but as elements of a plan. The question which is consequently put to the particular historical fact is not about its causal relation to other facts or to more general relations but about its teleological connection with this plan. Hence medieval historians use pragmatic explanations of behavior of individual persons, to be sure, but *historical phenomena on the mass scale never enter into a causal system for them.* This metaphysics of world history seeks meaning in it to explain its overall plan, just as we look for such a plan in a poetic epic.

And as a matter of fact Christian reflection first found itself compelled to interpret history teleologically because of objections from its opponents. Hence pressure of circumstances caused metaphysics of history to arise as early as the epoch of the church Fathers and the struggle between Christianity, ancient polytheism, and Judaism; the Middle Ages merely developed it further. Why, asked the foes of Christianity, did the law God gave to Moses have to be improved, for after all one improves only what has been badly done?[163] Why should a Roman abandon religious convictions on which society rests and the general education which binds together those reared in humanity?[164] Why, both Celsus and Porphyry ask in their polemics against Christianity, did it not occur to God to redeem men until after such a long course of history?[165] And from the time that the barbarians began to exert severe pressure on the Roman Empire—in fact the Christian Goths had conquered and devastated Rome—the question arose which penetrated still more deeply into interpretation of world history: Is not Christianity the cause of all the most recent disasters of the empire? Or how can one interpret this enormous political crisis so as to contradict reproaches of this sort?[166] The first of these questions called for interpreting the inner history of religious and philosophical ideas already planted in Christian historical consciousness.[167] The last question compelled Christians to bring the Roman Empire in the purview of this metaphysical consideration of history. To answer it, the first models of a comprehensive philosophy of history—Augustine's *The City of God* and *The Histories* of his student Orosius—made their appearance.

The Christian mind, essentially historical in makeup, brooded over these puzzles, looking back on now completed forms of spiritual life which were intrinsically over and done with and provoked one to world-historical reflections, because the night of barbaric rule over the Roman Empire appeared to be coming on. Thus the solution of these riddles emerged in the idea of an *inner development of the human race as a unity in a sequence* in which every earlier step was the necessary condition for succeeding ones. The steps are not determined like effects in a causal system, but are instead identified as components in the plan of God. And the idea of progress through them remains within the boundaries of a schema in which progress is achieved by adapting divine education to the human race's circumstances. *Tertullian* regarded the human race with respect to its religious education as a single man who, while learning and progressing in the various periods of his life, passes through necessary stages of his development. According to him, religious progress of the human race demonstrates organic growth. He uses the image of the organism, which had been used as a guide for understanding the relationship of parts to the whole in society, to shed light on how the earlier carries and determines the later in this case.[168] Clement also adapted Greek philosophy to this graduated course of education in his doctrine of the logos;[169] but so grandiose a doctrine had no effect on the subsequent course of metaphysics of history. And *Augustine* found changes which take place in revealed religion conditioned by a development of mankind comparable to the succession of stages in one's life.[170] So the same conception is dominant among these and other church fathers. Humanity is a unity like an individual who has to go through development in life but for whom, as for a pupil, the law of this development derives mainly from the system set up by the educator. Alongside this deeper ordering of the history of man goes the more external arrangement which divides it into historical ages corresponding to the days of creation.

Religious Conceptual Sphere

This idea of the inner structure of the history of humanity, which—volatile and elusive as it was among the hard facts of history—seemed that it must evaporate into thin air acquired a solid frame and body through the *connection into which it entered with religious and secular ideas. Separation of the religious sphere of society from the secular* was grounded in the autonomy of religous experience and the communal religious life based on it; that life stood up to the Roman world power itself and asserted itself with a feeling of invincibility. Christ first expressed this separation in the decision: Render to Caesar the things that are Caesar's and to God the things that are God's. This distinction divided God's law and state, which had been the last word of ancient Stoic philosophy, into a secular order of society and a religious structure. Accordingly, later development of the idea of the relationship of history and society now leaned on *two historical conceptual frameworks,* one of which dealt with the *church* and the other with the *Roman world empire* with its antecedents and denouement. Because this theory of society issued from the will and plan of God, it could not deduce the structure of history purely from rational content but had to interpret the plan of God from the great historical relations of his will. Not until later was the speculative construction added to this religious interpretation, as the gaps in it indicate.

But this interpretation worked with deficient material. We can understand the unscientific and superstition-dominated character of the medieval mind only by addressing historical facts and the historical tradition. For an abbreviated and falsified tradition about the ancient world was authoritative for the medieval mind, regardless of what the causes were that led it to such an uncritical posture. And because its condition with regard to historical sciences coincided with the state of its natural-scientific thought, deep shadows and fantastic beings spread out from here over the earth.

Among the elements one uses to explain the external organization of society in the Middle Ages, the most important was the idea of the *church.* It determined the theocratic character of the medieval conception of society. Spiritual beings of every order of rank are united in the church in a mystical body which extends from the Trinity and the angels standing closest to it to the beggar at the gates of the church door and the serf who humbly attends the sacrifice of the Mass on his knees from the remotest corner of the church.

The creative germ of this viewpoint lies in the epistles of the apostle *Paul.* Paul designates individual Christians as members of the body of Christ; under Christ as the head, individual members of the community are united into an organism through the unity of the Spirit. Within this organism individual members of the community have different functions, each one necessary for the life of the whole. Therefore, when any member suffers, all the other members also suffer. In this Pauline view of the life of the Christian community the use of the concept of an organism is a trope, and Paul never thought of degrading the structure of religious-ethical life of the community to the natural determinism of organic life. But this trope expresses here the state of a unity completely different in nature from unity in a political totality. For the *pneuma* is a real unity in the community, a real bond like the psyche in a human body. And so the trope of the organism acquires a more exact meaning in this application.

Because the legal and political organization of the Catholic church grew out of the communities to which Paul's profound vision addressed itself, a concept emerged in which one thought of God's state [*Staat*] as held together by a real bond, which had a kind of existence, as it were, alongside and between individuals. We can identify the moments which have shaped this concept. The idea of the church as a body animated by the single Spirit of God acquires support first of all in the conception of the Eucharist, which sees it as the *sacrament of incorporation* into the church. This conception, which we find completed in Augustine, is mediated by the fact that the church is understood as the body of Christ; hence in the Eucharist sharing in this body of Christ and in the church, which alone gives salvation, and incorporation of the individual in the church take place.[171] The idea acquires further support from the real bond which holds the church together through the idea of an actual transmission by which supernatural powers are passed down from above to the clergy in rites of consecration, indeed stream downward as though in steps; thus with ordination comes the spiritual capacity, distinguishing him from the laity, by which the cleric performs his functions. In this way the idea of the church as the mystical body of Christ acquires a graphic presence. But because at the same time this church becomes a *civitas Dei,* a quasi-political entity which enjoys extensive jurisdiction, the concept of the unity of the church organism passes over to this political body as well. A result of this is that the Spirit which works from above appears as the bearer of jurisdictions which are exercised through his body in the church. The office handed down to the cleric through ordinations includes in this aspect the right and the obligation to exercise church power in a definite material sphere and in a specific spatial region based on a constantly imparted commission. On the one hand, one can describe the jurisdiction of the church in society, as jurisdiction, in legal terms and one can accordingly arrange it in a legal system, canon law; on the other hand, as deriving from God, it enjoys the highest validity in human society. Thus arose the view of the totality of the church as consisting of head and members, a church in which, as the body of that totality, a unity dwells which is given it from the transcendent world and accomplishes a divine plan of salvation; as the soul of this body it realizes the highest purpose with the highest jurisdiction. Indeed, compared with this purpose all interests for which political orders exist are mere means and all political arrangements are subject to it.

This is the basic idea of the theocratic social order of the Middle Ages. The *theologians,* above all Augustine, presented this basic idea theoretically. Because they adopted a combination (first made by the Stoics) of natural law and teleological metaphysics,[172] natural law further coincided for them with divine law, whose bearer is the church. Hence they posited church law as something which issued from God's eternal plan of salvation, which was therefore valid and intrinsically immutable, in contrast with human statutes.[173] They regarded any ordinances and laws of the state which conflicted with the laws of the church as not obligatory.[174] In the context of the entire Christian theology just described they subordinated the state as means or as an instrument of service to the mystical body of Christ or to the church.[175] But though theologians developed this theory, the monarchical state authority of the Roman Empire held on to traditional foundations of Roman law. Only gradually did Christian-ecclesiastical ideas penetrate legal life, and it was the *canonists* who first introduced them with creative energy into the scientific framework of positive jurisprudence. We will call to mind only the basic idea. The corporation of the church rests on direct divine ordinance; it is ruled by the king of heaven; from that transcendent will the Spirit of God courses through it; in fact the manner in which that Spirit works in the church is set down by divine ordinance and is therefore specified in legal forms, to which communication of salvation and jurisdiction of the church based on it are bound; the form of this constitution legally expresses the fact that in it God's will is directed from the transcendent world into the earthly world and in the latter from the vicar of Christ downward in graduated steps. One perceives here that *an emanationist conceptual framework corresponds intrinsically to the hierarchical system;* indeed, the Areopagite's description of the heavenly and earthly hierarchy and the influence this description had in the Middle Ages confirms this kind of system. The idea of God is resolved into a living flux and process; a voluntary structure stretches out from God into the system of nature.

This theocratic ordering of medieval society puts the principle of *authority which stems from God* in place of former political principles of the West. The view operative in that ordering transformed the entire conception of society in the Middle Ages. In jurisprudence there now emerged a concept of a corporation by which natural individuals it binds together merely represent the actual legal person which, as incorporeal and invisible, can act only through its members. The important constitutional concepts of representation and of personal office expanded. In political science the theological grounding of concepts of the state came about and, connected with that, a first metaphysics of society which was grounded in general metaphysics and comprised the entire reality of historical and social phenomena known at that time.

Mundane Conceptual Sphere

But precisely this gave this theocratic theory of society its power and maintained it, and its fundamental idea combined with the most varied elements: from antiquity with concepts of Greek philosophy and Roman law as well as the fact of the Roman Empire; from the life of the Germanic peoples with legal and political ideas and institutions. A *secular conceptual framework* was established here which was in part subject to the theocratic system and thus fused together with it, and in part worked against it.

While the *Roman Empire* was still standing, even though already shaken by attacking Germanic barbarians, *Augustine* wrote his work *The City of God,* in which he opposed the secular state to that of God. According to this work, the Roman world empire represented the earthly city in its last and most powerful stage. The Romans received world rule from God because they subordinated all baser passions to the highest earthly passions, above all the desire for fame after death, "through which they wished to survive even after death, so to speak." Their self-sacrifice for the earthly state was a model for Christians of the self-sacrifice they owed the heavenly state.[176] After Polybius's political-philosophical discussions, the feeble manuals of Florus and Eutropius had corroborated the notion of the Roman world empire in the historical literature of the imperial period itself. In his construction Augustine now defined the significance which the Roman world empire claimed in the plan of providence and at the same time its limit, which from the standpoint of Christianity he believed he saw. When the church then put the imperial crown on the head of the great Germanic king, the idea of Roman world monarchy entered into closer relationship with a unified Christianity comprised by the church. A few years later (A.D. 829) two councils, at Paris and Worms, developed the idea, on the basis of the *one* body of Christianity, that this body is ruled on the one side by the priesthood and on the other by the monarchy.[177] Thus a fact and a conceptual system came together to construct a world monarchy. And people traced that idea back to the East by way of the influence of the passage in the book of Daniel about the four kingdoms: fable-ridden images of the four world monarchies became the schema of political history.

These historical and political realities, mixed together with fables about such, won their place in the theocratic system and an importance tied in with its deepest principles. The Stoics had already related divine monarchy with the Roman universal state; now, on the basis of the unified plan of God and the unity of the human race as its object, one deduced the *monarchy* in Dante's sense, that is, the world state, corresponding to the single spiritual state of the church. Dante described this connection most incisively in a multiplicity of arguments whose gist was the same. The human race, a part of the universe directed by God, has a single purpose, which consists in developing all the intellectual and practical powers in human nature. A single force is what directs a manifold to a *single* goal with the greatest assurance, just as reason guides all the forces of human nature, the head of the family his home, the particular prince his state, and finally God the world, which includes the human race. This is the only way to realize peace among men and to establish similarity with the most perfect, that is, God's rule over the world. It is the only way to fulfill the external condition for establishing justice, for a system of feuding states would possess no ultimate instance for decisions according to law. Finally, it is the only way to create an inner precondition which justice requires, for the emperor alone, whose jurisdiction is limited only by the ocean, can have no further wish, hence no desire inhibits justice in him. With the fullest outlay of the syllogistic resources of those days the great poet concludes that only the empire as a world state could produce a satisfactory condition of the human race.[178] Like all deductions of medieval metaphysics of society, this one too could be easily countered by opposed interests and replaced by other deductions. Defenders of the right of particular monarchies could interpret the will of God in the sense of the national idea on the basis of variety of conditions of life, of customs, and of the law of individual peoples.[179]

The more detailed ordering of the state into the theocratic system described varied, depending on various evaluations of the empire and of politics in general. We can distinguish here *three different ways of determining the value of the secular state.*

Augustine regarded only "the state whose king is Christ," that is, the church, as a divine foundation and as an expression of the moral world order grounded in God; but he attributed property and relations of domination to original sin. Hence to him the secular state, if it did not enter into the service of the heavenly one, was a creation of selfishness, a *civitas diaboli.*[180] So he established the hierarchical conception of politics, which considered the state an intrinsically worthless instrument in the service of the church for protecting the true faith and for combating infidels. Gregory VII and representatives of his papal politics held fast to the same viewpoint,[181] and it had its defenders in the extreme papal party throughout the Middle Ages. But among the most outstanding political metaphysicians of the Middle Ages there was another valuation of political life, one connected with the study of Aristotle. Thomas Aquinas and Dante mark the apex of this political metaphysics; both are far removed from the standpoint of Augustine. As different as their viewpoints are, even on this question, both deny the origin of political life in original sin and find it to be grounded instead in the moral nature of man.

And *Thomas Aquinas* is in fact the chief representative of this second direction in regard to evaluating political life. He defined its task as that of realizing the system of conditions with which the religious purpose of human existence is bound up. This view corresponds to the more general medieval idea of secular life as a means and a foundation for accomplishing the religious, a position given classical expression in the ethics of Albert the Great and Thomas Aquinas. According to Thomas's treatise *On the Rule of Princes,* the ultimate goal of human society is to come to the enjoyment of God through virtuous living. This goal cannot be reached by the powers of human nature, but only by the grace of God. Hence realizing virtuous life in political community is the means to attain a purpose which lies beyond the state's sphere of activity: the divine king himself realizes that purpose, using the priesthood to mediate the task. Secular sovereignty is thus subordinated to this hierarchy.[182] Picking up an analogy that originated as early as the period of the church Fathers and that medieval thinkers often used, Thomas finds a reflection of the relation of the body to the soul in the relation of the secular state to the church.[183] Among medieval writers this evaluation of political life was the most common one, and Thomas, the wisest of all mediators, successfully expressed the harmonizing formula here too.

A third standpoint came out of a higher evaluation of political life. It regards *imperium* and *sacerdotium* as two powers that stem with equal immediacy from God, and each performs an independent function in the moral world. Hence it recognizes equal sovereignty for the state and for the church. Literary representatives of imperial claims tried to establish this evaluation of *imperium* from the time of Henry IV.[184] *Dante* developed it penetratingly in his treatise *On Monarchy,* using ideas of Aristotle and Thomas, but demonstrating not only more powerful language but also greater style of thought than Thomas does. The purpose of every part of creation lies in the activity proper to it. An individual person cannot actualize what the power of reason contains; on the contrary, only the human race can completely develop the theoretical and, secondarily, the practical power of reason. The condition for achieving this goal lies in universal peace, and monarchy assures this; it maintains justice and directs the activity of individuals to a *single* goal.[185] Thus monarchy enters into the following relationship with the theocratic ordering of society. Among all things that exist, man alone stands in the middle between the transitory world and the unending one. Therefore, insofar as he is ephemeral he has a different final goal than he has insofar as he is immortal. An inexhaustibly profound providence has given him one goal in the happiness of this life, which consists in exercising the virtue appropriate to him, and the other goal in the happiness of eternal life, which consists in enjoying the vision of God. We attain the first goal along the path of philosophical insight through our intellectual and moral virtues, and we arrive at the other, final goal of revelation through the theological virtues. The emperor is responsible for leading the effort toward the first goal, and the pope is responsible for leading the effort toward the other goal. The empire directs the human race toward its temporal happiness by way of philosophical insight; the pope leads it to eternal life by way of truths of revelation.[186] This independent evaluation of the state, as we encounter it in Dante, led still further in a mind like *Marsilius of Padua*—given the need to overcome a dualism of this kind—to seeing *sacerdotium* as a component and function of the state. Marsilius drew the consequences of the ancient concept of the state; at root he was opposed to the progress contained in the assertion of Christ about the rights of Caesar and the rights of God.[187]

This division of valuation between spiritual and secular power found expression in *legal-historical fables* about the transmission of divine power, which make up an important element of the historical metaphysics of the Middle Ages. For where the will of God works together with wills of men to accomplish a plan supervised by providence, there appears the concept of an *institution* grounded in a *special divine act* and in which a part of the task of world rule is *transmitted* to an earthly person as representative of God. The hierarchy grounds its jurisdiction in the supreme authority of the vicar of Christ. Similarly, people predominantly regarded the office of king in the Middle Ages as an office conferred by God. And the question then arises as to whether the state authority derives its sovereignty directly from above by way of a transmission proceeding from ecclesiastical power. Among known discussions of this question, Dante's proof of the legitimate origin of the Roman world monarchy stands out because it comes extremely close to providing a historical basis of legitimacy. This proof finds legitimacy in the will of God, but it does not look for this will in specific theocratic acts. On the contrary, just as one can know the will of an individual person from the outside only from signs, so Dante interprets history as a system of signs of the will of God.[188]

Just as the theocratic system assigned the state its position in the external organization of society, so likewise it afforded a basis for defining the nature of the state. From the mystical body of the church the *idea of an organism* was transferred to the state in a new sense which transcended Aristotle. Probably the oldest extant execution of the comparison between members of the body and parts of the state, assuming that the basic features of organic structure actually recur in the state, was contained in the *Institutio Trajana* falsely ascribed to Plutarch—something we can find in part once again in the remarkable *Polycraticus* of John of Salisbury.[189] This harmony of the universe, according to which the structure of the state as a moral and political body is reflected in that of its parts, the individuals, forms the background of the medieval organic concept of the state. And writers of that time ingeniously used relations which we perceive to exist in an organic body to interpret the political organism.

Beyond this whole theocratic conception of history and social order an entirely opposite conception emerged ever more powerfully in the course of the Middle Ages. This idea originated in the free-city communities of antiquity: the *derivation of political unity of will and of the right of sovereignty from the particular wills* of persons united in an organization. This theory explained the rise of a unity of will in the external organization of society not as a conferral of God's sovereign right but through a pact of subjection [*pactum subjectionis*] based on particular wills, hence through a construction from below, from the elements of political life. It carried forward the basic idea of Greek natural law. But while the Greek view had conceived of the problem of a mechanical explanation of political will-units [*der politischen Willenseinheiten*] arising out of the anarchy of social atoms in a very general way (such that we could designate it as a metaphysics of society), the Middle Ages pursued the method initiated by the Romans of relating these Greek speculations to positive jurisprudence. In the hand of canonists and legalists [*Legisten*] the concept of corporation had become dominant in the sphere of external organization of society and was applied to the state as well as the church. Juristical construction of this concept regarded the unitary legal subjectivity of a corporation, which makes it a "person," as arising from a constitutive act. Thus the construction of the unity of will in a political totality became the focal point of every politico-journalistic [*publizistische*] theory through this sort of act, and the cooperation or the exclusive efficacy of united wills in the act that gives rise to the state gave this act the character of a contract. Fundamental ideas of ancient Germanic law; then the legal fiction about a constitutive act by which the Roman people gave sovereignty to the emperor; in addition the influence of Greek theories; and finally the self-rule of free communes in Italy (the most important country for political theory at that time): all this swelled the stream of natural law. From the turn of the thirteenth century into the fourteenth on, juristic construction based on particular wills and their contract took systematic form. Social contract, popular sovereignty, and limitation of positive law by natural law became part of public law. This further development of natural law through positive law strengthened its revolutionary force for a future period, but its immediate effect during the Middle Ages was its adaptation to other social ideas of the time. Not before Marsilius of Padua did this radical standpoint break with other social ideas of the Middle Ages, and that indicates the dawning of modern political ideas. The full unfolding of the force of natural law then began among modern peoples with the decline of the feudal orders. We have now reached the point in the development of modern society at which one could get serious about sovereignty of individuals, analogous to the point in the development of Greek society at which the natural law of the Sophists had won respectability.[190]

Thus the theocratic theory of society found its limit in natural law theory, and the latter in turn still lacked a general framework and the resources of analysis which might have made it possible for it to explain society adequately.

Finally, we are going to survey and test the connection between the principles developed in this theocratic metaphysics of society. This theory was superior to every earlier one inasmuch as it set out from the general structure of human social life, and this structure determined every principle regarding jurisdiction of political power as well as every assertion about the concept of virtue or of obligation. But medieval thinkers did not break down composite facts which present themselves to historical study and political observation into simpler individual contexts; on the contrary, they linked them together into a whole by way of teleological interpretation. The upshot of this could not possibly have been anything other than an arbitrary game were not the key to these ciphers of history and society available in revelation, for revelation established the beginning, middle, and end of humanity's course of life and defined its content. Hence, what constituted the basic characteristic of this metaphysics of society was this: Every conceptual construction is nothing but a subsequent attempt to describe conceptually and to prove what tradition and religious insight present. The dominant medieval theory of society was a theocratic system, to be sure, but this system was not free from contradiction. Corporative life contained another element, a right of the communality, which appeared to point back to a contractual relationship. The theocratic theory of society did not explain this element, and as natural-law theory of society developed, it indicated a limitation of the theocratic system's usefulness and a gap in its premises. Antinomies from the theory of metaphysical principles extended into the philosophy of society and inwardly tore this theocratic metaphysics apart. The deepest of these antinomies functions in social theory as the contradiction between the conception of God as an intelligence, for which only the eternal and the universal exist, and as a will, which undergoes changes in moving toward a goal, manifests itself in temporal acts, and is stimulated by the actions of free wills to countermeasures. *As principles of social order, eternal verities had the same meaning for antiquity in the world of men that substantial forms had in the realm of nature.* As Aristotle transferred Platonic Ideas into the world itself, he outfitted this world with eternity, both with regard to its stability and to its forms. In immutable identity with itself the living being arises out of the organic germ in that world, and the germ in turn arises out of life. According to Aristotle, the course of history achieves no deeper content for the soul and for the eudaemonism it actualizes. His descriptive science of politics developed a solid framework of concepts which contains the ever uniform law of political life and merely possesses its variable content in changing conditions of life in society. Despite how profoundly Aristotle conceived the relationship of conditions of the life of states to their political forms, he held that to develop purpose-complexes of human life does not require an ever new expression in political constitutions to correspond to the difference in content. On the contrary, conditions of society, which are like material for constructing a state, made it possible to have a lesser version here and a higher version there of the *same* ideal form. *To Christianity God became historical.* The medieval theory of society carried by Christianity first used the idea of a divine will which embraces an ascending series of changes as its purpose, and it accomplishes this purpose in the sequence of individual will acts and in interaction with other wills. The deity enters into time. So as often as medieval metaphysics seeks to reconcile the Greek system of eternal truths with the plan of God, the insolubility of the contradiction manifests itself. For one cannot harmonize the living personal experience of the will, which embraces needs and changes, with the immutable world of eternal ideas in which the intellect possesses necessary and universally valid truth.[191] Epistemologically speaking, speculative construction from concepts contradicts the arbitrary factuality characteristic of decisions of a free divine will. Hence Occam's theory of will dissolved the objective metaphysics of the Middle Ages. And if *nominalism* in its first stage had perished on account of its barren negativity with respect to the tasks facing medieval thought, in the mighty reality of the will it now found its higher justification even here in the theory of society. The intellectually powerful ecclesiastical-political writings of *Occam,* in a wide-ranging presentation of arguments and counter-arguments, destroyed every part of the rational system of philosophy of history and society.[192] And rightly so, because demonstration was truly incapable of grounding medieval theory of society in any measure at all. The logic of the argument fails where one is supposed to derive the dualism of state and church from the theocratic principle or to decide issues like the relation of state and church or world monarchy and individual state by syllogisms.

Section 4. Dissolution of the Metaphysical Attitude of Men toward Reality

1. Conditions of Modern Scientific Consciousness

The second generation of European peoples now experienced a transformation like the one which took place in Greece as a result of the dissolution of the ancient tribal constitution. As feudal orders and the organization of Christendom under pope and emperor fell apart, modern European society emerged, and in its midst *modern man*. He is the product of the gradual internal development which took place in the youthful period of this second generation of European peoples, the Middle Ages. What we look for in him is our own heartbeat, in comparison with what we can read in the souls of men of more ancient times, which is alien to us. Thus nothing is more relative, whether one looks to the gradualness with which it asserts itself or to the variety of personal feeling in the historian, which determines such an historical type. But the historian sees reality when he sees the first examples of modern man appear at certain points. In the midst of continuous development he perceives the outcome in graphically describable historical phenomena and seizes it. Nor does the fact that the point at which such a type appears in the evolutionary path of one people is far removed in time from the point at which this happens with another hinder him in doing this. It does not confuse him that special features of this form in one people diverge greatly from those in another. Petrarch is obviously such a type and we rightly think of him as the first representative of modern man as he emerges in clear outlines as early as the fourteenth century. It is not easy to find the same type again in the modern man of the North, in Luther and his independence of conscience or in Erasmus and that personal freedom of the inquiring mind which presses forward in an endless sea of tradition in search of enlightenment. Nevertheless, there is something in the one case as in the other which defines the whole substance of these men, something we share with them and separates them from everything people willed, or felt, or thought earlier.

Out of the context of what makes modern man we call attention to *one feature* which we saw unfolding slowly and laboriously in the course of intellectual history and is *decisive for the rise and the justification of modern scientific consciousness* in its opposition to the metaphysical attitude of man. In science the purpose-nexus of knowledge in Europe broke away from its foundation in the totality of human nature, just as art did, or, in another way, law. On this specialization rests not only the technical completion of the great purpose systems of human society but also, as the heart of the process, emancipation of all the powers of the individual soul from their original imprisonment. The soul becomes mistress of her powers, like a man who has learned to execute each movement of his limbs independently of the movements of others and to use them with more precise and assured estimation of their effect. The work of history is what first broke the original fettering of the powers of the soul. For feeling first possesses its manifold, changing, and rich life through art: Works of artists reflect feeling's own inner world to it in heightened form in images, perceptions, and ideas as though in a magic mirror. In the work of science the intellect first realizes the importance of its resources and the power of its method, and it now uses powers in itself with the technical virtuosity of a kind of logical athlete.

Medieval man had only incompletely held on to the specialization achieved in the ancient world. It is true that he had profoundly developed Christian experience. In the system of the Catholic church he possessed the autonomous power of religious life and of social consciousness bound up with it which united, strengthened, and defended all peoples, even though with frightful coercive measures. Under the protection and unfortunately also the compulsion of this church system the purpose-complex of science likewise grew to a larger organization in the universities, and in the midst of the corporative life of the Middle Ages it also struggled toward its own legal sphere of autonomy. But domination of religion, which lent all higher feelings and ideas a rare security and depth in the Middle Ages, nevertheless to a certain degree also confined all independent purpose-complexes. Alloying of Christianity with ancient science damaged the purity of religious experience. Corporative and authoritative restriction of individuals hindered the free relation of personal activities in areas which draw their life's breath in freedom, such as science and religion. Thus conditions of life in the Middle Ages intertwined the richness of higher existence into a structure directed by the church, in which Christianity surrendered itself to metaphysical science while science and art were shackled inwardly and outwardly. This system of formation was embodied in the external organization of the church. Compared to it, everything else which stirred in medieval man was secularity, which one had to destroy or subordinate. Thus the same separation which split apart society of those days into imperial and ecclesiastical power passed through the soul of medieval man. Natural growth of political life, continuance of individuals in their primordial relations to the soil, individuality, personal relations and personal association accompanied by removal of all general rules of law, and finally youthful impetuosity in the Germanic race and in the more ancient peoples they infused with new blood: All this resulted in an unbridled life of the senses and of the will in the man of that time. But in his soul there warred against this his faith in a transcendent realm which functioned in this world through the agency of church, clergy, and sacraments, and from which divine powers continually radiated. The ordering of medieval society intensified the force of this objective system. In it the individual was totally fitted into associations, of which the church and the feudal order were only the most powerful. The goals of society which seem to require freedom the most were carried and restricted by authority and the corporation. Medieval man's dependence was increased by his attitude toward the entire historical tradition, which confined his thought in something like a thick forest of traditions. And not the least among the reasons which hindered autonomy of individuals and independent unfolding of particular life goals in society consisted in a metaphysics which, given the state of the sciences, maintained itself victoriously in its basic outlines and provided a solid anchor point for the transcendent arrangement defended by the church. Thus even the intellectually most powerful medieval thinkers appear only as representatives of this worldview and ordering of life, comparable to the great feudal and hierarchical heads of society of those days. What was individual in them was subordinated to this system and this is the reason why the thinker was a world power. As lonely and gloomy as even Dante was in pursuing his path, his entire great soul was devoted to this objective system, just as much as were the souls of Anselm, Albert, or Thomas. Dante thereby became "the voice of ten silent centuries."

The substantial change which we designate as the appearance of *modern man* is a result of a composite formative process, and its interpretation would require comprehensive examination. Here, where the issue is the rise and justification of modern scientific consciousness, the most important thing to begin with is that the specialization and independence of purpose-complexes of society, which peoples of antiquity had previously achieved in piecemeal fashion, were now actualized in the new generation of European peoples. The spiritual formation of these peoples rests on self-certitude of religious experience, autonomy of science, and liberation of the imagination in art, in contrast with earlier religious constraint. Such a new constitution of the inner structure of culture is a higher step in developing the new generation of European peoples, for these nations had naturally started with their souls' powers restricted. But at the same time it restores what the Greeks had elaborated and what Christianity had achieved, and so Humanism and the Reformation are outstanding elements in the process by which our modern consciousness came into being. Besides this specialization, as another side of the historical movement which gave birth to modern scientific consciousness, occurred a change in external organization of society which released all individual powers and made the individual autonomous. This social and political transformation took place first of all in the cities. The classical picture which Jacob Burckhardt painted of the first appearance of modern man in Italy of the Renaissance fits harmoniously into the framework of our description. He says:

> In the Middle Ages both aspects of consciousness—that directed toward the world and that toward the interior of man himself—lay dreamlike or half-awake, as though behind a common veil. This veil first scattered to the winds in Italy with the awakening of an *objective* standpoint and treatment of the state and of all things in this world in general. But alongside it the *subjective* asserted itself with full power; man became a spiritual *individual* and recognized himself as such.

Acquisition of relative autonomy among particular spheres of existence is what first of all determined what Burckhardt here calls an objective treatment. As science ceases subordinating itself to the medieval schema of religious understanding, the bond is broken between religious ideas as means of construction, on the one hand, and reality on the other hand. One becomes aware of reality with unprejudiced understanding, and so objective examination and *positive science* came into being where, formerly, metaphysical derivation had kept the phenomenon linked to the profoundest level of the general life of the spirit. However, the changed position of the individual in the external organization of society effected a liberation of the individual's powers and his self-awareness. Thus *a new attitude of the knowing subject toward reality* came into being. Finally, with the growth of the individual sense of selfhood and the development of objective inquiry, a *free diversity in worldview increased*. In metaphysical thought and in poetical musing, all possibilities of worldview were developed. If the full light of this new period first struck Italy, nevertheless its first dawning in the North was a more powerful phenomenon. In Occam we find a deeper foundation of modern consciousness than in his younger contemporary

Petrarch: the self-certitude of inner experience. In contrast with authority, verbal demonstration, and experience-transcending syllogisms, he perceived in the will a mighty reality, an honest and true actuality.

Thus changes in the entire status of man, even in relatively independent intellectual development, prove to be influential, indeed even decisive. It is superficial to trace the transformation of the scientific spirit since the fourteenth century to Humanism. Throughout the Middle Ages an increase in knowledge of books and resources of antiquity took place.[1] If an intimate renewed understanding of the spirit of the ancient authors first came about in fourteenth century Italy and later among other peoples, this was a result of deeper underlying causes. Among modern peoples, especially in the cities, social and political conditions took shape which were analogous to those in the ancient city-states; this resulted in a personal sense of life and in dispositions, interests, and ideas that, through their affinity with those of ancient peoples, made it possible to renew their understanding of the ancient world. For the man who is supposed to recapture the past in his own person must be prepared for this through an inner elective affinity with it.

This altered condition of intellectual formation—as manifested in increasing autonomy of religion, science, and art and growing freedom of the individual as against communal life of man—is the deepest reason, located in the psychical constitution of modern man himself, why *metaphysics has now played out its former historical role*. Christian religion, as Luther and Zwingli related it to inner experience; art, as Leonardo now taught it to seize the hidden depths of reality; science, as Galileo directed it in analyzing experience—these made up modern consciousness in the freedom of its living expressions.

Metaphysics, as theology, had been the real bond that had held together religion, science, and art—the various aspects of intellectual life—in the Middle Ages; now this bond was broken. The intellectual life of modern peoples had progressed to such a state, and its understanding had been so disciplined by Scholasticism toward research for research's sake, that they began to set up and also accomplish more limited tasks, employing more rigorous methods. The time of *independent development of the special sciences* had arrived. One could take up again the achievements of the positive epoch of the ancient world. One could pick up the thread of positive research again where Archimedes, Hipparchus, and Galen had dropped it. Antiquity and the Middle Ages sought in science for the answer to the riddle of the world and in reality for the embodiment of the highest ideas; so people confused reflection on ideal significance of phenomena with analysis of their causal connections. But now that science was breaking away from religion (without wishing to replace it), causal research abandoned this false connection and came closer to the needs of life. People were fed up with abstract demonstrations of transcendent objects and with metaphysical cobwebs which had been spun from this world to the beyond, and yet the honest struggle for truth beyond appearances continued. So Latin man now turned to experiences of external nature and of life of the world; Northern man turned primarily toward living religious experience.

And now a *new class of persons* as carriers of this new tendency also appeared at this juncture of intellectual development: the cleric made way for the man of letters—the writer or perhaps the professor at one of the universities founded or newly reformed by the cities or enlightened rulers. In the cities where these men appeared, the distinction between a large, busy, but uneducated mass of slaves and a few free citizens who regarded every type of manual labor as unworthy of them did not exist. Although this condition had greatly hindered progress of invention in Greek cities, inventions of great significance were made in industry in modern cities. The broad theater of our continent and the enormous resources of this modern world produced a continuous organization of many workers. But nature did not confront them as a kind of intrinsically divine growth; the hand of man reached through it to seize the forces underlying its forms. The character of *modern science* arose in this movement: the study of reality as it is given in experience by way of the search for causal structure, hence by breaking down composite reality into its factors, especially through experiment. Search for laws of nature replaced the job of determining the constant element in changes in nature. The law of nature makes no claim to express the essence of things, and inasmuch as that defined the limits of positive science, the study of reality was expanded by a *theory of knowledge* which measured off the field of the sciences.

So, investigation of causal laws of reality in the sphere of nature and in the socio-historical world along with theory of knowledge emerged as the special products of modern science. These two have been carrying on a war of annihilation against metaphysics ever since, and their tendency now is to establish a system of special sciences of reality on the basis of epistemology.

And if *metaphysics has tried to defend itself* now in this modern world at whose inception we now stand, nevertheless *its character and its condition are gradually changing*. The *position* it seeks to maintain in the *system of the sciences* is a different one. For because positive sciences strive to analyze reality and to define its most general features in a system of elements and laws, and because they are becoming critically aware of the relation of these propositions to reality and to consciousness, metaphysics loses its position as the foundation for interpreting reality in the special sciences. The only possible task remaining for it is to round out the results of positive sciences in a general worldview. The degree of probability one can attain in such an attempt can be only a modest one. The *function* of such metaphysical systems likewise changes in *society*. Wherever metaphysics continued to exist, it was transformed into a mere private system of its originator and of the persons who found themselves attracted by this private system owing to similar temperament. This was determined by the change in circumstances which broke the power of monolithic monotheistic metaphysics. Changed basic ideas in physics and astronomy destroyed the arguments of monotheistic metaphysics. A *free multiplicity of metaphysical systems,* of which none is provable, now came into being. Thus the only task remaining for metaphysicians was to create centers in which one could gather together results of the positive sciences into a satisfactory general organization of phenomena in a formulation of relative value. As metaphysicians see it, positive science produces only particular words and rules for combining them; it takes metaphysics to make a poem of them. But a poem possesses no universally valid truth. In about the same time and place people heard Schelling proving his philosophy of revelation, Hegel his world reason, Schopenhauer his world will, and the materialists their anarchy of atoms—all of them with equally good or bad reasons. Could it be that one should seek out the true one among these systems? That would be a strange superstition. This metaphysical anarchy teaches the relativity of all metaphysical systems as palpably as possible. Each one represents as much as it contains. It contains as much truth as the limited facts and truths underlying its unlimited generalizations. It is an organ enabling one to see, giving conceptual depth to individuals, keeping them in contact with the invisible system. This, and much more like it, constitutes *the new function of metaphysics in modern society*. Hence these systems are expressions of important and intellectually wide-ranging persons. True metaphysicians lived what they wrote. Modern historians more and more consider Descartes, Spinoza, Hobbes, and Leibniz as key individuals whose broad souls reflect an aspect of the state of scientific thought. Precisely this representative character they possess proves the relativity of truth-content in their systems. Truth is not something representative.

But even *this function* of metaphysical systems in modern society can only be *transitory*. For once one recognizes the relativity of truth-content of these glittering magical palaces of scientific imagination, they can no longer deceive the disillusioned eye. And no matter how long metaphysical systems might influence educated circles, the possibility is irretrievably over and done with that such a system of relative truth, which stands alongside many others having the same truth-content, could ever be used as the foundation for the sciences.

2. Natural Sciences

Modern natural science originated in the general context just described. The mind of modern peoples had been disciplined in the scientific corporate bodies of the Middle Ages. Science, cultivated as a calling which passed on its legacy in the great corporate bodies, intensified its demands for technical perfection and limited itself to what it could master. And, indeed, it felt itself stimulated in the process by powerful impulses it encountered in society. To the extent that it freed itself from inquiring into ultimate grounds, it took its tasks from the progressing, practical goals of society: trade, medicine, and industry. The inventive mind of the industrious citizenry, which combined reflective thought and practical sense, created devices of incalculable importance for sciences of experiment and measurement. And from their Christian heritage these Romanic and Germanic peoples experienced a powerful feeling that mastery over nature was the mind's proper due, as Francis Bacon expressed it. Thus positive science of nature, sure of its limited goals, broke away with ever greater clarity from the compact totality of intellectual formation which, as metaphysics, had drawn its sustenance from the entirety of the soul's powers. Knowledge of nature became distinct from the general life of the soul. A constantly growing number of assumptions taken for granted in this totality was eliminated from knowledge of nature. Its foundations were simplified and reduced with ever greater exactitude to data given in sense perception. Natural science of the sixteenth century still worked with fantasies of psychical relations in the processes of nature. Galileo and Descartes started the successful battle against these surviving notions from the metaphysical period. And gradually even substance, cause, and force became mere auxiliary concepts for solving the methodological task of seeking out conditions underlying phenomena given in external experience, conditions which could explain their juxtaposition and succession and predict their occurrence.

Metaphysics of Antiquity and Middle Ages Is Dissolved by Natural Sciences

This modern science of nature gradually destroyed the *metaphysics of substantial forms*.
The rationally compelling system which modern natural science seeks as the ground of explanation for given reality, in accordance with the ideal of knowledge metaphysics has developed and prescribed for modern science, has for its material the concepts of substance and of causality (efficient cause), which metaphysics likewise abstracted from the

experience of total human nature and developed scientifically. As [philosophers] developed the concepts of ground of knowledge or rational necessity in metaphysics, they encountered both basic concepts already on hand as ideas which conduct human thought from the given back to its foundations. Accordingly, we see natural research striving to break down the apparent picture of changes and movements in objects into a chain of causes and effects and to grasp uniformities in them which will allow the mind to master them. It also tries to construct substances, as the carriers of this process, that are not subject to generation and corruption as material objects are. To this extent the mental labor of modern natural science is not at all distinct from the work of the Greeks, that is, to look for ultimate grounds of the given universe. And what is most characteristic of natural research among modern peoples now? What is the special device they have used to destroy the ancient theoretical structure of the cosmos?

Movement toward the true factors of nature was already evident in alchemy. Aristotle's doctrine of elements had made warmth, cold, moisture, and dryness the basis of characteristics given in simple perception. The stage of chemistry represented by Paracelsus used chemical analysis to push beyond this descriptive approach to the real factors which compose matter. Hence it distinguished three fundamental bodies (*tres primas substantias*): that which burns, or sulfur; that which smokes and is sublimated, or mercury; and that which remains behind as incombustible ash, or salt. Out of these basic materials—which the art of chemistry cannot describe in isolation, to be sure, but can distinguish in the process of combustion—Paracelsus first deduced the Aristotelian elements. Thus he trod the path which took man closer to chemical elements by way of actual decomposition of matter in experiment. It was precisely the process of combustion, with which Paracelsus began, that was to negotiate an entry into the quantitative method of investigation for Lavoisier. Yet long before chemistry acquired a solid foundation, mechanics became an exact science through Galileo. With respect to Galileo's achievement Lagrange has pointed out that, to discover satellites of Jupiter, phases of Venus, and sunspots, one needed only the telescope and some hard work; however, only an extraordinary mind could unravel the laws of nature in phenomena which one constantly has before one's eyes but has been unable to explain as yet. The simple, conceptually and quantitatively determined, ideas on which Galileo built presupposed breaking down the process of motion into abstract components, and precisely because of the simplicity of the fundamental relationships, those ideas made it possible to reduce motions to mathematics. The apparently obvious principle of inertia cut through the entire metaphysical theory we have described, which said a motion continues only through continued operation of the cause which produced it, hence one must posit a uniformly operative cause for uniformly continual motions. This theory, which recommended itself to our sense impressions of bodies set in motion and then returning to a state of rest, was the basis for assuming psychical entities as causes of a broad spectrum of changes in nature; however, the theory acquired its more lasting force from the rational orderliness of motions. But Galileo's principle now showed that the reason an object continues to move is because of its own need to persist in its state of motion. This necessity makes the object traverse every subsequent differential of its path because it has traversed the previous one. The foundation for the metaphysical view of nature was annihilated.

The first application of mechanics to a complex system of facts—at once the most brilliant and the most sublime application of which it is capable—was its application to the great motions of masses in space. Hence mechanics of the heavens came about.

Advances made by mathematics in analytic geometry and differential calculus made it possible. The mechanical way of viewing things through the theory of gravitation as the invisible bond of the starry universe now brought the intricate mechanism of the bodies orbiting in space under its control. And with that the celestial spirits of the metaphysical view of nature were over and done with and became fairy tales of a bygone age.

The immense change in man's view of the world which thus took place began when Copernicus—linking up with investigations of the Greeks, who had attempted the same thing—placed the sun in the middle of the world [*Welt*]. "For, after all, who could wish to assign this torch in the glorious temple of nature a different place?" he asks. Kepler's three laws graphically outlined the figures and numerical relationships of the heliocentric motions of the planets, in which Kepler, following in the footsteps of the Pythagorean school, saw the harmony of the heavens. Newton looked for the explanation of the motions whose form was thus determined. And he explained them by breaking them down into two factors. The one factor consists in an impulse which each planet has received in a direction tangential to its present path, the other in gravitation; thus one could calculate the curvature of their paths. In this way, in place of the spiritual beings whose perceptual power and mutual inner spiritual relationship had been the basis for explaining the complex forms of the apparent paths and their mechanically disconnected machinery, a mechanism appeared which was like the inner workings of an enormous clock. This took place once Copernicus's heliocentric standpoint had given the problem a simpler formation and Kepler had given it an exactly precisioned formulation. And the means behind all this was analysis, which traced form to the cooperation of factors conducive to explanation, whereas until this time people had studied form esthetically and teleologically.

We are not going to pursue the significance of advancing chemistry and physics in totally transforming previous metaphysics; in chemistry particularly, analytic method now seemed about to discover experimentally the substances which are linked together in the cosmos. But forms of organic life were the second major strong point in metaphysics of substantial forms, and it was about to lose that one as well. Using the concept of a living soul, or *anima vegetativa,* for a time the metaphysics of substantial forms withstood the demand to trace organic forms and behavior, the most complex of all the phenomena of nature, to physical and chemical mechanics. Then biology attributed at least the use of chemical and physical forces to this living soul until finally most biologists, especially in Germany, downgraded the concept of living soul and living force as useless for scientific progress and tried to eliminate it altogether. Here too, it was once again analysis of the *forma naturae,* which had previously been regarded as a living totality developed from something psychical, which brought down the ancient metaphysics. Thus the *method of analysis*—not mere conceptual analysis, but one which *delved into facts*—pressed forward toward first causes in nature and dissolved both psychical entities and substantial forms.

If *monotheistic doctrine* had been the focal point of metaphysics until now and if it had its principal strong point in rigorous science in *argument from facts of astronomy,* so now the stringency of even this argument was *undermined.*

Even *Kepler's* discoveries had led him only to the point of assigning the divine power which produces the movements of the planets to the sun as the middle point of all their paths, hence of already assuming a central power in the sun:

> We must assume one of two things: either that motive spirits become weaker the further they are removed from the sun or that there is a *single* motive intelligence at the midpoint of all these paths, i.e., in the sun, which imparts more accelerated motion to each heavenly body

the closer it comes to that midpoint but which wears down, so to speak, in the case of the more distant ones on account of distance and diminution of force.[2]

Even for *Newton,* then, only *one* ground for explaining motions of planets fell in the province of matter; besides it he needed to assume that a planet was thrown in a certain direction and with a certain velocity by external impulse. So he still needed a first mover, even though now in a subordinate role. What is more, Newton explained that planets and comets persist in their paths according to laws of gravity, to be sure, but they could not arrive at their original and uniform state through these laws. "This perfect framework of sun, planets, and comets could have come about only through the decision and sovereignty of an intelligent and powerful being."[3] His spiritual substance carries the interaction of parts in the universe. Thus for a time the force of the astronomical part of the cosmological proof for the existence of God persisted, though in a weakened state. Several important thinkers who had otherwise conducted a passionate war against the faith of the church were still convinced even by this weakened argument. But once one used the mechanical theory of *Kant* and *Laplace* to explain the origin of the planetary system, mechanism took the place of the deity in the new hypothesis.

From this point on, the *metaphysical argument* which has accompanied us throughout the entire history of metaphysics was *destroyed* as such. In addition, discoveries about changes in heavenly bodies, as well as the mechanics and physics of the heavens, now eliminated the distinction between a higher, immutable world and the world of change beneath the moon. What remains is the *metaphysical mind-set,* the basic metaphysical feeling of man which has accompanied him through the long period of his history from the time when sheepherding peoples of the East looked up to the stars and when priests in the observatories of temples of the Orient combined the cult of stars with their observations. This fundamental metaphysical feeling was everywhere intertwined in the human mind with the psychological origin of belief in God. It rests on the immensity of space, which is a symbol of infinity, and on the pure light of the stars, which appears to point to a higher world, but above all on the harmonious order which puts even the simple path which a star in the heavens describes into an arcane but vividly felt relationship to our geometrical view of space. All this is tied together in *one* frame of mind: the soul feels itself expanded, and a rationally harmonious and divine system stretches out in concentric circles from it into the infinite. One cannot break this feeling down into some sort of demonstration. Metaphysics remains mute. But when the stillness of night comes, even we can still hear the harmony of the spheres sounding from the stars, about which the Pythagoreans said that only the noise of the world drowned it out. This is an inextinguishable metaphysical disposition which underlies all arguments and will outlive them all.

Because modern natural science has thus dissolved the entire metaphysics of substantial forms and psychical entities previously described even to their innermost core which makes up the single spiritual cause of the world, the question arises, *Into what has science dissolved this metaphysics?*

Mechanistic Explanation of Nature Is Not a New Metaphysics, nor Can It Be Used as a Starting Point for One

What was it that put analysis of composite forms of nature in place of these *formae substantiales,* which had once been the object of a descriptive conception and of a reduction to quasi-spiritual entities? People have indeed said: a new metaphysics did. And, in fact, insofar as one is talking about a standpoint such as Fechner has recently depicted as the view of nature—one which holds that atoms and gravitation are metaphysical entities such as substantial forms used to be—then naturally one has merely exchanged an old metaphysics for a new one, and one could not even say a better for a worse one. Materialism was such a new metaphysics, and for that very reason current natural-scientific monism is its offspring and heir; for it, too, atoms, molecules, and gravitation are entities or realities just as truly as any object is which we can see and touch. But truly positive scientists are related to concepts they employ to know nature in a different way than metaphysical monists are. Newton himself saw in the force of attraction only an auxiliary concept to express the formula of a law, not knowledge of a physical cause.[4] Most leading natural scientists consider such concepts as force, atom, and molecule a system of auxiliary constructions which help us develop determinations of the given into a system which is clear to understand and useful for life. And this corresponds to the facts of the case.

We cannot demonstrate that *object* [*Ding*] and *cause* are components of sense perceptions. They also do not result from the formal demand for a rationally necessary connection between elements of perception, still less from their mere relations of coexistence and succession. For the natural scientist, then, they lack legitimacy of origin. They constitute content-laden ideas grounded in experience which lend a systematic form to our perceptions, and indeed appear in a development which precedes conscious recollection.

In the course of this historical survey we have seen the abstract concepts of *substance* and *causality* issue from those ideas. It is the distinction of object from action, passion, or condition—as well as from distinctions we rightfully derive from knowledge based on that distinction and which are given along with the concepts of substance and causality—that determines the form of judgment. Hence we can eliminate these concepts verbally, but not in actual understanding, and natural research can only aim at using these ideas and concepts to construct an adequate and self-contained system of determinations to explain nature. These ideas and concepts embrace the only system possible to us and appropriate to our consciousness.

Once again we are only drawing a conclusion from the historical survey when we particularly insist further: The concept of *substance* and the constructionist concept of *atom* derived from it have arisen from demands that knowledge directs to what we are to posit as an underlying solid foundation for change taking place in things. They are historical products of the logical mind struggling with objects, and are thus not entities of a higher rank than an individual object is; on the contrary, they are creations of logic which are supposed to make the object thinkable, and their cognitive value is subject to the condition of experience and observation in which we encounter the thing. The schema of these concepts has also been used to classify the great discoveries which, within the limits of our experiences in chemistry, prove the immutability of matter with respect to mass and properties in the midst of the transformations involved in chemical combinations and separations. Thus the possibility arises, on which all fruitful natural research depends, of retrospectively positing facts and relations given in observation as the foundation for what we take from observation, and in this way of carrying through a unified view of nature. The clear notions of mass, weight, motion, velocity, and distance, which have taken shape in connection with larger visible bodies and have proven themselves in studying masses in outer space, are also used in places where we must replace the senses by the power of imagination. Hence even the attempt of German idealism to drive off this fundamental idea from the constitution of matter has remained by an unfruitful episode, while atomic theory has been steadily advancing, even though at times with very baroque notions about elementary particles. These baroque notions do not conform to our ideal demands on the ultimate grounds of the cosmos, to be sure, but they are like visible phenomena and they make possible the most suitable conceptual system for explaining these phenomena in accordance with the state of science in the period. On the contrary, through their affinity with spiritual life, concepts of the idealist philosophy of nature appear to be eminently worthy of constituting the starting point for interpreting nature. But because they concocted an interior state heterogeneous to and beyond these visible objects, they were incapable of really explaining them and were therefore totally useless.[5]

The same results also ensue with respect to the cognitive value of the concept of *force* and its allied concepts of *causality* and *law*. Although the concept of substance was developed in antiquity, the concept of force first received its present form in connection with the new science. Let us look back again; we grasped the origin of this concept as a living experience still bound up in mythical thought. The nature of this experience will later be the object of epistemological investigation. Here we wish to point out only the following: As we discover in our experience, the will can direct our thoughts and set our limbs in motion, and it has this capacity even though it does not always use it; in fact an equal or greater force can use external restraint to keep it in check, but we still feel its presence. So we conceive the idea of a working capacity (or a faculty) which precedes the individual operative act; particular will acts and behavior issue forth from a kind of reservoir of effective force. We have already seen the first scientific development of this idea in the Aristotelian series of concepts of dynamis, energy, and entelechy. Yet, no one had yet distinguished productive force in Aristotle's system from the reason for the purposeful form of its operation, and we earlier recognized in this a characteristic hallmark as well as a limitation of Aristotelian science. This distinction first made the mechanical worldview possible. It divided the abstract concept of quantity of force (energy, work) from concrete natural phenomena. Every machine manifests a measurable motor power whose quantity differs from the form in which the power appears, and it shows at the same time how the impetus is used up in work: *vis agendo consumitur*. In this direction, discovery of the mechanical equivalent of heat and establishment of the law of conservation of energy realized the ideal of an objective and rationally comprehensive system of conditions for the given. Here too we have no a priori law before us; on the contrary, positive discoveries have brought natural science closer to the declared ideal. Because one natural force after another is resolved into motion, but motion is subject to the general law that every act is the effect of an equally large previous act and that every effect is the cause of a further equally large effect, the system is complete. Thus the law of conservation of force has the same function with respect to use of the idea of force that the principle of constant equivalence of the mass of the universe has with respect to matter. Together they use practical experiment to isolate the constant element in changes transpiring in the universe; the metaphysical epoch strove in vain to lay hold of that constant element.

This much is clear: One cannot more crudely misunderstand the mechanical interpretation of nature, which is the fruit of the marvelous work of the European mind in natural research since the end of the Middle Ages, than by thinking of it as a new kind of metaphysics, say one based on induction. Of course the ideal of explanatory knowledge of the system of nature broke away only gradually and slowly from metaphysics, and epistemological investigation first explained the total *opposition* between the *metaphysical spirit and the work of modern science*. Before we begin to present our theory of knowledge, epistemology might define that opposition provisionally in the following way.

1. *External reality* is given to us in the totality of our self-consciousness not as a mere phenomenon but as reality, inasmuch as it has an effect, opposes the will, and is present to feeling in pleasure and pain. In action and reaction of the will we are aware of a self in the system of our perception and an other which is separate from it. But this other is present to consciousness only with its predicate determinations, and predicate determinations illuminate only relations to our senses and to our consciousness: the subject or subjects themselves do not exist in our sense impressions. So we know perhaps *that* the subject is there, but certainly not *what* it is.

2. Mechanical *interpretation of nature* looks for *cognitively necessary conditions* for this phenomenon of external reality. And indeed man has always investigated external reality with regard to its substance and its underlying causality because it had been present to him as something in action. Also, thought remains linked through judgment, as its function, to the distinction between substance on the one hand and action, passion, property, causality, and finally law on the other hand. We can eliminate the distinction between the two classes of concepts which judgment separates and unites only if we eliminate judgment, hence thought itself. But for that very reason the concepts developed under these conditions can serve only as symbols for studying the external world; these symbols are introduced into the system of sensations as instruments the mind's structure uses to accomplish the task of knowledge. For knowledge cannot substitute a reality independent of experience in place of experience itself. It can only reduce the data of lived experience and experiment to a system of conditions which allow us to understand them. It can establish constant relationships of parts which recur in manifold forms of the life of nature. Thus if one abandons the sphere of experience itself, then one is dealing only with mentally fabricated concepts but not with reality, and from this point of view atoms, if they claim to be entities, are no better than substantial forms: they are creations of scientific understanding.

3. *Conditions* which *mechanical interpretation of nature* is looking for explain only *part of the content of external reality*. This intelligible world of atoms, ether, and vibrations is only a deliberate and extremely artificial abstraction of what is given in living knowledge and experience. The task was to construct conditions which allow one to derive sense impressions with the exactitude of quantitative determinations and accordingly to predict future impressions. The system of motions of elements in which this task is accomplished is only an excerpt from reality. For calculation of unchangeable and quality-free substances is in itself a mere abstraction, a scientific expedient. It is determined by the fact that all real change is shifted from the outer world into consciousness, which then frees the outer world from bothersome changes of physical properties. The medium of clarity—in which the leading concepts of force, motion, law, and element hover here— merely results from the fact that abstraction frees the objective situation from anything inaccessible to quantitative determination. And therefore this mechanical system of nature is in the first place surely a necessary and fruitful symbol which formulates the system of overall occurrences in nature in terms of quantity and motion. But what it might be

beyond this is something no natural scientist can pronounce on so long as he does not wish to abandon the ground of strict science.

4. For the time being, the *complex of conditions* which the mechanical intepretation of nature erects *cannot yet be demonstrated at all points of external reality*. Organic body is such a limit of mechanical interpretation. Vitalism had to acknowledge that physical and chemical laws do not cease to be operative at the boundary of organic body. But if natural science, assuming one eliminates living force, has posed for itself the comprehensive problem of deriving from the mechanical structure of nature the processes of life, its organic form, its laws of formation, its development, and finally the kind of specialization of the organic in types, then this problem remains unsolved even today.

5. From the nature of this process of searching for determinations of external reality a further conclusion follows. *One cannot be certain whether there are still more determinants* hidden in the facts, knowledge of which might make a totally different construction necessary. Indeed, if we possessed a broader range of experiences, then perhaps we would replace these conceptual objects we have constructed with some which lie still further back and are more elementary. *The still unexplained residue which has led metaphysicians to start out from the whole or the idea* in fact positively points in this direction. For if one regards elements as ultimate data, then reflection must fall into an abyss of questions whether these elements influence one another, demonstrate common behavior, and on its basis cooperate in constructing purposefully moving organisms. Mechanical interpretation of nature can regard the archetypal arrangement from which this harmonious system proceeds as merely accidental for the time being. Chance, however, means eliminating the cognitive necessity which the will to knowledge commits itself to find in natural science.

6. Natural science does not arrive in this way at a *unified system of conditions of the given*, which it had after all set out to discover. For we cannot explain laws of nature which govern all elements of matter as a whole by describing them as the behavior pattern of a particular material substance. Analysis arrived at the two terminal points of the atom and the law, and because one uses the atom in natural-scientific thought as an elementary magnitude [*Einzelgrösse*], there is nothing in it which one could bring into epistemological connection with the system of uniformities in nature. One cannot explain that one particle in the system of relations exhibits the same behavior as another one from its character as an elementary magnitude; indeed, it appears difficult even to comprehend it on that basis. In fact it is completely incomprehensible, now, how a causal connection is supposed to exist between immutable elementary magnitudes. Our understanding has to take the world apart like a machine to understand it; it breaks it down into atoms; but it cannot infer from these atoms that the world is a whole. Once again we draw a conclusion from the historical survey. This final report of analysis of nature in modern natural science is analogous to one we saw the metaphysics of nature arrive at among the Greeks: substantial forms and matter. *Natural law* corresponds to substantial form, and *elementary particle to matter*. Indeed, what finally emerges from these isolated findings is only the difference between *properties* which reveal themselves to unity of consciousness as uniformities and that which underlies them as a single *positivity* [*als einzelne Positivität*]; in short, the nature of judgment and consequently of thought.

Thus even for isolated reflection on nature, *monism* is only an *arrangement* in which the relationship of characteristics and behavior to that which exhibits them is a necessary one, for one rightfully derives it from the nature of the phenomenon of consciousness, which is reality. But establishing this relationship merely binds together what does not intrinsically belong together: the elementary magnitude of an atom and the rational, uniform structure which, to our consciousness, constantly points back to a unity. But if natural-scientific monism steps beyond the borders of the outer world and brings even the spiritual within the compass of its interpretation, then natural research now annuls its own precondition and presupposition: It draws its force from the will to knowledge, but its explanations can only negate this will in its full reality.

Residue Remaining from Natural-Scientific Explanation in the Form of Spontaneous Consciousness of the Comprehensibility of the Universe and of Life in Nature

The residue which thus remains for scientific interpretation is actually connected in consciousness with the whole relationship to nature which is grounded in the totality of our mental life and from which modern scientific investigation of nature has differentiated itself and declared its autonomy. We have shown that this differentiation did not yet exist in the mind of Plato or Aristotle, of Augustine or Thomas Aquinas. Consciousness of perfection and the harmonious beauty of the universe were still inextricably intertwined with their reflection on forms of nature. Removal of mechanical explanation of nature from this context of life in which we encounter nature was the first thing to eject the teleological idea from natural science. However, it remains part of the context of life in which we encounter nature, and if one recognizes teleology in the Greek sense as this awareness of the harmoniously beautiful system which corresponds to our inner life, then this idea of teleology is indestructible in the human race. The forms, genera, and species of nature express this immanent teleology, and even the Darwinists only push it further back. This awareness of purposefulness likewise stands in an inner relationship to knowledge of the rational harmony of nature by which it produces types in conformity with laws. This rationality is strictly demonstrable, however. For regardless of what our impressions are symbols of, the course of our knowledge of nature can analyze the coexistence and succession of these symbols, which stand in a fixed relationship to "the other" given in the will, into a system which corresponds to characteristics of our knowledge.

At the same time as the execution of the mechanical interpretation of nature and with the power of an irresistible natural phenomenon, profound awareness of life in nature as it is given to us in the totality of our lives expressed itself in poetry. This did not happen as a kind of beautiful appearance or form (such as representatives of formal esthetics would assume), but as a powerful feeling of life, first in the feeling for nature Rousseau had (his favorite predilections were natural-scientific) and then in Goethe's poetry and philosophy of nature. Without the benefit of clear discussion, Goethe fought with passionate anguish, yet in vain, the certain results of Newtonian mechanical interpretation of nature. This was because he considered it to be philosophy of nature and not what it was: development of a partial system given in nature as an abstract device for knowing and exploiting nature. Indeed, even Schiller compared the synthesis of esthetic reflection, as a method of a higher degree of quasi-metaphysical truth, to scientific analysis, which dissects and kills. And in his esthetics he correspondingly ascribed understanding of autonomous life in nature to the artist. Hence in the process of differentiation which the life of the soul and of society undergo, the holy, invulnerable, and all-powerful element we actually experience in our life as nature was something poets and artists loved and described, but it is inaccessible to scientific treatment. And we must despise neither the poet, who is filled with what cannot exist at all for science, nor the scientist, who knows nothing about what the happiest truth is for the poet. In the specialization of society's life a system like that of poetry has constantly modified its function. Since the introduction of the mechanical conception of nature, poetry has stood up for the self-contained, unexplainable, yet great, feeling of life in nature, just as it always protects what is lived, but cannot be conceived, from being volatilized by analytical operations of abstract science. In this sense what Carlyle and Emerson have written is a formless poetry. Therefore, though those popular descriptions of nature which sentimentally project a deceptive play of inner vivacity into the hard and clear ideas of analytic understanding of matter are a reprehensible hybridization; and though German philosophy of nature obfuscated knowledge of nature by introducing spirit into it and degraded spirit by leveling it down to nature, poetry nevertheless preserves its immortal task.

> Sublime Spirit, you granted me, gave me, everything
> I asked for. You have not turned your face
> Toward me in fire for nothing.
> You gave me glorious nature to be my kingdom,
> And the power to feel it and enjoy it.
> You did not permit me but a cold and gaping visit;
> No, you let me gaze into her deep breast
> As into the bosom of a friend.
> You lead the parade of the living before me,
> And you teach me to recognize my brothers
> In the quiet bush, in the air, and in the water.

3. The Human Sciences

Besides the natural sciences a second complex of sciences has emancipated itself from metaphysics, one that likewise deals with reality given in our experience and explains it on the basis of that experience alone. Here again analysis has destroyed forever concepts which the metaphysical epoch had used to interpret facts. Thus the metaphysical construction of society and history created by the Middle Ages perished not only because of the contradictions and logical gaps described above but also because actual analysis carried out among the special human sciences began to replace its universal ideas.

Metaphysical Construction of Society and History is Dissolved Analytically in Science of the Individual Person; in Special Sciences of Society; in Historical Science Founded on Them

This metaphysics had spread out the cords of its net of universal ideas to span the creation of Adam and the end of the world. Gathering of sufficient historical material, criticism of sources, and a philological method of working began in the humanistic epoch. In this way the real life of the Greeks became visible again through their poets and historians. Indeed, just as in climbing higher we catch sight of ever more distantly located landscapes and cities, so historical overview expanded more and more for the upwardly mobile peoples of the modern era. The mythical beginning of the human race now disappeared in the face of research that looked for historical features in the most ancient traditions. Added to this was the extension of the spatial geographical horizon of social reality. Peoples of lower cultural level and divergent type were already coming into contact with adventurers who pushed on into new continents beyond the ocean. Under the influence of these new impressions people here and there distinguished between a black, a red, and a white Adam. The historical framework of metaphysics of history collapsed. Historical criticism everywhere destroyed the web of sagas, myths, and legal fables that theocratic theory of society used to link human institutions with the will of God.

But was there not a metaphysical construction left over that would combine into a meaningful whole the facts which the work of philological and historical criticism had now cleanly established? The medieval mind had explained the unity of the human race through a real bond, just as such a bond as a soul unites the parts of an organism. Nor had historical criticism destroyed that kind of idea the way it had destroyed the idea of the Donation of Constantine. On the basis of its theocratic idea, the medieval mind had subjected the pattern of history to teleological interpretation, and the results of criticism had also not directly destroyed this view. But once the solid premises of this teleological interpretation in the historical tradition of the beginning, middle, and end of history as well as in the positive theological determination of its meaning had dissolved, the *boundless multiplicity of meaning of historical material* came to light. In the process the *uselessness of a teleological principle of historical knowledge* was demonstrated. In fact, for the most part, outmoded dogmas succumb not so much to direct argument as to a feeling that they no longer agree with what one has acquired in other areas of knowledge. Causal investigation and law were carried over from natural science into the human sciences. Thus the whole difference between the cognitive value of teleological explanations and real explanations became more distinct than through any argument when one compared discoveries of Galileo and Newton to the assertions of Bossuet. And the *application of analysis* to composite spiritual phenomena and the general ideas abstracted from them little by little dissolved these general ideas and the metaphysics of the human sciences fabricated from them.

But the pace of this dissolution of metaphysical ideas and of the establishment of an independent system of causal knowledge grounded in impartial experience was *much slower* in the human sciences than in the natural sciences, and we have to show why this was so. The relation of mental facts to nature suggested an attempt to subordinate especially psychology to mechanical science of nature. And the justified effort to comprehend society and history as a whole broke away only slowly and painfully from the originally medieval metaphysical expedients used to solve this task. Subsequent historical facts illustrate both of these things, but at the same time they show how in their common progress the study of man, of society, and of history destroyed the schemata of metaphysical knowledge and began everywhere to put living and effective knowledge in their place.

In analyzing human society we confront *man* himself as a living unity,[6] and so *breaking up this living unity* constitutes the basic problem for analysis.[7] One did away with the view of older metaphysics in this area first of all by going beyond teleological grouping of universal forms of mental life to *explanatory laws*.

Modern psychology therefore strove to know the uniformities by which one process in psychical life determines another. In doing so it showed the subordinate importance of psychology developed in the metaphysical epoch, which had looked for class concepts for individual processes and ascribed faculties or powers to them. It is extremely interesting to see this new psychology surface in the second third of the seventeenth century among countless works of classification. Of course, as one might expect, it was at first influenced by the dominant interpretation of nature, which was the first area to apply a fruitful method. Hence immediately following the introduction of the *mechanical interpretation of nature* by Galileo and Descartes came the *extension of this mode of explanation to man and the state* by Hobbes and then by Spinoza.

Spinoza's principle *mens conatur in suo esse perseverare indefinita quadam duratione et hujus sui conatus est conscia* stems from principles of the mechanical school[8]; it obviously subordinates the living element in expansive will to the concept of inertia in nature. Spinoza carried out the further development of mechanics of general psychical states (*affectus*) according to the same principles. He invokes principles which refer general psychical states to their causes, recalls them with respect to their identity and similarity, and transfers mental states of others into one's own life through sympathy. Of course this theory was extremely imperfect. The dead and rigid concept of self-preservation does not adequately express the force of life. If we supplement theory through the principle that feelings are an awareness of states of will, nevertheless we can subject only a portion of our states of feeling to this assumption. And one can deduce sympathy from self-preservation only by way of fallacious argument.[9] But the extraordinary importance of Spinoza's theory consisted in the fact that, in the spirit of the great discoveries in mechanics and astronomy, he tried to reduce apparently lawless and arbitrarily directed general conditions of psychical life to the simple law of self-preservation. He does this by sketching, as it were, the living individual, the mode of which is man and which strives to preserve himself, into the system of conditions which make up his milieu. A schema for a causal system of psychical states comes about because he deduces that self-preservation faces demands from without as well as restraints in this context, and he places the emotions thereby generated under basic laws connecting psychic states. He specifies the precise points at which particular psychical experiences are inserted into the mechanical system thus outlined. Definitions of general states merely pinpoint where such experiences fit in constructing the mechanism of self-preservation, and they lack only quantitative determination to correspond externally to demands of explanation.

David Hume, who continued Spinoza's work more than two generations after him, stands in exactly the same relationship to Newton as Spinoza did to Galileo and Descartes. His theory of association is an attempt to sketch out laws of association among ideas following the paradigm of the theory of gravitation. "Astronomers," he explains,

> had long contented themselves with proving, from the phenomena, the true motions, order, and magnitude of the heavenly bodies, till a philosopher at last arose who seems, from the happiest reasoning, to have also determined the laws and forces by which the revolutions of the planets are governed and directed. The like has been performed with regard to other parts of nature. And there is no reason to despair of equal success in our inquiries concerning the mental powers and economy if prosecuted with equal capacity and caution. It is probable that one operation and principle of the mind depends on another.[10]

Thus interpretive psychology began by subordinating spiritual facts to the mechanical order of nature, and this subordination has had its effect up to the present time. Two theorems were the foundation for the attempt to map out a mechanism of spiritual life. One treats ideas which impressions leave behind as fixed magnitudes that constantly enter into new relations but remain unchanged in them; one establishes laws governing their mutual behavior on whose basis one is supposed to deduce the psychical facts of perception, imagination, and so forth. In this way a kind of psychic atomism is made possible. Nevertheless, we shall show that both of these assumptions are false. Just as a new spring season does not merely make old leaves on trees visible once again, so neither are ideas of a bygone day resurrected, only rather more obscurely, in our own day. On the contrary, the renewed idea takes shape from a definite internal perspective outward, just as sensation does from an external perspective. And laws of reproduction of ideas designate the conditions, to be sure, under which psychical life functions, but it is impossible to deduce from these processes that shape the background of our psychical life either a line of reasoning or an act of the will. Psychical mechanics sacrifices what we experience in inner perception to a line of reasoning which plays around with analogies from external nature. And so interpretive psychology, which takes its lead from natural science (and in whose paths Herbart also moved later) destroyed the classifying school among older metaphysical schools and pointed out the true task of psychology as modern science saw it; but where that interpretive psychology itself was influenced by metaphysics of the natural sciences, it could not maintain its position. Even in this realm science annihilates metaphysics, ancient as well as modern.

The next problem of the human sciences consists of systems of culture which are interwoven with one another in society as well as their external organization, hence *interpretation and governance of society*.

Sciences which deal with this problem encompass totally different classes of statements: judgments expressive of reality as well as imperatives and ideals aimed at directing society. Reflection about society has its profoundest challenge in connecting one class of assertions with the other. Metaphysical and theological principles of the Middle Ages had made such a connection possible by the bond which joined God and the law residing in him with the organism of the state, the mystical body of Christendom. The current state of society, the sum of traditions accumulated in it, and the feeling of an authority of higher provenance permeating it were closely knit in this metaphysics with the idea of God. This association gradually unraveled. Here, too, this happened because *analysis now reached back beyond the external teleological system of form-concepts and looked for a system based on laws*. This was made possible by applying interpretive psychology and developing abstract sciences which work out basic characteristics of related aspects of particular areas of life (law, religion, art, and so on). Thus appropriate causal concepts replaced teleological notions of Aristotle and the Scholastics; laws replaced universal forms; and immanent grounding based on study of human nature replaced a transcendent one. With that the attitude of older metaphysics toward the facts of society and history was overcome.

As we illustrate how modern science has dissolved the theological and metaphysical conception of society, we limit ourselves to the first phase, which lies completely behind us in the eighteenth century. For the first thing to emerge was the natural system[11] of knowledge of human society, its purpose-complexes, and its external organization, such as the seventeenth and eighteenth centuries developed them; a creation which was just as imposing, though less tenable, than the founding of natural science.

For this *natural system* signifies that we will henceforth understand society on the basis of human nature from which it has sprung. In this system the human sciences first discovered their own proper center—*human nature*. In particular, analysis now went back to psychological truths of second rank (as we named them).[12] It discovered motives of practical behavior in the spiritual life of the individual as well and thus overcame the old opposition between theoretical and practical philosophy. The expression for this scientific revolution in systematic classification is that in place of the opposition between theoretical and practical philosophy that between the *foundation for sciences of nature and the foundation for sciences of the mind* appears. In the latter the study of interpretive grounds for judgments about reality is connected with that of interpretive grounds for value judgments and imperatives, for they are directed toward regulating the life of the individual and of society.

The *method* the natural system used in dealing with religion, law, ethics, and the state was *imperfect*. It was predominantly determined by mathematics, which had had such extraordinary results in mechanical interpretation of nature. Condorcet was convinced that the rights of man were discovered by a method which was just as certain as that of mechanics. Sieyès believed that he had perfected politics as a science. The basis of the method consisted of an *abstract schema of human nature* which established the interpretive basis for facts of man's historical life in a few general dimensions of the psyche. Thus a false metaphysical method was still mixed in with beginnings of fruitful analysis. But as feeble as this natural system might appear to us today, nevertheless these scanty principles of natural theology about religion, of theoreticians of moral sense about morality, of the physiocratic school about economy, and the like, *definitively overcame the metaphysical stage of knowledge of society*. For these principles develop the basic features of the homogeneous partial contents in these systems of society, relate them to human nature, and in this way open up insight into the inner functioning of factors of social life for the first time.

History constitutes the ultimate and most complex problem of the human sciences. People now applied analyses contained in the natural system to the historical process. Because they accordingly pursued that process in various relatively independent spheres of life, the theological one-sidedness and crude dualism of the Middle Ages vanished. Because one sought motives of historical movement in humanity itself, the transcendent conception of history ended. A freer and more comprehensive way of thinking emerged. Through the efforts of human sciences in the eighteenth century a *universal historical viewpoint,* whose core was the *idea of evolution,* broke away from medieval metaphysics of history.

The soul of the eighteenth century consisted of an inseparable union of enlightenment, progress of the human race, and the idea of humanity. These concepts saw and expressed from different aspects the same reality which animated the eighteenth century. The power of consciousness of the *unity of the human race,* such as the Middle Ages had expressed it in metaphysical terms, continued. In the seventeenth century consciousness of the unity of the human race was still based on religion for the most part and extended only to the scientific community; in the world at large *homo homini lupus* was the rule—an opposition which permeates Spinoza's system so remarkably. Now, especially through the agency of the school of economists and the general interest in enlightenment and tolerance, a solidarity even of secular interests surfaced in various countries. Thus the metaphysical basis of the unity of the human race was transformed into a gradually growing knowledge of real bonds which unite individual to individual.[13] On the other hand historical consciousness developed further. The idea of *progress of the human race* dominated the century. It too was rooted in the historical consciousness of the Middle Ages, which had recognized an inner and central advance in the *status hominis*. But considerable changes in thought and feeling were needed before it could unfold freely. As early as the seventeenth century people rejected the notion of a historical state of perfection at the start of human history. In that period, in conjunction with the Renaissance, people vigorously discussed the notion that modern peoples were superior to the ancient world in sciences and literature. And now the most important thing happened. For medieval ecclesiastical faith and to a lesser degree for the old Protestant church faith, the sublimest feelings of man, the realm of his ideas concerning the highest things, and the order of his life had been something complete and self-contained. Now, as this faith receded, it was as if someone drew back a curtain which had until now prevented a view of the future of the human race: the mighty and overpowering feeling of an immense evolution of the human race emerged. Of course the ancients already had a clear awareness of historical progress of mankind in arts and sciences.[14] Bacon was filled with it and emphasized that the human race had now entered into an age of maturity and experience, and therefore the science of the moderns was superior to that of the ancients.[15] Pascal had this passage of Bacon before him when he wrote: "Man is constantly learning in his forward progress, for he takes advantage not only of his own experience but also of that of his predecessors. In the sciences all men taken together constitute a single progressing organization in such a way that we must regard the entire succession of men during the course of so many centuries as a single man who always exists and constantly learns." Turgot and Condorcet now expanded these ideas, however, inasmuch as they looked on science as the guiding power in history and they linked the progress of enlightenment and of feeling of community with its progress. And in Germany people finally reached the point where the conception of society based on the system of nature passed over into genuine historical consciousness. Herder discovered in the makeup of the individual person the element that changes and constitutes historical progress. In Germany art, especially poetry, was the organ one used to study this progress, and Hegel extended the schema which thus came into being into a universal view of cultural development.

Thus *progress of the human sciences* proceeds by way of the *natural system toward the evolutionary-historical view.* "Does one wish to become acquainted with a brief history of almost our entire misery?" asks Diderot. "Here it is: There once existed a natural man, and people have introduced an artificial man into his inner core. This has enkindled a civil war between the two which lasts until death." This sort of juxtaposition of the natural and the historical demonstrates in glaring light the limitations of the constructionist method of the natural system. And when Voltaire wrote: "It will be necessary to convulse the earth to bring it under the rule of philosophy,"[16] the one-sidedness of unhistorical understanding, which makes the natural system the counterpart to reality, was unfolding its destructive consequences in him. But that same natural system first subjected the great object of the spiritual world to factor-oriented analysis. It went beyond class concepts through a genuine resolutive process, which analysis of the idea of national wealth in political economy shows most clearly. And the resolutive process has of itself led the scientific mind beyond the limits of the natural system and paved the way for modern historical consciousness.

The metaphysical mind of course entwines the facts of history and society at innumerable points with still much finer threads; these stem from the natural way of conceiving and thinking. For in the study of society the same situation repeats itself which we have perceived in that of nature. On the one hand analysis affects individuals as subjects; on the other hand it affects predicative determinations which as such must remain general. Hence what the latter determinations contain appears as an entity between and beyond individuals and is substantiated as such in concepts like law, religion, and art. These more subtle and unavoidable deceptions of natural thought are something epistemology fully resolves for the first time. Epistemology will show the following: At this point in our self-awareness where we are certain of these subjects and their autonomy, indeed where we know the forces which underlie their predicative determinations, the relation of subjects to these general predicates differs from the relation which obtains in natural science between elements and laws. Concepts which one here forms out of predicates are different in their makeup from those of the natural sciences.

If one tears away the gray web of abstract substantial entities, what remains is—*man,* that is, men related variously to one another amid nature. We see every piece of writing and every series of actions as located on a man's periphery, and we seek to press on toward his center. I am supposing that this man is Schleiermacher and that his *Dialectics* lies before me. Apart from whatever ideas this book contains specifically, I find in it the thesis of the presence of the sense of God in all psychical acts, and at this deepest point *Dialectics* makes contact with his *Discourses on Religion.* So I pass on from work to work, and though I admittedly cannot know the center toward which all these peripheral statements are oriented, I can understand them. I find that Schleiermacher belongs to a group in which Schelling, Friedrich Schlegel, and Novalis, among others, find themselves. Such a group behaves in a manner analogous to a class of organisms: if an organ in such a class undergoes a change, then the corresponding ones also change; if one increases, others atrophy. I go on from group to group, to ever wider circles. The life of the soul has differentiated itself in art, religion, and so on, and we now face the task of finding the psychological foundation of this process and then of comprehending the process, both in the soul and in society, in which this specialization takes place. Furthermore, taking a cross section of history I can study the society of a certain time in general or among a specific people. I can match such cross sections against one another and compare man from the time of Pericles with man from the time of Leo X. Here I am approaching the profoundest problem: What is changeable in human nature in history? Nevertheless, in all these twists and turns of method man is always the object of investigation, sometimes as a totality, sometimes in part or in his relationships. To the extent that one carries through this standpoint, society and history will attain to the kind of treatment that corresponds in this autonomous area to mechanical explanation in the study of natural phenomena. At that point the metaphysics of society and history has really passed away.

Has it perhaps happened that the human sciences, having driven away the metaphysics of a realm of spirits through analytical investigation, now *find a gateway into a new metaphysics in man,* the initial and final point of their analysis? Or has a metaphysics of spiritual facts become impossible in every form?

As for metaphysics of science, the answer is yes. For the course of intellectual development has shown the concepts of substance and causality developed gradually out of living experiences under the demands of knowledge of the external world. Thus to one who is at home in the world of inner experience those concepts can say no more about the world than what has been taken from it. Whatever they say beyond that is merely an auxiliary device for knowing the external world and is therefore not applicable to the psychical. Furthermore, one can neither prove nor refute the thesis of metaphysical psychology which maintains the autonomous substantial and indestructible status of the soul; indeed, proof based on unity of consciousness has only a negative significance. Unity of consciousness underlies every comparative judgment, for in it we must possess different sensations—say, two shades of red—at the same time and in the same indivisible unity; otherwise how could we be aware of the difference? But we cannot infer this fact of unity of consciousness from the construction of the world as the mechanical science of nature discloses it to us. Even if we were to imagine that molecules of matter were equipped with psychical life, the upshot of this situation could still not be unitary consciousness for the whole of a composite body. Hence the result is that mechanical science of nature must regard unity of the soul as an independent entity over against itself, but this does not exclude the possibility that a system of nature existing beyond these auxiliary concepts formed for the world of appearances contains the origin of the unity of the soul in itself; these are completely transcendent questions.

Residue Remaining from Human Sciences in the Form of Spontaneous Consciousness of the Metaphysical in Human Nature and in Life

But the meta-physical [*sic*] dimension of our *life* as personal experience, that is, as moral-religious truth, remains. Metaphysics—and here we want to draw a long, spun out thread to its end—which traced the life of man to a higher order had not derived its force, as Kant in his abstract and unhistorical mode of thought assumed, from arguments of theoretical reason. The idea of the soul or of a personal God would never have issued from these. On the contrary, these ideas were grounded in inner experience; they developed along with it and reflected on it; and they maintained themselves in direct defiance of conceptual coercion, which knows only a system of ideas and thus can attain to panlogism at most. But experiences of a person's will are exempt from a universally valid presentation, which would be coercive and obligatory for every other intellect. This is a fact which history preaches with a thousand tongues. Therefore we also cannot liken them to compelling metaphysical arguments. Although psychological science can use the comparative method to establish common elements among psychical individuals in the life of the soul, the content of the human will remains nevertheless in the inner freedom [*Burgfreiheit*] of the person. No metaphysics can change any of this; on the contrary, every metaphysics has had to struggle against the protest of clear religious experience in this area, from the earliest Christian mystics who set themselves apart from medieval metaphysics (and were no worse Christians for it) to Tauler and Luther. It is not by force of logical compulsion that we accept a higher system with which our life and death are intertwined; we shall soon see where this logical coherence leads us if we extend it to such a system. On the contrary, from the depths of self-reflection which encounters the experience of dedication and free renunciation of our egoism and thus demonstrates our freedom from the system of nature, the awareness arises that the natural order cannot determine this will. The will's life does not correspond to natural laws; only something which leaves that natural order behind corresponds to it. But these experiences are so personal and so special to the will that the atheist is capable of *living* this metaphysical reality while the *concept of God* in a believer can be a mere worthless shell. Liberation of religious faith from its metaphysical bondage through the Reformation is the expression of this state of affairs. In the Reformation religious life attained autonomy.

And so besides vision into the immeasurable space of the heavenly bodies, which shows the harmony of the cosmos, we also have vision into the depths of our own heart. How far analysis can penetrate with certainty in this area is something the following books will show. But whatever they will turn up, wherever a man by his will breaks through the structure of perception, desire, impulse, and pleasure, and is no longer self-interested, here we have the meta-physical [*sic*] element, which the history of metaphysics we have described has merely reflected in countless images. For metaphysical science is a historically limited phenomenon, but the meta-physical [*sic*] consciousness of the person is eternal.

4. Final Consideration Concerning the Impossibility of a Metaphysical Status of Knowledge

At this conclusion of the history of the metaphysical attitude of mind, a history of a metaphysical science not yet broken by that mind's epistemological standpoint, we are going to try to bring together the facts that have gradually come to light in this history through a general evaluation.

Logical World Structure as the Ideal of Metaphysics

It is inherent in the unity of human consciousness that experiences it contains are conditioned by the context in which they appear. From this ensues the *universal law of relativity which governs our experiences of external reality*. A sensation of taste obviously depends on the sensation which preceded it, and the image of a spatial object depends on the observer's position in space. Thus the task at hand is to define these relative data through a system that is self-sufficient and solid. For incipient science this task was, so to speak, enveloped in an orientation toward space and time and by search for a first cause, and it was intertwined with ethical-religious motives. Thus the term *principle* (*arkhē*) meant, indiscriminately, first cause and explanatory ground of appearances. If one proceeds from the given to its causes, one can achieve certitude through inference of this sort only on the basis of the conceptual necessity of reasoning; hence some degree of logical consciousness of a ground was always connected with the scientific search for causes. The doubt of the Sophists first led to logical awareness of the method of finding causes or substances, and this method was then defined as one of inferring back from the given to its conceptually necessary assumptions. Because knowledge of causes was thus tied to rational argument and the conceptual necessity inherent in it, this knowledge presupposes that logical necessity prevails in the system of nature; without it knowledge would have no foothold. Hence a *theorem concerning the logical system of nature* corresponds to the calm faith in knowledge of causes which lies at the root of all metaphysics. As long as one resolves its logical form into individual formal ingredients as its components, but does not pursue it beyond these through truly analytical investigation, development of this theorem can consist only in describing an extrinsic relation between the form of logical thought and that of the system of nature.

Thus the *monotheistic metaphysics* of the ancients and of the Middle Ages regarded the rationality of nature as a given, and looked on human logic as a second given; a third datum consisted of the correspondence between the two. For this entire state of affairs, then, what one had to find was a dependency relationship [*Bedingung*] in a system that would combine them. This was accomplished by a viewpoint which Aristotle had already sketched out in its basic outlines, namely, that divine reason produced the link between the rationality of nature (grounded in that reason) and human logic which sprang from it.

As the state of knowledge of nature more and more dissolved the coercive force of the theistic foundation, the simpler *formula of Spinoza* emerged, which eliminated divine reason as the middle term. The foundation of Spinoza's metaphysic is the pure self-certitude of the logical mind which subjects reality to itself with methodical deliberateness in the process of knowing, just as in Descartes it designates the first stage of a new attitude of the subject toward reality. From the standpoint of content Descartes' conception of the mechanical structure of the natural universe evolved here into a pantheistic worldview, and so a general animation of nature was transformed into an identity of spatial movements with psychical processes. Regarded epistemologically, knowledge was interpreted here on the basis of identity of the mechanical structure of nature with the logical connection of thoughts. Hence this theory of identity further includes explaining *psychical* processes according to a mechanical, hence logical, system: *the objective and universal metaphysical significance of the syllogism* [*Logismus*]. In this respect the theory of attributes expresses the *immediate* identity of the causal system of nature with the logical connection of truths in the human mind. Spinoza *eliminates the middle term* of this connection, which had previously been a God distinct from the world; the order and connection of ideas is identical with the order and connection of things.[17] In sharp assertion of this identity Spinoza thinks of even the order of succession in the two series as in correspondence: knowledge of the effect depends on knowledge of the cause and includes it.[18] He devises a system of axioms and definitions one can use to construct the world system. This takes place through obviously fallacious arguments, for from Spinoza's premises one can infer a multiplicity of independent entities just as readily as unity in the divine substance. For, after all, unity of world order and multiplicity of solid atomic particles at its basis are merely two sides of the same mechanical, that is, logical world system. Thus Spinoza had to asssume his pantheism at the outset to enable him to deduce it. Nevertheless, in his system the consistency of the metaphysical principle of sufficient reason appears with a fullness which did not yet exist among the ancients. If the ancients had allowed human will to stand as an *imperium in imperio,* the formula of panlogism now annulled this sovereignty of spiritual life. "In the nature of things there is nothing contingent; rather, everything has been determined by necessity of divine nature to exist and function in a certain way."[19]

In the *principle of sufficient reason Leibniz* has devised a formula for metaphysics that expresses the necessary system in nature as a principle of thought. In positing this principle metaphysics reaches its formal conclusion. For the principle is not a logical but a metaphysical principle, that is, it does not express a mere law of thought but at the same time a law of the structure of reality and therefore also the rule for the relationship between thought and being. Its final and most perfect formulation is one which occurred in the correspondence with Clarke not long before Leibniz's death. "This principle is that of the need for a sufficient reason as to why a thing should exist or an event should transpire or a truth should exist."[20] With Leibniz this principle always appears alongside the principle of contradiction; in fact the principle of contradiction is the ground for necessary truths, whereas that of sufficient reason is the ground for facts and actual truths. But even here the metaphysical significance of this principle betrays itself. Although factual truths go back to the will of God, nevertheless intellect ultimately directs this will according to Leibniz. And so behind the will, once again, the visage of a logical world ground appears. Leibniz expresses this with full clarity:

> It is true, as they say, that there is nothing without a sufficient reason why it is and why it is thus rather than in some other way. But they add that this sufficient reason is in accordance with the simple will of God; just as when one asks why matter was not placed otherwise in space or why the same locations continue to be maintained among bodies. But this is precisely to maintain that God wills something without there being any sufficient reason for his will, contrary to the maxim or the general rule for everything that transpires.[21]

According to this, the principle of sufficient reason signifies that one asserts an unbroken logical system which comprises every fact and accordingly every principle. It is the formula for the less comprehensive principle set down by Aristotle,[22] which now comprises not only the structure of the cosmos in concepts, that is, eternal forms, but also the ground of every change, indeed even in the spiritual world.

Christian Wolff traced this principle to the fact that something cannot come into being from nothing and accordingly to the principle of knowledge from which we have seen metaphysics draw its theorems [Sätze] since Parmenides.

> If an object A contains something within it that explains why B exists, whether B is something in A or outside A, then one calls what one encounters in A the ground of B; A itself is called the cause, and one can say of B that it is grounded in A. This is to say that the ground is that which explains why something is and the cause is an object that contains within it the ground for something else.

> Whenever something is present which explains why it exists, then it has a sufficient ground. Hence when such a ground is not on hand, then there is nothing which explains why something exists, that is, why it can really come to be, and so it must arise out of nothing. Therefore whatever cannot arise out of nothing must have a sufficient ground why it exists, just as something must be possible in itself and have a cause which can bring it to actuality when we speak of objects which are not necessary. Because it is impossible that something should come from nothing, then everything which exists must also have its sufficient reason why it exists.[23]

Thus we now recognize retrospectively in the principle of sufficient reason the expression of the principle which has guided metaphysical knowledge forward from its beginning.

And if we look forward beyond Leibniz and Wolff, we find finally that *Hegel*, disdaining any fear of paradox, has developed the assumption contained in the principle of sufficient reason concerning the logical world system into a principle of all reality in his system. There have not been lacking persons who question this assumption and yet wish to hold on to metaphysics; Schopenhauer did this in his theory of will as the ground of the world. But an inner contradiction in its foundation condemns every metaphysics of this sort from the start. We cannot make intelligible what lies beyond our experience, even by way of analogy, much less can we prove it, if one denies ontological validity and meaning to the means for such grounding and proof, that is, to the logical system itself.

Reality's Contradiction of This Ideal and the Untenability of Metaphysics

The *"great principle"* *of sufficient reason* (as Leibniz repeatedly designates it), the ultimate formula of metaphysical knowledge, is however *not a law of reasoning* to which our
intellect would be subject as though to its fate. Inasmuch as *metaphysics pursues its demand
for knowledge* of the subject of the world's course in this principle all the way *back to its first
premise, it demonstrates its own impossibility.*

The principle of sufficient reason, in Leibniz's sense, is not a law of the mind; we
cannot place it on a par with reason's law of contradiction. For reason's law of contradiction is valid at every point in our knowledge. Whenever we assert something, it must be
in harmony with this law, and if we find an assertion to conflict with it, that assertion is
thereby annulled for us. Hence this law of reasoning controls all knowledge and certitude. The question never arises for us as to whether we wish to apply it or not; on the
contrary, as surely as we assert something, we subject our assertion to it. It can happen
that we might not notice the conflict of an assertion with reason's law of contradiction at
a given point. But as soon as one calls the attention of even a totally uneducated person to
this contradiction, he does not escape the consequence that, of assertions which contradict each other in this way, only one can be true and one must be false. In contrast, the
principle of sufficient reason, as understood by Leibniz and Wolff, obviously does not
have the same position in our thought, and it was therefore not right when Leibniz
juxtaposed the two principles as principles of equal value. The entire history of human
thought teaches us this. During the epoch of mythical thought man saw himself as
confronted by will-endowed powers which behaved with unpredictable freedom. It
would have been a waste of time if a logician had approached this man caught up in
mythical ideas and had explained clearly to him that the necessary system of the world is
canceled where his gods prevail. That sort of insight would never have destroyed his
convictions about his gods but would only have clarified further for him the element that
transcends the logical system of the world and his sort of faith embraces as a mighty
force. At the dawning of science man looked for inner coherence in the cosmos, but his
faith in the free power of the gods in its midst persisted in him. In the heyday of
metaphysics the Greek regarded his will as free. What he possessed here in living and
immediate knowledge did not become less certain because he was likewise aware of
rational necessity; on the contrary, it seemed to him that holding fast to what he felt as
freedom in his immediate experiences was compatible with this logical awareness. Medieval man displays an exaggerated tendency toward logical considerations, but this never
prompted him to give up the religious-historical world in which he lived and which
allowed him to miss the ubiquitously compelling conceptual structure. And experiences
of daily life confirm what history has shown. The human mind does not find it intolerable to see the logical system, which lets the mind go beyond the immediately given,
interrupted when it experiences freedom of will and action in living and immediate
knowledge.

If the principle of sufficient reason as formulated by Leibniz does not possess the
absolute validity of a law of reason, how can we define its position in the context of
intellectual life? While we search out its *locus,* we are also testing the *legal footing* of every
really *consistent metaphysics.*

If we distinguish the logical ground from the real one and the logical system from the
real one, then we can express the fact of thought's logical consistency, as displayed in

reasoning, through the principle: posit the ground, and you posit the effect too; remove the effect, and you remove the ground. In fact we find this necessity of linkage in every syllogism. It can be shown that *we can perceive and comprehend nature* only insofar as we search for this *structure of conceptual necessity* in it. We cannot even imagine the external world, much less know it, without ultimately searching out a conceptually necessary structure in it. For we cannot recognize particular impressions and images which make up the given as an objective reality in themselves. In the actual framework in which they exist in consciousness, because of its unity, they are relative, hence one can use them only in this framework to establish an external state of affairs or a natural cause. We relate every spatial image to the position of our eye and of our hand, with which we seek to grasp it. Every passing impression is relative to the mass of impressions in the percipient and to their organization. The relation in which stimuli of the external world stand to our senses determines the qualities of sensation. We cannot directly judge intensities of sensation and express them in numerical values; on the contrary, we merely designate the relation of one intensity of sensation to another. Thus producing a system is not a process which follows on one's grasping of reality. On the contrary, no one takes a fleeting image in isolation as reality; we possess it in a context by which we seek to establish reality even in advance of any scientific activity.

Scientific activity introduces method into this process. It shifts the focal point for the system of determinations which organizes impressions away from the mobile and changeable ego into this system itself. It develops an objective space in which individual intelligence is located in a specific place; an objective time on the continuum of which the present of the individual occupies a point; and an objective causal structure and fixed elementary units between which that structure is located. The entire thrust of science is to replace fleeting images, in which a multitude of things struggle with one another, with objective reality and objective system by means of the relations thought pursues among those images present in consciousness. And every judgment about the existence and condition of an external object is ultimately determined by the conceptual structure in which this existence or condition is posited as necessary. The fortuitous coincidence of impressions in a changing subject constitutes merely the starting point for constructing universally valid reality.

Consequently, the principle that every given stands in a ratiocinatively necessary framework in which it is conditioned and itself conditions first of all controls the solution of the task of establishing universally valid and fixed judgments about the external world. Scientific analysis is *conscious of relations* which determine what is given in perception when it describes the *relativity* in which the given appears in the external world. Thus every perception of objects of the external world is already subject to the principle of sufficient reason.

This is one side of the matter. On the other side, however, *critical application of the principle of sufficient reason must renounce metaphysical knowledge* and be satisfied with the conception of external dependency relations in the external world. *For, because of their differing origins, components of the given are heterogeneous, that is, incommensurable.* Consequently, they cannot be reduced to one another. One cannot bring a color into direct inner relationship with a sound or with the impression of density. Thus study of the external world must leave unresolved the inner condition of what is given in nature and must content itself with arranging an organization based on space, time, and motion, that combines experiences into a system. Thus the conception and knowledge of the external world is subject to this law: Everything given in sense perception finds itself in a ratiocinatively necessary framework in which it is conditioned and itself conditions, and only in this framework is it useful for understanding what exists. But conditions of consciousness restrict use of this law merely to creating an external system of conditions which assigns facts their place in the complex of experiences. Precisely the scientific requirement of producing such a ratiocinatively necessary structure has led people to overlook the inner substantial structure of the world. A system of mathematical-mechanical nature took its place and only then did sciences of the external world become exact. Thus, because of their own inner requirements, these sciences rejected metaphysics as barren, even before the epistemological movement turned against it in Locke, Hume, and Kant.

But the *relation of the epistemological law of sufficient reason to human sciences is a different one* than to sciences of the external world; this, too, makes it impossible to have a metaphysical system govern all of reality. Something I am aware of, as a condition of myself, is not relative in the way an external object is. The truth of an external object does not exist as a conformity of image with reality, because this reality is not given in any consciousness and it therefore eludes all comparison. One cannot pretend to know how an object appears when no one is conscious of it. On the contrary, what I experience in myself as a fact of consciousness is therefore present for me because I am aware of it; a fact of consciousness is nothing other than something I am aware of. Our hoping and striving, our wishing and willing: this inner world as such is the whole thing. Regardless of what view one might entertain about components of these psychical facts—and Kant's entire theory of inner sense can appear logically justified only as such a viewpoint—the fact that such facts of consciousness exist is not thereby affected.[24] Therefore what we are aware of, as a condition of our very self, is not given to us relatively as an external object is. Not until we wish to bring this immediate awareness to more distinct knowledge or to communicate it to others does the question arise how far we are thereby transcending what is contained in inner perception. Judgments we express are valid only on condition that our cognitive acts do not modify inner perception and that this dividing and combining, judging and inferring, contains identical facts under the new conditions of consciousness. Hence the principle of sufficient reason, which says that every given exists in a logically necessary system which conditions it and which it conditions in turn, has never had the same standing relative to spiritual facts that it is entitled to claim with respect to the external world. It is in this case not the law which governs every conception of reality. Only insofar as individuals occupy a place in the external world, appear at a certain time, and produce perceptible effects in the external world do we insert them into the web of this system. Thus, to be sure, a comprehensive conception of mental facts assumes their external ordering into the system fashioned by natural science, but spiritual facts confront one as actuality and possess its full reality independently of this system.

So we have recognized in the principle of sufficient reason the logical root of every consistent metaphysics, that is, of the science of reason, and we have recognized in the relationship of the ensuing logical ideal toward reality the origin of the difficulties of this science of reason. This relationship makes a large portion of previously described *phenomena of metaphysics comprehensible to us from a most general point of view*. Only metaphysics which is a science of reason, that is, which tries to demonstrate a logical world system, is consistent. The science of reason has therefore been the backbone of European metaphysics, as it were. But the logical system of a universally valid science could not exhaust the authentic, naturally strong person's feeling for life nor that segment of the world which was especially his own. Thought could not manage to transmit particular contents of experience, that were separate from one another in their origins, to one another. But every attempt to demonstrate something other than a logical system in reality destroyed the form of science in favor of its content.

The entire phenomenology of metaphysics has shown that metaphysical concepts and principles have not arisen out of the pure relationship between knowledge and sensation but out of the labor knowledge expends on a system created by the totality of the mind. In this totality we encounter not only the ego but also an "other" that is independent of it: It is present to the will, which this other resists (though the will has no power to change impressions), and to feeling, which suffers from it—immediately, therefore, and not through some sort of argument, but as life. From a natural standpoint, the will to knowledge would like to prevail over and master this subject and active cause which we encounter. At first the will to knowledge is not conscious of the connection between self-consciousness and the subject of the course of nature. Self-consciousness confronts the will independently in external sensation and seeks to comprehend the subject with the available means of concept, judgment, and argument, that is, as a logically necessary system. But we can never entirely reduce to ideas what is given in the totality of our being. Either the content of metaphysics became inadequate to the demands of living human nature or the proofs turned out to be inadequate inasmuch as they tried to go beyond what understanding can establish from experience. Thus metaphysics became a playground for specious reasoning.

In the sphere of the given, whatever derives from an independent origin possesses an indestructible core for knowledge, and we cannot reduce to one another contents of experience which differ from one another in their provenance. That is why metaphysics has been filled with false deductions and antinomies. Thus there arose first the antinomies between intellect, which reasons with finite magnitudes, and intuition—antinomies which belong to knowledge of external nature. Their battleground, indeed, existed in the metaphysics of antiquity. One cannot reach the constant element in space, time, and motion by way of conceptual construction. One cannot explain the unity of the world and its formulation in the rational system of universal forms and laws through analysis, which breaks things down into elements, and synthesis, which assembles things out of these elements. The self-contained element in an intuitive image is always annulled once again through the limitless will to knowledge which transcends that self-contained element. In addition other antinomies appear, for imagination [*das Vorstellen*] wants to include living psychical individuals woven into the world process, and knowledge wants to subject them to its system. That is how the theological and metaphysical antinomies of the Middle Ages mainly came about, and when the modern period undertook to understand psychical behavior itself in its causal context, contradictions between ratiocinative thought and inner experience also appeared in metaphysical treatment of psychology. These antinomies cannot be resolved. For positive science they do not exist, and for epistemology their subjective origin is obvious. Hence they do not disturb the harmony of our mental life. But they have pulverized metaphysics.

If metaphysical thought, in defiance of such contradictions, really wishes to know the subject of the world, then for it this subject can be nothing other than—rationalism [*Logismus*]. Every metaphysics which claims it seeks to know the subject of the world's process but looks for something other than logical necessity in it falls into an obvious contradiction between its goal and its means. *Thought cannot discover any other than a logical system in reality.* For because only the state of our own self-consciousness is immediately given to us, hence we cannot look directly into the inner core of nature, if we wish to fashion an idea of that core independently of a rational process [*Logismus*], all we are doing is transferring our own inner self into nature. But this transference can only be a poetical play of analogical understanding, which at one moment introduces the abysses and dark powers of our spiritual life, at another moment its placid harmony, lucid free will, or creative imagination into the subject of the process of nature. Accordingly, metaphysical systems of this tendency, taken in a rigorously scientific sense, amount simply to a protest against the logically necessary system. So they lead to the view that the world contains more things and other things than just this system. In this point alone lay the temporary importance of the metaphysics of Schopenhauer and of writers akin to him. Fundamentally, it was a nineteenth-century brand of mysticism and a life-and-will-powered protest against all metaphysics as logical science. When, on the contrary, knowledge based on the principle of sufficient reason decides to take possesssion of the subject of the world process, it discovers only logical necessity as the core of the world; hence neither the God of religion nor the experience of freedom exists for it.

Understanding Cannot Univocally Define the Bonds of Metaphysical World Structure

Let us go further. Metaphysics can produce a link between inner and outer experiences only by using notions about an inner material connection between them. And if we focus on these notions, the result is the impossibility of metaphysics. For these ideas are not susceptible of clear and univocal definition.

We have seen that the process of specialization in which science distinguishes itself from other systems of culture is constantly going forward. The purpose-nexus of knowledge did not free itself all at once from the compact state of all the forces of the mind. How great a similarity still persisted between nature, which passes over from one inner state into another in virtue of its own inner vivacity, or the limiting principle at the heart of the world, which attracts matter to itself and shapes it, and the divine forces of Hesiod's theogony! And how long a time did the view remain dominant which traced the harmonious ordering of the universe to a system of psychical beings! Intelligence freed itself from this inner togetherness with difficulty. It accustomed itself gradually to manage with less and less life and soul in nature and to trace the system of the world's course to ever simpler forms of inner connection. Finally, even purposefulness as the form of inner material structure was called into question. *Substance and causality* remained behind as the two *inner bonds* which hold together the world's course in all its parts.

And if we recall the fate of the concepts of substance and causality, the upshot is: metaphysics as science is impossible.

The conceptually necessary system posits substance and causality as fixed magnitudes in the chain of successive and simultaneous impressions. Now metaphysics experiences something wonderful. In this period in which epistemology has not yet broken its self-assurance, metaphysics is convinced that it knows what one means by the terms *substance* and *causality*. In reality its history demonstrates constant change in defining these concepts and unsuccessful attempts at developing them to a point of clarity free from contradiction.

Indeed, we cannot clarify even our concept of an *object* [*des Dinges*]. How can we distinguish the unity to which manifold characteristics, conditions, action and passion inhere from these latter things? Or the constant element from changes? Or how can I determine when one and the same object is still undergoing change and when it ceases to exist at all? How can I distinguish what remains in it from what changes? Finally, how can I think of this continuing unity as being located somewhere in a spatially extended locale? Everything spatial is divisible and therefore nowhere contains a cohesive indivisible unity; on the other hand, if I prescind from space, all sensible qualities of the object disappear. Nevertheless, one cannot explain this unity by the mere coming together of different sensations (in perception and association); for unity expresses an inner coherence precisely in contrast with that.

Prompted by these difficulties, the *concept of substance* emerges. As we have shown historically, it arose out of the need to grasp conceptually the constant element we assumed to exist in every object as its stable unity and to use it in solving the problem of relating changing impressions to a permanent something in which they are bound together. But because that concept is nothing more than the scientific elaboration of the idea of an *object,* it just makes all the more explicit the difficulties inherent in that. We have seen even Aristotle's metaphysical genius struggle in vain to solve this. It is also useless to replace substance with *atom*. For along with it one transfers its contradictions as well into this indivisible spatial element, this mini-object. Natural science must be content—insofar as it fashions a concept of something we cannot further break down in our process of nature—with simply excluding these difficulties; it renounces any hope of solving them. Thus the metaphysical concept of atom is transformed into a mere regulatory concept for ordering experience. Nor do we solve the difficulties if *we shift the substance of objects to their form.* We have seen the whole metaphysics of substantial forms grapple unsuccessfully with difficulties in this concept; so here too science, observing its limitations about what it cannot research, must ultimately be content with treating this concept as a mere symbol. It stands for a condition which knowledge encounters in its quest to organize facts around an objective unity among them; but no one can explain its actual content.

And at the core of the concept of substance itself, whether one refers it to atoms or to forms in nature, an insuperable difficulty remains. Science of a logically necessary system of the external world suggests that we treat substance as a fixed magnitude and therefore transfer change, becoming, and alteration into relationships among these elements. But as soon as one takes this procedure as something more than an auxiliary construction of conditions needed to conceptualize the system of nature, and as soon as one derives from that a determination about the metaphysical essense of the substantial, a kind of Chinese puzzle results. Inner change now slides over into physical event; it is here that the color now flashes and the tone sounds. The only choice we have then is to oppose the rigid mechanism of nature with the inner vitality of psychical events and thus to give up the metaphysical unity of the world system we were looking for or to understand the unchanging elements at their true value as mere auxiliary concepts.

It would be tedious if we now wished to show how the concept of *causality* succumbs to similar difficulties. Here too mere association cannot explain the idea of an inner connection, and yet understanding cannot devise a formula in which a concept composed of sensible or conceptually clear elements would describe the content of the causal idea. And so causality likewise ceases being a metaphysical concept and becomes a mere auxiliary means for mastering external experiences. For natural science can recognize as a component of its conceptual framework only something it can prove by elements of external perception and conceptual operations which employ them.

Thus if we cannot comprehend substance and causality as objective forms of the course of nature, then the next best thing at hand for a science which works with abstract logically prepared elements would be at least to hold on to *a priori forms of intelligence in them*. Kant's epistemology, which used abstractions of metaphysics for epistemological purposes, thought that it could rest content with that. Then these concepts would at least make possible a solid, although subjective, framework of appearances.

If they were such forms of the intelligence itself, then as such they must be totally transparent to that intelligence. Instances of such transparency are the relation of the whole to its parts and the concept of identity and difference. In them there is no quarrel over interpretation of concepts: B can think only the same as A about the concept of identity. Concepts of causality and substance are obviously not of this type. They possess a murky core of factuality which we cannot reduce to sensible or intelligible elements. Unlike concepts of numbers they cannot be univocally broken down into their elements; in fact their analysis has led to endless controversy. Or how can one imagine, say, a permanent substratum in which characteristics and behavior change, without this active element itself undergoing any change? How can one make that comprehensible to the mind?

If substance and causality were such a priori forms of intelligence, hence given together with the intelligence itself, then it would be impossible to give up any components of these forms of thought and exchange them for others. But in reality, as we saw, mythical thought assumed a free vivacity and spiritual power in causes which, given our concept of causes, we no longer encounter in the natural order. Elements that people originally imagined in a cause have undergone continual diminution and others have replaced them in a process of adapting the original idea to the external world. These concepts have a history of development.

In this phenomenological treatment of metaphysics, we can advance the precise reason why ideas of substance and causality prove to be incapable of univocal and clear definition only as a possibility; epistemology will have to demonstrate it later on. The living origin of both concepts lies in the totality of the powers of our soul, in the fullness of living self-consciousness which experiences the activity of an other. We need not assume here a subsequent transference from self-consciousness to the *per se* lifeless external world by which that world receives life in mythical thought. The other can be given as a living, functioning reality in self-consciousness just as originally as the self can. But intelligence can never completely explain what is given in the totality of the powers of the soul. The process of specialization of knowledge in the course of scientific progress, as a process of abstraction, can therefore prescind from ever more elements of this living being; yet the irreducible core remains. In this way one can explain all the features which these two concepts of substance and causality have exhibited in the course of metaphysics, and one can see that even in the future every device of understanding will prove powerless against these features. Therefore genuine natural science will treat these concepts as mere symbols for an X, which its reasoning requires. The expansion of this process then consists in analysis of consciousness, which points out the original value of these symbols and the reasons why natural-scientific reasoning requires them.

The human sciences are related altogether differently to these concepts. From concepts of substance and causality they legitimately hold on only to what has been given in self-consciousness and inner experience, and they give up what has stemmed from their adaptation to the external world. Hence they may make no direct use of these concepts to designate their objects. Direct usage has often harmed them and has never been of use to them at any point. For these abstract concepts have never been able to tell the student of human nature more about it than what was given in self-consciousness from where they have issued. Even if we could apply the concept of substance to the soul, it could not serve as the basis for immortality, even in a religious order of ideas. If one traces the origin of the soul to God, then what has come into being can also perish, or whatever has separated itself in a process of emanation can revert to unity. But if one excludes the assumption of creation or of emanation of soul-substances from God, then the soul-substance calls for an atheistic world order; in that case souls, whether they exist alone without God or independently alongside God, are nonactualized gods [*ungewordene Götter*].

A Content-Bearing Conception of the World's Structure Cannot Be Demonstrated

As metaphysics continues about its business, its assumptions lead to new difficulties which make it impossible to accomplish that business. *It is not possible to demonstrate a definite inner objective structure of reality, such that remaining possible structures are excluded.* At still another point, then, we establish that metaphysics as a science is impossible.

For either one will deduce this structure from a priori truths, or one will demonstrate it from the given. *A priori deduction* is impossible. Kant drew the final conclusion of metaphysics in the direction of increasing abstractions when he actually developed a system of a priori concepts and truths such as had already hovered before the minds of Aristotle and Descartes. But he proved irrefutably that even under this condition "employment of our reason extends only to objects of possible experience." But perhaps the state of metaphysics is not even as favorable as Kant assumed it was. If causality and substance are in no way univocally definable concepts but rather express irreducible facts of consciousness, they disqualify themselves entirely from any role in logically deducing a world structure. Or else metaphysics proceeds *from the given back to its presuppositions.* In that case, if one disregards the arbitrary notions of German philosophy of nature, there is unanimity about the course of nature: Its analysis leads one to particles that interact with one another according to laws as the ultimate necessary conditions of natural science. But we saw that for us no sort of connection exists between the condition of these atoms and the facts of their interplay, the law of nature, and the forms of nature. We saw that no similarity exists between such atoms and the psychical units that enter into the world's course as unique individuals, actively experience inner changes in it, and vanish from it again. Consequently, the ultimate concepts attained by sciences of the real do not embrace the unity of the world process. For after all neither atoms nor laws are real subjects of the process of nature. For subjects which make up society are given to us, whereas the subject of nature or most subjects of nature are not; on the contrary, we possess only the image of the course of nature and knowledge of its external organization. However, this process of nature itself together with its organization is only a phenomenon for our consciousness. Subjects that we ascribe to it as particles therefore likewise belong to phenomenality. They are only auxiliary concepts for the idea of structure in a system of predicative determinations which make up nature: properties, relations, changes, and motions. They are therefore only part of the system of predicative determinations whose real subject remains unknown.

Metaphysics, which knows how to resign itself and only *seeks to link into a conceivable whole the ultimate concepts to which empirical sciences attain,* can never hope to overcome either the relativity of the sphere of experience which these concepts describe or that of the standpoint and makeup of intelligence which unifies experiences into a whole. And as we show this, it becomes clear from two more points of view that metaphysics as a science is impossible.

Metaphysics does not overcome the relativity of the sphere of experience from which it has drawn its concepts. The ultimate concepts of the sciences lay down conditions of their conceivability for the specific number of given phenomenal states which make up the system of our experience. But accumulation of experiences has caused our notion of these conditions to change. Thus antiquity had no knowledge of a structure of changes according to laws, which today combines our experiences into a system. Hence such an idea of conditions always has only a relative truth, that is, it does not designate a reality but *entia rationis,* conceptual objects which make it possible for thought to govern and to intervene in a given limited range of phenomena. If one supposed a sudden expansion of human experience, then the *entia rationis* which are supposed to express premises for these experiences would have to accommodate themselves to its expansion. Who can say how far this change would extend? And if one seeks now for a unifying framework for these ultimate concepts, the epistemological value of the thus ensuing hypothesis cannot be greater than that of its foundation. The metaphysical world which reveals itself behind auxiliary concepts of natural science is—though to the second power, so to speak—an *ens rationis.* Does not the entire history of modern metaphysics confirm this? Spinoza's substance, the monists' atoms, Leibniz's monads, and Herbart's reals confuse natural sciences because they introduce elements from inner psychical life into the process of nature and they degrade spiritual life because they look for natural structure in the will. They cannot eliminate the duality which permeates the history of metaphysics, that between the mechanical-atomistic worldview and the worldview which proceeds from the whole.

Metaphysics is just as incapable of overcoming the limited subjectivity of the life of the soul, which underlies every metaphysical combination of ultimate scientific concepts. This assertion comprises two propositions. A unitary conception of the subject of the world's course comes about only by way of what the life of the soul contributes to it. This life of the soul, however, is in constant development, is incalculable in its further developments, is historically relative and limited at every point, and is thus incapable of combining ultimate concepts of special sciences in an objective and conclusive manner.

For what does it mean that one can *represent* or *conceive* those ultimate facts which special sciences strive for, that is, as metaphysics tries to produce them? If metaphysics wishes to combine these facts in a comprehensible idea, the chief thing it has at its disposal for this purpose is just the principle of contradiction. But where contradiction exists between two determinations of the structure of experiences, then one needs a positive principle to decide between the contradictory propositions. When a metaphysician maintains that he is using only the principle of contradiction to combine in comprehensible fashion the ultimate facts to which science attains, one can nevertheless always point to positive ideas which are secretly guiding his choices. Hence conceivability must mean something more here than freedom from contradiction. In fact metaphysical systems also produce their organization by means which differ altogether in strength of content. Conceivability is here just an abstract expression for representability, which however means nothing more than that *thought, when it abandons the solid ground of actuality and analysis,* will nevertheless be *guided by residues of that actuality.* Within this range of representability it often happens that contrary things appear to be equally possible, even compelling. A famous statement of Leibniz says: "The monads are without windows." But Lotze rightly observes on this point: "It would not surprise me if Leibniz had used the same figurative expression in a contrary sense to teach that the monads *did* have windows which would enable their inner states to communicate with one another, and this assertion would have had about the same justification, or perhaps more, than the one which he preferred."[25] Some metaphysicians hold that each one of their molecules can act or be acted on; others believe that mutual interplay under common laws is conceivable only in a consciousness which binds together all particular beings. Everywhere in such matters metaphysics, as queen over a realm of the dead, deals only with the shades of bygone truths, some of which forbid her to think something while others command her to think it. These shades of beings which covertly guide our representations and make representability possible are either images from matter provided by the senses or representations from psychical life given in inner experience. Modern science has recognized the phenomenal character of the first, and for that reason materialistic metaphysics, as such, has fallen into decline. Where it is really a question of the subject of nature and not merely predicative determinations, such as motion and sensible qualities give us, then for the most part, either secretly or consciously, representations of psychical life decide what we can or cannot conceive as a metaphysical system. It is all the same whether Hegel wants to make world reason the subject of nature, or Schopenhauer makes it blind will, or Leibniz makes it perceptive monads, or Lotze makes it overarching consciousness which mediates all interaction, or the most recent monists see psychical life flashing forth in each atom: It is images of one's own self, images of psychic life, which have guided the metaphysician as he decided on what is thinkable, images whose secretly operative power have transformed the world for him into a monstrously fantastic reflection of his own self. For this is the final outcome; the metaphysical mind perceives itself, fantastically magnified, as though in second sight.

Thus *at the terminus of its path metaphysics coincides with epistemology,* which deals with the comprehending subject itself. Transformation of the world into the knowing subject through these modern systems is in effect the euthanasia of metaphysics. Novalis tells a tale of a young man seized by a yearning for the secrets of nature. He forsakes his beloved, travels through many lands in search of the great goddess Isis and the vision of her wonderful countenance. Finally, he stands before the goddess of nature, lifts the light, shining veil and—his beloved sinks into his arms. When it seems that the soul is about to succeed in perceiving the subject of the course of nature itself, without its masks and its veil, then it discovers in that subject—itself. In fact, this is the final word of all metaphysics, and one can say—now that that word has been expressed in all languages, whether of understanding, or of emotion, or of the depths of the soul in recent centuries—it seems that metaphysics even in this respect has nothing more of importance to say.

We reason further with the help of the second proposition. This personal content of the life of the soul changes continually through history, is unpredictable, is relative, and is limited, and so it cannot make a universally valid unity of experiences possible. This is the deepest insight to which our phenomenology of metaphysics has attained, in contrast with constructions of the epochs of humanity. Every metaphysical system is representative only for that situation in which a soul has caught sight of the riddle of the world. It has the power to recapture for us this situation and this period, the state of the soul, and the way men see nature and themselves. It does this more profoundly and comprehensively than poetic works, in which the life of the soul governs persons and objects in accord with its own law. However, spiritual content changes with the historical setting of the life of the soul, and it is the spiritual content which gives unity   I life to a metaphysical system. We can neither define this change within boundaries nor predict its tendency.

The Greek in the period of Plato or Aristotle was bound to a specific mode of representing first causes. The Christian view evolved, and then it was as though a wall had been removed, behind which one saw a new way of representing the first cause of the world. For the medieval mind, knowledge of divine and human things was complete in its basic outlines, and no one in eleventh-century Europe had a notion that empirical science was destined to transform the world; but then something happened which no one could have foreseen, and modern empirical science came into being. And thus we too must tell ourselves that we do not know what lies behind the walls which surround us today. The life of the soul itself, not just this or that idea, changes in the history of humanity. And this awareness of the limits of our knowledge, which issues from historical insight into evolution of the life of the soul, is a different and a deeper awareness than Kant had, for whom, in the spirit of the eighteenth century, metaphysical consciousness was without any history.

Skepticism, which has dogged metaphysics like a shadow, furnished the proof that we are locked up in our impressions, so to speak, so that we do not know their cause and cannot say anything about the real constitution of the external world. All sense impressions are relative and permit no conclusion as to what produces them. Even the concept of cause is a relation which we foist upon objects, and we have no justification for applying it to the external world. Moreover, the history of metaphysics has shown that with respect to the relationship between thought and objects we can formulate no clear idea, whether we label it identity or parallelism or correlation or correspondence. For a representation can never be identical with its object, as long as we conceive of that object as a reality independent of it. A representation is not an object inserted into the soul, and we cannot make it coincide with an object. If we water down the concept of identity to one of similarity, we cannot, strictly speaking, apply even this concept here; the representation of agreement is diverted in this way into the indefinite. The rightful successor of the skeptic is the epistemologist. Here we have arrived at the boundary where the next book will begin: at the epistemological standpoint of humanity. For modern scientific consciousness is conditioned on one side by the fact of relatively independent special sciences and on the other by the epistemological attitude of man to his objects. Positivism has built up its philosophical foundation predominantly on the first side of that consciousness; transcendental philosophy has done so on the other side. At the point of intellectual history where the metaphysical attitude of man ends the next book will begin and will describe the history of modern scientific consciousness in its relation to human sciences insofar as it is determined by its epistemological stance towards objects. This historical description will still have to show how the residues of the metaphysical epoch were overcome only gradually so that people drew the consequences of the epistemological attitude only very slowly. It will make clear how in the metaphysical foundation itself the abstractions which the depicted history of metaphysics has left behind have been swept away only at a late date and even to this day still very incompletely. Thus it should lead us to the psychological standpoint, which undertakes to solve the problem of knowledge not by the abstractions of isolated intelligence but by the entirety of the facts of consciousness. For Kant accomplished only the self-dissolution of abstractions which the history of metaphysics we have described has created; now it is time calmly to become aware of the reality of inner life and, taking it as a point of departure, to determine what nature and history are to this inner life.

Appendix: Supplementary Material from the Manuscripts

[*Translator's Note:* The following material was appended to volume I of the *Gesammelte Schriften*. The preliminary remarks, arrangement of the text, and notes are by Bernhard Groethuysen, editor of the 1923 edition of volume I.]

Preliminary Remarks

Among Dilthey's literary remains from the years 1904–1906, when he was considering a new edition of the first volume of the *Introduction to the Human Sciences,* there are some sketches for a preface and for supplementary materials, which we are printing here. Insofar as the supplementary materials relate to the first book of the volume, they contain declarations on the one hand about how Dilthey sought to justify his own methodological position as against Windelband and Rickert and on the other hand about how he made his rejection of sociology more specific with respect to Simmel. For the controversy with Windelband, presented here only briefly, there is among the literary remains a further statement from an earlier period (1896), which is published in volume 5 ("The World of Spirit") of this edition. The supplements to the second book mainly offer a plan for two new historical segments Dilthey wished to insert ("The Fusion of Greek Philosophy with the Worldview and Life Concepts of the Romans" and "The Fusion of Greco-Roman Philosophy with Oriental Revealed Faith"). In the further course of his historical research Dilthey had acknowledged more and more the independent significance of the Roman view of life for the spiritual evolution of the West. He had set down his thoughts on the subject in the essay "The Interpretation and Analysis of Man in the Fifteenth and Sixteenth Centuries" published in the *Archiv für Geschichte der Philosophie* in 1891 and spun them out still further, in part, in his lectures. They were then supposed to be worked into the text of the new edition of the *Introduction* to supplement the picture of ancient-medieval development at a crucial point. The plan was not carried out. The sketch for it is being printed here along with a reference to the treatise published in the second volume of this edition. The remaining supplements offer expansions of particular points in the historical section.

Preface[1]

Because this volume has been unavailable in the book trade for some years now, at the request of the publisher I have agreed to a second edition even before its sequel can appear. The first, introductory book of the volume appears unchanged. It arose from an effort to gain recognition for the independence of the human sciences, their inner coherence, and their life from their own resources. And so a number of expressions in this polemic could well be toned down today when younger, hardy combatants strive to solve the same problem in their own way. And yet it did not seem advisable to me to destroy in it the coloring of the period which first gave rise to the entire enterprise. And so I want only to repel some misunderstandings here that have appeared in controversy concerning this volume, confessing that I have occasioned them in some measure through the energy of my expression.

The second book, which contains the history of the metaphysical conception of spirit, society, and history in antiquity and the Middle Ages, has been improved and expanded in many ways. Two entirely new sections have been added. I had to maintain necessary limits in organizing the whole that much the more rigorously. For, after all, it was not a history of philosophy. I wanted to show how the human mind conceives the historico-social world as a problem at a specific point in that world's evolution and how, on the basis of varying presuppositions, it introduces anticipations of the conception of this world, so to speak. Among these the greatest and most influential was the metaphysical conception of the spiritual world in its various modifications.

At the end of this period man's mind freed itself from the illusion that the metaphysical conception of the spiritual-historical-social world entails just as much as the metaphysical conception of the physical world does. Behind this illusion of course there are truths hidden that the experiential standpoint of the human sciences expresses more appropriately. For in this matter the scientist is like the artist: the artist's style—as the expression of a power of experiencing and seeing personalities, periods, and trends in just such a way and of receiving precisely these impressions of feeling about reality—is always one-sided when compared with unfathomable reality; but that style makes it possible to experience, see, and describe in a new way. It is always the case that a specific kind of movement in the soul brings to light certain aspects of the reality of objects and opens up possibilities for gaining impressions of them. This two-sidedness of methods and procedures also exists in research. And the human sciences, since the general state of the scientific mind has conditioned them, have been the instruments that gave the mind the power to see certain aspects of objects for the first time. I wished to describe only this connection in which the historical world gradually surfaces above the horizon of the human mind and one experiences viewpoints that make certain aspects of that world visible. Two added chapters also serve this purpose. And their brevity, despite the interest and importance of their subject matters, is determined by the fact that they serve only this epistemological and methodical purpose.

Addenda to the First Book

The standpoint[2] of the first book of the *Introduction to Human Science* [*sic*] has been discussed often in the literature of this theme, both polemically and supportively. Since then, on the basis of other logical-epistemological foundations, people have offered new solutions to questions concerning the concept and interpretation of the human sciences. The most important of them, those of Windelband and Rickert, are, to be sure, at one with me in the effort to assert the independence of the human sciences, as opposed to subordinating them to the natural sciences or rather to their method. We also agree on two further points. They, too, seek recognition for the singular and the individual in human science.[3]

And they, too, recognize in the connection of facts, theorems, and value judgments a further characteristic feature of the human sciences (p. 91). But because our logical-epistemological points of departure are totally different, a completely different concept of the human sciences and an entirely different definition of their task emerge for these two outstanding researchers. Hence it seems necessary for me to describe my own epistemological foundation as clearly as I can do it here in brief compass. This supplement thus expands what the first book of this work contained. My intent there was to prepare the way for the history of the human sciences. This history must assume some basic ideas among its readers about the task of the human sciences, their limits, their concept, and their parts. The purpose of the first book was to supply these. And now I also find myself obliged to my readers to defend and clarify my positions to the degree necessary to prepare them for the history of the human sciences.

If in the meantime I have had to delve into problems of the logic and epistemology of the human sciences, this will work to the advantage of the historical presentation. We see more clearly into the process by which, based on its conceptual conditions,[4] consciousness forms the entire human-social-historical world.

Organization of the Introduction to the Human Sciences[5]

I

1. The starting point of my work is the sum total of research which probes into man, history, and society. I am not beginning with an object, that is, human-social-historical reality, and the relationship of knowledge to this object. These are conceptual abstractions, necessary in their place; indeed, this reality is only an ideal concept that indicates a goal of knowledge we can never fully reach. The factual element given as the foundation of every theory consists of intellectual efforts which have issued from the purpose of knowing man or history or society or mutual relations among these moments.

Each of these efforts is defined by the relation of a knowing subject and its historical horizon to a specific group of facts likewise limited in its range by a fixed horizon. For each of them the object exists only from some point of view. Each is thus a definitie relative way of seeing and knowing its object. To one who enters into these labors they confront him as a chaos of relativities. *Subjectivity [is] the modern way of viewing things.*

2. Thus the task arises of elevating oneself to a historical consciousness in which one can explain the system by which particular tasks fit together, their resolutions become presuppositions for posing new questions, these questions probe ever more deeply, and links between various questions emerge which make it possible to generalize problems. [This is] a system in which we gradually understand the principles we have discovered with greater certitude and universality through their connection with new experiences, for the horizon of accessible experiences is, at first, a smaller one: a system in which we generalize propositions on the basis of their connection and so forth. [It is] a system in which illusion and anticipations that hinder knowledge in this area, just as they do in the natural sciences, are gradually dissolved. In particular, linking concepts of being and concepts of value in metaphysical thought and a priori construction of this system is such

an illusion. Finally [it is] a system in which analysis gradually breaks down the complexity of the web in these various areas and allows us to grasp the necessities of the case in the isolated areas amid the juxtaposition or the succession of facts.

In this process a selection takes place through constant testing, just as in the natural sciences. Assumptions and methods are thoroughly tested, and the immanent measure of their worth is precisely the success of knowledge: the same as in the natural sciences. Specialization produces rigorous knowledge; combination produces challenges and broad views. Connection with nature teaches laws of development; immersion into higher phenomena produces value-concepts. Comparison, study of causes, and reflection on values have their special strength in perceiving spiritual realities. But all these presuppositions with which we approach this class of realities are inwardly related to one another. This determines their order of succession in the history of these sciences. Deepening of knowledge gradually gives them their place in the structure of knowledge of this reality.

3. I am making a comparison not only to shed light on this matter but also to call attention to the deeper problem that lies beyond it.

Personality, style, and inner form of the artist as means of new perceptions, possibilities of impressions, etc. No single work sees nature as it is but only something of it. The subjective horizon conditions the constant illusion of ultimate comprehension, and precisely this limitation gives it its energy.

Is it possible in the realm of science to use this relationship which exists here too for objective knowledge? History will show that we are actually coming closer little by little to objective knowledge and that we are creating ever more instruments to make knowledge more certain, more universal, and more objective with respect to these objects.

The most important instrument is forming concepts in the special human sciences. Therein lies the possibility for the historical mind to summarize the previous yield of thought and research and to use it for problems or groups of facts. Thus the history of this concept-formation [is] an important part.

On the other hand, critically tested knowledge of facts and selection of those that assume a place in the value-formative structure of history—in short, universal history—is growing.

4. Now, however, we must recognize the most important forms in which researchers have conceived the value-formative structure of the human-social-historical world they have isolated. Here is the true core of the history of these sciences. Here is also the focus of enlightenment regarding the boundaries of this science, its parts, and its inner structure.

(*Introduction to the Human Sciences*, p. 142ff.)

(1) We must resolve history analytically into particular contexts.

(2) Laws of formation within those contexts which demonstrate the necessity of the matter in the *process* itself.

(3) Relations between simultaneous facts in different areas.

II

1. These methods; positively, the principles discovered and, negatively, the dissolution of appearance in this world; insight into the direction and tendency of this entire class of studies; increasing knowledge of the system and inner ordering of that knowl-

edge: all this constitutes now the sum total of history we have understood, which should make systematic construction possible. The concrete, historically realized concept of such a complex of research and knowledge is the essential kernel of experience on which one can erect a theory. Theory must satisfy the essence of this experience. Division, determination of boundaries, organization, and response to the problem of the possibility of knowledge in this area has its experiential foundation here.

The goal is to lay the foundation of and to organize the human sciences. We can reach this goal only on the basis of what the history of this knowledge has gradually brought to light.

The situation is exactly the same with respect to how laying the foundation of and organizing the natural sciences is possible only through insight into laws discovered in nature and into the developmental history of the universe as well as into theory of the forms of nature. Only natural scientists of philosophical power or philosophers with a comprehensive knowledge of nature can solve this task.

But therein consists the difference between human sciences and natural sciences. These values have an altogether different character, their own special kind of indissolubility from subject, standpoint, and object, and consequently from history and system. History must offer at least enough to call attention to the dissolution of illusion, the most important moments of the formation of concepts, and so forth.

2. But now inasmuch as this historical development demonstrates at every step a relation between this research and the great attitudes of human consciousness and, issuing from there, a grounding and organization of pertinent sciences, and inasmuch as research depends on these great attitudes of consciousness and acquires its position according to how they are expressed (i.e., as worldviews),[6] the most important task which the history we are attempting here has to fulfill emerges for the first time.

Just as for its part this task had its great historical background in grasping these attitudes of consciousness and the possibilities they contain for securing standpoints and methods of research, such history also reveals an insight into the necessity of laying a foundation, its steps, and finally a grasp of the situation in which such foundation-laying and ordering has now become possible. Thus this history must also describe those moments of the progress of the philosophical spirit that make it possible to become increasingly preoccupied with the conditions and organization of these sciences insofar as they lie beyond these sciences in universal philosophical standpoints. And the negative side of scientific work nowhere else achieves such importance as it does precisely in this area. The issue at stake here is the gradual dissolution of the illusion of a metaphysics which combines ontological and axiological forms of the cosmic structure and its purpose—a metaphysics which has hung like a foggy mist between objects in question and the human mind for so long.

3. The reader of such a history will find it much to his advantage, however, if he has first made clear to himself some basic features inherent in this class of sciences in accordance with the stage of their current development. This is the intent of the first, introductory, book. It distinguishes human sciences from natural sciences. It permits one to see their independence with respect to natural sciences. At the same time, however, it shows their foundation in natural sciences (p. 85ff.) and then the relation of knowledge to this material and the procedural modes by which analysis breaks down and isolates the

complex phenomena of the human sciences, the classification of special sciences that emerges in this analysis, and their relation to one another. Finally, in contrast with false metaphysical constructions of these sciences, which seek to solve their basic problem, we posit the modest insight into their development (which goes beyond us as well) and into the task of laying their epistemological foundation.

On page 77ff. [we made] the express statement that we can ultimately establish and ground the concept of human sciences only in the work itself and that here we are using only the concept of fact which these sciences in question contain in order to ascertain the limits of the human sciences.

III

1. Only a grounding, ordering, and cautious immanent critique based on them of this sum total of work that has become a part of man, history, and society can lay a foundation and provide organization as a system.

The main proposition regarding this procedure is on page 78:

> These intellectual data which have developed historically among men and to which general linguistic usage has applied the designation of sciences of man, of history, and of society constitute the reality which we wish not so much to master as mainly to comprehend. Empirical method demands that we draw from this stock of sciences themselves to analyze historically and critically the value of the individual procedures which thinking uses in solving its problems in this area; it demands further that we clarify, through observation of that great development whose subject is humanity itself, what the nature of knowledge and understanding is in this field.

2. I illustrate this with the natural sciences. Laying their foundation must deal with the question whether a relation to objective reality is inherent in our images of bodies given in sensation. Of course this question demands logical and epistemological investigations, and I maintain their necessity with the greatest emphasis. We can prove it by actually analyzing logical forms. But we can solve the question itself only on the basis of the innermost core of the natural sciences themselves. These sciences show that objective ordering according to laws, which makes appearances possible for us, is the objective factor accessible to us.

3. Thus we can solve the question concerning the delimitation of the human sciences only on the foundation of logical-epistemological facts, but ultimately really only by using this foundation to penetrate into the inner structure in which these investigations require one another and relate to one another. If Rickert were right in saying that historical thought had no relation to systematic psychology, then excluding it from the grouping of the human sciences would of course by justified. But one has to concede to him that the first question is, after all, whether we can establish such a psychology with sufficient certainty.

Insight into the structural complex of the life of the soul is also the permanent key for understanding the organization of functions in an organic historical totality. If we can formulate this insight in clear concepts, then the historian thereby obviously acquires an important instrument for clarifying the forms of organization in such a totality through a combination of relatively simple concepts.

Similarly, the question whether the object of human sciences is the particular (their idiographic character) or whether one can transcend those sciences and know conceptually describable general causal structures from the necessity of the case here (their nomothetic character)[7] is something one can really solve only when one has seen whether this latter thing has already been acomplished to any extent. If this question is answered affirmatively, then the affair is decided. And not until it is denied would one have to fall back to general epistemological determinations.

The situation is the same with respect to the question concerning meaning and value in history.

IV

From this standpoint, laying the foundation of philosophy acquires a character opposed to epistemological factions associated with Fichte and presents itself on the contrary as a continuation of the real direction taken by Kant.

The possibility of this lies in annulling Kant's erroneous theory of categories, according to which actuality, being, and reality are categories of the understanding. Likewise the assumption of an arrangement of consciousness in which one would understand the relation of subject and object as psychologically primordial. It is possible to eliminate these things, however, only if one begins from life and totality in making psychological deductions. Riehl (*Kantstudien* IX, pp. 511–12) correctly discerns in Kant the distinction which makes psychological analysis take place at a certain point, in fact where the given comes into question.

1. The supreme rule in laying a foundation is that one use only such propositions in it which one can clearly describe and that one should use all propositions of this kind, whether they belong to empirical sciences or to epistemology and logic. In laying the foundation, just as many errors arise because one fails to use established propositions as because one employs shaky ones. The epistemological systematic which proceeds from conditions of consciousness and uses them to try to demarcate the sphere of validity of experience and of knowledge and only then proceeds to empirical sciences (for it assumes that one has assured their existence only then for the first time) is the fundamental error of the entire Fichtean party in epistemology. Kant himself avoided this one-sidedness because he assumes the existence of an affecting factor just as much as he does the existence of conditions of consciousness. This existence of an affecting factor, however, rests for him on the contents of mathematical natural science.

2. Orderly deduction from analysis of consciousness which first seeks to construct experience in order then to use its results is the illusion of the theory of knowledge which we must dissolve.

Such a procedure is impossible because:

(1) Vicious circle

(2) Presupposition of experiences

(3) True or false exists only in judgment. But every judgment already contains concepts which presuppose some kind of division of the given content of experience and selection from it through disjunctions (Schleiermacher's dialectic). So there is no legitimate beginning, no independently established judgment of experience; on the contrary,

every beginning is arbitrary. The various epistemological starting points always bear this note of arbitrariness and always have presuppositions on which they rest.

I conclude thus: epistemology is never something definitive. It will always have validity only to the extent that it can do justice from its very beginning to what empirical sciences have established.

Rule: Extremest epistemological rigor with regard to all appearance in experiences and strictest justification of the value of the concepts of reality, object, immediately given, and so on, must work together with understanding of what the empirical sciences establish as reality.

In one-sided fashion the first leads to an idealism that is either subjective or that constructs, as the only valid thing, a transcendental universal subject that functions in the norms of thought.

3. All thought consists in relating things; all relating presupposes contents which are related. We have hereby established the difference between thought and something given to this thought as to a discursive activity: the contents, in other words, Kant's form and matter.

"Given" is taken here only in the sense that it is given to discursive thought. In this sense something is immediately given which discursive thought finds present to inner awareness as external observation or something perceived. This is the standpoint from which logic, as the theory of discursive thought, draws this distinction.

But this concept of the immediately given contains this problem: Because it is clear that this given itself comes into being through logical operations, givenness slides back a notch. So a second concept of "given" or "immediate" becomes necessary.

But we can resolve this problem only if we first carry the theory about what relational thought accomplishes beyond discursive thought. And in fact it is not a matter of the psychological question as to what the nature of the processes is whereby the given comes into being. At present this question allows for a variety of answers. Hence we cannot use it in laying the foundation.

Sociology[8]

1. My polemic against sociology concerned the stage of its evolution characterized by Comte, Spencer, Schäffle, and Lilienfeld. The idea of sociology contained in their works was that of a science of the social communal life of men, that also included law, ethics, and religion in its purview. It was therefore not a theory of the forms that psychical life assumes when affected by social relations of individuals. Simmel has set up such a concept of sociology. Sociology then deals with the form of society as such, a form that remains the same amid change. According to him, this societal form as such manifests itself in a number of separable modes of combination among men. Examples of such are superiority and inferiority, imitation, division of labor, competition, self-preservation of the social group, formation of hierarchies, representation, and formation of parties. And the task now is to establish these forms inductively and to interpret them psychologically. Society is only the sum of these particular combinatory forces that exist between such elements. Society as such would no longer exist if these combinatory forces were eliminated.

Demarcation of such a scientific sphere is something I must naturally acknowledge; it rests on the principle that says that one can study in their own right relations that remain constant as forms of communal life amid variation among its purposes and content. In fact, in my *Introduction* I myself (before Simmel) already characterized external organization of society as a special sphere in which, viewed psychologically, relations of dominance and dependence and community relations are operative. My view is different from Simmel's principally inasmuch as I cannot simply trace these combinatory forces to the psychical moments mentioned; on the contrary, I regard the natural organization of the sexual community, procreation, the ensuing homogeneity of the family and race, and on the other hand communal living in the same place as equally important.

My rejection of sociology cannot therefore refer to that kind of discipline, but is aimed at science which tries to summarize everything which de facto occurs in human society in a *single* science. The principle which underlies this summarization would be: Whatever transpires in human society in the course of its history we must bring together into the unity of the same object.

This would amount to the kind of argument which says: Because mechanical, physical, chemical, and vital processes are bound up together in nature and pursue their course in the same material physical world, we must put them together into *one* science. As a matter of fact natural sciences draw only this conclusion: Special sciences must always be prepared to subordinate general truths they discover to still more general ones, say, astronomical truths to mechanical ones and physiological truths to chemical ones, or conversely to look for applications of mechanical truths in astronomy and so on. But a general science of nature is always only a problematical perspective, not the point of departure. And human sciences likewise strive to establish the relations of truths they discover through subordination and application, but they cannot start by constituting such a general, still entirely problematical, science.

2. If one imagines such a science in action, then either, lacking a principle of unity, it is a composite of all the human sciences which have separated themselves from the mesh of societal life as special sciences. And then, as Simmel correctly observes, it is the great common pot on which the label sociology is pasted: a new name, but no new knowledge. Or else it is an encyclopedia, compiled from epistemological-logical-methodical standpoints, of special sciences which have arisen on the basis of psychology. In that case sociology designates only philosophy of the human sciences in its second part.

But this is not the meaning of sociology as developed by Comte, Spencer, and others. Their view, on the contrary, sees in society—in the specialization and integration operative in it, in the solidarity of interests, in its progress toward an order which answers to the common good—the principle which explains religiosity, art, ethics, and law. It is in this sense that I have called sociology "metaphysical."

The errors one finds here are the following: (1) We encounter individuals in social relationships. This basic fact has two aspects. The individual constitutes a self-contained totality through his structural unity. We can reduce neither the basis nor the purpose of individual existence to society through any sort of demonstration. And from this it is clear that it is a metaphysical hypothesis to think that we can. (2) In purpose-complexes in society we can deduce a great deal from the mere fact of sociality. But even a structure like the development of philosophy, with respect to foundation and purpose, is just as inherent in the individual in himself as it is in society. This two-sidedness is still more obvious in religion and art. If one could imagine a solitary individual making his way in the world, that individual would develop these functions out of his own resources, in total isolation, if he lived a life long enough to develop them. (3) But even in law a principle of linkage to the oppositely established side exists, that does not function merely through social compulsion and whose utilitatrian derivation is an unsatisfactory hypothesis. And the situation is the same for ethics. (4) Accordingly, this sociology is not at all scientific knowledge that one might define by its sphere, but is a certain orientation of viewpoint that asserts itself in the nineteenth century in a given situation. And, determined by this orientation, it is a method which, based on an assumed principle of explanation, explains the largest possible number of facts by its interpretation. This sort of method is heuristically valuable, and evolutionist theory of society has in fact had an invigorating effect. But because the method clashes with the facts mentioned, which one can explain just as well individually as socially, their inability to constitute a science becomes clear. Thus sociology is ultimately just a name for a number of works that treat social facts in accordance with one great principle of interpretation or for an orientation of the interpretive process; it is not the name of a science.

Addenda to the Second Book[9]

To page 151. Division.

(1) Objective metaphysics of the Greeks. Their achievement is that they created the principal metaphysical categories. These are not obvious. They are discovered in the world of objects as substance and what is asserted about substance through categories. This can also be found in Plato, but is grounded most profoundly in Parmenides. Subordination of categories of affective behavior and voluntary behavior to objective [categories].

(2) Roman metaphysics of will. The Roman worldview arises as one traces concepts of life to a priori dispositions of a practical sort. Therefore, consciousness of law, freedom of will, and so on, are innate. They constitute another world, for the relation of subordination of the categories, hence their determination, is different. Now comes the decision that man is born for action, from which the practical nature of his talents follows. Is not his highest metaphysical objectification of life's rank [*Lebensstand*] the ethical community, in which the inherently benevolent divine will binds individuals together?

(3) Metaphysics of religious experience was possible only on the foundation of skepticism. Only so could the subjectivity of the religious viewpoint convince the educated as the only thing possible.

In the experience of revealed religions man intuitively creates truth out of the need to satisfy his feeling (happiness). The guarantee of the union of life [*Vereinigung des Lebens*] (=happiness) lies in loving relationship with the eternal. Removal of distance from God in the relation of law and obedience, in the relation of obligation, and so on, through the melting feelings of union [*durch die schmelzenden Gefühle der Vereinigung*].

To page 165: The Pythagoreans are, even formally, founders of the dominant tendency in Greek thought. For they constructed out of mathematical units.

To page 185: In Plato the decisive moment of the dominant Greek philosophy occurs. This consists in a conceptual construction out of mathematical elements, which is different from temporal derivation. The procedure is cosmic here; it is subjective in Kant. Thus Euclid later constructs on the basis of a mathematical point and continues to regular bodies, which then provide the basis for physics and astronomy.

To page 206ff. Distinguish: the concept of human science according to the concept of causality, for example, Democritus, from the spiritual notion of purpose in Attic philosophy.

Deeper reasons why Attic thinkers discovered the cardinal concepts of a historical organism. There is a metaphysical stage in both.

Beginning of the human sciences. Metaphysical epoch.

If Aristotle won a victory, this was partially because his metaphysics was applicable to the human sciences that had sprouted up mightily from the time of the Sophists. For the concept of form, which as a purpose is an operative cause and thus contains a law of formation in itself—unfruitful in the sphere of nature—answered to man's teleological structure and to purpose-complexes based on it. And likewise the comparative method, which was oriented toward laws of formation, proved itself capable and so forth. Finally, these metaphysical concepts themselves contained the possibility for clearly distinguishing and inwardly connecting purpose-complexes which had acquired distinct status in vocational life.

Politics. The science of politics has its foundations in Aristotle, but in him lie also its limitations, that to this day have hindered its establishment as a historically comparative science. From Aristotle on, the starting point is the individual state. The individual state is just as much an abstraction as individual man is. States live only under conditions of pressure, expansion, contrast, and equilibrium; even peace is only a transitory constriction of living expansive energy, which is always very strong in any state. And this relationship determines the inner development of the particular state. This is the most general condition to which the dynamics of the inner conditions of the individual state is subject. The highest law of this inner dynamics consists in the fact that amid competition of individuals and their interests the state is held together through forces powerful enough as motives in individuals to maintain a continuing state order and state power. It is not first and foremost a question of which forces have produced the state's life but which ones can now be shown to be keeping it in existence. As in all human affairs, they are manifold: habitual obedience and consciousness of authority, economic interest in the power of the state, awareness of advantages which accrue to a particular class from the prevailing order, most fundamentally the mutual affinity of persons bound together by language and descent, which asserts itself more and more as the only unshakeable foundation. For in the most extreme crises of a political totality this affinity has always proven itself and it is intensified through history, which has ultimately linked individuals of a political body ever more closely to one another.

To page 222: To skepticism. Its cause. Critique of the concept of cause is basic in skeptical thought. But it is also applied to grammar and history. Here arises the problem whether justification of the concept of cause, which Stoic philosophers undertook against the skeptics, has also been adopted by the historians.

Essentially, carrying through the causal concept in the Stoical concept of the world is the factual answer to skepticism. For history, therefore, the work of Polybius. One wonders whether he had a theoretical awareness of that.

To page 228 above:
Section 3
(Worldview and concepts of life of the Romans) Fusion of Greek philosophy with the view of life and concepts of life of the Romans (*Archiv* IV, p. 612–23)[10]

(1) Opposition to Greek metaphysics (pp. 612–15)

(2) Dominant concepts in the Roman mind

(3) From this practical attitude toward the world results incapacity for systematizing of worldviews (p. 616)

(4) Roman religiosity, arising out of the practical attitude of life of the Romans; theology, however, from the Greeks.

(5) Roman philosophy
   (a) History of transmission of Greek philosophy to Rome (*Grundriss*, [11] pp. 50–58)
   (b) Roman society around the younger Scipio (*Archiv*, p. 619)

(6) The three directions of Roman philosophy (*Grundriss*, p. 58ff.)

(7) The solid elements, etc. as a foundation (*Archiv*, p. 619ff.)

(8) Philosophical, juridical, and political structure

(9) The historians

Section 4
Fusion of Greco-Roman philosophy with oriental revealed faith.
(*Grundriss*, p. 64ff. to link up with *Introduction to the Human Sciences*, pp. 228–39).
At the beginning [see] *Archiv* IV, 4, p. 604ff.[12] as a general introduction which shows the universal-religious meaning of the concepts now used.

Notes

1. In the *Manuscripts*, fasc. C7: 58–62.

2. Last manuscript of the beginning. In the *Manuscripts*, fasc. C47: 126–29.

3. "In the human sciences (because they are a standing refutation of Spinoza's principle '*omnis determinatio est negatio*') the idea of the singular or the individual constitutes a *final goal* as much as the development of abstract uniformities does." See page 91.

4. Here the manuscript breaks off.

5. Fasc. C47: 12–46.

6. [See volume 8, pp. 73–118, of Dilthey's *Gesammelte Schriften* for his well-known description and typology of worldviews.]

7. [In 1894 Wilhelm Windelband gave an address on "History and the Natural Sciences" in which he distinguished between the natural sciences and the "historical sciences" (his designation for the human sciences). Whereas the natural sciences try to establish the *general laws* operating in nature (hence are "nomothetic" = "law-positing"), the historical sciences stress the unique and the individual features of the specific event (hence are "idiographic" = "describing one's own"). Of course Windelband acknowledged that an occurrence could be described or approached by both methods.]

8. Fasc. C7: 22; 24–30.

9. Fasc. C7:17–18; 15; 12; 7; 8–11; 5; 2–4.

10. *Archiv für Geschichte der Philosophie*, vol. IV (1891): "Auffassung und Analyse des

Menschen im 15. und 16. Jahrhundert." Printed in this edition, vol. II, p. 1ff. Vol. II, pp. 7–16, corresponds to the pages given in the text.

11. The *Grundriss der Allgemeinen Geschichte der Philosophie,* printed in manuscript form, for Dilthey's lectures.

12. See the *Gesammelte Schriften,* vol. II, p. 1ff.

Notes

Translator's Note: [Most of the notes given here are Dilthey's. When Dilthey quotes texts in languages other than German, the original is quoted first and followed by an English translation in square brackets. Because Dilthey's notes are extensive in their own right and the complex material affords virtually endless opportunities for further commentary, I have severely restricted myself to a few notes of clarification or explanation. They are indicated as such in each instance by being enclosed in square brackets. The more important larger issues that require commentary have been addressed in my introduction.

Unfortunately, it has not been possible to pursue a fully consistent and comprehensive practice in amplifying some of Dilthey's often arcane and highly abbreviated source citations. A small number of these references have been recorded just as they stand in Dilthey's original text.]

Book I. Introductory

1. Pascal expresses this feeling for life very imaginatively in the *Pensées,* article I: "Toutes ces misères—prouvent sa grandeur. Ce sont misères de grand seigneur, misères d'un roi dépossédé. Nous avons une si grande idée de l'âme de l'homme, que nous ne pouvons souffrir d'en être méprisés, et de n'être pas dans l'estime d'une âme." *Oeuvres* (Paris, 1866) I, 248,249. ["All these miseries—prove (man's) grandeur. They are the miseries of a great lord, the miseries of a dispossessed king. We have such an exalted idea of the soul of man that we cannot bear to be despised and to be considered nothing in the estimation of another soul."]

2. *Summa Contra Gentiles* (cura Uccellii, Rome, 1878) I, chap. 22. Cp. II, chap. 54.
3. Liber II, chap. 46ff.
4. [Dilthey's description of the "double sense" in which the human sciences differ from the natural and the "double significance" of the concept of the boundaries of knowledge is somewhat opaque at this point. He goes on to explain that the respective contributions of the senses and of our intellectual apparatus are different in origin and (pp. 81–83) in kind. Difference in origin of material vs. intellectual data might not prevent the full adaptation of the latter to the former, but difference in kind will prevent one from reducing either one to the other. Data regarding the world of nature remain different in our minds from data regarding our own psychic states; they differ in their respective origins.]
5. Emil Du Bois-Reymond, *Über die Grenzen des Naturerkennens,* 1872. Cp. *Die Sieben Welträtsel,* 1881.
6. Laplace, Marquis Pierre Simon de, *Essai sur les Probabilités* (Paris, 1814), 3.
7. [Dilthey's epistemology was never fully developed, but his general epistemological outlook was similar to Kant's to the extent that both of them agreed that human knowledge and experience are limited to the contents of consciousness; we have no ontological knowledge. "Objectivity" for both of them is ultimately a consistent ordering of the elements of our own subjectivity, limited to the sphere of "possible experience." In the last analysis there is no real way to get outside the mind and its contents in knowledge.]
8. The proof begins on p. 28 (4th ed.) of *Über die Grenzen.*

9. Loc. cit., 29, 30, cp. *Du Bois-Reymond, Welträtsel* 7. Moreover this line of argument is cogent only if metaphysical validity, as it were, is attributed to atomistic mechanics. One might wish to compare its history as touched on by Du Bois-Reymond with the formulation given by the classicist of rational psychology, Mendelssohn. For example (*Schriften,* Leipzig, 1880: I, 277): 1. "Everything which differentiates the human body from a block of marble can be traced back to movement. But movement is nothing other than the alteration of place or position. It is manifestly clear that all possible changes of place in the world, no matter what sort they are, do not afford us any perception of these changes in place." 2. "All matter is made up of a number of parts. If individual ideas were isolated from one another in the soul as objects in nature are, we would be unable to find the whole anywhere. We could not compare impressions of the various senses with one another nor could we match up our ideas with one another; we could perceive no proportions nor could we know any relationships. From this it is clear that a lot of things have to come together into a single whole not only in the case of thought but also of sensation. But since matter never becomes a single subject . . . etc." Kant develops this "Achilles heel of all dialectical conclusions in the doctrine of the pure soul" as the second paralogism of transcendental psychology. Lotze develops these "acts of relational knowing" as "an unimpeachable basis on which the conviction of the independence of the soul can rest securely" in several of his works (most recently in *Metaphysik,* 476) and he makes them the foundation for this part of his metaphysical system.

10. Du Bois-Reymond, *Welträtsel,* 8.

11. [Perhaps those who maintain that we come to a knowledge of ourselves, even initially, by way of contact with what is not a part of us would reject the view Dilthey here expresses.]

12. ["For nature is not overcome except by obeying her."] *Baconis Aphorismi de Interpretatione Naturae et Regno Hominis,* aphorism 3.

13. Mommsen, *Römisches Staatsrecht* I, 3ff.

14. For the purposes of such a restricted overview of particular areas of the human sciences the following encyclopedias may be consulted: Mohl, *Enzyklopädie der Staatswissenschaften* (Tübingen, 1859); 2d (rev.) ed., 1872; 3d ed., 1881—new title page. Cp. his review and evaluation of other encyclopedias in his *Geschichte und Literatur der Staatswissenschaften,* vol. 1: 111–64; Warnkönig, *Juristische Enzyklopädie oder Organische Darstellung der Rechtswissenschaft,* 1853; Schleiermacher, *Kurze Darstellung des Theologischen Studiums,* 1st ed., Berlin, 1810; 2d (rev.) ed., 1830; Böckh, *Enzyklopädie und Methodologie der Philologischen Wissenschaften,* pub. Bratuschek (1877).

15. An overview of the problems of the human sciences in accordance with the inner connections linking them together methodically (and in which, consequently, their dissolution may be brought about) may be found sketched out in Auguste Comte, *Cours de Philosophie Positive,* 1830–1842, vols. 4–6. His later works, which have a different point of view, cannot be used to the same purpose. The most significant counterproposal for a system of the sciences is that of Herbert Spencer. The first attack on Comte in Spencer, *Essays,* 1st series (1858), was followed by a more precise presentation in *The Classification of the Sciences* (1864). (Compare the defense of Comte in Littré, *Auguste Comte et la Philosophie Positive.*) Spencer's *System of Synthetic Philosophy* also gives us his detailed description of the organization of the human sciences. The first part of this book appeared in 1855 as *The Principles of Psychology;* [*The Principles of*] *Sociology* has been published since 1876 (with reference to the work *Descriptive Sociology*); the concluding part, *The Principles of Ethics* (about which he himself declares that he considers it "the one for which all the preceding works were intended solely as groundwork"), takes up "The Facts of Ethics" in its first volume, 1879. Besides this attempt to establish a theory of socio-historical reality, the one by John Stuart Mill is also noteworthy. It is contained in the sixth book of the *Logic,* which deals with the logic of the human sciences or the moral sciences, as well as in the work by Mill called *Auguste Comte and Positivism,* 1865.

16. Discussions about the concept of society and the task of the sciences of society were the point of departure for these efforts—discussions which aimed at expanding the political sciences. The stimulus in that direction was supplied by L. Stein, *Der Sozialismus und Kommunismus des heutigen Frankreich,* 2d ed., 1848, and R. Mohl, *Tübinger Zeitschrift für Staatswissenschaften,* 1851. It was carried forward in Mohl's *Geschichte und Literatur der Staatswissenschaften.* We single out two attempts at organization as especially remarkable: Stein, *System der Staatswissenschaft,* 1852, and Schäffle, *Bau und Leben des Sozialen Körpers,* 1875ff.

17. ["Every determination is a negation." This principle alludes to the logical principle that the

larger the number of specific predicates one attaches to a class of things, the smaller the class becomes. Thus the class "animal" by itself is larger than "rational animal," which in turn is larger than "male rational animal," etc.]

18. [Dilthey gives no reference for his use of the principle "the individual is ineffable." The *Historisches Wörterbuch der Philosophie* (vol. 4, no. 312, Darmstadt: Wissenschaftliche Buchgesellschaft, 1976) notes that Goethe used the expression in a letter to Lavater (September 20, 1780) and adds: "One might be inclined to regard this citation, although its origin is still obscure, as a polemically secularized form of the ancient and well-known statement: 'God is ineffable.'" Friedrich Meinecke's *Die Entstehung des Historismus* (Munich, 1936) cites Goethe's words to Lavater immediately following the title page: "Have I already written you the statement 'Individuum est ineffabile,' from which I derive a world?"]

19. [Dilthey is forcefully opposed throughout his writings to what he calls "constructionism" or "constructivism." This is but a reflection of his strong opposition to metaphysics, which is in his opinion the capital sin of western philosophy in general and such systems as Hegelianism and Comtean positivism in particular. Dilthey's whole thrust and emphasis in the human sciences is on description and analysis, which he regularly contrasts with the hypothetical foundations of the natural sciences and the synthetic a priori constructs of the metaphysical systems. In his view any form of constructionism tries to say what a thing is in itself, whereas our only grip on reality is epistemological/critical in character.]

20. [Dilthey cites Carlyle in German: "Weises Erinnern und weises Vergessen, darin liegt alles." I cannot find an exact equivalent for this in Carlyle's work. It is possible that Dilthey is just paraphrasing some of what Carlyle has written, both in his essay "On History" (1830) and especially "On History Again" (1833). See, for example, pp. 410–11 of the latter essay in *The Works of Thomas Carlyle*, vol. 14 (*Critical and Miscellaneous Essays*), New York: Peter Fenelon Collier, Publisher, 1897.]

21. The concept of sociology or science of society (such as Comte, Spencer, etc. understand it) must be entirely distinguished from the concept which society and science of society has signified for German constitutional lawyers. These lawyers distinguish society from state in a given period, because they begin with the need to designate the external organization of communal life as something which constitutes the presupposition and foundation for the state.

22. [Note that *Verstehen* (understanding) is for Dilthey a special mode of knowing that is proper to interior experience or psychic life. He contrasts it with *Erklären* (explanation), i.e., that mode of knowledge by which we know the external world through natural science.]

23. [Johann Heinrich von Thünen (1783–1850) was a north German specialist in agricultural matters generally and in questions of social justice for farm workers particularly. His economics classic *Der Isolierte Staat in Beziehung auf Landwirtschaft und Nationaloekonomie* (1825ff.) contains his ideas about the effect of distance from markets as an important factor in agricultural production.]

24. Johannes Müller, first in his *Schrift über die Phantastischen Gesichtserscheinungen* (Koblenz, 1826). I have tried to explain poetic imagination through a combination of historical, psychological, and psychophysical facts: "Über die Einbildungskraft der Dichter," *Zeitschrift für Völkerpsychologie und Sprachwissenschaft*, vol. X, 1878, pp. 42–104. (Reworked into "Goethe und die Dichterische Phantasie," in *Das Erlebnis und die Dichtung*, pp. 175–267. See p. 468 for a statement about the reworked version.)

25. [Rudolf von Ihering (1818–92) was a professor of Roman Law at the universities of Giessen and Göttingen. He is best known for his legal philosophy of "social utilitarianism" in which, in contrast to Bentham's individualist utilitarianism, the needs of individuals and society would be coordinated and, if the need arose, precedence would be given to societal needs over individual ones.]

26. *Ulpiani Fragmenta Principalia*, no. 4 (Huschke). [Ulpian's statement in English reads: "a tacit consent of the people established through long usage."]

27. Aristotle, *Politics*, Book I, chap. 1. [Aristotle's text reads in English: "Every community is established with some good in mind."]

28. See Gierke's presentation in the first volume of his work, *Das Deutsche Genossenschaftsrecht* (Berlin, 1868).

29. Schäffle, *Bau und Leben des Organischen Körpers* I, 213ff.

30. See p. 107ff.

31. See p. 105ff.; pp. 107–8; pp. 119–20.

32. See p. 107ff.

33. See p. 108ff.; p. 110.

34. This stage of Greek thought about law and the state is still preserved in the fragment of Heraclitus: *trephontai gar pantes hoi anthrōpinoi nomoi hupo henos tou theiou; krateei gar tosouton hokoson ethelei kai exarkeei pasi kai periginetai.* ["For all human laws are nourished by the law of God. It holds sway as much as it wills, is addressed to all, and remains supreme over all."] Stobaeus, *Florilegium* III, 84) and in related passages in Aeschylus and Pindar. The passage in Pindar—*kata phusin nomos ho pantōn Basileus,* etc. ["By nature the law is the king of all," etc.] (fr. XI, 48)—is especially worthy of note for the development of the concept. A passage of Demosthenes in which the *nomos* [law] is conceived of primarily as an *heurēma kai dōron theōn* [invention and gift of the gods] and secondarily as *poleōs sunthēkē koinē* [the common agreement of the polis], which passage also explains the obligatory nature of the law, has found its way into the Pandects through Marcian (1. 2 *Digesta de Legibus* 1, 3).

35. I have found the influence of his archaeological studies on such a comparative collection in Clement, *Stromata* VI, 624. The account of the conversation between Hippias and Socrates (Xenophon, *Memorabilia* 4, 4) is doubtless authentic, but it is distorted and confused, because Hippias's view was developed quite clearly at the beginning of the discussion, as the preface also shows us; consequently, the conversation must be considered to have been different.

36. To avoid misunderstanding I point out the following: One must distinguish this natural-law theory from the completely different one that developed in the negative school of the theoreticians of power and interest. Thrasymachus was its chief representative in antiquity, and Plato has left us a systematic description of this school.

37. This notion, which stems from the abstraction implicit in the concept of the state, is in agreement with Mohl's definition (drawn from the judicious empiricism which was so characteristic of him): "The state is a permanent unitary organism of those *institutions* which—guided by a *general will* and maintained and executed by a *general power*—have the task of furthering the respective legitimate life goals of a specific, territorially circumscribed people, from the individual to the societal level, insofar as these life goals cannot be satisfied by the personal resources of those concerned and are the object of a common need." From this definition it follows that political science can comprehend that part of reality which it has for its proper subject matter only in relation to this reality.

38. [Among the ancient Greeks the *phylae,* or "tribes," were kinship groups making up the entire citizenry and constituting the largest political divisions in the state. The *phratriae,* or "brotherhoods," were smaller kinship groups which were subdivisions of the *phylae* and contained a number of families. The *demes,* or "country districts," were not a kinship designation. The term indicates the commoners, or plebeians, or citizenry in general or, specifically, the hundred townships or administrative districts into which Cleisthenes divided Attica in his reforms of ca. 509 B.C.]

39. See the law ascribed to Solon in the *Corpus Juris* 1, 4 *Digesta de Coll.* [*sic*] 47, 22.

40. To the thorough review of the literature in Mohl's *Geschichte und Literatur der Staatswissenschaften* (I, 1855, p. 67ff.) I would add that the first (and most fruitful) outline (which Mohl did not call special attention to on p. 101) goes further back than 1850 and may be found in Stein's *Sozialismus Frankreichs,* 2d ed. (1848), p. 14ff.

41. For example, after he had eliminated the community from his science of society because of Treitschke's objections (*Gesellschaftswissenschaft,* 1859). On this issue see the *Enzyklopädie der Staatswissenschaften,* 2d ed. (1872), p. 51ff.

42. Mohl, *Staatswissenschaften,* p. 51.

43. Stein, *Sozialismus* (1848), p. 24.

44. Stein, *Volkswirtschaftslehre* 2d ed. (Vienna, 1878), p. 465

45. Stein, *Gesellschaftslehre,* part I, p. 269.

46. Mohl, *Literatur der Staatswissenschaften* I (1855), p. 82

47. The following ideas in the sociology of Comte can be traced with certainty to Saint-Simon: the concept of society (vs. that of the state) as a community unrestricted by boundaries of states;

see his essay, "Réorganisation de la Société Européene, ou de la Nécessité et des Moyens de Rassembler les Peuples de l'Europe en un Seul Corps Politique, en Conservant à Chacun sa Nationalité" ["Reorganization of European Society, or on the Necessity and the Means of Collecting the Peoples of Europe into a Single Political Body, While Preserving the Nationality of Each"] (written in collaboration with Augustin Thierry), 1814; then the idea that, if decay of society occurs, it is necessary to organize it anew. This is to be done by a guiding intellectual power which, as a philosophy of the positive sciences, has the task of discovering the truths connecting these sciences and of deriving the social sciences from the connection; see *Nouvelle Encyclopédie*, 1810, as well as the *Mémoire* on the same, etc.; finally, his plan—whereby beginning in 1797 he first studied mathematical-physical sciences at the polytechnical school, and then biological sciences in the school of medicine—was actually carried out in a scientific spirit by his colleague and student Comte. With this foundation Comte combined Turgot's theory, developed since 1750, about the three stages of understanding and de Maistre's theory about the necessity of a spiritual power which, in opposition to the destructive tendency of Protestantism, would hold society together.

48. I have dealt with universal history in detail in my essay on Schlösser in the *Preussische Jahrbücher* (April 1862).

49. Scholium to proposition 40 of the second book of the *Ethics*, as well as *De Intellectus Emendatione*.

50. "Ex. gr. qui saepius cum admiratione hominum staturam contemplati sunt, sub nomine hominis intelligunt animal erectae staturae; qui vero aliud assueti sunt contemplari, aliam hominum communem imaginem formabunt," etc. ["For example, those who generally look on the stature of man with admiration understand by the term man an animal erect in stature; but those who are used to regarding something else will form a different general notion of man," etc.]

51. See the fourth and fifth books of the *Ideen* [*zur Philosophie der Geschichte der Menschheit*], with which later the fifteenth book links up, as well as the outline of the last volume given us by Johannes Müller, toward the end.

52. Kant, *Werke;* Rosenkranz, vol. VII, p. 321.

53. Kant, *Werke;* Rosenkranz, vol. VII, p. 320ff.

54. Lessing, *Erziehung des Menschen* [*geschlechts*] nos. 92, 93. For my more detailed view of the connection between the doctrine of metempsychosis and Lessing's system, I call attention to my investigations in "Lessing," *Preussische Jahrbücher* 1867 (now in *Das Erlebnis und die Dichtung*), along with the discussion by Konstantin Rössler in the same place, and my reply to it.

55. *Ideen*, Book 14, 6: "The philosophy of purposes has brought no advantage to natural history; on the contrary, it has satisfied its devotees with specious delusions instead of research; how much more so the thousand-purposed intricacies of human history."

56. Lotze, *Mikrokosmos* 3, 52 (1st ed.).

57. This connection [*Zusammenhang*] was expressly acknowledged as decisive for the development of sociology in *Philosophie Positive* 4, 225.

58. Thus Hitzig, once again, in *Untersuchungen über das Gehirn*, p. 56, passim. Cp. Wundt's *Physiologische Psychologie*, section 6 of the second volume, 2d ed., 1880.

59. Vol. 4, p. 631.

60. *Philosophie Positive* 5, 45. [The original, which Dilthey gives in the text, reads thus: "Nous avons reconnu, que le sens général de l'évolution humaine consiste surtout à diminuer de plus en plus l'inévitable prépondérance, nécessairement toujours fondamentale, mais d'abord excessive, de la vie affective sur la vie intellectuelle, ou suivant la formule anatomique, de la région postérieure du cerveau sur la région frontale."]

61. *Philosophie Positive* 4, 623ff.

62. Mill, *Logic* 2, 436 [*sic*]. [Dilthey translates Mill into German in his text; I have supplied the original Mill from *A System of Logic—Ratiouative and Inductive*, vol. 2, 4th ed. (London: John W. Parker & Son, West Strand, 1856), pp. 406–7.]

63. Comte, *Philosophie Positive* 4, 623ff.

64. This is especially evident in *Schleiermacher's* marvelous *Ethics*, for here "the action of reason on nature, on the basis of their interpenetration, whereby that interpenetration is constructed as conceptually manifold" (no. 75ff.) first acquires its content through its relation to systems which make up the life of society and through the discoveries of the special sciences concerning society.

65. Cp. the final wording of *Tatsachen in der Wahrnehmung* (1879), p. 27.

66. In the first volume of his *Logik* (1873), which was then followed in the second volume (1878) by the *Methodenlehre*.

67. See p. 87.

68. Ibid.

69. See p. 131ff.

70. See p. 134ff.

71. See p. 141ff.

72. See p. 95ff.

73. See p. 90ff.; p. 40ff.; p. 132ff.

74. See p. 129ff.

Book II
Section 1. Mythical Thought and the Rise of Science in Europe

1. [Dilthey's citation is from *Faust*, part 2, act 1, "Dark Gallery," in which Faust and Mephistopheles visit "the Mothers."]

2. See p. 102.

3. Bonitz, *Aristotelis Metaphysica* II, p. 3ff., argues exhaustively that Aristotle designated this science as *prōtē philosophia* ["first philosophy"], that the expression *meta ta phusika* ["after the physical matters"] for this part of the writings of Aristotle first appears in the period of Augustus (probably traceable to Andronicus), indicating first of all the essence of the writings [*den Schrifteninbegriff*] which followed the natural-scientific writings in the collection and in the systematic context which Aristotle clarified sufficiently, but which then—in line with the tendency of the period—was interpreted as a science of the transcendent.

[The confusion surrounding the nominal definition of the term *metaphysics* is based of course on the word *meta*, which means (among other things) both "after" and "beyond" or "transcending." We appear not to know substantially more about the matter than Dilthey's source, Bonitz, did. The *Historisches Wörterbuch der Philosophie* (Joachim Ritter and Karlfried Gründer, eds.; Darmstadt, 1980) says in vol. 5, no. 1188, under the rubric "Metaphysik": "For a long time people believed that [the term *metaphysics*] was due entirely to a librarian's accident: *Andronicus of Rhodes* (first century B.C.) was supposed to have put Aristotle's writings in order and in so doing placed what we today understand by Aristotle's 'metaphysics' after the 'physics.' And in this fashion the library designation *ta meta ta phusika* is supposed to have come about. But *Kant* surely did not believe that the term 'arose by chance in this way, because it is so precisely appropriate to the science itself.'. . . In fact we must suppose that this appellation had deeper and more objective grounds. Accordingly, the term 'metaphysics'—which might have been coined in immediate proximity to Aristotle and can first be proven to have been used by *Nicholas of Damascus*, a peripatetic of the second half of the first century B.C.—indicates the sequence of writings which, for their part, were grounded in the Aristotelian path of knowledge from the 'physical,' i.e., sense objects, to the trans-physical. . . . *Aristotle* himself calls this discipline 'first philosophy,' 'wisdom,' or 'theology.' "]

4. This definition of the *prōtē philosophia* [first philosophy] of Aristotle is derived by way of its connection particularly with the *Metaphysics* I, 1. 2. III, 1ff. VI, 1. With respect to the relation of the concepts of *sophia*, *prōtē sophia*, and *holos sophos* to *prōtē philosophia*. [wisdom, first wisdom, wholly wise, first philosophy] I refer the reader to Schwegler's *Kommentar zur Metaphysik*, p. 14, and to Bonitz's index—see *sophia*.

5. Thomas Aquinas, *Summa de Veritate* 1. I, chap. 1.

6. Kant's *Werke* (Rosenkranz) 2, 63ff.—1, 486ff.

7. Trendelenburg, *Logische Untersuchungen* (3d ed.) I, 6ff.; Überweg, *Logik* (3d ed.), p. 9ff. Schelling, who in his latest works likewise goes back to Aristotle—see his *Philosophie der Offenbarung*, W. W. II, 3, 38. Lotze, *Metaphysik*, p. 6ff.

8. Kant II, 350 (*Werke*, Rosenkranz).

9. Ibid., 648 and I, 490.

10. Apelt, *Metaphysik,* p. 21ff.

11. Kant I, 558.

12. Kant I, 493.

13. See p. 156.

14. Kant II, 241ff.

15. Turgot first tried to unravel what conformed to law in the development of intelligence, since Vico's *Scienza Nuova* (1725) related to the development of the nations. He begins correctly with language; for him mythical ideas indicate the first step in research aimed at causes. "La pauvreté des langues et la nécessité des métaphores, qui résultoient de cette pauvreté, firent qu'on employa les allégories et les fables pour expliquer les phénomènes physiques. Elles sont les premiers pas de la philosophie' (*Oeuvres,* II: 272 [Paris, 1808], based on Turgot's papers which related to his *Lectures on History* from 1750). "Les hommes, frappés des phénomènes sensibles, supposèrent que tous les effets indépendans de leur action étoient produits par des êtres semblables à eux, mais invisibles et plus puissans" (II:63).

[Turgot's texts read: "The poverty of languages and the necessity for metaphors which results from this poverty lead one to employ allegories and fables to explain physical phenomena. They are the first steps in philosophy." "Human beings, struck by sense phenomena, suppose that any effects that are independent of their own activity are produced by beings similar to them, but invisible and more powerful."]

16. Lubbock, *Entstehung der Zivilisation* (German edition, 1875), p. 172; cp. p. 170.

17. Spencer, *System der Philosophie,* vol. VI, p. 504ff. (summarized).

18. [See note 19, page 341, on "constructionism."]

19. [*Erlebnis,* or "lived experience," is a term which acquired philosophical status in the mid-nineteenth century and played a basic role in Dilthey's philosophy of the human sciences. It is crucial to his position that the epistemological basis of the human sciences differs essentially from that of the natural sciences. In contrast to the merely hypothetical relations established among phenomena or external reality and which we term "experience" (*Erfahrung*), the "lived experience," or *Erleben,* is an immediate inner awareness of reality by the totality of the mind's powers. Our most original knowledge is acquired by living contact with reality in our inner lives; our natural-scientific knowledge, on the other hand, is acquired only by way of analysis and synthesis, through a series of steps, logical progressions, and verification procedures.]

20. Max Müller, *Ursprung and Entwicklung der Religion,* p. 41.

21. *Schleiermacher* has unassailably established the starting point for this psychological condition. This is his imperishable merit: he has demonstrated that the intellectualistic grounding of religion on logical reasoning which functions by way of the concepts of cause, understanding, and purpose is a secondary issue; he has shown how self-awareness contains facts which constitute the starting point of all religious life. See his *Dogmatik,* no. 36, 1 (3d ed.): "We always find ourselves only in a state of continuing existence, and our being is always already in process; consequently, so long as we prescind from all else and posit ourselves only as finite being, our self-consciousness can also represent this finite being only in its continuing existence. And we would do this so completely—since in fact our absolute feeling of dependence is such an all-pervading element of our self-consciousness—that we can say that no matter what our general situation might be or at what particular point in time we happened to find ourselves, whenever we had our wits about us we would always find ourselves only in that condition, and can say further that we would also always extend this feeling to all of finite being." [Schleiermacher's] error lay in the fact that this profound insight did not lead him to break with intellectualistic metaphysics at this point and to give philosophy a psychological foundation which corresponded with his point of departure. Thus he fell victim to Platonism and to the powerful current of the philosophy of nature of his time.

22. Mimnermus, fragment; Bergk II (4th ed.), 26.

23. *Arkhe.* Simplicius, *In Physicam,* f. 6r, 36–54. Hippolytus, *Refutatio Haeresium* I, 6. Going back to Theophrastus, cp. Diels, *Doxographi,* 133, 176; Zeller I (4th ed.), 203.

24. [In accordance with an ancient notion or feeling, Anaximander saw *temporality* itself as a root cause of disorder, dissolution, and even injustice in the world order. For him only *to apeiron*—which is a substance infinite, eternal, and all-encompassing—is perfect; all else is partial and one-sided, something demonstrated by the phenomena of generation and corruption which mark all temporal beings.]

25. See note 17, pages 340–41.

26. Pseudo-Plutarch, *De Placitis Philosophorum* II, 1. See also *Stobaei Eclogae* I, 21; p. 450 in Heer. See Diels, 327.

27. *Nomos* and *logos*.

Section 2. Metaphysical Stage in the Development of the Ancient Peoples

1. Because of the state of the documentation regarding Parmenides, the discussion of his outstanding position in the history of metaphysics unfortunately can take place only through a kind of subjective reproduction which would ordinarily not be allowed.

2. This explains the meaning of the much discussed proposition: *to gar auto noein estin te kai einai.* ["For to know and to be are the same."] (in Mullach, *Fragmenta Philosophorum Graecorum* I, 118, vol. 40). When Zeller (vol. I, 4th ed., 512) reads *estin* and translates "for the same thing can be both conceived of and exist," one would expect *noeisthai* ("to be known"), but the "can" also hardly corresponds to the thought of Parmenides. And the meaning of the declaration is corroborated through verse 94: *touton d'esti noein te kai houneken esti noēma* ["It is the same to be and therefore to be thought."] and the immediately following grounding for it.

3. We are providing the oldest version of this idea, which became so important for natural science: Parmenides, vol. 77 (in Mullach: *Fragmenta Philosophorum Graecorum* I, 121): *tōs genesis men apesbestai kai apistos olethros* ["Thus coming to be is eliminated and perishing unbelievable."] and vol. 69: *touneken oute genesthai out' ollusthai anēke dikē* ["Therefore justice never experiences birth or destruction."]

4. Simplicius, *In Physicam,* f. 7r, 6ff. (Diels, *Doxographi,* 483), borrowed, to be sure, from Theophrastus: *Leukippos de ho Heleatēs ē Milēsios . . . koinōnēsas Parmenidēi tēs philosophias ou tēn autēn ebadise Parmenidēi kai Senophanei peri tōn onton hodon.* [Leucippus of Elea or Miletus . . .an associate of Parmenides in philosophy, did not follow the same path as Parmenides and Xenophanes with respect to existing things.]

5. Aristotle, *Physics* IV, 6.

6. Simplicius, *In Physicam,* f. 35r. (Mullach I, 251, fr. 15). Cp. *Zeller's* clear demonstration that Anaxagoras was referring to Leucippus with polemical intent (I, 4th ed., 920ff.).

7. Plutarch, *Adversus Colotem,* chap. 4, p. 1109A. Cp. Sextus Empiricus, *Adversus Mathematicos* VII, 389.

8. Zeller, 857ff.

9. *Eudemian Ethics* I, 5; cp. *Nichomachean Ethics* X, 9.

10. Apart from the recognized passages in Plutarch, see Plato's *Phaedrus,* p. 270A.

11. Simplicius, *In Physicam,* f. 33v. (Mullach I, 248,fr. 1).

12. Simplicius, *In Physicam,* f. 34v. (Mullach I, 251,fr. 17).

13. Simplicius, *In Physicam,* f. 35v. (Mullach I, 248, fr. 3.): *spermata pantōn chrēmatōn* ["the seeds of all things"].

14. It is noteworthy that he used the oldest experiment on *sense deception* about which we have any information as a proof in this connection. If one adds a dark-colored fluid drop by drop to white, our sense perception cannot distinguish the gradual changes in color even though these changes are actually taking place. His paradox of the black snow belongs in the same context. For other experiments of Anaxagoras see Aristotle's *Physics* IV, 6.

15. This conclusion of Anaxagoras from Silenus is preserved in Diogenes Laertius II, 11f. With respect to what follows one may note that the purpose of this presentation leaves aside the question whether Anaxagoras was the first to posit these theories.

16. Hyppolytus, *Philosophumena* VIII, 9 (Diels, 562). In fact Hippias combines in his report: that Anaxagoras first exactly determined eclipses and phases of the moon and: that he explained the moon as an earthlike body and also admitted mountains and valleys on it.

17. Cp. Parmenides, however, v. 144 (Mullach I, 128).

18. In *Cratylus,* 409A.

19. [Nemea was a valley in northern Argolis in ancient Greece. Greek mythology cites the first of the labors of Heracles (Hercules) as the slaying of the Nemean lion by strangling.]

20. Diogenes Laertius, ibid.

21. See Humboldt, *Kosmos* (1st ed.) II, 348, 501; cp. I, 139 among other places based on Jacobi's manuscript notes on the mathematical knowledge of the Greeks. Humboldt mentions these notes, but they have been lost or lie hidden somewhere. See Plutarch, *De Facie in Orbe Lunae*, chap. 6, p. 923C and Ideler, *Meteorologia Veterum Graecorum et Romanorum* (1832), p. 6.

22. Simplicius, *In Physicam*, f. 33v., 35r (Mullach I, 249 fr. 6).

23. This is in agreement with the manner in which the pole is mentioned in Diogenes' article on Anaxagoras; see Diogenes Laertius, II, 9. Indeed, the part of the heavens at which one finds this location was especially important from the time of Homer: "Ursa, which is otherwise called the Great Bear, which revolves at the same spot. . .and alone never sinks into Oceanus's bath." Aratus remarks (*Phenomena*, 37ff.) that the Greeks used the Great Bear in their navigation because it is brighter and can be seen more easily at the onset of night. The Phoenicians go by the Small Bear, which is admittedly darker but is more useful to sailors because it describes a smaller circle.

24. It is valuable to me to find this combination, which I have been setting forth for a number of years now in my lectures, in the *Mémoires de l'Institut* vol. XXIX, p. 176ff.: Martin, "Hypothèses Astronomiques des Plus Anciens Philosophes de la Grèce Étrangers à la Notion de la Sphéricité de la Terre" ["Astronomical hypotheses of the ancient Greek philosophers unacquainted with the sphericity of the earth"].

25. Anaxagoras says: with no *khrēmati*, or particle.

26. Simplicius, *In Physicam* f. 33v. (Mullach I, 249, fr. 6).

27. Ibid.

28. Aristotle, *De Anima* I, 2, p. 404b 1 says of Anaxagoras: *pollakhou men gar to aition tou kalōs kai orthōs ton noun legei.* ["He tells us in many places that mind is the cause of the beautiful and the orderly."] Anaxagoras himself says (Mullach I, 249, fr. 6): *kai hokoia emelle esesthai kai hokoia ēn kai hassa nun esti kai hokoia estai, panta diekosmēse noos.* ["And whatever things were future or past or now are or will be, the mind *has ordered them all.*"]

29. [The work referred to here is the statue of Zeus at Olympia, executed by Phidias from 437 to about 433 B.C., perhaps the greatest work of the master sculptor of Greece.]

30. Diels, 337ff., for parallel passages in Plutarch and Stobaeus; cp. Diogenes Laertius, II, 9. That according to Anaxagoras the earth was inclined toward the south (and not, on the contrary, that the celestial axis and pole were inclined) must be understood according to the wording of parallel passages and the declarations of the atomists about the theory in question. *Humboldt* (*Kosmos* 3, 451) appears to relate the passage to the inclination of the ecliptic. He says "Greek antiquity was much preoccupied with the inclination of the ecliptic. . . .According to [Pseudo-] Plutarch (*De Placitis Philosophorum* II, 8) Anaxagoras believed 'that the world, after it had come into being and had brought forth living beings from its womb, inclined of its own accord toward a southern direction. . . .The coming about of the inclination of the ecliptic was taken as a cosmic event.' " This misconception doubtless arose through relating this inclination of the earth's surface to the emergence of climates.

31. This is the tradition concerning the sun and the moon. But one may no doubt assume that he also traced the other irregular motions he perceived in the heavens to the same cause which he assumed in reference to the sun and moon. He and his contemporaries distinguished the planets as stars which changed their location (Aristotle, *Meteorologia* I, 6, p. 342b 27) and he explained the comets by their conjunction. But even Democritus still did not know their number and their motions any more exactly (Seneca, *Naturales Quaestiones*, 7, 3. Cp. Schaubach, *Anaxagoras,* fr., p. 166f.)

32. Report of Sosigenes in Simplicius, *De Caelo,* Scholium, p. 498b 2: *tinōn hupotetheisōn homalōn kai tetagmenōn kinēseōn diasōthēi ta peri tas kinēseis tōn planōmenōn phainomena.* ["What even and ordered movements we must assume to maintain the phenomena relating to the movements of the planets."]

33. See page 173ff.

34. See note 3 to page 346.

35. [A body's *Aggregatzustand* refers to one of the three phenomenal forms of matter: gaseous, liquid, or solid.]

36. On this important point Protagoras rendered assistance in establishing a more precise foundation for atomism.

37. As Zeller did (I, 3d ed., 779, 791), and his view has been decisive (see, for example, Lange, *Geschichte des Materialismus,* I, 2d ed., 38ff.). I can only point out why his reasons do not convince me. The passages in Aristotle (*De Caelo* IV, 2, 308b 35) and Theophrastus (*De Sensibus* 61, 71 [Diels, 516ff.]) only prove the passages given in the text regarding the connections between atoms. But one is not justified in transferring the weight and vertical fall of these composite bodies to the behavior of atoms revolving in the *dinos* (whirling). If one avoids doing that, these passages are in harmony with those that exclude the vertical fall of atoms as the initial condition and as such establish the *dinos:* Aristotle, *De Caelo* III, 2, p. 300b 8 and *Metaphysics* I, 4, p. 985b 19. See Theophrastus in Simplicius, *In Physicam,* f. 7r, 6ff. (Diels, 483ff.) and Diogenes Laertius IX, 44, 45. See [Pseudo-] Plutarch, *De Placitis Philosophorum* I, 23 with parallel passages (Diels, 319); Epicurus, 2d letter, in Diogenes Laertius X, 90; Cicero, *De Fato* 20, 46.

38. Indeed, Sextus Empiricus labels him a relativist in *Adversus Mathematicos* VII, 60: *phēsi . . . tōn pros ti einai tēn alētheian* ["He says . . . that relativism is the truth."]

39. The connection between Protagoras' theory of perception and Heraclitus and the explanation of perception as a coming together of movements, hence a contact, seems indeed to be assured by the fact that Protagoras could have provided clarity to his theorem only by probing into the process of perception; but it is out of the question that he did provide such clarity and that Plato would impute to him an altogether different explanation. This [explanation of Protagoras' theory of perception] is corroborated by the account of Sextus Empiricus (*Hypotyposes* I, 216ff.; *Adversus Mathematicos* VII, 60ff.), which cannot be traced back to Plato as its exclusive source (Zeller I, 4th ed., 984). Apart from this difference, I refer the reader also to the account in Laas, *Idealismus und Positivismus* I (1879).

40. Aristotle, *Metaphysics* IV, 4, p. 1007b 22.

41. Pseudo-Aristotle, *On Melissus, Xenophanes, and Gorgias,* p. 979b 21ff.

42. Lange's conception of the structure of Greek intellectual development arrives at the antithesis: "We have shown above how, *taken abstractly,* the standpoint of the Sophists *could* have been developed still further, but if we had to demonstrate the motive forces that might have accomplished that without the intervention of the Socratic reaction, then we would encounter difficulties" (*Geschichte des Materialismus* I, 43). Thus, according to Lange, the premises of modern theory of knowledge were available in the fifth century B.C.: all that was lacking was the persons who might have drawn the conclusions!

43. The critical difficulties which arise out of the difference between the account of Xenophon and the picture given by Plato are not adequately resolved by the canon set up by Schleiermacher and accepted by most researchers since then (cp. also the literature in Zeller II (3d ed., 85ff.); (they will be adequately resolved) only if one uses Plato's *Apology* of Socrates in rendering a critical decision between Xenophon's account and the other Platonic writings. The defense made sense only if it gave a true picture of Socrates, at least with respect to the matters he was accused of. Fidelity of presentation is thus guaranteed in this case, whereas in all Plato's other works it can be established only by an investigation more open to discussion.

44. With respect to this fundamental state of affairs the direct description in the *Apology,* the overall position Plato ascribes to his Socrates, and the principal passage in Xenophon agree about the conduct of Socrates (*Memorabilia* IV, 6). Cp. especially at no. 13: *epi tēn hupothesin epanēgen an panta ton logon* ["he would lead the whole discussion back to the point at issue. . ."] and at no. 14: *houtō de tōn logōn epanagomenōn kai tois antilegousin autois phaneron egigneto talēthes.* ["Through argumentation of this kind the truth became clear even to those who quarreled with him."] He sought for *asphaleian logou* (no. 15) ["the certainty of an argument"].

45. This situation is described with Socratic irony in Plato's *Apology,* p. 21B f.; cp. Xenophon, *Memorabilia* IV, 5, no. 12.

46. Plato, *Apology,* 22–24.

47. Compare Xenophon's account of the individual conversations as well as his awkward but sincere characterization of Socrates' conduct (in IV, 6) in deciding moral and political questions by tracing them to concepts which were proven on the epistemological basis of moral consciousness. One has to evaluate the special nature of these value-concepts—which contain theses as well—in

this connection. Compare further Aristotle (passages in Bonitz, *Index Aristotelicus*, p. 741). If Aristotle (*Metaphysics* XIII, 4, p. 1078b 27) ascribes induction and definition (and not merely the latter) to Socrates, one must take account of the fact that Aristotle was not familiar with analytical method as a component in a logical operation and therefore had to classify Socrates' whole method under induction.

48. Plato, *Sophist*, 242CD. Compare the related presentation in the *Theaetetus*, 180f. and the corresponding transition to the task of going back from the *assertions of the older schools* to their *epistemological grounds*.

49. *Timaeus*, 51E; *Meno*, 97f.; *Republic* VI, 506.

50. *Sophist*, 243ff.; *Theaetetus*, 181ff.

51. *Republic* VI, 511 sketches out this problem of the theory of knowledge for the first time in the history of the sciences; then in the *Republic* VII, 523–34, we find a synopsis of these positive sciences and emerging from that the problem of dialectic: "The dialectical method alone, setting aside hypotheses (*hupotheseis*), goes directly to the source itself to establish its ground solidly" (533c).

52. In the *Republic* VII, 527B, the *art of measurement* is designated as a "science of the permanently existing" and is accordingly set *alongside the development of the ideas*. Plato's purely theoretical thought is guided by mathematics, which was the already established science of that period. If number, especially, was for him the palpable schema for the purely conceptual, the logic of his system pushed him toward subordinating mathematical quantities and the Ideas to an overarching concept which would then be the most universal expression of the conditions for the conceivability of the world. He later discovered such a concept in a more abstract notion of number: accordingly, he distinguished between numbers in a narrower sense, which consist of uniform units such that each one of these numbers differed from the others only with respect to magnitude, and ideal numbers, each of which differs in kind from the others.

53. *Phaedo*, 100f.

54. *Meno*, 82ff. Cp. *Phaedo*, 72ff.

55. At any rate it is impossible in the nature of the case to establish precisely the boundary between the mythical and the scientific in this proof of Plato's. In his *Geschichte der Philosophie* (p. 101) Schleiermacher therefore reinterpreted it in this sense: "Plato called this timeless indwelling derived from primordial intuition a *mnēmē* [recollection]." But even in the sphere of timelessness the assumption behind the theory of ideas remains the relation of an always and everywhere identical knowledge to a timeless and everywhere identical being that constitutes its real object. For the rest see Zeller, II (3d ed.), p. 555ff.

56. It could be demonstrated how any such rigorous establishing of the theory of ideas presupposes the idea of a contact with the object (the immaterial ideas) in intuitive thought [*in dem anschaulichen Denken*]. And it is in conformity with this inner structure grounding the theory of ideas that the *Phaedrus*—on the basis of completely different, i.e., literary/historical grounds, developed by Schleiermacher, Spengel, and Usener—must be recognized as one of Plato's early writings and contains precisely this structure of the theory of ideas (though in rough draft), setting out in fact from tracing moral consciousness to such a contact.

57. Plato, *Philebus*, 28E, cp. 30 also and especially the *Timaeus* and the *Laws* at various passages.

58. See page 190ff.

59. Aristotle, *De Anima* I, 2, p. 403b f.

60. Cp. Theophrastus, *De Sensibus* 3 (in Diels, p. 499).

61. Aristotle, *De Anima* I, 2, p. 404b 17: *ginōskesthai gar tōi homoiōi to homoion*. ["For like is known by like."] He appeals in this matter to the *Timaeus* and to his treatise *peri philosophias* [*On Philosophy*] in which he reports Plato's teaching on the basis of lectures he delivered. On the whole passage see Trendelenburg, *On Aristotle's De Anima* (1877, 2d ed.), p. 181ff.

62. The wording has been carefully chosen on account of the notorious difficulties relating to the position of the divine *nous* [mind] vis-à-vis substantial forms and stellar spirits [*Gestirngeister*].

63. This is in the polemic against the theory of ideas. See *Metaphysics* I, 9, p. 993a I.

64. Cp. the passages and detailed discussion in Zeller, II, (3d ed.), 188ff.

65. *To d'aisthētikon dunamei estin oion to aisthēton ēdē entelecheiai* ["what has the power of sensation is, potentially, like what the perceived object is actually."] in *De Anima* II, 5, p. 418a 3.

66. *De Anima* III, 1, p. 424b 22.

67. Cp. the conclusion of the main logical treatise we have available to us in the form of the two *Analytics;* see the *Posterior Analytic* II, 19, p. 100b.

68. Cp. p. 186ff.

69. Cp. the noteworthy observations of Simplicius on *De Caelo,* scholium, p. 491b 3.

70. *Posterior Analytics,* II, 19, p. 100b 14: *ei oun mēden allo par'epistēmēn genos echomen alēthes, nous an ein epistēmēs arkhē. kai hē men arkhē tēs arkhēs ein an, hē de pasa homoiōs ekhei pros to hapan pragma.* ["If, therefore, it is the only other kind of true thinking except scientific knowing, intuition will be the originative source of scientific knowledge. And the originative source of science grasps the original basic premise, which science as a whole is similarly related as originative source to the whole body of fact." Translation by G. R. G. Mure in *Introduction to Aristotle,* ed. Richard McKeon (New York: Modern Library, 1947)]

71. He explains this himself with justified self-esteem in *Sophistici Elenchi,* 33, p. 183b 34 and p. 184b 1.

72. In his *Commentary on Euclid* (see Friedländer, p. 70) Proclus reports that Euclid wrote a special treatise on logical fallacies, which proves his extensive preoccupation with logical theory.

73. Aristotle, *Metaphysics* IX, 10. p. 1051a 34; cp. IV, 7, p. 1011b 23.

74. Aristotle, *Metaphysics* V, 7, p. 1017a 23 [24]: *hosakhōs gar legetai, tosautakhōs to einai sēmainei.* ["For 'to be' has as many meanings as there are ways of speaking."]

75. Sigwart, *Logik* I, 394.

76. A great merit of *Prantl* is that he was the first to show in thorough detail the relation of Aristotle's logic to his metaphysics and accordingly the correct meaning of Aristotle's logic. *Sigwart* went on from there to provide a critical demonstration of the limits to the value of Aristotle's syllogistic theory.

77. *Arkhē* is the term which encompasses both meanings. *Metaphysics* V, 1, p. 1013a 17, the division: "Thus everything which is *arkhē* bears the general characteristic that it is the first thing by which something is, or becomes, or is known."

78. Cp. p. 174ff.

79. *Metaphysics* I, 3 and 10, with which one should compare the step-by-step derivation of principles in the *Physics* (esp. Books I and II).

80. Aristotle, *Physics* I, 2, p. 185a 12.

81. Aristotle, *Physics* I, 1, p. 184a 21: *esti d'ēmin prōton dēla kai saphē ta sugkekhumena mallon; husteron d'ek toutōn ginetai gnōrima ta stoikheia.* ["What is manifest and obvious to us at first are, instead, indiscriminate masses of things; later on their rudiments become clear to us."]

82. On this tripartite division into *ousia* [substance], *pathos* [passivity], and *pros ti* [purpose] see Prantl, *Geschichte der Logik* I, 190.

83. Aristotle, *Metaphysics* IV, 1, p. 1003a 21.

84. Ibid., 2, p. 1003a f.

85. *Metaphysics* VII, 1, p. 1028a 11, 18.

86. Cp. VII, 1, p. 1028 a 13; p. 1028b 6; IX, 1, p. 1045b 27; XII, 1, p. 1069a 18.

87. To complete the enumeration of the ten categories one must add to those mentioned *ekhein* [*habitus,* or possession] and *keisthai* [*situs,* or position]. See the general survey in Prantl's *Geschichte der Logik* I, 207.

88. Plato, *Sophist,* 247D E.

89. "Ipsam rerum substantiam in agendi patiendique vi consistere" ["The very substance of things consists in the power of acting and being acted upon"]: Leibniz, *Opera Philosophica* I, 156 (Erdmann).

90. *Katēgorountai kata tōn ousiōn.* ["They signify in accordance with their substances."] Cp. Bonitz, *Index Aristotelicus* under *ousia.*

91. *Categories,* 5, p. 2a 11.

92. *Physics* III, 3, p. 202a 25: *epei oun amphō kinēseis.* ["Since then they are both motions."] Cp. *On Generation and Corruption* I, 7, p. 324a 24 and *Metaphysics* VII, 4, p. 1029b 22. In the last-cited passage *kinēsis* [motion] is inserted as a category in place of *poiein* [activity] and *paskhein* [passivity].

93. *De Anima* II, 5, p. 416b 33.

94. Aristotle, *On Generation and Corruption* I, 7, p. 323b.

95. The same metaphysical way of treating the problem is the source of the unfortunate and

insoluble question whether substance is to be sought after in form or in matter or in the individual object. Cp. Aristotle, *Metaphysics* VII, 3, p. 1028b 33 and the telling exposition in Zeller, op. cit., 309ff.; 344ff.

96. Aristotle, *De Generatione Animalium* V, 1, p. 778a 30.

97. Aristotle, *De Generatione Animalium* III, 11, p. 762a 18.

98. Aristotle, *Metaphysics* XII, 8, p. 1073b 4.

99. Aristotle, *Metaphysics* VI, 1 p. 1026a 10.

100. This line of argument has been carried out with masterful rigor in the eighth book of the *Physics*, which thus leads into the *Metaphysics*.

101. *Metaphysics* XII, 7: In popular fashion and without using metaphysical concepts and the middle term of the astronomical facts of the case, Simplicius (in *De Caelo*, scholium, p. 487a 6) provides the argument which leads back to the most perfect being.

102. Aristotle, *De Caelo* II, 12, p. 292b 18; *Metaphysics* XII, 7, p. 1072b 3.

103. Cicero, *De Natura Deorum* II, 37, 95.

104. Op. cit., p. 1073b 16.

105. The enduring power of these ideas can be deduced not only from proof based on the well-known passages but also because the sophistic enlightenment could view religion as an invention of the art of politics (Critias in Sextus Empiricus, *Adversus Mathematicos* IX, 54; Plato, *Laws* X, 889E).

106. Cp. Plato's *Theaetetus*, 167, 172A; *Protagoras*, 334.

107. Cp. Aristotle, *Politics* I, 18, p. 1260a 24 with Plato's *Meno*.

108. Cf. p. 123ff.

109. The passages from Plato must be used in accordance with this rule: Where he personally makes inferences, this is indicated by the way in which they are drawn out from an opponent through reasoning; on the other hand, where propositions are put before Socrates—such as those of Thrasymachus and Glaucon in the first and second books of the *Republic*—we have a report of someone else's theory. With respect to the theoretical presentations made by Glaucon, Plato would not have put that into the mouth of a youth if it were an independent further development.

110. Cp. especially the discussion between the Melians and the Athenian legates in Thucydides V, 85ff., from the year 416.

111. See p. 124ff.

112. See p. 179ff. and p. 194ff.

113. The derivation of the *polis* from division of labor and from trade (*Republic*, 369ff.) merely confirms this. For it shows that Plato did consider the bearing of particular interests on the communal good, but did not believe he could establish the unity of will in his state on it.

114. Cp. the description of the same error in the *Philosophie der Geschichte*, p. 109ff.

115. See p. 141ff.

116. Cp. further Aristotle's *Politics* I, 2, p. 1252b 30 and p. 1253a 19.

117. Cp. p. 133ff.

118. Cp. p. 118ff.

119. The purpose of the state is the realization of eudaemonism, of the *eu Zēn* ["good life"] or also of the *Zoēs teleias kai autarkous* ["fullness and perfection of life"].

120. See p. 117ff.

121. Aristotle, *Politics* III, 3, p. 1276b 1.

122. Aristotle, *Politics* VII, 4, p. 1325b 40.

123. Aristotle, *Politics* III, 6, p. 1278b 8.

124. Aristotle, *Politics* III, 1, p. 1275a 22.

125. *Nichomachean Ethics* III, 7, p. 1113b 6. For more see Trendelenburg, *Historische Beiträge* II, 149ff.

126. Diogenes Laertius IX, 103: *peri men ōn hōs anthrōpoi paskhomen, homologoumen.* ["We admit that as men we suffer in these areas."]

127. Ibid.

128. Sextus Empiricus, *Hypotyposes* I, 19f.

129. Ibid., as well as Diogenes Laertius, IX, 103

130. *Kai gar hoti hēmera esti kai hoti zōmen kai alla polla tōn en tōi biōi phainomenōn diaginōskomen; peri d'ōn hoi dogmatikoi diabebaiountai tōi logōi, phamenoi kateilēphthai, peri toutōn epekhomen hōs adēlōn, mona de ta pathē ginōskomen.* ["For we can see that it is daytime and that we

are living and many other things which are evident in life. But with respect to the things the scholars argue about with so much noise, saying they are sure about them, we make no judgment about them, for all we know is what we sense."] Diogenes Laertius, IX, 103.

131. Sextus Empiricus, *Hypotyposes* I, 13, 20.

132. Diogenes Laertius IX, 102–8.

133. Sextus Empiricus, *Hypotyposes* I, 15.

134. The first four tropes of Sextus Empiricus (*Hypotyposes* I, 40–117) are summarized in this paragraph.

135. Likewise the fifth to the seventh trope, *Hypotyposes* I, 118–34.

136. For the 8th trope, see 135ff.; cp. 39 as well as Gellius, *Noctes Atticae* XI, 5, 7: Omnes omnino res, quae sensus hominum movent, *tōn pros ti* esse dicunt. ["They say that absolutely all things which affect the senses of men are purely relative."]

137. Sextus Empiricus, *Adversus Mathematicos* IX, 204ff.

138. Nevertheless, Carneades also did not wish to deny the existence of the gods. Cicero, *De Natura Deorum* III, 17, 44: Haec Carneades aiebat, non ut deos tolleret, sed ut Stoicos nihil de diis explicare convinceret. ["Carneades said these things, not to eliminate the gods, but that he might convince the Stoics to explain nothing concerning the gods."]

139. Cp. the outstanding treatment in "Recherches Historiques sur le Principe d'Archimède" by M. Charles Thurot (*Revue Archéologique* 1868–69).

140. On Asclepiades cp. Lasswitz, *Vierteljahrsschrift für Wissenschaftliche Philosophie* III, 425ff.

Section 3. Metaphysical Stage of Modern European Peoples

1. This according to Jacob Burckhardt, who has most profoundly portrayed the first centuries after the birth of Christ in his work on the period of Constantine the Great. See that work, p. 140ff.

2. Schleiermacher, *Psychologie,* p. 195.

3. Cp. p. 185.

4. The main passage on this is in Philo, *De Ebrietate,* p. 382–88 (Mangey).

5. Philo, *Legum Allegoriae* I, p. 62 (Mangey).

6. Augustine, *Contra Academicos* III, chap. 11.

7. Augustine, *De Civitate Dei* XI, chap. 26.

8. Cp. p. 185 and p. 231.

9. Augustine uses this division of philosophical problems in *De Civitate Dei* XI, chap. 25; cp. VIII, chaps. 6–8.

10. Ibid., chap. 25.

11. Augustine, *Epistolae,* 118, chap. 3; *De Civitate Dei* II, chap. 7.

12. *De Civitate Dei* XI, chap. 26.

13. Augustine, *De Divinis Quaestionibus LXXXIII. Quaestio* 46 defines the concept of the idea as it then passed over into the Middle Ages: "Sunt ideae principales formae quaedam vel rationes (wobei er ausdrücklich bemerkt, dass dieser Begriff die ursprüngliche Ideenlehre überschreite) rerum stabiles atque incommutabiles, quae ipsae formatae non sunt, ac per hoc aeternae ac semper eodem modo sese habentes, quae in divina intelligentia continentur." ["The principal ideas are certain permanent and unchanging forms or essences (whereby he expressly remarks that this concept goes beyond the original theory of ideas) which have not been created themselves, hence are eternal and always identically disposed, and which are contained in the divine intelligence."]

14. The most important passages can be found in the tenth book of *Writings on the Trinity.* Cp. *De Genesi ad Litteram Libri Duodecim* VII, chap. 21.

15. *De Genesi ad Litteram Libri Duodecim* VII, chaps. 20, 21; *De Vera Religione,* chap. 29; *De Libero Arbitrio* II, chap. 3ff.

16. *Sermones,* 241, chap. 2; *Epistolae,* 166, chap. 2; *De Vera Religione,* chaps. 30, 31.

17. Augustine, *De Trinitate* XI, chap. 6.

18. *De Civitate Dei* XIX, chap. 18: Civitas Dei talem dubitationem tanquam dementiam detestatur. . . .creditque sensibus in rei cuiusque evidentia, quibus per corpus animus utitur,

quoniam miserabilius fallitur, qui nunquam putat eis esse credendum. ["The City of God despises such skepticism as a kind of madness. . . .it believes in the report of the senses which the mind uses to its own purposes because the man who thinks we should never trust them is more seriously mistaken."]

19. See the beautiful presentation of the doctrine of the Highest Good in *De Civitate Dei* XIX, chaps. 3 and 4.

20. Besides the last-cited passage, see ibid., VIII, chap. 8.

21. Ibid., V, chaps. 10 and 11.

22. See the digression in his autobiography, the *Confessions* VII, chaps. 10–15.

23. Augustine, *De Libero Arbitrio* II, chap. 3ff.

24. *Confessions* I, chap. 6.

25. *De Musica*, esp. in the 6th book.

26. Augustine, *Confessions* XI, chaps. 11–30.

27. More significant than the external literary elements (confessions, soliloquies) is the internal form of writing: Augustine alternates between monologue, prayer, and speech making, and the captivating power of his writings partially rests on this living relationship, at times to himself, at times to the spiritual experience of others, at times to God. His lack of talent for the composition of large-scale works goes hand in hand with this.

28. See Flügel in the *Zeitschrift der Deutschen Morgenländischen Gesellschaft,* vol. XIII, p. 26.

29. See p. 239ff.

30. As was shown in the case of Augustine, p. 233ff.

31. One finds this combination of the two standpoints (for the first of which proofs are superfluous) in the famous statement of Bernard of Clairvaux: "Quid enim magis contra rationem, quam ratione rationem conari transcendere? Et quid magis contra fidem, quam credere nolle, quicquid non possis ratione attingere?" ["For what is more contrary to reason than to strive to transcend reason by reason? And what is more contrary to faith than to refuse to believe whatever you cannot attain by reason?"] For the second part see, e.g., Hugh of St. Victor, *De Sacramentis* I, part 10, chap. 2.

32. Anselm, *De Fide Trinitatis,* preface and chaps. 1, 2; *De Concordia Praescientiae Dei cum Libero Arbitrio,* question III, chap. 6. The solution of the apparent contradictions lies for Anselm in the assumption that even the inaccessible mystery of faith is a rational structure in God. Although Anselm hereby separates himself from the mystics, he makes contact on the other side on this point with Scotus Erigena and Abelard. See Eadmer, *Vita Sancti Anselmi* I, chap. 9.

33. For the meaning offered here of the treatise *Sic et Non* by Abelard, the conclusion of the prologue is decisive. For the rest, see the description (based on John of Salisbury, Richard of St. Victor, Abelard, etc.) of the rationalistic factions in Reuter, *Geschichte der Aufklärung* I, 168ff.

34. This was the outcome of the last-mentioned tendency. It can be deduced from the well-known formula of Scotus Erigena in *De Divisione Naturae* I, chap. 66, p. 511B (Floss). But neither Scotus Erigena's nor Abelard's rationalism was unbounded. The theory one finds in both of them, that restricts the relation of concepts and judgments of understanding to finite reality, which they were designed to deal with (for after all a sentence, with its indispensable verb, includes temporality as a limit), is an attempt to defend the actual transcendence of God against rationalists. See Abelard, *Theologia Christiana* I; III, p. 1246B, 1247B (Migne) as well as the parallel passage of the introduction and Scotus Erigena, *De Divisione Naturae* I, chap. 15ff. 463B, chap. 73; p. 518B.

35. For the historical proof of this we are indebted mainly to Cousin, Jourdain, Hauréau, and Prantl.

36. See Hauréau, *Histoire de la Philosophie Scolastique* I, 42ff. and Prantl on Porphyry in the *Geschichte der Logik* I, 626ff.; on Boethius, 679ff.; on the disputed question II, 1ff., 35ff.

37. Scotus Erigena, for example, in *De Divisione Naturae* I, chap. 29ff., p. 475B; IV, chap. 4, p. 748; William of Champeaux according to the report in the treatise *De Generibus* (*Ouvrages Inédits d'Abélard,* Cousin), p. 513ff. and in Abelard's *Epistolae* I, chap. 2, p. 119.

38. Abelard belonged among them. See his *Introductio ad Theologiam* II, chap. 13, p. 1070.

39. In the *Glossulae Super Porphyrium* according to the excerpt from Rémusat, *Abälard* II, p. 98. In addition there was the logical untenability of this realism, which was developed in *De Generibus,* p. 514ff.

40. After the controversy in which Gottschalk destroyed human freedom by means of the

concept of the immutability of God while Scotus Erigena identified that freedom with necessity, Anselm has offered the profoundest treatment of this problem in the two treatises *De Libero Arbitrio* and *De Concordia Praescientiae et Praedestinationis cum Libero Arbitrio.*

41. Mutazila designates a sect or a band that separates itself from a larger whole. The name was transferred to the most important among the sects of Islam. See Steiner, *Die Mutaziliten,* p. 24ff. With respect to the content of the controversy, the defenders of human freedom of will were called Kadarija. See ibid., 26ff. and Munk, *Mélanges de Philosophie Juive et Arabe,* p. 310. There is an account of them in Shahrastani's *Religionsparteien und Philosophenschulen,* trans. Haarbrücker I, 12ff., 40ff., 84ff.; II, 386ff., 393ff.

42. The comparison of sectarian life from all sides forces this view upon us, and the historical situation makes it probable. See Munk, *Mélanges,* p. 312.

43. Shahrastani I, 55, 59. The differences among the factions of the Mutazila are not taken into account here.

44. Ibid., 53ff.

45. Ibid., 88ff.

46. Ibid., I, 77; cp. Steiner's rendering of the content of this difficult passage, p. 70.

47. Ibid., 98ff., esp. 102ff., on which see Steiner, p. 86.

48. In his *Spekulative Dogmatik;* see *Philosophie und Theologie des Averroës,* trans. Müller, p. 45. Under this title and pagination I am citing the two treatises joined in the translation: *Harmonie der Religion und Philosophie* and *Spekulative Dogmatik.*

49. *Philosophie und Theologie des Averroës,* trans. Müller, p. 98ff.

50. Anselm, *De Concordia,* question I: beginning; II: beginning. *Opera,* pp. 507A, 519C (Migne). See the theses and antitheses in Abelard, *Sic et Non,* chaps. 26–38 in this connection. *Opera,* p. 1386Cff. (Migne).

51. The older Scholastics simply ascribed the preservation of the world to creation; the thesis developed above was convincingly presented by Thomas in the *Summa Theologiae,* p. 1, q. 103, 104, "De Gubernatione Rerum," etc., esp. q. 104, art. 1: Conservatio rerum a Deo non est per aliquam novam actionem, sed per continuationem actionis, quae dat esse, quae quidem actio est sine motu et tempore, sicut etiam conservatio luminis in aere est per continuatum influxum a sole. ["The conservation of things by God is not through some new action but through continuation of the action by which he grants existence, which action to be sure is without motion and time, just as the conservation of light in the air is through continued influx from the sun."]

52. Hence from this standpoint (which conflicts with moral consciousness) evil must be regarded as relative and the totality of reality as good. Let us not be deceived by words here. Thus teach Scotus Erigena (deviation is surely accommodation), the most important of the Sufis and the mystics of the Christian Middle Ages and also, very beautifully, Jacob Böhme: "In such lofty speculation one finds that all of this issues from and out of God himself and that it belongs to his very nature that he exist himself and that he thus created out of himself, and that evil belongs to [our] formation and our instability [*Bildung und Beweglichkeit*] and good to love, etc." *Beschreibung der Drei Prinzipien,* foreword, no. 14.

53. *Averroës,* trans. Müller, p. 99.

54. Thus in *Kusari,* p. 414 (trans. Cassel): "Only the stubborn hypocrite, who speaks of something he does not believe in, denies the nature of the possible. When he prepares for something he hopes for or fears, you can see from that that (he believes that) the thing is possible, hence his preparation is useful." Maimonides says in *More Nebochim* T. III, 102 (trans. Scheyer): "It is a basic principle of the laws of our teacher Moses and of all his disciples that man has perfect freedom, that is, that by his very nature he does everything that he is capable of doing with free choice and self-determination, without anything new being produced in him in the process. In like manner all the species of unreasoning animals move about as they will. This is the way God wanted it. . . .It is unheard of that men of our nation and our faith have ever contradicted this basic principle."

55. *Kusari,* p. 416.

56. Anselm, *Dialogi de Casu Diaboli,* chap. 4. *Opera,* t. I, p. 332ff.; *De Concordia,* etc., q. III, chap. 2ff.; *Opera,* t. I, p. 522ff.

57. Thomas, *Summa Theologiae,* p. I, q. 49, art. 2: Effectus causae secundae deficientis

reducitur in causam primam non deficientem, quantum ad id, quod habet entitatis et perfectionis, non autem quantum ad id, quod habet de defectu. . . .Quicquid est entitatis et actionis in actione mala, reducitur in Deum sicut in causam, sed quod est ibi defectus, non causatur a Deo, sed ex causa secunda deficiente.

["The effect of a deficient secondary cause is traced to the primary and nondeficient cause with respect to whatever of being and perfection exists in it, but not with respect to any defect in it. . . .Whatever there is of being and action in an evil action is reduced to God as to its cause; but whatever there is of defect is not caused by God but is from the secondary deficient cause." Dilthey concludes by saying: "With which old-Protestant dogmatics agree."]

58. Thomas, *Summa Theologiae*, p. II, 1, q. 10, art. 4.

59. Anselm, *De Concordia*, etc., q. I.

60. Especially in the presentation of Duns Scotus, *In Sententias* II, dist. 42, 1ff.

61. Occam, *Quodlibeta Septem* I, q. 16.

62. The *thesis* is expressed so often that proofs are superfluous; the *antithesis* passed on particularly from the Neoplatonic school by way of Dionysius the Areopagite to Scotus Erigena and other older medieval writers. See Scotus Erigena, *De Divisione Naturae* I, chap. 15ff., p. 463B; chap. 73ff., p. 518A; Abelard, *Theologia Christiana*, Liber III, p. 1241B ff.; Anselm, *Monologion*, chap. 17, p. 166A. The *antinomy* was very clearly *formulated* from older materials by Thomas, *Summa Theologiae*, p. I, q. 13, art. 12.

63. Besides the passages which follow, see Abelard, *Sic et Non,* chap. 31–38, p. 1389C ff.

64. Augustine *De Trinitate* V, chap. I: ut sic intelligamus Deum, si possumus, quantum possumus, sine qualitate bonum, sine quantitate magnum, sine indigentia creatorem, sine situ praesidentem, sine habitu omnia continentem, sine loco ubique totum, sine tempore sempiternum, sine ulla sui mutatione mutabilia facientem. . .("that we may thus understand God if we can and to the degree we can as good without quality, great without magnitude, creator without need, presiding without a seat, containing all things without possession, entirely ubiquitous apart from a place, everlasting without time, causing changes without any change in himself. . .")

65. Shahrastani I, 13: "The Mutazilites go to such extremes in maintaining [God's] unity, that through their disputing of attributes they arrive at a total emptying out [of God]."

66. Shahrastani (I, 69ff.) reports this thus with an energetic expression of disapproval.

67. See the controversy of Averroës with the Mutazilites over this issue in the "Essay on the Region" in his *Spekulative Dogmatik: Philosophie und Theologie,* p. 62ff. and Shahrastani I, 43.

68. See Averroës' *Philosophie und Theologie,* p. 53ff. and the corresponding presentation of Maimonides in Kaufmann, *Geschichte der Attributenlehre,* p. 431ff. According to the latter, only the existence of God can be known, but not his essence, for the concept of every object is composed of a genus and a specific difference, but these do not exist for God; accidents are likewise excluded from God.

69. See note 62.

70. This double division is in Maimonides I, chap. 58 (Munk, *Le Guide des Egarés* I, 245); in contrast, Jehuda Halevi uses a tripartite division, which is, to be sure, very incomplete—see Kaufmann, *Attributenlehre,* p. 141ff., and also *Kusari* (trans. Cassel), p. 80ff. Like the Arab division, see likewise the double division in *Emunah Ramah* by Abraham ben David (trans. Weil), p. 65ff.

71. Freudenthal, *Hellenistische Studien* III, 285ff.

72. Durandus, *In Petri Lombardi Sententias* I, dist. 3, p. 1, q. I: Triplex est via investigandi Deum ex creaturis: scilicet via eminentiae, quantum ad primum; via causalitatis, quantum ad secundum via remotionis, quantum ad tertium. ["There is a threefold way of investigating God from his creatures: namely, the way of eminence, with respect to the first; the way of causality, with respect to the second; the way of removal, with respect to the third."]

73. *Emunah Ramah,* trans. Weil, p. 70.

74. Maimonides, *More Nebochim,* trans. Scheyer, volume III, 130.

75. Thus, as Augustine already said in *De Trinitate* VI, chap. 7: Deus multipliciter quidem dicitur magnus, bonus, sapiens, beatus, verus, sed eadem magnitudo ejus est, quae sapientia etc. ["God is spoken of in many ways as great, good, wise, blessed, and true, but it is his same magnitude which is his wisdom, etc."]

76. The self-contradictory position of Thomas on this question appears most clearly in the *Summa Theologiae*, p. I, q. 3 and q. 13, as well as in his treatise *Contra Gentiles* I, chap. 31–36; see particularly in the first treatise q. 13, art. 12.

77. *Contra Gentiles*, I. chap. 36. *Summa Theologiae*, p. I, q. 13, art. 12.

78. Occam (*Quodlibeta Septem* III, q. 2) says: Attributa (divina) non sunt nisi quaedam praedicabilia mentalia, vocalia vel scripta, nata significare et supponere pro Deo, quae possunt naturali ratione investigari et concludi de Deo. ["The (divine) attributes are nothing more than certain mental predicables, spoken or written, come into being to signify or stand for God, things which can be investigated and concluded about God by natural reason."]

79. On the disruptive activity of skeptical sects in Islam, see Renan, *Averroës* (3d ed.), p. 103ff.

80. Shahrastani I, p. 3.

81. Jehuda Halevi, *Kusari*, p. 323ff.

82. Munk, *Mélanges de Philosophie Juive et Arabe*, p. 313ff.

83. There are only vague guesses in Renan, *Averroës* (3d ed.), p. 92ff.

84. Sédillot, *Matériaux pour Servir à l'Histoire Comparée des Sciences Mathématiques* I, 236.

85. On the transmission of the system which is expressly designated as "Indian" by the Arabs, see Wöpcke, "Mémoires sur la Propagation des Chiffres Indiens," *Journal Asiatique*, 183, I, 27. On the possibilities of ascertaining the origin of algebra, see Hankel, *Zur Geschichte der Mathematik*, p. 259ff. and Cantor, *Geschichte der Mathematik* I, 620ff.

86. There is more information on the practical knowledge of Arab chemists in Kopp, *Geschichte der Chemie* I, 51ff.

87. For more information on the accomplishments of the Arabs in mathematics, see Hankel, *Zur Geschichte der Mathematik*, pp. 222–93; on their achievements in mathematical geography, see Reinaud, *Géographie d'Aboulféda*, t. I, introduction; on their accomplishments in astronomy, Sédillot, *Matériaux pour Servir à l'Histoire Comparée des Sciences Mathématiques Chez les Grecs et les Orientaux*. In connection with the latter work: with respect to Sédillot's assertion that Abul Wefa anticipated Tycho's discovery of the variation in the course of the moon, one should take account of the objections made by Biot.

88. See p. 203.

89. Cp. the contrast in methods between these ancients and Plato, p. 186ff.

90. Gabir ben Ablah already adopts a more independent attitude toward Ptolemy's hypotheses; then the astronomer the Latins called Alpetragius disputed Ptolemy's theory of epicycles (Delambre, *Histoire de l'Astronomie du Moyen Âge*, p. 171ff.) and so did Averroës.

91. On this question see Renan, *Averroës* (3d ed.), p. 93

92. Thurot in the *Revue Archéologique*, n. s. XIX, 111ff. (*Recherches Historiques sur le Principe d'Archimède*)

93. For more details, see Jourdain, along with his research in his *Philosophie de Saint Thomas* I, 40ff.

94. For more information, see the fundamental investigations in Libri, *Histoire des Sciences Mathématiques*, vol. II.

95. Augustine, *Retractationes* I, chap. 3. Nec Plato quidem in hoc erravit, quia esse mundum intelligibilem dixit, si non vocabulum, quod ecclesiasticae consuetudini in re illa non usitatum est, sed ipsam rem velimus attendere. Mundum quippe ille intelligibilem nuncupavit ipsam rationem sempiternam atque incommutabilem, qua fecit Deus mundum. Quam qui esse negat, sequitur ut dicat, irrationabiliter Deum fecisse quod fecit, aut cum faceret, vel antequam faceret, nescisse quid faceret, si apud eum ratio faciendi non erat. Si vero erat, sicut erat, ipsam videtur Plato vocasse intelligibilem mundum. ["Nor was Plato in error in saying that the world is intelligible if we pay attention not to the word, which is not the one used in church practice on this issue, but to the matter itself. For what he called the intelligible world was the eternal and immutable reason by which God made the world. And if anyone denies this, it follows that he is saying that God made what he made in an irrational fashion or that when he created or before he created he did not know what he was doing, if indeed no reason for creation was in him. But if in fact there was, as there was, it seems that this is what Plato called the intelligible world."] [Dilthey continues:] See further the passage cited on p. 331 [*sic* in Dilthey. I cannot find what this refers to.]. See also Leibniz's *Monadologie*, nos. 43, 44: "The eternal truths or the ideas on which they depend" must have their basis in a real, existing being.

96. See page 193ff.

97. On the origin of this formula in its logical aspect, see the detailed account in Prantl, *Geschichte der Logik* II, 305ff.; 347ff.; III, 94ff. On the insertion of the *rationes* into this formula, e.g., of reason's principle of contradiction, see p. 331.

98. Duns Scotus, *In Sententias* I, dist., q. 2 and 3.

99. Epistle to the Romans I:19ff. and Acts of the Apostles XIV:15ff. and XVII:22ff. [Although Dilthey is talking about *proofs* for God based on the world here, it is odd that he does not mention the Hebrew monotheistic tradition predating Greek monotheistic arguments.]

100. [The "utterances" in question are given in Latin in Dilthey's text: "quod sermones theologi sunt fundati in fabulis" and "quod sapientes mundi sunt philosophi tantum."]

101. The *Chronica Fr. Salimbene Parmensis* (Parma, 1857) speaks on p. 169 of the "destructio credulitatis Friderici et sapientum suorum, qui crediderunt, quod non esset alia vita, nisi praesens, ut liberius carnalitatibus suis et miseriis vacare possent. Ideo fuerunt Epycurei. . . ." ["the destructiveness of the rash confidence of Frederick and his wise men who believed that there is no other life but the present one so that they would be freer to give themselves to their physical pleasures and miseries. Thus they were Epicureans. . . ."]

102. In the beautiful description, based on personal observation, of the *Chronica* mentioned in note 101, it says (p. 166) of Frederick the Second: "de fide Dei nihil habebat" ["of faith in God he had none"], but this *fides Dei* is clearly to be understood in the sense of the faith in God of a Christian.

103. Ibid., p. 182.

104. On the scholastic debates about the existence of God in the monasteries, see Thomas de Eccleston's *De Adventu Fratrum Minorum in Angliam* (*Monumenta Franciscana,* London, 1858), p. 50: "Cum ex duobus parietibus construatur aedificium Ordinis, scilicet moribus bonis et scientia, parietem scientiae fecerunt fratres ultra coelos et coelestia sublimem, in tantum, ut quaererent an Deus sit." ["Because the edifice of an order is built up of two walls, namely, good morals and knowledge, the brothers made the wall of knowledge sublime beyond the heavens and the celestial, inasmuch as they took up the question of whether God exists."]

105. At the head of the *Summa Theologiae* of Thomas stands part I, q. 2: De Deo, an Deus sit ["On God, Whether God exists"] (q. 1 treats only of the concept of Christian knowledge); in the third article of the same question five individual proofs are distinguished: (1) from motion; (2) from the links between causes and effects; (3) from the relationship of the possible—which can exist but does not have to exist and which comes into being, undergoes change, and perishes—to the necessary (the later proof from the contingency of the world); (4) from the relationship of gradations in things to an absolute; (5) from purposefulness. Cp. Duns Scotus (*In Sententias* I, dist. 2, q. 2) with this.

106. [Dilthey gives the Italian from Dante: "l'amor che muove il sole e l'altre stelle."]

107. Albertus Magnus, *De Causis et Processu Universitatis,* Book I, tract 4, chaps. 7, 8; Book II, tract 2, chaps. 35–40. Thomas, *Contra Gentiles* III, chap. 23ff. Bonaventure, *In Librum II Sententiarum,* esp. dist. 14, p. 1 (the premises of the argument are given most clearly in art. 3, q. 2: an motus coeli sit a propria forma vel ab intelligentia ["whether the motion of the heavens be from their own proper form or from an intelligence"]). Duns Scotus, *Quaestiones Subtiles in Metaphysicam Aristotelis,* Book XII, qq 16–21.

108. Albertus, *Summa Theologiae* II, tract I, q. 3, m. 3, art. 4, part. 1, p. 28a.

109. The assumption of the arguments which conclude from the world to a God distinct from the world, that an infinite regress is impossible, was dissolved by Occam.

110. From out of the vast material we cannot highlight any individual proofs. Thomas expressly excludes this reasoning from his demonstration only because it does not permit any universally valid formulation; see *Summa Theologiae,* p. 1, q. 2, art. 1. The development from a striving after the highest good to its satisfaction in God as a rule followed the Augustinian format (see p. 237) in the Middle Ages; the mystics follow suit, among whom *Hugh of St. Victor already distinguished the proof from the world from grounding based on religious experience.*

111. The assumption of the ontological proof, which concludes from an *esse in intellectu* ["intellectual existence"] for the being *quo majus cogitari non potest* ["than which nothing greater can be conceived"] to its *esse et in re* ["actual existence as well"], appears most clearly in Anselm's *Apologeticus,* chaps. 1, 3. In Anselm's earlier proof the proposition in the *Monologion,* chap. 1, is

especially noteworthy: Quaecunque justa dicuntur ad invicem, sive pariter sive magis vel minus, non possunt intelligi justa nisi per justitiam, quae non est aliud et aliud in diversis. ["Whatever things are said to be just with respect to one another—whether equally so, or more or less so—cannot be understood as just except through justice, which is not a different thing in diverse instances."] Thomas's fourth proof (*Summa Theologiae*, p. 1, q. 2, art. 3) is linked to this earlier argument of Anselm's.

112. Nemesius, *De Natura Hominis*, chaps. 2, 3.

113. Plotinus, *Enneads* IV, Book 7, p. 456ff., is directed against the Epicureans (p. 457), some Peripatetics (p. 458), and the Stoics (p. 458ff.). He gives a splendid proof of the impossibility of deducing psychical facts unless they are presupposed in the grounds of explanation.

114. Cp. p. 80ff.

115. Plato, *Theaetetus*, 185ff.

116. Aristotle, *De Anima* III, 2, p. 426b 15.

117. Plotinus, *Enneads* IV, Book 7, p. 461ff. The parallel argument from physical feeling (p. 462) is also noteworthy. If we think of the single spot at which we locate a pain, in the process of feeling it and communicating that condition we would feel the pain in all the places suffering along with it, thus something multiple. Of less value are the demonstrations from thought, virtue, etc. On the merely *negative value of the inference,* see pp. 9ff. and 383ff.

118. Augustine, *De Genesi ad Litteram* XII, chap. 33.

119. Page 236ff.

120. I have cited texts in evidence from Augustine, p. 236, above. The chief discussion of this was in the first book of *De Libero Arbitrio.*

121. Thomas, *Contra Gentiles* II, chap. 49ff.; p. 197ff.

122. Averroës, *Destructio Destructionum* II, disputation 2 and 3; fol. 135Hff.; 145Cff. (Venice, 1562). *The principal argument in the form given it by Avicenna* can be found particularly in the opposing observations of Averroës on the *ratio prima* for an immaterial soul-substance. Further proofs argue from the inconceivability of what would follow from the assumption that a corporeal organ, say the brain, thinks; that would make a knowledge of our knowledge impossible, for example. A very corrupted composite passage made up of proofs commonly used by the Arabs can be found in the letter of Ibn Sab'in to emperor Frederick the Second, a letter that also answers the emperor's questions about immortality.

123. Thus Thomas, *Contra Gentiles* II, chap. 49–55, p. 197ff.

124. This type of argument is summarized well in Bonaventure, *In Librum II Sententiarum,* dist. 19, art. 1, q. 1.

125. Thomas, *Contra Gentiles* II, chap. 46, p. 192a.

126. On Amalrich of Bene and David of Dinant, see Hauréau, *Histoire de la Philosophie Scolastique* II, 1, p. 73ff.; cp. p. 260ff. above. The important *attack on the demonstrability of personal immortality* as *Duns Scotus* introduced it into Christian scholasticism is in Duns Scotus, *Reportata Parisiensia,* Book IV, dist. 43 and in the corresponding presentation in *In Sententias.*

127. Aristotle's third book of psychology was the point of departure for the doctrine of the unitary intellect; Alexander of Aphrodisias, Themistius, and the pseudo-Aristotelian theology developed it, and the Arab Peripatetics used the theories of the active and passive intellect in Alexander and Themistius.

128. Thomas Aquinas already recognized the limited validity of the principle *ex nihilo nihil fit:* the principle is not applicable to the transcendent cause—cf. *Contra Gentiles* II, chaps. 10, 16, 17, 37.

129. Averroës, *Destructio Destructionum* II, disputation 3, fol. 145 (Venice, 1562): nam *plurificatio numeralis individualis* provenit *ex materia* ["for individual numerical plurification arises out of matter"].

130. Averroës, *De Animae Beatitudine,* chap. 3, fol. 150ff.

131. *Destructio Destructionum* II, disputation 3, fol. 144K. Averroës on the ratio decima: Igitur necesse est ut sit non generabilis, nec corruptibilis, nec deperditur, cum deperdatur aliquod individuorum, in quibus invenitur ille. Et ideo scientiae sunt aeternae et nec generabiles nec corruptibiles, nisi per accidens, scilicet ex copulatione earum Socrati et Platoni. . .quoniam intellectui nihil est individuitatis. ["Therefore it is necessary that (the understanding) should not be generable nor corruptible, nor does it perish when one of the individuals in which it is found

perishes. And therefore knowledge is eternal and neither generable nor corruptible, except per accidens, by way of its being joined to Socrates or Plato. . .for there is nothing individual about the understanding."]

132. *Destructio Destructionum* I, disputation 1, fol. 20M: Et anima quidem Socratis et Platonis sunt eaedem aliquo modo et multae aliquo modo: Ac si diceres sunt eadem ex parte formae, et multae ex parte subjecti earum. . .anima autem prae ceteris assimilatur lumini, et sicut lumen dividitur ad divisionem corporum illuminatorum, deinde fit unum in ablatione corporum, sic est res in animabus cum corporibus. ["And the soul of Socrates and of Plato to be sure is identical in one sense and plural in another sense: As if you said that they are the same as to form and multiple as to their subject. . .for the soul, more than other things, is like the light, and just as light is divided in accordance with the division of the bodies it illuminates and becomes one if the bodies are taken away, this is also the case of souls with bodies."]

133. See Albertus Magnus, *De Unitate Intellectus Contra Averroëm,* chap. 4. The arguments are reproduced loosely in the text, for they presuppose the nuances of Averroistic metaphysics in their precise formulation. In addition, see Leibniz, *Considérations sur la Doctrine d'un Esprit Universel,* which indeed links Averroës to Spinoza.

134. Averroës, *De Animae Beatitudine,* chap. 2, fol. 149G. [Dilthey gives the Latin text: "Ex necessitate est, ut sit aliquis philosophus in specie humana."]

135. Averroës, *Destructio* II, disputation 3, fol. 145ff.

136. See further discussion on this in Renan, *Averroës* (3d ed.), p. 152ff. and more exactly in Munk, *Le guide des Égarés, Traité de Théologie et de Philosophie,* t. I, p. 434, note 4. The shifting of proofs whereby Averroës principally bases himself on the fact of abstract science is indicated and demonstrated on p. 316.

137. *Philosophie und Theologie des Averroës* (Müller), p. 79ff.

138. [Dilthey has: ". . .und das Gegründetsein der Ursachen auf die Wirkungen." Evidently the opposite is meant.]

139. Thomas Aquinas persists in viewing the *will* as under the sway of *intellectualism:* see *Contra Gentiles* I, chap. 82f., p. 112a. But he shifts the antinomy to the will of God himself inasmuch as he distinguishes the necessity by which the will wills his own being [*Inhalt*] as his purpose from the freedom with which it chooses that purpose's means in the contingent world, for after all it could preserve its own perfection even without these means; see the *Summa theologiae,* p. 1, q. 19, art. 3. And in fact, according to him, such a will contains no imperfection because it always has its object within itself; cp. ibid., art. 2. Thus God eternally wills what he wills, namely, his own perfection, hence in a necessary way; ibid., art. 3. Accordingly, according to Thomas's view of this matter, God's will is evidently essentially necessary, just as his knowledge is.

140. I am using especially Duns Scotus, *In Sententias* I, dist. 1 and 2; dist. 8, q. 5; dist. 39, esp. q. 5; II, dist. 25, 29, 43.

141. Duns Scotus, *In Sententias* I, dist. 2, q. 7.

142. Cp. with Aristotle, p. 268. Duns Scotus, *In Sententias* II, dist. 25, q. 1.

143. Duns Scotus, *In Sententias,* dist. 8, q. 5: Et si quaeras, quare igitur voluntas divina magis determinatur ad unum contradictoriorum, quam ad alterum, respondeo: indisciplinati est, quaerere omnium causas et demonstrationem. . . .Principii enim demonstrationis non est demonstratio: *immediatum autem principium est, voluntatem velle hoc.* ["And if you ask why it is then that the divine will is more inclined to one of two contradictories rather than its opposite I answer thus: It is a mark of an undisciplined person to search for the causes and demonstration of everything. . . .There is no way of demonstrating the principle of a demonstration: *but the immediate principle is that the will wants this.*"]

144. Duns Scotus, *In Sententias* I, dist. 2.

145. *In Sententias* II, dist. I, q. 2: Sicut non est ratio, quare voluit naturam humanam in hoc individuo esse et esse possibile et contingens: ita non est ratio, quare hoc voluit nunc et non tunc esse, sed tantum quia voluit hoc esse, ideo bonum fuit illud esse. ["Just as there is no reason why he willed that human nature in this individual should exist and be possible and contingent, so likewise there is no reason why he willed that this thing should exist now rather than then; on the contrary, it is only because he willed this thing to exist that it was good for it to exist."] In connection with this point and with his entire teaching on the will, see Duns Scotus, *Quaestiones Quodlibetales,* q. 16.

146. The parallel phenomenon in the Orient is not lacking here either. The *Mutakallimūn* substituted immediate special acts of God for the causal system of nature and thus traced the course of the world, as an accidental thing, to the divine will.

147. See page 205.

148. Renan (*Averroès*, 3d ed., 108ff.) presents, in translation, a discussion by Averroës from his great *Commentary* on the metaphysics of Aristotle (Book XII) which adequately deals with this thesis.

149. Thomas, *Contra Gentiles* I, chap. 81ff., p. 111a; IV, chap. 13, p. 540a: Deus res in esse producit non naturali necessitate, sed quasi per intellectum et voluntatem agens. ["God brings things into being not by natural necessity but as though acting through intellect and will."]

150. The formula "ex nihilo" is the translation of II Maccabees VII: 28. In the passage named it is possible that "nonexistent" is to be understood in a Platonic sense; Hermas in the first mandate (*The Shepherd of Hermas*, edited by Gebhardt and Harn., p. 70) wrote: *ho poiēsas ek tou mē ontos eis to einai ta panta.* ["Who brought all things into being out of nothing."] For the establishment of the antithesis, namely, the doctrine of creation, see, for example, Thomas, *Contra Gentiles* II, chap. 16, p. 145a. [II Maccabees VII: 28 reads: "I beseech thee, my son, look upon heaven and earth and all that is in them: and consider that God made them out of nothing, and mankind also." (Confraternity of Christian Doctrine translation)]

151. Albertus Magnus, *Summa Theologiae* II, tract. 1, q. 4, m. 2 art. 5, part. 1, p. 55a ff. Cp. Kant II: 338ff. (Rosenkranz). There is a good discussion in *Kusari*, where the first principle of the Medabberim (i.e., of the philosophizing Arab theologians) was worded thus: "First one must establish the created status of the world and confirm this by a *refutation* of the faith in its uncreated status. If this time were without a beginning, then the number of existing individuals in this time until the present would be infinite; but what is infinite does not become actual, and how did those individuals become actual since their number is infinite? . . . Whatever becomes actual must be finite, but whatever is infinite cannot become actual." Therefore the world has a beginning. See *Kusari* (trans. Cassel, 2d ed.), p. 402. The matter was in fact determined in the same way by Saadja, *Emunot* (trans. Fürst, p. 122) and, used differently, by Maimonides (*More Nebochim* I, chap. 74, 2; see Munk, I: 422).

152. Averroës, *Destructio Destructionum* I, disputation 1, fol. 15ff.

153. See esp. Thomas, *Contra Gentiles* II, chap. 10, p. 140b; chap. 16ff., p. 145a; chap. 37, p. 177a and the *Summa Theologiae* I, q. 45, art. 2: Antiqui philosophi non consideraverunt nisi emanationem effectuum particularium a causis particularibus, quas necesse est praesupponere aliquid in sua actione. Et secundum hoc erat eorum communis opinio, ex nihilo nihil fieri. Sed tamen hoc locum non habet in prima emanatione ab universali rerum principio. ["The ancient philosophers did not consider anything except the emanation of special effects from special causes, which require one to presuppose something in their operation. And accordingly their general view was that nothing comes from nothing. But this does not apply to the first emanation from the universal principle of things."]

154. Duns Scotus, *In Sententias* I, dist. 8, qq. 4, 5. The will is the will precisely because one cannot establish a reason for the structure from which the act of the will proceeds; cp. ibid., II, dist. 1, q. 2. The distinction between a first and a second understanding in God (ibid., I, dist. 39) does not resolve the antinomy which thus arises.

155. Thomas, *Contra Gentiles* II, chap. 46, p. 192a; chap. 49ff., pp. 197, 198.

156. This is developed in the same frame of argument, ibid., from p. 199b on.

157. See page 268ff.

158. Thomas, *Contra Gentiles* III, chaps. 66–73, esp. pp. 364a, 367a, 371a, 375a.

159. See page 218.

160. See page 216ff.

161. This is most clearly developed in Thomas Aquinas, *Summa Theologiae* II, 1. q., 90ff. (where his philosophy of law begins): 1. lex = quaedam rationis ordinatio ad bonum commune, ab eo qui curam communitatis habet, promulgata (q. 90, art. 4); 2. lex aeterna = (da Gott als Monarch die Welt regiert) ratio gubernationis rerum in Deo sicut in principe universitatis existens (q. 91, art 1); diese lex aeterna ist *bindende Norm oberster Art und Ursprung jeder anderen bindenden Norm;* 3. lex naturalis = participatio legis aeternae in rationali creatura; durch eine Partizipation

des Menschen an dem ewigen Gesetz ensteht aus der lex aeterna in Gott die lex naturalis, welche die überall gleiche Norm der menschlichen Handlungen bildet (q. 91, art. 2). ["1. law = a certain ordinance of reason for the common good, made by one in charge of the community, and promulgated (q. 90, art. 4); 2. eternal law = (because God rules the world as its king) the reason of the governance of things existing in God as in the ruler of the universe (q. 91, art. 1); this eternal law is the *binding norm of the highest order and the source of every other binding norm;* 3. natural law = a sharing in the eternal law by a rational creature; natural law arises out of the eternal law in God through a participation by man in the eternal law; natural law constitutes the ubiquitously uniform norm of human activity (q. 91, art. 2).]

162. Augustine, *De Civitate Dei* V, chap. 11; cp. Origen, *Contra Celsum* II, chap. 30. This leading idea appears over and over in Augustine's *De Civitate Dei,* e.g., IV, chap. 33; V, chap. 21.

163. A question put to Augustine by Marcellinus: in Augustine's correspondence, epistle 136.

164. This occurs frequently, e.g., Celsus in Origen's *Contra Celsum* V, chap. 35ff.

165. Celsus in Origen's *Contra Celsum* IV, chap. 8; Porphyry in Augustine's epistle 102 (*Sex Quaestiones Contra Paganos Expositae,* q. 2: "De Tempore Christianae Religionis").

166. Augustine's chief work, *De Civitate Dei,* was directed against this objection; see Book I and Book II, chap. 2. *The Seven Books of Histories against the Pagans* by Orosius are likewise directed against it. See I, prologue: He is responding to the injunction of Augustine to combat the notion of a confusion of the world and of human society as a consequence of Christianity. Therefore he pulls together a complete catalogue of disasters. "Praeceperas ergo, ut ex omnibus, qui haberi ad praesens possunt, historiarum atque annalium fastis, quaecumque aut bellis gravia aut corrupta morbis aut fame tristia aut terrarum motibus terribilia aut inundationibus aquarum insolita aut eruptionibus ignium metuenda aut ictibus fulminum plagisque grandinum saeva vel etiam parricidiis flagitiisque misera, per transacta retro saecula repperissem, ordinato breviter voluminis textu explicarem." ["Thus you gave orders that, using all the extant materials in the records of histories and annals, I should find out everything which has transpired in previous centuries: whatever has been crushed by wars or racked by diseases or made wretched by famine; or terrors of earthquakes or uncommon deluges of water or fearful outbreaks of fire or lightning bolts or cruel lashings by hailstones; or even miseries caused by parricides and disgraces. And I am to explain these things briefly in the text of a book."] That was an unsalutary model for the historiography of the Middle Ages.

167. See page 229ff.

168. Tertullian, *De Virginibus Velandis,* chap. 1.

169. Clement, *Stromata* I, chap. 5, p. 122 (sylb.) says of philosophy: *epaidagōgei gar kai autē to Hellēnikon, hōs ho nomos tous Hebraious eis Xriston.* ["For it guided the Greek world, just as the law did the Hebrews, to Christ."]

170. Augustine, epistle 138, chap. 1, toward a solution of the problem posed by Marcellinus (see note 163): Quoties nostrae variantur aetates! Adolescentiae pueritia non reditura cedit; juventus adolescentiae non mansura succedit; finiens juventutem senectus morte finitur. Haec omnia mutantur, nec mutatur divinae providentiae ratio, qua fit ut ista mutentur. . .aliud magister adolescenti, quam puero solebat, imposuit. ["How often do our stages in life not vary! Childhood gives way to adolescence, never to return again; youth succeeds adolescence, without itself abiding; terminating youth, old age is itself ended by death. All these things are changed, but the reason of divine providence which causes them to change is not changed. . .The teacher has imposed something different on the adolescent than he used to impose on the boy."]

171. According to the ancients [*Nach Älteren*], Augustine, sermon 57, chap. 7; sermons 227 and 272; *De Civitate Dei* XXI, chap. 19ff.

172. Cp. page 224ff.

173. *Augustine, Tractatus* VI, 25 to chap. 1 of John, V:32: Divinum jus in scripturis divinis habemus, humanum jus in legibus regum ["We have divine law in the sacred scriptures, human law in the laws of kings"]: see epistle 93, chap. 12. Cp. Isidore, *Etymologiae* V, chap. 2: Omnes autem leges aut divinae sunt aut humanae. Divinae natura, humanae moribus constant; ideoque hae discrepant, quoniam aliae aliis gentibus placent. ["But all laws are either divine or human. Divine laws are such by nature; human laws are such by custom. Hence there are differences among the latter, because different laws suit different peoples."] For the concept of natural law, which as

legislation from God embraces the moral as well as the legal sphere, *Abelard* holds an especially important place between Augustine and Thomas Aquinas with his *Dialogus Inter Philosophum, Judaeum et Christianum.*

174. Augustine, epistle 105, chap. 2; sermon 62, chap. 5. On the concept of natural law in Thomas Aquinas and his distinction between eternal law and natural law, see note 161.

175. In Augustine's presentation in Book XIX of *De Civitate Dei,* see esp. chap. 14: The goal of the earthly city is peace on earth, while that of the heavenly city is eternal peace, and the purpose of man lies in the latter.

176. Augustine, *De Civitate Dei* V, chap. 12ff.

177. Council of Paris, 829 (Mansi, t. XIV, p. 537ff.). Constitutio Wormiensis. (*Monumenta Germaniae Legum* I, p. 333, rescript c. 2, 3): 2. Quod universalis sancta Dei ecclesia unum corpus ejusque caput Christus sit. ["That the holy universal church of God is one body whose head is Christ."] This is proven by the passages from Saint Paul touched on above on page 279. 3. Quod ejusdem ecclesiae corpus in duabus principaliter dividatur eximiis personis. Principaliter itaque totius sanctae Dei ecclesiae corpus in duas eximias personas, in sacerdotalem videlicet et regalem, sicut a sanctis patribus traditum accepimus, divisum esse novimus. ["That the body of this same church is divided in principle between two main persons. Thus we know, as handed down to us by the Holy Fathers, that the body of the entire holy church of God is divided in principle between two main persons, namely, the priestly and the royal."]

178. Dante dedicates the entire first book of his treatise *De Monarchia* to the development of these propositions. Here too one can find in Occam an incisive weighing of grounds and countergrounds that no longer recognizes the logical force of the metaphysical construction: see Occam, *Dialogus,* p. III, tract. 2, book I, chap. 1–9.

179. Thomas Aquinas also emphasizes in his *Commentary on Aristotle's Politics* (Book VII, lesson 3) that a modest territorial extent of a state is required for order in it. Cp. John of Paris, *De Potestate Regia et Papali,* chap. 3 (in Goldast, *Monarchia* II, p. 111) and the most all-sided treatment of the problem in Occam, *Dialogus,* p. III, tract. 2, book 1, chap. 1ff. Occam rejects every metaphysical solution of the problem and admits only one in accordance with the historical situation, chap. 5.

180. Augustine, *De Civitate Dei* XIV, chap. 28; XV, chaps. 1–5; XVI, chap. 3, 4; XIX, chaps. 15–23. The comparison of the state to a wild animal, such as we find in Plato and Hobbes, is also made by Augustine, following the lead of the Apocalypse (*De Civitate Dei,* 20, chap. 9).

181. Gregory VII, in Jaffés, *Bibliotheca* II (1865), book VIII, epistle 21 a. 1081, p. 457: Quis nesciat, reges et duces ab iis habuisse principium, qui, deum ignorantes, superbia rapinis perfidia homicidiis, postremo universis paene sceleribus, mundi principe diabolo videlicet agitante, super pares, scilicet homines, dominari caeca cupidine et intolerabili praesumptione affectaverunt? ["Who is ignorant of the fact that kings and leaders derive their origin from those who—ignorant of God, with pride, pillage, perfidy, and homicides, in short, with almost every type of crime, obviously moved by the devil, the prince of the world—have aspired to rule their equals, i.e., men, with blind lust and intolerable presumption?"]

182. Thomas, *De Regimine Principum* I, chap. 15. In agreement with this is the *Summa Theologiae* II, 1, q. 93, esp. arts. 3 and 6.

183. Thus already in the *Apostolic Constitutions* II, chap. 34, p. 681C (Migne) and in the *Oratio* 17 of Gregory Nazianzen, chap 8, p. 976B (Migne) as well as in many medieval writers, including Thomas, *Summa Theologiae* II, 2, q. 60, art. 6: Potestas saecularis subditur spirituali, sicut corpus animae. ["The secular power is subject to the spiritual as the body is to the soul."]

184. See the passages in Gierke, *Deutsches Genossenschaftsrecht* III, 534.

185. Dante, *De Monarchia* I, chap. 1ff.

186. Ibid., in the third book.

187. Marsilius of Padua, *Defensor Pacis* I, chap. 4: the definition of the task of the state according to Aristotle's *Politics;* then chap. 5, 6: insertion of the priesthood into the state in accord with Christian prescription; the priesthood is designated as a part of the state [*pars civitatis*].

188. Dante, *De Monarchia,* at the start of the second book.

189. Cp. esp. book V. There in chap. 2: Est autem res publica, sicut Plutarcho placet, corpus quoddam, quod divini muneris beneficio animatur, et summae aequitatis agitur nutu, et regitur quodam moderamine rationis. Ea vero qua [*sic*] cultum religionis in nobis instituunt et informant,

et Dei (ne secundum Plutarchum deorum dicam) ceremonias tradunt, vicem animae in corpore reipublicae obtinent. ["The commonwealth, as Plutarch says, is a certain body which is informed by the privilege of divine office, is moved by the imperative of the highest justice, and is governed by a direction of reason. Now those things which establish and inform the cult of religion among us and communicate the ceremonies of God (lest I should speak of 'Gods,' as Plutarch does) have the role of the soul in the body of the state."] At this point one directly perceives the carryover from the concept of the church.

190. Of this *second* historical *formation of natural law, the medieval one*, we have a first thorough description with proof texts in Gierke's *Genossenschaftsrecht* III, 627ff. and in his *Althusius*, p. 77ff.; 92ff.; 123ff.

191. Augustine, *De Civitate Dei* XI, chap. 10: Neque enim multae sed una sapientia est, in qua sunt immensi quidam atque infiniti thesauri rerum intelligibilium, in quibus sunt omnes invisibiles atque incommutabiles rationes rerum etiam visibilium et mutabilium ["There are not many wisdoms, but only one, in which there exist the immense and infinite treasures of intelligible things which contain all the invisible and immutable reasons of things, even of the visible and the mutable"]; *De Trinitate* IV, chap. 1: Quia igitur unum verbum Dei est, per quod facta sunt omnia, quod est *incommutabilis* veritas, ibi principaliter et incommutabiliter sunt omnia simul ["Therefore, because there is just one word of God through which all things have been made and which is *immutable* truth, all things exist simultaneously, in principle, and immutably in it."] Augustine looks in vain for a resolution of this in the proposition in *De Trinitate* II, chap. 5: "Ordo temporum in aeterna Dei sapientia sine tempore est. ["The temporal order is atemporal in the eternal wisdom of God."]

192. Occam's principle, which put the moral order into a psychological relationship with the will and made a sharp separation between what is of value to the will and what is true for the understanding (and thus eliminated any metaphysics of the moral world), first appeared in an admittedly exaggerated form of expression, e.g., *In Sententias* II, q. 19: Ea est boni et mali moralis natura ut, cum a liberrima Dei voluntate sancita sit et definita, ab eadem facile possit emoveri et refigi: adeo ut *mutata ea voluntate, quod sanctum et justum est possit evadere injustum*. ["This is the moral nature of good and evil, that when it is ratified and defined by the most free will of God, it can also easily be removed and demolished by that same will: in such a way that *if that will is changed, what is unjust can become something holy and just*."] Occam's extreme supernaturalism was thus determined by this.

Section 4. Dissolution of the Metaphysical Attitude of Men toward Reality

1. In his *Geschichte der Logik im Abendlande*, 1855ff., Prantl has provided an exhaustive proof of this important thesis for a particular branch of the scientific literature.

2. Kepler, *Mysterium Cosmographicum*, chap. 20. [Dilthey's citation is in German. The original reads:". . .duorum alterum statuendum est: aut motrices animas, quo sunt a Sole remotiores, hoc esse imbecilliores: aut unam esse motricem animam in orbium omnium centro, scilicet in Sole, quae, ut quodlibet corpus est vicinius, ita vehementius incitet: in remotioribus propter elongationem et attenuationem virtutis quodammodo languescat." See Johannes Kepler, *Opera Omnia*, ed. Christian Frisch (Hildesheim: Verlag Dr. H. A. Gerstenberg, 1971).]

3. From the famous general observation on the third book of Newton's *Principia Mathematica*. [Dilthey's citation from the *Scholium Generale* is in German. The original reads: "Elegantissima haecce solis, planetarum & cometarum compages non nisi consilio & dominio entis intelligentis & potentis oriri potuit." See *Isaac Newton's Principia*, vol. 2, ed. Alexandre Koyré and I. Bernard Cohen (Cambridge: Harvard University Press, 1972).]

4. Newton, *Principia*, def. VIII: Voces autem attractionis, impulsus vel propensionis cujuscunque in centrum, indifferenter et pro se mutuo promiscue usurpo; has vires non physice, sed mathematice tantum considerando. Unde caveat lector, ne per hujusmodi voces cogitet me speciem vol modum actionis causamve aut rationem physicam alicubi definire vel centris (quae sunt puncta mathematica) vires vere et physice tribuere, si forte aut centra trahere, aut vires centrorum esse

dixero. ["I use the words attraction, impulse or propensity of anything toward the center indifferently and in mutually exchangeable fashion; I am not considering these forces physically but only mathematically. So let the reader beware lest he think that by the use of words of this kind I am defining the kind or mode of action or the cause or physical reason at any point or that I am really and physically attributing forces to the centers (which are mathematical points) if I should perchance say that either the centers or forces of the centers are exercising an attraction."]

5. See Fechner, *Über die Physikalische und Philosophische Atomenlehre* (2d ed.) Leipzig, 1864.

6. See p. 85ff.; p. 92ff.; p. 97ff.

7. See p. 92ff.

8. This source of the *Ethics* III, props. 6–9, is clearly shown by the reasoning in prop. 4: Nulla res nisi a causa externa potest destrui ["Nothing can be destroyed except by an external cause"], a proposition which can be valid only with respect to simple elements, hence cannot be simply applied to the mind. Spinoza proves it only by transferring it from the logical to the metaphysical plane in accordance with his fallacious basic assumption. [Spinoza's principle as given in the text reads in English: "The mind strives to continue in its existence for an indefinite duration, and it is conscious of this striving."]

9. Spinoza, *Ethics* III, props. 16 and 27.

10. Hume, *Inquiry Concerning Human Understanding*, section 1.

11. With this term we are designating those theories which advertise themselves as natural law, natural theology, natural religion, etc. Their common characteristic was the deduction of social phenomena from the causal structure in man, regardless of whether man was studied by a psychological method or was explained biologically in terms of the system of nature.

12. [See p. 100ff.]

13. When Condorcet entered the French Academy in 1782 he declared: "Le véritable intérêt d'une nation n'est jamais séparé de l'intérêt général du genre humain, la nature n'a pu vouloir fonder le bonheur d'un peuple sur le malheur des ses voisins, ni opposer l'une à l'autre deux vertus qu'elle inspire également; l'amour de la patrie et celui de l'humanité" (Condorcet, "Discours de Réception à l'Académie Française," 1782: *Oeuvres* VII, 113) ["The true interest of a nation is never separate from the general interest of the human race. Nature could not have wished to establish the happiness of one people on the unhappiness of its neighbors nor to set in opposition to one another the two virtues which it equally inspires: the love of country and that of humanity." (Condorcet, "Discourse upon Reception into the French Academy," 1782: *Works* VII, 113).]

14. *Para men gar eniōn pareilēphamen tinas doxas, hoi de tou genesthai toutous aitioi gegonasin.* ["From some of (those who have philosophized about the truth) we have received certain teachings; others made it possible for the first ones to appear."] Thus wrote the Pseudo-Aristotle, *Metaphysics* II (a), I, p. 993b 18; cp. the entire chapter.

15. Bacon, *Novum Organum* I, 84.

16. [Dilthey cites Voltaire in French: "Il faudra bouleverser la terre pour la mettre sous l'empire de la philosophie."]

17. Spinoza, *Ethics* II, prop. 7. [Dilthey gives the Latin in the text: "Ordo et connexio idearum idem est ac ordo et connexio rerum."]

18. Ibid., I, axiom 4. [Dilthey gives the Latin in the text: "Effectus cognitio a cognitione causae dependet et eandem involvit."]

19. Ibid., prop. 29. [Dilthey gives the Latin in the text: "In rerum natura nullum datur contingens; sed omnia ex necessitate divinae naturae determinata sunt ad certo modo existendum et operandum."]

20. In Leibniz's fifth letter to Clark, no. 125. One may find less complete formulations in his *Théodicée*, no. 44, and his *Monadologie*, no. 31ff. [Dilthey gives the French in the text: "Ce principe est celui du besoin d'une raison suffisante, pour qu'une chose existe, qu'un événement arrive, qu'une vérité ait lieu."]

21. [Dilthey gives the French in the text: "Il est vrai, dit on, qu'il n'y a rien sans une raison suffisante pourquoi il est, et pourquoi il est ainsi plutôt qu'autrement. Mais on ajoute, que cette raison suffisante est souvent la simple volonté de Dieu; comme lorsqu'on demand pourquoi la matière n'a pas été placée autrement dans l'espace, les mêmes situations entre les corps demeurant gardées. Mais c'est justement soutenir que Dieu veut quelque chose, sans qu'il y ait aucune raison suffisante de sa volonté, contra l'axiome ou la règle générale de tout ce qui arrive."] Third letter to

Clarke, no. 7. And as a matter of fact Leibniz expressly rejects the assumption that the cause of a state of affairs in the world can be found in the mere will of God. "On m'objecte qu'en n'admettant point cette simple volonté, ce seroit ôter à Dieu le pouvoir de choisir et tomber dans la *fatalité*. Mais c'est tout le contraire: on soutient en Dieu le pouvoir de choisir, puisqu'on le fonde sur la raison du choix conforme à sa sagesse. Et ce n'est pas cette fatalité (qui n'est autre chose que l'ordre le plus sage de la Providence), mais une fatalité ou nécessité brute, qu'il faut éviter, ou il n'y a ni sagesse, ni choix." (no. 8) ["People object to me that in not admitting this simple will I am depriving God of the power to choose and am plunging into *fatalism*. But it is completely the other way around: we are supporting the power of choice in God, for we are establishing it on the rationality of choice in conformity with his wisdom. And this is not that kind of fatalism (actually it is nothing other than the most wise order of providence), but a fatalism or brute necessity which one must avoid, where there is neither wisdom nor choice."] If in rejoinder Clarke appealed to the view that the will itself can be regarded as a sufficient reason in its own right, Leibniz replied peremptorily: "Une simple volonté sans aucun motif (a mere will), est une fiction non-seulement contraire à la perfection de Dieu, mais encore chimérique, contradictoire, incompatible avec la définition de la volonté et assez réfutée dans la Théodicée." 4th letter to Clarke, no. 2. ["A simple will without any motive (a mere will) is a fiction that is not only contrary to the perfection of God but is furthermore chimerical, contradictory, incompatible with the definition of the will, and sufficiently refuted in the *Theodicy*."] It is clear that in this fashion Leibniz ends up with an executive power which carries out an idea, not with a true will.

22. See page 193ff.

23. Wolff, *Vernünftige Gedanken von Gott,* etc., nos. 29 and 30.

24. Kant, *Kritik der Reinen Vernunft* I, 1, no. 7: "In any case time is something real, namely, the actual form of inner intuition. It has therefore subjective reality with respect to inner experience, i.e., I really have the representation of time and my determinations in it." In these assertions one recognizes what I am principally maintaining above, only in connection with a theory about the components of inner perception.

25. Lotze, *System der Philosophie* II, 125.

Index

Ramon J. Betanzos received his Ph.D. in intellectual history from the University of Michigan. He is currently Associate Professor of Humanities at Wayne State University. Professor Betanzos has translated individual essays for the Princeton University Press six-volume translation of Dilthey, *Selected Works,* currently in preparation.

The manuscript was prepared for publication by Thomas B. Seller. The cover was designed by Joanne Elkin Kinney. The typeface for the text and the display is Galliard. The book is printed on 50-lb. Glatfelter text paper. The cloth edition is bound in Holliston Mills' Roxite Linen over binder's boards.

Manufactured in the United States of America.